WAR IN ENGLAND
1642–1649

A fresh approach to the English civil war, *War in England 1642–1649* focuses on answering a misleadingly simple question: what kind of war was it to live through? Eschewing descriptions of specific battles or analyses of political and religious developments, Barbara Donagan examines the 'texture' of war, addressing questions such as: what did Englishmen and women believe about war and know about its practice before 1642? What were the conditions in which a soldier fought—for example, how efficient was his musket (not very), and how did he know where he was going (much depended on the reliability of scouts and spies)? What were the rules that were supposed to govern conduct in war, and how were they enforced (by a combination of professional peer pressure and severe but discretionary army discipline and courts martial)? What were the officers and men of the armies like, and how well did they fight?

The book deals even-handedly with royalists and parliamentarians, examining how much they had in common, as well as discussing the points on which they differed. It looks at the intimacy of this frequently uncivil war, in which enemies fought at close quarters, spoke the same language and had often been acquainted before the war began, just as they had often known the civilians who suffered their presence. A final section on two sieges illustrates these themes in practice over extended periods, and also demonstrates the integration of military and civilian experience in a civil war.

Drawing extensively on primary sources, Donagan's study illuminates the human cost of war and its effect on society, both in our own day as well as in the seventeenth century.

Barbara Donagan is a graduate of the University of Melbourne. She is an independent scholar at The Huntington Library, California

War in England
1642–1649

BARBARA DONAGAN

OXFORD
UNIVERSITY PRESS

OXFORD

UNIVERSITY PRESS

Great Clarendon Street, Oxford OX2 6DP

Oxford University Press is a department of the University of Oxford.
It furthers the University's objective of excellence in research, scholarship,
and education by publishing worldwide in

Oxford New York

Auckland Cape Town Dar es Salaam Hong Kong Karachi
Kuala Lumpur Madrid Melbourne Mexico City Nairobi
New Delhi Shanghai Taipei Toronto

With offices in

Argentina Austria Brazil Chile Czech Republic France Greece
Guatemala Hungary Italy Japan Poland Portugal Singapore
South Korea Switzerland Thailand Turkey Ukraine Vietnam

Oxford is a registered trade mark of Oxford University Press
in the UK and in certain other countries

Published in the United States
by Oxford University Press Inc., New York

British Library Cataloguing in Publication Data

Data available

Library of Congress Cataloging in Publication Data

Data available

Typeset by Laserwords Private Limited, Chennai, India
Printed in Great Britain
on acid-free paper by
Biddles Ltd, King's Lynn, Norfolk

ISBN 978–0–19–928518–1 (Hbk.)
ISBN 978–0–19–956570–2 (Pbk.)

1 3 5 7 9 10 8 6 4 2
2 4 6 8 10 9 7 5 3 1

In memoriam
Alan Donagan

Preface

This book has been many years in the making, and over those years the landscape of armed conflict has undergone a seismic change. Technology has continued to grow more sophisticated and individual weapons of choice have evolved from guns to suicide bombs, but the change in attitudes to rules governing conduct between enemies and between soldiers and civilians has been more significant and unsettling. The twentieth century had more than its fair share of the horrors of war, yet most nations acknowledged the legitimacy of the rules promulgated in the Geneva and Hague conventions as norms for conduct in war. Observance was imperfect, and no nation, however self-righteous, could assert that it had not lapsed from the ideal. Nevertheless there remained a consensus that recognized rules of war should be observed and that failure to do so deserved condemnation. There was a sense that their formulation and the degree of success in observing them represented progress on an upward path of humanity and civilization. The wars of the twenty-first century, however, have tested that assurance, for they have seen the decay or rejection of restraints on conduct between enemies in, for example, the rise of killing and torture of prisoners and the rejection of restraints intended to protect the traditionally 'innocent'—women, children, and the old—and abandonment of the mutuality of codes of conduct that made for a degree of respect and trust between enemies. The march of progress has stalled and indeed become regressive.

War in England may therefore qualify as a period piece. The voluntary restraints that marked the English civil war, like faith in the evolutionary progress of enlightened international conduct, may now seem like a relic of a more benevolent past. The book is not only a study of the war's conditions, personnel, and mental world, but also of the ways in which unwritten but mutually recognized codes of conduct shaped a seventeenth century war in which, indeed, the majority of participants hoped, despite differences of politics and religion, to preserve an organic society without radical structural change. Yet consideration of the elements—human, technical, and natural—that shaped the ways in which the war was fought reveals that civil war England faced its own set of dangers to soldiers, civilians, and to a cohesive social and political state, and that it too could descend into savagery. The English experience in the seventeenth century retains its interest not only for the political and religious issues that opponents sought to resolve, or for the clash of battle, but also for the way in which the consequences of now familiar divisive issues such as race, religion, and revenge were circumscribed by a combination of principle, prudence, and luck.

In the writing of this book I have incurred more debts of kindness and scholarly assistance than I can acknowledge here. To all those who have helped and supported me in good times and in bad I am truly grateful. My greatest debt is both institutional and personal: it is to the Huntington Library and its community of scholars, both resident and visiting. The library's collections of early modern British books and manuscripts, unrivalled in the United States, and its knowledgeable and helpful staff, make research easy as well as a constantly stimulating exploration. I am particularly indebted to Robert C. Ritchie, the W. M. Keck Foundation Director of Research, for his support in the face of my many delays, and to his predecessor as Director of Research, Martin Ridge. Like all those who come to the Huntington, I owe an incalculable debt to Mary Robertson, William A. Moffett Chief Curator of Manuscripts, whose expertise, interest, and friendship have smoothed my path and that of many others.

I have benefited from the collections of many libraries and record offices on both sides of the Atlantic and from the patience and skill of their staffs. As well as to the Huntington, my thanks go to the following libraries: the Bodleian Library, the British Library, the National Library of Wales, the Regenstein Library of the University of Chicago, and the William Salt Library, Stafford. I am grateful to the governing bodies of the following colleges for allowing me access to their libraries: in Cambridge, Magdelene College (for the Pepys manuscripts); in Oxford, Christ Church (for the Walker manuscripts), Lincoln College, Wadham College (for the Waller manuscripts), and Worcester College (for the Clarke manuscripts). The staffs of the record offices of Chester, Cheshire, Derbyshire, Devon (Exeter), East Sussex, Essex, and Staffordshire have been unfailingly helpful. I owe particular thanks to Frances Henderson, who shared her unequalled knowledge of the Clarke papers at Worcester College and helped me with their interpretation and exploration, and to Christopher Whittick, who rightly insisted in the face of my doubts that I would find the Danny papers in the East Sussex Record Office interesting and who has pointed me towards many other unexpected sources of material. In both cases, the rewards of scholarship have been enhanced by the pleasures of friendship and enthusiasm. At Worcester I must also thank Joanna Parker for her help in providing access to the Clarke papers, and at Kingston Lacy I thank Kate Warren and the National Trust staff for making my visit both profitable and enjoyable. Bernard Horrocks at the National Portrait Gallery, Steven Tabor and William Frank at the Huntington, and Kate Heard at the Ashmolean Museum all helped me greatly in my search for illustrations.

Many friends have listened to, read and commented on aspects of *War in England*. I have benefited enormously from Ian Gentles's vast and generously shared knowledge of all facets of civil war armies, from battles to politics. Blair Worden has provided support, friendship, and discussions of topics that range far beyond the seventeenth century and that have helped me think about the civil war in its wider context. Cynthia Herrup and Linda Levy Peck have listened, read, clarified, and broadened my horizons on many occasions from the beginning of the project. Among the many others whose interest and stimulating friendship have been one of the joys of scholarship are Michael Braddick, David

Cressy, Lori Anne Ferrell, Paul Hammer, Felicity Heal, Clive Holmes, Mark Kishlansky, Jason Peacey, Ian Roy, and Kevin Sharpe. The comfortable and sociable hospitality provided by Margaret and John Ackrill, Marie and Rupert Hall, and Lincoln College made possible much of my Oxford research. I am grateful for the support of the National Endowment for the Humanities, the British Academy, and the Huntington Library, whose grants helped me to undertake research in England.

I have also been very fortunate in my family. My sister and brother-in-law Norah and Colin Forster have selflessly provided rest, relaxation, encouragement, and interesting conversation on everything from history and politics to cricket. My sister-in-law Enid Donagan has been a constant and hospitable support.

The book is dedicated to the memory of Alan Donagan, a philosopher with a wide knowledge of military history, with whom I first walked battlefields. I hope that he would have enjoyed the military details and would not have found the moral and legal framework that underlies much of the discussion in *War in England* too far removed from the rigour of his own arguments in philosophical ethics.

Battle
Siege or other site mentioned in the text

N

SCOTLAND

Dundee
Edinburgh
Berwick
Newcastle on Tyne
Carlisle

Scarborough
Marston Moor York
Pontefract Castle Hull
Preston Leeds
Adwalton Moor
Lathom House

Rowton Moor Winceby
Chester Newark
Beeston Castle Nantwich
Hopton Heath Nottingham

ENGLAND

Shrewsbury Lichfield Leicester King's Lynn Yarmouth
Severn Birmingham Norwich
Coventry Naseby Bury St Edmunds
Powick Bridge Cropredy Bridge Cambridge
Worcester Newport Pagnell

WALES Hereford Edgehill Colchester

Raglan Castle Gloucester Boarstall House
Pembroke Oxford

St Fagans Bristol London
Reading Thames Turnham
Lansdown Newbury Green Canterbury
Roundway Basing House Maidstone Dover
Bridgwater Down Winchester
Taunton Wardour Cheriton Arundel
Torrington Langport Castle Castle
Exeter Lyme Regis Portsmouth
Stratton Corfe Castle
Lostwithiel Plymouth
Braddock Down
Pendennis
Castle

0   50   100 MILES

0   50   100   150 KM

MAP. I

Contents

Preface vii
Map x
Abbreviations xiii
Note xiv
Acknowledgements xv

Introduction: '[T]his *Insanum Bellum*, this mad Warre' 1

BEFORE THE WAR

1. God's Wars 15
2. Man's Wars 24
3. Military Educations 33

THE TEXTURE OF WAR: THE SOLDIER'S WORLD

4. An Integrated War 65
5. The Means of Violence 74
6. Knowledge and Confusion 94

SLAY IN LOVE: THE MORAL AND JUDICIAL ECONOMY OF CIVIL WAR

7. War and Civil War 127
8. Soldiers' Law 134
9. Theory and Practice 157
10. Outside the Law? 196

THE PROTAGONISTS

11. Armies 215
12. Officers 225
13. Men 258

CASE HISTORIES: TWO SIEGES

14. Boarstall House 1645–1646   295

15. Colchester 1648: 'The Mournfull City'   312

16. Colchesters Teares: Fire, Hunger, and Atrocity   330

17. Reciprocity, Negotiation, and Surrender   347

18. Colchester: The Aftermath   369

    Conclusion   389

Bibliography   404
Index   433

Abbreviations

Add. MSS	Additional Manuscripts
AHR	*American Historical Review*
BIHR	*Bulletin of the Institute of Historical Research* (now *Historical Research*)
BL	British Library
Bodl.	Bodleian Library
CAM	*Calendar of the Committee for the Advance of Money*
CCC	*Calendar of the Committee for Compounding*
CJ	*Journals of the House of Commons*
Clarendon, *History*	Hyde, Edward, earl of Clarendon, *The History of the Rebellion and Civil War in England* (Oxford, 1702–4)
CSPDom.	*Calendar of State Papers Domestic*
CSPVen.	*Calendar of State Papers Venetian*
DNB	*Dictionary of National Biography*
EHR	*English Historical Review*
EL	Ellesmere manuscripts
HA	Hastings manuscripts
Harl.	Harleian manuscripts
HEH	Henry E. Huntington Library
HJ	*Historical Journal*
HMC	Historical Manuscripts Commission
HR	*Historical Research*
JBS	*Journal of British Studies*
JSAHR	*Journal of the Society for Army Historical Research*
LJ	*Journals of the House of Lords*
NS	New series
PP	*Past and Present*
ODNB	*Oxford Dictionary of National Biography*
PRO	Public Record Office (now National Archives)
Rushworth	John Rushworth, *Historical Collections*, 8 vols. (1680–1701)
SP	State Papers
STT	Stowe-Temple manuscripts
TLS	*Times Literary Supplement*
TRHS	*Transactions of the Royal Historical Society*
VCH	Victoria County History

Note

Dates are given according to the old-style calendar, but the year is taken to begin on 1 January instead of 25 March.

The spelling of quotations from manuscripts has been modernized. All other quotations are given as they appear in their printed source.

Acknowledgements

I am very grateful to the following institutions for permission to reproduce illustrations from their collections: the Ashmolean Museum, Oxford, for numbers 1–4, 9, 10, 20; the Henry E. Huntington Library, San Marino, California, for numbers 5–8, 11,12, 21; the National Portrait Gallery, London, for numbers 13–19, 22.

I also thank Carol B. Pearson for her expertise and patience in preparing the index.

Introduction: '[T]his *Insanum Bellum*, this mad Warre'

'The residence of an army is not normally pleasant to any place.'[1]

Like Tolstoy's unhappy families, every war is miserable in its own way. But it also shares miseries common to virtually all wars. In seventeenth-century England they were characterized as God's arrows of plague and famine, fire and the sword, and these age-old mixed disasters of the wounds and death of battle, of sickness and hunger for soldiers and civilians, of loss and destruction of property and ensuing poverty and homelessness, have continued in varying proportions in later wars. Acts of cruelty and atrocity also recur with universal and depressing frequency, yet the virtues of war are equally unconfined by time and place: courage, self-sacrifice, and kindness, restraint and attempts to adhere to norms of conduct that protect at least some potential victims, are to be found across centuries and cultures.

The English civil war shared both the sufferings and the mitigations of suffering of other European wars of the first half of the seventeenth century, but it also had distinctive characteristics. This distinctiveness was not confined to its character as a civil war rather than one against foreigners. Because it was a civil war enemies were countrymen, but links of family, institution, and property were not wholly sundered or forgotten. They survived as strongly as they did in part because of the kinds of civil war it was not. It was not a class war, despite the emergence of powerful radical elements, despite the outlet it provided for populist violence, and despite the fashion at one time for Marxist interpretations of its causation and course. It was not a regional war; there was no basic geographical division as there was, however untidily, in the American civil war, nor was there anything comparable to the sense of invasion of one sovereignty by denizens of another of the kind that citizens of the state of Virginia could feel when confronted by northern troops. It was not a confessional war comparable to the French wars

---

[1] *Mercurius Elencticus*, 36 (26 July–2 Aug 1648), 279; 'His Maiesties Speech at Shrewsbury on Michaelmas Eve last, to the Gentry and Commons of the Countie of Sallop. There Assembled', in *The True Copie of a Letter written by Captain Wingate, now a Prisoner in Ludlow* (1642), [6].

of religion, although religion has properly been reinstated as crucial among its complex of causes and although it released unprecedented expressions of religious diversity. The clash of political ideologies was blurred by the anxiety of both sides, but particularly the parliamentarians, to establish themselves as the true conservators of traditional constitutional theory and practice and, until fairly late in the conflict, to reject innovative political formulations. The 1640s indeed saw striking expressions of genuine radicalism, but what is also striking is the success of the political establishment and the army high command, riven though they themselves were by divisions, in containing them. The absence or weakness of divisive ideological absolutes was complemented by a common interest that crossed partisan lines, namely anxiety that established, orderly, hierarchical social and property relations should not suffer radical breakdown and restructuring through the disruptive forces temporarily liberated by war.

These moderating conditions did not mean that the war was fought half-heartedly or softly. Its protagonists used the arms and tactics of European wars with determination; they modelled their practice on European expertise, and many of them had learnt their craft abroad. So, like contemporary war in the Low Countries and Germany, it was fought intimately, brutally, and at short range, and like other wars was often confused and unpredictable. Yet, again, it had distinctive features. It was extremely mobile and ranged across much of the country. Despite the importance of garrisons and the frequency of sieges, its practice was not determined by existing sophisticated fortifications, for England's strongholds dated back to an earlier military age. There was no strategic network of modern *trace italienne* fortresses; instead there was strong native distrust of garrisons as a means of oppression. When war came old works were updated and new ones thrown up, but although with time some defences, such as those at Oxford and Colchester, became admirably complex and up to date, on the whole English fortifications remained ad hoc strengthenings of old works or improvisations to meet current needs. The unavoidable mingling of civilians and soldiers in creating these works and in the daily life of garrisons and besieged strongholds was another aspect of the war's distinctive integration. This was equally visible in the countryside that soldiers passed through and on which they depended for supplies, lodging, and money. Fellow-countrymen and fellow-Protestants lived together, fought each other, and, linguistically, understood each other.

England and Europe differed in another way. As wars go, the English civil war is of only moderate interest to military historians. Despite the high proportion of English men and women actively engaged in it, its real scale was small when compared with contemporary European conflict. Total numbers of troops and, with the exception of Marston Moor, numbers involved in particular actions did not rival those in Germany. More significantly, although Cromwell, Fairfax, and Rupert were very good generals, they were not in the class of Gustavus Adolphus or Tilly. They were supported by many able officers, but the war did not produce notable military innovations, nor did either side demonstrate powerful strategic thinking.[2] Probably the closest to a true strategist in the first civil war was Prince Rupert, whose early, unsuccessful proposal that the royalists should conduct a garrison-based war to counter parliament's superiority in numbers revealed an ability, rare on both sides, to analyse a large problem and then to offer a tactical policy. Much of the war's fighting reflected opportunistic challenge and hurried response rather than overall design.[3] To the extent that guiding plans can be discerned, the chief were to take or keep London, and to interdict supplies by land and, particularly, by sea. With hindsight, we can see that the two crucial events of the war came very early: the earl of Warwick's seizure of the fleet for parliament, and the turning back of the king at Turnham Green, which frustrated his last, best chance to take London. These, with the later entry of the Scots into the war, rendered royalist military victory almost impossible. None is an event of military distinction. Of the two greatest battles of the war, Marston Moor put the seal on the effect of Scottish participation; Naseby's major long-term significance probably lay in the king's loss of a large part of his officer corps. Neither was a model for the textbooks. With hindsight we can also see that parliament's ultimate victory owed much to its superiority off the battlefield, where innovations in administrative planning and bureaucratic oversight enhanced its ability to mobilize the 'sinews of war'.

If the war lacked theoretical military interest compared with that of the conflicts between Spanish and Dutch or Imperialists and Swedes, it nevertheless shared much with them beyond matters of military technique. The laws of war were international, and the 'rules' that should guide the conduct of soldiers to each other and to civilians were as well known in England as on the continent. Practice frequently failed to live up to theory, but when Englishmen loudly accused their enemies of failing to observe humane, Christian, and professional standards, or regretted the failures of their own side, they consciously appealed to rules of conduct that transcended national and temporal boundaries. In what follows I shall look primarily at the particularities of English habits, both moral and practical. We should, however, retain a sense of perspective unavailable to most combatants in England. Much that appears distinctive, localized, and particular has counterparts far from western Europe and the seventeenth century. So when we consider the powerful tradition, derived from Christian and classical teaching, that women, children, and the old should be protected, or that promises should be inviolable, or that military honour demanded mercy in

---

[2] Although a case can be made for Cromwell and Lambert in the Worcester and Dunbar campaigns of 1648 and 1651. B. H. Liddell Hart, *Strategy: The Indirect Approach* (3rd edn. 1954), 88–91; Austin Woolrych, *Britain in Revolution 1625–1660* (Oxford, 2002), 485–7.

[3] In explaining the 'indecisiveness' (in their long-term strategic effects) of civil war battles, Liddell Hart commented that 'the military campaigns took the form of repeated direct advances by one side or the other, interspersed with . . . "mopping up" operations, which had only a local and transient effect—at the price of a drain of strength'. *Strategy*, 85.

certain circumstances, and that failure to observe such norms was evidence of breakdown of standards that bound and protected a larger society, we should also remember that comparable rules are to be found far from Europe. In the world of the Oghuz Turk Dede Korkut, ferocious and devious though it was, women and children retained special status and breach of oaths merited revenge. In twentieth-century Los Angeles gang wars, survivors of an older generation saw the abandonment of codes that had once, for example, protected a man from attack while he walked with his family, as a sign of the rise of a lawless, normless, affectless society. In New England in 1704 John Williams told the Indian captor who threatened to kill him that 'death, after a promise of quarter, would bring the guilt of blood', and lived to report the exchange. Even details that at first seem of little more than picturesque and antiquarian interest, such as identification by coloured rags and scarves in the absence of formal identifying uniforms, have counterparts in the blue and red of modern urban street gangs, and in both contexts serve to demonstrate the likeness of enemies. Similarities across space and time are endless.

If a study of the English conflict of the 1640s is necessarily minor and local on the scale of the world's wars, and if it shares many characteristics with other times and places, it nevertheless has value beyond its undeniably powerful anecdotal and national interest. Just as studies of its politics and religion raise issues of wide principle and cast a broad as well as a microscopic light, so a study of its codes and practices illuminates methods of success and failure in restraining excesses in many wars. It reveals attempts to 'humanize' war, or at least to prevent its dehumanization to a degree that would barbarize its practice and endanger a reconciled and stable postwar society. Yet few of those touched by the civil war were concerned with theoretical issues of just war or legitimation of war itself. Even the objections of neutralists were largely pragmatic, while protagonists, even when reluctant, were usually convinced of the justice of their cause. The civil war has a place in the history of attempts to control war, but not in that of attempts to abolish it.

The present study tries to look at the kind of war the English civil war was: how brutal, how humane, how restrained, and to consider the effect of the presence of armies on civilians. It confines itself to war in England, for the 'British wars' of the mid-seventeenth century, although linked by issues of religion, sovereignty, interest, and personnel, differed in kind. Scotland and Ireland had their own civil wars, but for the English their war against the Scots was conducted as a foreign war; that in Ireland could best be described as a colonial war. Only in England were they engaged in war against each other, and forced to confront the problems peculiar to civil war. How a war is fought and how combatants treat each other and civilians reverberates long after peace returns. We have tended to take for granted, in the aftermath of the civil war in the Interregnum and Restoration, the absence of rigid feuds and postwar divisions along lines dictated by wartime allegiance. This is in part because of the fluidity of commitment to causes between 1640 and 1660, as former leaders grew disillusioned or were dropped or moved to outer darkness and new stars rose, in part because the flourishing life of factions and parties after 1660 has diverted attention from the possibility of more intransigent, older enmities, and in part because the relatively few incidents of bloody retribution such as the brief but horrible period of post-Restoration executions seemed to fulfil the requirements of revenge. Yet it is nonetheless noteworthy that in general Englishmen managed to live together in the 1650s and 1660s without the crippling intranational bitterness that has followed some other civil wars, and without wounds such as those they left on contemporary Ireland. This book is an attempt to provide part of the answer to the question of how they managed to do so.

The English civil war has been fortunate in its historians. Any account of its historiography begins with the great figures of Clarendon and Gardiner. In recent decades the study of its political, social, intellectual, religious, and regional character has been transformed. Its military history has long attracted expert and professional interest, and there is valuable prosopographical work on its officers. What has attracted less attention is the integration of the war of armies and fighting with the war of civilians and a continuing society, despite invaluable local and regional histories and despite pioneering studies of supply, command, and military conduct. Much remains to be done. Only recently have topics such as taxation, the economy, social policy, and the evolution of the state begun to receive the attention they merit as matters of national importance profoundly influenced by the fact of war. Although writing on the civil war is voluminous, it has tended to fall into one of two categories: general historians' history—primarily political, religious, and social—and military historians' history. And when the two approaches have been synthesized, as in Sir Charles Firth's study of Cromwell's army, another factor that has shaped much work on the period comes into play, namely a tendency to focus on the New Model army. The political and religious importance of the New Model, the coherence of its planning, and the eminence of its commanders have resulted in disproportionate attention to its role in the war and its influence on the life of contemporary Englishmen. The war began in the summer of 1642, but the New Model was not formed until the spring of 1645 and even then remained one among other parliamentary armies, although the most important. By the summer of 1646 the first civil war was over. The next period of action in England began in the spring of 1648 and, although some pockets of trouble persisted into 1649, the second civil war was effectively an affair of a few months. The so-called 'third civil war' of 1650–1 was essentially a Scottish campaign until the brief incursion of Scots and royalists that ended in their disastrous defeat at Worcester. The New Model's fighting life in England therefore covered a limited portion of total fighting time. Its political life and its contribution to victory were another matter, but in the context of the war itself it must be studied with the other armies, both royalist and parliamentarian; it should not colour our whole picture of the nature of the war nor of the impact of armies on society.

Perceptions of the character of the war have shifted over time. English decency, good sense, and social cohesion, it was once believed, imparted to it an admirable and distinctive moderation. In retrospect Englishmen congratulated themselves on 'the very few cruel and unnecessary deeds which disgraced our civil wars', which were conducted with 'great and remarkable humanity . . . in an age not generally distinguished by a too squeamish delicacy'. These 'humane principles' had shaped 'a contest between men of the same race and creed, not . . . a *guerre à outrance*'; fortunately 'Englishmen, then as now, were devoted to fair play'.[4] This confidence has faded, and it has become more fashionable to find atrocity than restraint or kindness, but traces of these earlier beliefs still linger and the issues they raise are still valid. One of the purposes of this book is to throw light on the question: how benign was the English civil war?

Contemporaries did not share the confidence of later commentators. King Charles foresaw a 'dark equal chaos of confusion'.[5] The Speaker of the House of Commons, when reminded of the miseries of the people, admitted that war's 'bitter effects' were felt by friends as well as enemies and that it brought burning, spoil, destruction, cold-blooded killing, and the collapse of law and morality.[6] In May and June 1642 the earl of Northumberland, a future parliamentarian, wrote to Sir John Bankes, a future royalist, of the misery that would follow a resort to force, and asked, 'what can be so mischievous, so destructive to all as a civil war?' By 1646 England seemed 'A Kingdome burning'.[7]

Pre-war knowledge and experience of war had led English men and women to expect the worst if war came close to home. In what follows more attention than is usual in accounts of the civil war will be paid to England's pre-war military formation, through which actual and potential soldiers acquired the elements of professional education and the broader public became familiar with the practices and consequences of war abroad and, to some degree, with its moral issues and norms of conduct. Anxiety about what war would entail derived more from

---

[4] J. H. Round, 'The Case of Lucas and Lisle', *TRHS* ns 8 (1894), 159, 168, 170; Charles Thomas-Stanford, *Sussex in the Great Civil War and the Interregnum 1642–1660* (1910), 195. For Victorian romanticization of the civil war, see Roy Strong, *Recreating the Past: British History and the Victorian Painter* (1978), 136–51, on 'Cavaliers and Roundheads' and 'Oliver Cromwell'.

[5] John Rushworth, *Historical Collections of Private Passages of State*, 8 vols. (1680–1701), 4. 732. Charles linked war, constitutional collapse, and social breakdown. He predicted the vesting of all power in the House of Commons and then, by a logical progression, the triumph of the 'wild Humours' of the common people who would 'set up for themselves, call Parity and Independence Liberty', and destroy all rights, property, and distinctions of family and merit. Many conservative parliamentarians, when confronted by Levellers and other radicals, later came to hold similar views.

[6] Bodl. MSS Tanner 62/1B, fos 168–168ᵛ.

[7] Kingston Lacy, Bankes MSS, 'Autograph Letters', I, no foliation, Northumberland to Bankes, 19 May and 14 June 1642; HMC, *Bath MSS . . . Longleat*, 5(1980), 288, verses in memory of the earl of Essex.

perceptions of the intrinsic nature of war than from the issues over which it was to be fought. Furthermore, if the issues that were propelling the country towards armed conflict seemed clear-cut matters of black and white to some, to many they were complex and, between moderate men of good will, negotiable in the cause of preventing the disaster of civil war.

We will see many degrees of commitment and enthusiasm, from reluctance that might evolve into dutiful and devoted service or alternatively lead to departure from England, to an apparently instinctive loyalty with no evidence that any process of choice was required. For many, however, active commitment to war on behalf of one side or the other involved difficult choices and often brought wrenching changes in social relations. The issues over which they were forced to divide did not offer simple alternatives, and if the fortunate saw black and white many saw only grey. Difficulties were further compounded by a long war in which both causes and fortunes changed. Northumberland and Bankes have already introduced us to these complexities. In the early summer of 1642 they and a group of sympathizers exchanged letters that anxiously and fruitlessly sought a compromise that would stave off war. Yet when choice could no longer be postponed each would be actively engaged on his chosen side. For some English men and women allegiance was a simpler matter. One mother 'joy[ed] she had a son to fight his majesty's quarrel'. The earl of Norwich, an old courtier, wrote simply, 'I had all from his Majesty, and he hath all again.'[8] For others, however, as John Wallace pointed out, the choice demanded by the civil war presented them with 'the most colossal case of conscience' of their lives.[9] Many tried to evade decision, to be 'merely passive in this great difference', but in a war that ranged widely and lasted long few succeeded.[10] Any account of the war as a national phenomenon must incorporate its effects for such would-be 'neuters', for the unenthusiastic and undecided, and for the passive and ignorant, who suffered from the presence and the demands of the committed of both sides. The records are littered with the punitive consequences of their attempts to be unengaged and inconspicuous as they were fined and expropriated. Friendship contended with the belief that those who were not for us were against us, and both sides joined to excoriate the 'neuter'. In 1642 the preacher John Sedgwick cited with approval '*Solon's* Law to the *Athenians* who adjudged him to die, and unworthy to live that in time of civill Garboyles . . . withdrew himselfe, and became a neuter'.[11]

As the war went on the strains on bonds of friendship and kinship grew greater. 'What person is sorrowful for the Destruction of inveterate Enemies?' observed

[8] Bodl. MS Carte, 7, fo. 177; *CSPDom. 1644*, 261.

[9] John M. Wallace, *Destiny his Choice: The Loyalism of Andrew Marvell* (Cambridge, 1968), 10.

[10] Bodl. MS Tanner 64, fo. 26.

[11] John Sedgwick, *Englands Condition Parallell'd with Iacobs For Troubles/Salvations/Hopes* (1642), A2, 'Epistle Dedicatory'.

the king's secretary Sir Edward Walker.[12] Yet the distinction between friend and
enemy was not always clear. As we shall see, the allegiance of ordinary soldiers
was often flexible and problematic, for desertion was chronic in civil war armies
and prisoners were frequently re-enlisted in the armies of their former enemies.
Even the locally prominent could puzzle observers. After more than a year of
war Sir William Brereton, the parliamentary commander in Cheshire, had to
write to the Speaker of the House of Commons to inquire whether the earl of
Bridgewater, a regional magnate, was or was not a 'delinquent'. In this war of
interlocking families and communities and of sometimes uncertain ideological
boundaries, perceptions of persons and actions could remain fluid. On the one
hand there was a vociferous polemical literature that credited the enemy with
few virtues and uncountable vices, on the other the pragmatic recognition of
links and similarities and even of shared middle ground. In seeking allegiances
and parties later historians must find their way across terrain that shifts under
their feet.

   This book thus addresses a dual world in which violence and enmity were
set against moderation and established associations. Although it cannot explore
the political and religious contexts of the war, these both shaped and were
shaped by the experiences of its military protagonists and civilian victims. Yet
neither politics nor religion presents a simple face. In the war's early years
few of the leaders on either side claimed to want fundamental constitutional
change. If some of the king's supporters were more absolutist than others and
a few of parliament's had a republican gleam in their eye, most in both parties
accepted the formula of government by king and parliament. The problem
lay in which had precedence, but most parliamentarians evaded an explicit
claim to the sole supremacy of parliament for as long as they could. In 1645
Sir Thomas Fairfax could still write to Prince Rupert, 'Sir The Crown of
England is & will be where it ought to be. We fight to maintain it there,
but the King misled by evil Counsellors or through a seduced Heart hath
left his Parliament & his People.'[13] The fiction that they fought for king
and parliament grew ever harder to sustain, and it had been dismissed by
many royalists from the start. At Edgehill in 1642, said one, 'that maske
of fighting for the King [was] blowne off with their owne priming powder'.
They had, said another, 'the desperate impudence to shoot at the King, and
say it is to save his life'.[14] Even some royalists, however, recognized that evil
councillors were a valid cause of concern. Yet if root and branch constitutional
radicalization came late to parliamentarians, their practice from the beginning
of the war asserted the supremacy of parliament. On the king's part, the belated

---

[12] Sir Edward Walker, *Historical Discourses, upon Severall Occasions* (1705), 246.

[13] BL Stowe MS 184, fo. 110ᵛ.

[14] *The Anti-Covenant, Or a sad Complaint Concerning the new Oath or Covenant* (Oxford,
1643), 7; *The Round-Heads Remembrancer: or, A true and particular relation of the great defeat
given to the Rebels by . . . Sir Ralph Hopton . . . May 16. 1643* (n.pl., 1643), 1.

establishment of an Oxford assembly attempted to impart a parliamentary gloss to his government. Yet superficial similarities of constitutional formulae did not disguise basic differences in the way power could be exercised, and these affected the way in which each side conducted its war and its politics. The royal armies, faction-ridden though they were, offered no challenge to the ultimate authority of the king. Parliament, less secure in its claims to supremacy, was to be challenged by its own army. On one point of law and constitution, however, both sides could agree: each branded the supporters of the other as 'rebels and traitours'.[15]

On the religious and moral front, one of the most striking characteristics of the massive output of print during the war years is its vituperative nature. Royalists were 'the spirit and spawne of Satan', agents of the devil, vermin, atheists (or worse, popish), heretics, men of blood and sin who would shortly 'ravish our virgins, defloure our wives, cut our throates, and divide our estates', declared a puritan minister in 1642.[16] Against this 'base, swearing, whoring, stealing and murderous company, who stinke in all places where they come', were pitted 'the *Parliament* . . . men of piety, fidelity, gravitie, goodnesse, and loyalty', the defenders of liberty, religion, property and England's glory, and the proponents of 'publique Reformation'.[17] The royalists replied in kind, and dismissed 'reformation' as a 'stalking horse' that had thrown 'our English world quite off the wheeles': the whimsies of religion had lead to rebellion and treason, to abrogation of the laws and tyranny. 'Nothing is more frequent with the Agents in this Rebellion', wrote a royalist pamphleteer, 'than to fasten their Treasons on *God* and *Religion*.'[18]

There were irenic voices on both sides, but they were few and little heard amid the noise of conflict. Indeed, the language of both parties was remarkably similar, and each believed that the God of battles was on their side and that they were his agents. Puritans' conviction that God sent victory and defeat, encouragement and chastisement, to men who were his instruments and whose cause, because it was his, would ultimately triumph, has long been recognized as one of their defining characteristics, an energizing incentive to action and a comfort in failure. Royalists were in the main less strident, but they too saw God's hand on the battlefield and traced divine providence in the king's successes and defeats. So some royalists suggested that the fall of Bristol in 1645 had perhaps

---

[15] *A most true Relation Of divers notable Passages of Divine Providence in the . . . wonderfull victory . . . of the Earle of Stamford . . . against . . . Sir Ralph Hopton and his adherents, rebels and traitours . . . 25. April. 1643* (1643). See Ian Roy, 'The Royalist Council of War, 1642–6', *BIHR* 35 (1962), 150–68, for an account of royalist decision-making and administration. He concludes that the king, 'more completely than parliament, retained ultimate authority in his own hands' (p. 168). This authority, however, coexisted with and pandered to faction and to inconsistent execution of policies in the absence of effective administrative oversight.

[16] Sedgwick, *Englands Condition Parallell'd*, 'Englands Troubles', 8–[9], 20, 40.

[17] Ibid., 'Englands Troubles', 40; 'Englands Hopes', 14.

[18] *Mercurius Aulicus*, 3 (21 Aug. 1648), 19; *Round-Heads Remembrancer*, 1.

been ordained by God for the best, since it led to the dismissal of Prince Rupert, while even in those dark days, said another, God had 'raised . . . a miraculous deliverance' through Montrose's success in Scotland: 'are not these miracles of providence able to make an atheist superstitious?' God was clearly 'carrying us through with his own immediate hand, for all the work of Montrose is above what can be attributed to mankind'.[19]

There were thus levels of language and belief, both political and religious, at which the two sides converged, but there were also 'sticking-points' even for their moderates. A conservative parliamentarian like Fairfax may have wished for only limited church reform and to preserve the life of the king, but he did not waver in his belief in the primary authority of parliament. A moderate royalist like Sir John Bankes regretted the king's provocative policies in 1642 and was no Laudian, but he followed the king to Oxford without hesitation. If there was less evolutionary change on the royalist side, where policy remained ultimately in the hands of one man, the king, and was marked by a kind of devious intransigence, 'parliament' was both hydra-headed and protean. Its radicalization in politics, and even more notably in religion, induced a conservative reaction among many of its supporters. Fluctuations in parliamentary policy and personnel contrasted with the relative if squabbling stability of royalism. If some of the royalists mentioned in the following pages retired from the stage through death, disfavour, or faction, their opponents more often made their exits declaring their loyalty to parliament but complaining that the cause, not they, had changed.

The constitutional and religious contexts of the civil war were volatile and untidy. Their twists and turns were no mere passive backdrop to its campaigns. They affected its armies—their leadership, their money and supplies, their choice of officers and the disposition of their men—as well as the civilian population who paid for those armies and suffered their presence, and whose familiar law, religion, and social networks seemed under threat.

The treatment of the civil war that follows is unconventional in that it is neither narrative nor strictly thematic. Instead it provides a kind of environmental study of the war's armies that considers their habitat and the factors that shaped their actions. It attempts to illuminate the experience of soldiers and, to a lesser extent, civilians (to whom a later study will be more specifically devoted). It assumes that the mental and moral formation of soldiers, the means and conditions of warfare, the training and discipline imposed on troops, and the nature of relations between enemies shaped the actions and capabilities of armies, and that their success or failure in the field and their demands—for pay, for indemnity, for political rights—in turn influenced the options available to the armies' putative

---

[19] *Certain Observations, Upon the New League or Covenant, As it was explained by a Divine of the New Assembly* (Bristol, 1643), 40–1; Kingston Lacy, Bankes MSS, 'Autograph Letters', I, 21 Sept. 1645, letter to Lord Jermyn.

masters in wider matters of policy. It hopes to deepen the understanding of political or religious or social historians as to the nature of the body they are talking about when they discuss 'the army', and to suggest a need for greater attention to the social interactions of military and civilian society.

The book is divided into sections each of which addresses an important aspect of army formation and experience. They can be read independently, for example for information on the officer corps or military law and custom or the nature of siege warfare, but they are also intended, taken together, to provide a detailed picture of the components of military experience in civil war England. They do not provide a narrative of the military or political progress of the war, but although the book lacks a chronological framework, most of the events discussed are dated so that they can be placed within the span of the years 1642 to 1649.

The book assumes that both the physical and the intellectual contexts of war affect its character, and hence it will look at normative codes as well as material conditions. It will consider the pre-war background that established familiarity with the practices and codes of contemporary warfare. It will examine the conditions of war, including the limitations imposed by such factors as the quality of weapons, supply, and intelligence, and will also look at the nature of officers and men. It will describe the codes that in theory governed the conduct of soldiers in the field, to each other, and to civilians, which differed little between opponents. Along the way it will become evident how inextricably the military and civilian experiences of war were intertwined, for armies conducted their affairs in the midst of the civilian population, on whom they were dependent in many ways; the economic and social lives of those civilians were often radically disrupted and they could easily become victims of predatory brutality if ordinary law was overridden and army law and codes were weak. Finally it will examine the interplay of all these factors through case histories of two sieges, one obscure and relatively benevolent, the other both famous and infamous. The emphasis on the codes, conditions, and conduct of the civil war and on the interaction of military and civil society rather than its battles means that this is a book in which Fairfax will be mentioned more often than Cromwell, desertion more often than tactics, and destruction more often than victory, while some of the war's most famous issues, notably the religion of godly soldiers and the rise of army radicalism, must be largely ignored. The sum of the parts, it is hoped, will nevertheless constitute a step towards an overall picture of the nature and experience of the civil war for soldiers and for the civilians among whom they fought and lived, and to whose society most veterans returned at the end of the war.

This war was fought in a country in which the greater part of the population would almost certainly, if they could, have negotiated an inactive and unmolested way between the adversaries, and in which active partisans of each side shared more than divided them in constitutional theory, social practice, economic interest, and even a moderate national Protestantism. They were enmeshed in networks of kinship, obligation, and friendship. If initial choice was difficult for many, war nonetheless hardened differences and often strained the sense of commonalty to breaking point. It created a history of death, suffering, and outrage that was nurtured by the extremism of much public rhetoric. A major unwritten part of the history of the English civil war is the survival, however beleaguered, of moral and professional norms and social bonds, so that a recognizable English Humpty Dumpty could be put together again. If these enemies were to live to be friends, as those old friends and new enemies Sir Ralph Hopton and Sir William Waller hoped, much depended on their conduct to each other during the war.

BEFORE THE WAR

This section will not discuss the convergence of political and religious grievances in the years before 1642 that, by a progress that now seems at once unnecessary and ineluctable, culminated in civil war. Nor will it deal with the processes of conscience, loyalty, and interest by which sides were chosen or choice evaded. Instead it will describe attitudes to and beliefs about war in general, and knowledge in particular of the contemporary wars with which English men and women were most familiar in France, the Netherlands, and Germany. Together these shaped the way in which their own war would be fought. From Europe they learnt techniques, tactics, and weaponry, but the prospect of contemporary Europe also instilled fears of a descent into social, moral, and economic chaos when enemies ceased to observe the laws of war that traditionally, if minimally and erratically, moderated the conduct of soldiers to each other and to civilians, and when civilians themselves, loosed from the bonds of order and hierarchy, might revert to a predatory and feral society.

For many Englishmen the 1630s were halcyon days of peace. Domestic divisions paled when they looked abroad to a continent wracked by war; accounts of the cruelty and barbarism of the Thirty Years' War in Germany both frightened and fascinated English readers. Yet, although they rejoiced in England's peace, the country was neither as resolutely civilian, nor as utterly unprepared for war, nor as unsupplied with modern, educated soldiers, as tradition would have it. The novelty of the 1640s, whether in the emergence of a new officer class and disciplined troops, or in attitudes to war, or in the religious rhetoric used to justify it and its agents, has been exaggerated. A preliminary look at the 1620s and 1630s helps to clarify what was new and distinctive in the 1640s, what represented evolution from pre-existing conditions, and what remained unchanged, traditional, and international. When we examine attitudes to war—to both its legitimacy and its nature—and the military education of Englishmen, it becomes clear that future royalists and future parliamentarians shared a common heritage. Recognition of this fact helps to explain much in their wartime relations; it also helps us to discern more clearly the ways in which they differed.

1

God's Wars

Any war raises two kinds of questions. Is it legitimate to go to war? And how should soldiers conduct themselves in it? The law of war thus has two parts. The first, *ius ad bellum*, addresses the theory of just war, of the occasions on which it is morally permissible to resort to arms. The second, *ius in bello*, addresses conduct in war and the rules intended to regulate and moderate it. The application and observance of the rules that nominally governed conduct will be one of the major topics of later sections of this book.

The first part of the law of war, *ius ad bellum*, need not detain us long. Its chief interest here lies less in its substantive arguments than in the ways in which they were presented and in the use made of them. If there was some defensiveness about the legitimacy of war as an institution—did it perhaps flout gospel teaching? should Christians kill?—it was easily dispelled. Although mid-seventeenth-century English men and women thought about these problem in terms largely shaped by religious apologists, religious and secular justifications differed little.[1] The greatest secular theorist of the age, of course, was Hugo Grotius, but although his work, like that of the professor of civil law at Oxford, Alberico Gentili, was known to an educated elite, it did not capture hearts and minds as did that of their clerical contemporaries. Religious and secular theorists alike, moreover, dismissed pacifism as a romantic dream. The injunction to beat swords into ploughshares was 'somewhat *hyperbolicall*', said the preacher William Gouge, while Gentili even-handedly demolished condemnations of war by pagan Cicero and Seneca and Christian Tertullian and Gregory, and pronounced Erasmus a 'flighty dilettante'.[2] Those who denied that Christian princes could lawfully make war or that their subjects could lawfully serve as soldiers were 'both hereticall and phrenetical persons' said Matthew Sutcliffe, whose *Practice, Proceedings, and Lawes of armes* appeared in 1593 and remained a respected

---

[1] See discussion of this topic in J. R. Hale, 'Incitement to Violence: English Divines on the Theme of War, 1578 to 1631', in J. R. Hale, *Renaisssance War Studies* (1983), 487–517.

[2] Richard Bernard, *The Bible-Battells: Or The Sacred Art Military* (1629), 25; William Gouge, *The Churches Conquest over the Sword* (1631), in William Gouge, *Gods Three Arrowes: Plague, Famine, Sword, In Three Treatises* (2nd edn. 1631), 212; Alberico Gentili, *De Iure Belli Libri Tres* (Classics of International Law, 2 vols., Oxford, 1933; ii, tr. John C. Rolfe, introd. Coleman Phillipson), 2. 27–31. And see [George Wilde], *A Sermon preached . . . In St Maries Oxford. Before . . . the Members of the Honourable House of Commons There Assembled* (Oxford, 1643) 2, for a royalist dismissal of pacifism.

authority for decades.[3] Pacificism was in fact of little practical significance.[4] It should not be confused with the widespread neutralism of the 1640s, which did not deny the legitimacy of war so long as it was waged elsewhere. Most Englishmen who wished to do so, as in other times and places, readily persuaded themselves that their cause was just and that it was only the arguments of the other side that were specious and hypocritical. As Gentili observed, 'It is the nature of wars for both sides to maintain that they are supporting a just cause.'[5]

The ringing terms in which war was legitimated and righteous purpose attributed to its agents have long been seen as notable characteristics of the English civil war. They are part of the familiar picture of godly parliamentarians urged on to battle by their preachers, singing psalms as they advanced in brave and orderly ranks, and led by that prime instrument of the Lord, Oliver Cromwell. Even the royalists, when not merely represented in dashing cavalier mode, are credited with loyalty to church and prayer book as well as to their king, and when they justified war and claimed to act in the service of God they shared arguments and rhetoric with parliamentarians. A glance at earlier decades shows that it was the quantity and audibility of righteous justification for war that changed in the 1640s rather than its quality and content. The trumpets of the Lord that exhorted parliamentarians to victory and reform were very loud, but their tune was not new; it formed part of the shared heritage of both parties and of Christian western Europe, Protestant and Catholic alike. The law of God and the secular law of nature and nations converged, and together they had long been deployed in support of righteous violence. Arguments that allied reason of state, the duty to obey constituted authority, and Christian killing were already familiar parts of the apologetics of war.

War still had to be justified. Christianity was not nominally a militaristic religion. And the soldier's vocation had to be rendered honourable and religious; it was not to be confused with that of necessary but shameful functionaries like executioners. English apologists followed in the footsteps of Catholic fathers and early modern European theorists. 'Warre is warrantable', said the respected mentor William Gouge, as he denied apparent conflict between the messages of the New and the Old Testaments. Soldiers had 'good warrant', for shedding blood in a just war was 'warrantable equity' not 'unlawfull cruelty'. 'The martialist may be a good Christian', Thomas Adams had insisted in 1617, and in 1649

---

[3] Matthew Sutcliffe, *The Practice, Proceedings, and Lawes of armes, described out of the doings of most valiant and expert Captaines, and confirmed both by ancient, and moderne examples, and praecedents* (1593), 1.

[4] See Barry Reay, *The Quakers and the English Revolution* (1985), 41–3, on 'ambiguity' and limitations in Quaker views on pacificism in the 1650s.

[5] Gentili's further conclusion that 'a war may be waged with justice on both sides' was harder for his contemporaries to accept. He admitted that justice might derive either from 'reality' or from 'justifiable ignorance'. *De Iure Belli*, 2. 31. Cf. Stephen Gosson (in 1598) on the 'uncharitable and unjust' wars of England's enemies, compared with the charity and justice of her own, quoted in Hale, 'Incitement to Violence', 496–7.

Sir Balthazar Gerbier was to remark in the course of a lecture on military architecture that 'even the Apostles were commanded by the Prince of Peace to provide Armes for defence'.[6] In 1629 Richard Bernard, contemplating endangered continental Protestantism, cited St Augustine: '[T]he true servants of God make warres, that the wicked may be restrained, and good men be relieved. Warre upon just cause undertaken is undoubtedly lawfull.' All should seek peace, but just and necessary war must not be condemned.[7] His list of thirteen 'just causes and true grounds of making warre' would leave no intending belligerent at a loss.[8] If even offensive war was lawful when it met their elastic criteria, the case for defensive war was virtually self-evident to the writers on *ius ad bellum*. 'If the Enemie begin,' said Bernard, 'let us stand for our Religion and lives with courage. Christ will take our parts and give us glorious victorie in the end.'[9] In 1643 George Wilde could explain the relation between peace and war to his royalist congregation in Oxford in familiar terms: 'The only Masculine Logick now lies in the Sword; and we must haste unto the Camp for a true definition of Peace.'[10] A parliamentarian banner announced more simply, 'That Warre is Iust Which is Necessary.'[11]

Clearly no war need ever be unjust in the representations of its protagonists. Nonetheless it must not be undertaken lightly, for its miseries were 'unutterable':

Lusts of unruly Souldiers raigne, without respect of friends, or foes, many times. The battle of the warriour (saith *Esa*) is with confused noise, and garment rolled in blood; and hee telleth the people that the sword hath made the world a wildernesse and destroyed Cities; yea children have been dashed to peeces, houses spoyled, Temples robbed, strong men slaine, and women ravished, and crueltie committed without pittie.[12]

For Englishmen, this description depicted more than biblical history; it conjured up the Europe they saw across the Channel. Such miseries required that war be necessary as well as just. An imbalance between justice and necessity, rather than pacifism, was to trouble many neutralists in the 1640s, who saw miseries overwhelming benefits, false conceptions of just cause, and at least some soldiers who loved violence for its own sake or for its profit. Unfortunately the permissive

---

[6] Gouge, *Churches Conquest*, 209–10, 294–5; Tho[mas] Adams, *The Souldiers Honour. Wherein By divers inferences and gradations it is evinced, that the Profession is iust, necessarie, and honourable* (1617), 23; Sir Balthazar Gerbier, *The First Publique Lecture, Read at Sr. Balthazar Gerbier his Academy, Concerning Military Architecture, or Fortifications* (1649), 7.

[7] Bernard, *Bible-Battells*, 24–7.

[8] Ibid. 38–47; for Bernard's use of Sutcliffe, see p. 43; and see Sutcliffe, *Lawes of armes*, dedication. For Gouge's categorization of just wars, see *Churches Conquest*, 214–16.

[9] Bernard, *Bible-Battells*, 53–4; and see Gouge, *Churches Conquest*, 293–4; W[illiam] B[edell] (tr.), *The Free Schoole of Warre, or, a Treatise, whether it be lawfull to beare armes for the service of a Prince that is of a divers Religion* (1625), I/ii–K/ii; John Everard, *The Arriereban: A Sermon preached to the Company of the Military Yarde, At St. Andrewes Church in Holborne on St. James his day last* (1618), 22, 29–30, 31, 33; and compare Gentili, *De Iure Belli*, 2. 30.

[10] [Wilde], *Sermon . . . In St Maries Oxford*, 7.   [11] BL Sloane MS 5247, fo. 20.

[12] Bernard, *Bible-Battells*, 52.

side of the apologists' analysis was more memorable than the cautionary, and despite its miseries a just and necessary war was held to be preferable to an unjust peace. Then as now justice and necessity tended to lie in the eye of the beholder.

Nevertheless, despite these generous justifications for war, apologists still felt the need to defend the soldier's profession and to render his killing Christian. This proved simple enough for a generation adept at seeking and finding useful biblical texts, yet it remained difficult to reconcile uplifting rhetoric with the popular stereotype of soldiers as the scum of society, a stereotype that gains some support from accounts of recruiting in England that reveal the mixture of cynicism and despair with which Falstaff and his recruits have made us familiar. '[I]s God walking among us?' asked Samuel Bachiler, preaching to English troops in Holland in 1629, as he contemplated the gap between ideal and reality. He advocated choice of the 'best men', neither 'tatred outside' nor 'ragged' in mind, 'to make a holy Campe', but at the same time he lamented the rarity of 'stayed, sober, religious men, fearing *God* and eschewing evill'. Instead, he conceded, the camp was filled with '[t]he skumme of men, fitter to fill *prisons* and *Iayles*, then an armie of *Saints*'.[13] Bachiler's plea for an army of saints foreshadowed the reformist rhetoric of the 1640s that hoped to produce soldiers worthy of God's service, while in 1643 the royalist Henry Ferne was to echo his hope for a holy camp, and his dismay at the reality.[14] More to the immediate point, Bachiler exemplified one of the reasons for defensiveness about the soldier's vocation even when his cause was unequivocally 'good and sure', just and Protestant. England indeed had its military heroes like the Vere brothers, with their years of Low Countries service, and it was dazzled by Gustavus Adolphus, 'that *Caesar* and *Alexander* of our times' who was 'beloved for his virtues both *Christian, Morall, & Military*', but the stereotype of the soldier remained closer to Bachiler's model—and Falstaff's recruits—than to that 'reliever of the wronged' Gustavus Adolphus.[15]

It was the nature of the vocation itself, however, rather than the habits of its practitioners that most exercised pre-war apologists. The law of nature permitted forcible defence 'against violent enemies' and the Bible and the classics offered honourable examples of soldiers engaged in this task.[16] Thomas Barnes, arguing

---

[13] Samuel Bachiler, *The Campe Royall, Set forth in briefe Meditations on the words of the Prophet Moses . . . preached in the Army at the Laager* (1629), 46. Compare [Thomas Barnes], *Vox Belli, or, An Alarum to Warre* (1626), 14–15; Alexander Leighton sensibly observed that soldiers were undervalued in normal times because their 'esteem . . . dies and lives with the necessitie of their service', *Speculum Belli sacri: or the Lookingglasse of the Holy War* ([Amsterdam], 1624), 253. See also C. G. Cruickshank, *Elizabeth's Army* (Oxford, 1966), 23–30.

[14] Henry Ferne, *The camp at Gilgal. Or, a view of the King's army, and spirituall provision made for it* (1643), 2–3, 9, 13–15, 21.

[15] *The Swedish Intelligencer. The first part . . . Now for the third time, Revised, Corrected, and augmented* (1632), 'Preface to the Reader', 3; A[lexander] Gil, *The New Starr of the North, Shining upon the Victorious King of Sweden* (1632), 44.

[16] Adams, *Souldiers Honour*, 23; Bernard, *Bible-Battells*, 29, 31–7.

that it was a duty to be active in God's business through one's calling, concluded that the soldier's duty lay in 'workes of bloud, (he being a *man of Warre*)' and quoted Jeremiah's 'terrible' text: 'Cursed be he that keepeth backe his sword from bloud.'[17] Other less sanguine texts and cases were marshalled to show God's approval. How else could the plethora of references to soldiers in the Old Testament be explained, or the presence of the religious centurion in the New Testament? Why should St Paul have told the Hebrews that they had 'not yet resisted unto Bloud' if it was not to urge them to prepare for war?[18] The arguments may seem less than compelling, but they reveal on the one hand the apologists' sense that there was a case to be answered, and on the other a belief that the present age formed part of a 'History of Holy Warres' that self-evidently validated the soldier's vocation. In 1643 the royalist Wilde declared that 'the Incense at the Altar burnes the sweeter for the Gunpowder in the Field. The smoak of the Cannon is good or bad, as the cause is so.'[19] Parliamentarians might balk at the incense, but they shared the sentiment.

In much of the justification of war and soldiering the metaphorical and the real converged to strengthen the sense of righteous action in God's cause. In this the pre-war decades were forerunners of the 1640s, when both sides exploited the merging of real and metaphorical holy war. Patrick Collinson has noted the 'affinity, as mental and rhetorical structures, of religion as conflict and the actual violence of real warfare'.[20] Certainly the language of warfare shaped conceptions of the Christian's God and of his own path through the world, and the Bible was mined for terms and images of violence and belligerence. Not only was God a man of war and lord of hosts, but the life of the individual Christian was war: 'Whosoever is a profest Christian, he is a profest Souldier', and Christians 'continue [Christ's] faithfull Souldiers to [their] lives end'.[21] In 1643 Henry Ferne conflated the 'Christian Life' and the 'Spirituall warfare' of the royalists, chosen by God to be soldiers, 'Israelites', and 'Christians'.[22] The image has not died, of course; it survives in the Salvation Army and wherever Christian soldiers march onward as to war. What is today a metaphor, however, was both metaphor and fact to Englishmen before their civil war, and apologists slid from one mode to the other. Spiritual

[17] [Barnes], *Vox belli*, 2.

[18] See e.g. Everard, *Arriereban*, 21–2; Bernard, *Bible-Battells*, 25–[2]6, 28, 34–5; Gouge, *Churches Conquest*, 211; I. Leech, *The trayne Souldier. A Sermon Preached Before the worthy Societie of the Captaynes and Gentle men that exercise Armes in the Artillery Garden* (1619), 1.

[19] [Wilde], *Sermon . . . in St Maries Oxford*, 2.

[20] Patrick Collinson, *The Birthpangs of Protestant England: Religious and Cultural Change in the Sixteenth and Seventeenth Centuries* (1988), 134.

[21] Leech, *trayne Souldier*, 26; John Davenport, *A Royalll Edict for Military Exercises: Published in a Sermon preached to the Captaines, and Gentlemen that exercise Armes in the Artillery Garden at their generall meeting* (1629), 25. Exod 15. 3 was a favourite text, e.g. Adams, *Souldiers Honour*, frontispiece: 'The Lord is a man of warre'.

[22] [Ferne], *Camp at Gilgal*, 4, 22.

and material worlds merged to form a transcendent whole, for in both they fought 'under the colours of our great General Jesus Christ . . . [in] this mystical warre'.[23]

It was not only the character of the religion of Protestants but the character of the threatening world they saw around them that enabled Englishmen so comfortably to accept this mystical conjunction of metaphorical and real war, and to see the latter as both just and godly. The wars so conjured up were fought abroad and primarily by others, but England's treasured domestic peace did not reduce the sense of imminent danger. Although causes and campaigns that mesmerized English attention over the pre-war decades—the disasters of the Palatinate, of Ré and La Rochelle, the mixed fortunes of Germany—varied from year to year, there was one constant: fear of Catholic designs on England. This gave both apologetic and descriptive discussion of war a religious cast that foreshadowed the 1640s. Spain was still invoked as a primal enemy, to be joined by the Austrian Habsburgs and their allies as they became the great field adversary of European Protestantism. In 1619 Jeremy Leech warned of the designs of Spain and Rome: '[W]e heare of great *preparations* that others make abroad . . . it cannot be amisse for us to have an eye to our owne safetie.'[24] Where 'cruell and bloudy Rome' prevailed, declared Thomas Jackson in 1622, an 'iron yoke of captivitie' brought 'murders and massacres' and 'the incredible havocke of thousands and millions'.[25] The representation of contemporary war was tied to anti-Catholicism, and placed in the tradition of just and holy wars.

For the godly party, England and Israel had already, before the civil war, become metaphorically interchangeable and prototypes of the cause of God and Protestantism. The executants of their just, holy, and anti-Catholic wars should aspire to be 'devout men, fearing God', 'the *Lords Worthies, Christian Souldiers*'.[26] Like the Israelites in their struggle against the Canaanites, they fought for 'the defence and propagation of Religion'. If the most vociferous enthusiasm for 'mysticall Warre' conducted by the Christian soldier came from the 'puritan' wing of the English church, these themes were nonetheless already familiar in the 1620s and 1630s to a broad spectrum of English society, both civilian and military. While to modern eyes they may appear hackneyed by overuse, familiarity had not then dimmed their power. They were bipartisanly appealed to in the civil war, as royalist preachers like Ferne and Wilde reveal. The ideas of just war against an ungodly foe and of service in the cause of right religion extended far beyond any narrowly 'puritan' or clerical faction.

If God and the law of nature and nations approved just war in terms readily appropriated by royalists and parliamentarians alike, and if it could be undertaken by Christian soldiers, the terms of approval nevertheless incorporated

---

[23] Adams, *Souldiers Honour*, A3.   [24] Leech, *Trayne Souldier*, 50–1, 57.
[25] Thomas Jackson, *Judah must into Captivitie. Six Sermons On Ierem. 7.16* (1622), 97, 105–6.
[26] Leech, *Trayne Souldier*, second dedication, to Hugh Hammersley; Davenport, *Royall Edict*, 26.

one dangerous element, for they implied that the individual should reflect on whether the cause was truly God's and raised the spectre of private judgement and private conscience. In the 1640s both sides were to wrestle with the consequences. In armies the issue was most commonly one of military discipline, but in and out of the army obedience also raised issues of principle relating to duties not only to military superiors but also to the central authority in the state and hence, by an unavoidable corollary, to a decision about the location of its sovereign power. The problems and arguments were familiar before domestic war made them acute, but responses to this issue of obedience, which often weighed heavily in decisions as to where allegiance properly lay, were to reveal crucial differences between royalists and parliamentarians as they debated the rival claims of king and parliament to ultimate supremacy.[27]

What if private conscience concluded that a war was unjust? Pre-war theorists admitted that the problem was age-old, but they were not dismayed. Their resolution was twofold. First, knowledge might be imperfect, for private men were not privy to reasons of state.[28] Second, and more important, God had granted sovereignty to the ruler for preservation of the common welfare, and decreed the superiority of public to private good. To argue the contrary was 'the ruine of the State, and the perversion of all Lawes both Divine and Humane'.[29] Although the volunteer was indeed free to choose his cause, the conscript was bound by the duty of obedience. Once in arms, both should obey superiors. Many, although by no means all, Englishmen who fought abroad before their own war chose their vocation, their master, and thus the cause they served, but armies of the 1640s were increasingly, after the early days, composed of conscripts and of those—like re-enlisted prisoners—whose choice was hardly free. For conscripts, the question of moral choice—over whether to serve or how to serve—was moot: 'They who are sent by lawfull authority unto lawfull warre, must go.' That authority was 'the comma[n]d of such as God hath set over us', and was exercised for the benefit of the state: 'Souldiers owe to common peace and safety the service of executing their Governors commands of waging warre.'[30] Here of course the problem of the evil ruler arose, but it was briskly resolved, for in virtually every case—even when the ruler was an infidel—the duty of obedience to constituted authority overrode that to private conscience. The soldier might fight for a sacrilegious king, obeying him without scruples unless he was ordered to do something that clearly and certainly contravened God's command. Mere doubt and moral discomfort did not justify disobedience, and God's commands and the laws of war between them admitted a wide range of

---

[27] For a comparison of royalist and parliamentarian approaches to the issues of obedience, allegiance, and sovereignty within the context of God's overarching design, see B. Donagan, 'Casuistry and Allegiance in the English Civil War', in Derek Hirst and Richard Strier (eds.), *Writing and Political Engagement in Seventeenth-Century England* (Cambridge, 1999), 89–111.

[28] Everard, *Arrierban*, 31–2.   [29] Bedell, *Free Schoole of Warrre*, K/ii(2).

[30] Gouge, *Churches Conquest*, 247; Bernard, *Bible-Battells*, 63–7.

dismaying actions. The king might be guilty through 'iniquity of commanding, but the order of serving may prove the souldier to be innocent'.[31] We have arrived at the Nuremberg defence. As Sutcliffe had said, 'if the iniustice of warres be not notorious, the subject is bound to pay and serve, and the guilt shall be laid to his charge that commandeth him to serve . . . the injustice of the commandement shall bind the Prince, as the dutie of obedience doth make the soldier innocent'.[32]

The problem of notorious injustice remained but in practice civil war guides to soldiers' conduct were to emphasize the Nuremberg defence over anxieties of conscience. In the political sphere, the problem of 'lawfull authority' grew more vexing, as parliamentarians were forced to allow a larger place to 'right intention' and first to fudge and ultimately to redefine 'right . . . authority',[33] but in the armies of both sides discipline and effective action required the subordination of private moral responsibility to the proper authority of superiors. Pre-war apologists had already made it clear that God's authority supported the obvious military necessity for obedient soldiers.

Much in pre-war theory thus usefully prepared the way for the circumstances of civil war. It was part of the shared heritage of future enemies. Yet if war against infidels was readily acceptable the awkwardness of war against Christians was compounded when they were Protestant countrymen. William Gouge had reassured his readers, however, not only that some Christians (notably papists) could be as great enemies to the true faith as infidels, but also that the cause of a war was more significant than the identity of those against whom it was waged. This was a useful principle when it was waged against fellow Protestants. Yet Gouge further argued that papists were to Protestants as the Amalekites were to the Israelites, a parallel that raised horrible possibilities given the fate of the Amalekites. It was possible to offend so deeply that a people or group moved into the category of 'other' for whom humane and Christian restraints were waived; they were 'hateful to God' and 'by God devoted to utter destruction'.[34] This argument opened the way for relegation of the Irish to a category to which normal restraints need not apply.

These issues of whom one could legitimately fight and how one could fight them haunt study of the civil war and raise a broader question about seventeenth-century England: how was ideology to be adapted to suit social needs and inclinations? Here too a pre-war theorist had prepared the way. In 1625 that moderate and cosmopolitan cleric William Bedell published a translation of the Venetian Paolo Sarpi's *Free Schoole of Warre* that addressed the problem of military service across confessional lines (specifically, of Italians in Dutch service). It distinguished between aid to heretics in support of their doctrine,

---

[31] Gouge, *Churches Conquest*, 248.
[32] Sutcliffe, *Lawes of Armes*, 12; see Bernard, *Bible-Battells*, 66–7, for Bernard's appropriation of Sutcliffe's argument.
[33] Davenport, *Royall Edict*, 2–3.
[34] Gouge, *Churches Conquest*, 213, 271, 292, 295; on the Amalekites, see 1 Sam. 15.

and aid to heretics for reasons of friendship, kindred, gratitude, good nature, want, or need. To deny aid of this latter kind would be a 'flat prohibition of all offices of humanitie and good workes'.[35] The persistence of such 'offices of humanitie and good workes' between enemies, as of the ties of kin and kindness, will be evident in the pages that follow. Once again, pre-war apologetics had foreshadowed wartime issues in asserting that opposition to a principle did not entail inhumanity to its adherents. If just war was legitimate, and if its justified practices included the draconian and the cruel, it nonetheless did not override private obligations of charity and relationship—but only if they could be safely indulged without military disadvantage.

The enthusiastic embrace of traditional justifications of just war in England in the first half of the seventeenth century was in part a consequence of national perception of embattled Protestantism. The rhetoric of godly warfare and saints in arms was already familiar, as was the call for radically changed, morally reformed soldiers that was later to be heard in the armies of both sides. The nature and terms of legitimation of war reflected the country's integration into international military and intellectual culture. That integration was apparent not only in shared apologetics but in interest in and knowledge of its contemporary continental practice. It is time now to turn to these aspects of pre-war 'formation'.

---

[35] B[edell], *Free Schoole*, F iii. Venice, engaged in a struggle against the papacy, offered the opportunity to indulge in anti-papist rhetoric while supporting a Catholic power. Sarpi had justified the Protestant Dutch against the Spanish, his fellow Catholics, on the ground that the Dutch were engaged in a defensive and therefore just war. Ibid., I ii–iii.

2

Man's Wars

When Englishmen looked back sadly to their 'former Halcyon days of peace' they saw them through a golden haze that intensified their sense of loss: '*England* . . . the Paradise of the world, is now become our *Babylon* And by these waters of *Morah* do we sit down, and weep to remember thee, our Brittish Sion.'[1] If some had found the 1630s less than idyllic, all could agree, when they looked across the Channel, on their good fortune in not being as others were: England, enjoying 'the Sun-shine of true quiet' and 'blessed fruits of peace', was the envy of 'forraine Nations'.[2] This sense of English exceptionalism was not isolationist or hermetic. Rather it reflected intense awareness of and anxiety about continental events, as Clarendon clearly saw:

the Happiness of the times . . . was invidiously set off by this distinction, that every other Kingdom, every other State were entangled, and allmost destroyed, by the rage and fury of Arms; those who were engaged in an ambitious contention, with their Neighbours, having the view, and apprehensions of their Miseries, and Desolation, which they saw other States suffer by a Civil War.[3]

The prospect of contemporary Europe fostered recognition of the fragility of peace and order and of vulnerability to foreign and Catholic threat. The chorus

---

[1] Daniel Featley, *Roma Ruens, Romes Ruine* (1644), 'To the unknown reader'; see also R[ichard] H[arwood], *The loyall Subiect's retiring-roome. Opened in a sermon at St Maries, on the 13th day of Iuly, . . . 1645* (Oxford, 1645), 2. Nostalgia was not confined to royalists; see e.g. the presbyterian Eleazar Gilbert, *The Prelatical Cavalier Catechized, and Protestant Souldier incouraged. By a Missive sent to King Charles in the name of the Protestants beyond Seas* (1645), 27. I owe the latter citation to Ian Green.

[2] *The German History Continued. The Seventh Part* (1634), XI. 1; Huntington Library, EL MS 6879. Recognition of England's good fortune was not new, but it grew more intense in the 1630s. For the 1620s see Samuel Buggs, *Miles Mediterraneus. The Mid-land Souldier*, bound with Philemon Holland, *A Learned, Elegant, and Religious Speech Delivered unto his Most excellent Maiestie* (1622), publisher's preface: '(alas) wee see all Christendome be up in armes, besides our selves'; and Jackson, *Judah must into Captivitie*, 95, 97, 105–6. See also David L. Smith, 'The Fourth Earl of Dorset and the Personal Rule of Charles I', *JBS* 30 (1991), 271–2, for Dorset on England's happy and blessed 'dissimilitude' from '[o]ur neighbour countrys'. For shadows on this picture, see ibid. 277–85, and Graham Parry, 'A Troubled Arcadia', in T. Healy and J. Sawday (eds.), *Literature and the English Civil War* (Cambridge, 1990), 38–41, 46–50. For Clarendon's famous assessment of the 'Blessings' and 'Tranquillity' of the 1630s, see Clarendon, *History*, i. 59–60. See also Kevin Sharpe, *The Personal Rule of Charles I* (New York, 1992), 603–25, for a discussion of 'felicity' and infelicity in the 1630s.

[3] Clarendon, *History*, i. 58–9.

of publication, both religious and secular, urging military preparedness at home while regaling readers with the sufferings of Protestant brethren abroad, swelled after the outbreak of the Thirty Years' War in 1618. Reports that revealed the power of the worst in human nature and the frightening consequences when the restraints of law, custom, and charity were broken, shaped English fears when war came to Britain. If the Scottish wars, ill-managed and unsuccessful as they were for England, offered little more than the usual disasters of war, the Irish rebellion of 1641 appeared to bring the horrors of Germany close to home and to inflict them on English Protestants. When, in the 1640s, England experienced her own excesses, perpetrated by Englishmen, it was the spectre of La Rochelle and Germany that rose before them. This section will look at some of the elements that contributed to this domestic anxiety.

English views of war, as we have seen, derived from a common European tradition, on to which were grafted strident Protestant and nationalist overtones. Even as English apologists legitimated war and preached Protestant crusade, however, they conceded that war brought the abandonment of Christian standards and that its soldiers were all too likely to be 'corrupted men, *to whom it is a sport to destroy houses, to rob Churches, to ravish virgins, to ruinate cities*'.[4] In the 1620s and 1630s this was not mere rhetoric. English men and women knew in gruesome detail that contemporary Europe exemplified all these horrors and more. Wars in the Low Countries, France, and Germany were vividly described in print, letters, and conversation at home, and provided a school of arms abroad. In one sense indeed their horrors were not new. Shakespeare's audience had needed no gloss to understand what was going on in *Henry V*: 'waste and desolation . . . heady murder, spoil, and villainy', fire, rape, and massacre, were all part of popular knowledge of war.[5] For each generation however there are particular events that by their immediacy have special vividness, poignancy, and power to shock.

France and Germany had this quality for British audiences before war was domesticated on home ground. In the 1620s the fate of the Palatinate, renewed war in the Low Countries, and the fortunes of English troops engaged in those and related campaigns, aroused deep public anxiety and controversy, while the impact of England's own war with France, from 1627 to 1629, was sharp and intimate. Not only was England's role inglorious, but the fate of soldiers and civilians alike aroused outrage, pity, and horror that extended beyond London and the political classes.[6] The expedition to the Isle of Ré took a terrible toll and losses of officers and men resonated through the families of great and

---

[4] [Barnes], *Vox belli*, A2, 14; Leech, *Trayne Band*, 46–7; and see generally Gouge, *Gods Three Arrowes*.

[5] *Henry V*, 3. 3. See Theodor Meron, *Henry's Wars and Shakespeare's Laws. Perspectives on the Law of War in the Later Middle Ages* (Oxford, 1993) for discussion of stage war as a reflection of the laws and practices of real war.

[6] *William Whiteway of Dorchester: His Diary 1618 to 1635*, ed. David Underdown, Dorset Record Society, 12 (1991), 89, 92, 90–9.

humble alike. In a single engagement, according to one report, colonels like Sir Charles Rich and Sir Alexander Brett died with their men to the number of two thousand; another set the total at four thousand.[7] If many died ignominiously and by accident instead of at the hands of the enemy, this too educated as to what really happened in war, for the 'miscarriages' of the Ré expedition were notorious.[8]

The war with France brutally reminded Englishmen of the costs of war in soldiers' lives and money, while the fate of Protestant La Rochelle brought home what could happen to civilians. Accounts of its prolonged siege and the consequences in famine, broken taboos, and indiscriminate suffering both fascinated and horrified. Nehemiah Wallington, a London turner, recorded in his diary a cousin's graphic eye-witness report from the fallen, starving city, where the survivors 'looked like anatomies', and where engrained taboos—against eating human flesh and against mutilation of the dead—were breached when poor people were driven by hunger to cut off the butttocks of dead men as they lay unburied in churchyards. Wallington believed that some sixteen thousand had died of famine and that suffering was prolonged by scarcity and inflation. Such knowledge was not limited to London or those—like Wallington or the Barrington family in Essex—with relations in La Rochelle. In Dorchester, for example, William Whiteway reported that when the city surrendered there were 'but 4000 Persons alive in it, 18000 being dead with famine'.[9] Knowledge of England's humiliating and ineffectual intervention was thus joined to knowledge of the suffering war had brought to French Protestants. The fate of civilians in prolonged civil war sieges such as Pendennis and Colchester only confirmed fears shaped well before 1642. When the earl of Norwich joked at Colchester in 1648 that the starving inhabitants might eat their children, he evoked memories of continental barbarities. The decade after 1618 reminded forcefully not only that God's arrows did not discriminate as to their targets, killing civilians as readily as soldiers, but also that courage and bloodshed did not ensure the triumph of his cause.

[7] *CSPDom. 1627–1628*, 419; Whiteway, *Diary*, 92. See BL Add. MS 46,188, fo. 104 for a list of officer casualties.

[8] Magdelene College, Cambridge, Pepys MS 2099, fos. 33–34ᵛ; BL Add. MS 46,188, fo. 104, and see fos. 30, 32; *CSPDom. 1627–1628*, 419–20, 422–3, 438–9, 474, 535: one writer observed that his 'soul melt[ed] with tears to think that a state should send so many men and no provision at all for them'. See also Whiteway, *Diary*, 92, and for detailed and damning reports of the expedition, Magdelene College, Cambridge, Pepys MS 2099, fos. 26–36ᵛ (an account of 'that untoward service'), and HEH, HA 45148, 'Relation of the Occurrances happening . . . in the Isle de Ree'.

[9] BL Add. MS 21935, fos. 80–80ᵛ; Whiteway, *Diary*, 99; *Barrington Family Letters 1628–1632*, ed. Arthur Searle, Camden Society, 4th ser. 28, (1983), 41, 253; HEH, HA 45148 (a volume containing MS copies of accounts of Ré and La Rochelle; no pagination), 'The State of Rochell at the King's entrance thereinto, 1628' (an account setting the death toll from starvation at 15,000 and estimating that when the siege ended there were only 3,000–4,000 survivors, of whom many had since died); he too reported that the flesh of the dead had been eaten.

The struggle that began in 1618 and ranged across 'Germany', that vast central European area that stretched from the Baltic to the Alps and from Holland to Hungary, evoked even more sustained interest and fascinated horror. Like the struggle against Spain, it was a Protestant crusade against Rome, Antichrist, the whore of Babylon and Habsburg aggression. It had a royal, British, and Protestant heroine in James I's daughter Elizabeth, the Winter Queen, driven from her husband's rightful domain, the Palatinate. In Gustavus Adolphus it had a dazzling Protestant hero whose star was prematurely eclipsed. And it had an extensive and sensational literature of misery, terror, and titillating sadism that overlapped with sober narratives of current history and works of military instruction. The anxieties and emotions of a wide public were deeply engaged. '[T]he whole Nation', said Clarendon. 'was sollicitous to know what pass'd weekly in *Germany* and *Poland*, and all other parts of Europe', and they found their information in many ways.[10] Print was reinforced by stomach-turning illustrations and confirmed by letters and word of mouth, and this mosaic of information fed and sustained public interest.[11] William Whiteway of Dorchester began his diary in 1618, and as the year ended he wrote: 'It was Reported that there was a great stir in Bohemia about choosing them a king, who it is hoped shall be a Protestant.' In 1635, in the last entry before his death, he summarized the latest moves in the war that sprang from the events behind that innocent sentence.[12]

Virtually all English consumers of this news were fervently committed to the Protestant cause, whether or not they favoured official and military intervention and whether or not they originally had reservations about the Elector Palatine's claim.[13] Despite this pro-Palatine bias political, military, and diplomatic news was subjected to critical examination, but the response to news of another kind was less analytic and more complex. Accounts of social breakdown and atrocity were on the whole taken at face value. We may now recognize that many of the stories had a formulaic similarity to atrocities reported in many wars and all ages, but at the time they were widely circulated, luridly illustrated, and uncritically received; at their further edge they joined the literature of prodigies, portents,

---

[10] Clarendon, *History*, i. 88.

[11] See Richard Cust, 'News and Politics in Early Seventeenth-Century England', *PP* 112 (1986), 62–6. The title-page of [P. Vincent], *The Lamentations of Gemany. Wherein, As in a Glass, we may behold her miserable condition, and reade the woefull effects of sinne* (1638), noted that it was 'illustrated by Pictures, the more to affect the Reader'.

[12] Whiteway, *Diary*, 24, 159.

[13] The Habsburg incumbent represented *de facto* power and magistracy and hence raised issues of obedience to established power, whereas support for the Elector introduced a destabilizing element into foreign policy. For James I's reservations in 1621 see Glyn Redworth, 'Of Pimps and Princes: Three Unpublished Letters from James I and the Prince of Wales relating to the Spanish Match', *HJ* 37 (1994), 403–4, 407–8; and see Smith, 'Fourth Earl of Dorset', 271–7, for a non-interventionist position. See also Walker, *Historical Discourses*, 321–2, and note the dissemination of manuscript discussions as to 'whether the cause of the state of Bohemia be just or not', e.g. Derbyshire RO, Gell MSS, D258, 31/80.

prophetic comets, and 'Battailes in the Ayre'.[14] In December 1642 observers reported another heavenly battle, now between royalist and parliamentarian armies, 'with Ensignes displayed Drums beating, Musquets going off, Cannons discharged, Horses neyghing', and accompanied by the groans of the dying. The reporter was quick to draw the parallel between these 'strange and portentous Apparitions' and their German forerunners. Parliamentarian propagandists in particular were to exploit the themes of atrocity and portents as they assimilated past to present, emphasizing the continuum of suffering and of Catholic threat. In 1646 John Vicars called up the past:

[W]itnesse, O witnesse, the Oceans of Christian blood shed all over desolate *Germany*, and in speciall the ruine of the *Palatinate*, . . . witnesse . . . the blood of most wofully ruinated *Rochell*, and all the brave *English* blood spilt in the Isle of *Ree*, . . . witnesse . . . the late most lamentable *Irish Massacres*, of almost 200000 *English* innocent soules there. Yea, witnesse all the (still) fresh gashes and bleedings, or rather gushing streams, nay floods of blood, of *Scotland* and *England* to this day.[15]

More important, however, than the sensationalism of the reports from Germany was their unrelenting picture of social, economic, and demographic collapse. It was uncritically accepted, but much was nonetheless true. Edward Walker, a traveller in Germany in 1636 and King Charles's wartime secretary believed that only eye-witnesses could comprehend the reality and that those who brought war upon England might have been deterred 'had [they] but seen . . . the Calamities the War . . . brought upon . . . all . . . Places of *Germany*'.[16] Yet if accounts of Germany appalled English men and women, there was an element of enthusiastic enjoyment of the horrible, a conjunction of excitement and fear, that combined with anti-Catholicism to blunt critical faculties. War in Germany, as seen from England, embodied all the conventional horrors of war and added new elements of atrocity and terror.[17] In all wars, admittedly, Christian standards and the unwritten laws of war that should protect the weak, helpless, and holy and moderate the conduct of soldiers to each other were at risk, but horrors reached their apogee in Germany. Soldiers perpetrated appalling atrocities against

---

[14] [L. Brinckmair], *The Warnings of Germany. By Wonderfull Signes, and strange Prodigies* (1638)**4 and ff. ('Preface', #11), and B–B3; Vincent's *Lamentations* (ch. 2, pp. following B2), shows 'the blazing starre 1617' appearing as portentous warning above a group of sociable, prosperous citizens enjoying al fresco food and drink in a vine arbour. The accompanying pictures on this page chart the decline to a world of horror: one is captioned 'burgers and ministers . . . in prison', and the last graphically portrays 'a divine tortured with a Catt'.

[15] John Vicars, *The Burning-Bush not Consumed*, 322–3, in idem, *Magnalia Dei Anglicana. Or, Englands Parliamentary Chronicle* (1646).

[16] Walker, *Historical Discourses*, 215.

[17] The frontispiece to the volume containing [Vincent], *Lamentations of Germany*; [Brinckmair], *Warnings of Germany*; and *Lacrymae Germaniae: or, The Teares of Germany. Unfolding her woefull Distresse by Jerusalems Calamity* (1638) shows a map of Germany surrounded by armies in massed combat before a once peaceful city; mothers driven by hunger to cannibalize their children; men, women, and infants fleeing a burning town; and a skeletal death stalking a pestilential land.

each other and against civilians; plague, famine, and violence depopulated the country; humankind reverted to cannibalism and desecration of the dead.[18] The linked pleasures of revulsion and attraction that were to be enthusiastically and bipartisanly exploited in the cause of God and right by civil war publicists were already present in the production and reception of accounts of contemporary European war.

Modern scholarship has revised the traditional accounts of universal German horror and devastation, but the accuracy of these contemporary English perceptions is irrelevant here; they were strong and widespread, and they did not derive only from propagandist Protestant sermons or feverish atrocity publications.[19] In 1637 an account of the earl of Arundel's diplomatic travels the previous year conveyed a sense of quotidian horror through its repetitive catalogue of burnt, plundered, depopulated, famished towns and villages. Robert Monro's account of his ten years' service in Denmark and Germany with Scottish regiments joined matter-of-fact narration of military and diplomatic affairs to reports of massacre, sack, and burning.[20] The earliest forerunners of English newspapers kept the miseries of Germany before the public eye. They celebrated the triumphs of Gustavus Adolphus, but they also spread news of the 'annihilation' of Magdeburg in 1631, a city of 20,000 that Gustavus failed to save, which was sacked, burnt, and razed and whose fate echoed throughout Europe.[21] In these narratives a country once prosperous and peaceful had become a scene of death, cruelty, and 'universall desolation'.[22] Present peace and prosperity, it was clear, did not protect against the consequences of future war.

The Thirty Years' War thus represented an exceptional concentration of the conventional miseries of war, but it also seemed to differ qualitatively from other wars in its reversion to atrocity, barbarity, and lawlessness. The bonds of civilization had broken for soldiers and civilians alike, and those who traditionally merited special protection were equally victims with combatants. 'I have seene [the Croats] beat out the braines of poore old decrepid women, as in sport',

---

[18] *German History Continued*, II. 11–12, 49–51; IV. 56, 59–60, V. 1–2; [Vincent], *Lamentations*, 26, 29, 53, and illustrations *passim*.

[19] For discussions of the realities of the Thirty Years' War in Germany, see Henry Kamen, 'The Economic and Social Consequences of the Thirty Years' War', *PP* 39 (1968), 44–61; C. R. Friedrichs, 'The War and German Society', in Geoffrey Parker, *The Thirty Years' War* (1984), 208–15. See also Ian Roy, 'England Turned Germany? The Aftermath of the Civil War in its European Context', *TRHS* 5th ser. 28 (1978), 127–44.

[20] William Crowne, *A True Relation of all the Remarkable Places and Passages Observed in the Travels of the right honourable Thomas Lord Howard, Earle of Arundell and Surrey . . . 1636* (1637), 5, 9, 12–14, 17–25, 27–38, 46, 58; [Robert Monro], *Monro His Expedition with the Worthy Scots Regiment (called Mac-Keyes Regiment) levied in August 1626* (1637), *passim*.

[21] On Magdeburg see ibid. 2. 43, 45: some five years later Monro reported that Magdeburg's houses could not 'this day be seen, what for houses they were'. See also Gil, *New Starr of the North*, 22–4; Parker, *Thirty Years' War*, 125; *The Swedish Intelligencer. The first part* (1632, 'Now for the third time, Revised, Corrected, and augmented'), 117–19.

[22] [Vincent], *Lamentations*, 33–4; see also Crowne, *True Relation*, 39.

reported Philip Vincent, but the numbing of the moral sensibilities of victims
horrified him almost as much:

It is now growne so usuall with the poore people to see one slaine before anothers
face, that (as though there were no relation, no affection of neighbourhood, kindred or
friendship among them) none compassionateth almost, none crieth out, oh my father, or
oh my brother![23]

Germany and the Thirty Years' War, as represented in England, thus combined
the traditional miseries of war with a new reversion to moral and social chaos. A
lurid and breathless catalogue of 1638 epitomized the 'warnings' that Germany
offered to England:

How many fruitfull Countries, Dominions, and Territories are . . . totally ruinated; the
Cities, Towns, and Villages therein spoiled, and made pillars of fire and smoke; the
Churches lying desolate, the woods being cut down, the earth untilled, and lying waste.
The bloody and cruell dealing of inhumane souldiers, especially of the *Crabats* [Croats],
in many goodly Townes and Cities, is scarce credible, which furiously have plundered the
places, torturing the Inhabitants most barbarously; ravished women even to death; . . . and
generally used them with such barbarous cruelty, that many begged to be shot or slain
instantly, rather than to live, and be partakers of such misery. Some they have rosted alive,
and sacked the Cities miserably, that they spoiled what they could not carry away . . . and
left the places so bare, that many of the best rank, . . . were glad to feed upon roots and
water: spoiled the Inhabitants of their garments, exposed them to that nakednesse, that
neither man, woman, nor childe have had clothes to put on. No man indeed can be
ignorant of the miserable condition of all *Germany*.[24]

Like other accounts of atrocities the passage raises questions of truth and
exaggeration, but it contains incidents that became familiar through frequent
repetition and illustration. It shows the tendency to find a scapegoat, a worst
among the bad, to whom any wickedness can be attributed: here the Croats
played a role later assigned to the Irish. And it reveals an awareness that there are
laws of war, for the list assumes that 'rules' have been breached.

The final and perhaps most disturbing component in this view of Europe was
that horrors were inflicted bipartisanly. Atrocity was not defined by confession or
nation. 'We' as well as 'they' could lapse into barbarism and inhumanity. Protestant Englishmen of course emphasized Catholic evil, but they acknowledged
the '[i]nfinite and unspeakable . . . cruelties, which have . . . beene exercised by
the furious Souldiers on all sides'.[25] The war gave new force to old recognition

---

[23] [Vincent], *Lamentations*, 30, and see 3–13, ch. 3, 'Of Tortures and Torments'. For other
characteristic 'atrocities', see e.g. [Brinckmair], *Warnings of Germany*, 52, and compare *Swedish
Intelligencer*, 1. 124.

[24] [Brinckmair], *Warnings of Germany*, 4–5. See also the appalling report of the fate of Hochstadt
in Swabia, *German History . . . The Seventh Part*, ch. IV. 49–51, which prefigured English accounts
of the Irish rebellion.

[25] [Vincent], *Lamentations*, 11. Sir Thomas Barrington characterized a Swedish general as a
'careless and bestiall man . . . a salvage beast . . . crewell'. *Barrington Family Letters*, 243.

that civilized and Christian standards were fragile and that, under pressure, 'the *Protestants* (the more the pity) as [well as] the *Papists*' abandoned them.[26] In Dorchester in 1635 Whiteway, reporting a collection for relief of the Palatinate, noted that its purpose was to offset the effects of Protestant 'protection' of inhabitants who had 'suffred far more under the Swedes and French who came to helpe them, then ever they did under the Spaniards and Imperialists, so that they longed for their Government again'.[27] The English civil war was to confirm that friends could be as dangerous as enemies. Meanwhile, when Englishmen looked at Europe they saw not only 'natural' calamities of war such as battle and disease, but also dangers of a spiral of barbarous reprisal that threatened future as well as present society.[28] The horrors of Germany were not forgotten in the 1640s.

This English knowledge of continental war during their own halcyon days of peace deserves attention. On the one hand it habituated a large public to detailed, informed, often highly coloured reports of political and military operations in war. On the other, it formed expectations as to the nature of war and contributed to the anxiety and nervousness of civilians as war approached at home. Sensational news from Germany may well have conditioned the English public to heightened response to reports of cruelty, sexual outrage, and broken taboos, and contributed to the violence of the reaction to the Irish rebellion of 1641, which in turn cast a long shadow over the civil war years. Certainly the literature of Irish atrocities echoed that of Germany with which Englishmen were already familiar. The accounts of Germany, by suggesting that it was not only Protestant Christianity that was threatened but the bonds of civility and society, evoked singular fear and dismay. They heightened awareness, once war came to England, of the need to observe the codes that could moderate its worst excesses and preserve the conditions that could render post-war reconciliation feasible. The narratives of Europe that had made the horrors of uncontrolled war disturbingly familiar haunted memory. La Rochelle and Germany became preludes to the 'lamented . . . *Massacres*' of the Irish rebellion and hence, to parliamentarian propagandists, to their own civil war.[29] When Birmingham burnt in 1643, one gentleman confessed to 'the deepest Apprehensions . . . as presenting to my view a picture of the present estate of *Germany*, and as by a prospective shewing me (not very farre off) the Scene translated from thence

---

[26] [Vincent], *Lamentations*, 'Preface Exhortatory' and 33. Reprisal, as always, raised awkward problems but although e.g. the Swedes burned 2,000 Bavarian villages 'in revenge of the *Palatine* cause', in Protestant eyes they remained better than the Imperialists. For a private report of such Swedish retaliation, see BL Add. MS 46,188, fo. 143; and Gouge, *Churches Conquest*, 271, 344–5, for oblique approaches to this issue.

[27] Whiteway, *Diary*, 158.

[28] See [Vincent], *Lamentations*, 63, on 'wounds [that] will not in haste be recured, and perhaps posterity for some generations will see the scarres'.

[29] Vicars, *Burning-Bush*, 322–3; and see Samuel Kem, *The Messengers Preparation For an Address to The King For a Well-grounded Peace* (1644), 10–11.

hither'.[30] The siege of Colchester evoked the 'smoaky ruines of Magdeburgh', established in popular memory as a paradigm of war that spared neither civilian nor soldier, and as a disaster that rivalled the destruction of Troy or Jerusalem.[31] When precarious restraint between native enemies threatened to break down, warnings of 'animosity and cruelty' destructive of 'charity, compassion and brotherly affection' recalled earlier 'German' literature.[32] An appeal for peace in 1644 drew its title from the literature of the Thirty Years' War. The *Teares of Germany* had become *England's Teares*, for '[t]he German . . . hath now a Co-partner in his miseries'.[33]

In England's halcyon days, then, war was vividly present in English minds although still absent from English soil. A literature of cruelties and social breakdown, its message intensified by anti-Catholic polemic, had shaped national consciousness of war. La Rochelle and Magdeburg and countless towns and villages warned that civilians would not be spared. The fates of innumerable officers—many of them from families soon to be deeply engaged in the civil war—and of legions of humbler men, and indeed of the great Gustavus Adolphus himself, reminded of the end awaiting the soldier. Yet while England looked abroad with horror and dismay, the practice of war in contemporary Europe prepared English soldiers to fight at home.

[30] 'A Letter written from Walshall by a Worthy Gentleman to his friend in Oxford, concerning Burmingham', in *Four Tracts relative to The Battle of Birmingham Anno domini 1643*, ed. L. Jay (Birmingham, 1931), 21.

[31] e.g. *Pond's almanack for the yeare of our Lord Christ 1649* (Cambridge, 1649), A4; J[ean] Parival, *The History of this Iron Age: Wherein is set down the true state of Europe, as it was in the year 1500 . . . till this present year 1656*, tr. B. Harris (1656), 131–2, 135, on the city's 'utter ruine' and 'the smoaky ruines of Magdeburgh'.

[32] BL Add. MS 11,331, fos. 75^v, 76^v.

[33] [James Howell], *England's Teares, for the present Wars* (1644), A3–A3^v, 3–4.

3

Military Educations

Englishmen in the 1620s and 1630s thought about the justification and nature of war in terms that prefigured the 1640s, and they knew about its practice in contemporary Europe, but such familiarity did not necessarily prepare them to fight a war of their own. It has been common, from Clarendon's day to our own, to assume that pre-war England was unmilitary, a 'land utterly unprepared for war'. In 1642, said Clarendon, the country was 'unapt' as well as 'uninclined' for war.[1] More recently, some historians have seen England's halcyon days as a new chivalric heyday, in which residual feudal displays gave way to a more refined, more idealized, less military expression of political culture. In this view, such military experience as there was reflected an old-fashioned chivalric romanticism rather than modern, practical professionalism. In fact, however, England was far better prepared to embark on a war than either contemporary self-congratulation at the rapid emergence of capable soldiers from so pacific an environment or modern revisionism have suggested. This pre-war preparation was of two kinds. The first was literary and intellectual, the second practical and professional. Yet even the first was no ivory tower entertainment. The interest of authors and readers, civilians and soldiers, was rooted in the real military world of their own day and closely linked to preparation of the second kind, for the profession of arms was alive and well in pre-war England despite the fact that its practitioners had to pursue their vocation abroad.

'AMMANUENSES OF THE SWORD': WRITING WAR

The literature of war educated many men and women in halcyon, peaceful England in aspects of war that ranged from its moral economy to the minutiae of infantry drill. It was at once cosmopolitan, Protestant, and insular. It comprehended current history and accounts of atrocity and social breakdown, but also the most pragmatic of soldiers' manuals. It appealed to ancient and modern wisdom, to Alexander and Caesar as well as Maurice of Nassau and

[1] Edward N. Luttwak, 'Au-dessus de la mêlée', *TLS*, 29 Jan. 1994: review of L. Freedman *et al.* (eds.), *War, Strategy and International Politics*; Clarendon, *History*, i. 421; and compare G. M. Trevelyan, *History of England* (New York, 1928), 408, on 'that most civilian of societies'.

Gustavus Adolphus. It was exotic and domestic, focusing as readily on Bavarian peasants as on members of the Yarmouth artillery company. Personal narratives and atrocity literature, some at first sight only marginally military, recounted strategy, tactics, and reasons for success and failure.[2] Interest in this news from Europe's multiple fronts, with its mixed social and military message, was not confined to an educated elite or the political world of London and the court.

English works formed part of that 'flood of books dealing with the conduct and technology of war' that Hale has noted in sixteenth- and early seventeenth-century western Europe.[3] They translated, commented on and re-presented French, Dutch, Swedish, and classical writers: the upholders of the modern 'science of war' did not ignore the wisdom of the ancients, whose authority derived from the sensible and universal military truths they dispensed and their instruction in practices that had become rare in the contemporary military landscape. This conjunction of ancient and modern, practical and theoretical authority was not new. Fluellen, we recall, had technical objections to the way the walls of Harfleur were being mined (the 'concavities . . . [were] not sufficient' so that the mines were 'not according to the disciplines of the war'), but he also argued for 'the discipline of the pristine wars of the Romans'.[4]

The diverse military literature of the decades before the war ranged from the narrative to the broadly prescriptive to the minutely didactic. Some works, like John Cruso's *Militarie Instructions for the Cavallrie* of 1632, or Robert Monro's *Monro His Expedition with the Worthy Scots Regiment* of 1637, were large, elegant, sophisticated, and demanding. Others accommodated less affluent and less educated readers. Thomas Fisher's *Warlike Directions* of 1634 came in a handy pocket size, its hundred pages designed 'to instruct . . . an unexperienced Souldier' and to be accessible 'to the lowest and meanest capacity'. Some were little more than pamphlets, like the government-sponsored *Instructions for Musters and Armes* of 1631, a strictly practical craft manual designed for wide distribution in the hope of raising the lamentable standards of county trained bands.[5] Yet these and many similar works shared a common instructive purpose and drew on a common subject matter: the art and science of war

---

[2] See B. Donagan, 'Halcyon Days and the Literature of War: England's Military Education before 1642', *PP* 147 (1995), 65–100.

[3] John Hale, 'The Military Education of the Officer Class in Early Modern Europe', in Hale, *Renaissance War Studies*, 233.

[4] Shakespeare, *Henry V*, 3. 2.

[5] [John Cruso], *Militarie Instructions for the Cavallrie: or Rules and Directions for the Service of Horse, Collected out of Divers Forrain Authors Ancient and Modern, and Rectified and Supplied, According to the present Practice of the Low-Countrey Warres* (Cambridge, 1632); Monro, *Expedition*; T[homas] F[isher], *Warlike Directions: or the Souldiers Practice. Set forth for the benefit of all such as are, or will be Scholars of Martiall Discipline. But especially for all such Officers as are not yet setled, or rightly grounded in the Arte of Warre* (2nd edn. 1643), A2 (published with minor corrections to the 1st edn. of 1634); *Instructions for Musters and Armes, And the use thereof: By order from the Lords of His Maiesties most Honourable Privie Counsaile* (1631; earlier versions appeared in 1623 and 1626). The titles of Cruso and Fisher make their didactic purpose clear.

as recently and currently practised in Europe, particularly the Low Countries and Germany, so that even Caesar and Alexander were viewed through a modern prism.[6] They shared a professional, practical approach that was both self-consciously modern and designed for use. Cruso demonstrated high technical expertise, while the old soldiers Monro and Fisher were part of a brotherhood of European veterans of whom a remarkable number passed on their accumulated experience in print: Henry Hexham's *Principles of the Art Militarie* of 1637 reflected four decades of service in the Netherlands, and the artillery expert John Roberts' *Compleat Cannoniere* of 1639 drew on his own experience in the Low Countries to set out 'the Chiefe grounds and principals of the whole Art' of gunnery.[7]

Civilian publicists like William Gouge and old soldiers like Fisher shared the belief that preparedness was a country's best defence.[8] They held that the way to military proficiency was through a combination of books and experience, of 'Theoricke [and] Practicke'; that there was a progressive 'science' of war; and that their own age was one of notable advance on the past. War was amenable to reason and knowledge—hence '[a] Souldier without letters is like a ship without a Rudder'—but at the same time one should never forget the fickleness of 'good Fortune, Lucke, or chance'. One should hope for a leader with 'wisdom and understanding' but also for one who fought with 'good lucke & victory'.[9] Indeed, the pre-war years gave added weight to the attractive concept of the lucky general. Gustavus Adolphus was 'fortunate' and 'invincible' until he became terminally unlucky at Lützen; later Sir William Waller in his civil war heyday was to be hailed as 'Victorious and Fortunate'. Yet skill and luck were not divorced.[10] Military writers introduced a wide public, from fellow professionals to interested potential soldiers to ordinary civilians, to the idea of a rational approach to war dually based on application of the wisdom of the past and new knowledge of the present and on acquisition of necessary physical and technical skills, but they recognized that theory and rational planning did not necessarily ensure success. In the civil war years, the unpredictable tended to be interpreted as the providential intervention of God, but the language of the divine hand coexisted with that of secular fortune with which soldiers were already familiar.

This varied military literature was directed to equally varied audiences. Narratives obviously had the broadest appeal, but even narrative, as in the weekly

---

[6] For the extent of military publication in pre-war England, see Maurice J. D. Cockle, *A Bibliography of Military Books up to 1642* (2nd edn. 1957), *passim*.

[7] Henry Hexham, *The Principles of the Art Militarie; Practised in the Warres of the United Netherlands* (1637), 2; John Roberts, *The Compleat Cannoniere: or, The Gunners Guide. Wherein are set forth exactly the Chiefe grounds and principals of the whole Art, in a very briefe and Compendious forme, never by any set forth in the like nature before* (1639), 36.

[8] Fisher, *Warlike Directions*, A2ᵛ.   [9] Monro, *Expedition*, 2. 151, 170.

[10] Ibid. 2. 151, 200; B. Donagan, 'Understanding Providence: The Difficulties of Sir William and Lady Waller', *Journal of Ecclesiastical History*, 39 (1988), 442.

'Corantoes', was mingled with precept.[11] Monro's *Expedition* told a professional's inside story of great and small operations and of the persons involved, from Gustavus Adolphus to that hard-drinking old general Sir Patrick Ruthven (later King Charles's chief commander) and the author's 18-year-old kinsman Andrew Monro, indefatigable, 'little . . . merry, and sociable without offence', who died of plague.[12] Monro also, however, offered general 'observations' about the conduct of war (for example, on the workings of 'Panicke feare' and the importance of reconnaissance), all illustrated by particular German examples. To these were added specifically didactic sections of 'Instruction' and 'Observations' for 'the Younger Souldier'. Some partook of the platitudes characteristic of advice to princes, but they too were reinforced by illustrations from Germany.[13] Works like Cruso's or Monro's were not addressed to a broad popular audience, but they were widely known among the classes from which future officers were drawn.

Works that educated in high strategy and tactics or in high theory and politics did little directly to prepare for field service. A mass of books filled this gap. Some provided general instruction and information—for example, on how to starve out a fortress or on the duties of each rank of officers. Others focused on the details, minutely deconstructing the physical actions of pikemen and musketeers. No aspect of war escaped these military authors. From victualling to fortification to the quality of horses, from the duties of pioneers to the uses of spies, from orders of march to the 'postures' of the pikeman, there was 'no want of books'.[14] Their common aim was to reduce the time in which the 'tyro' ranked as a 'novice or fresh water souldier', and to improve the performance of the experienced.[15] Their approach was intensely practical. Petardiers, for example, were offered general encouragement—'in this businesse diligence doeth all'—but also specific directions as to how to perform their notoriously risky assignments, directions that were clarified by diagrams of equipment and illustrations of petardiers at work. Authors reassured their readers that their precepts were 'both *solid* and *serviceable*' and that they worked. The technique described in William Barriffe's chapter on '*Captaine* Wallers Triple firing to the Front' had, he claimed, 'the approbation of good and well experienced *Souldiers*'.[16]

---

[11] For the impact of early newspapers, note Gil, *New Starr of the North*, 23–4: 'we shall not need here to describe the particulars of [Gustavus Adolphus's] Achievements blowne abroad by the Trumpet of publique Fame, and echoed unto us by the weekly tell-tale *Corantoes*'; see also Joseph Frank, *The Beginnings of the English Newspaper 1620–1660* (Cambridge, Mass., 1961), 3–16.

[12] Monro, *Expedition*, 2. 10, 75, 167.

[13] Ibid. 2. 109, 151–2, 194, 200. 'Trust never thy selfe rashly to a reconciled enemy' was proved by Gustavus's wisdom in not doing so at Frankfurt.

[14] Cruso, *Cavallrie*, 29–31, 98.

[15] J[ohn] C[ruso], *The Art of Warre, or Militarie discourses . . . by The Lord of Praissac* (Cambridge, 1639), 131 and 123–50, bound with *A short Method for the Easie Resolving of any Militarie Question propounded. By the Lord of Praissac. Englished by I.C.* (Cambridge, 1639), an early exercise in decision theory.

[16] Cruso, *Cavallrie*, 'To the Reader'; C[ruso], *Art of Warre*, 58 and 50–8; William Barriffe, *Military Discipline: or, the Young Artillery Man* (1635), 254.

The most immediately practical and influential print education was probably that for infantry officers, particularly that offered by the drill manuals that instructed officers on how to teach their men to perform instantaneously and without conscious thought complex exercises and manœuvres. The rationale for military drill has not changed: the more automatic and skilled the movements, the greater troops' effectiveness in battle and the less the chances of panic and confusion. So soldiers were to learn how to march, countermarch, and wheel, how to keep distances on the march, how to handle musket and pike, how to fire and care for musket and powder, how to recognize, interpret, and obey orders. No detail was too small. 'When you will countermarch to the right hand', said the *Instructions for Musters and Armes*, 'The first Ranke of Leaders only must advance one step forward with the right leg, and then turne.'[17] Instructions must often have strained understanding; Cruso's directions for one form of countermarch demanded close attention:

The . . . countermarch by files is when the file-leaders facing to the rear, cause all the rest of their file to follow after them, and lead them to another ground, leaving that ground behind them where they formerly stood; or rather, the bringers-up face about, and every man of the file placeth himself before his bringer-up, in their due places, until the file-leader come up to the front.[18]

Not surprisingly, such detail lent itself to contemporary satire. In the 1640s the author of *The Country Captaine* (probably the marquis of Newcastle) had Captain Underwit's servant buy 'all the bookes [that] can be bought, of martiall discipline which the learned call Tacticks', and there followed much knockabout comedy as the captain employed his new learning in a stream of incomprehensible and contradictory commands.[19]

Unskilled readers may well have foundered, and we should not exaggerate the benefits of military reading. Authors, recognizing the problem, tried to resolve it graphically. Cruso accompanied his prose with a picture of four files of troops, with dotted lines plotting each man's movements. Barriffe provided detailed lettered plans that resembled cryptographers' tables. Hexham explained the difference between files and ranks—puzzling to the novice—with pictures of rows of little musketeers and pikemen. As one authority observed, 'small Maps' enabled the written word to be 'better conceived and fixed in . . . memories'.[20] Indeed, illustrations enhanced explanations of virtually every aspect of war. Large-scale plans and panoramic views showed how to lay out a camp or deploy an army. Notations for 'The Posture tune' and 'The Falling of[f] Tune'

[17] *Instructions for Musters and Armes*, A3–3ᵛ.   [18] Cruso, *Art of Warre*, 171.

[19] [William Cavendish], *The Country Captaine, And the Varietie. Two Comedies written by a Person of Honor* (1649), 5, 25, 50–1.

[20] William Barriffe, *Military Discipline: or the Yong Artillery Man* (2nd edn., revised and enlarged, 1639), 308–9 and *passim*; C[ruso], *Art of Warre*, 170–1, 196–7; Fisher, *Warlike Directions*, A2ᵛ, 67–93 *passim* (and contrast p. 43 for the opacity of the written word alone); see also Hexham, *Principles of the Art Militarie*, 21–2.

familiarized the musically literate with orders conveyed by fife and drum. Most impressive of all were the elegant and detailed strip cartoons that showed step by step how to use musket, pike, and pistol. Cruso, for example, offered double fold-out folio pages containing twenty-four frames that progressively showed the cavalryman how to mount his horse and then to draw, load, and fire his pistols.[21]

Thus in the decades before 1642 England was well provided with literature that addressed every aspect of war, and did so analytically and pragmatically, but if it is easy to establish its existence it is difficult to find hard evidence about readership and influence. The regular presence in private libraries of the *Swedish Intelligencer* and the *German History*, and the zeal with which English men and women sought the 'Corantoes' and 'books' that retailed the shifting fortunes of war, indicate widespread familiarity with serious war reporting.[22] The steady production of more narrowly military books of all kinds throughout the 1620s and 1630s suggests that authors, from the prolific hack Gervase Markham to the Low Countries veteran Thomas Fisher, judged that there was a promising market.[23] The reissues of Barriffe, Fisher, Hexham, Markham, and others when domestic crises erupted in 1639 and 1642 suggest that they were already accepted as tried and true authorities, useful and applicable in new circumstances. Barriffe's *Militarie Discipline* was reissued three times in 1643, and these later editions reveal a process of modernization and adaptation, for the stocky Low Countries soldiers of his earlier frontispiece have been streamlined into fashionable figures with the arms and clothing familiar to us from civil war portraits. Five editions between 1635 and 1648 attest to Barriffe's reputation and usefulness.[24]

While evidence of dissemination remains serendipitous, dedications indicate that it was geographically extensive and socially diverse, with patrons ranging from Prince Charles and peers to gentry and townsmen. Cruso chose the deputy lieutenants of Norfolk, the colonel of a Suffolk regiment (the future royalist commander Thomas Glemham), and members of the Norwich artillery

---

[21] Cruso, *Cavallrie*, 66, 104, and see e.g. 38–41, 52–3, for information by combined text and plan; Hexham, *Principles of the Art Militarie*, 11–19; *Instructions for Musters and Armes*; William Barriffe, *Mars, his Triumph: or, The Description of an Exercise Performed the XVIII of October 1638 in Merchant-Taylors Hall by Certain Gentlemen of the Artillery Garden*, (1639), 10, 15.

[22] For libraries of the Harley and Hastings families, see BL Add. MSS 70001, between fos. 230–1; 70109, Misc.54; HEH, Hastings Inventories, Box 1, Item 13, fos. 18 ff.; Hastings F[inancial] 12, Items 10, 38; and 13, Item 46 (I am grateful to James Knowles for introducing me to the Hastings inventories); and see Donagan, 'Halcyon Days', 93 n. 95.

[23] Fisher, *Warlike Directions*; Markham's three books appeared in 1625–7, had a 2nd edn. in 1639, and were reprinted in 1643: see e.g. G. Markham, *The Souldiers Exercise: in Three Bookes* (2nd edn. 1639), containing *The Souldiers Accidence*, *The Souldiers Grammar*, *The Second part of the souldiers Grammar*. And see Cockle, *Bibliography of Military Books*, 82–3, 86–7.

[24] Barriffe's *Militarie Discipline* was first published in 1635; a 2nd revised edn. appeared in 1639, followed in 1643 by 3rd and 4th editions and a reprint of the 4th. The 5th edn. appeared in 1647 and was reprinted in 1657, and a sixth in 1661. See listings in *Short Title Catalogue*.

company. Those to whom books are dedicated do not necessarily read them, but we can at least assume that Cruso's *The Art of Warr* and *A short Method for the Easie Resolving of any Militarie Question* made their way to Norfolk and Suffolk. We know that Philip Skippon, already a professional soldier and later a much loved parliamentary commander, was interested in the books, for Cruso translated them at Skippon's request. Inventories of seventeenth-century libraries also bear witness to the dissemination of a broad range of military literature. Narrative and descriptive works were common, but we also find more strictly military works, as in the earl of Huntingdon's purchases in response to national anxieties early in 1640.[25]

In 1624 Sir John Gell, later a parliamentary commander in Derbyshire, lent a 'training book'—probably one of the Privy Council's authorized drill books—to his neighbour Peter Frescheville, who found it useful. Gell also owned Thomas Styward's *Pathwaie to Martiall Discipline*, published as long ago as 1581 and partly Spanish in origin, but still apparently valued in a new military age.[26] Young Edward Harley's bookseller's bill for March 1642 offers testimony to the relevance and reputation of this pre-war literature, for more than a third of its thirty odd named works were directly military. They included such standard authorities as Monro's *Expedition* and *The Swedish Discipline*, Hexham's 'Military Discipline' (probably *The Principles of the Art Militarie*), and Cruso's *Cavallrie*, but they also ranged more widely to Machiavelli, Caesar, and an account of the siege of Breda, while Markham's *Souldiers Accidence*, Fisher's *Warlike Directions*, and Cruso's *Art of Warre* provided practical help on topics from drill to building forts.[27] The foundations for Harley's speedy transformation from young man about Lincoln's Inn to parliamentary colonel had been well laid. John Lambert, who began the war as a cornet of dragoons under Sir Thomas Fairfax and became one of Cromwell's major-generals, may have been such another. Local legend in Yorkshire had it that he trained for war by riding at a makeshift ring in the lane near his home, but his preparation may also have come from books. The library that he took into exile in Guernsey after the Restoration was strongly religious, but it also contained Barriffe's *Military Discipline* and John Bingham's *The Tactiks of Aelian*, one of the most respected military works of the seventeenth century.[28] There is no knowing when Lambert acquired them—they may have

[25] See n. 22 above.

[26] Derbys. RO, Gell of Hopton MSS, D3287, Peter Frescheville to John Gell, 21 Aug. 1624; Thomas Styward, *The Pathwaie to Martiall Discipline* (1582) and [Luis Gutierrez de la Vega], *A Compendious Treatise entituled, De Re Militari* (1582) are bound together; Gell's copy is among the Gell of Hopton MSS, D3287; a slip in the book reads, '[T]he stain is blood & may [sic] have been from Gell's doublet when he was wounded.' Styward's work had been sufficiently regarded to have edns. in 1581, 1582, and 1588 and to be quarried in 1591. See Cockle, *Bibliography*, 25–6, 46–7.

[27] Bodl. MS Eng. Hist. c. 308, fo. 76.

[28] William Harbutt Dawson, *Cromwell's Understudy: The Life and Times of General John Lambert* (1938), 28, 425–8, and see plate facing p. 432; other 'military' works in the collection were Grotius's *De jure belli* and a 'Collection of Articles' of war; and see [Io. Bingham], *The Tactiks of*

been old or new favorites—but they attest to the enduring reputation of pre-war English military writers.

Learning war from the printed page had obvious advantages. As one laudatory versifier remarked in 1639, 'Here, you may fight by Booke, and never bleede.' A later poem elaborated:

> Lo, in one *Volume*, here thou dost explain
> What *Germany, Italy, Netherlands* or *Spain*
> Can render us; and to our doors has *brought*
> What many thousands have so deerly sought.[29]

'The Souldier and the Scholler' met in the pages of these 'Ammanuens[e]s of the Sword' and readers could become 'skilfull, at least in the *Theory* of a Souldier'.[30] In many cases this theoretical skill was complemented by modern training at home that was shaped by some of the same veterans who wrote the books. Yet theory and book-learning were no substitute for experience. 'The *Campe's* a *Schole* . . . Where *practise* perfects, what in bookes we learne', wrote an anonymous poet in 1629 of the army in the Netherlands.[31] In the years before the civil war, a large number of Englishmen gained their experience in the camps of Europe.

NURSERIES OF SOLDIERY

Experience meant above all continental Europe, the great school of war. In the first four decades of the seventeenth century natives of England, Wales, and Scotland who wished to learn a soldier's trade at first hand had to go abroad, either to continental Europe or to Ireland. Ireland was the less attractive option, militarily less interesting and offering slender hopes of promotion; it was, said a European veteran at The Hague in 1637, 'not an active place'.[32] At home there was neither a standing army nor any formal institution that taught how to be a soldier. The age of military academies had not yet dawned, and the apprentice soldier learnt from the practitioners of his métier. 'A campe continuallie maintained in

---

Aelian. Or art of embattailing an army after ye Grecian manner Englished & illustrated with figures [1616], Iohn Bingham, *The Art of Embattailing an Army. Or, the Second Part of Aelians Tacticks* (1629), and Cockle, *Bibliography*, 70–2, 79.

[29] Robert Ward, *Anima'dversions of Warre: or, A Militarie Magazine of the Truest Rules, and Ablest Instructions, for the Managing of Warre* (1639), Edmund Plumme, 'To our Countrymen imployed in Forraine Service'; Richard Elton, *The Compleat Body of the Art Military: Exactly Compiled, and Gradually Composed for the Foot, in the Best Refined Manner, According to the Practice of the Modern Times* (2nd edn. 1659), prefatory poem by Johannes Hunnings. Elton's book reflected civil war experience. The 1st edn. appeared in 1650.

[30] Ibid., prefatory poem by Captain Samuel Jervis.

[31] Bachiler, *Campe Royall*, B.

[32] Sir Jacob Astley, quoted in Paul Hardacre, 'Patronage and Purchase in the Irish Standing Army under Thomas Wentworth, Earl of Strafford, 1632–1640', *JSAHR* 67 (1989), 102.

action', said Sir Roger Williams, 'is like an universitie continuallie in exercises.'[33] There was no deep divide between the literary education so far considered and the education of the camp. Both were predicated on the duality of war as a science and war as a trade, and on the need to apply a trained mind to both its aspects.

Early in the century the Dutch armies provided 'the learnedst Schoole for that kind of discipline, that . . . is in all *Europe*', and they remained a 'Nurcery of Souldierie' even when Gustavus Adolphus and the Swedish army outshone them.[34] There were also valuable lesser arenas. English regiments were dispatched to Denmark in the 1620s and English soldiers found their way to Poland and Russia.[35] In Italy young William Waller had the first of his many providential escapes from the hazards of war as he served under the banner of Venice. Later he moved to Prague, was present at the battle of White Mountain, and had another miraculous escape, this time from the Cossacks, while serving the Elector Palatine.[36] Many English Catholics found a comfortable niche in French armies, where they could fight alongside co-religionists but against the Habsburg enemy of England's Protestant heroine, Elizabeth of Bohemia. Others, like Henry Gage, later a distinguished royalist officer, joined the Spanish in the Low Countries. Catholic Venice was sufficiently anti-papal to satisfy good Protestants, but some Englishmen were restrained neither by confession nor geography. Protestant Sir Thomas Lunsford, a future royalist, served in France. Sydenham Poyntz, a future parliamentarian, began in the Low Countries and moved steadily east to Hungary and the Turkish lands, and moved as well from Protestant to Catholic service; his masters and mentors included Mansfeld, Wallenstein, and Bethlen Gabor, and he seems to have felt little discomfort at alliance with the Turks, at least until he was captured and enslaved by them. The Catholic Arthur Aston served Sweden, Poland, Russia, and Charles I before his death in the massacre at Drogheda. There were Protestants as well as Catholics in Spanish service. The norm, however, remained service with English regiments in the Netherlands and Germany, often alongside Scottish colleagues, and the

---

[33] Quoted in Hale, 'Military Education of the Officer Class', 230, and see 227–30 on failed projects for military academies.

[34] B[edell], *The Free Schoole of Warre*, B iii(2); Hexham, *Principles of the Art Militarie*, dedication to the earl of Holland.

[35] For Polish and Russian campaigns see Paul Dukes, 'New Perspectives: Alexander Leslie and the Smolensk War, 1632–1634', and Robert I. Frost, 'Scottish Soldiers, Poland-Lithuania and the Thirty Years' War', in Steve Murdoch (ed.), *Scotland and the Thirty Years' War* (Leiden, 2001), 173–213; although primarily concerned with Scottish service, they also reveal English participation in the 'Northern Wars'. Note also John Barrington's comments on the severe English losses at the hands of 'the Polanders' in June 1629, *Barrington Family Letters*, 101.

[36] 'Recollections, by General Sir William Waller', in *The Poetry of Anna Matilda* (1788), 108–9. A manuscript version of Waller's 'Recollections' in the library of Wadham College, Oxford, records his multiple providential escapes from European dangers, 'Sr Wm Waller's Remarks—Experiences', 9, 27, 37. I am grateful to the Warden and Fellows of Wadham College for permission to consult this manuscript.

apprenticeship one in the Dutch and Swedish military traditions.[37] Soldiers, both famous and obscure, who were later to fight against each other learnt their trade side by side.

This common pre-war education bears on two vexed questions. The first is that of the confessional intensity of the civil war, the second that of professionalism. For the first we may note here the intermingling of national, professional, pragmatic, and religious considerations in pre-war military careers. Unlike Poyntz, who was unusual in the diversity of his masters, most Englishmen who served abroad did so in an unambiguously Protestant cause, whether at the Isle of Ré, in the Netherlands, or ranging through Germany in the service of the Palatinate and Sweden. They did not need to risk, as Monro put it, 'shipwracke of [their] consciences'. Nor did Catholic officers like Colonel Gage and Colonel Richard Gerard, who served Spain.[38] Yet we also find Catholics who learnt their trade with Protestant armies. The future royalist and 'grand Papist' Charles Gerard, for example, went from the university of Leiden to the armies of the United Provinces. As the Italian Sarpi had explained, scruples of conscience were redundant in the face of the higher good of military expertise.[39] Monro took it as a sign of virtue that so few Scots had been 'induced to serve . . . Catholique Potentates', but in fact by his day Protestant armies offered the best training, good hope of profit, and the comfortable presence of fellow countrymen.[40] When civil war came it was notable that, despite sometimes abusive rhetoric, relations between Protestant and Catholic officers were based on shared professional and social standards rather than confessional difference. Their relationship was foreshadowed in the pre-war milieu in which those who served Catholic masters did so within the same context of international professional codes as those who served Protestants.

---

[37] *ODNB*, 'Sir Thomas Lunsford'; *The Relation of Sydnam Poyntz 1624–1636*, ed. A. T. S. Goodrick (Camden Society, 3rd ser., 14, 1908), 45–50, 55; Ian Roy, 'The Profession of Arms', in Wilfrid Prest (ed.), *The Professions in Early Modern England* (1987), 192–3. Poyntz's 'mutabilitie' in the 1630s foreshadowed his career in the 1640s. For Venetian service, see John Adair, *Roundhead General: A Military Biography of Sir William Waller* (1997), 7: in 1618 Sir Thomas Peyton commanded a regiment of 500 English foot for Venice. See also *Barrington Family Letters*, 41. For Aston see P. R. Newman, *Royalist Officers in England and Wales, 1642–1660: A Biographical Dictionary* (1981), 10; Alexia Grosjean, 'Scotland: Sweden's Closest Ally', and Frost, 'Scottish Soldiers, Poland-Lithuania and the Thirty Years' War', in Murdoch (ed.), *Scotland and the Thirty Years' War*, 146, 201–2, 204, 208, 211.

[38] *Relation of Sydnam Poyntz*, 75–6, 145; Monro, *Expedition*, 2. 75; Newman, *Royalist Officers*, 146–7, 153; and see Bodl. MS Clarendon, 15, fos. 86–87ᵛ, 105, 128ᵛ–129, 140ᵛ, 173, for the quarrels of English Catholic officers in Spanish service.

[39] Newman, *Royalist Officers*, 151; Roy, 'Profession of Arms', 193; Sarpi (who was translated into English by a sound Protestant) observed that 'it would have been . . . an *Asinine* ignorance' for Italian gentlemen not to serve the States of Holland with 'a meere intent to learne the art of Warre' in 'the learnedst Schoole . . . in the whole world'. B[edell], *Free Schoole of Warre*, Biii (2), Fiii (2). See Jack Binns, 'Captain Browne Bushell: North Sea adventurer and pirate', *Northern History*, 27 (1991), 92, for an apparently Protestant officer who served Philip IV of Spain.

[40] Monro, *Expedition*, 2. 75.

This leads to the second issue. Officers who fought in Europe were self-consciously members of a profession. So were many non-commissioned officers. Admittedly the case of the rank and file, as in most wars, was more problematic, for many had little choice in the matter. In 1631, for example, an observer reported 'a great deal of unwillingness of the common people' to volunteer for Danish service and the consequent need to resort to 'a press' to raise troops.[41] Contemporaries were not kind about the quality of such common soldiers. The charitable called them 'untamed colts'; the less charitable, as we have seen, called them 'skumme'.[42] Officer careers, however, raise the question of soldiering as a profession. It was more informal in its career paths than law, medicine, or religion, and this has made it difficult to assimilate to modern preconceptions of professionalism. Yet it is clear that well before the civil war military practitioners saw themselves as belonging to a profession requiring education and training, one with a strong corporate sense of expertise, identity, and solidarity, and with a distinctive ethos. We can also see that accusations that men who served in Europe were mere mercenaries and soldiers of fortune, men who were 'here today and God knows where tomorrow' in the words of a royalist grandee—a charge that will recur in the following pages—should be treated cautiously.[43] Until 1639 soldiers had to practise their profession abroad, and not until 1642 did career opportunities at home rival those overseas.

If the emergence of soldiering as a professional option for Englishmen comparable to the law or the church has not been widely recognized, the existence of a confident body of practitioners has nevertheless long been familiar to historians. Ian Roy noted that the wars at the end of Elizabeth's reign and in the 1620s were 'formative years in the development of the officer corps in England', and that 'those who made good in the European wars, alongside or fighting against the best soldiers of the age, took ... an undoubted pride in their craft'.[44] In part they acquired their education the hard way, for it did not pay to make a dangerous mistake twice, but they also learnt from mentors like the officer who 'had both the Theorie and Practick befitting a Commander', so that '*Cavalieres* under his command, could learne by him much good order and discipline'.[45] In other cases, particularly when those sent abroad to gain a military education were young, the mentorship was more personal. A Lieutenant Coke supervised William Gell's progress in the Low Countries and dispensed

---

[41] BL Add. MS 18,979, fo. 25.   [42] BL Add. MS 4275, fo. 68; Bachiler, *Camp Royall*, 46.

[43] The second marquis of Worcester, in a post-Restoration report of his service to Charles I. HMC, *Twelfth Report, Appendix, Part IX* (1891), 'Beaufort MSS', 60.

[44] Roy, 'Profession of Arms', 187, 191; see also Simon Adams, 'A Puritan Crusade? The Composition of the Earl of Leicester's Expedition to the Netherlands, 1585–1586', in *The Dutch in Crisis, 1585–1588: People and Politics in Leicester's Time* (Leiden, Sir Thomas Browne Institute, 1988), 10–11, on development of the English officer corps from the 1570s. He notes the 'pride (if not arrogance) of the Low Countries officers in their own professional superiority'.

[45] Monro, *Expedition*, 2. 10. In the 1630s 'Cavalier' had not acquired its later partisan connotation.

money sent out for the boy. William wrote anxiously to his father in Derbyshire that he hoped Coke sent back a good report for, he said, 'I strive according to his directions to behave & carry myself.'[46] When 17-year-old Thomas Fairfax persuaded his family to let him go to Holland, he went to Lord Vere's company at Dort and 'Lord Houghton promise[d] his best care over him whilst he [was] there'.[47] As soldiering offered a career open to talents, it was particularly attractive to younger sons and younger brothers. They were not cast adrift by their families, however, many of whom provided financial support and personal oversight. Sir Thomas Wentworth intervened to get a commission for his younger brother Michael, a 'freshwater soldier', and sent him money and affectionate, nagging advice on how to conduct himself in the 'Profession and Vocation' he had undertaken.[48] A number joined existing kin groups: the English Vere and Scottish Monro cousinages in European armies were extensive. Even young Gell, who had deeply displeased his father, continued to be an object of irritated care.[49] Many of those who went to learn became, if they survived, mentors in their turn.

The men who went to Europe to learn their trade were not a homogeneous group. The most obvious distinction was that between short-term and long-term soldiers, between those like young Thomas Fairfax and young William Waller who, after their stints abroad, returned to the life of country gentlemen, and those who made a career of it. Yet this distinction was not always clear cut. Fairfax wanted a second tour of service for he had an 'earnest desire to see the army of Swede', and he grew 'melancholy' when his grandfather did not grant permission.[50] Even that unmilitary figure the earl of Holland, later to be an incompetent commander against the Scots, 'betook himself to the war in *Holland*, which he intended to have made his Profession: where . . . he . . . made two or three Campaigns' until, back in England one winter, he realized that the prospects for a handsome young man were better at court.[51] As for young men

---

[46] Derbyshire RO, Gell MSS, D258, 41/31 (g), (n), 60/68 (b).

[47] BL Add. MS 18,979, fo. 15ᵛ, and see John Wilson, *Fairfax* (New York, 1985), 8; Fairfax was accompanied by another young Yorkshireman, the ill-fated John Hotham. Lord Houghton, Vere's son-in-law, was the second generation of the Holles family to serve abroad; his father had ranged as far as Hungary, while his brother Francis died in Dutch service in 1622. See *ODNB*.

[48] William Knowler, *The Earl of Strafforde's Letters and Dispatches* (2 vols. in one, 1739), 1. 18; Lady Burghclere, *Strafford* (2 vols., 1931), 1. 42; *Wentworth Papers 1597–1628*, ed. J. P. Cooper (Camden Soc., 4th ser. 12, 1973), 34–6, and compare 171–2.

[49] P. R. Newman, 'The Royalist Officer Corps 1642–1660: Army Command as a Reflexion of the Social Structure', *HJ* 26 (1983), 947; Roy, 'Profession of Arms', 189–91; Monro, *Expedition*, 1. O 2–O 3 (appendix following the table of contents), 2. 12, 109, 180; Derbyshire RO, Gell MSS D258 41/31 (g), and see 47/19 (k).

[50] Bodl. MS Fairfax, 31, fos. 15, 40, and see Wilson, *Fairfax*, 9. Fairfax went to the Low Countries in the spring of 1629; in 1631 he was in France where, he wrote, he 'only learned the language and knew war only by an uncertain relation'. He returned to England early in 1632 to seek permission from his grandfather to serve with the Swedish army; old lord Fairfax apparently refused his permission. Ibid., and see BL Add. MS 18,979, fos. 23–23ᵛ.

[51] Clarendon, *History*, i. 49.

like Waller and Fairfax, their experience was not that of some dilettante grand tour. They learnt, rather, the advanced theory and practice of the modern 'science of war' from its leading exponents and in the company and under the tutelage of professionals: Waller served with Sir John Vere in the army of Venice, while Fairfax was under the eye of a Holles and another Vere in the Low Countries. They returned to an England deeply interested in the course of the wars, where there was ample opportunity to follow both their events and their technicalities. They had received a military grounding on which they could build by reading and reflection.

Like length of service, motivation varied. Some were drawn by a combination of adventure, religion, technical interest, and a sort of glamour, particularly—as for Fairfax—that attached to service of Gustavus Adolphus.[52] Others, including many whose names were to become familiar in the 1640s, were less idealistic. Some went just ahead of the law, like George Monck, while Thomas Lunsford escaped from imprisonment on a charge of murderous assault. Some were in effect remittance men, like profligate George Goring, whose family bought him a commission in Dutch service because he was too expensive at home.[53] Yet as the later careers of Monck and Goring were to demonstrate, professional ability did not depend on virtuous motivation. Above all, however, war offered an opportunity to improve financial and even social standing for younger brothers and sons of families in economic trouble or of marginal status. It was said that military service was 'the only way of living well' for younger sons 'that have not estates'.[54] Sydenham Poyntz, whose family had fallen on hard times, claimed that he ran away from his apprenticeship because he prefered the noble life and death of a soldier to being 'bound an Apprentice [a] life I deemed little better than a dogs life and base'.[55] Ian Roy has commented that 'if a man was not a gentleman before becoming an officer he became one after'.[56] Even for those whose status was less shaky than that of the Poyntz family, soldiering offered the incentives of pay and sometimes large profit. Lieutenant-Colonel Prude of Kent did well out of war before his death at Maastricht in 1632. George Fleetwood gained a Swedish barony and Swedish estates. If most fell short of such substantial success, they could still hope for a good if not remarkable

---

[52] See e.g. Parival, *Iron Age*, 209, on England's years of peace: 'such as were not content to live in such delicious idlenesse, betook themselves to the warre, either in *Germany*, or in the *Low Countries*'.

[53] For Lunsford, Goring, and Monck, see *ODNB*.

[54] Algernon Sidney, quoted in Clive Holmes, *The Eastern Association in the English Civil War* (Cambridge, 1974), 285 n. 109.

[55] Poyntz's story of free and heroic choice is not supported by other witnesses. His master's widow claimed he was a pilfering runaway while his brother, in defence, declared that he had been driven to fraudulently obtaining a halfpenny loaf and a halfpenny cheese by near-starvation and that his 'sudden departure' followed a cruel and inhuman whipping. *Relation of Sydnam Poyntz*, 45, 140.

[56] Roy, 'Profession of Arms', 189, 191.

income. John Barrington, contemplating Swedish service, observed, 'A captain's meanes is good theare which is twentie five pounds a month, ten to a lieutenant, as much to an ensigne.'[57] Furthermore, as the future royalist Sir Jacob Astley wrote from the Hague in 1637, '[S]uch gentlemen as are of any merit here none but hath some hopes from one colonel or another for their preferment.'[58] Monro warned against the dangers of profligacy, but the warning reveals some of the flashier charms of his profession for needy younger sons and 'meanely risen' men:

[S]ome fantastick Officers that cannot governe themselves nor their wealth, they will hunt and hawke, . . . thinking themselves equall to Princes, . . . and they will have their silver plate, their gold, their silver, their Iewells, their Coaches, their horses, their traines, and Officers of household counterfeiting greatnesse and great men, having, it may be, but little worth besides.[59]

One can see why a Scottish presbyterian disapproved, but one can also see the attractions.

In real life, most advancement came by the familiar means of patronage and connection, aided by merit and the mortality of others, and the process could be slow. If few equalled Fleetwood's barony and estates, the preacher at Prude's funeral nonetheless offered his career as an answer to the problem of 'what course men noble in birth, & quality of mind, yet oppressed with poverty, should take to live by, and to be fruitful members of the Commonwealth'.[60] This more modest aspiration—to maintain or improve status, to earn suitable income, and to find an interesting vocation—remains familiar in the choice of profession; in the seventeenth century a military career was one option among others. As William's father John Gell wrote to his brother, 'The motion you write of for my son I like very well . . . .I pray you send Will into the Low Countries if you can.' If not, he could 'sail into Virginia'.[61] For John Barrington, service under Gustavus advanced the Protestant cause to which his family was committed, but also offered a solution to financial difficulties. As he wrote to his mother, '[M]y desire is greate to be in inployment, yet I ought to loake for such an one as I may be able to live by.'[62] Yet although the professional life of these long-term soldiers was in Europe, many retained and cultivated their roots at home, their comings and goings between

---

[57] *Barrington Family Letters*, 79; 'Letter from George Fleetwood to his father giving an account of the battle of Lützen and the death of Gustavus Adolphus', ed. Sir P. de M. Grey Egerton, *Camden Miscellany*, Camden Soc. 39 (1847), 3. Compare Monro's strictures on undeserving officers in Germany who were 'making up estates for their posteritie', Monro, *Expedition*, 2. 96. Wages, of course, were only part of the hoped-for profit of war.

[58] Quoted in Hardacre, 'Patronage and Preferment', 102.   [59] Monro, *Expedition*, 2. 20.

[60] F. Rogers, *A Sermon preached on September the 20. 1632. In the Cathedrall Church of Christ at Canterbury at the Funerall of William Proud, a Lieutenant Colonell, slaine at the late siege of Mastricke* (1633), 'Dedication'.

[61] Derbys. RO, Gell MSS, D258 47/19 (k).   [62] *Barrington Family Letters*, 101, 151.

England and the continent governed by the seasons and the availability of employment.[63]

We can never know exactly how many of them there were. Even for officers total numbers remain a puzzle, but we can note with certainty the existence of 'officer cadres' and, from at least the mid-1580s, trace military dynasties and affinities whose members, well before 1642, shared tradition, expertise, and familiarity with each other and with the practices of modern war.[64] The old soldier Henry Hexham in 1637 listed a roll-call of honour of great military families who had served the Protestant Netherlands: Norrises, Sidneys, Willoughbys, Veres, Morgans. Fathers and sons, brothers and cousins, served Protestant God and country while making careers abroad.[65] Vagaries of mortality and the age and sex of heirs precluded any simple succession from Elizabethan to Caroline service, but it is clear that in some families soldiering abroad was a family avocation comparable to law, medicine, or the army in later days. Lesser men clustered around the great names, and they too contributed to the sense of professional coherence and continuity. Lord Vere kept twelve full-length portraits of his Low Country captains at his house in England, a visible statement of solidarity and distinctiveness, of membership of a 'band of brothers'.[66] The two great Veres, Sir Francis and Sir Horace, were gone from the scene by the mid-1630s, but less distinguished kin remained in the field and professional as well as biological lineage persisted. Hexham had followed the Veres from his youth; by 1637 he saw his colonel, Goring (the remittance man), as their true successor. A more plausible case could be made for Thomas Fairfax, who had not only served under Lord Vere but remained his protégé and later married his daughter. She in turn was the cousin of the redoubtable Brilliana Harley (their mothers were sisters), whose name memorialized the service of her father, Sir Edward Conway, as governor of Brill in Holland. Generations of Conways served in Europe, and through Brilliana the lineage descended to her son Edward the parliamentary

---

[63] On the fluctuations in employment opportunities, see John Barrington's hopes and disappointments in 1629–30. After his return from La Rochelle he spent nearly two years (punctuated by illness) trying to secure a company. In Nov. 1629 Gustavus Adolphus 'remitted the leavie of the English and Scottish nacion', leading Barrington to seek alternative employment; by Jan., however, the 'bussines for Swethland' and his hopes were 'revived againe'. Finally in May 1630 he left England to join Lord Vere at Dort, and died in the Netherlands in 1631. Ibid. 79, 97, 101–2, 113–14, 122, 151–2, 253. For Essex's seasonal continental campaigns in the 1620s, see Arthur Wilson, 'Observations of God's Providence, in the Tract of my Life', in *The Inconstant Lady, a Play* (Oxford, 1814), 116–24; *Relation of Sydnam Poyntz*, 65.

[64] Roy, 'Profession of Arms', 193.

[65] Hexham, *Principles of the Art Militarie*, dedication to the earl of Holland. See also Adams, 'Puritan Crusade?', 20–1, on Leicester's expedition of 1585. For reappearance of the same names in action after action from the 1570s to the 1630s, see Clements R. Markham, *The Fighting Veres* (1888), *passim*; and note the reunion of Veres and Devereux in 1620, Whiteway, *Diary*, 28.

[66] G.E.C., *Complete Peerage*, 12. 259, lists Vere's twelve captains, as well as other officers who served under him and whose portraits were in his collection. Compare the fresco portraits of the leading officers of the Swedish general Karl Gustav Wrangel (including three Scots) that decorate the upper cloister of his palace at Skøkloster.

colonel. Fairfax himself did not depend on the Vere connection for his military heredity, for both his Fairfax and his Sheffield grandfathers were old European officers. When his Fairfax grandfather made a brief return to European service in the 1620s his sons, also soldiers, observed that it greatly improved his notoriously irascible disposition.[67] Similar direct and indirect descents can be traced in less prominent families. The practice was already well-established, over several generations, of military careers in Europe undertaken at a serious professional level.

Some of the old families were militarily on the wane in the 1630s, but many of the actors of the 1640s had already been in the field. They included such notable commanders as Astley, Essex, Goring, Leslie, and Skippon, but most were and remained obscure, their unremarkable presence earning no special comment. We hear, for example, as a routine matter that at the taking of Creuznach, Lieutenant-Colonel Talbot died of his wounds, that Lord Craven, Sir Francis Fane, Robert Marsham, and Henry Wynd (the last two gentlemen volunteers) were wounded, and that Nicholas Slaning later joined the survivors of the action. Three of these five were to serve in the royalist armies, Wynd as lieutenant-colonel to another old European hand, Sir Lewis Kirk, while Slaning was to die storming Bristol.[68] Some old hands indeed had been in service for so long that they might normally have been approaching retirement; Gustavus Adolphus liked to retire his generals at 60 but 'old Generall Major *Ruthven*' was close to 70 when he became Charles's chief general. Sir Jacob Astley went to the wars in Europe in 1599; he was 67 when he surrendered the last royalist field army at Stow on the Wold in March 1646. Length of similar service was in itself a bond for those old professionals.[69]

The Scots made up the largest group in the British contingents in Europe. While they maintained a separate identity—English and Scottish regiments were distinctly recruited and organized—they have a place in discussion of professional education and preparation for the English civil war on two grounds. First, Scottish officers were later to be found in the armies of both sides, bringing their own expertise and passing it on to newer recruits. Only with Scottish entry

---

[67] For the Conways as a military family, see Markham, *Fighting Veres*, 253; and see Monro, *Expedition*, 2. 13. For the elder Sir Thomas Fairfax and his sons, see BL Add. MS 30305, fos. 29–29ᵛ, 31, 33, and for Lord Vere's continued support of the younger Thomas Fairfax see Bodl. MS Fairfax 31, fo. 40.

[68] *Swedish Intelligencer*, 2. 81–2, 138; Newman, *Royalist Officers*, 126, 216, 343, 425. The *Swedish Intelligencer* reported Talbot's death, but Newman lists a John Talbot who returned from military service in Europe in 1639, was a captain in 1640, and a royalist colonel in 1643. Ibid. 366–7. Craven entered Dutch service at 17 and remained a devoted and active supporter of the cause of the Palatinate; he spent the war years with Elizabeth of Bohemia's court at The Hague, contributing lavishly to her support and to the royalist cause. See *ODNB*, 'William Craven'.

[69] *Swedish Intelligencer*, 2. 77; *Ruthven Correspondence: Letters and Papers of Patrick Ruthven, Earl of Forth and Brentford . . . 1615–. . . 1642*, ed. W. D. Macray (Roxburghe Club, 1868), ii; Monro, *Expedition*, 2. 75 (for Monro's pleasure at serving with his old friend Colonel Hepburn in 1630, as well as for his admiration for Ruthven's hard head).

into the war in support of parliament in 1644 and the formation of the New Model army was there a significant decline in their numbers as some joined their national army, or faced a crisis of national loyalty, or were excluded. Sir John Urry, not unfairly described as 'of turncoat memory', who served Scots, king, and parliament in a side-changing career after his return from Europe, is only one of the most visible.[70] Second, while still in Europe, English and Scots together made up 'Britaines forces'. They fought in many of the same actions, and off the field they quarrelled, fraternized, and remained consciously different: Monro claimed that Gustavus showed special favour to the Scots, treating them more as friends than servants. When Sir Henry Vane came to Wurzburg as ambassador, however, 'the whole Officers, whoe were there of both Nations, *Scots* and *English*' were 'courteously and kindly . . . entertaine[d], with such respect as became his Honour to give unto *Cavaliers*', while his followers 'did also keepe familiaritie alike with both Nations'.[71] In the 1640s, in the armies of both sides, a shared past and current professional opportunities, often allied to religious sympathies, were to make the presence of Scots like Andrew Potley, Waller's major-general of foot and a Swedish veteran, a continuation of pre-war 'familiaritie'. The 'officer cadres' described by Roy, around which 'new English forces could be built', were Scottish as well as English.[72]

Estimates of total numbers of English and Scottish troops who served in Europe are confusing and elastic, and they vary according to the times and places on which they are based. Roy has suggested that 6,000 to 8,000 Scots served Gustavus under their own commanders, a carefully circumscribed figure, for although most were in Scottish regiments, not all were; nor was Germany the only field of service.[73] Parker suggested that twenty-five thousand Scots 'fought for the Protestant cause in Germany during the war'. A more recent estimate suggests that for the whole period 1618 to 1648 some one hundred thousand British soldiers served in assorted anti-Habsburg armies from the Low Countries to Russia, of whom fifty thousand were Scots and fifty thousand English, Welsh, and Irish. All estimates must be treated with caution.[74] Nor should we visualize a

---

[70] Newman, *Royalist Officers*, 383–4; *Ruthven Correspondence*, 151, 157–66. In Europe Sir John had been part of a long-serving Urry and Erskine kin group that did not sever its European ties when members served in England. Henry Urry had Rupert's licence to return to the Low Countries in 1644; in 1668 William Urry, once a cornet under the Swedes, later a captain under Essex, later still an officer of Scottish forces under Charles II, and married to a Dutch wife, sent her back to manage family affairs in the Low Countries. Sir John, less fortunate, was captured while serving with Montrose in 1650 and executed.

[71] *Swedish Intelligencer*, 2. 79, 82, 3. 30–2, 71; Monro, *Expedition*, 2. 75, 85, 108, and 2. 93 on 'my deere Camerades of the British Nation'.

[72] John Adair, 'The Court Martial Papers of Sir William Waller's Army, 1644', *JSAHR* 44 (1966), 213; Roy, 'Profession of Arms', 193.

[73] Ibid. 192. See Monro, *Expedition*, 2. 108–9, on officer movement between Scottish, Dutch, and Swedish forces.

[74] Parker, *Thirty Years War*, 193–4; Murdoch, 'Introduction', in *Scotland and the Thirty Years War*, 19–20, and see his discussion of the difficulties in estimating these numbers. He distinguishes

'steady state' volume of British troops in German and Dutch service. Forces were rarely at full nominal strength; at one point, for example, Gustavus Adolphus 'cashiered' English and Scottish regiments because of the 'extreame weaknesse' of their numbers.[75] Overall we can safely but unhelpfully say that the numbers, from early in the century, were large, but we must also remember that the number of soldiers officially authorized in warrants to raise regiments normally exceeded the number actually raised; that individual and unofficial enlistments were not necessarily in English or Scottish regiments; that attrition rates were high; and that some enlisted men—like the companies drowned on their way to Denmark under Sir Thomas Conway—never reached the front.[76] Furthermore, estimates like those given above do not account for the men who served in Catholic armies; although they were fewer than those who served with Protestants they were not insignificant in numbers or influence, and many—like Gage and his officers—returned to fight in England.

Once in Europe the usual causes of troop attrition operated: death, wounds, sickness, accident, desertion, capture. Overall losses are, again, unquantifiable but they were high. Many of those young enough to have come home to fight in England were already dead by 1642. In the 1620s two Fairfaxes died fighting for the Palatinate and a third at La Rochelle; Waller's younger brother survived service under Mansfeld only to die as a captain in Ireland; a Holles younger son, a soldier like his father and brother, died in the Netherlands; the disastrous Ré expedition, where Buckingham's obstinacy and ignorance brought protests from the old professionals on the spot, killed off young officers.[77] In November 1629 John Barrington had to force himself to think the best even of Gustavus: 'Moste parte of the English which went over last sommer into Swethland being placed in the front of the king's army weare cut of by the Polanders . . .; although the kinge is very much blamed for placing such younge souldiers in the front, yet wee thinck the best.' A few days later, after talking to an English captain returned from Sweden, he added: '[A]llmost all the English officers are dead, some slayne others by famine and pestilence.' He was dead himself by 1631.[78] Monro presented a similar picture of mixed mortality and a reminder that disease was as dangerous

---

between proposed 'enlistments'—the numbers authorized in formal warrants (112,700, of whom 61,000 were to be Scots)—and actual numbers who joined the colours (100,000); see also 9–14 for additional discussion.

   [75] *The Swedish Intelligencer. The Third Part* (1633), 71, and ibid. 30–2 and Monro, *Expedition*, 2. 12–13, for fluctuations in regimental composition and command.

   [76] Ibid. 2. 13.

   [77] Bodl. MS Fairfax 30, fos. 152, 156, 163; Wilson, *Fairfax*, 6; Adair, *Roundhead General*, 17–18. See HEH HA 4158, 'Relation of the Occurrances happening . . . in the Isle of Ree', for an account of the unanimous 'soldier like' advice to Buckingham from 'the colonels. . . by whom he ought to be governed'. They cited Spinola's example to prove that withdrawal would be perfectly honourable. For another, equally damning, version see Magdelene College, Cambridge, Pepys MS 2099, fos .26–36ᵛ.

   [78] *Barrington Family Letters*, 101, 253.

as battle when he recalled young Andrew Monro, dead of plague, and his cousin John Monro, 'without feare . . . and of a merry and quicke disposition', who died of a 'burning Feaver'.[79] Monro named 103 Scottish officers of the rank of major and above who served the king of Sweden in 1632. By the time he wrote—his book appeared in 1637—twenty-nine were dead. A death rate of just on 30 per cent over four or five years is a warning that we should not expect a high rate of personal professional survival from continental Europe to England.[80] Monro did not attempt to calculate how many junior officers and men died; unlike those of the young Monro cousins, most of their deaths went unrecorded.

The other side of the question—how many members of civil war armies had pre-war military experience?—remains equally difficult to resolve. Newman, in a pioneering survey, estimated that 'perhaps a good half' of the 1629 royalist officers of the rank of major and above whom he was able to identify, 'had sound military experience prior to the civil wars', although that experience included service against the Scots and in Ireland.[81] No such calculation has been made for their parliamentarian counterparts, but the distribution of veterans in the armies of both sides appears to have been similar.[82] In 1639 some old European hands had hurried home to England to fight an enemy whose army was filled with their Scottish counterparts. Stephen Hawkins, for example, 'hearing of the insurrection in Scotland, . . . forthwith repaired home and raised for his majesty's service there 100 foot'.[83] Others remained in continental service. At home their places were filled by the throng of nobility and gentry—'ye greatest part . . . of this kingdom was personally engag'd'. For most of them and their troops, the Scottish war was their first campaign, and it was hardly triumphal.[84] The education it offered proved cautionary, for the English armies were notoriously incompetent and disorganized. Sir Edward Walker, appointed secretary to the earl of Arundel who commanded the first expedition, listed its leading officers and commented drily, 'The Army thus composed, any Man of Reason might have doubted the Event.'[85]

---

[79] Monro, *Expedition*, 2. 10, and see 2. 12 on the 'divers brave Souldiers of the Regiment' buried at Stettin in 1630 when 'the Pest raged so'.

[80] Ibid. 1. O 2–O [4] (appendix following the table of contents); in addition, two of the five English colonels noted by Monro were dead. Compare Rogers's lament in 1632 for 'many . . . worthy Souldiers' lost in recent years: Rogers, *Sermon . . . at the Funerall of William Proud*, [C3 (2)].

[81] Newman, *Royalist Officers*, pp. vii–viii.

[82] Given the larger number of Scots in Europe, both absolutely and in proportion to the total population of the country, the proportion of European veterans in Scottish armies was probably higher than in English.

[83] BL Harl. MS 6852, fo. 253; Newman, *Royalist Officers*, 182.

[84] National Library of Wales, Chirk MS F 7442, and see HMC, *Second Report* (1871), 'Myddelton-Biddulph MSS', 73; *The Diary of Sir Henry Slingsby of Scriven*, ed. Daniel Parsons (1836), 31.

[85] Sir Edward Walker, 'A Short View of the Life of the Most Noble and Excellent Tho. Howard, Earl of *Arundel* and *Surrey*, Earl Marshall of *England*', in Walker, *Historical Discourses, upon Several Occasions* (1705), 216.

Despite its failure, however, this 'first Army that had then for many Years been raised in *England*' gave domestic employment to foreign veterans who were to become civil war commanders, from royalists like Astley and Goring to parliament's general the earl of Essex. It also educated the less experienced. Sir Henry Slingsby, after six weeks as a soldier, approved the life as 'a commendable way of breeding for a young Gentleman', improving him morally and physically. Walker observed that most of those who were later to be the king's generals and senior officers were in this war 'but private Captains or Gentlemen Volunteers', while Fairfax was no more than captain of a troop of horse.[86] The Scottish campaigns in fact offered opportunities to learn by mistakes and to begin the 'socialization' of an English army of professional colleagues operating together on home ground, and forced them to focus attention on problems of supply and logistics. The Irish rebellion of 1641 offered another, more dangerous lesson, for reports of its atrocities brought a German terror close to home and accustomed civilians in England as well as soldiers in Ireland to habits of reprisal and a rhetoric of barbarity. These campaigns thus began the practical domestic education of future opponents, but they also killed off experienced soldiers who might otherwise have contributed their European expertise to England's war. One such casualty was Sir Simon Harcourt, whose career epitomized the professional and family formation described so far. His mother was a Vere; at 16 he went to the Low Countries as lieutenant to his uncle Sir Horace Vere, and continued a soldier for twenty years. In 1638 he was at The Hague; in 1639 he was back at home with the English army at Berwick; in 1640 he returned to the Netherlands but foresaw 'benifitiall' opportunities in the king's service, and by January 1641 he was in Ireland. Just over a year later he was killed in a minor action near Dublin. Yet old military tradition and connection did not end with his death; his widow, a cousin of the earl of Essex, later married Sir William Waller.[87]

The professionalism of European veterans therefore combined with military literature to condition the nation for war even in its 'halcyon' years. Nor was conditioning by experience confined to soldiers. Civilian travellers observed and listened. William Crowne, after his travels with the earl of Arundel, brought the practices of continental war home to the English reader. Sir William Brereton, later an able parliamentary commander, went to Holland in 1634 as a civilian tourist. He recorded everything that piqued his interest, from tulips to the prince of Orange's baby elephant, from the ways of the Amsterdam Jewish community to murder and natural history, but he also dined with the young Prince Rupert, Colonel Goring, and other English soldiers and clergy, and heard accounts of siege, famine, and disease. Along the way he had met some of those who were to

---

[86] Slingsby, *Diary*, 38; Walker, *Historical Discourses*, 217.

[87] *The Harcourt Papers*, ed. Edward William Harcourt (14 vols. Oxford, [1880–1905]), 1. 104, 111, 113, 118, 129–35, 138–62.

be eminent enemies.[88] Many others, from the boys sent to France to refine their education to the merchants who travelled to Germany with their servants, had seen countries at war.

We should not exaggerate or romanticize this pre-war exposure to real war. Those who served abroad made up a very small part of the population, and those who survived an even smaller one. By the end of the 1630s the population of England numbered just over five million, and even if we add those who served Catholic powers and those who served further afield to the suggested total of fifty thousand English, Welsh, and Irish who enrolled, over a thirty-year period, against the Habsburgs, together they clearly made up a tiny fraction of total population, nor did their death or absence bring devastating demographic consequences comparable to those experienced by Sweden.[89] Furthermore, continental experience did not infallibly produce professional competence, discipline, or courage. The desertion, mutiny, and 'tumults or mischief' against civilians that were to be familiar aspects of the civil war were part of that experience. In 1627, when English regiments in Holland were to be transferred to Denmark, half of Sir Charles Morgan's five thousand men deserted before they could be embarked, and an angry Morgan attributed the débâcle to the 'ill usage' of their officers who could 'hardly be made fit to know what belongs to command'.[90] Monro's disapproval of flamboyant, extravagant officers confirmed the survival of the swaggering, vainglorious soldier of traditional stereotypes, and although such men might prove effective field officers it is unlikely that many applied themselves to the higher theory of warfare or that they served as prototypes for the New Model army. Nor were all who went to Europe enthusiastic soldiers even when they did not desert; if John Barrington was eager to serve, Will Gell returned to Germany reluctantly.

Yet despite uneven quality, high attrition rates, and enlistments that were lower than the Scots' in numbers and even lower in proportion to total population, there remained a nucleus of experienced, seriously professional officers and other ranks whose influence exceeded their numbers. As war between England and Scotland loomed in January 1639 some were already training domestic troops and offering seasoned advice, but both countries recognized the need to bring home more of the professionals who could command and train their raw levies. Many of the latter were unwilling recruits, and all needed professional help. A correspondent from the north of England reported unskilled soldiers who were nonetheless

---

[88] Sir William Brereton, *Travels in Holland the United Provinces England Scotland and Ireland M.D.C.XXXIV–M.D.C.XXXV*, ed. Edward Hawkins, Chetham Society, 1 (1844), 28, 30, 33–40, 47, 60–1.

[89] E. A. Wrigley and R. S. Schofield, *The Population History of England 1541–1871: A Reconstruction* (Cambridge, 1993), 209; Parker, *Thirty Years War*, 193.

[90] Quoted in E. A. Beller, 'The Military Expedition of Sir Charles Morgan to Germany, 1627–9', *EHR* 43 (1928), 530, 533. Morgan complained that most of the officers had come from the Inns of Court, where they had 'learned to play the mauvais garçon'. He hoped in time 'to bring them to better experience, or else I'll show them the way to break their necks'. The delinquent officers were presumably fairly new recruits.

willing to learn, but added, 'the greatest want is of serjeants, corporals, and such as should teach them'.[91] Meanwhile the Scots, in their more systematic master plan for the war, specified the regimental structure for their army. They allowed that the captain and ensign might be noblemen or gentlemen, but their criteria were more stringent for the men who mattered in commanding and training the regiment. The colonels and the major, 'being prime officers, ought to be men of skill'; they and the lieutenants and sergeants—the men responsible for the hands-on transformation of recruits into soldiers—must all be 'sent for out of Germany and Holland'.[92] Some of these seasoned soldiers came back to Britain and were to be found on both sides in the Anglo-Scottish wars, but in England their success in producing disciplined and effective soldiers, amid the chaos and disorganization of the country's war effort, was admittedly limited. Once these wars were over there was a widespread desire to disband all the British armies 'with all convenient Expedition', and many soldiers, like Sir Simon Harcourt, dispersed again to the continent and to Ireland. Some, however, had recognized the danger of dependence in a crisis on the expertise of English soldiers based abroad. In a little noticed speech on 14 April 1641 the earl of Essex moved that parliament should consider

How a Provision may be made for the preserving and maintaining of able Commanders, experienced in the Wars, and a Supply and Pension to be paid them, whereby they may be encouraged and induced to remain ready upon all Occasions to serve the Kingdom, and not be inforced to serve Foreign Princes for Maintenance, and so this Kingdom to be deprived of their Assistance and Service in Time of Need.[93]

Nothing came of the proposal, and events soon overtook the need for it, but the conjunction of habitual professional service abroad and domestic crisis had produced a first plea for the establishment of a standing English army.

Finally, we should note that professionals were not the only Englishmen to bear arms in the decades before the civil war. These years also saw another form of preparation, in the training of amateur soldiers in England. Its best known but usually least effective mode was through the militia or trained bands. Although intermittently fostered by the central government and by local magnates, enthusiasm and energy were sporadic. Official encouragement for employment of experienced old soldiers to manage musters and drill, for modernization of equipment, and for dissemination of updated training instructions, tended to reflect temporary crises or personal interest rather than sustained policy, and encountered local inertia and dislike of soldiers and military authority. Nevertheless, the employment of veterans like Thomas Fisher, who came home after twenty-six years in the Dutch army to instruct the trained bands of Kent, meant that their men learnt modern European military practice. Standards probably improved overall under James and Charles but progress was

[91] *CSP Dom. 1638–1639*, 370.   [92] Ibid. 409.   [93] *LJ* 4. 216.

uneven; units with soldierly skills and enthusiasm were outnumbered by those that were to be the despair of their officers when they came to arms as 'freshwater men' in 1642.[94] One discouraged military writer in 1639 proposed ways to improve the trained bands, but concluded that 'the *parched barrennesse* of our *Militia*' left the country '*dull and snoring* in the *lap of stupid security*; and . . . *ridiculous*, in the *eyes* of our *enemies*'.[95]

More important for the future dissemination of modern military skill were the various military companies, some civic, some private, that flourished in the decades before 1642. Scattered through England, mainly in towns, they trained citizen-soldiers and represented an embourgeoisement of soldierly expertise that was to have a profound influence on English armies, on the spread of officer skills beyond traditionally trained military men and rural gentry, and hence, later, on developments in the New Model army. They nurtured the idea that citizenship and soldiership were not divorced.

The most famous companies were those of the Artillery Garden and the Military Garden in London. These 'publique Gardens' in Bishopsgate and St Martin's Fields were supplemented by 'Private Meetings' such as those of Christ Church, Townditch, and Cripplegate. All, their supporters claimed, had produced 'able and . . . learned Souldiers' for service at home and abroad, but the Artillery and Military Gardens provided the most advanced education. The private London companies, indeed, often served as feeders to them, giving basic training and arousing ambition for higher skills. Members of the Cripplegate company did not acquire the more recondite military arts, but they learnt the fundamentals of drill and formations and how to handle a musket, although only with '*false fire* in their pans'. Even those who went no further became 'Souldier-like', 'able knowing' men who could move correctly and manage their arms, and who were familiar enough with military discipline to be 'silent *and* obedient Souldiers'.[96] Nor was this training confined to London. Provincial towns like Norwich, Derby, Yarmouth, and Colchester had their own companies. In Kent the old veteran Sir Ralph Bosvile was captain of 'a Select Company of Foot' and employed the expert William Barriffe as his lieutenant.[97]

---

[94] See Ian F. W. Beckett, *The Amateur Military Tradition 1558–1945* (Manchester, 1991), 34–9, and see p. 38 for his muted defence of the trained bands in his warning against 'too ready acceptance of the universal failure of the exact militia'; he suggests that in 1639 'the 99,000 or so men in the trained bands . . . were in relatively good order'. For a more flattering account of the pre-war militia than that given here, see James Scott Wheeler, *The Making of a World Power: War and the Military Revolution in Seventeenth-Century England* (1999), 71–3. For a government attempt to disseminate modern military directions, see *Instructions for Musters and Armes . . . 1631*. Fisher's detailed drill book *Warlike Directions: Or the Souldiers Practice* was reissued in new edns. in 1643 and 1644. Cockle, *Bibliography of Military Books*, 99.

[95] Barriffe, *Military Discipline* (2nd edn. 1639), 313.

[96] Ibid., dedications to captains and gentlemen of Cripplegate meeting and to Captain William Geere; Elton, *Compleat Body of the Art Military*, 68.

[97] Barriffe, *Military Discipline* (2nd edn. 1639), dedication to Sir Ralph Bosvile; Cruso, *Art of Warre*, dedication to 'The Gentlemen of the *Artillerie* and *Militarie* companies in the Kingdome,

We may wonder how extensive and how effective this training was, particularly as much of the evidence comes from those predisposed in its favour. Even they sometimes admitted to discouragement and felt that society failed to appreciate their efforts on its behalf. '[N]one more *neglected* and less *countenanced* . . . nor none more *scrued-up* in the places of their abiding' than practitioners of the military art, said Barriffe. 'Souldiers (though never so poore)' were taxed 'like Gentlemen', he complained, for 'The common speech [is] (oh let him pay) he hath money enough to spend upon his exercises of Souldiery.'[98] Nevertheless the sense of ill usage was accompanied by self-confidence, and the experts were almost certainly correct in their belief that they had improved England's military expertise through basic training and by familiarizing their citizen soldiers with new European developments. Cruso believed that the basic training prepared companies for advanced instruction, and that the 'Garden, Yarde, City, Home, and Countrie trialls' offered innovative lessons for 'new', modern soldiers. At the Military Garden in London, for example, the professional Major Henry Tillier (later to be Prince Rupert's major-general at Marston Moor) was the first to demonstrate 'the marching of the Souldiers in a *Regimentall* way'.[99] When Lieutenant Hammond visited the Isle of Wight in 1635 the highest praise he could offer its garrison of 'ready exercis'd, and well disciplin'd, trayn'd men' was that they were 'as expert in handling their Armes, as our Artillery Nurseries'.[100]

The lessons thus presented undoubtedly took in varying degrees, and although they were offered on a regular basis the number who availed themselves of them fluctuated. In 1614 the London Artillery Garden was authorized to raise membership from two hundred and fifty to five hundred to meet the demand for places, but in 1626 this 'number was not full', and William Gouge lamented in a sermon that there were 'no more of your Company'.[101] In the mid-1620s the company had in fact enrolled healthy numbers of new members—85 in 1624, only 33 in 1625, but 107 in 1626—but by the early 1630s, partly as a

---

and particularly that in *Norwich*'; Cockle, *Bibliography of Military Books*, 112; see Beckett, *Amateur Military Tradition*, 35, and G. A. Raikes, *The History of the Honourable Artillery Company* (2 vols. 1878–79), 1. 58, 89–90, for companies in Colchester, Bury St Edmunds, Norwich, Bristol, Gloucester, Yarmouth, Derby, Coventry, Ipswich, and Nottingham.

[98] Barriffe, *Military Discipline* (2nd edn. 1639), 257.

[99] Cruso, *Art of Warre*, dedication to gentlemen of artillery and military companies; Elton, *Compleat Body of the Art Military*, 67; G. M[arkham], *The Second Part of the Souldiers Grammar: Or A Schoole for Young Souldiers* (1639), 45. The London Artillery company also provided serious apprenticeship training in gunnery, granting certificates to candidates for appointment as naval gunners. Raikes, *History of the . . . Artillery Company*, 1. 81.

[100] *A Relation of a Short Survey of the Western Counties Made by a Lieutenant of the Military Company of Norwich in 1635*, ed. L. G. Wickham Legg (*Camden Miscellany*, 16, 1936), 58.

[101] Raikes, *History of the . . . Artillery Company*, 1. 43–4; William Gouge, *The Dignitie of Chivalry, Set forth in a Sermon Preached before the Artillery Comapny of London, Iune xiij. 1626* (2nd edn. 1631), 426–7, 432. Gouge had high standards of military preparedness. He believed that every town and village should have its own artillery company, and offered King Jehosophat's army of 1,160,000 'in so small a Kingdome as *Iudah*' as a model for England.

result of squabbles between the Company and the City government, it fell on hard times, recruiting only 12 in 1632. In 1635, however, new membership shot up to nearly 350 and remained at a respectable level: in 1640 it was 112, in 1641 188.[102] In these years immediately before the war, membership must have outrun the statutory limit of five hundred, and by 1641 the Company had succeeded in acquiring a new Artillery Garden at Bunhill Fields to meet its needs.[103] Nevertheless, although at times it was clearly fashionable to be enrolled, it seems unlikely that all the mayors, sheriffs, and aldermen of London who belonged to the Artillery Company were equally diligent in its exercises.[104] Yet some of those who resorted to the London Military Garden apparently did so daily, and not surprisingly they showed 'great improvement'. A more modest and attainable ideal was a weekly meeting like that at Christ Church, while the two companies that had met at Cripplegate since the late 1620s exercised for an hour every Thursday, ending in summer at 7 a.m. and thus, as an admirer pointed out, did so without hindrance to their more necessary callings.[105] For citizen soldiers, a balance between military keenness and economic responsibility was demanding, but in the 1630s throughout England many townsmen succeeded in acquiring a basic military education.

There were clearly elements of fashion, sport, and entertainment in this domestic preparation. Gouge had likened such 'delightsome preparations for war' to 'the *Olympian* games' and '*armed dancing*', and he defended them as useful as well as pleasant recreations.[106] Practitioners in turn entertained the public with their skills. Participation in military spectacles bolstered pride and solidarity as performers of a fashionable art while disseminating to the civilian populace a superficial familiarity with its picturesque detail. The unmilitary D'Ewes recorded, for example, a public training exercise in Tothill Fields led by Buckingham in 1622, at which spectators included the king and Prince Charles. Three years later curiosity took him to view the skill of the pikemen 'double-armed' with a combined pike and bow, as demonstrated at the Artillery Yard. In 1638 the 'Artillery men' of Yarmouth conducted manœuvres according to the most modern principles that ranged through the town, involved many of its citizens, and won their universal commendation. The fashion even spread to Ireland, where at annual

[102] These figures cover the old-style year from March to March. *The Ancient Vellum Book of the Artillery Company, being the Roll of Members from 1611 to 1682*, ed. G. A. Raikes (1890), 36–63.

[103] Raikes, *History of the . . . Artillery Company*, 1. 93–9.

[104] Raikes, *Ancient Vellum Book of . . . the Artillery Company*, 2–3. By late 1638, their historian believed, the Artillery Company was so flourishing that 'but few citizens of eminence . . . were not members'. Raikes, *History of the . . . Artillery Company*, 1. 95. Barriffe told Captain William Geere, to whom he was lieutenant, that his presence would encourage soldiers, which suggests that it was irregular. Barriffe, *Military Discipline* (2nd edn. 1639), dedication to Captain William Geere. Geere was enrolled as a captain in the Artillery Company in Nov. 1632, *Vellum Book of the . . . Artillery Company*, 45.

[105] Elton, *Compleat Body of the Art Military*, 67, and prefatory poem by John Hayne; Barriffe, *Military Discipline* (2nd edn. 1639), 313, and dedication to captains and gentlemen of Cripplegate.

[106] Gouge, *Dignitie of Chivalry*, 429.

exercises in Dublin in 1637 Wentworth, with other peers and officers, played their parts as members of model companies commanded by professionals.[107]

A performance in the Merchant Tailors' hall in October 1638 epitomized the educational, social, and entertainment attractions of military companies, although its elaborate and exotic presentation must have outshone most such displays. Part tattoo, part masque, it combined music, drill, and drama. Eighty members of the Artillery Company, some representing Saracens, some 'moderne Armes', marched into the hall, where they paid their respects to the assembled nobility, aldermen, and gentry; performed ceremonial marches 'demonstrating [their] dexteritie'; went through the complex steps of preparing and firing muskets and of coordinating the movements of musketeers and pikemen in battle formation, to the accompaniment of the appropriate 'posture tunes' on fife and drum; and finally staged a rousing battle between Christians and Saracens in which, after many changes of fortune, the Christians were victorious.[108] It must have been a splendid show. When Captain Mulli-Aben-Achmat and his Saracens marched into the hall, 'their musick was a *Turky Drumme*, and a hideous noise making *pipe* (made of a *Buffolas* horn:) . . . some of the chiefest of them had broad *Turky daggers* at their girdles, and all of them habited after the *Persian* and *Turconian* manner'. The captain and lieutenant carried large pole-axes and were hung around with scimitars, battle axes, and daggers. The ensign's azure blue colours, on a ten-foot pole surmounted by a steel crescent, proclaimed in Arabic characters 'Bismi-Alli Val Mahomet', or as Barriffe helpfully explained, 'In the name of *Alli and Mahomet*'. At the end of their preliminary display, they took their leave 'after the *Persian* maner: putting their *left hands* upon the *tops of their Turbans* and *Shashes*, bowing their *bodies forward*'. It was a hard act to follow, but Captain John Venn's men reasserted the superiority of the west, coming in to 'a lofty *English march*', and proceeding to dazzle with modern military expertise and good tunes, and to win the ensuing battle.[109]

The event contained messages that went beyond spectacle to the establishment of a domestic military education without benefit of formal academies and to the social formation of soldiers. Some were made explicit in the speech delivered to the assembled worthies by one of the musketeers, who extolled the value of a nucleus of officers with skill both to instruct and to command. These talents, he emphasized, were now native and no longer a matter of foreign expertise, and his insistence on this change tells us much about the spread of military education in England before the war:

---

[107] *The Diary of Sir Symonds D'Ewes (1622–1624)*, ed. Elisabeth Bourcier (Paris, 1974), 88, 190; Cockle, *Bibliography of Military Books*, 112; Hardacre, 'Patronage and purchase', 42.

[108] Barriffe, *Mars, his Triumph, passim*. The work includes musical notation for the posture tunes. It was reprinted in 1645 and 1661. The last leaf of the Huntington Library's copy of the 1639 edn. (bound with the 2nd, 1639 edn. of Barriffe's *Military Discipline*) is inscribed 'Ensigne Will. Harvye his Booke 1660.' The show-business element may have contributed to its longevity.

[109] Barriffe, *Mars his Triumph*, 2–6, and 10 ff.

The time has been, the rugged mayne *was crost*
To both the Germanies *with care and cost*
To finde a Souldier, *whose experience might*
Teach our Commanders *how to* form a fight.
But now, that trouble's *sav'd.*[110]

He also reiterated the theme of the soldier-citizen: '*Behold the* Souldier *and the* Citizen / Make but *one man.*' This integration into the life of the city was one of the implicit messages of the occasion, for as Barriffe observed of the defeated Turks, they were 'now either *Merchants* or *Shopkeepers* for the most part'.[111] Many of those present would shortly be allies or enemies in real war, but their professional formation, technically and morally, had come as colleagues. Like the professionals who came back from Europe, home-grown soldiers had learnt their trade together. The pre-war military companies formed long-standing bonds of 'friendly . . . society' among 'loving Gentlemen' who were then still amateurs, and of sociable camaraderie among experts like 'a Captain, a Lieutenant, and an Ancient, all three of the Military Company of Norwich' who together made a tour of western counties in 1634.[112] Meanwhile the audiences who watched such shows were exposed not only to modern military practice but, as at Yarmouth, to military conventions ranging from the treatment due to prisoners to the etiquette of drum and parley.

It would be satisfying to trace exactly the dispersal of these pre-war soldiers to wartime armies, but often the trail is lost. Captain John Venn of the Merchant Tailors' Hall exercise had by October 1642 become colonel of a regiment and parliamentarian governor of Windsor castle, but the future careers of some of his fellow performers are more obscure and uncertain. We can only say that John Alford, for example, probably commanded a troop under Manchester and became a major in the New Model, and that Henry Slayde was probably a captain in Warwick castle in 1644 and later a major who died in Ireland in 1650.[113] Many from the London companies and trained bands of course were soon to be found in the London regiments, like Captain Thomas Juxon, formerly of the Artillery Company, killed at Newbury serving with the London Green Regiment.[114] Some moved upwards, like Randolph Manwaring and Rowland Wilson, members respectively since 1613 and 1614, captains in the Artillery Company in 1639 and lieutenant-colonels in City regiments by 1643, and

---

[110] Ibid. 7–9.   [111] Ibid. 7.

[112] Barriffe, *Military Discipline* (2nd edn. 1639), dedication to the officers and gentlemen of the Cripplegate meeting; Elton, *Compleat Body of the Art Military*, 68, and third dedication to officers and men of the Christ Church meeting; [Hammond], *Relation of a Short Survey of the Western Counties*, iii, [xv], and note Hammond's convivial sense of military fellowship, 3, 20, 58.

[113] For Venn's lengthy command at Windsor (1642–5), see PRO SP 28/126, fos. 5–85 *passim*; Barriffe, *Mars, His Triumph*, 2, 9; Sir Charles Firth, *The Regimental History of Cromwell's Army* (2 vols. Oxford, 1940), 1. 143–5; 2. 632.

[114] Raikes, *Ancient Vellum Book of the . . . Artillery Company*, 54; Raikes, *History of the . . . Artillery Company*, 1. 137.

some had moved outwards as well, like Samuel Carleton, also a lieutenant-colonel by 1643 but no longer with a London regiment. For others the change was more radical. Nicholas Crispe, one of the king's custom farmers, and Marmaduke Rawdon, a member of the Clothworkers Company, were Artillery Company captains in 1639 and royalist colonels by 1643. By 1643, indeed, the parliamentarian Barriffe made a number of politic changes to the dedicatory sections of a new edition of his *Military Discipline*.[115] His own old 'Much Honored Captaine' William Geere of Cheapside was one of those dropped, a suggestive omission in view of Geere's troubles in 1644, when he appeared in custody for failure to pay his assessment. Yet although Geere was still stigmatized as a delinquent in 1646, his post-war survival within the nexus of City and government financial affairs is a further reminder of the ties that continued to bind old citizen soldiers as well as country neighbours across partisan lines of combat.[116]

England before the civil war was not a militarized country. On the other hand, it was a country that knew a great deal about war and its social and moral effects, and furthermore was accustomed to thinking about it in religious and confessional terms, that is, to seeing God's approving hand at work and to seeing war as a conflict between true and false religions. There were civilians who had thought seriously about the practice of war, and professional soldiers who had been engaged with the most advanced practitioners of their day. All of this was not enough to prevent humiliating, muddled defeat in their first wars after the halcyon decade. In the Scottish wars command was feeble, troops were ill disciplined and untrained, logistical planning was piecemeal, and delivery of supplies fortuitous, while civilians experienced disorder and predation at the hands of their countrymen as well as the enemy. The opening months of the civil war seemed to offer little improvement, but as national organizations were pulled into shape and command structures were established the lessons of the 1630s began to take effect and the experience of pre-war soldiers, amateurs, and enthusiasts began to shape the forces engaged—although as we shall see all civil war armies, including the New Model, could be volatile, disorderly, and unpredictable.[117]

---

[115] Raikes, 1. 70, 74, 111, 133, 136, 149; Raikes, *Ancient Vellum Book of the . . . Artillery Company*, 20, 22; Barriffe, *Military Discipline* (2nd edn. 1639), dedication 'To all the worthy captaines of the city,' and cf. 4th revised edn. (1643), prefatory material *passim*; Newman, *Royalist Officers*, 92, 311.

[116] Barriffe, *Military Discipline* (2nd edn. 1639), dedication to Geere; for Geere's tax troubles, see *CAM* 1. 385. In 1640 Geere had been Receiver-General of Crown Revenues in Worcestershire, Shropshire, and Staffordshire; for hearings in the late 1640s and early 1650s relating to his complex and sometimes politically suspect financial dealings, see *CCC* 2. 949–51, 3. 2106.

[117] See Keith Roberts, 'Citizen Soldiers: The Military Power of the City of London', in Stephen Porter (ed.), *London and the Civil War* (1996), 90–101; he comments that, while exercises of the kind taught at artillery gardens provided useful training for set battles, they did not prepare troops for mobile campaigns in which skirmishes and small actions predominated. Ibid. 107.

One of the themes of this chapter has been the common military past of royalists and parliamentarians, but the campaigns in which the English were engaged in the decades before 1642 reveal one feature that was to differentiate royalist from parliamentarian conduct in their domestic war and to be crucial to its outcome, namely the managerial weakness of the royalist state. In these pre-war decades when they learnt the best and worst of war, the successes of the Dutch or Gustavus Adolphus were offset by the long roll-call of death, disease, drowning, and defeat, but it cannot have escaped attention that the most ignominious episodes for the English were ventures under the direction of the crown and its officials. The skills of English professional officers were no match for the ineptitudes of a royal state that proved unable to manage planning, command, supply, or pay, and these failures in turn led to the most shameful—and widely publicized—losses of English lives. The management of the Scottish wars confirmed the weaknesses of the old system. It was not that the crown lacked sound professional advice. In January 1639, for example, Sir Jacob Astley toured the north of England and sent back to London an admirably practical survey of the military situation there, with sensible soldierly recommendations for improvement.[118] The difficulty lay in converting advice to effective action through the customary means of court and council. One of the striking features of the civil war, and one which contributed powerfully to parliamentary victory, was the divergence between the state systems of the two parties. Royalist weaknesses of oversight, planning, and organization that had been evident in the military ventures of the past twenty years persisted, and were exacerbated by factional quarrels among royalist officers. Parliament too had notable quarrels, but it managed to cobble together a system of centralized oversight and planning and to secure execution of its plans to a degree that, if far from perfect, marked a great leap forward from the pre-war administration of war to which the royalists still clung. If military preparedness was greater than tradition has suggested, the administrative lessons of the pre-war decades had still to be learnt.

[118] *CSP Dom. 1633–1639*, 383–6.

THE TEXTURE OF WAR: THE SOLDIER'S WORLD

The conditions of war affect the relations of combatants to each other and to the civilian population. What follows is an attempt to reconstruct some of the limitations and peculiarities that shaped the acts, attitudes, and expectations of participants in the English civil war. In this as in other wars, factors as diverse as inadequacies of weapon design, the formation of officers, the patterns of disease, the shape of the landscape, and the vagaries of weather affected military outcomes, civilian sufferings, and the ways in which countrymen behaved to one another.

Some of the conditions to be considered were peculiar to civil war in an essentially monolingual country. With the exception of Welsh, Cornish, and Irish speakers, most of the enemies who fought in England and Wales shared a common tongue; even the Scots, unless they were highlanders, were in theory comprehensible. Other conditions were common to any seventeenth-century European land war. The capacities and unreliability of weapons, proximity of opponents, difficulties of troop movement when topographical information was uncertain and roads bad, persistent shortages of supplies, pay, and horses—all presented problems that dogged every early modern army. Confusion, accident, sickness, and bad weather combined, individually or in unpredictable conjunction, with heroism, cruelty, cowardice, stupidity, chutzpah and ignorance, to subvert the best laid plans or grant undeserved success, to ennoble defeat or corrupt victory. The confusion and incomprehension of Stendhal's Fabrizio or Tolstoy's Prince André, the corporate courage of Pickett's charge, the brutality of Mai Lai, and the moral uncertainties over the deaths of women and children in countless modern wars, all had their counterparts in the civil war.

This examination of the texture of war emphasizes both the unpredictable hazards of military experience and the degree to which that experience was enmeshed in civilian society. It stresses the contingency of war rather than its intentionality, and looks at some of the ways in which military planning was at the mercy of uncontrollable events and circumstances. By examining factors that shaped the experience of soldiers and civilians in England in the 1640s, it seeks to illuminate the context of the military actions and political and religious manœuvres that are the stuff of much narrative and analytical history. It will explore the deadliness and the limitations of weapons, the uncertainties of intelligence, and the consequent difficulties of planning and execution that thickened the fog of war. It will address the ways in which a war without a front line and fought between countrymen was intimate, integrated, and, in its national reach, a forerunner of more modern 'total' wars. Succeeding sections will consider the rules intended to govern military conduct, the character of the troops, and indicate in passing their dependence on the civilians among whom they lived and marched and who, in their turn, were vulnerable to soldiers' volatile moods and discipline.

4

An Integrated War

The civil war was thus in many ways both intimate and domestic. Its protagonists shared space and language. Its technology reduced physical distance, just as common language reduced psychological distance. Consequently it was difficult to forget that the enemy was a man all too like yourself, and that he was a fellow-countryman. The war was also wide-ranging, so that few parts of the country escaped untouched. Its effects—material, psychological, financial—extended far beyond the sites of military engagements. Maps showing civil war battlefields present a heavily fought over area running south from Yorkshire roughly down the middle of the country and then veering to the south-west. In the far north and Wales isolated significant sites—such as Newcastle and Pembroke—are more scattered, while in the east and south-east an arc running through most of East Anglia to London and Kent appears virtually unscathed until 1648.[1] Some regions, such as the western royalist supply corridor and the approaches to Wales and Ireland, the south-western ports, and the midland areas above Oxford, were of a strategic importance that rendered them 'cockpit' war zones: Ian Roy has remarked of the Severn valley that 'no region was more populated with warring troops throughout the year, none was more overrun by field armies in the summers'.[2] The peace of other places such as Norwich, described as having 'a quiet Civil War', was marred only by an occasional outbreak of military violence or random explosion.[3] Many English men and women probably never heard a shot fired in anger. Yet military engagements are a misleading criterion for measuring the impact of the war and give only a partial view of the ways in which it was planned, administered, fought, and experienced.

By modern standards, this war was a curious mixture of the static and the extremely mobile, for it combined innumerable sieges, large and small, with peripatetic armies engaging in minor skirmishes and major battles. In 1642 Prince Rupert had urged a royalist strategy of garrisoned fortresses in order to divide parliament's forces and counter their numerical superiority, but his

---

[1] See e.g. maps in Austin Woolrych, *Battles of the English Civil War* (1961),[14]; Peter Young, *Civil War England* (1981), [6]; Anthony Baker, *A Battlefield Atlas of the English Civil War* (1986), 4.

[2] Roy, 'England turned Germany?', *TRHS* 5th ser. 28 (1978), 133–4.

[3] Peter Gaunt, *The Cromwellian Gazetteer* (Gloucester, 1987), [110].

plan was not adopted and in practice both sides employed the mixed tactics of marching armies and garrisoned strongholds. Both installed garrisons over much of the country. They ranged from small strongholds like Bletchingdon House near Oxford, a manor house modified for military purposes, or Beeston Castle, a minor but virtually impregnable fortress in Cheshire, to the sprawling city of Bristol, whose long lines of circumvallation and virtual indefensibility were the undoing in turn of Nathaniel Fiennes and Prince Rupert. It has been estimated that in 1645 England held close to 160 royalist and parliamentarian garrisons.[4] Even those parts of the country where a quiet war only intermittently flared into action, like Bedfordshire or Kent or Norfolk, sustained local strongholds as well as enduring the passage of marching troops. The effects of these resident garrisons, furthermore, extended far beyond the towns and castles where they were quartered, for neighbouring areas were designated as sources of men, taxation, supplies, and livestock. The competition of commanders of the same side for these resources sometimes led to bitterness that rivalled that towards their enemies, while for civilians there was little to choose between the takings of royalists and parliamentarians. The worst hardship was to suffer both indiscriminately.[5] For both parties, moreover, larger strategic plans, such as they were, whether directed against the central power-house of London or the royalist western axis from Chester to Cornwall, or towards control of important entry and supply ports, were regularly submerged by the pragmatic needs of local garrisons and commanders.[6]

The wide dispersal of garrisons and their effect on surrounding civilian life reduced the contrast between 'peaceful' and 'war-zone' regions of the country. Nor should we exaggerate the ease and security of what we now know to have been the more fortunate parts of England. By contrast with Newark, which had the misfortune to lie at a vital crossing of land and water routes, or with Chester and Nantwich, which were in the middle of active warfare from 1642 to 1646, the peace of Essex seemed little disturbed until the notorious siege of Colchester in 1648. Yet the county took anxious emergency steps against the 'very hot' alarum of the enemy's approach in 1644, suffered from unruly soldiers and civil disorder early in the war, raised troops for service inside and outside its borders,

---

[4] *A Speech Spoken by His Excellence Prince Rupert To his Sacred Majesty, and the Lords of his Privie Councell . . . Wherein is freely delivered his opinion concerning the present Warre* (1642, first printed in Oxford), 3–6; Geoffrey Parker, *The Military Revolution: Military Innovation and the Rise of the West, 1500–1800* (1988), 41.

[5] Ross Lee, *Law and Local Society in the Time of Charles I: Bedfordshire and the Civil War*, Bedfordshire Historical Record Society, 65 (1986), 45–6; Devonshire RO, Seymour of Berry Pomeroy MSS 1392 M/L 1643/61, 1644/25; BL Add. MSS 11,331, fos. 14ᵛ–15; 18,981, fo. 86; 29,319, fos. 29, 31; Bodl. MS Tanner 303, fos. 120–120ᵛ. Beeston changed hands twice, but only as the result of treachery (or possibly incompetence), BL Harl. MS 2125, fo. 135ᵛ.

[6] Royalist defeat at Naseby was partly attributable to the king's refusal to augment his army by calling in troops from Leicester, Newark, and other garrisons. Parker, *Military Revolution*, 41.

supported garrisons and fortifications against threats—real or imagined—to the coastline, and paid war taxes.[7] A county that remained under the control of one party might nevertheless suffer raids by the enemy, like the royalist raids on Ampthill, Bedford, and Dunstable in parliamentarian Bedfordshire in 1643 and 1644. Kent suffered a series of royalist revolts, successfully suppressed, from 1642 to 1648, culminating in the battle of Maidstone. Cornwall was generally regarded as safely royalist beyond its debatable eastern borders, at least until the royalist Lord Goring's depredations changed the popular mind, yet from Braddock Down in January 1643 through the Lostwithiel campaign of 1644 to the fall of Pendennis Castle in August 1646 it suffered intermittently from marching and fighting troops on land and attempted blockades at sea.[8] Oxford was perpetually manned and fortified, and royalist civilian and military government was inextricably mingled. It was overcrowded and full of troops, quarrelling officers, and parliamentarian prisoners; it was at the centre of a web of battles, raids, and marches; it was devastated by epidemics and fire; and the enemy was as close as Cassington and Islip even before it was seriously besieged in 1645. Unthreatened Cambridge, on the other hand, counted as having an uneventful war, but it was nevertheless the base of the county parliamentary committee and a centre of military administration; it housed soldiers and prisoners (the latter barely segregated from the townspeople), and it was the resort of sick soldiers and of needy wives and widows seeking relief. Its defences, no less than those of endangered Chester, were secured by the destruction of civilian property.[9] Even London's safety could not be taken for granted. The royalists got as close as Brentford and Turnham Green in November 1642, and thereafter royalist threats to Newbury to the west and Newport Pagnell to the north prevented complacency and relaxation. The city was surrounded by a complex and extensive system of defences; defence industries throve, as did ancillary businesses such as specialist brokers in high-end plundered goods; and the visible presence of war was reflected in orders that attempted to remove soldiers

[7] In 1644 anxiety was so great in Essex that the county committee ordered that the trained bands be sent to the rendezvous on horseback 'because of the pressing expectation'. BL Stowe MS 189, fos. 30–1; Wilson, 'Observations of God's Providence', in *The Inconstant Lady*, 134–7; HMC, *Report on the Manuscripts of Lord Montagu of Beaulieu* (1900), 153; HMC, *Seventh Report, Part I* (1879), Appendix, 'Manuscripts of Geo. Alan Lowndes, Esq., of Barrington Hall, Co. Essex', 560; HMC, *Manuscripts of the Duke of Portland*, 1 (1891), 187; *CSPDom. 1641–1643*, 420; *The Victoria History of the County of Essex*, 2 vols. (1907), 2. 283–4. See J. S. Morrill, 'Mutiny and Discontent in English Provincial Armies 1645–1647', *PP* 56 (1972), 52, on the costs 'in quarter and in the forcible distraint of provisions' even in 'areas remote from the fighting'.

[8] Alan Everitt, *The Community of Kent and the Great Rebellion 1640–60* (Leicester, 1986), chs. 6 and 8 *passim*; Mary Coate, *Cornwall in the Great Civil War and Interregnum 1642–1660* (Oxford, 1933), 118, 184.

[9] See e.g. the report of a 'fearful fire in Oxon. October 6, 1644', Bodl. MS top. Oxon. c. 378, p. 408; for Cambridge, see PRO SP 28/21, fos. 41, 54; SP 28/23, fos. 109, 158; SP 28/24, fo. 52; SP 28/25, fo. 361.

who were there unofficially and to protect civilians from those legitimately present.[10]

The other face of war was that of soldiers on the move, and indeed for many of them war brought wider knowledge of their own country. The rector of Ducklington, near Witney, recorded men from Cheshire, Lancashire, Staffordshire, Suffolk, Yorkshire, and Wales among the troops who for years washed through his small village. Some soldiers wanted only to go home but others, like Richard Symonds and Nehemiah Wharton, combined soldiering with tourist curiosity.[11] Army mobility meant that even places that escaped garrisons or battles were likely to endure the passage of marching armies or foraging parties or the presence of billeted troops. For most of the year armies were constantly in motion, through a landscape peopled by civilians. Although traditionally they retired to winter quarters to avoid the worst snow and mud, winter was not infallibly peaceful, and at best the off-season only lasted from December to March.[12] A soldier's life, it was said, was 'to march up and down in England'. A detailed log of one soldier's progress from November 1643 to December 1644 shows him for more than half of that period in constant, often daily movement, frequently criss-crossing the same area, a routine only interspersed by limited winter cessations and by some eleven weeks in a garrison town.[13] The log of Prince Rupert's marches, from September 1642 to his departure from England in July 1646, demonstrates a similar mobility. The first month, beginning on 5 September, saw twelve transfers of place, including at least two night marches. Then followed a pause of two weeks, but from 10 October to the end of the month he was on the move every day but three. The pattern was sustained for another three and a half years, broken only by seasonal declines in winter and stationary interludes such as the period at Bristol, or by particularly intensive episodes such as the 'York march' before Marston Moor, when Rupert's army covered nearly 50 modern miles in three days. A week in May 1644 gives the flavour: '16. Thursday, to Petten, near Wem. 18. Satterday, to Whitchurch.

---

[10] Adair, 'Court Martial Papers . . . Waller', *JSAHR* 44 (1966), 209–10; C. H. Firth and R. S. Rait, *Acts and Ordinances of the Interregnum 1642–1660*, 3 vols. (1911), 1. 986–7; Victor Smith and Peter Kelsey, 'The Lines of Communication: The Civil War Defences of London', in Stephen Porter (ed.), *London and the Civil War* (1996), 117–48. See *Considerations upon The present state of Affairs of this Kingdome* (1642), 5, on the royalist advance on London in Nov. 1642: 'if the Cavaliers were defeated, they marched within seven miles of the Parliament after their Defeat, [and] there stood in Battell again'.

[11] Bodl. MS top. Oxon. c. 378, pp. 238–9, 359, 409; *Richard Symonds's Diary of the Marches of the Royal Army*, ed. C. E. Long and Ian Roy (Cambridge, 1997), 14–22; [Nehemiah Wharton], 'Letters from a Subaltern Officer of the Earl of Essex's Army, written in the Summer and Autumn of 1642', *Archaeologia*, 35 (1853), 2.317, 325, 328, 332–3.

[12] For winter campaigns 'in January, the worst of the winter season', see Josiah Ricraft, *A Survey of Englands Champions* (1647), 3, 7, 18. Conventional military wisdom was expressed by a parliamentarian in Feb. 1645: '[N]ow, the spring is coming on . . . we shall go into the fields', Derbys. RO, Sanders MSS, 1232 M/024.

[13] Bodl. MS Carte 74, fos. 39, 159–60.

20. Munday, to Draiton. 21. Tuesday, to Betlye in Staffordshire. 22. Wednesday, to Sandbach, in Cheshire. 23. Thursday, to Knotsford.'[14]

The 'Iter Carolinum' reveals a less frenetic but similar pattern for the king himself when he was away from Oxford, and provides more evidence of the symbiotic relation between combatants and civilians. Daily movements were usually in the 5 to 12 mile range, but marches of 28, 30, and 32 miles were by no means uncommon.[15] Sometimes, for weeks on end, he moved almost nightly.[16] On occasion he 'lay in the field all night in his coach', at other times his lodgings ranged from the earl of Huntingdon's house at Ashby de la Zouch to the 'mean Quarter' of Mr Philips of Bow in Devon, and he took his meals in equally diverse locations, from the house of the earl of Cork at Stalbridge to 'a little Lodge' and a yeoman's house.[17] Many of the king's subjects, of many social levels and in many parts of the country, experienced the king's presence in their own houses. Many more saw and felt the presence of the army that accompanied him. Parliamentary armies were equally mobile and their presence equally widely felt. The pattern for Fairfax's army in 1645–6 differed little overall from the king's or Rupert's. In October 1645, by no means his army's most strenuous month, it quartered in thirteen towns or villages.[18] Civilians did not merely watch these armies pass by. They provided, voluntarily or involuntarily, food, lodging, horses, and information, and their property and sometimes their lives were at risk.

Long marches could not be avoided. Some resulted from a blind man's buff search for the enemy in the absence of certain intelligence as to his whereabouts, but the apparent aimlessness of some of the frequent movement that so often seems to lack any clear purpose was also due to the need to tap new resources. This

[14] Woolrych, *Britain in Revolution*, 285; C. H. Firth (ed.), 'The Journal of Prince Rupert's Marches, 5 Sept. 1642 to 4 July 1646', *EHR* 52 (1898), 730–41; for a corrected version for Mar. 1645, see BL Add. MS 11,331, fo. 141, and R. N. Dore (ed.), *The Letter Books of Sir William Brereton, Vol.1, January 31st–May 29th 1645*, Record Society of Lancashire and Cheshire, 123 (1984), 142 n. 1.

[15] The estimates of miles covered are those of the 17th-cent. recorders. A 17th-cent. mile was a flexible unit, often longer than the modern mile; common measurements ranged from 1,760 to 2,428 yards, but less formally there were 'little myles' and 'good miles'. For differences in measurements of miles, see E. G. Box, 'Kent in Early Road Books of the Seventeenth Century', *Archaeologia Cantiana*, 44 (1932), 9–11. In the last two weeks of Sept. 1645 the 'Iter Carolinum' records daily marches of 26, 28, 14, 20, 14, 20, 20, 18, 26, and 30 miles. The 50-mile march after the second battle of Newbury was achieved by 'marching all night' and part of the next day. 'Iter Carolinum; being a succinct Relation of the necessiated Marches, Retreats, and Sufferings of his Majesty Charles the first', in John Gutch (ed.), *Collectanea Curiosa; or Miscellaneous Tracts*, 2 vols. (1781), 2. 428, 438, 446. In the 1620s the Privy Council stipulated marches of 12 to 15 miles a day for conscripts on their way to join the army, i.e. for unencumbered small groups. See Stephen J. Stearns, 'Conscription and English Society in the 1620s', *JBS* 11 (May 1972), 4.

[16] 'Iter Carolinum', in Gutch (ed.), *Collecteana Curiosa*, 2. 428, 435, 440. 446.

[17] Ibid. 2. 434, 436–7, 441, 443.

[18] Ioshua Sprigge, *Anglia Rediviva; Englands Recovery* (1647), 331–5. For further evidence of army mobility, see maps showing Cromwell's routes from 1642 to 1648, in Gaunt, *Cromwellian Gazetteer*, [228–32].

high mobility intensified the perpetual problems of care and control of troops, but it also intensified problems of quartering, supply, forage, and requisition. Advance agents sought out promising sites, such as the 'fruitful valley of corn and pasture grounds, a great circuit fit to quarter an army in', that had caught the eye of a European veteran in 1639.[19] Yet even such prosperous neighbourhoods could quickly lose their prosperity under army occupation, and were unable to support and supply large bodies of troops for unlimited periods of time. Furthermore, short marches of a few miles that left troops fresh were less fortunate for the civilian population, for they restricted the area from which the army derived sustenance and lodging.

In theory, orderly provision was made for an army on the move, with the quartermaster acting as an advance guard who, in cooperation with the local constable or headborough, sought out lodgings that were then hierarchically assigned by rank. Alternatively, when the army was forced to camp in the open, he oversaw the laying out of well-regulated quarters and streets.[20] The distance between theory and practice is evident in the narrative of Sir Thomas Hyde, a hapless civilian prisoner with Essex's army in the summer of 1643. In fifty-six peripatetic days, Hyde lodged in twenty-two towns. Two weeks were spent in Kingston and one in Uxbridge, but the rest of the time he and the army were in rapid motion; in one week he lodged in six places. He was marched and counter-marched close to London, then taken on a great loop west for the relief of Gloucester before returning to the battle of Newbury. He covered most of the distance on foot, received bad and inadequate food, and was quartered—in conditions that ranged from discomfort to acute squalor—in houses, churches, and jails, in churchyards, tents, and barns; when all else failed, he passed the night on a wagon in the rain. Admittedly the welfare of prisoners came low in the army's priorities, but what emerges from Hyde's account is the ad hoc nature of provision of accommodation and food for this mobile army and the extent to which, as it traversed large areas, it was in the midst of and dependent on the civilian population for lodging and sustenance. Hyde's complaints about his food and lodging in Uxbridge indicate the pressure on local resources when the army came to town. Even his sojourns in jail, which also occasioned angry complaint, were another aspect of the mingling of army and civil life, bringing together military and civilian flotsam.[21]

Experience of war was thus widely diffused, and the impact of soldiers and strangers on local populations was intensified by the fact that most of the communities that experienced their presence were small: it has been estimated that nearly half the population of south-east England 'dwelt in parish communities

---

[19] *CSPDom. 1638–1639*, 384.   [20] Elton, *Compleat Body of the Art Military*, 179–80.
[21] HEH STT Personal Box 10(5); see Henry Foster, *A True and Exact Relation of the Marchings of the Two regiments of the Trained Bands of the City of London, being the Red and Blew Regiments* (1643), printed in [John Washbourn], *Bibliotheca Gloucestrensis* (Gloucester, 1825), 251–71, for a soldier's view of the same march.

of fewer than 500 residents', while their mean size was under three hundred.[22] London indeed was a metropolis of 375,000 by 1650, but its fabric too was permeated by the war.[23] The other small cities of England and its villages lacked London's absorptive power. Relations between soldiers and civilians, like those between soldiers of opposing sides, were necessarily intimate. Garrisons lived among and depended on the civilian population, and even small and isolated strongholds held civilians as well as soldiers and women as well as men. Nor were civilians insulated from military engagements. Inhabitants of besieged towns became part of the action. Country people sometimes observed battles from the sidelines. At Alresford they were close enough to hear the horse exhort the flying foot, 'Face them, face them'. At Naseby they converged to strip and bury the dead, and village tradition had it that a boy of 9 or 10 'was keeping cows in the field during the whole time of the battle'.[24] Richard Baxter's congregation was distracted from his sermon on 'The Kingdom of Heaven suffereth violence' by the cannon at Edgehill, and the next day Baxter and a friend, riding out to inspect the field of battle, 'saw the dead Bodies of English Men slain by one another'.[25] Survivors too reinforced the sense of an integrated war for prisoners talked to locals, often with remarkably little constraint. As the royalists were paraded through London after Naseby they were free to talk to their friends in the crowd, some publicly airing 'dangerous speeches', while others sought sympathy by declaring they were pressed men forced to fight for the king.[26]

The lack of linguistic barrier between fellow English speakers enhanced and made distinctive the physical closeness characteristic of seventeenth-century war. Even between enemies, communication was easy. The common language of most soldiers not only complicated problems of identification in action, to which we shall return, but also made for informal eavesdropping and conversation. Military manuals, reflecting another kind of war, continued to specify the ability to speak several languages as a desirable attribute of 'drums' and 'trumpets', the official envoys between enemies, but in the civil war it was unnecessary.[27] In camp, battle, and siege, proximity allowed opponents to talk and overhear. The armies encamped before the battle of Alresford were 'so neer that the Sentinels

[22] Mary J. Dobson, 'The Last Hiccup of the Old Demographic Regime: Population Stagnation and Decline in Late Seventeenth and Early Eighteenth-Century South-East England', *Continuity and Change*, 4 (1989), 399–401. The mean figure for the 1720s was 274, which Dobson notes was similar to, although perhaps lower than, that for the 1640s and 1670s. 'Most communities', she notes, 'could be numbered in tens and hundreds rather than thousands and tens of thousands.' Ibid. 399.

[23] Ibid. 408.

[24] [E.A.], *A Fuller Relation Of the Great Victory obtained (through Gods Providence) at Alsford* (1644), [4]; John Mastin, *The History and Antiquities of Naseby, in the county of Northampton* (Cambridge, 1792), 117.

[25] Samuel Clark, *The Lives Of sundry Eminent Persons in this Later Age* (1683), 'Epistle'.

[26] *The Kingdomes Weekly Intelligencer*, 105 (17–24 June 1645), 841.

[27] Markham, *Second Part of the Souldiers Grammar*, 3; Elton, *Compleat Body of the Art Military*, 177–8.

could heare one another talk'.[28] Besiegers and besieged could do likewise. They may have disapproved of what they heard, like the defenders of Brampton Bryan, who deplored the 'rotten language' and 'poisoned words' of the royalists in the adjoining gardens, or of Lyme, who were subjected to 'railing language' from the enemy's siege works, but the language of offence was shared.[29]

Common language aided communication between enemies but it also added to confusion. It simplified intelligence gathering, although it did not always ensure correct interpretation. Information could be passed, for example, by cryptic messages, but the risk of error was considerable in the absence of an agreed code. Edmund Ludlow and the defenders of Wardour Castle in March 1644 puzzled over the intent of the sentence loudly uttered by their friend who had been pressed into royal service, but had to admit, '[W]e were mistaken in the interpretation.'[30] Common language also had its dangers on the battlefield. The 'word' adopted by each side was one of the most important means of distinguishing friend from foe in the confusion of battle, but it too could be a fallible guide. On at least one occasion both sides chose the same word, 'God with us.'[31] Given the need for brief and memorable words and commanders' limited imaginations—'God with us' remained a parliamentary favorite—soldiers sometimes mistook foe for friend. Even when the 'words' were phonetically distinct—'God our strength' and 'Queen Mary' at Naseby, 'Truth' and 'King and Kent' at Maidstone in 1648—they were readily borrowed, so that in the absence of other identifying signs the borrower could make an escape through his enemies, as some parliamentary horse did at Leicester, 'having gotten the enemies word (which was *God and the Prince*)'.[32] Parliamentarians claimed that merely changing speech habits constituted a disguise; if they swore, they could pass for royalists. On at least one occasion a successful physical disguise,

---

[28] [E.A.], *Fuller Relation Of the Great Victory . . . at Alsford*, 3.

[29] HMC, *Calendar of the Manuscripts of the Marquess of Bath*, 1 (1904), 6, and see 3–4 for the defenders' response to intimidating 'shouts' and abuse; *CSPDom. 1644*, 205.

[30] *The Memoirs of Edmund Ludlow Lieutenant-general of the horse in the army of the commonwealth of England 1625–1672*, ed. C. H. Firth, 2 vols. (Oxford, 1894), 1. 70–1.

[31] John Vicars, *Gods Ark Overtopping the Worlds Waves* (1646), 193, in Vicars, *Magnalia Dei Anglicana*. God showed whose side he was on 'by the successe of the battell', said the parliamentarians.

[32] Sprigge, *Anglia Rediviva*, 35; *A Perfect Relation of the taking of Leicester: With the severall marches of the Kings Army* (1645), 2; *An Exact and Perfect Relation of the Proceedings of the Army under the Command of Sir Thomas Fairfax . . . near Langport* (1645), 7; and see [Tho. Ellis], *An Exact and full Relation of the last Fight, Between the Kings Forces and Sir William Waller* (1644) 7. John Syms's account of the siege of Plymouth reveals the confusions that 'words' could give rise to. For one engagement, he says, the royalist word was 'The town is ours', the parliamentarian 'God with us'. A little later he notes that 'the enemy's word was "if God be with us, the town is ours"'. If he was referring to the same occasion it suggests that even a careful narrator like Sym had difficulty in keeping 'words' straight; if to a different one, the conflation could be dangerously confusing. BL Add. MS 35,297, fos. 11, 24. For the importance of remembering the 'word', and the fallibility of soldiers' memories, see the case of the soldier at Leicester 'casually hurt by Colonel Grey, because he forgot our word, which was "God prosper us," the enemies word being, "For the King"', J. F. Hollings, *The History of Leicester during the Great Civil War* (Leicester, 1840), 32–3.

the adoption of parliamentary colours, was subverted by a royalist captain's absent-mindedly falling into a quarrel with opponents who had to that point accepted his false colours; shared language could be a trap for the foolish or hot-headed.[33] It also increased the anxiety caused by fraternization between victorious and defeated troops, and rendered side-changing easier, for language was no barrier to understanding new orders or new comrades. Opposing soldiers could 'parley' as they did at Oxford in 1646, while at the siege of Chester officers intervened to stop 'friendly' and 'familiar' debate between the opposing troops.[34] Nor were officers immune to the unsettling effects of easy communication. Faced by reverses at Plymouth, a royalist major-general 'called to a [parliamentary] officer . . . & told him that he thought God fought against them, & said, if he could be convinced that he was not in the right, he would hang himself at his door, ere he would take up arms again in the quarrel'.[35]

Shared language thus had its military disadvantages. It enhanced ideological and physical volatility, facilitated exchange of ideas, information, and insults, and eased migration of persons. Yet it was also a constant reminder of the fact of *civil* war between compatriots. It could moderate and maintain links as well as give free rein to quarrels. When the time came for conciliation, it reduced occasions for misunderstanding, and made possible an exchange such as that between members of the two armies in Cornwall in 1646. Royalist soldiers, anxious for peace, mistakenly believed that a truce had been arranged; the parliamentarians pointed out their error and urged them to retire to safe positions; they were in their turn 'kindly thanke[d] . . . for their civilitie'.[36] One party had rejected the opportunity to take a bloody advantage; the other had expressed appreciation of this reconciling intention. If shared language aided subversion and added a gratifying edge to vituperation between parties it could also, as on this occasion, be the vehicle by which benevolent intentions and a desire to refrain from further bloodshed was expressed.

---

[33] *The Exchange Intelligencer*, 6 (15–24 June 1645), 45; Walker, *Historical Discourses*, 91.

[34] BL Add. MS 11,332, fo. 94; Ludlow, *Memoirs*, 1. 71; R. T. Lattey, E. J. S. Parsons, and I. G. Philip, 'A Contemporary Map of the Defences of Oxford in 1644', *Oxoniensia*, 1 (1936), 172; at Oxford officers joined in such 'parleying'. At Lostwithiel in 1644 Skippon tried unsuccessfully to have a proviso against fraternization included in the surrender terms. Walker, *Historical Discourses*, 77.

[35] Major-general Thomas Basset, on Christmas Day 1643, BL Add. MS 35, 297, fo. 10ᵛ. Basset survived, but there appears to be no record of military activities after 1643. Newman, *Royalist Officers*, 19, no. 81.

[36] Sprigge, *Anglia Rediviva*, 213; [J.R.], *Sir Ralph Hoptons and All his Forces comming in* (1646), 3–4.

5

The Means of Violence

The war, then, left few parts of the country untouched, was integrated with civilian life, and was fought by and among people who, with some exceptions, understood each other. It was also conditioned by factors that ranged from matters beyond human control such as weather to the nature of the material and man-made means of war, such as the weapons that limited and shaped the activities of their users. The means of violence most commonly employed in the civil war demonstrated in acute form the chanciness of death and destruction common to all wars. This in turn enhanced the attraction of a providential faith that endowed often inexplicable human misfortune with divine purpose.

It used to be argued that the introduction of firearms made war more impersonal and less savage because they reduced its bloody immediacy: an impersonal death occurred off-stage, as it were, at 'discreet distances'.[1] The technology of the nineteenth-century rifle and its successors may have made such a theory attractive, but it had little relevance to civil war muskets, pistols, and other miscellaneous weaponry. Hostilities were still conducted at close quarters and even artillery often dealt death at short range. The process of killing and wounding was intimate; death was rarely distant. Guns were limited in range and accuracy and a pike was ideally 18 feet long but usually 16 feet or less. Articles of war that forbade flight in battle before 'push of pike' or 'dint of sword' did not use the phrases accidentally, and informal weapons were little more remote.[2]

Civil war armies still employed a transitional mixture of firearms and 'muscle-powered weapons' that ranged from heavy artillery to clubs. Even the bow and arrow marginally survived, although they seem to have been most useful as a means of sending propaganda messages in and out of besieged strongholds.[3] Artillery was widely deployed although variably effective. It weighed as much as 8,000 or as little as 120 pounds and varied in length from 12 feet to 3, while

[1] J. U. Nef, *War and Human Progress* (Cambridge, Mass., 1952), 251–3.

[2] BL Add. MS 11,810, fo. 11a; C. H. Firth, *Cromwell's Army* (1962), 73–4. In Europe soldiers often shortened their pikes for greater ease in marching, e.g. to 13 feet in the Thirty Years' War. Monro, *Expedition*, 2. 191; Woolrych, *Battles of the English Civil War*, 100; Parker, *Thirty Years War*, 198.

[3] George Raudzins, 'Firepower Limitations in Modern Military History', *JSAHR* 67 (1989), 137; Peter Edwards, *Dealing in Death: The Arms Trade and the British Civil Wars (1638–52)* (Stroud, 2000), 4–5; Firth, *Cromwell's Army*, 117.

the weight of the shot ranged from 63 pounds to three-quarters of a pound. One day's bombardment at Worcester sent in shot that varied in weight from 17 to 31 pounds, but it did 'no hurt to man or house'.[4] Personal weapons revealed more clearly the transitional nature of arms. Officers carried pistols and swords, as did the cavalry, and royalist cavalry sometimes added a small pole-axe; dragoons—mounted foot soldiers on inferior horses—usually carried firelock muskets or carbines as well as swords; and foot regiments were composed of musketeers (normally with less advanced matchlock muskets) and pikemen, both of whom also carried swords.[5] When the war began, the desirable infantry balance was regarded as one-third pikemen to two-thirds musketeers although in practice the proportions depended on levels of recruitment, supply, degrees of desertion or less permanent absenteeism, and the preferences of officers. In February 1643, for example, a royalist officer was provided with forty muskets and thirty pikes to arm one company of foot, but with time the preponderance of musketeers increased. When Essex set out to re-equip his foot from scratch in the autumn of 1644 after the débâcle at Lostwithiel, he put in a request for 6,000 muskets, 6,000 swords, and 1,000 pikes; a resupply order for Fairfax's troops early in 1646 specified only 761 pikes to 2,980 muskets and 4,826 swords.[6] In addition to these 'official' arms, both sides at times took to even more traditional weapons, from scythes to stones.

Homely weapons played a larger part early in the war than they did after it had settled down and supplies and logistics had improved. Many of the early skirmishes in which Englishmen accustomed themselves to killing each other were conducted with makeshift weapons and 'handy blows'. As the parliamentarians moved to take Leeds early in 1643 Sir William Fairfax's foot consisted of 1,000 musketeers to 2,000 clubmen, while in Lancashire the earl of Derby's royalist army also contained 2,000 clubmen and only 1,000 horse and other foot. The parliamentarians' 'quick and violent entry' into Preston in February 1643 was

[4] See tables in A. R. Hall, *Ballistics in the Seventeenth Century* (Cambridge, 1952), 168, and Ian Roy (ed.), *The Royalist Ordnance Papers 1642–1646*, Oxfordshire Record Society, 43, 49 (1964, 1975), 43. 6; Ronald Hutton and Wylie Reeves, 'Sieges and Fortifications', in *The Civil Wars: A Military History of England, Scotland and Ireland, 1638–1660*, ed. John Kenyon and Jane Ohlmeyer (Oxford, 1998), 209–10; *Diary of Henry Townshend of Elmley Lovett, 1640–1663*, i, ed. J. W. Willis Bund, Worcestershire Historical Society, 1915 (1920), 24. The biggest guns—cannon royal, cannon, and demi-cannon—while powerfully destructive were relatively few in number and slow and difficult to move into action. A demi-cannon required 'an average hundred men, or thirty or forty animals, to move it'. Hutton and Reeves, 'Sieges and Fortifications', 205.

[5] For the arms of infantry and cavalry, see Firth, *Cromwell's Army*, chs. 4 and 5, and see 117 n. 3 for royalist use of the pole-axe.

[6] Essex's request included 260 partisans and halberds in addition to pikes. Bodl. MS Tanner 61, fo. 149; *The Royalist Ordnance Papers*, ed. Ian Roy, Oxfordshire Record Society, 43 (1963–4) and 49 (1971–3), 43. 7, 198; PRO SP 28/126, fo. 3. Cf. HMC, *14th Report. Appendix 2. Portland MSS* (1894), 3. 119, where 800 muskets, 400 pikes, and 1,200 swords were requested for a regiment of 1,200 foot in Nov. 1643; and *CJ* 3. 587 (12 Aug. 1644), 1,200 muskets to 300 pikes, for Irish service.

achieved 'chiefly by sword and clubmen'.[7] In December 1642 Bradford men had pursued the enemy with a medley of swords, scythes, sickles attached to long poles, flails, and spits.[8] Even when more professional weapons largely replaced makeshifts, harms remained intimate, short-range, and, often, domesticated and informal. At the storming of Shelford, logs of wood sufficed to 'sweepe off a whole ladder full of men at once'. In 1645 the parliamentarians at Saltash defended themselves with stones, while soldiers at Sherborne were so close that they threw stones rather than fire their muskets.[9] More exotic was the 'Herculean club' used by defenders at Newcastle against the Scots in 1644 which 'grimely looke[d] like to the pale face of murther' and consisted of an iron-bound staff 'with a round falling head (like to a Pomegranate) . . . set with sharpe iron pikes . . . with a long poynted pyke of iron' in its 'forehead'. This ferocious object was used 'to slay or strike' at short range as soldiers came up storming ladders.[10]

Firearms did not radically change the situation. Pistols were of doubtful accuracy beyond about seven yards, and body contact was ideal. Trained troops would hold their fire until the enemy was nearly upon them for, as the parliamentarians found at Powick Bridge in September 1642, if they discharged 'at too uncertaine a distance, [they] did no execution'. On that occasion they were routed by Rupert's cavalry who held their fire until they could 'discharge . . . just at their breasts'.[11] The maximum range of the matchlock musket, the most common musket of the war years, remains a matter of controversy. It may have been as much as 400 yards but was usually closer to 250, while its 'killing range' with some degree of accuracy was only 40–100 yards. In a public lecture in 1649

---

[7] *The Memoirs of General Fairfax* (Leeds, 1776), 32, 116, 122, 127. This edn. of Fairfax's 'A short Memorial of the Northern Actions' was 'improved' by the addition of material from 'Noted Historians of those Times', so that it contains a few passages that do not appear in *Short Memorials of Thomas Lord Fairfax* (1699). The volume also includes accounts of actions at Manchester, Preston, and Bradford. Sir William was Sir Thomas Fairfax's cousin.

[8] *The Autobiography of Joseph Lister, of Bradford in Yorkshire*, ed. Thomas Wright (1842), 15 n.; *Rider of the White Horse And His Army* (1643), reprinted ibid. 65.

[9] Lucy Hutchinson, *Memoirs of the Life of Colonel Hutchinson with the fragment of an autobiography of Mrs. Hutchinson*, ed. James Sutherland (1973), 162; BL Add. MS 35,297, fo. 47ᵛ; *A True Relation of The taking of Sherborn-Castle* (1645), 4; A. R. Bayley, *The Great Civil War in Dorset* (Taunton, 1910), 286. See also *Journal of Sir Samuel Luke*, 2, ed. I. G. Philip, Oxfordshire Record Soc. 31 (1950), 139; Worcester College, Clarke MSS, 114, fo. 59. At the siege of Chester in 1645 'when the Enemy came under the walls, [stones] did more execution than muskets could have done'. 'John Byron's Account of the Siege of Chester 1645–1646', *The Cheshire Sheaf*, 4th ser. 6 (1971), 15 (repr. from Bodl. MS Rawlinson B.210).

[10] William Lithgow, *An experimental and exact relation upon that famous and renowned siege of Newcastle* (Edinburgh, 1645), in *The Siege of Newcastle* (Newcastle, 1820), 25. Lithgow admitted that hand grenades caused more slaughter than 'either Musket, Pyke, or Herculean clubs', but a grenade lobbed at soldiers 'climbing up . . . steep . . . breaches' was also an intimate weapon.

[11] *True But Sad and Dolefull Newes from Shrewsbury . . . October 10, 1642* (York, repr. London, 1642), 4. At Edgehill, the royalists said, the parliamentarians 'discharged their carabines and pistols at an unskilful distance, without any mischief to our men'. Tho. Carte, *A Collection of Original Letters and Papers Concerning the Affairs of England From the Year 1641 to 1660* (2 vols. 1739), 1. 10.

Sir Balthazar Gerbier put the best case possible for the common musket when he observed that it 'carireth but point blanck 200 Geometrical paces, . . . with that force as to serve the killing of a man'. Volleys of fire from these weapons, he concluded, could be 'more terrible than damageable'.[12] In confused mêlées, furthermore, a bullet was as likely to kill friend as foe. Reloading was slow and complex—a round a minute was a good rate of fire—so a rapidly advancing enemy might leave no time or space to reload. Furthermore, in wet weather the lighted match needed to ignite the powder that fired the bullet in a matchlock musket did not stay lit. Pistols and muskets became weapons of battery as well as firepower, and English musketeers were skilled at 'clubbing . . . down'.[13] Rupert's early success at Brentford in 1642 demonstrated the combination of firepower and hand combat; there, after one volley, his men advanced smartly 'up to push of pike and the butt end of muskets'.[14] At Naseby the heroic defence of the royalist Blue Regiment, which stood 'like to a wall of brasse', forced the parliamentarians 'to knock them down with the But-end of their Musquets'.[15]

Even the use of artillery did not necessarily distance. The larger cannon had a range of up to 2,000 yards, but the ability to induce terror at medium range (particularly in sieges) and short range blasting power were equally prized. Sustained artillery attack could lay defences low if terrain and soil were favourable, and we shall see its power in siege warfare, but at short range artillery was valued for its ability to blast men as well as walls. At the siege of Plymouth in 1643 royalists planted batteries within pistol shot of a parliamentarian outer fort and the barrage from their demi-cannon and culverin forced its surrender. A month later guns were set up within musket shot of royalist gunners to 'counter-batter' them away from their pieces.[16] In battle, proximity to artillery might be closer still, for soldiers fought at

[12] Sir Balthazar Gerbier, *The First Publique Lecture . . . Concerning Military Architecture, or Fortifications* (1649), 9–10. As a 'Geometrical pace' was 5 feet and 'point blanck' indicated the horizontal flight of a projectile before it began to fall, Gerbier extended the killing range of muskets to over 300 yards (to be distinguished from their accurate range). He admitted that many were killed at greater distances than 200 paces; inaccurate shots could be as fatal as any others. See also *True But Sad and Dolefull Newes from Shrewsbury*, 4; Walker, *Historical Discourses*, 92, on the ineffectiveness of musket fire at the relief of Basing House in 1644; HMC, *14th Report. App. 2. Portland MSS*, 3. 119, for the desirability of a proportion of more advanced firelock muskets; David Smurthwaite, *Battlefields of Britain* (New York, 1984), 135; David G. Chandler, *Atlas of Military Strategy* (New York, 1980), 37. See Raudzins, 'Firepower Limitations', 132–3, on the deficiencies of even the more efficient flintlocks.

[13] Firth, *Cromwell's Army*, 104–5.

[14] BL Add. MS 11,810, fo. 11a. Compare 'Memoirs of Captain John Hodgson', in *Original Memoirs, Written during the Great Civil War, being the Life of Sir Henry Slingsby and Memoirs of Capt. Hodgson* (Edinburgh, 1806), 147.

[15] *Kingdomes Weekly Intelligencer*, 104 (10–17 June 1645), 838; in 1654 troopers in Scotland were instructed that, after firing their pistols, they should throw them in the enemy's faces before falling on with their swords. Firth, *Cromwell's Army*, 141–2.

[16] Peter Young and Wilfrid Emberton, *Sieges of the Great Civil War 1642–1646* (1978), 4; BL Add. MS 35,297, fos. 4, 9v.

the cannon's mouth.[17] The royalist assault on Leicester in May 1645 demonstrated the limited distancing between opponents offered by standard weapons
of all kinds. Defenders of a breach in the wall pulled pikes out of the hands of the
attackers, who nevertheless came to 'push of Pike' four times; Colonel St George
and his men, 'in a bravery', came up to the cannon's mouth and were 'by it shot-
ter'd into small parcels'; and when Colonel Sir Henry Bard tried to scale the walls,
he 'was beaten down with the butt-end of a Musquet'.[18] There was little remote-
ness, and often little anonymity, in the harm compatriots inflicted on each other.

The distribution of harm, moreover, was unpredictable as well as intimate.
The design of weapons, both large and small, was not standardized nor was
their performance reliable. Each cannon, by the nature of its manufacture, was
an individual piece; its mould was literally broken. It was tested before use, but
once the absence of flaws of design or metal had been established, a gunner had
to come to terms with the quirks of his cannon much as a rider did with the
ways of his horse. Hence, perhaps, the survival of individual names for some
guns, like 'Roaring Megg' or the 'Great Piece of Ordnance called "Sweet-lips"'
(named for a well-known whore) taken at Newark in 1646.[19] Contemporaries
indeed recognized the dangers of lack of uniformity. In the 1630s the Ordnance
Office had tried to impose a 'Standard Arm' of uniform pattern, while the
chartering of the Gunmakers' Company had signalled an attempt at officially
authorized quality control for handguns, for the company was empowered to
search out, inspect, 'prove', and mark all those either manufactured in the London
area, or brought there for sale.[20] If such regulations indicated recognition of
deficiencies, they did not necessarily cure them, and any potential improvement
was overwhelmed by the demands first of the Scottish wars and then of the civil
war. These led to urgent attempts to procure weapons from many sources. In
February 1639, demand was such that the London armourers and gunmakers
were unable to supply the earl of Bridgewater with the arms he had been
ordered to send the king at York. Others complained of delays and low quality,
and alternative sources in the Low Countries were stretched beyond capacity.

---

[17] See Mrs Hutchinson's tribute to the 'valliant dreadfulnesse' of the cavaliers attacking
Nottingham castle who, 'when one of their leading files fell before them all at once, . . . marcht
boldly over the dead bodies of their freinds under the mouth of their enemies cannon'. Hutchinson,
Memoirs, 114.

[18] *Narration of the Siege and taking of the Town of Leicester* (1645), 7; and compare Hutchinson,
Memoirs, 162, on the storming of Shelford. Bard (whose daughter became Prince Rupert's mistress)
survived, to die instead in 1660 in a sandstorm on his way to become ambassador to the Persian
court. Newman, *Royalist Officers*, 16.

[19] W. Y. Carman, *A History of Firearms from Earliest Times to 1914* (1956), 45; HMC, *Bath
MSS*, 1. 40; Hutton and Reeves, 'Sieges and Fortifications', in Kenyon and Ohlmeyer (eds.), *Civil
Wars*, 209.

[20] Hall, *Ballistics*, 12–13; Charles M. Clode, *The Military Forces of the Crown; their Administration
and Government* (2 vols. 1869), 2. 231; Richard Winship Stewart, *The English Ordnance Office: A
Case Study in Bureaucracy* (1996), 99–101; 'The Charter of the Company of Gunmakers, London',
printed in *JSAHR* 6 (1927), 79–92, and see p. 87 for provisions concerning inspection and proof.

Eighteen months later Bridgewater's London suppliers could meet his needs, but slowly 'for they [had] few ready'. Meanwhile they offered arms for light horse at two prices: at 45s. 'if proof', but otherwise at 40s., a distinction that did not bode well for the reliability of the cheaper guns.[21] These pre-war difficulties of supply and standards vastly increased after 1642.

Parliament's seizure of the great national armouries, including those at the Tower of London and Hull, gave it an initial advantage in armaments over the royalists. At Chatham Dock ('the Kingdomes store-house', its captors boasted), the parliamentarians acquired 300 pieces of ordnance as well as ammunition that the royalists had planned to spirit away by night.[22] Royalist attempts to gain control of county armouries, which were in any case of variable quality, met with limited success, and they were forced to rely heavily at first on the private armouries of supporters.[23] The supplies from these sources were mixed in kind and age, for they were sporting and historical as well as strictly military repositories. Few, perhaps, could rival the famous collection at Wilton—which in the luck of the draw of allegiance fell to parliament—but its contents in 1635 revealed the miscellaneous and heirloom character of private armouries. The Wilton armoury held sufficient arms to fit out a thousand horse and foot, but it also contained '30. Welsh Hookes, 60. Black Bills, 20. Holy Water Springers, and 60. Staves', coats of mail, arms dating from the reigns of Henry VIII and Edward VI, the arms of Lord William Herbert, the victor of St Quentin (including his Turkish scimitar), and other antiquarian riches.[24] Such repositories also offered a plentiful supply of sporting guns that were widely used by both sides. In Bradford at the beginning of the war there were some thirty fowling, birding, and smaller sporting pieces to forty muskets and calivers. Sporting guns should not be dismissed as dilettante peacetime holdovers, however, for although less 'robust' they were usually more accurate than muskets and in the hands of experts they delivered valuable sniper fire. At Bradford the royalist master-gunner fell to a parliamentarian fowling piece, and at Sherborne in 1645 the royalists used two former park-keepers as expert marksmen, 'who with long fowling-pieces, take aim through the loop-holes in the wall—for the most part at commanders'.[25]

[21] HEH EL MSS 6571, 6576, 6601, 6604 (facsimiles), and 6603; BL Add. MS 29974.2, fo. 287; and see Edwards, *Dealing in Death*, 68–79.

[22] *A perfect Diurnall of the severall passages in our late journey into Kent, from Aug. 19 to Sept. 31 1642* (n.pl., n.d.), 3–4.

[23] Ronald Hutton, *The Royalist War Effort 1642–1646* (1984), 29; Roy, *Royalist Ordnance Papers*, 43. 11–13.

[24] [Hammond], 'Short Survey of the Western Counties', *Camden Miscellany*, 16: 67–8; and see Roy, *Royalist Ordnance Papers*, 43. 15. Compare the '50 old calivers with rottten stocks and rusty barrels, useless . . . and of little service' from the Sheffield armoury lent to Sir John Gell in the autumn of 1642. HMC, *9th Report. Part 2. App.* (1884), 'Chandos-Pole-Gell MSS', 387.

[25] Bayley, *Dorset*, 284; Hall, *Ballistics*, 8; Smurthwaite, *Battlefields*, 134; Lister, *Autobiography*, 15 n.; *Rider of the White Horse*, 65. See Firth, *Cromwell's Army*, 90, for Monck's advocacy of army snipers with fowling pieces 'to pick off the officers of the enemy'.

Efficient weapons should be reliable, sturdy, and standardized for mass use. Civil war weapons did not meet these criteria. Officers might try to specify kinds and standards of weapons and ammunition—that they be 'proved' before receipt, well-made, and serviceable, and that the match and gunpowder be English, but they were at the mercy of circumstances and suppliers.[26] In December 1643 Prince Maurice had hoped for a windfall of some sixty carbines, pistols, and 'long firelock guns', all good merchant-supplied weapons from a captured Dunkirk frigate. Instead a few second-rate weapons were palmed off on him, including 'two old pistols & fourteen old unfit carbines, but none of the merchants' carbines'. 'I much wonder at it', wrote Maurice stiffly, and demanded the rest of the carbines and, especially, the firelocks. Another shipment was characterized as 'old trash'.[27] From the other side Sir Samuel Luke complained when 'the snaphances or firelockes' were missing from an arms shipment, for their superiority in action and 'saveing in Match' were 'knowne to every one'.[28] Even when sound weapons were dispatched, damage and spoilage could occur before they saw action, as a request that pistols and carbines be packed in a chest 'and well fenced against rain' acknowledged.[29]

Both sides faced problems of quality control and lack of standardization. Parliament inherited the pre-war infrastructure of English armament manufacture, which had been dominated by London, and this gave a strong initial advantage. A partial estimate suggests that between August 1642 and September 1651 London arms makers produced over 30,000 pikes, 102,000 swords, and 111,000 firearms. The success of parliament's weapons programme is indicated by the drop in prices: a matchlock musket cost £1 in 1642 and 10s. in 1645, and the price of a sword fell from 6s. 8d. or 7s. to 4s. 2d.[30] Parliament also controlled major areas supplying raw materials and goods, notably the Weald with its iron supplies and cannon foundries. It retained the services of experienced manufacturers, managers, and workmen, and although the royalists tried to entice 'skilful workmen for all sort of arms' by promises of pay, housing,

[26] See Hopton's efforts to specify the quality of light artillery—'of the best lengths, and extraordinarily fortified', Bodl. MS Firth c. 6, fo. 294ᵛ. See also Devonshire RO, Seymour MSS 1392 M/L 1644/28, for Colonel Edward Seymour's dependence on merchant suppliers of pistols, bandoliers, and musket rests in Apr. 1644; for an attempt to regulate kinds of weapons, see *CJ* 3. 587, specifying 500 flintlocks and snaphances out of a total order of 1,200 muskets; for detailed specifications, including insistence on English match and powder, see PRO SP 28/18, fos. 399–434 (possibly for naval supplies). See also Bodl. MS Clarendon 22, fos. 137–137ᵛ, for Van Haesdonck's contract with the royalists of 26 Oct. 1643, by which muskets, pistols, and carbines were to be tested by a proof of a double charge of powder and one bullet, within three days of delivery; defective weapons were to be repaired at Van Haesdonck's expense.

[27] Devonshire RO, Seymour MSS 1392 M/L 1643/37, 1643/39; Parker, *Military Revolution*, 68; and see Seymour MS M/L 1644/22, for commanders' attempts to stipulate kinds and quality of weapons.

[28] 'The Civil War Papers of Sir Will. Boteler, 1642–1645', ed. G. Herbert Fowler, *Publications of the Bedfordshire Historical Record Society*, 18 (1936), 11.

[29] Devonshire RO, Seymour MSS 1392 M/L 1644/19.

[30] Edwards, *Dealing in Death*, 71–2.

and good iron, few arms makers left London to join the king.[31] Even so, parliament had to rely on a motley collection of armaments, especially early in the war; in 1643 we find Lieutenant-Colonel Thomas Gell paying for two muskets here, a fowling piece there, or a job lot of three muskets, a fowling piece, and three swords.[32] Despite its control of major English manufacturing centres, parliament had to seek continental supplies. At first domestic suppliers were heavily engaged in repairing and refurbishing existing stocks of arms, and consequently imports were extremely heavy; they remained important even as domestic production rose.[33]

Although the royalists had some success in developing new production sites, as at Oxford and Bristol, the loss of existing national armouries, limited capacity, and the military vulnerability of their chief alternative areas of supply such as the Forest of Dean and Shropshire, led to heavy dependence on supplies from Europe.[34] Both sides suffered from the depredations of Flemish privateers as their shipments were in transit, but in addition the royalist position was made more difficult by parliament's dominance at sea. Nevertheless, despite the best efforts of the earl of Warwick and his fleet, the royalists managed to maintain an adequate supply of continental arms. The queen's efforts in raising money and negotiating sales for this purpose are well-known, and she was supported by agents like the old courtier Lord Goring (later earl of Norwich) and Newcastle's lieutenant-general of ordnance, Sir William Davenant. Not all their efforts were successful, but they had some spectacular coups, like the 20,000 muskets shipped through Dunkirk and the 2,000 barrels of powder sent from France early in 1644.[35] There were also private entrepreneurs like Sir Nicholas Crispe and John Van Haesdonck of London and Yorkshire. The scale of their operations appears in Van Haesdonck's contract of December 1642, when he took the first step into a long spiral of royal debt that ultimately ruined him. He agreed to supply the king with over £12,000 worth of arms imported through Tynemouth. The shipment was to include 3,000 muskets, 2,000 pairs of pistols, and 1,000 carbines. A subsequent contract of October 1643 for southern delivery to Weymouth was of similar

[31] Ibid.; BL Harl. MS 6804, fo. 160ᵛ; Roy, *Royalist Ordnance Papers*, 43. 13–14. Both sides used foreign experts but royalist need was greater; for domestic production they often had to establish manufacture and recruit workers from scratch, as in the foundry, forges, and workshops set up in Oxford at Christ Church and Magdelen. Ibid. 26–7.

[32] Derbys. RO, Gell MSS, D258, 31/30 (aa).

[33] Edwards, *Dealing in Death*, 199–201; and see Peter Edwards, 'Logistics and Supply', in Kenyon and Ohlmeyer (eds.), *Civil Wars*, 239–46.

[34] Edwards, *Dealing in Death*, 201; Roy, *Royalist Ordnance Papers*, 43. 7–9, 13–14, 39–41; G. E. 69 Aylmer, *The King's Servants: The Civil Service of Charles I 1625–1642* (1961), 341; H. R. Schubert, *History of the British Iron and Steel Industry* (1957), 249–55. See Roy, *Royalist Ordnance Papers*, 43. 34, 36, on the low quality of some European supplies and their high price, and on alternative royalist supply sources, especially the Forest of Dean; and see BL Harl. 6804, fos. 160–60ᵛ and Bodl. MS Firth c. 6, fo. 294, on artillery from the Forest of Dean and Shropshire.

[35] William Salt Library, Stafford, Salt MS 561/2; Roy, *Royalist Ordnance Papers*, 43. 39–40; *CSPDom. 1644*, 260; *CSPVen. 1643–47*, 65, 79.

magnitude.[36] Such substantial orders required purchase of unstandardized arms from assorted European makers.

An even larger parliamentarian requirement in 1644 did not herald uniformity. The resupply of Essex's shattered forces after Lostwithiel demonstrated the pressure that an emergency placed on the army's supply system. By the terms of surrender the only arms kept by the defeated were officers' pistols and swords, necessitating resupply from scratch. The wish-list for the foot submitted to the Committee of Both Kingdoms on 27 September 1644 included, as we have seen, 6,000 muskets, 6,000 swords, and 1,000 pikes, as well as 120 barrels of powder, and 20 pieces of ordnance, to replace the more than 5,000 miscellaneous arms, 36 cannon, and 100 barrels of powder that were officially forfeited, as well as losses through weapons abandoned and broken in the frenzy to surrender. There may have been more time to select and inspect the 500 pairs of pistols needed to re-equip the cavalry, who had escaped earlier, but arms for the foot were unmistakably a rush job involving many suppliers that raised the issue of quality control in acute form.[37] Even in less urgent circumstances, the weapons supplied met specifications erratically and came from a variety of sources. One consignment of French pistols led Sir Samuel Luke to complain first of slow delivery, and then that they had arrived without their holsters.[38]

As the examples above suggest, continental and English guns mingled on the field, and their provenance was unstable. Arms routinely changed owners after battles and sieges. One of the most important points of negotiation when towns and strongholds surrendered was the disposal of personal and public weapons. The transfer after Lostwithiel was unusual in its scale but not in its attention to the disposition of matériel. The enumeration of captured arms was part of the public assertion of any victory. The taking of cannon and ammunition, noted the king's secretary, Sir Edward Walker, was 'in all Battels . . . the greatest sign of victory'. Even common soldiers were known to 'fall on' enthusiastically to seize enemy ordnance, while its safe removal signified an orderly withdrawal.[39] Personal weapons were even more volatile. Soldiers lost their arms when wounded, threw them down as they surrendered or fled leaving them to be retrieved by pursuers, and sometimes sold them as they ran: after a skirmish in 1642

---

[36] *CSPDom. 1641–43*, 418–19; *CSPDom. 1661–62*, 226, 630; *CSPDom. 1663–64*, 261, 283, 396; Bodl. MS Clarendon 22, fos. 137–8. Van Haesdonck and his associates thereafter received letters of marque and turned their attention chiefly to privateering, but retained a subsidiary obligation to supply arms. Maritime operations and the acquisition and transportation of arms were rationally linked enterprises. Bodl. MS Clarendon 23, fos. 4–5; 25, fos. 7, 176–77ᵛ, 180.

[37] Bodl. MS Tanner 61, fos. 149–149ᵛ.

[38] BL Egerton MS 787, fos. 3, 16, 74; cf. Hopton's requests specifying Dunkirk pistols and muskets out of royalist stores, Bodl. MS Firth c. 6, fo. 294ᵛ.

[39] Sir Edward Walker, 'His Majesty's Happy Progress . . . 1644', in Walker, *Historical Discourses*, 7; BL Add.MS 35,297, fo. 10.

royalist foot 'fled and offered the[i]r armes in the townes adjacent for twelve pence a peece'.[40] The ebb and flow of arms, as of horses, between sides was a reality of campaigns but a nightmare to bureaucrats and accountants.[41] Even when troops were not in action, commanders on both sides had continually to threaten punishment of soldiers who sold, pawned, or lost their arms.[42] The king ordered all arms to be registered and regularly inventoried, and it was one of the duties of a gentleman at arms to keep a record of his regiment's marked weapons, but it is clear that weapons not only changed owners but, like soldiers, changed sides.[43]

There were thus many impediments to building up expertise in handling predictably uniform weapons. They were compounded by the limitations of the weapons themselves. These were sometimes overcome by talented experts, but more commonly their intrinsic deficiencies joined with carelessness and unfamiliarity on the part of their users to add another element of danger and unpredictability to war. The lighted match with which matchlock muskets were fired, for example, was awkwardly held in the musketeer's left hand, gave away his presence at night, and went out in wet weather, while the pouches of powder on his bandolier rattled revealingly in the wind and sometimes caught fire.[44] 'Negligence' tended to keep firearms in 'disordered' disrepair—hence the importance of regimental gunsmiths—but muskets, pistols, and artillery all had technological weaknesses that made their performance uncertain. In the 1620s the preacher William Gouge had hailed guns as 'the sure and sore messenger of death', but he exaggerated.[45] Although pre-war efforts to test in order to maintain standards of safety continued, as did provisions to repair and 'fix' weapons, they were working against the technological grain. Barrels

---

[40] [Wharton], 'Letters from a Subaltern Officer', *Archaeologia*, 35 (1853), 2. 316; BL Add. MS 70109 (unfol.), Misc. 67. Six men were detailed to look for abandoned arms after Naseby. Edwards, *Dealing in Death*, 67.

[41] See PRO SP 28/260, fos. 380–90, for Commissary Lionel Copley's defence against charges of fraud, with its recital of arms lost, spoilt, 'broke', and decayed in the natural course of events during and after action.

[42] For royalists, see *Military Orders and Articles, Established by His Maiestie* (Oxford, [1643]), [5, 9, 14–15], nos. 24, 60–2, and 'A Proclamation prohibiting all Persons whatsoever, from buying or receiving Horse or Armes of any kind from any Souldiers of His Majesties Army'; see also the proclamation of 10 Mar. 1643 designed to remedy the spoiling, losing, and negligent care of arms 'Notwithstanding Our many Proclamations'. J. A. Larkin (ed.), *Stuart Royal Proclamations* (Oxford, 1983), 2. 872. For parliament, see *Lawes and Ordinances of Warre, Established for the better Conduct of the Army by His Excellency The Earle of Essex Lord Generall of the Forces raised by the Authority of the Parliament, for the defence of the King and Kingdom* (Sept. 1642), B3–B3ᵛ, 'Of a Souldiers Duty touching his Armes', nos. 1–7.

[43] BL Harl. MS 6804, fos. 160–160ᵛ. Neither the problem nor the attempted solution was new; see Larkin, *Stuart Royal Proclamations*, 2. 190–2, 'A Proclamation prohibiting the Buying and Selling of any of His Majesties Armes or Munition', 9 Mar. 1628. See also Elton, *Compleat Body of the Art Military*, 178–9; the duties of the gentleman at arms also included safeguarding the arms of the dead, wounded, and demobilized, and distributing powder and match.

[44] Firth, *Cromwell's Army*, 81–2.

[45] BL Harl. MS 6804, fo. 160ᵛ; Gouge, *Dignitie of Chivalry*, 430–1.

were unrifled, making accurate ballistic calculation of the trajectory of bullets and balls virtually impossible. Muskets varied in bore, so that bullets had to be 'shaved' to fit and consequently 'flew a less way, and more uncertainly'.[46] Skilled operators, such as sharpshooters, who could overcome these deficiencies were highly valued and were called on for special service. At Chester in 1645 they successfully cleared an area under the city walls for the royalist defenders, and their parliamentary counterparts killed the royalist sheriff 'dead with a bullet out of St. John's church steeple'. At Worcester, as his colleagues were picked off by the parliamentarians, a royalist complained, 'The Enemy are very good marksmen.'[47] Skilled gunners were also highly valued although always in short supply, and like Black Will, the cannoneer of Thomas Gell's regiment, they often earned special rewards. The good artilleryman, it has been suggested, was an empirical practitioner of a variable art, rather than the operator of a precisely accurate machine, but he could achieve impressive results. At Hereford in 1645 the besieged royalists declared that one of their 'excellent cannoneers . . . spent but one shot in vain throughout the whole seidge'.[48] Not only were some practical artillerymen highly skilled, but theoretical mathematical artillerists also claimed successes, and brash young Nathaniel Nye dazzled his readers with science as he explained the triangulation and calculations that had led to the successful battery of Worcester. Innovative backroom experts, like the royalist 'fire-worker' M. de la Roche, were encouraged despite reservations about the practical 'fitness' of their inventions.[49]

Skill, intelligence, and ingenuity helped to transcend innate technical weaknesses, but another common characteristic of civil war arms and ammunition added a further element of unpredictability. Much was made, recycled, and repaired on the spot, and the resulting local variations increased problems of uniformity and reliability. At the siege of Hereford in late 1642 and early 1643 the governor of the town, Fitzwilliam Conyngsby, noted that he '[b]ought and made in [his] garrison . . . arms & ammunition of all sorts' for his 700 men. The presence in the royalist army of a mill for boring ordnance suggests practical efforts to keep the bore of cannon true in the face of the warping brought

[46] Hall, *Ballistics*, 32–3; BL Harl. MS 6852, fo. 89; PRO SP 28/26, fo. 672; Roger Boyle, earl of Orrery, *A Treatise of the Art of War: Dedicated to the Kings Most Excellent Majesty* (1677), 29.

[47] BL Harl. MS 2155, fo. 124ᵛ; BL Add. MS 11,332, fos. 69ᵛ, 75; Townshend, *Diary*, 1. 175; and note the 'best marks-men' placed in the Bradford church steeple, *Rider of the White Horse*, 65, and the two musketeers called on by Colonel Hutchinson to pick off a particularly effective royalist defender at Shelford. Hutchinson, *Memoirs*, 162.

[48] Derbys. RO, Gell MSS D258, 31/30 (aa); BL Stowe MS 189, fo. 31; John Duncumb, *Collections towards the History and Antiquities of the County of Hereford*, 3 vols. (Hereford, [1804–82]), 1. 279. Note the regret at the death of '[o]ne of the Best Gunners the Garrison had' at Colchester in 1648. HMC, *Fourteenth Report. App. Pt. 9*, 'Round MSS' (1895), 286.

[49] Nathaniel Nye, *The Art of Gunnery: Wherein is described the true way to make all sorts of Gunpowder, Gun-match, the Art of shooting in great and small Ordnance* (1647), 50; BL Harl. MS 6802, fos. 137, 140, 141; Roy, *Royalist Ordnance Papers*, 43. 32–3.

about by use, but it seems unlikely that regulations requiring that all arms be proved or 'fixed' were meticulously observed in local garrisons or on active service.[50]

Arms, ammunition, and their raw materials were in chronically short supply. Shortages encouraged ingenious inventions such as the 'Engine' to salvage cannon from sunken ships in England's seas and rivers. On a more practical level, the need to manufacture arms and ammunition locally increased civilian involvement in the war. At Leicester in May 1645 the townsmen, having obtained 200 new muskets and 70 carbines from Sir Arthur Hesilrige, made 100 barrels of powder and 'match proportionable' themselves.[51] Oxford made and repaired guns, ammunition, pikes, and swords and provided auxiliary supplies such as powder and cannon baskets.[52] In the midst of the siege of Chester in 1645, Lord Byron laboured to maintain satisfactory supplies from the city's powder mills and took 'oakam and old cordage from a ship' for match.[53] The war demonstrated, however, the hazards of unregulated and often inexpert manufacture and handling of dangerous substances. The unpopular pre-war monopoly of manufacture of gunpowder—which had never in fact been watertight—had been swept away by the Long Parliament in the interest of free trade and the private right of every man to make or import his own. Gunpowder and match did not require large capital investment and so lent themselves to small-scale, ad hoc production, and although much manufacture, especially in and around London, remained in the experienced hands of large-scale producers, there were many small provincial powder makers, while inadequate domestic production forced both sides to rely on imports. Such varied and fortuitous sources of supply did not contribute to reliable, uniform quality, although there was no mystery about the specifications for either powder or match.[54] Nathaniel Nye explained that match should be made from hemp or tow boiled with lye, ashes and saltpetre, and that the common formulae for gunpowder ranged from a strong blend of six parts of saltpetre to one of brimstone and one of charcoal for pistols, to a weaker four:one:one ratio for cannon that put less pressure on the piece. In practice, factors from the age of the powder to the quality of the saltpetre and the skill of the mixers affected reliability, and the risks were magnified by the shortages, inexperience,

---

[50] Bodl. MS Tanner 303, fo. 115; BL Harl. MS 6804, fo. 160[v]; and see BL Harl. MS 6852, fo. 89 for royalist conversion of the boring mill to a mill for grinding sword blades; and Bodl. MS Firth c. 6, fo. 294[v], for Hopton's 'fixing of arms' in 1643.

[51] *Narration of the Siege and taking . . . of Leicester*, 4.

[52] Bodl. MS Add. D.114, fo. 92; Roy, *Royalist Ordnance Papers*, 43. 26–7; Edwards, *Dealing in Death*, 76–9, 115–16.

[53] 'John Byron's Account of the Siege of Chester 1645–1646', *The Cheshire Sheaf*, 4th ser. 6 (1971), 12, 15–16 (from Bodl. MS Rawlinson B210).

[54] Roy, *Royalist Ordnance Papers*, 43. 9–10, 12; Edwards, *Dealing in Death*, 110–17. For royal efforts to regulate manufacture in the interests of quality, security, and monopoly, see e.g. James I's proclamation of 1623, 'for prevention of abuses touching Gunpowder and Saltpeeter', James F. Larkin and Paul L. Hughes, *Stuart Royal Proclamations*, 1 (1973), 565–8.

and urgency of war.[55] A prudent commander like Sir Ralph Hopton preferred to use the experts he sent for from Oxford, but they too were in short supply.[56] The lack of effective quality control over the manufacture of gunpowder, difficult at the best of times, increased the already high potential for accidents.

Bullets too were variable. Some were commercially supplied 'for money', but they were also made on the spot. Troops carried moulds and nippers for the purpose, and they were among the items listed for re-equipment of Essex's army in 1644. The expenses of Venn's regiment at Windsor included 10s. 10d. for bullet moulds and 10s. for melting and casting 1,000 pounds of bullets. Waller's troops had to 'melt lead and cast bullets' as they besieged Hereford. Lead for this purpose was sought wherever opportunity offered. Roofs were useful, while Sir Thomas Myddleton's claimed purpose in breaking up the church organ at Wrexham was utilitarian, not ideological: its pipes would provide bullets for his men. Some sources of supply were more risky. The shortage of shot at Sherborne in 1645 was so great that soldiers were paid for every bullet they retrieved with 'great adventurousness . . . from under the very Walls'.[57] They might find in the midst of battle, however, that their home-made ammunition did not fit their muskets, and the subsequent 'gnawing' or 'shaving' of bullets to fit took valuable time, rendered them less efficient, and caused a tumbling motion that produced tearing wounds and led to accusations of atrocity.[58]

Guns and ammunition of the kind described here could kill as dead as any other, but the relation between intent and effect was often fortuitous. In this admittedly the civil war did not differ from other wars, and technical advances have changed the picture surprisingly little. 'Human factors', it has been said, 'cancel out technological potentialities.' Many Second World War soldiers preferred not to fire their advanced 'individual arms at the enemy in combat'; they had their counterparts in civil war soldiers who chose to fire their non-uniform bullets from their technologically backward muskets into the air.[59] Randomness and intrinsic

---

[55] Nye, *Art of Gunnery*, 4, 7–9. Nye also set out the methods for mixing and making powder, including corning it, i.e. producing granules to give a stronger charge, by rubbing damp powder through a sieve; Edwards, *Dealing in Death*, 107–20; Firth, *Cromwell's Army*, 81–6; and see Roy, *Royalist Ordnance Papers*, 43. 11, 29–33, and 43 (on inferior 'old cannon powder' stored for years before being palmed off on the English by European suppliers); Hall, *Ballistics*, 55, 60 (who notes that 'powder varied in strength from barrel to barrel by as much as twenty per cent'), and 59–62.

[56] Bodl. MS Firth c. 6, fo. 294.

[57] Bodl. MS Tanner 61, fo. 149ᵛ; Tanner 303, fo. 125; PRO SP 28/126, fos. 34–5 (on the variable costs of casting); *Chirk Castle Accounts A.D. 1605–1666*, comp. W. M. Myddleton (St Albans, 1908), p. x; Rushworth, 6. 63; Devonshire RO, Seymour MSS 1392 M/L 1644/22. At Sherborne 200 bullets were retrieved in one day; and see similar payments for bullets retrieved at Pontefract. *True Relation of The taking of Sherborn-Castle*, 5; Nathan Drake, 'A Journal of the first and second sieges of Pontefract Castle 1644–1645', in *Miscellanea*, Surtees Soc. 37 (1860), 9

[58] Orrery, *Art of War*, 29; HMC, *14th Report. App. Pt 9*, 'Round MSS', 286, 288.

[59] Firth, *Cromwell's Army*, 98; Raudzins, 'Firepower Limitations', 132: he estimates that up to three-quarters of American troops in elite units in the Second World War did not fire at the enemy; compare the American soldier in Iraq in 2003 who said, 'I could go home a happy man without firing at anyone', reported in *USA Today* (4 Apr. 2003), 4A. In the Franco-Prussian War it was

cost inefficiency were also striking characteristics of civil war artillery and here too firepower and results were often vastly disproportionate. The defenders of Brampton Bryan claimed that 513 'great bullets' were shot against them, most of them falling within the castle, and that the royalists had expended £6,000 on powder there and at nearby Hopton Castle, yet only four men were killed at Brampton Bryan. At the siege of Manchester, it was calculated that 4,000 cannon and musket bullets were shot into the town, but total casualties were four killed (of whom two died by accident) and four wounded.[60] Nevertheless the civil war is not necessarily shamed by modern progress. Twentieth-century figures suggest that while artillery inflicted proportionately more casualties than small arms (perhaps a ratio of 6.7 to 2 for British forces in the Second World War), the process remained expensive; according to one estimate it took 250 rounds of artillery fire to hit one German defender in Normandy.[61]

The English civil war did not see the use of massed artillery on the scale developed by Gustavus Adolphus on the continent and imitated by Imperialist armies. The integration and mobility of an unsettled war in which there were relatively few areas securely dominated by one side or the other meant, as Geoffrey Parker has noted, a high risk of attack on a field train of artillery on the move. Parliament, indeed, suffered the effects of such an unwise concentration of artillery in 1644 when it lost nearly forty heavy guns to the king after Lostwithiel.[62] Yet if big guns were dispersed in England, and if the outcome of major battles and of many sieges did not depend on an artillery barrage, such guns and their skilled gunners were widely employed and highly valued. Given the old-fashioned nature of most pre-existing English fortifications they could inflict dramatic damage. Tall old castle walls of vertical stone, unprotected by the bastions and other developments of the *trace italienne*, were vulnerable to breaches, and in fact hastily thrown-up earthworks usually provided better protection against cannon fire for they absorbed the shot instead of shattering. At Worcester in 1646 the defenders recorded that one heavy cannon ball buried itself two feet deep in a mud wall.[63]

estimated that 'a ton of iron was expended for every man killed'. Some killing rates were more expensive than others: at Vitoria the British fired 459 shots for every enemy hit; in the Crimea the French fired 1,000 shots for every hit; a British patrol in the Cape of Good Hope in 1851 achieved a rate of 32,000 rounds per hit. Raudzins, 'Firepower Limitations', 147. Compare the civil war claim that the many hundreds of shot the royalists sent into Plymouth from one fort over two months harmed no one, did little damage to houses, and succeeded only in shooting off one arm of a windmill, which was quickly repaired. BL Add. MS 35,297, fo. 5.

[60] HMC, *Bath MSS*, 1. 33 (the surrender of Hopton Castle was followed by a massacre, changing the cost−benefit ratio); Fairfax, *Memoirs*, 109−10; Foster, 'True and Exact Relation', in [Washbourn], *Bibliotheca Gloucestrensis*, 26.

[61] Raudzins, 'Firepower Limitations', 150−1.

[62] Parker, *Military Revolution*, 23−4, 28. At Breitenfeld in 1631 Gustavus had 51 heavy guns and every regiment was reinforced by 4 light field pieces. Ibid. 23.

[63] Townshend, *Diary*, 1. 124.

Artillery produced dramatic effects even when it did not bring victory. Offensively it was valuable for making breaches for siege assaults and breaking formations before battle. At Banbury 'great Shot' made a 30 yard breach in the walls of the castle, although the storm two days later failed. Basing House, however, having withstood earlier bombardments, was finally damaged beyond defensibility by Cromwell's six-day assault with heavy siege guns and an ample supply of ammunition.[64] The effectiveness of artillery varied not only with size and number of guns and skill of gunners but also with the nature and strength of fortifications against which it was directed. Some, like Beeston Castle, were virtually impregnable geographically; others were blessed by exceptionally thick stone walls or protected by a tricky river crossing. Clay soil in particular hardened to make earthworks that were notoriously 'a grave to Cannon balls'. Yet if sustained heavy bombardment could shatter the walls of Arundel castle and assert the destructive force of seventeenth-century siege artillery, the ruins of Corfe castle, slighted after surrender but still massively formidable today, are witness to the limits of contemporary power to destroy.

There were other constraints on the use of heavy artillery. It was expensive of manpower, horsepower, and cash; moving it was at best cumbersome and slow, at worst it was immobilized by rain and mud. In 1647 it was estimated that a train of 36 guns required the support of 200 labourers, 600 pioneers, and 100 'mattrosses' or assistant gunners, as well as a retinue of 'officers, artificers and attendants' ranging from the general, the chief engineer, and the master-gunner to miners, clerks, rope-makers, and servants. At Edgehill the royal horse and foot had to delay action for two hours until the king's artillery lumbered into position. Nor, once in place, was artillery necessarily effective in battle, as the parliamentarians observed at Marston Moor and Naseby.[65] And once enemies closed with each other at close quarter it was useless; then, a royalist noted at Colchester in 1648, 'our Cannon were obliged to cease firing, least we hurt our own Troops, as well as the Enemys'.[66] Nevertheless its skilful use could interdict enemy action, as when the royalists at Alresford fired their drakes 'so thick' that they rendered a valuable wood untenable, or when at Alton in 1643 a field gun fired at close range devastated advancing enemy horse. In this chancy business, both sides paid tribute to expertise. The augmentation of arms granted to the royalist comptroller general of the artillery

---

[64] Walker, *Historical Discourses*, 89; Gaunt, *Cromwellian Gazetteer, passim.*

[65] Townshend, *Diary*, 1. 124; Gerbier, *First Publique Lecture*, 9; [T.R.], *The Souldiers Accompt. Or, Tables Showing the Personall Allowance of Pay to all Officers and Souldiers belonging to an Army, either Foot or Horse . . . Also, To all Officers and Attendants on a Train of Artillerie* (1647); Ricraft, *Englands Champions*, 3; *A Relation of the Battaile lately fought between Keynton and Edgehill* (1642), 2; *A True Relation Of a Victory obtained over the Kings Forces . . . betweene Harborough, and Nasiby* ([1645]), A3: when the royalists had advanced within cannon shot, the parliamentary 'Ordnance began to play, but that being found at *Marston*-Moore and other places but a losse of time', trumpets and drums promptly sounded a charge.

[66] HMC, *14th Report. App. Pt.9*, 'Round MSS', 282.

train included 'two pieces of Canon mounted Sable' as symbolic recognition of his value.[67]

One of the chief uses of artillery was as an instrument of terror. It worked against troops, as at Alresford, when the sight of the 'execution' done by a single gun led one body of royalists to flight.[68] It was also a calculated tactic against civilians under siege. Bombardments opened breaches that might pave the way to successful assault or negotiated surrender, but they also joined with food shortage, prolonged discomfort, and dislocation of normal life as factors inciting civilians to unrest that complicated the task of defending commanders. At Chester, Lord Byron faced increasing difficulty in restraining 'mutinous' civilians in the face of heavy terror bombardment by the parliamentarians. These planned attacks, concentrated at night, used mortars and grenades much as flying bombs and missiles were used in a later age. After the range had been found with stone balls, the town was terrified by huge balls that battered and set fire to houses; fire, smoke, and noise joined to frighten and demoralize as well as kill the inhabitants. A spy inside the town had advised that 'a great shoot . . . be made that will so terrify people that their greatest aim will be to fly and also setting torches on the steeple which also will be a great terror'.[69] Yet such terror tactics, although they frightened and exhausted, were not necessarily effective. In October 1645 a Chester man complained that they had been kept 'waking' all week by day and night bombardment, but a few weeks later he noted that a twenty-four-hour barrage that sent in 300 great cannon shot and made two large breaches in the defences had led to no more than 'a brave attempt' at assault and a damaging repulse. A Chester woman wrote to reassure her husband, 'You need not fear [for] me for I am so fearful I go no whither out of doors', but she also observed, '[H]ere is more killed in looking on than those that are on service.'[70] On other occasions the softening up effects of artillery were more successful, as in Rupert's bombardment of Leicester in 1645, or Cromwell's night-long 'hot' barrage with cannon and mortars at Devizes a few months later.[71] Artillery was clearly valued not only for planned destructive effects on fortifications and soldiers, but also for random physical and psychological effects on civilians.

[67] BL Add. MS 14,294, fo. 31ᵛ; Gaunt, *Cromwellian Gazetteer*, 73. Artillery and musket fire in combination could be devastating, as the Imperialist casualties of 7,600 dead inflicted by the Swedes at Breitenfeld had demonstrated. Parker, *Thirty Years War*, 126.

[68] [E.A.], *Full Relation . . . Alsford*, 3; and see Fairfax, *Memoirs*, 28; Foster, 'True and Exact Relation', in [Washbourn], *Bibliotheca Gloucestrensis*, 257: 'we fired some drakes at them, they retreated: then . . . we fired two great pieces of ordnance at them, and then they retreated . . ., and drew up . . . facing us; then we let flye two or three of our greatest ordnance at them; they all fled'.

[69] BL Add. MS 11,332, fo. 49; 'John Byron's Account', *Cheshire Sheaf*, 4th ser. (1971), 18–19, 21.

[70] BL Add. MS 11,332, fos. 80, 81ᵛ, 82ᵛ.

[71] *Narration of the Siege and taking . . . of Leicester*, 6; [Ralph Norton], *A Letter Concerning The Storming and Delivering up of the Castle of the Devises* (25 Sept. 1645), 4; see also BL Add. MS 11,810, fo. 21ᵛ, on the 'close siege' at Devizes: 'incessant peals of muskets, great guns and mortar pieces played upon us day and night'.

There were other terror weapons. 'Hot bullets' started fires where they landed, and were countered by foresighted commanders who ordered household watches, had combustible materials removed to cellars, and required that hides and tubs of water be placed at the doors of houses.[72] The royalists besieging Lyme combined incendiary and fragmentation missiles when they loaded their artillery with red hot shot, shanks of anchors, and bars of iron. At Newbury in 1643 they used 'chain shot and all ways that would murder most cruelly'. Case shot and shrapnel were also employed without, it seems, incurring the odium attached to chewed or poisoned bullets.[73] Even the pike could become a terror weapon when combined with fire; neither men nor horses could face Rupert's fire-pikes at Bristol.[74] Mines joined more advanced technology with terror. The first mine in England was 'sprung' by Rupert's troops at Lichfield in April 1643. Preliminary mining, in the sense of undermining, frightened townsmen when it reached their defensive walls, but it also gave opportunities for reciprocal cruelties. At Hereford, for example, after a counter mine was sunk, boys were sent out at night to 'fire' the miners' works, and 'what . . . fire could not perfect (though it burnt far and suffocated some of their miners) . . . water did, breaking in upon them and drowning that which the fire had not consumed'.[75]

We should not exaggerate the effect of lack of technological uniformity and predictability. Soldiers often found ways to get around the deficiencies of their weapons, and there were experts and dilettanti who delighted in the challenges of innovation and translated them into effective action. Charles I himself had been an aficionado of 'great artillery' in the 1630s, while the skills of Wemyss, his former master-gunner, were valued by both sides. John Gwyn revealed pride in professional skill in his account of calculations, based only on 'a flash of fire . . . and the help of a perspective glass', that enabled him to determine the height of musket loopholes so that he could send in his men to deliver decisive volleys of fire.[76] There were also fortunate commanders, whose luck combined with skill to bring success. Sir William Waller enjoyed a reputation for both until his luck deserted him. Ingenious soldiers, furthermore, found unconventional ways to exploit unpromising military matériel, as when the royalists laid a train of

---

[72] Fairfax, *Memoirs*, 65; 'John Byron's Account', *Cheshire Sheaf*, 4th ser. 6 (1971), 19; Q.F., 'Red Hot Shot', *JSAHR* 5 (1926), 206–8.

[73] HMC, *Twelfth Report. Appendix. Part 3. Manuscripts of the Earl Cowper. Vol. 3* (1889), 141; *CSPDom. 1644*, 227; at Lyme a day's intensive barrage succeeded in starting fires (which were quenched), but only three casualties resulted. See also Bodl. MS Tanner 303, fo. 121ᵛ, on 'one brass piece which carried half a peck of musket balls'; A. Norris Kennard, 'A Civil War Hand Grenade', *The Bradford Antiquary*, NS 8/39 (1958), 192.

[74] Carman, *History of Firearms*, 10.

[75] Duncumb, *Collections towards the History and Antiquities . . . of Hereford*, 1. 278; 'Prince Rupert's Journal', *EHR* 13 (1898), 733; BL Add. MSS 11,331, fo. 113ᵛ; 11,332, fo. 75ᵛ; Bayley, *Dorset*, 282, 285.

[76] BL Add. MS 11,810, fo. 30ᵛ. For Charles's interest in artillery, see e.g. HEH EL MSS 6520, 6521; for Wemyss and his 'very serviceable' leather guns, see BL Add. MS 11,810, fo. 22ᵛ; *CSPDom. 1644*, 351–2.

powder on the sand near Exmouth, lit it, and 'scalded' pursuing parliamentarians. And homely materials, such as logs and stones or mud, woolsacks, and beds (which strengthened ramparts), could be turned to effective use.[77] Finally, the fact that weapons were unpredictable did not make them less frightening. Gwyn's recollection of the file of six dead men lying on the battlefield, their heads struck off by a single cannon ball, evoked a mythic terror.[78]

Clearly war was conducted with even less precision then than now. If training, discipline, and morale all reduced the degree of randomness, a large and irreducible minimum remained, and problems of volatility of material, lack of quality control, inadequate training, and carelessness contributed to the large number of accidents. Death and injury did not require the agency of an enemy. Stores of gunpowder, for example, were a constant hazard and the resulting disasters, deadly and dramatic, were sometimes seen as providential, sometimes as man-made. Enemies tried to exploit the known dangers, as when the royalists employed a 'Fellow . . . to blow up the Rebels Ammunition, who . . . put his lighted Match tyed to a Bag of *Wildfire* into a Cart of their Powder'. On that occasion, the fuse of one device went out of its own accord—a further example of the unreliability of matériel—but the other, by a providential dispensation, was discovered in the nick of time, within an inch of detonation, and the dastardly red leather-covered 'Engine' was dispatched to parliament.[79] On other occasions, magazines exploded when hit by random shots.[80] On yet others, causes were no more than a loose spark or remained veiled in confusion. The wagonload of powder that blew up after the battle of Lansdown disabled the royalist general Sir Ralph Hopton, and in so doing contributed to his army's failure to exploit its success. At Torrington in Devon the spectacular explosion of the powder stored in the church killed royalists and parliamentarians indiscriminately but—providentially—preserved the Bible. Norwich's peaceful war was interrupted in 1648 by the explosion of its magazine, killing forty people.[81] And simple negligence had its victims, as in the casually horrifying

---

[77] BL Add. MS 35,297, fos. 4, 16; BL Harl. MSS 2125, fo. 135ᵛ; 2135, fos. 91–4; 2155, fo. 114ᵛ; Bayley, *Dorset*, 286; Hutchinson, *Memoirs*, 162; *Colonel Joseph Bamfeild's Apologie, Written by himselfe and printed at his desire* ([The Hague?], 1685), 6 (for an example of successful exploitation of technological weakness: the need for lighted match to fire muskets led defenders to expect to see attackers' lighted match in the dark; ergo, surprise could be achieved by forgoing the advantage of pre-lighted match).

[78] BL Add. MS 11,810, fo. 24ᵛ; John Vicars, *Jehovah-Jireh. God in the Mount* (1644), in Vicars, *Magnalia Dei Anglicana*, 375.

[79] Vicars, *Burning Bush*, in *Magnalia Dei Anglicana*, 17; BL Add. MS 35,297, fo. 4, and fo. 44ᵛ for a plot to blow up the magazine at Plymouth by carts of 'fireworks' and lighted match, aborted when the match went out for lack of air. Walker, *Historical Discourses*, 68–9.

[80] Fairfax, *Memoirs*, 28; *A great and bloudy Fight at Colchester* (1648), title-page.

[81] Adair, *Roundhead General . . . Waller*, 87; Gaunt, *Cromwellian Gazetteer*, [110]; John Heydon, 'The Discovery of the wonderful Preservation of his Excellency Sir Thomas Fairfax, the Army, the Records . . . of Torrington in Devon' (1644) in *Somers Tracts*, ed. Walter Scott (2nd edn. 13 vols. 1809–1815), 4. 70. Such risks were already familiar before the war, e.g. the disaster at a trained

story of 'the careless Soldier, [who] in fetching Powder (where a Magazine was) clapt his hand carelessly into a Barrel of Powder, with his Match lighted betwixt his Fingers, whereby much Powder was blown up, and many kill'd'.[82]

Besides major disasters, there was a constant run of lesser accidents. Casualty lists included victims of malfunctioning weapons as well as of the enemy. At Worcester a 'great culverin of iron . . . broke to pieces', hurt 'our best canonier', and killed one of his assistants. At Brampton Bryan, the greatest gun of each party broke, respectively killing the royalist cannoneer and severely wounding one of Lady Harley's garrison. The garrison saw God's punishing hand in the blowing up of the royalist gun, but chose to see his mercy in the absence of fatality in their own case.[83] Artillery and handguns alike were sources of accidents, often fatal, through defects of the guns themselves and their powder, and through careless handling. The only parliamentary casualty in one skirmish at Plymouth was a soldier killed 'by shooting off his own musket as 'tis thought'. And then as now friendly fire had its victims. One of the four fatalities at Manchester resulted from a comrade's gun 'flying off unawares'. A soldier forgot his gun was loaded and 'shot a maide through the head, and she immediately died'. Another 'shot at randum' while exercising and killed one of his fellows.[84] In battle, malfunctions cost some soldiers their lives and saved others. Joseph Bampfield escaped death from a pistol 'fyred in vaine' although—another example of a firearm's conversion to weapon of battery—he sustained a dangerous wound to the eye inflicted 'by the blowe of [the] pistol'.[85] Given the hazards in routine handling of routine weapons, it is not surprising to find reluctance to use those that were even more intrinsically risky. Some soldiers refused to 'meddle with hand Granadoes, the using of them being somewhat dangerous', a reasonable position in view of the instructions for users: '[B]e sure when you have fired the Fuse, suddenly to cast it out of your hand'.[86]

In the circumstances of early modern war negligence, instability, terminal stupidity, bad luck, and God's providence could all lead to disaster. On occasion, providence was very visibly at work, as in the case of the disgruntled soldier who intended to shoot Sir William Waller but whose musket failed to fire. In such

band display in London in 1631, when a barrel of powder blew up 'through the negligence of some careless fellows which were going to receive munition', leaving six dead on the spot and forty or fifty badly burned. HEH EL MS 6547 (FAC).

[82] Richard Bulstrode, *Memoirs and Reflections upon the Reign and Government of King Charles the Ist. and K. Charles the IId.* (1721), 84; East Sussex RO, Frewen MS 4223, fo. 72.

[83] Townshend, *Diary*, 1. 117; HMC, *Bath MSS*, 1. 3–5.

[84] Fairfax, *Memoirs*, 110; [Wharton], 'Letters from a Subaltern Officer', *Archaeologia*, 35 (1853), 2. 313–14, 332; BL Add. MS 35,297, fo. 26; and see Foster, 'True and Exact Relation', in [Washbourn], *Bibliotheca Gloucestrensis*, 253, 259, for accidental deaths at the hands of fellow soldiers.

[85] *Colonel Joseph Bamfield's Apologie*, 10.

[86] Nye, *Art of Gunnery*, 75; the petardier's was also a 'desperate service', Edwards, *Dealing in Death*, 9. Petardiers were paid 4s. a day and their attendants 2s. 6d., against 2s. or 1s. 6d. for gunners and 1s. for labourers and pioneers. [T.R.], *Souldiers Accompt*.

cases interpretation owed much to predilection, so when a 'pistol only fired in the pan, and did not discharge', thus saving the life of Sir John Reresby, his son saw providence clearly at work. When destruction was in some sense self-induced, however, a severer approach was legitimate, as in the account of the death of a soldier 'slaine by our owne cannon through his owne negligence'.[87] To modern eyes the weapons of the seventeenth century appear primitively unreliable and imprecise, but the failings of their human operators are not unfamiliar. Together they heightened the sense of uncertainty and vulnerability brought by civil war. Faith in divine providence gave a sense of purpose to this mutable world, but that faith was strained when God's instruments, like his enemies, proved also to be the victims of chance.

[87] *Memoirs of Sir John Reresby of Thrybergh*, ed. Andrew Browning (2nd edn., ed. Mary K. Geiter and W. A. Speck, 1991), xlii; Foster, 'True and Exact Relation', in [Washbourn], *Bibliotheca Gloucestrensis*, 258: *A Narration of The great Victory, (Through Gods Providence) Obtained by the Parliaments Forces Under Sir William Waller, At Alton* (n.pl., 16 Dec. [1643]), 7, on wounded men 'scorched with powder by reason of their owne negligence'.

6

Knowledge and Confusion

'Intelligence, as ever, was less than perfect.'[1]

Knowledge in war is of multiple kinds. Some is public and open, available to all those interested enough to seek it in print, manuscript, or verbal report. Some is private, specialized, and—if possible—protected from penetration by the enemy. Some is directly military in application, some is part of the general world of contemporary information that, through its effects in civilian politics, has consequences for the conduct of war. Some is sought in order to shape future events—to know, for example, where to send troops to forestall an enemy strike—and some records and draws morals from those that have already happened. Some is acquired and disseminated by 'legitimate' agents, by army scouts or news reporters; some is a clandestine affair of spies and turncoats. Some is freely offered by local populations; some is extorted. Some is true, and some is false. All these strands were interwoven in the information world of the English civil war.

The circumstances of civil war both facilitated and complicated intelligence gathering and analysis. The process revealed again the distinctive intimacy of this war in which language formed no barrier, troops were volatile, prisoners regularly exchanged, and clothing a shaky guide to affiliation, and in which civil society, with its poor transients, messengers, and travelling civilians coexisted alongside armies, as did family links and friendship between enemies. Commercial, legal, and social communication between royalists and parliamentarians continued despite hostilities. The blurred boundaries between civil and military society aided information gathering, while the technological limits of communications and the confusions of war reinforced the need for it. When the renegade, the spy, or the disloyal civilian was only certainly identifiable by his actions, not by speech, manner, or clothing, suspicion was easily aroused. Readiness to suspect and condemn spies is a common enough form of war hysteria; public revulsion against spying and subversion, of the kind expressed in the heated denunciations and terminal punishments of the 1640s, has had a long life, as has the odium against the spy's breach of personal and professional honour and affront to social

---

[1] R. W. Apple, 'A New Way of War', *New York Times* (20 April, 2003), B1.

norms. Civil war, while it made many things easier for the spy and the turncoat, also fostered anxiety about their subversive presence. This made for caution even among the apparently committed. The security of Fairfax's council of war itself could not be taken for granted: before a letter from a spy in the royalist camp was read, 'first the name was torne out'.[2]

FINDING OUT

We have already seen that the weapons with which the war was fought reinforced its intimacy and enhanced the sense of vulnerability to the unpredictable common to all wars. Bungled intentions and failures of information and control compounded uncertainties. How could commanders and their soldiers know where they were? In battle, how could they act with knowledge and according to plan? How could they identify friend or foe? Problems of intelligence joined the material means of waging war and the character and professional abilities of officers and men in shaping its nature. We shall return to the soldiers, but first we shall look at two aspects of intelligence: at the ways in which knowledge was acquired, and at some of the difficulties of translating it into action. Sources of information ranged from 'public' items reported in the wartime flood of print news or available in pre-existing maps and descriptions to reports from a very mixed bag of human agents. Its acquisition and application demonstrated yet again the ad hoc, provisional elements of the English civil war, but here too similarities to modern wars persist. For all their technological aids to navigation and identification modern armies too offer plentiful examples of erroneous intelligence and of troops who get lost or fail to distinguish friend from foe.

Armies needed many kinds of information but the most basic related to their physical environment. They needed to know where they were going and where the enemy was, and they needed to understand the topographical strengths and weaknesses of positions and details of military fortification. Information came from direct observation, printed or manuscript representation, and local knowledge. Direct observation was a relatively simple matter, although it was subject to vagaries of weather, smoke, or eyesight (the latter sometimes supplemented by the use of telescopes or 'perspective glasses'). The other two sources of knowledge have been little explored, but they were crucial in the design and execution of military plans. The ability to use maps and plans was a basic military skill. The human informants have a shadowy survival on the military margins, but they were valued if not honoured in their day.

The use of maps and plans is rarely specifically documented, but it was part of the arcana of the professional officer. In 1639, for example, the old soldier

---

[2] 'The Proceedings of the New-moulded army from . . . 1645, till . . . 1647. Written by Col. Edward Wogan, till then an Officer of the Army', in Carte, *Letters*, 1. 139.

Sir Jacob Astley, surveying the military defences of the north of England, sent
'cards' of Berwick and Carlisle to London to demonstrate their strategic importance.[3] If the new officers of the war years did not already possess some skill with
maps, they rapidly acquired it. Familiarity with schematized representation of
topographical space was already common among the educated, who had both general geographical interests and long-standing acquaintance with maps and plans of
property for estate and legal purposes. A more specialized recent development was
the market for manuals full of diagrams of fortifications and military formations.
Sophisticated 'carto-literate' map- and plan-readers probably made up no more
than a subclass of the literate, but representations like the 'True Mapp' of Plymouth that accompanied the *True Narration* of its siege in 1644 or the overview
of Colchester that formed part of a broadsheet *Diary* of events there in 1648,
with their skilled depictions of the towns and their topographical settings, their
fortifications and troop dispositions, argue for the existence of a popular familiarity with maps and their meanings.[4] The habit of abstraction and visualization, of
mental connection between pictorial representation, place, and movement, did
not need to reach a cartographically sophisticated level to be militarily useful.[5]

England already had a distinguished cartographic tradition. The maps of
Saxton, Norden, and Speed were frequently reprinted before the war. Saxton's
wall map of England and Wales was a favoured decoration in great houses by
the late sixteenth century, a fashion that made publicly visible the topographical
articulation of the country, and there was a market for large tapestry wall maps
of English counties. Statesmen, soldiers, and gentlemen were familiar with maps
for business and pleasure. It is not surprising to find that the 'Great Chamber'
of Essex's house at Chartley held thirteen maps at his death, for he was a soldier
with European as well as English experience; it is more notable that an obscure
William Fiske of Pakenham, Suffolk, bequeathed his 'globe, mapps, . . . and the
great mappe' to his son in 1648.[6] Saxton's county maps had even appeared on
a set of playing cards in 1590, while the banner of Sir Richard Grenvile, in his

---

[3] *CSPDom. 1638–1639*, 384.

[4] 'A True Mapp and description of the towne of Plymouth and the Fortifications thereof, with
the workes and approaches of the Enemy, at the last Seige; Ao 1643' is a large sheet folded to fit a
pamphlet-sized publication, *A True Narration Of the most Observable Passages, in and at the late Seige
of Plymouth, from the fifteenth day of September 1643, untill the twenty fist [sic] of December following*
(1644); *A Diary of the Siege of Colchester by the Forces under Command of his Excellency the Lord
Generall Fairfax* (1648). And see J. B. Harley, 'Meaning and Ambiguity in Tudor Cartography', in
Sarah Tyacke (ed.), *English Map-Making 1500–1650* (1983), 45 n. 103. For a discussion of the
increasing use of maps by 'statesmen, landowners, military engineers and others' from the mid-16th
cent., see Sarah Tyacke, 'Introduction', ibid. 16–18, and note pls. 3–11, 20–9, 35, 44.

[5] Such 'visualization' was not new, nor was it confined to landed property or war: see e.g. the
'Plot' of Mendip lead mines (probably dating from the late 1650s) made for the virtuoso and
entrepreneur Thomas Bushell. BL Add. MS 5207.A, fos. 70, 77–8.

[6] *Wills and Inventoriues from the Registers of the Commissary of Bury St. Edmunds*, ed. Samuel
Tymms, Camden Society, 49 (1850), 209. At his death in 1637 Sir Thomas Puckering owned
twenty-four maps of towns and cities. Ann Hughes, *Politics, Society and Civil War in Warwickshire,
1620–1660* (Cambridge, 1987), 36. The Victoria and Albert Museum displays a fragment from a

brief parliamentary phase, depicted a map of England, its counties marked and identified by initials, with the legend, 'England Bleeding'. The practical ability to visualize the relations between parts of the country, between villages within a county, and between streets within a town, was as significant as the symbolic, metaphorical, and literary implications of these maps to which much attention has been drawn.[7] The military use of maps and civilian concern to follow the course of war probably enhanced the English sense of a national topography.

Travellers' guides had an overtly practical intent. Jacob Van Langeren's *Direction for the English Traviller*, which had three editions in 1635 and 1636, was 'the earliest English road book with maps'. The purpose was to enable the traveller 'to Coast about all England and Wales', to inform himself of his present location and future direction, to establish the orientation of towns, and to find the distances between towns in each county by means of detailed distance tables. The county maps in the first three editions remained tiny, simple, and basic, but in 1643 a revised edition was issued with new, larger, more detailed maps, and in 1644 a significant addition was made to the title-page: 'Usefull for Quartermasters, Brief-Gatherers, and all such as have to doe the Shires of England.' These books were small, roughly $6\frac{1}{2}$ by $5\frac{1}{2}$ inches; the quartermaster's edition was even more pocket-sized, 5 by $2\frac{1}{4}$ inches. Their modern rarity, it has been suggested, is evidence of their constant use in the seventeenth century.[8] The deficiencies for war use of the maps in the *Direction* were compensated for not only by reissues of Speed's and Saxton's maps in standard forms, but by their adaptation to war needs. In 1644 Saxton's large wall map of England appeared, shorn of decorations, in an $8\frac{1}{2}$ by $3\frac{3}{4}$ inch format 'Portable for every Mans Pocket', bound in calf and containing six folded map sheets, 20 inches wide and from $10\frac{3}{4}$ to 16 inches high. Its title-page claimed that it was 'Usefull for all Comanders for Quarteringe of Souldiers, & all sorts of Persons, that would be informed, Where the Armies be.'[9] Its publisher was a London parliamentarian, but Wenceslas Hollar, a royalist, had worked on its plates, while an Oxford bookseller revised Saxton's county atlas and published it in 1645. Cartographic

tapestry map showing features of Surrey and Middlesex; such maps were a speciality of the Sheldon workshops.

[7] R. A. Skelton, *Saxton's Survey of England and Wales, With a facsimile of Saxton's wall-map of 1583* (Amsterdam, 1974), 10, 12; R. A. Skelton, *County Atlases of the British Isles 1579–1850*, 1 (1970), 16–17 and *passim*; Harley, 'Meaning and Ambiguity', 27; Victor Morgan, 'The literary image of globes and maps in early modern England', in Tyacke, *English Map-Making*, 46–56; Richard Helgerson, 'The Land Speaks: Cartography, Chorography, and Subversion in Renaissance England', *Representations*, 16 (1986), 51–85; for Essex and Grenvile, see HEH HA Inventories Box 1 (20), and BL Sloane MS 5247, fo. 73.

[8] Skelton, *County Atlases*, 63–6, 68–70, and see pls. 20a and b; Van Langeren's book was preceded by John Norden's *England: An Intended Guyde, for English Travailers* (1625), which printed distance tables without maps. See Box, 'Kent in Early Road Books', *Archaeoligica Cantiana*, 44 (1932), 1–2, 8–9, and pls. I and II.

[9] Skelton, *Saxton's Survey*, 12, 14–15, 22. I am grateful to Richard Helgerson for drawing my attention to the Quartermaster's Map.

knowledge was bipartisan. 'Saxton's maps . . . fought on both sides', as did travellers' guides and more restricted and local maps and 'descriptions'.[10]

The value of such knowledge was described by an old soldier and quartermaster, Henry Hexham, in 1636:

[W]hat Generall is there, which conducts his armies through passages, over Rivers, Brookes, Mountaines or Woods, quarters or lodges them, or besieges any Citty, Towne or fort, but he must have continually a Topographick description, and Map of that Countrie, town or place in his hand, to advance his intended designe.[11]

That such knowledge extended a long way below generals and was part of daily military life in the civil war is evident from the record of John Syms, the refugee puritan minister who became deeply engaged in the defence of Plymouth. In the course of his many detailed accounts of new defence-works, he noted that one was 'called in the map, Lipson-Mill-Work', an indication that maps were progressively updated to reflect new conditions. Ability to 'read' and produce a diagrammed representation of the physical world among those who were not military professionals was also reflected in Syms's quick, crude sketch maps of Portland castle and Weymouth.[12]

Maps and guides were detailed and informative. Maps showed rivers, hills, and woods, houses, forts, ruins, and assorted items of interest. They indicated market towns, and made it possible to find 'the smallest Village . . . *Henxey* or *Botley* as well as *Oxford*'.[13] Printed guides indicated distance and orientation. Many local and specialized maps were part perspective view, and their incidental charms—such as the inclusion of a maid milking her cow in a field—do not disguise their practical usefulness for they sometimes provided astonishing detail, naming lanes, fields, and gates and showing the houses that lined the streets. Some dated from well before the civil war, but Speed's 1610 maps of Reading and Leicester, for instance, gave precisely the 'Topographick description' and the representation of roads, streams, churches, houses, gateways, and bridges that Hexham advocated, for two towns that were later to suffer much attention from soldiers.[14]

---

[10] Skelton, *Saxton's Survey*, 12. It has been suggested that the order in which maps were revised reflected the movements of the armies.

[11] Henry Hexham, quoted in Skelton, *Saxton's Survey*, 12. Monro, in his 'Practicall Observations' for the 'Younger Officer', took a commander's use of 'his land mappe' for granted, merely commenting that it should be confirmed by peasant informers (by 'the Boores intelligence'). Monro, *Expedition*, 2. 201.

[12] BL Add. MS 35,297, fos. 9, 179–83ᵛ. For plans of Oxford's fortifications, of varying degrees of sophistication, see R. T. Lattey *et al.*, 'A Contemporary Map of the Defences of Oxford in 1644', *Oxoniensia*, 1 (1936), 161–6.

[13] Skelton, *Saxton's Survey*, 17, and see the facsimile plates of Saxton's wall-map; Skelton, *County Atlases*, pl. 30.

[14] For Speed's maps of Leicester and Reading, see Basil L. Gimson and Percy Russell, *Leicestershire Maps: A Brief Survey* (Leicester, 1947), [7], pl. 3, and Charles Coates, *The History and Antiquities of Reading* (1802), pl. 6; for familiarity with detailed local topographical representations, see 16th-century examples in Tyacke, *English Map-Making*, pls. 5 and 7.

Topographical information, then, was not strange or esoteric, for many were accustomed to the diagrammatic abstraction of maps and plans and could conceptualize relationships of space and distance. What this meant to Rupert's or Fairfax's soldiers as they marched 'up and down in England' remains conjectural. What they did know were roads that were often bad and muddy. And roads were strikingly absent from most of the county and national maps, although they were meticulously detailed on local plans. Neither of the pocket-sized books specially targeted at the needs of quartermasters and other soldiers showed roads; they were not added to the 'Quartermaster's Map' until 1671.[15] Hence the importance of human guides who, together with scouts and spies, provided armies with information.

All three had important parts to play in an army's information system, as Richard Elton acknowledged when he grouped guides, scouts, and spies together in *The Compleat Body of the Art Military*, a book that had the imprimatur of 'diverse . . . most experienced commanders'. 'Intelligences' were a standard item among the 'charges incident' to maintaining an army; in Sir John Gell's claim for reimbursement, for example, expenses for horses, arms, and intelligence were lumped together. The informants who earned this money were various. When parliament authorized £10 in payments to Colonel Venn's regiment at Windsor, some went to official agents such as scouts, and some to unofficial sources who provided supplementary information, such as 'Mr. Wilson a minister', who received £1 'for intelligence'.[16] Armies could not in fact dispense with the help of such local civilians, and the value of information freely volunteered by a sympathetic, or at least benevolently neutral, local population was acknowledged in a revealing comment by Sir Edward Walker. When the king's army moved into Cornwall in 1644 they suddenly found themselves surrounded by a loyal populace, while the parliamentarians were 'utterly deprived' of information. '[N]ot till now', wrote Walker, 'were we sensible of the great and extraordinary Advantage the Rebels have over His Majesties Armies throughout the Kingdom by Intelligence (the Life of all warlike Actions).' In Cornwall, instead, it was the royalists who received 'hourly Notice' of the enemy's movements.[17] Nevertheless,

---

[15] Skelton, *Saxton's Survey*, 22; Box, 'Kent in Early Road Books', 7. Maps showing roads existed, like Norden's for Essex, but unlike Saxton's, and Van Langeren's *Direction*, they were not converted and distributed for military use. The large, regular pre-war network of carriers, 'foot-posts', waggons, hoys, etc., for transmission of passengers, letters, and goods, was presumably another source of information about routes, even if the network was intermittently disrupted by war. See John Taylor, *The Carriers Cosmographie; or A Brief Relation of The Innes, Ordinaries, Hosteries, and other Lodgings in, and neere London, where the Carriers, Waggons, Foote-posts and Higglers doe usually come, from any ports, townes, shires and countries* (1637); this brief but comprehensive work, an embryo timetable, is all text and contains no maps or diagrams.

[16] Firth and Rait, *Acts and Ordinances*, 1. 399; PRO SP 28/126, fos. 22, 35; Derbys. RO, Gell MSS, D258, 30/16; Elton, *Compleat Body of the Art Military*, 185–6. Soldiers from a locality or who had spent enough time there to know the country were also valuable sources of information. Hutchinson, *Memoirs*, 129.

[17] Walker, *Historical Discourses*, 50.

although local people were useful auxiliary informants even when not formally employed by an army, civilians were unpredictable commodities, and armies had greater control over men who were formally enrolled for service and therefore subject to the rigours of military law. [18] The articles of war of both sides legislated penalties for delinquent guides, spies, and scouts.[19]

Elton's analysis of the roles of an army's intelligence gatherers reflected his own civil war experience, and much of it retains a remarkably modern ring. The first category, the guides, were not normally regular, long-term soldiers but were employed as needed for their local expertise. Their work complemented the printed materials described above, for although Elton acknowledged that '*Maps* with the right use and knowledge of them, are great helps towards the finding out of the best and most convenient ways', he immediately added a requirement for '[s]kilfull and expert Inhabitants of the Countrey' as guides. It was the wagon-master's responsibility to screen them, to ascertain their knowledge of

all passable *By-paths, Crosse-ways, &.c* . . . of the distance of places, of the evennesse, and streightnesse of them, whether they be plain, or crooked, hilly or stony, and difficult of passage; what *Rivers, Hedges, Ditches*, and *Bridges*, lye in the way, and which way (if there shall be severall ways) is the safest and shortest.

The guide was also responsible for information about water and forage supplies and practicable routes for baggage. This degree of dependence had its risks, for guides could wilfully mislead or be mistaken. When conflicting advice was offered, it fell to officers and others with local knowledge to adjudicate. Faithful service deserved a reward, but it must never be forgotten that guides could also lead soldiers into 'danger and great hazards, if not utter ruine'—as at Colchester in 1648 when 'good Guides' enabled one party of horse to escape from the blockaded town but another was forced to retreat, 'misled' by guides who ran away. As a general warning, 'they [were] many times caused to ride halter'd about the neck to put them in mind of capitall punishment, if they shall mislead . . . for the terrour of others'.[20]

The case of one of the earl of Essex's Staffordshire tenants demonstrates how justified this nervousness was and how easily an army might be misled. Civilians were vulnerable to military demands for help and information, but a guide's coerced cooperation was not always reliable. Ralph Baxter, after being plundered to the point of ruin by the royalists, was ordered to guide the king's army to Essex's manor of Chartley. Parliament condemned him for collaboration but

---

[18] At Langport in 1645, Fairfax knew the enemy's intentions through 'Scouts and other countrymen'. *An Exact and Perfect Relation of the Proceedings of the Army under . . . Sir Thomas Fairfax . . . near Langport* (14 July 1645), 2.

[19] *Military Orders . . . Established by his Maiesty* (1643), 16, nos. 116–17; *Laws and Ordinances of Warre . . . Essex* (1643), [A*ᵛ*], 'Of Duties in generall', no. 1.

[20] Elton, *Compleat Body of the Art Military*, 185–6; HMC, *Fourteenth Report, Appendix. Part IX* (1895), 'Round MSS', 287–8.

fellow-tenants, petitioning on his behalf, said that instead he had risked his life to save the house and its park and deer, and had also 'by [his] provident care' preserved their own estates, 'All of which had been lost and destroyed if the said Ralph had not guided the army another way.'[21] Ralph survived to receive a modest reward, but such defiance by misdirection could be dangerous. Royalist articles of war mandated death without mercy for a guide 'found false in [his] charge'.[22]

Unlike guides, who were employed according to need, scouts were regular members of the army, sent out to reconnoitre and report. They were therefore unambivalently subject to its discipline, but Elton's insistence that they should be incorruptible as well as courageous, and that a scout's performance reflected on the reputation of his officer, suggested similar anxiety about treachery or incompetence. Commanders needed scouts to warn of possible enemy attack and to improve their own 'infesting of [the] Enemy'. Brave, trustworthy, discreet, observant scouts were to move by highways and by 'private unsuspected passages', reconnoitring all 'accessible' places, and to report 'nothing but what they can give *ocular* proof of'—for error could lead 'the whole *Army* possibly . . . into an irreparable ruine'.[23]

The civil war provides ample evidence of Elton's scouts in action as they sought to discover the enemy's whereabouts and facilitate action by their own side, and to report on militarily significant developments such as large-scale troop movements. The scale of this activity is revealed in the vast correspondence of the parliamentarian scoutmaster Sir Samuel Luke and in the tireless comings and goings of his agents. A good and lucky scout did not mislay the enemy, did not reveal his own presence, and enabled his army to remain undiscovered. The secrecy of an army concentration was a credit to the scouts who made it possible, as was prevention of surprise to their own forces. Essex urged that scouts be sent out continually to prevent surprise by Hopton at Wareham in 1644, and a few months later Waller's scouts were so 'diligent' that the royalists were unaware of the concentration of his forces and their secret approach to Alton, for Waller's men took prisoner anyone likely to pass on news of the parliamentary army's presence, while captured royalist scouts became themselves supplementary sources of information.[24] Not all operations were so fortunate, for a success for the scouts of one side usually entailed a failure for those of the other. They could also be incompetent, like the 'straggling scouts' observed before Hawarden in 1645. The relevant royalist article of war ordered discretionary punishment for scouts who were merely sluggish in their duties, but if their failings were due to sleep, drink, or intentional misdirection they became, like drunk or sleeping

[21] BL Add. MS 46,189, fo. 131.

[22] *Military Orders . . . Established by his Maiesty* (1643), [11], no. 77.

[23] Elton, *Compleat Body of the Art Military*, 186.

[24] BL Add. MS 29,319, fo. 11; *Narration of The great Victory, (Through Gods Providence) Obtained by the Parliaments Forces Under Sir William Waller, At Alton* (n.pl., [1643]), 3.

sentinels, subject to the death penalty.[25] Scouts were also vulnerable to capture. The parliamentarian Walter Erle, lamenting the earl of Caenarvon's success in Dorset in 1643 and noting his 'sudden and private' arrival, added a self-justifying marginal note: 'I had 2 scouts upon the way that he came but they were both intercepted.'[26] When action seemed imminent, forlorn hopes were deployed for advance reconnaissance to supplement the efforts of the scouts, but despite their fallibility scouts remained the basic and irreplaceable element in planning military movements. Some of the abrupt and apparently random changes of direction and backtracking of army marches can be explained as reaction to news suddenly received from scouts.

Finally, there were spies, 'at all times necessary for an *Army*, and . . . of all men they . . . deserve to be most certainly and liberally rewarded' for, as Elton recognized, their willingness and trustworthiness in this dangerous trade depended on generous and reliable payment. Spies, he said, were of three kinds. First were selected soldiers, preferably cavalry because of their wider opportunities to gather intelligence, who under pretence of discontent or lack of pay crossed to the enemy, whence they were to report on plans and events. The more of such spies the better, although they should be unknown to one another; they were to be fully briefed, and drops for exchange of information and orders carefully set up: only in emergencies should face-to-face meetings be necessary. Second (and in real life probably more important), there were 'Cursary Spies', bringing current intelligence. Transients 'of meanest rank, and quallity' were best fitted to act as these mobile messengers and observers: '*Peasants, Pedlers, Sellers* of *Strong-waters*, or *Tobacco*, and the like'. The civil war's women spies seem largely to have fallen into this humble category. Lastly, there were 'Doubles', who after their trustworthiness had been fully established, might be allowed to feed true information to the enemy in order to '*insinuate* . . . themselves into the private service of . . . Prime Officers'.[27] Elton's analysis of spying was not novel; it merely provided an unusually lucid account of traditional wisdom, applied to English conditions. As it makes clear, many of the practices of espionage are timeless, from autonomous cells and management by spy-handlers to moles. Other aspects of the civil war experience, however, such as the assumption of a large, homogeneous pool of side-changing soldiers to provide cover, were peculiar to Elton's circumstances. The nature of the war provided fertile ground both for the spy's deceptions and for pervasive suspicions about his undetected presence.

[25] BL Add. MS 11,331, fo. 18ᵛ; *Military Orders . . . Established by his Maiesty* (1643), [11], nos. 76, 78.

[26] Bodl. Tanner MS 62/1B, fo. 218. See Ludlow, *Memoirs*, 1. 66, for a scout's 'turning' of a friendly enemy soldier to transmit information that he could not deliver himself.

[27] Elton, *Compleat Body of the Art Military*, 186; for pre-war views, see e.g. Monro, *Expedition*, 2. 201–4, on intelligence, reconnaissance, and prisoners as sources of information; [Cruso], *Militarie Instructions for the Cavallerie*, 57–8.

The 'ordering [of] . . . Scouts and spies' to acquire reliable intelligence remained a major duty of commanders, but if guides and scouts had sensitive, risky jobs, a spy's danger, if caught, was even greater.[28] His fate, once guilt was established—usually by court martial—was routine. As Richard Symonds noted laconically on Sunday, 30 June 1644, 'Nothing of any moment done all this day. A spy hanged.'[29] The punishment of soldiers who proved double agents or who were suborned into giving intelligence to the enemy was a simple matter of military law. Nevertheless the cases of many spies were less clear-cut. They might claim to be messengers protected by passes, or officers on parole, or innocent civilians. If their claims had any technical defects, these protections were worth little, as the unfortunate Richard Smith discovered when he was captured by the parliamentarians four miles from Arundel Castle. He claimed that he was a messenger from the castle, sent to seek aid from Sir Ralph Hopton, but his inability to corroborate his story—he said he had lost the letter—was taken as proof of guilt: 'So that it appearing that he had been an arch Spie in our Army, and was now going to betray it into the hands of the Enemy, he was condemned to be hanged upon the Bridge in the view of the Castle'.[30] Justice was sometimes tempered by discretionary mercy, but even then the message as to what a spy could expect remained clear. In 1648 John Goforth escaped hanging, but only after the terror of reprieve as he stood on the ladder with the rope around his neck.[31] A parliamentary ordinance of August 1644 prohibited unauthorized civilian as well as military communication with the enemy, but civilians suspected of spying were already at risk. A Mistress Spurwill, for example, had been seized as a traitor at Plymouth and confined to the castle for 'correspondency' with the royalists. It is not clear whether she escaped a traitor's fate, but the puritan John Syms looked forward with pleasure to the heavy 'shame & doom' he foresaw for her partner in crime, 'the other virago'.[32]

When siege lines were porous, when soldiers lived and fought among civilians, when men, women and goods still travelled the roads, and when the party affiliation of fellow countrymen was not apparent unless they chose overtly to signal it, the mark of Cain was invisible and the kind of quarantine of information that parliament's ordinance hoped to impose was impossible. The suspicions

[28] Hutchinson, *Memoirs*, 68.   [29] Symonds, *Diary*, 24.

[30] [Daniel Border], *A Wicked Plot against the Person of Sir William Waller* (1644), A3. For a messenger taken for a spy in the nervous summer of 1648, see Essex Record Office D/DQ s18, fo. 39ᵛ. A case in which a countryman recruited as a guide was given a soldier's red coat may indicate an attempt to give him protection as a military agent. [Wharton], 'Letters from a Subaltern Officer', *Archaeologia*, 35 (1853), 2. 322.

[31] PRO ASSI 44/3; and see Rushworth, 5. 749–51 (misnumbered for 750): in Apr. 1644 one spy was hanged in the Palace Yard at Westminster, 'he having been once before Pardon'd by the General', but another was 'brought to the Gibbet, but being his first Attempt in that kind, Reprieved'.

[32] Firth and Rait, *Acts and Ordinances*, 1. 487–8; BL Add. MS 35,297, fos. 26–27ᵛ; and see the case of Sybell Meese, committed to the Marshallsea of Dartmouth for giving information to the king's enemies, HMC, *Fifteenth Report, Appendix 7*, 'Manuscripts of the Duke of Somerset' (1898), 80.

nurtured by the identity problems of civil war meant that soldiers and civilians were constantly alert for betrayal or transmission of dangerous intelligence, while employers were quick to suspect their own agents of duplicity. Hence the doubts implicit in Sir Arthur Aston's letter from Reading shortly before its fall in 1643: 'I think some evil fate hangs over our designs, for no sooner is a business spoke of but either by information, or inspiration, the enemy hath notice thereof.'[33] That such suspicions were not unreasonable is suggested by the parliamentarian spy who, signing himself only 'Your very humble & careful servant', wrote somewhat uncarefully from Oxford, 'I am now lodged at the Maidenhead over against Lincoln College'; he hoped shortly to move to Christ Church, to 'the court itself'. He was, he reported with satisfaction, 'taken for a high cavalier', and he confidently expected 'opportunity for effectual service in due time'.[34] Yet if infiltration was easy, accusers were quick to act, however slight the evidence. In one case a captain and a soldier of Waller's army were court-martialled for spying on evidence so thin that the court peremptorily dismissed the charges and ordered restitution of their confiscated property. Once aroused, however, suspicion died hard. Years later the story was still being repeated that the royalist Colonel Fielding, although ultimately pardoned for his surrender of Reading, had been seen going surreptitiously into Essex's tent and that nothing was more certain than that the garrison had been betrayed.[35] As we shall see in the account of the siege of Boarstall, in this internecine war the claims of old friendship conflicted with caution lest one be thought a traitor, and a careful man might ask to have his most innocuous letters burnt. Communication and surrender were always likely to arouse suspicion of treachery, of being the action of a long-planted mole or a new renegade.

Yet once an intelligence source had been placed or found it was likely that he or she would have access to useful information and that its dispatch would not be effectively monitored. When an ingenious and determined man devoted his full energy to spying, it was even more difficult to withhold intelligence. Colonel Joseph Bampfield, who spied for Cromwell as well as the king, was one of the war's more dashing spies, at least by his own account. He 'wanted neither means, nor assiduitie', he said, in carrying out his missions for the king, whether gathering intelligence of parliamentary politics, suborning presbyterians, or rescuing the duke of York, by methods that included infiltration, family influence, disguise, and manipulation of gentlemanly and soldierly obligations. On one occasion, after he had been exchanged from a previous imprisonment, he was captured for a second time when he was already acting as the king's agent carrying 'papers of importance and cyfers in [his] clothes and sadle'. He secured his release by

---

[33] William Salt Library, Salt MSS 477, 1 March [1643]. The speed with which news of Aston's injury in Apr. was later disseminated gives some support to his suspicions. Ibid. 564 (20 Apr. [1643]).

[34] Bodl. MS Carte 103, fo. 138.

[35] Adair, 'Court Martial Papers', *JSAHR.* 44 (1966), 219; BL Add. MS 11,810, fo. 16.

some speedy sleight of hand that persuaded his captors to accept an outdated pass and parole that Essex had previously issued. An ingenious agent could exploit the codes of soldierly honour and reciprocal observance of obligations and conventions, but such slippery practices were seen as endangering a mutually beneficial system.[36]

The number of 'professional' spies like Bampfield was probably fairly small, although the more successful they were the less likely we are to know of them unless they took to print. In general, spying reflected inevitable looseness of security when civilians mingled constantly with soldiers, so that a parliamentarian captain could observe of the Scottish invasion of 1648, 'We had spies amongst their army daily, that brought us true intelligence of their numbers, as near as could be computed, and their postures and demeanours.'[37] Elton's 'Cursary Spies', moving round the country and between armies, were among the most difficult to monitor. Not surprisingly, few names have come down to us. Many, it seems, were women, who often passed with some degree of freedom even through siege lines. Parliament Joan had a long and varied career and Bess, a maidservant, carried many letters from one of the spying 'viragos' of Plymouth. Others remained more anonymous. 'I pray you send the woman that lodges in Capt. Booth's quarter [to] Worcester to gain intelligence', wrote Lieutenant-Colonel Jones to Brereton in November 1645. The terms of the request suggest that she was not a novice, an impression reinforced by her capable report on her return two weeks later. In Worcester and Bridgenorth she had been cross-examined by senior officers, Prince Maurice among them, and successfully fended off their questions. She relayed purported royalist plans to relieve Chester but noted that she saw no signs of troop movements, while her report on the debriefing of a prisoner newly released by the parliamentarians enabled Brereton to discover the nature of the intelligence the royalists were receiving.[38] Other women may have been less expert but were similarly useful, in part because their movements were so routine that they became invisible unless special vigilance called them to attention. So at Plymouth, women revealed details of a planned attack. At Chester, Thomas Welchman's wife was turned out of town and promptly became a source of intelligence to the parliamentary enemy. At Chester, too, women brought in the news of parliamentarian mining of St Werburgh's (although subsequent royalist countermining was in turn promptly reported to Brereton by one of his own spies). Meanwhile the mayor's maid was able to pass through the lines, gathering information for the royalists as she went.[39]

---

[36] *Colonel Joseph Bamfeild's Apologie*, 10, 12; *DNB*, 'Joseph Bampfield'.

[37] Hodgson, 'Memoirs', in Slingsby, *Original Memoirs*, 113–14.

[38] BL Add. MS 11,333, fos. 12ᵛ–13; see also Add. MSS 11,332, fo. 105ᵛ and 35,297, fos. 27–27ᵛ.

[39] BL Add. MSS 11,331, fo. 146; 11,332, fos. 49, 75ᵛ; 35,297, fo. 38ᵛ. See also Hutchinson, *Memoirs*, 93–4; William Salt Library, Salt MS 544.

Guides, scouts, and spies were specifically employed to secure intelligence. Other important sources of information were more accidental; they included prisoners, escapers, renegades, and deserters. Waller lumped together 'prisoners, and spies' among the sources on which he based a decision in 1644.[40] In all cases credibility was a problem, as Elton had pointed out. If you knew you had planted renegades in the enemy's ranks, how could you be sure of the sincerity of the deserter who 'came in' to you? Would your prisoner tell the truth? Could you be certain that a returning prisoner had not been turned in his absence? One solution lay in careful, extensive cross-examination; another was to refuse to accept persons of suspect status.

In spite of such doubts, it was conventional wisdom that prisoners could supply valuable information. A pre-war manual, noting that spies were not always available, gave instructions on how to send out parties to take prisoners, 'from whom there may be drawn a relation of the estate of the adverse part, and this exploit is called taking of intelligence' or, by the French, 'prendre langue'.[41] There is little evidence of prisoner-raids in the civil war, but ample evidence of extracting information from those prisoners who came to hand. Examinations were conducted up to the highest levels; on occasion the king himself intervened in questioning. The resulting information might be significant enough to lead to serious action, as in Rupert's decision to attack Newark, or it might be of trifling local value.[42] Returned prisoners were also carefully debriefed, as in the case of the released prisoner whose report to Prince Maurice was, as we have seen, in turn reported back to Brereton by his female spy.[43]

The case of Lieutenant Philemon Mainwaring, a prisoner of the royalists in Chester, shows how useful an observant and ingenious prisoner could be. Mainwaring sent out his letters of information and advice in December 1645 when Brereton's noose was tight around the city. He had earlier been allowed out on parole in an unsuccessful attempt to seek an exchange and had then returned to Chester according to his word as 'gentleman and soldier', but this did not prevent purveyance of clandestine intelligence by routes presumably arranged during parole. It is clear that there was little difficulty in getting his reports out of the city. Indeed, a disillusioned royalist, himself a prisoner in Brereton' quarters, wrote bitterly of the plentiful, certain intelligence received from Chester.[44] As a prisoner in the castle, Mainwaring's sources were ample, for imprisonment rarely entailed isolation. Friends and informants reported to him from market square and council hall, so that news of citizen morale, military expectations, and political divisions mingled with his first-hand report of an alarum that set

   [40] *CSPDom. 1644,* 301.   [41] [Cruso], *Cavallrie,* 57–8.
   [42] BL Add. MSS 11,331, fos. 59–59ᵛ; 11,810, fo. 23; Bodl. MS Tanner 303, fo. 121; Sprigge, *Anglia Rediviva,* 28; Thomas Bailey, *Annals of Nottinghamshire. History of the County of Nottingham including the Borough,* 4 vols. ([1853]), 2. 719.
   [43] BL Add. MS 11,333, fo. 13; William Salt Library, Salt MS 482.
   [44] BL Add. MS 11,333, fos. 4, 80–80ᵛ, 89ᵛ.

the city by its ears: 'I could not sleep in my bed for their crying, Arms, Arms, up and down the streets.'[45] Nor was he the only prisoner-informant in Chester. A letter from the Marshallsea on the state of the city was addressed to friends but included recommendations for transmission to Brereton.[46] Practical everyday needs such as food, laundry, and medical care meant that armies could neither throw a *cordon sanitaire* around their own activities nor quarantine prisoners from civilians. Royalist prisoners at Yarmouth could spread subversion as well as gather information as they talked to their friends in the town.[47]

Prisoners remained tricky properties. While imprisoned they were often in a position to gather useful news and to spread misinformation or disloyalty (like the parliamentarian colonel who tried to suborn his royalist captors to 'come in' to parliament). When they returned to their own armies, however, they might find themselves distrusted, and some commanders saw them as potential Trojan horses.[48] Lord Byron, for example, flatly refused to take back prisoners who had taken the Covenant while held by parliament, even when they had done so under duress, while Colonel Butler faced trial in London for his suspect conduct after his return from imprisonment just before the collapse at Lostwithiel.[49] Renegades, deserters, and escapers presented similar problems. Their information might be valuable, like that of the foot soldiers who 'came over' to the royalists with news of the parliamentarian cavalry's plan to break out at Lostwithiel.[50] But while such information could not be ignored, it demanded scepticism. Careful cross-examination and, where possible, confirmation from other sources could not always prevent successful deception or simple error.[51]

All intelligence, it is clear, was not equal, and it was not accepted uncritically.[52] Even intelligence provided in good faith could be faulty or misleading. In 1645, faced with conflicting reports of the movement of enemy forces, a royalist was driven to lament 'the king's ill intelligence'.[53] And even a report 'from a very good hand', a trustworthy supplier of 'certain intelligence', was better if supported

---

[45] Ibid., fos. 80–80ᵛ.   [46] BL Add. MS 11,332, fos. 75–75ᵛ.

[47] Bodl. Tanner MS 62/1B, fo. 213, and see fo. 220 for a similar complaint about prisoners at Cambridge.

[48] *The Bloody Treatie: or, Proceedings between the King and Prince Rupert* (1645), 8.

[49] Bodl. Tanner MS 62/1B, fo. 213; BL Add. MSS 11,332, fo. 75; 11,333, fo. 4; *The Kingdomes Weekly Intelligencer*, 74 (24 Sept.–1 Oct. 1644); *The London Post*, 7 (1 Oct. 1644); Rushworth, 5. 710–11. Another colonel, whose regiment fled at Lostwithiel, was suspected of pretending to be taken prisoner although in fact he 'went willingly to the King's Forces'. He too faced trial when he returned to London. Ibid.

[50] Walker, *Historical Discourses*, 70; and see Bailey, *Nottinghamshire*, 2. 719.

[51] For information from 'escapers' and turncoats, see BL Add. MSS 11,331, fo. 157; 11,333, fos. 27, 35ᵛ, 64. For reasons for scepticism about their intelligence, see Hodgson, 'Memoirs', in Slingsby, *Original Memoirs*, 150, on the Scottish campaign in 1650: 'We had spies sent out amongst them . . . pretending to run away from us, and they were coming in continually with intelligence.'

[52] See Mrs Hutchinson on the superiority of her husband's intelligence network to Sir John Gell's: the 'chiefe commanders', she implies, weighed reports from both and found Gell's wanting. Hutchinson, *Memoirs*, 68.

[53] Symonds, *Diary*, 244.

by confirmatory evidence. Interpretation was difficult, and commanders had ultimately to back their own judgement, as when Colonel Gerard was told in April 1644 that the enemy was within five miles of Hereford but plausibly concluded that their true objective was the relief of Brampton Bryan. Even information from an apparently impeccable source, such as the letter taken from the pocket of a captured officer of the king's own troop, and 'so be-bloodied over' that the original was 'not fit' to be sent to London, still left uncertainty as to the 'design' and how best to counter it.[54] The importance of confirmation and assessment was characteristically reflected in the royalist attitude to the deserters' information at Lostwithiel: 'This Intelligence was very particular, and being confirmed from other Parts, it was believed.'[55] On the other hand, a boy's news of the landing of Irish troops for the relief of Chester late in 1645 was not supported by other reports, and one of the besieged tartly observed, 'I think the boy babbles.'[56] Even confirmation could not always be trusted. Rupert's precipitate action at Naseby was attributed to the fact that the officer sent to ascertain the truth of intelligence about the disposition of parliamentary forces 'returned with a Lye in his Mouth'. The problems arising from such uncertainties were revealed at a council of war held by Fairfax in 1645. A letter of intelligence from the prince of Wales's army urged speedy advance, but the officers 'had no confidence in him that wrote that letter'; Fairfax overrode their doubts, however, with assurance 'that all was true'.[57] Ultimately much depended on a commander's hunch or judgement.

Fears of subversion, impersonations, false pretences, and the easy spread of rumour all led to wariness about the information that was so assiduously gathered, a wariness increased by persistent, often ingenious, attempts to spread false or discouraging news.[58] Furthermore, the need to keep a watch on the machinations of one's own side did not foster a spirit of trust. Royalist quarrels showed this in its bitterest form. In the course of a feud between Colonel Leveson and Colonel Bagot, fellow royalists, only intelligence received enabled Leveson to move his men out of the way of an attack by Bagot's. And Lord Capel, his friends believed, was intentionally given false information by rivals and only alerted to their duplicity by news from captured scouts. Meanwhile parliamentary commanders in the provinces anxiously maintained links with correspondents in London lest they fall by the wayside of political manœuvre.[59] Colonel Goodwin's warning in 1643 that letters to the general

---

[54] William Salt Library, Salt MSS 477 (23 June 1643); 518 (12 Apr. 1644); 550/1, 550/14; BL Add. MS 11,331, fos. 139ᵛ–140.

[55] Walker, *Historical Discourses*, 70.

[56] BL Add. MS 11,332, fo. 80, and see Dore (ed.), *Letter Books*, 2. 81, 83; Bailey, *Nottinghamshire*, 2. 709, 719; *Narration of the Siege and taking . . . of Leicester*, 3; BL Add. MS 11,332, fo. 80.

[57] Walker, *Historical Discourses*, 130; Wogan, 'Proceedings of the New-moulded army', in Carte, *Letters*, 1. 139.

[58] BL Add. MSS 11,332, fo. 85ᵛ; 11,333, fo. 24; Walker, *Historical Discourses*, 62.

[59] William Salt Library, Salt MS 546 (reprinted in 'Some letters of the civil war', *Historical Collections. Staffs.* [1941], 143); HMC, *12th Report. App. Pt. IX. Manuscripts of the Duke of Beaufort*

'sure are intercepted' can be interpreted as applying to action by friend or enemy.[60]

The methods of transmitting intelligence, like those for obtaining it, were largely traditional and common-sensible. There were few of the exotica beloved of intelligence communities. Messages on occasion were passed by signs—a fire, or blowing one's nose—and at Colchester, in a propaganda exercise designed to hasten surrender, parliamentarians used kites and arrows to spread news that would undermine morale and 'undeceive' the besieged. Nevertheless the enthusiastic pre-war expert who recommended a kind of long-distance planchette table, or an embryo morse code transmitted by torches, or carrier pigeons, found few followers. If his observation that 'the secret conveying of Letters is of great consequence in time of Warre' was generally accepted, his unbreakable codes were not.[61] Instead codes were usually simple numerical or substitution ciphers, many of which could have been read with relative ease, although a few defeated codebreakers; Essex sent up to London a 'letter we cannot decipher'. Often, however, the purpose seems to have been delay, should a message be intercepted, rather than real concealment, particularly as many were written part en clair and part in code.[62] Alphabetic codes that interchanged letters and numbers were flexible enough for any messages, if laborious, but random substitutions of groups of numbers, letters, or words were restricted in the information they could convey to what their creators had foreseen a need for. In Sir John Gell's case this enabled him to refer to the Scots (201) and martial law (218), to pray to God (260), and to characterize men as religious or debauched (240, 265).[63] Encoding took time that was often not available in emergencies. 'I have not time to write in ciphers. If I had, I should say more', wrote one officer to Rupert in 1645.[64] Codes were also vulnerable not only to being broken but to loss of the key or its acquisition by the enemy. In his imprisonment in 1647 Sir Lewis Dyve was unwilling to 'let the cipher goe out of [his] hand' without the king's express order, refusing it (mistakenly, it proved) to a 'messenger . . . being

(1891), 'Beaufort MSS', 40; BL Egerton MS 787, fo. 74; and see Brereton's letter to John Glyn at Westminster defending himself and his officers against the false 'aspersions' of an informer. BL Add. MS 11,331, fos. 19ᵛ–20ᵛ.

60 Bodl. MS Carte 103, fo. 91.

61 Ward, *Anima'dversions of Warre*, 1. 143–6; for assorted signals see BL Add. MS 11,331, fo. 59; Ludlow, *Memoirs*, 1. 71; *Diary of the Siege of Colchester*, 25 July 1648; HMC, *Twelfth Report. App. Pt.9*, 'Beaufort MSS', 30.

62 Bodl. MS Nalson, 3, fo. 244; and see William Salt Library, Salt MS 517, for a letter to Rupert in June 1645 concerning troop strengths and movements; the interpretations of the coded passages have been written above in a different hand. For the relative simplicity of interpretation, note that 15, 23, 23, 28; 28, 30, 23; 13, 26, 10, 16, 23, 23, 22, equals *foot*; *two*; *dragoon*; i.e. a = 9 or 10. See also BL Add. MS 11,331, fos. 80ᵛ; and Dore (ed.), *Letter Books*, app. V, 1. 530–3, for discussion of Brereton's ciphers and the limited secrecy they provided.

63 Derbys. RO, Gell MSS, D258, 44/39; and see 42/29 (d) for a more subtle and comprehensive code.

64 Eliot Warburton, *Memoirs of Prince Rupert, and the Cavaliers*, 3 vols. (1849), 3. 60.

a young man and a stranger to me'.[65] It seems remarkable that Dyve retained the cipher in captivity; possibly his captors were as able as he to read his ciphered correspondence with the king.

More effort went into securing unintercepted dispatch and delivery of letters than into obfuscation of their content.[66] Army messengers appear to have been significantly well paid; their risks and the opportunities for subornation made it only prudent. A humble but trusty civilian appointed to carry messages between Fairfax and the Scots, who 'faithfully discharged' the 'dangerous designs' entrusted to him, earned a long-term reward out of sequestered Catholic lands.[67] Messengers travelled alone, often through enemy territory, and as we have seen they were open to suspicion of spying. Brereton's 'foot post', taking a message to one of his officers, shared the fate of Richard Smith and was hanged in Chester.[68] Messengers were employed for routine transmission of information, such as that sent to and from Luke, and that between officers, such as the mutually beneficial exchanges agreed on between Brereton and Vermuyden in 1645 that by-passed any central clearing-house. In urgent times the pace of messages became hectic and demands on the numbers and courage of messengers heavy. A late royalist push to relieve Beeston castle in 1645 produced a rush of messages—'this night', '5 at night', '8 at night', 'at night'—of warning, organization, and advice dispatched between parliamentarian officers. In 1643 four messengers in two days turned back because of the 'danger of the way' from Warwick to Lichfield.[69] Besides these official messengers there was a large, amorphous army of unofficial carriers of information—officials, sailors, officers, civilian men and women—travelling English roads with letters on every subject from the course of battle and deficiencies of troops to a grandchild's legacy and care of cattle. There were also purely clandestine carriers, often unnamed for security's sake, like the 'convenient and trusty messenger' who transmitted Mainwaring's spy

[65] 'The Tower of London letter-book of Sir Lewis Dyve, 1646–47', ed. H. G. Tibbutt, *Publications of the Bedfordshire Historical Record Society*, 38 (1958), 75–6. In Jan. 1649 William Legge still had Rupert's cipher but wrote to him en clair, 'doubting you have lost the copy'. William Salt Library, Salt MS 544.

[66] Ingenuity intended to make messages secure could be self-defeating. In 1644 two messengers sent out by the royalist governor of besieged Banbury castle were captured. The governor had 'writ a letter in a shred of paper close written and cut in the middest, that if but one of them had beene taken we had not known what to have made of it'—but the message would have been equally opaque to Prince Rupert had only one messenger got through. C. D. and W. C. D. Whetham, *A History of the Life of Colonel Nathaniel Whetham: A Forgotten Soldier of the Civil Wars* (1907), 80.

[67] Christopher O'Riordan, 'Thomas Ellison, the Hixson Estate and the Civil War', *Durham County Local History Society Bulletin*, 39 (1987), 4–5. See also *CSPDom. 1660–1661*, 153.

[68] BL Add. MSS 11,331, fo. 146. In Manchester's army in 1644, a messenger was paid £2 a week; in a foot regiment, a lieutenant's pay was £2. 2s. 0d., an ensign's £1. 1s. 0d., a common soldier's under 5s. PRO SP 28/26, fos. 22, 319, 455, 486; 28/25, fos. 140, 228, 230. For the peril incurred by messengers, see ERO D/DQ s18, fo. 39ᵛ; *CSPDom. 1660–1661*, 153.

[69] BL Add. MSS 11,331, fos. 154ᵛ, 164ᵛ–165; 11,332, fos. 101ᵛ–102ᵛ; Derbys. RO, Gell MSS D258, 31/30 (j).

reports out of Chester.[70] Finally, even the official envoys between opponents, the drums and trumpets who carried messages of threat or negotiation and were protected by the laws of war, had an unofficial intelligence function, for they were expected to be observant as well as discreet and to pick up what information they could while giving nothing away.[71] Both parties tried to prevent transmission of any unauthorized communication from their own territory, as in parliament's ordinance of August 1644. The victims of severity could be pathetic, like the old yeoman Francis Pit, a 'great Professor' of religion, who was prevailed on by his Catholic landlord to carry a letter offering a bribe to the governor of a parliamentary garrison. Beguiled by the governor into continuing negotiations, Pit was trapped and confessed. Mitigating circumstances were no help, and he was executed at Smithfield.[72]

Attention to the interception of intelligence was not confined to purely military information or authorized messengers. In the 1640s England became to a remarkable degree a country under surveillance. Informers passed on to the authorities the rash and often drunken remarks of the unlettered, and the communications of the lettered were vulnerable to unfriendly seizure. The evidence for parliamentary interceptions is more plentiful than that for their opponents, but the royalists too provided for 'secret service', and it seems safe to assume that they too read suspect correspondence.[73] It was widely recognized that sending letters expressing frank opinions on public issues or persons, or passing on news beyond unexceptionable domestic matters or information that was clearly in the public domain, entailed risk. Although it is obvious from the material cited in this book that the English did not become a close-mouthed race and that the dangerous 'loose talk' of a later war was already familiar, it is also obvious that there was much self-censorship that reflected the state's success in interdicting unfettered communication and in gathering intelligence from incautious letters. In January 1643 Elizabeth of Bohemia wrote to Sir Thomas Roe in Essex, 'When you think how subjects' letters are to be opened you will not wonder you hear no oftener from me.' Even the use of a cipher would not help, for the sight of an enciphered letter could arouse suspicion that it said 'something against the parliament'.[74] One correspondent passed on general news from London but added, 'When I remember my letters never

---

[70] BL Add. MS 11,333, fos. 80–80ᵛ. Although Mainwaring was confident of the bearer's trustworthiness, he still urged Brereton to 'encourage' him—presumably financially.

[71] Elton, *Compleat Body of the Art Military*, 177; Thomas Venn, *Military Observations or Tacticks put into Practice for the Exercise of Horse and Foot, Military & Maritime Discipline in Three Books; Book I* (1672), 5. Venn's work, although finished in the 1660s, drew on material from 1641–2 as well as from Sir Francis Vere's much earlier experience. Cf. BL Add. MS 11,332, fo. 75ᵛ, for the assumption that a drummer would expand verbally on the written report he carried; and see Wharton, 'Letters from a Subaltern Officer', 2. 330, for Rupert's trumpeter 'led blindfold' through Worcester to Essex's presence.

[72] Rushworth, 5. 777–8, 781–2; Firth and Rait, *Acts and Ordinances*, 1. 487, and see 1. 327–8.

[73] *CSPDom. 1641–43*, 504.   [74] Ibid. 436.

come to you, I can go no further.' Another simply declared, 'News I dare not write.'[75]

Some of these interceptions were carefully organized. In May 1643 parliament ordered that all prisoners in the Tower of London were to be searched for letters and papers, which were then 'to be perused by such as shall be thereunto authorised'; such authorized analysts included men like Sir Samuel Luke, whose intelligence network is well-known, and the parliamentarian scoutmasters Leonard Watson and Thomas Scott. In less formal quests for intelligence prisoners' pockets were routinely searched for letters, as were the bodies of the dead. A roster of intercepted letters coming out of Chester in 1645 indicates how valuable an active programme could be.[76] Many interceptions however were more opportunist than systematic. Travellers knew that merely to be found carrying letters could be grounds for suspicion so they sought passes that would enable them 'to pass quietly' on their journeys; unfortunately these did not reliably ensure that they would not be stopped by enthusiastic soldiers, who were often energized as much by opportunities to pilfer as by zeal to intercept suspect messages.[77]

Clearly many messages and letters never reached their intended recipients. Others were sent on after reading, in a kind of intelligence double play leaving the recipient in ignorance of the information now held by the enemy. In the best tradition of spy literature, one messenger was made drunk and the letter he carried was opened, copied, resealed, and replaced in his pocket.[78] Yet for all the energy and success of the interceptors, the mass of surviving correspondence from the 1640s makes it clear that caution and inhibition did not silence English letter writers. It is also clear that both soldiers and civilians recognized that letters put them at risk and that, while a rich source of intelligence, they could also be a danger to those who wrote them and those who carried them.

Clandestine and military sources were not the only ones enabling armies to move and plan or inducing betrayals. The steady output of printed newsletter and pamphlet accounts of military and political affairs, published within days of the events they described, were read by soldiers and civilians alike, and were supplemented by private letters in which personal and public affairs mingled. Sir Samuel Luke, notwithstanding his large and sensitive information network, acknowledged their value even as he complained to his London agent and friend Samuel Moore, '3 lines of your wise news would have been 100 times more acceptable than your 3 pennyworth of diurnals.' A week later, however, he was transmitting news from his scouts together with 'the Aulicus', with a comment, 'I send you nothing but what I believe to be true'. Bad news, however, as Luke

---

[75] *CSPDom. 1641–43*, 507; BL Add. MS 29974.2, fo. 388.
[76] *CSPDom. 1641–43*, 463; BL Add. MS 11,331, fo. 18ᵛ; BL Add. MS 11,332, fos. 80–5, 96–7ᵛ; William Salt Library, Salt MS 550/14.
[77] Derbys. RO, Gell MS D 258, 31/10 (qa); BL Add. MS 11,331, fo. 22.
[78] *CSPDom. 1641–1643*, 415, 473.

recognized, was less likely to appear in London newsletters than good, and here private letters came into their own.[79] The correspondence between Luke and Moore covered political moves in London, the armies' reconstitution into the New Model, victories and defeats, and orders for wheelbarrows, crowbars, drums, and colours. A weekly letter did not satisfy Luke, whose complaints revealed the level of information he expected. 'Forgetful Mr. Moore,' he wrote, 'I have received your letter of 2 sides of paper written, wherein you answered 5 of mine at once, but not satisfied me in any one particular.'[80]

Luke's network was exceptional in scale but not in nature. Sir George Gresley's 'intercourse of intelligence' provided Sir William Brereton with detailed news from this Derbyshire landowner. Colonel Edward Seymour's friends sent letters into Dartmouth filled with jokes, gossip, news of troop movements, and predictions of military actions.[81] Arthur Trevor wrote his own news to Rupert's headquarters but added, 'The printed papers will tell you how things stand.'[82] Commanders and officers on both sides clearly had varied and extensive knowledge on which to base their actions. Their troops, too, had access to informative and—allowing for bias—surprisingly accurate newsletters to supplement word-of-mouth fact and rumour. Rumour itself had, as usual, a life of its own, which was particularly robust on the most inflammatory topics such as the Irish. It was also consciously manipulated, as in the stories of imminent relief that kept Chester soldiers from mutiny in December 1645.[83]

Old ways of disseminating information survived and contributed to knowledge of the war. They spread into the far corners of the country and made it difficult for Englishmen to escape a sense of involvement, however unwilling, in a divisive and destructive process. Messengers talked; taciturn correspondents counted on the bearer to recount what they were afraid to write; carriers, traditionally bearers of news, still travelled the country.[84] Conversations between opposing troops spread news. Distribution of the voluminous pamphlet and newsletter output crossed party lines. Traditional means, often telegraphic and symbolic, transmitted information to civilians and soldiers. Proclamations and ordinances were read aloud, bells warned, drums announced the coming of further news, flags—red for defiance, white for truce—sent wordless messages, and 'cries', whether of 'Arms, Arms' or for a stray horse, alerted local populaces. In Chester the coming of war was announced when 'they drummed in behalf of the parliament'. In Hereford, the 'common bell' called citizens to work on the defences; its ringing

---

[79] BL Egerton MS 787, fos. 16, 27ᵛ, 36ᵛ, and see *The Letter Books 1644–45 of Sir Samuel Luke, Parliamentary Governor of Newport Pagnell*, ed. H. G. Tibbutt, Publications of the Bedfordshire Historical Record Society, 62 (1963), *passim*.

[80] BL Egerton MS 787, fos. 3, 36ᵛ, 52–3.

[81] BL Add. MS 11,332, fo. 112; Devonshire RO, Seymour MSS 1392 M/L 1644/9, 24, 47.

[82] William Salt Library, Salt MS 600.

[83] BL Add. MS 11,333, fos. 47 (the Irish are landed 'for certain'), 80ᵛ.

[84] BL Add. MS 29974.2, fo. 388; Taylor, *Carriers Cosmographie*, *passim*.

was 'the strictest summons that [could] be given to the citizens, . . . upon which they [were] bound by oath to appear'. Significantly perhaps for the royalist cause, it was ineffectual in April 1643 and 'very few came'. Nonetheless the message was plain even if ignored. We should not forget that simple and traditional means of communication persisted even if they seldom entered the records.[85]

Armies gathered information as a basis for military action and sought to disseminate those parts of it that served their purpose. Civilians sought it to understand what was going on in the nation, to know what had happened to friends and kin, and to prepare for the next blow. The variety of means is less important than their demonstration of the ways in which professional and lay contributions to intelligence were inextricably entangled; they were yet another aspect of the interpenetration of military and civil society. Once again the unprofessional civilian and the military expert confronted the uncertainty of war, despite the best efforts to turn armies into bodies so well primed with knowledge that they could predictably take successful action. Even when intelligence did not fail the soldier's venture often did, and he was once again forced to contemplate the puzzling ways of providence, God's foresight, or luck.

FROM KNOWLEDGE TO ACTION

Intelligence, once obtained, had to be translated into purposive military action. Decisions must be reached, understandable orders given and preparations made, but the civil war did not differ from other wars in the probability that the best laid plans would go agley. Generals and their councils of war made the best plans they could on the basis of information received, and as needs changed they dispatched aides de camp with revised orders. For the troops on the ground the means employed to reduce military chaos and achieve military success remained traditional. In retrospect they may appear picturesque, but their survival in seventeenth-century war reflected their continued usefulness in contemporary conditions. So visible and audible signs—colours and drums and trumpets—continued to direct action, to provide focus and coherence, and to bolster morale. Like their more advanced modern counterparts, they were imperfectly effective.

In action and on the march these traditional methods transmitted orders, provided rallying points, and enabled distinction of friend from foe. The better trained troops were, the fewer the orders required for the performance of fundamental manœuvres, but when special commands were needed the strongest human voice had its limits and the drum, aided by the fife for infantry and the

---

[85] For communication by conversation, signal, and drum, see BL Add. MSS 11,332, fo. 94; 35,297, fo. 4; BL Harl. MS 2155, fo. 108. For the bell's failure to produce action, see Duncumb, *Hereford*, 1. 249–50; for a charge of 6d. 'For crying [a stray] horse', see PRO SP 28/23, fo. 129.

trumpet for cavalry, served as the basic means of communication. Soldiers should be able to respond instantly. The 'posture tune', the 'troop', the 'falling of[f]', played on drums and fifes, had directed the drills of musketeers and pikemen that beguiled pre-war audiences at military displays. In preparation for real action, it was the duty of every soldier to learn 'all the severall beats of the drum', from the call, at which he must repair to the colours, to the tattoo, which gave notice for taking up night stations. Elton listed eight 'beats' in all. The directions for the fifth, the 'Battle' or 'Charge', reveal how—it was hoped—trained men would automatically respond: on hearing it the soldier was 'undauntedly to move forward, boldly steping in good order into the place of his fellow souldier that shall happen to fall down dead before him'. On the march, drummers were spaced through the regiments and organized so that, instead of beating in unison, they spelled each other. 'The English March', which had once accompanied English armies on the continent before falling into disuse, had been revived by Prince Henry, the king's martial elder brother, and now moved armies through the country, as the other 'beats' transmitted commands in action.[86] Drummers and trumpeters were essential to communications, and careful attention was paid to their needs. Drums, trumpets, and colours were part of the army's working equipment, and only secondarily ceremonial and decorative.[87]

Colours were a practical rallying-point for troops in action as well as symbols of honour whose capture was enumerated and flaunted as evidence of the enemy's humiliation.[88] They enabled soldiers to find their own side in confused situations, and to find that part of the army to which they were attached. At least one royalist disaster was attributed to 'want of colours [the soldiers] being thereby made incapable of rallying when they were dispersed'. The enemy, equally dispersed, had been able to rally to its colours but the royalists, in a classic confusion of war, 'mistaking the enemy for [their] own party', were captured.[89] Great attention was paid to the design, colour, and message of banners, as the roll-call of victory in the Naseby parade through London in 1645 indicated, when the trophies extended from the royal standard and the colours

---

[86] Magdelene College, Cambridge, Pepys MS 2874, fos. 591–2; Barriffe, *Mars, His Triumph*, 9–10, 15; Elton, *Compleat Body of the Art Military*, 176–8; G. Derbridge, 'A History of the Drums and Fifes 1650–1700', *JSAHR* 44 (1966), 50–1, and 53 for a suggestion that parliamentary armies banished the fife. For use of the drum to call civilian labourers to work on fortifications and 'to encourage the workers at the Work' during the day, see Bodl. MS Add. D.114, fos. 22, 87.

[87] BL Egerton MS 787, fo. 53, for dispatch of a drum to the painter for decoration with arms: honour, identification, and communication came together; PRO SP28/18, fos. 386–386ᵛ; SP 260, fos. 7–8, for the purchase of sixteen drums from Mr Tench of Hounsditch at 23s. each; SP 28/26, fo. 672, for a new drum at 30s.; Derbys. RO, Gell MSS D258, 31/30 (aa), for expenditure on drums and colours; *Chirk Castle Accounts*, ed. Myddelton, 32, for 1651 repair of drumheads at 2s. per parchment per drum.

[88] Ian Gentles, 'The Iconography of Revolution: England 1642–1649', in Ian Gentles, John Morrill, and Blair Worden (eds.), *Soldiers, Writers and Statesmen of the English Revolution* (Cambridge, 1998), 91–113.

[89] Bodl. MS Clarendon 34, fo. 26ᵛ.

of the king, queen, and Prince Rupert down to those of the cornets of horse. Their designs ranged from Rupert's sky-coloured ensign with a red cross and a cornet's orange damask with uplifting Latin motto to the green flowered damask ensign announcing 'Cuckold we come', directed at the maritally unlucky earl of Essex.[90] Parliamentary banners revealed similar diversity, from the military and secular ('Vincere spero' and 'Sans craindre') and the constitutional ('For king and parliament' and 'Viva el rex y muerra il mal govierno') to the religious, which in turn ranged from the restrained ('Deus Nobiscum' and 'Only in Heaven') to the combative ('Antichrist must downe: if you support him he will fall upon you' and 'Nay but as a captaine of the hoste of the Lord am I now come'). In action the refinements of message and picture, often a detailed representation of a complex idea, must frequently have been no more distinctive than Lord Willoughby of Parham's simple, wordless black and silver brocade, but they contributed to corporate and ideological solidarity.[91] Colours served as symbol, morale-builder, and signal, but the latter capacity could be literally obscured by the fog of war.

Identification of colleagues and enemies also presented problems. Watchwords, as we have seen, were indispensable but fallible guides, subject to appropriation and betrayal.[92] Clothing was equally uncertain. From early in the war regiments wore coats in a colour of their colonel's choice; in October 1643, for example, the earl of Manchester ordered 2,100 'coats of green cloth lined with red'.[93] On the battlefield, however, the resulting rainbow coalitions did not necessarily help to distinguish enemies from friends when regiments on both sides wore green or blue or red. Parliamentarian 'Grey-coats' and Kentish 'Redcoats', Irish 'yellow-coats' and the 'Codlin Colour' of the king's regiment, although helpful, were not an infallible guide to adherence, especially when soldiers on both sides wore the useful, protective leather buff coat. The New Model army brought greater uniformity, for from its inception its men wore red coats with facings of different colours indicating regimental affiliation, but the system was still imperfect and in July 1646 Rainsborough's forces at Pontefract were still only described as 'Most Red coats'. At all times the usefulness of uniforms was diminished by pillage and trade in the clothing of prisoners and the dead, which dispersed ownership among enemies and civilians. It was worthy of remark that, in the procession in London after Naseby, many of the prisoners still had their own clothes and coats.[94] Anecdotes suggest that the absence of visual distinction between enemies was commonplace. So John Gwyn noted without comment that 'a party of the

---

[90] *The Kingdomes Weekly Intelligencer*, 105 (17–24 June 1645), 840–1.

[91] BL Sloane MS 5247, fos. 7, 14, 15, 19, 20ᵛ, 28ᵛ, 37, 64, 71.

[92] '[T]he designe and the word (*now or never*) were betrayed', lamented a royalist of a plan to take Abingdon in 1646. 'Journal of Prince Rupert's Marches'. *EHR* 13 (1898), 740.

[93] HMC, *Seventh Report* (1879), 'Lowndes MSS', 565.

[94] BL Add. MSS 35,297, fos. 38ᵛ, 46ᵛ; 11,810, fos. 22ᵛ, 26; Townshend, *Diary*, 1. 170; *The Kingdomes Weekly Intelligencer*, 105 (17–24 June 1645), 841; Ludlow, *Memoirs*, 1. 72; Firth, *Cromwell's Army*, 231–3. In Sept. 1642 Nehemiah Wharton already spoke generically of 'a soildier's red coate', of 'the blew coats of Colonell Cholmley's regiment', and of 'a soildier's sute for winter'

enemy's horse went amongst us as some of our own', and John Syms related that royalists gained entrance to Wareham simply by telling the sentinel that they were a troop of Fairfax's horse.[95] At Shelford, when Colonel Hutchinson removed his identifiable, musket-proof, 'very good suit of armor' because it was too hot and heavy for action, he was indistinguishable in his buff coat from his royalist opposite number, and nearly paid for this interchangeability with his life.[96] Disguise, when it was attempted, need not be sophisticated. As late as 1648, at the siege of Colchester, a party of royalist soldiers equipped with spades and posing as workmen passed parliamentarian guards without difficulty, 'they conceiving them to be their own men', and despite the fact that they were accompanied by a body of musketeers. Unfortunately their luck ran out at the next guard post.[97] Nor was conduct an infallible identifier. Parliamentarian troops who harrowed, plundered, and terrified near Whitchurch in 1645 'pretend[ed] themselves to be cavaliers'.[98]

Neither language, clothing, nor demeanour was a sure guide to allegiance. Other aids were needed. In some contexts the civilian and peacetime practice of detailed description for identification of malefactors and property could be turned to war use, for example in pursuit of an escaped prisoner: 'He is a slender black haired man in a grayish suit with a little hair on the upper lip, he hath one club foot being born so, and useth to wear boots fast buckled with leathers about his heels instead of spurs.'[99] In action, however, some more immediate means of identification was needed, whether formal devices like scarves and hatbands or makeshift signs such as a bough in the hat or a white handkerchief tied above the elbow. After Essex had designated 'The Gospel' as the identifying 'word' for his men in one operation, he recognized the need for something more: 'And for distinction, I would have you wear a piece of white tape, ribband, or thread, or paper upon your breasts.' When the parliamentary horse escaped from Cornwall in 1644, their many needs included new scarves because of 'great inconvenience we find that upon service we cannot know one another from the enemy'.[100] The extravagant Sir William Myddelton spent £23 on 'ribbands & scarves for his

for himself (its colour was not specified, but it was to be edged with gold and silver lace). Wharton, 'Letters from a Subaltern Officer', 2. 323.

[95] BL Add. MSS 11,810, fo. 22; 35,297, fo. 106; for similar incidents in 1648, see Bodl. MS Clarendon 31, fo. 214ᵛ; 34, fo. 27ᵛ. Fleeing royalists at Marston Moor nearly strayed into the clutches of parliamentarian horse, 'For they only knew them . . . to be the Parliament soldiers by their singing of Psalmes. A blessed badge and cognisance indeed.' Quoted in Firth, *Cromwell's Army*, 330–1.

[96] Hutchinson, *Memoirs*, 163.

[97] *Diary of the Siege of Colchester* (31 July 1648); *Mercurius Elencticus*, 40 (23–9 Aug. 1648), 329.

[98] BL Add. MS 11,331, fo. 34ᵛ.

[99] BL Add. MS 11,331, fo. 43; note also descriptions of horses as means of identifying riders, ibid., fo. 22ᵛ, and note the common formula 'X saw Y on a black horse at Z', *Calendar of the Proceedings of the Committee of Compounding, &c. 1643–1660*, 1 (1889), 260.

[100] Bodl. MS Tanner 61, fo. 149; Bodl. MS Carte 103, fo. 98; Walker, *Historical Discourses*, 92; *The Coppie of a Letter from Sir Thomas Fairfax his Quarters to the Parliament, concerning the great*

regiment'. Scarves and ribbands, however, were an easily appropriated disguise, as royalists demonstrated as they marched from Oxford to relieve Basing House, 'passing through the Country for Parliament Men, with *Orange* Tawny Scarfs and Ribbands in [their] Hats'.[101] Fairfax, in the midst of enemies at Marston Moor, escaped by pulling the signal out of his hat and passing through them as one of their own commanders.[102]

Unfortunately ingenious methods of communication and distinction were not enough to ensure victory in the face of other uncontrollable factors that distorted the plans of commanders and conduct of troops. The chief of these was weather, usually bad, which affected the movements of armies and their ability to come to battle and, once they were in action, might make intrinsic confusion worse confounded. 'February-fill-dike' could be fairly reliably counted on to inhibit campaigning, but it was less predictable that a November night would be 'so sharpe, the soldjers could not Marche', aborting Rupert's expedition to surprise Abingdon in 1644.[103] A 'dark and tempestuous night' allowed the enemy to slip past royalist guards for a successful raid on Ellesmere.[104] The 'glut of rain' and 'most miserable, tempestuous rainy weather' of the late summer of 1643 contributed to royalist failure to take Gloucester and to the fatigue and debilitation of troops who 'lay pickled . . . all night' in wet clothes. In September 1642 Nehemiah Wharton's regiment, 'wet to the skin' and 'up to the ankles in thick clay', was sustained by a night of psalm-singing, but not all parliamentarian troops were so piously hardy. In the autumn of 1643 Waller wrote to the Speaker of the House of Commons of 'a night so foul that I could not possibly keep my men upon their guard', and added that 'the coldness of the night, with foul weather was a great discouragement to the London Regiments, who were not used to this hardness'. In the summer of 1644 the 'very clothes' of the parliamentary horse were 'worn & rotten upon their backs, with constant service abroad night & day for 6 weeks together in very wet weather'.[105] When 'the weather [was] ill for marching' it not only hindered deployment of troops but sapped their physical strength, increased their disinclination to action and encouraged desertion and mutiny. In the 'extreme and violent, [c]old and wet' November of 1645 Brereton, a sensible commander, observed that his mutinous, unpaid soldiers could not be

---

Battell . . . at Langport ([1645]), i2–3 (*sic*). For a scarf and a hatband as gifts, see Wharton, 'Letters from a Subaltern Officer', 2. 323.

[101] PRO SP 28/18, fo. 386; 28/260, fos. 7–8; Derbys. RO, Gell MSS D258, 31/30 (aa); Walker, *Historical Discourses*, 91.

[102] Fairfax, *Memoirs*, 85–6.

[103] *Swedish Intelligencer*, ii. 104; 'Journal of Prince Rupert's Marches', *EHR* 13 (1898), 738. See also the abrupt revocation of the orders for a march in Dec. 1645 because of a sudden cold change and consequent hardship to the troops. BL Add. MS 11,333, fos. 63ᵛ–64.

[104] HMC, *12th Report. App. Pt.9*, 'Beaufort MSS', 41.

[105] BL Add. MS 11,810, fos. 20–1; Wharton, 'Letters from a Subaltern Officer', 2. 325–6; Bodl. MS Nalson, 3, fo. 159; Bodl. MS Tanner 61, fo. 149; see also Luke, *Letter Books*, 30–1.

expected to endure the 'extremity of hardship [of] this weather unless they be well paid'.[106]

When action was joined, wind and light became important. In an age before smokeless powder (a nineteenth-century invention) each side tried to have the wind with them to gain the advantage of visibility. At Naseby, both sides sought 'to gain the Hill and the wind', although the parliamentarians, magnifying their victory, claimed that when battle began the royalists had 'all the points of the wind for them, and their advantage'.[107] Yet although commanders routinely manœuvred for such advantages, action was at any time noisy, smoky, and confusing: in the words of one captain, 'there was nothing but fire and smoke'. To the smoke of gunpowder was added that of fires, intentional or accidental, although God, riding 'on the wings of the wind', might blow the smoke away from his chosen. God and the weather, indeed, could hardly be separated. Providential explanations abound in accounts of mists that permitted escapes or of clear nights for marching.[108]

Seeing what one was doing was sometimes as much of a problem as knowing where one was going, particularly at night—and night marches and night actions were not the preserve of the 'night owl' general Sir William Waller but were common to all civil war armies. After the second battle of Newbury the royalists were able to march away by moonshine, while a 'very light' night enabled the defenders of Leicester to rake enemy foot with musket and cannon fire as they endeavoured to move a battery up to the town wall. On the other hand, a wet dark night at Plymouth allowed the enemy to build fortifications unobserved, and the setting of the moon enabled a fugitive to slip by enemy guards. A dark misty night let the parliamentary horse pass undetected 'within Pistol Shot' of the royalist guards at Lostwithiel, in spite of the prior intelligence about the planned escape. Only with the coming of daylight were the horse pursued.[109] Battles, too, were at the mercy of light, although most major battles were fought when days were long. The royalists claimed that at Edgehill the tide had turned in their favour, but by then 'it was grown so dark that [their] chief Commanders durst no[t] charge for feare of mistaking friends for foes'. Had there only been enough light, they declared, one more charge would have routed the parliamentary

---

[106] BL Add. MSS 11,332, fo. 77^v; 11,333, fo. 24^v.

[107] *A Relation Of the Victory obtained by Sr. Thomas Fairfax . . . neer Harborough, on Saturday, June 14. 1645* (1645), 2; *The Weekly Account*, XXIII week, 4–11 June 1645, A2^v; [G. Bishop], *A More Particular and Exact Relation of The Victory obtained by the Parliaments Forces under . . . Sir Thomas Fairfax* (1645), A2. Cf. the account of Langport: 'the Enemy had a Hill, and the Winde, we another Hill', *Exact and Perfect Relation of the Proceedings of the Army . . . near Langport*, 5.

[108] Fairfax, *Memoirs*, 99, 116; 'Memoirs of Captain John Hodgson', in Slingsby, *Original Memoirs*, 113; Waller, *Recollections*, 112; see also Bamfeild, *Apologie*, 8, on his successful march to take Arundel, 'being favoured by a great mist, without any discovery'.

[109] BL Add. MSS 11,810, fo. 26; 35,297, fos. 9^v, 22^v; *Narration of the Siege and taking . . . of Leicester*, 5; Walker, *Historical Discourses*, 70–1. For Waller's night marches, see e.g. *Narration of The great Victory . . . Under Sir William Waller, at Alton*, 3–4.

army.[110] In this as in other matters there was little a commander could do to outwit nature.

The range of factors that could disorder plans and enhance confusion was infinite. They could be as simple as unfavourable terrain, like the hedges and enclosures of Gloucestershire that hampered royalist horse in 1643, or as aggravating as the mutual incomprehension of a French artillery expert and his English gun crews.[111] Timing and coordination were problematic when only some officers had watches. The difficulties of getting forces to the rendezvous at the same designated hour for a planned operation continued to bedevil commanders of both sides, and uncertainties about time compounded those caused by dilatoriness or bad weather or other providential interventions. A prudent commander added 'God willing' as he scheduled any conjunction of forces.[112]

Some disorders were merely wartime versions of timeless muddles that endlessly defy explanation, such as messages delayed or never received or wrong roads taken. Royalists fleeing from Torrington early in 1646, for example, escaped when their parliamentary pursuers, 'mistak[ing] one bridge for another', found themselves entangled in the narrow, enclosed lanes of Devonshire.[113] Some fiascos came close to low farce, as in the case of Major Sanders, who keenly sounded the trumpet and roused his men, 'every man to horse and away', then found his own stable door locked and his friend's empty, so that he finally trudged out on foot. Royalist seizure of Pontefract castle in 1648 was preceded by a comedy of mistaken identity, a drunken corporal, a lost ladder, and guards who left their post to fetch ale with which to drink the health of the enemies they mistook for friends.[114] Some contretemps were peculiar to war. Explosions such as that in Torrington church, caused by 'accident...unknown', led to panic flight and chaos. A covey of recruits vanished in terror after the 'fearful crack...and the sad aspect' when a bargeload of men and munitions was blown up; the accidental firing of a guard's bandolier in the nervous period just before dawn produced 'incredible confusion...being so near day'; a carelessly fired musket was enough to betray a planned ambush.[115] Unthinking attachment to routine could be equally dangerous, offering opportunities to enemies with luck and an eye for opportunity. It is perhaps not very surprising that in August 1642,

---

[110] *Relation of the Battaile lately fought between Keynton and Edgehill*, 4.

[111] William Salt Library, Salt MSS 477, 19 [June 1643], 7 Aug. 1643.

[112] Bodl. MS Carte 103, fo. 98; Adair, 'Court Martial Papers', 215–16.

[113] HMC, *12th Report. App. Pt.9*, 'Beaufort MSS', 4; Walker, *Historical Discourses*, 7, for royalist horse who 'took the wrong way in their retreat' from Alresford in 1644. For delayed messages, see William Salt Library, Salt MS 518, 20 Oct. 1644: Rupert's commands came too late for Gerard to send forces to Hereford by the time required.

[114] Derbys. RO, Sanders MS 1232 M/025; Bodl. MS Clarendon 34, fos. 25–25ᵛ.

[115] HMC, *12th Report. App. Pt.9*, 'Beaufort MSS', 43; *A most true Relation Of divers notable Passages of Divine Providence...in...Devon* (1643), 4; BL Add. MSS 11,332, fos. 92ᵛ, 94; 11,810, fos. 12, 22; 35,297, fo. 39.

when the war had barely begun, Colonel Sandys could seize Upnor castle in Kent because most of the defenders were 'forth' at the harvest and the captain was playing bowls. It is more surprising to find Brereton being advised in 1645, in the middle of the siege of Chester, that he could profitably attack at 6 p.m. because there was then a hiatus in the defence, when the halberdiers had not been brought to the walls for the night watch and commanders and cavalry were at supper. Even the routines of virtue did not always bring their own reward: attendance at church delayed soldiers' response to a successful royalist raid at Plymouth.[116] At other times errors of judgement were so inexplicable that they must be due to divine intervention, as when 'god . . . besott[ed] the enemies ould Souldiers' so that they were 'engaged contrary to their intentions' at Langport.[117]

Shock, habit, and negligence all opened the way for the breakdown of discipline and for flight, dangers that were never far away. Officers tried to counteract them by building up the morale of their own troops while breaking down that of the enemy. The intimidating effect of the psalm-singing advance of the New Model army is well-known, but the other side employed variations on this technique. It was traditional wisdom that 'The use of *Musicke* in the warres, is partly to direct the *Souldier*, partly to encourage him.'[118] A royalist raiding party laid successful plans to attack Waller's rearguard at Marlborough, 'all to march in order and unanimously to sing a brisk lively tune (being a great part of the design) and so to fall on singing as they did'. The words may have differed—although psalms too were often sung to popular tunes—but intent and effect were similar, and were consciously reinforced by shouts so vociferous that the fleeing, demoralized parliamentarians were convinced that the whole royalist army was in pursuit.[119] The effect of the ancient practice of '*Shouting* to the Battel' was both well understood and a national speciality. 'The English are . . . much inclined to it', wrote an experienced commander, adding that 'such shoutings bring . . . a kind of Terror' as evidence of the 'great joy' of the attackers, 'but also it stirs up the blood and spirits before, and heats them during the Fight'.[120] Stirring and heating were necessary, for the tendency to flight and panic was ever present in the minds of military planners. It was to be exploited against the enemy and countered among your own but it was a common and understandable failing.

Like flight and panic, wounds and sickness were a normal part of war that nonetheless destabilized and overturned the best of plans. Epidemics periodically threatened the armies of both sides, affecting capacity to act and command. When

---

[116] *Perfect Diurnall of . . . our late journey into Kent, . . . 1642*, 3; BL Add. MSS 11,332, fo. 49; 35,297, fo. 39ᵛ.

[117] *Exact and Perfect Relation of the Proceedings of the Army . . . near Langport*, 7.

[118] Leech, *Trayne Souldier*, second dedication.   [119] BL Add. MS 11,810, fo. 28.

[120] Orrery, *Art of War*, 186; 'deep silence' was of course necessary up to the moment of attack; otherwise commands were inaudible. See also the intimidating pursuit of fleeing royalists after Alton in 1643, when Waller's troops 'made the woods ring with a shout'. *Narration of The great Victory, . . . Under Sir William Waller At Alton*, 5.

Maurice and two of his senior officers 'fell all three at one time dangerously sick, [it] caused disorder and delay', while in December 1645 Fairfax and his army were criticized for inaction when in fact his officers were dying of 'the *New Disease*', half his foot was sick, and he was forced to move his headquarters away from an infected town where soldiers and civilians were dying daily.[121] Wounds and death similarly affected outcomes, and not only in the obvious correlation between casualty rates and ability to undertake action. Sir Arthur Aston's head wound, from a roof tile dislodged by a cannon shot, put him in a coma and ultimately led to the surrender of Reading. The effect of Hopton's injuries from exploding gunpowder has already been noted, while the death of an officer in action could trigger the rout of his men.[122]

In the course of this chapter, we have moved from investigation of the means by which participants in the civil war attempted, with some success, to shape their actions in accordance with knowledge and reason, to a reassertion of the inevitable presence of chance and confusion. The effort to control has always coexisted in war with the irruptions of chance, but in the civil war the response to this conjunction was distinctive in two ways. First, providential explanations of victory and defeat flourished bipartisanly. They were characteristic of royalist as well as parliamentarian apologists, but the power of the belief of many parliamentarians that they were God's agents and his special care endowed them with a force and confidence that significantly strengthened their military actions and, given the adaptability of such doctrines, lent resiliency in coping with disasters.[123] Cromwell and the godly officers and men of the New Model provide the most famous example of the alliance of faith, morale, and victory, but commanders like Waller and Brereton equally drew strength from their conviction that God was not only on their side but intimately concerned in their every action. Second, unpredictable disasters, if not providential or the consequence of stupidity, were often seen as conspiratorial. This remains a familiar reaction, but in the circumstances of civil war it sowed suspicion even among allies and potentially embittered relations with civilians, prisoners, and other suspected sources of betrayal. It strained social bonds in ways that did not occur in more straightforward combat with a foreign enemy. It intensified the quarrels among officers that were so damaging to the royal cause and, among parliamentarians, it hastened the creation of the New Model army. Readiness to suspect contained the seeds of dangerous divisions.

War remained uncontrollable in spite of the best professional efforts to impose a connection between intent and outcome by the exercise of mind and will. Sir Thomas Aston noted in 1643, 'The intelligence failed not, but was seasonable',

---

[121] Bamfeild, *Apologie*, 7; Sprigge, *Anglia Rediviva*, 155.

[122] BL Add. MSS 11,810, fos. 13–14; 35,297, fos. 7ᵛ–8.

[123] For royalist providentialism, see e.g. an interpretation of Chester's fate as a manifestation of God's judgements, mercies, and warnings. BL Harl. MS 1944, fo. 99.

but the remark came in a recital of defeat.[124] Marston Moor was a famous victory, but an eye-witness account revealed the chaos that lurked near the military surface, the shared experience that distinguished little between winners and losers, and conduct by troops that was common to both sides:

[I]n the fire, smoke and confusion of that day, I knew not for my soul whither to incline. The runaways on both sides were so many, so breathless, so speechless, and so full of fears, that I should not have taken them for men, but by their motion which still served them very well; . . . both armies [were] mingled, both horse and foot; no side keeping their own posts.

In this horrible distraction did I coast the country; here meeting with a shoal of Scots crying out *Weys us, we are all undone*; and so full of lamentation and mourning, as if their day of doom had taken them, and from which they knew not whither to fly: and anon I met with a ragged troop reduced to four and a Cornet; by and by with a little foot officer without a hat, band, sword, or indeed any thing but feet and so much tongue as would serve to enquire the way to the next garrisons, which . . . were well filled with stragglers on both sides within a few hours, though they lay distant from the place of fight 20 or 30 miles.[125]

It is now time to turn to the laws that endeavoured to impose order on these armies and to the officers and men who, in these intractably chancy circumstances, experienced victory and defeat, whose conduct shaped much of the civilian experience of the war, and who, if they survived, remained fellow-countrymen when peace came.

[124] BL Harl. MS 2135, fo. 103ᵛ.
[125] Arthur Trevor to Ormonde, 10 July 1644, Carte, *Original Letters*, 1. 56.

SLAY IN LOVE: THE MORAL
AND JUDICIAL ECONOMY
OF CIVIL WAR

[E]ven in the heat of our Fury give us Pitty, that we may rather spare then
spoile; . . . Confound their Devices, but Convert their soules.

> If thou canst grieve to spoile the plow-mans Village,
> And make it not thy aime to fight for pillage;
> If in the furious sacking of a Towne
> Thou canst avoid to cast their women downe
> With their young new-born infants; if thou fly
> From all base actions of red cruelty;
> The Lord will sure protect thee from all harmes,
>   And I my selfe will say,—Stand to your Arms.[1]

The protagonists in the English civil war faced insoluble problems common
to all wars. How was a war to be fought hard and at the same time, if not
humanely, at least decently? The reasons for fighting hard—victory and self-
preservation—were simple and self-evident. The question of how the war was
to be fought was more complex, and the grounds of choice were both moral
and utilitarian. The laws of God, nature, and nations required that soldiers
should not 'delight . . . in blood', and that they '[p]ut on . . . bowels of mercies,
[and] kindnesse'. They should '[s]lay in love'.[2] This left the way open for a
wide range of permissible, violent, and sometimes appalling actions. Nevertheless
self-interest prompted mutual restraint and observance of the conventions of
war, lest reciprocity decline into vindictive reprisal. In addition, fear of social
chaos prompted controls on the conduct of one's own soldiers as well as the
enemy's. An examination of shared norms of conduct in war and of the degree

---

[1] T[homas] J[ordan], *The Christian Souldier. Or, Preparation for Battaile* (1642), 14, 'The
Souldiers Prayer'; [T. Swadlin], *The Soldiers Catechisme, Composed for The Parliaments Army*, 8th
edn. (*sic*), (1645), 6; this is the royalist parody version of the parliamentarian Robert Ram's *Souldiers
Catechisme*, of which the 7th edn. appeared in 1645.
[2] Gouge, *Churches Conquest*, 279, 295, 296.

to which they were observed can help us to understand English fears during the Interregnum for the order and cohesion of society, and also the factors that helped or hindered the reconciliation of former enemies.

The difficulties encountered in mid-seventeenth-century England in attempting to impose constraints on the conduct of war, and the military and civilian reverberations of success and failure, remind us of moral and judicial issues that remain sadly familiar. Modern wars may have been transformed exponentially in scale, but they still raise issues of cruelty, hunger, disease, death, and destruction, of the legitimacy of actions, and of moral and legal responsibility. This section will examine some of the means by which seventeenth-century English men and women sought to maintain the delicate balance between war and decent conduct, and their responses to lapses from ideal standards. Future chapters will demonstrate in more detail the rules applicable in particular circumstances and the playing out of laws and conventions in individual cases.

7

War and Civil War

War had long been blessedly absent from English soil, and even when the Scottish wars of 1639 and 1640 broke this domestic peace their humiliating and manifestly incompetent campaigns remained, for most Englishmen, distant as well as short, their significance more political than military. Yet as we have seen, domestic peace did not mean ignorance. By the time the Thirty Years' War ended in 1648 England had for decades been presented with, on the one hand, narratives of political and military events that greatly diminished isolationism and amateurism and, on the other, with horrifying pictures of war and disorder that had unleashed atrocities against soldiers and civilians alike, and that had broken the bonds of humanity and civility. The Irish rebellion of 1641 brought echoes of Germany closer to home in the narratives of atrocity and barbarity that flooded from English presses. By 1642 war elsewhere, from eastern Europe to England's Celtic margins, had already involved kin, friends, and the national government, and the English knew much not only about the practice of war but about its consequences.[1] They knew that religion ignited unstable passions, that controls on conduct were fragile, and that their breakdown could lead to a moral and material wasteland. In the words of Charles I in 1642 war, like political turmoil, was 'destructive to Publick Happiness'. When the 'wild Humours' of 'the common People' were loosed the king foresaw 'a dark equal chaos of confusion'. Many parliamentarians shared his fear, and the rhetoric of 'German' horrors and the destruction of all 'Rights and Proprieties, all Distinctions of Families and Merit', continued to mingle in civil war polemic.[2] The royalist preacher George Wilde lamented:

take away the Boundary of the Lawes, & what is this but to erect a Tyranny within every breast? . . . *Lust will be a law unto it selfe, Incest will be a law, and Rapine will be a law, and Murther will be a Law* . . . . Yes, these are the unlucky, the illegitimate brats and Spawne of our teeming Rebellion . . . . we may behold . . . the High-noon of Violence and Oppression.[3]

---

[1] See e.g. Rushworth, 4. 405–21, 'A Breviate of some of the Cruelties, Murders, &c. committed by the Irish Popish Rebels, upon the Protestants'; B. Donagan, 'Codes and Conduct in the English Civil War', *PP* 118 (1988), 65–95, and 'Halcyon Days', *PP* 147 (1995), 65–100.

[2] Rushworth, 4. 732 (Charles I's response to the Nineteen Propositions of 1 June 1642).

[3] Wilde, *Sermon . . . In St. Maries Oxford*, 16–17.

The Thirty Years' War had demonstrated the dual dangers of the breakdown of civilian law and of the laws of war that regulated relations between combatants and between soldiers and civilians. In this chapter I shall look at the ways in which laws of war applicable between nations were justified, adapted, and sustained in a civil war, and then at the regulations designed to produce an orderly and effective fighting force.

Both the unwritten conventions of conduct in war and its written disciplinary ordinances were already established and familiar to many before 1642. This familiarity extended beyond ideal soldierly norms, such as courage, expertise, and magnanimity, to awareness of the moral, constitutional, and religious problems entailed by engaging in any war, and particularly in a civil war. We have already noted the intermingling of the language of warfare and the language of religion in legitimating Christian war, and how awkwardly the resulting fusion of concepts coexisted with Christian precepts of love and charity. The man who endeavoured to act as a soldier, a Christian, and a gentleman struggled to reconcile them, but he was supported by the belief that despite its horrors, war was still a legitimate course of action. The Bible was a source of comforting justification for royalists and parliamentarians alike; it provided ample support for the bellicose. New Testament injunctions to turn the other cheek and to live at peace with all men, and the warning that those who lived by the sword would die by the sword, did not present obstacles to serious Christians. The scriptures proved satisfactorily that just war was 'agreeable to common equity'. In victory the parliamentarian minister Joseph Caryl declared that 'God is called a *man of warre*, but nothing shews him *more a God then warre*'; in defeat the royalist Richard Harwood would not 'perswade any man to fly from his Colours. Christianity is no such *cowardly Religion*'.[4] Both parties fought in the conviction that God sanctioned war, and that they fought in his just cause.

War should of course be just, and this could present a problem in a civil war. It was often easier to dismiss the cause of a foreign enemy as unjust than that of one's neighbour or brother. Some theorists indeed now argued that even in international conflicts each side should at least be given the benefit of the doubt as to the justness of their cause, and that the conduct of both sides should be governed by the codes applicable in a just war. Wartime propagandists, however, rarely acknowledged the possible justice of the enemy's cause; the parliamentarian *Souldiers Catechisme*, for example, rejected the possibility of good or Protestant royalists, declaring that they were 'siders with Antichrist; and so our eye is not to pitie them, nor our sword to spare them'.[5] Nevertheless in practice the military and social benefits of reciprocity outweighed the satisfaction of vengeance against

---

[4] Joseph Caryl, *Ioy Out-joyed: or, Joy in overcoming evil spirits and evil men, Overcome by better Joy* (1646), A2ᵛ; Harwood, *The loyall Subiect's retiring-roome*, 16; Gouge, *Churches Conquest*, 212–13.

[5] G. I. A. D. Draper, 'Grotius' Place in the Development of Legal Ideas about War', in Hedley Bull, Benedict Kingsbury, and Adam Roberts (eds.), *Hugo Grotius and International Relations* (Oxford, 1992), 183; Ram, *Souldiers Catechisme*, 14–15.

the unjust and ungodly, and it was the utility of reciprocity and predictability in their dealings with the enemy and their sense of obligation to adhere to professional standards, rather than high theory, that led serving soldiers to observe—often, admittedly, controversially and imperfectly—the laws of war. There were some enemies however to whom these benefits did not apply, and there were circumstances in which they might be suspended.

If contemporary Christian theorists offered an imprimatur for belligerence, it nevertheless came with the rider that war should be conducted in a manner befitting Christians, not Turks and infidels. To the admonitions of religion were added the secular norms of conduct to be expected of 'a gentleman . . . a soldier and an honest man'.[6] '[T]he faith of Christians and the honour of gentlemen' joined the professional self-respect and expertise of soldiers to make up the standards by which civil war soldiers judged their own and others' conduct.[7] The consequence, as John Pym had told a group of unruly soldiers in October 1641, should be 'that as . . . Gentlemen and Souldiers, [they would] scorne to wrong any of the Kings Subjects'.[8] In the years that followed his hope often proved vain, but the ideal standard was neither abandoned nor revised to vacuity. Its survival shaped not only the way in which the war was fought but also the way in which Englishmen were able to live together after it.

The codes of war that covered *ius in bello*, the law of conduct in war, were of three kinds, although they overlapped and intermingled. First, the laws of God, nature and nations covered the conduct to be expected of reasonable, moral men. Their authority crossed national and confessional boundaries, but it particularly behoved Christians to observe them. They were equally relevant to Catholic and Protestant, English and foreigner. Second, the laws of war, professionally specialized and largely customary, were also international, although there might be local variations of detail. Both the laws of God, nature, and nations and the laws of war were uncodified and unwritten. Only the third category of rules, those covering internal army discipline—the articles or ordinances of war—constituted a body of written law. Although we think of the seventeenth century as the great innovative age in the formulation of international law and the law of war and peace, the English civil war in fact, like other wars of the first half of the century, was conducted according to traditional codes. The works of Alberico Gentili and even Hugo Grotius, admired as they were by an elite, were not guides to the soldier in his daily round.[9] Instead the guides to conduct in England as on the continent were mutually recognized norms that combined

---

[6] Sir Ralph Hopton's recommendation of Colonel Francis Hawley to Prince Rupert in 1643, quoted in Newman, *Royalist Officers*, 182.

[7] Worcester College, Oxford, Clarke MSS 114, p. 33ᵛ.

[8] *The Heads Of severall Petitions delivered by many of the Troopers against the Lord Generall . . . With the Answer which Mr. Pym made . . . October 5. 1641* (1641), 4.

[9] B. Donagan, 'Atrocity, War Crime, and Treason in the English Civil War', *AHR* 99 (1994), 1143–4. Grotius' work on war and peace was not published in English until 1654.

virtue and utility. In the English civil war both sides hoped, sometimes vainly, to maintain them.

For the present we may note their mutuality and the moral and social reasons for observing them, but before turning to their substance one further problem must be addressed: the legal status of the conflict. Were the rules applicable to rebellion or to war to apply? When hostilities began in the summer of 1642, that status was not self-evident. If, as royalists claimed, they faced rebellion then civilian law, particularly the law of treason, applied, and captured parliamentarian soldiers could be tried and executed. If they were engaged in something comparable to foreign war, then the laws of war between nations covered the combatants of both sides and prisoners, for example, were subject to a recognized set of protections and restrictions.

Why then were the rules of foreign war observed? The obvious answer is utilitarian: it did not pay to do otherwise and to set the stage for a war of reprisal, of *lex talionis*. Yet although both sides recognized this danger, they were slow to address the problem formally. From the early days of the war each claimed that the other was engaged in rebellion. Parliament stigmatized enemies as 'Traytors', while the king's articles of war declared that parliament's troops were 'disloyall and Rebellious Subjects'.[10] Charles I argued forcefully that the actions of his opponents were 'literally and expressly' treasonable and assured his followers that they would 'meet with no Enemies but Traytors'. Sir Edward Walker, the king's secretary, declared that parliament could only execute those taken in arms as traitors 'by an arbitrary power' or by an intrinsically ridiculous claim to prosecute for statutory treason. Parliamentarians, on the other hand, argued that the king's soldiers were engaged 'in the Act of War against the Parliament, which, by the Laws and Statutes of this Realm, is Rebellion and High treason against the King and Kingdom'.[11] Parliament long continued to declare its loyalty to a misguided king, and that its army was raised 'for the necessary Defence of the true Protestant Religion, the King, Parliament, and Kingdom', but it claimed that 'Rebellions and Insurrections in this Kingdom of England' incited by cunning papists and malicious counsellors had forced it to take up defensive arms. Its claim was revolutionary: soldiers and commanders owed their first obedience to parliament, not king. If the primary duty of obedience in the state was to parliament, the king's soldiers could be guilty of rebelling against that sovereign power. Parliamentary logic may have been strained, but each side put a case for its own constitutional legitimacy.[12] What constituted treason and therefore merited punishment was a matter of partisan judgement.

---

[10] *A Catalogue of the Names of the Dukes, Marquesses, Earles and Lords, that have absented themselves from the Parliament, and are now with His Maiesty* (n. pl., 1642), 16; *Military Orders and Articles, Established by His Majesty* (Oxford, 1642), 1; this rare early edn. of royalist articles is in the library of Lincoln College, Oxford.

[11] Rushworth, 5. 6, 20; Walker, *Historical Discourses*, 248; *LJ* 5. 497.

[12] Ibid.; Firth and Rait, *Acts and Ordinances*, 1. 1, 5, 14–16.

At first both parties exercised restraint. Early in the war the king's secretary recorded 'a serious Debate in Council' in which it was objected that the exchange of prisoners—that is, countenance of a practice governed by conventions of war between nations—'tacitely impl[ied] the Justice of the War', thus granting it the status of war rather than rebellion. The king, out of concern for his imprisoned followers, agreed to exchanges, but Walker observed, 'He might by the known and ancient Laws of the Kingdom have executed such as He took in Arms as Traytors and Rebels.'[13] He did no more than repeat conventional views such as those of the respected sixteenth-century Spanish theorist Balthasar Ayala, who had argued that 'it is more correct to term the armed contention with rebel subjects execution of legal process, or prosecution, not war.... For the same reason the laws of war, and of captivity,... which apply to enemies, do not apply to rebels.'[14] This issue hardly died with the seventeenth century. It was only in 1977 that Protocol I, an addition to the 1949 Geneva Conventions, extended the rules and protections of international conflicts to internal wars of 'national liberation', and even then some countries refused to sign.[15]

In December 1642 a crisis precipitated an informal protocol between the parties to the civil war. The royalists in Oxford indicted three prisoners for treason, one of whom was the future Leveller John Lilburne. Instead of treating them as prisoners of war they proposed to try them by the processes of civilian law; conviction in the court of King's Bench would speedily be followed by execution. Lilburne's wife delivered a dramatic last-minute appeal to parliament, and the House of Commons at once mustered all its legal talent to respond to the threat. Within two days a joint declaration by Lords and Commons confronted the charge of treason and, more to the immediate point, warned of consequences. If the royalists proceeded from indictment to trial, or if these officers or any other agents of parliament were harmed, not only would judge and officials be held responsible but exact reprisal would follow: 'the like Punishment shall be inflicted, by Death or otherwise, upon such Prisoners as have been, or shall be, taken by the Forces raised by Authority of both Houses of Parliament'.[16] Parliament's 'declaration of Lex Talionis' (in Lilburne's phrase) formalized

---

[13] Walker, *Historical Discourses*, 247–8.

[14] Quoted in Geoffrey Parker, 'The Etiquette of Atrocity: The More Things Change, the More they Stay the Same', *MHQ: The Quarterly Journal of Military History* (1993), 13; Draper, 'Grotius' Place in . . . Legal Ideas about War', in Bull *et al.*, *Hugo Grotius and International Relations*, 189–90.

[15] Ibid. 204–5. John Keegan, linking honour and reciprocity, has argued that refusal to sign the 1977 protocol was justified on the ground that it 'undermines the code of honour, for [freedom] fighters are usually unable, even if they are willing, to reciprocate the practices of fair fight or proper treatment of prisoners on which the whole concept of restraint in warfare rests'. John Keegan, 'If you won't, we won't', review, *TLS* (24 Nov 1995), 11.

[16] *LJ* 5. 283, 497; *CJ* 2. 891–2; Pauline Gregg, *Free-Born John: A Biography of John Lilburne* (1961), 101–3; Clarendon, *History*, 3. 391; Ludlow, *Memoirs*, 1. 35. Ludlow's account conflated two incidents, that involving Lilburne in Dec. and the earlier case, in Aug 1642, of Captain Robert Ludlow and Dr Bastwick, in which the legal issues—of habeas corpus and parliamentary privilege—differed from those in Dec.

mutual restraint, but it did so on utilitarian rather than abstract moral grounds: a war of reprisal did not pay. Furthermore, although restraint had prevailed, both sides had established a reserve claim to regard the enemy as traitors to a civil state, even as they refrained from implementing treason's penalties. Nevertheless their operating principle had been made explicit. The laws of war rather than the laws of the civil state were applicable, and Englishmen confronted each other as 'lawful enemies'.[17] In the first civil war and its aftermath, the codes of war on the whole, if not infallibly, prevailed over the law of treason. Yet warning had been given of the inherent danger of civil war. Each side had defined the other as traitorous, and a shadow of the state's more ruthless law hovered over relations between victor and defeated. Its presence was acknowledged in 1642; it grew darker in 1648.

Recognition that hostilities were to come under the rubric of war rather than rebellion made civil war only a little more tolerable. It remained 'the most uncharitable mischiefe that a Common-wealth can be ingaged in'. It was self-destructive: 'wee. . . execute the designes of our enemies upon our selves'.[18] Enemies were not Turks or Spaniards but brethren and countrymen. It was demographically wasteful and overturned proper religious and social hierarchies of value:

Alas, in *Ireland* the Papists kill the Protestants, the *Irish* murder the *English*, but here the *English* kill the *English*, the Protestant murders the Protestant, there the greatest part of them that are kill'd, are women and children, heere the best men are pick'd out, and arm'd to kill one another.[19]

Many of those who lamented England's 'civill uncivill warres' and prayed for peace, freedom 'from the noise of terrifying alarums', and an end to 'cruell bloody warres' had nonetheless accepted war as the way to righteous peace.[20] Others, under no illusion as to the personal tragedy and the destruction of social cohesion wrought by civil war, were less certain that the end would justify the means:

the father sending his bullet at a venture, may kille his sonne, or the sonne his father; this is probable enough: but it is impossible, that brothers, kindred and friends should not mingle in one anothers blood, (and, perhaps, purposely) wee see such an eager division in all Families. And it is so universall, that no Countie, scarce any Citie or Corporation is so unanimous, but they have division enough to undoe themselves. And it is evident enough, that this Rent will encrease untill wee shall be quite torne in pieces.[21]

---

[17] Richard Zouche, *Iuris et Iudicii Fecialis, sive, Iuris Inter Gentes*, ed. Thomas Erskine Holland, 2 vols. (Washington, DC, 1911), 2. 37–8. Zouche succeeded Alberico Gentili in the chair of civil law at Oxford; his Latin synthesis of Grotius and Gentili was published in 1650.

[18] *The Moderator expecting Sudden Peace, or Certaine Ruine* (1642 [1643]), 11.

[19] *The Earle of Strafford's Ghost. Complaining Of the Cruelties of his Countrey-men, in Killing one another* (1644), 7; Gilbert, *Prelatical Cavalier*, 20.

[20] Kem, *Messengers Preparation For . . . Peace*, 30.

[21] *Moderator expecting Sudden Peace, or Certaine Ruine*, 11.

It was, said a young Yorkshireman, an 'Uncivil War that shed so much English blood'.[22] Fear of the consequences of that incivility, heightened by observation of Ireland and continental Europe, joined with hope that an organic and reconciled society might yet survive to foster adherence to norms of conduct in war. The parliamentary general Sir William Waller expressed the ideal: 'I constantly endeavoured to express all the civilities I could to those of the adverse party, that so our differences might be kept in a reconcilable condition; and we might still look upon one another, according to Aristotle's rule, as enemies that might live to be friends.'[23]

Reality proved more complex and civilities hard to sustain. It is now time to turn to the nature of the 'laws' that, ideally, should govern the conduct of war and that permitted both civilities and draconian severity.

[22] *Autobiography of Joseph Lister*, 10.
[23] *Vindication of the Character and Conduct of Sir William Waller, Knight; Commander in Chief of the Parliament Forces in the West, Explanatory of his conduct in taking up Arms against King Charles the First* (1793), 8.

8

Soldiers' Law

Soldiers' law was of three kinds, of which only that which regulated internal army discipline incorporated a formal machinery for enforcement and punishment. The others, which governed relations between enemies, depended on the power of opinion or recognition of the right of the aggrieved to exact revenge, to secure adherence to norms the validity and worth of which both sides acknowledged. The result, in the absence of effective force, was a system that depended heavily on the efficacy of social, peer pressure to maintain these bipartisanly accepted standards. The process would be familiar to students of the 'social norms' approach to modern law, who have observed the usefulness of '[f]ollowing the law, because you'd be too embarrassed not to'.[1] In the seventeenth century as in our own day 'embarrassment' and shame derived from multiple sources, from infringement, for example, of professional as well as moral norms, and could rarely be divorced from prudence and utility. The assumption that benefits to others carried an expectation of reciprocity had long been familiar.[2]

The resulting 'system' of laws of war in the seventeenth century undoubtedly mitigated ferocity, but it was hardly universally benevolent. Then as now military necessity and reprisal provided legitimate reasons for bending humane precepts. As Geoffrey Parker has observed, 'a certain amount of brutality is inevitable in all conflicts, given that the business of the military in war is killing people and breaking things'.[3] The exceptions to the rules can be as revealing as the rules themselves. Furthermore, in seventeenth century as in modern hostilities, the tension between what was lawful because it could be done with legal impunity and what was lawful because it was 'right and just' remained unresolved. Later chapters will show the uneasy coexistence of 'morality, the nature of law, humanity, and sheer necessity'.[4] Then as now, permissible cruelties existed side by side with humane protections.

---

[1] Jeffrey Rosen, 'The Social Police. Following the Law, Because you'd be Too Embarrassed Not to', *The New Yorker* (20–7 Oct. 1997), 170.

[2] See e.g. [Robert Cashman], *A Sermon Preached at Plimoth in New England* (1622), 4.

[3] Parker, 'Etiquette of Atrocity', *MHQ* (1993), 13.

[4] Draper, 'Grotius' Place in . . . Legal Ideas about War', in Bull *et al.*, *Hugo Grotius and International Relations*, 205; Edward Dumbauld, *The Life and Legal Writings of Hugo Grotius* (Norman, Okla., 1969), 70.

The English civil war represents a stage on the way to modern codified rules that regulate, still with very partial success, conduct in war. English practice in the 1640s, with its striking mixture of harshness and restraint, reflected a reality that later codifiers and theorists have continued to grapple with; the demands of 'military necessity' and of moral criteria have continued to coexist uneasily. Lieber's Code of 1863 for the Union army in the American civil war, the direct ancestor of modern international codes of war, struggled to distinguish between what 'military necessity admits' and 'does not admit', and the secular humanitarianism of the nineteenth century, like the biblical culture of the seventeenth, accepted starvation and bombardment of civilians as weapons in the service of military necessity.[5] The preamble to The Hague Convention No. IV of 1907 recognized the intractability of the problem in its declaration of purpose, which was 'to diminish the evils of war, so far as military requirements permit'.[6] The codes of war forbade many evils, but they also sanctioned many.

One of the dismaying lessons of war is that 'we' as well as 'they' can lapse into barbarism and inhumanity, and modern examples have shown the difficulty of accepting such a concept of ourselves. Part of the horror and fear that they arouse stems from recognition of how easily the veneer of civilization can be lost.[7] The Thirty Years' War had forced Englishmen to admit that good Protestants could behave as badly as depraved Catholics. This sense of the fragility of the standards and bonds of society, civilian as well as military, lay behind the pervasive rhetoric of the civil war that reiterated a basic and universal standard of human conduct derived from God and nature that was endangered by war and above all by the actions of one's enemies.

This universal standard was held to be specially applicable to Christian Englishmen, and failures were enthusiastically seized on by the busy propaganda mills. Reports from Germany had recounted 'barbarous . . . and inhumane' usage of civilians that was 'against all reason . . . and . . . all colour of right and justice . . . contrary to all Lawes and rights of nature; as also against the peace of Religion and of policy', and that lacked 'any Christian compassion'.[8] In the 1640s such accusations came home to England and suggested that the English too could become no better than 'the heathenish Turkes or Caniballs'. At the beginning of the war Prince Rupert's troops were accused of 'enormities' that violated 'all lawes both human and divine', while in 1647 parliament's treatment of the captive king

---

[5] Richard Shelly Hartigan, *Lieber's Code and the Law of War* (Chicago, 1983), 48–9. Lieber's code allowed 'destruction of life and limb' of soldiers and, when 'unavoidable', of civilians; deception was permissible but breaking faith, cruelty in cold blood, poison, and torture to extort information were not.

[6] Quoted in G. I. A. D. Draper, 'Wars of National Liberation and War Criminality', in Michael Howard (ed.), *Restraints on War: Studies in the Limitation of Armed Conflict* (Oxford, 1979), 137.

[7] James Dalrymple and Adam Sage, 'The War Crimes the Allies Chose to Forget', *Independent* (27 Mar. 1990), 4.

[8] [Vincent], *Lamentations of Germany*, 37–8, and see pp. 11, 30 on the deadening of the moral sense among Protestants as well as Catholics and among victims as well as soldiers.

was said to demonstrate 'monstrous injustice and cruelty whereof we may well wish had rather been found amongst Turkes and Heathens than us; and grieve that it should pollute any Christian and English Story'. The popularity of such language, however, serves to warn against giving all accusations of Turkish and unchristian conduct equal credence. While discomfort, inferior food, unwanted company, exposure to danger, or treatment deemed inappropriate to the status of the king—or other victims—might be demeaning, insensitive, or frightening, they were not necessarily atrocious. The pervasive polemical language of cruelty, injustice, and unchristianity may obscure the fact that all offences were not equal and that breaches of the laws of nature, nations, and war might lie in the eye of the partisan beholder. There was a significant difference between the king's captivity on the Isle of Wight and that of parliamentarian prisoners in Oxford castle. Habits of language and vituperation elevated lesser 'cruelties' to equality with undoubted atrocities.[9]

The borders between the three kinds of codes intended to regulate and moderate conduct in war were porous, and we should be wary of over-systematizing them. Daily practice and common usage rarely cited the finer distinctions of legal theorists. Together, however, they made up a known standard of conduct to which both sides appealed. Some aspects of the law of nature and nations and professional 'laws of war' were incorporated into armies' written articles of war, but at other times the laws of 'nature and nations' became part of a virtuous mantra appealing to a generalized standard of decency.[10] Some distinctions, however, can be made.

UNWRITTEN CODES: THE LAWS OF GOD, NATURE, AND NATIONS

The laws of God and nature were both the most general of the laws applicable to war, in that they stated basic principles not tied to specific circumstances, and the least open to exceptions, although even their benefits were compromised by the claim that necessity might render otherwise forbidden actions legitimate. The moral standards they asserted derived from reason as well as God, and therefore could be shared by reasonable non-Christians and Christians alike, a

---

[9] R. Andrewes, *A perfect Declaration Of The Barbarous and Cruell practises committed by Prince Robert, the Cavalliers, and others in his Majesties Army* (1642), A2ᵛ, [A4]; *An Antidote against An Infectious Aire* (n.pl., 1647).

[10] 'Code' may indicate an unwritten set of norms, as in 'a code of honour' or 'the pirates' code', but in modern usage it is more commonly applied to a written, 'codified' set of laws as in 'U.S. Code' or 'Code Napoléon'. Here it is used in both senses: the overarching codes of war—its primary norms of conduct—were unwritten, while the written articles of war provided legislation for the specifics of military discipline. The absence of a formalized, written code governing relations between enemies did not preclude an extensive and influential printed literature that discussed the unwritten laws of war, knowledge of which was also disseminated by manuscript, word of mouth, and professional example.

view reinforced by the influence of Roman thought and history. In practice, however, Englishmen tended to see the law not only of God but also of nature as a European preserve; they thought in terms of the duties of the moral and Christian person, not of the rights of all human beings. There were 'others', moreover, who had either removed themselves from, or had never known, the laws of God and nature. In England in the 1640s the Irish were allotted this role.

The laws of God and nature largely coincided, although their precise relationship had long prompted scholastic debate.[11] The law of nature demanded 'justice [and] righteousness' and 'provide[d] a moral framework within which all human laws must operate'. It was the 'higher law which every man already knows in his conscience'.[12] In the context of war it required that faith be kept, and that soldiers abstain from gratuitous acts of cruelty. Blood lust, pleasure in killing, private vengeance, and unnecessary bloodshed were alike indefensible. The weak and harmless should not be killed, and protection was expressly extended to 'weake women, aged men, and youn[g] children'. God and nature alike required that the weak and innocent should be treated with kindness. Those who acted with 'bowels of mercies, kindnesse' acted acceptably to God and might themselves be the beneficiaries of others' kindness, for virtue might bring rewards on earth as well as in heaven. The reciprocal calculus was rarely forgotten.[13]

Early medieval attempts to extend the law of God by establishing a peace of God that would protect not only the weak and harmless but whole classes of persons, property, and periods of time from the ravages of war had proved ineffectual, for they were both unrealistically comprehensive and powerless. Ultimately the peace of God had come to apply, in theory at least, not only to women, children, and the old but also to clerics, merchants, pilgrims, men at work, churches and church property, cattle and horses, and to feast days and even long weekends, but its only sanction, excommunication, was devalued by overuse.[14] Despite the movement's 'administrative futility', many of its provisions survived in the unwritten laws of war and some were incorporated in the earliest known articles of war, thus acquiring physical as well as spiritual sanctions. Some survived residually in civil war articles. We shall return to the content of the latter, but we may note that these protections derived not only from God and right reason but also from unacknowledged anthropological, economic, and ecological aspects of the law of nature.[15] Horror at harm to women in childbed echoed

[11] For the debates of medieval and early modern theorists over conceptions of the law of nature as 'right reason' and as the embodiment of the will of God, see Quentin Skinner, *The Foundations of Modern Political Thought*, 2 vols. (Cambridge, 1978), ii. 148–51.

[12] Ibid. ii. 149. Debate largely centred on the issue of whether reason alone could formulate this law of justice and righteousness or whether reason necessarily acted under divine direction.

[13] Gouge, *Churches Conquest*, 295, and see 278–9, 294–6.

[14] Julius Goebel, Jr., *Felony and Misdemeanour: A Study in the History of English Criminal Procedure*, i (New York, 1937), 299–309.

[15] Ibid. 307.

ancient taboos; prohibition of unauthorized destruction of crops and woods recalled memories of waste and famine as well as care for property.

The war's polemical literature exploited to the full the combination of fear and revulsion aroused by actions that offended against God and nature. The account of the 'bloudy & cruell practices' of Prince Rupert's troops in 1642 interspersed its feverish catalogue of 'pillaging, burning, and spoyling' with incidents of 'killing of men women and children that were unable to defend themselves', of cruelty to 'little Infants', and of torment and murder of harmless civilians: a pregnant woman was shot in the back 'with a brace of bullets . . . upon which she immediately dyed', and another woman was 'driven into the high way, she being in her smock with her child in her armes, though she had laine in but a week, who suddenly dyed after it'. Corn, woods, and 'plants which the earth is bringing forth' were destroyed. It was 'no disparity', said the pamphleteer, 'to parallel the present distractions of England with the Warrs of Germany'.[16] The laws of conduct in war embodied in the laws of God and nature were not mere abstract theory but vividly present in the minds of civilians and soldiers embroiled in the civil war, and they were polemically exploitable.

The law of nations had a more limited reach and less emotional resonance. It was made up of laws common to all nations, although there was much theoretical debate as to whether it was the embodiment in human law of the law of nature or merely 'a collection of widely-held judgments, not . . . a series of deductions from (or instances of) right reason itself'.[17] Its applications in war tended to be more particular and pragmatic than those of the law of nature, but it was nevertheless invoked in strongly moral terms, and many of its provisions depended on the sanctity of good faith that was part of the law of nature. It included the idea of compacts between nations, written and unwritten, and hence also the idea of a polity of nations. Unlike the laws of God and nature, which should govern the actions of individuals and nations alike, it applied in particular to the more formal relations between nations and by extension to those who were their official agents. Its 'rules' required that war be declared before military action was begun, that treaties be observed, that hostages be safeguarded in accordance with prior agreements, that ambassadors and official messengers be protected, and that ambassadors be exempt from local laws. The combination of reciprocal utility and good faith is again evident, and its major provisions remain familiar. Accusations of breaches of the law of nations suggested that Englishmen had fallen away from the standards of civilized nations; royalists, for example, found

---

[16] Andrewes, *Perfect Declaration, passim.*

[17] Skinner, *Foundations*, ii. 152. Grotius held that the 'law of nature derives directly from immutable human nature as an independent basis, and is therefore . . . valid even if God did not exist; whilst the law of nations proceeds from human will and is therefore merely 'positive' and mutable'. Peter Haggenmacher, 'Grotius and Gentili: A Reassessment of Thomas E. Holland's Inaugural Lecture', in Bull *et al., Hugo Grotius and International Relations*, 171. See also Dumbauld, *Grotius*, 69–71.

parliamentarians' treatment of the French ambassador, intercepted on his way to Oxford, 'barbarous'.[18] Like the law of nature, the law of nations was not wholly benevolent. If it did not allow enslavement of prisoners, as unfitting between Christians, it might sanction assassination (so long as faith was not broken); its stand on rape was uncertain; and it allowed the killing of captives (opinions differed as to the circumstances in which this was acceptable), and extensive rights to seize the property of the defeated.[19] Appeals to the law of nations in the English civil war were, often implicitly, a recognition of its status as a 'lawful war' in which both parties should be held to the standards governing hostilities between sovereign states.

UNWRITTEN CODES: THE LAWS OF WAR

The laws of war or arms, in the narrow and professional sense, were a set of customary rules governing the conduct of soldiers to each other and to civilians. Unlike the laws of nature and nations they were specific and practical. Detailed knowledge was a mark of professional expertise, and young soldiers learned them from their mentors; many civilians had at least a nodding acquaintance with them before the civil war began and perforce became more expert as it progressed. As I have already noted, the amount that Shakespeare did not need to explain in *Henry V* illuminates popular acquaintance with the ways of war. The different consequences to be expected from surrender and storm as conclusion to a siege; the rules for preserving or killing prisoners; the punishment for sacrilegious plunder; the protections due to the young; even the joke of Fluellen's pride in his insider's knowledge of soldierly proceedings, could all be presumed to be part of the baggage of a knowing audience. New officers and recruits may not have been experts in its details, but they became assimilated into a military ethos that was already familiar as a part of the larger national culture, and they recognized customary norms of conduct that went beyond the regulations set out in each army's formal articles of war.

The laws of war incorporated aspects of the law of nature and nations. When Fluellen protested the killing of the 'boys'—the young, unarmed servants and attendants in the English camp—he demonstrated the mingling of professionalism, interest, and humane principle: 'Kill the poys and the luggage! 'tis expressly against the law of arms.' It was an offence against the laws of God and nature to kill harmless boys; if the suggestion that the baggage too was protected by conventions of war was less persuasive, there was nevertheless an assumption

---

[18] Bedell (trs.), *Free Schoole of Warre*, Dii; Sutcliffe, *Practice, Proceedings, and Lawes of armes*, 295, 297; *Mercurius Belgicus* (n.pl., 1646), 18 Oct. 1643.
[19] Draper, 'Grotius' Place', in Bull *et al.*, *Hugo Grotius and International Relations*, 197–9.

that real soldiers should know the rules.[20] In the civil war 'the general sense and practice in all Wars' continued to govern both parties. Breaches of the 'old law of warr' were both unprofessional and 'perfidious'. There was conduct that became 'Soldiers to one another' and, in Edmund Verney's words, there was 'a civill and honourable custome, and so authenticke that it may not improperly be called a lawe amongst souldyers'.[21] That law, as we shall see, permitted actions that appeared to offend against the more humane precepts of the law of nature, which itself allowed uncomfortable exceptions. None of the codes of conduct in war was simple or monolithic; they interacted and adapted to each other, and those who claimed to follow them did so with flexibility, discretion, and a lawyerly turn for self-justifying interpretation.

The laws of war had a long history. Although the practice of war had evolved, the principles of behaviour between enemies had remained essentially unchanged for centuries. So surrenders were negotiated, paroles granted, prisoners exchanged, towns stormed, and property plundered, according to rules as familiar to those who fought with longbows as to those who fought with muskets. There had been, however, some significant developments. The importance of the customary rules for division of ransom faded as war became less a matter of private entrepreneurial profit and more national in its organization and financing. In the English wars civilians were more likely to be the objects of cash-for-release transactions than soldiers. Other obligations, however, such as those implicit in the grant of quarter to a surrendering enemy, did not change. The same rituals continued to govern certain actions, such as the dispatch and reception of drummers and trumpeters sent as emissaries between enemies, or the ceremonies of surrender with their carefully calibrated allocation of the symbols of honour to the defeated, such as colours flying or furled and arms carried out or confiscated. These have sometimes been taken as evidence of the survival of a chivalric mentality. Rather, while they reflected consciousness of membership of a historic profession, they survived because they were a familiar part of the procedures of war and useful to both parties to a conflict.[22]

The conduct required by the laws of war was that befitting 'a souldier, as well as a man of honour'.[23] Honour and military utility were closely connected but, beyond utility, the personal integrity of the honourable man was preserved by his adherence to the code of arms. The institution of parole for prisoners, for example, depended on the trustworthiness of the given word, and so on the basic moral and religious duty to keep faith, but the particular ways in which parole

---

[20] For legal and factual problems raised by Shakespeare's handling of this incident, see Theodor Meron, *Henry's Wars and Shakespeare's Laws* (Oxford, 1993), 155–60.

[21] Shakespeare, *Henry V*, 4. 7; Rushworth, 7. 1233, 1303; Vicars, *Burning-Bush*, 20; Round, 'Case of Lucas and Lisle', *TRHS* NS 8 (1894), 169.

[22] On the origins and practices of the laws of war, see generally M. H. Keen, *The Laws of War in the Late Middle Ages* (1965), and Meron, *Henry's Wars and Shakespeare's Laws*.

[23] *Declaration of his Highness Prince Rupert: . . . Bristoll*, 4.

operated, its terms and purposes, were matters of military convention. Strict observance of its terms benefited both sides, but at the same time reassured the individual as to his own moral worth. Later chapters will demonstrate the extent to which soldiers managed to live up to their professional code of honour and the strains to which broad precepts were subject in practice. Nor should we idealize the laws of war. The rules could be brutal as well as generous or, as in those governing plunder, more commercial than chivalric. An example demonstrates the legalism with which such unwritten rules could be used to adjudicate not only major issues such as the execution of prisoners, as at Colchester, but the most commonplace military affairs. A dispute about the ownership of a horse captured by the enemy, then recaptured by another soldier, was settled by appeal to the rule that captured property must be retained for 'twelve or twenty-four houres' before the rights in the property were transferred from the original owner to the taker. In this case, the horse was returned to its original owner, because the initial transfer did not last long enough to satisfy the time criterion. Had more time passed, the first taker of the horse would have had 'property in him, and he that then had taken the horse might have owned him by this old law of warr'.[24]

The laws of war were thus no mere matter of honour, courtesy, and chivalry. Instead they made up a system of customary law that governed many of war's minor and quotidian transactions as well as exchanges between heroes and commanders. For the moment we may note that the primary function of the laws of war in the seventeenth century was as a kind of etiquette of belligerence. They provided each party with a framework of expectations as to the conduct of others, and as to the kinds of contract, written and unwritten, into which they would enter. 'The Custom of War in like Cases' regulated crucial activities from surrender to plunder but, as a nineteenth century historian of the army said austerely, 'as a rule of right or wrong—of reward or punishment—in the most favourable view of it, [it] is uncertain'.[25]

WRITTEN LAW

The Evolution of English Articles of War

English ordinances or articles of war, the predecessors of modern military regulations, had a long history, but they underwent a revolutionary change in the later sixteenth century. They offer an invaluable guide to the hoped-for nature of army discipline but they also reveal the persistent problems of achieving an orderly and effective fighting force.[26] They addressed specific disciplinary issues

---

[24] Symonds, *Diary*, 245.   [25] Clode, *Military Forces of the Crown*, 1. 174.
[26] See e.g. Cruickshank, *Elizabeth's Army*, ch. 10, 'Discipline'.

and were heavily weighted towards prohibitions, but the severity of their content was mitigated by the discretionary element in enforcement. Military punishments for breaches of military law were shaped by principles of flexible, exemplary, and 'in terrorem' administration of justice.

The earliest systematic set of English regulations to survive is that issued by Richard I in 1189 to maintain order on a crusading voyage to the Holy Land. They were pithy, brutal, and narrowly practical: at sea killers were to be lashed to the body of the victim and thrown overboard, on land they were to be buried alive with the body; an assailant with a knife lost a hand, one who merely hit another was ducked three times; thieves were shaven, tarred and feathered, and set ashore; abusive language was fined.[27] Over the next two hundred years articles moved beyond these crude basics. By 1385 Richard II's were already very close to the notable formulation issued by Henry V, which had sufficient fame to be translated into Latin before 1450, whence its articles were retranslated into English verse in about 1500, and reappeared in an elegant edition in 1654. By then their interest was antiquarian, but they had remained the basis for English military ordinances to the end of Henry VIII's reign.[28]

The evolution of articles from Richard II to Henry VIII was largely a matter of clarification and adding details in response to immediate practical needs—for making ladders, for instance, or burying 'carren and bowells' to prevent pestilence—but the basics changed little. All began with a prohibition of sacrilege. Henry VIII's still protected 'holy churche', forbidding not only touching the sacrament and the pyx that contained it but also iconoclasm: no man was to be 'so hardy to burne or cut any images'.[29] All legislated against rape and murder of women, but also against the presence of women in the army although the penalties for such 'common women' showed, perhaps, some progress. Fifteenth-century articles provided that an offender's money be confiscated and that she be driven from the camp with a staff and her arm

---

[27] Printed in J.H.L., 'Articles of war', *JSAHR* 5 (1926), 202–3.

[28] Francis Grose, *Military Antiquities Respecting A History of the English Army, from the Conquest to the Present Time*, 2 vols. (1786–8), 2. 57–65 (Richard II); idem, *The Antiquities of England and Wales*, 8 vols. (new edn. [1783–7]), 1. 33–51 (Henry V, 1415, with additions by the earl of Salisbury); [Samuel Bentley], *Excerpta Historica, or Illustrations of English History* (1833), 28–43 (Henry V reissued under Henry VI, with additions by the earl of Shrewsbury); HEH HA MS 30662 (a variant of Henry V's articles collected by Sir Robert Cotton in the 1620s); Magdelene College, Cambridge, Pepys MS 2871, pp. 158–70 (Henry VI, 1437); [Edward Bysshe], *Nicolai Uptoni De Studio Militari, Libri Quatuor. Iohan. de Bodo Aureo, Tractatus de Armis. Henrici Spelmanni Aspilogia* (1654); Francis Pierrepont Barnard, *The Essential Portions of Nicholas Upton's De Studio Militari. Before 1446. Translated by John Blount. Fellow of All Souls* (c.1500) (Oxford, 1931); *Hereafter Ensue certayne Statuts and ordinau[n]ces of warre made . . . by . . . our moste dreade Souerayne lorde Kynge Henry the. viii* (1513); *Statutes and ordynances for the Warre* (1544). Henry VII's ordinances of 1493 (STC 9332) appear to exist only in fragmentary form; leaves are held at the Lambeth Palace, Society of Antiquaries, and Huntington libraries. A comparison of the five leaves held at the Huntington with Henry VIII's articles of 1513 reveals only minor variations.

[29] *Statutes and ordynances for the warre* (1544), Aii.

broken; Henry VIII merely mandated burning on the cheek for a first offence.[30] The overwhelming impression, however, is not one of religious or moral concern but of military practicality. The articles legislated against free enterprise raids not authorized by commanders, against captains who transferred themselves and their men to service in another army, against running away or advancing too far and too fast, against false musters (the popular practice of counting non-existent soldiers in order to claim their pay). They regulated the granting of safe conducts. They tried to ensure that captains paid their men according to contract and to preserve the army's supplies by protecting merchants, victuallers, and ploughmen. They forbade unauthorized destruction. They prohibited quarrels, affrays, and gambling.[31] The basic problems addressed by these late medieval and early modern articles of war did not go away. As the eighteenth-century antiquarian Francis Grose observed of Henry V's ordinances:

These laws do not differ so greatly from those now in force, . . . subordination, good order in camp and quarters, the preventing of desertion and false musters, with safety for persons bringing provisions to the army, being immutably necessary to the very existence of every army, must therefore always be strongly enforced, both by rewards and punishments, and will give a very striking similarity to the chief articles in the military code of every age and every nation.[32]

Henry V's language and specific details might have seemed archaic to the civil war soldier but much of the content would still have been familiar and useful.

In one area, however, there was a fundamental change. These early articles were obsessively concerned to regulate the distribution of the profits of war, but by the mid-seventeenth century only slender relics of the relevant substance or language remained. From Richard II to Henry VIII, the allocation of property rights in prisoners, and hence the share of their ransoms due to individual soldiers and officers, were meticulously regulated by a complex set of provisions that distributed these 'winnings of war' according to a strict formula. At each stage of this trickle-up process of profit-sharing, soldier-captor, commander, and king took his legislated and traditional cut.[33] In 1544 nearly a quarter of Henry VIII's ordinances, some four pages out of seventeen, was devoted to the topic, and the Bodleian Library's copy shows that the regulations were not mere antiquarian survivals, for the only marginal notations occur in the sections on taking prisoners and dividing the resultant spoils. The attention paid to property rights and distribution of profits shows that we are still in the age of entrepreneurial war, of indenture between sovereign and entrepeneurs who undertook to provide bodies and service in return for profits that would, it

---

[30] Ibid. Bii; Grose, *Antiquities of England and Wales*, 1. 51.
[31] Ibid. 1. 36–7; *Hereafter Ensue certayne Statuts* (1513), B2, nos. 14, 15; no. 14 is headed 'For good rule to be kept.'
[32] Grose, *Antiquities of England and Wales*, 1. 33.
[33] *Statutes and ordynances for the Warre* (1544), [Biii^v–B^v].

was hoped, accrue to them, their men, and the prince.[34] The winnings of war, most notably in the form of plunder, continued to provide incentive in civil war armies, but military prisoners had ceased in normal circumstances to be a significant source of private profit.[35] The changes in the profit rules of war are indicators of ways in which relations between the sovereign power in the state and its armies had evolved by the mid-seventeenth century. While war still offered profits for the fortunate, they were no longer part of a private entrepreneurial contract of entering into service. Instead a centralized and bureaucratized state, whether royalist or parliamentarian, attempted to control both the finances and the loyalty of its soldiers.

The Civil War

The military revolution of the late sixteenth and early seventeenth century transformed the ordinances as well as the practice of war. Regulations were still directed to the age-old problems of discipline and efficiency, but language reflecting 'modern' military theory and practice was added, old provisions relating to profit disappeared, and formats changed.

The shift in emphasis was already evident by 1562 in the orders issued for English troops on their undistinguished expedition to Le Havre, and confirmed by the earl of Leicester's *Lawes and Ordinances* of 1585–6, issued for the queen's forces in the Low Countries. These revealed the cosmopolitanism of English military culture, for they were not only designed for but influenced by Dutch experience.[36] They systematically addressed order in camp and discipline in battle, mutiny and the administration of military justice, moral discipline and duties to God. These Elizabethan articles arguably mark the entry of an aggressively Protestant note into army ordinances, and Leicester's preface foreshadowed the rhetoric of the civil war. The army's cause was now God's: 'martiall discipline'

---

[34] See e.g. Gilbert J. Millar, 'Henry VIII's Preliminary Letter of Retainer to Colonel Frederick von Reiffenberg for the Raising of 1500 Men-at-Arms: An Explication of a Sixteenth-Century Mercenary Contract', *JSAHR* 67 (1989), 220–5.

[35] The fees that could be extorted from prisoners by their keepers were not ransom but a custodial charge and part of keepers' remuneration. See Parker, *Thirty Years' War*, 196, on the problems of allegiance created by the continental system of 'military enterprisers'; Philippe Contamine, 'The Growth of State Control. Practices of War, 1300–1800: Ransom and Booty', in P. Contamine (ed.), *War and Competition between States* (Oxford, 2000), 163–93 (on continental and particularly French experience); and see *passim* Fritz Redlich, *De Praeda Militari: Looting and Booty 1500–1815* (Vierteljahrschrift für Sozial- und Wirtschaftsgeschichte, 39; 1956).

[36] *Lawes and Ordinances, set downe by Robert Earle of Leycester, the Queenes Maiesties Lieutenant and Captaine General of her armie and forces in the Lowe Countries* ([1585/1586]). The Public Record Office dates its copy of these ordinances to 25 Dec. 1585. For supplementary regulations see PRO SP 84/05, fos. 80, 58a. For the cosmopolitanism of English military culture, see Styward, *The Pathwaie to Martiall Discipline*, A.ii; he claimed to draw on the expertise of Italians, Germans, 'Swizzers', French, and English, as well as his own experience. Spanish expertise was added in 1582 when the book was reprinted in conjunction with a translation of Luis Gutierrez de la Vega's *De Re Militari*.

was designed to 'governe this Armie in good order', but it also served 'for the advancement of Gods glorie'.[37]

Leicester's articles set the pattern for succeeding decades.[38] After a hiatus in the pacific years of James I, the 1620s brought a return to war and to further ordinances. In 1625 a set containing only twenty-four articles was designed to control an army within the kingdom and to regulate its relations with a civilian population rather than the enemy; they provided, for example, for the erection of gibbets and strappados in market towns in the hope that 'such a remembrance will do good in a [soldier's] wicked mind'.[39] By contrast the sixty succinct articles almost certainly designed for the expedition to the Isle of Ré in 1627 were, after standard prohibitions of blasphemy, rape, murder, and harm to women and children, briskly military. In passing they asserted the commander-in-chief's control over all prisoners and prizes of war.[40]

There followed another period of 'halcyon' peace for England, but anxieties over continental wars and the presence of English and Scottish soldiers abroad maintained interest in their laws as well as their campaigns. The future parliamentarian commander Sir John Gell owned Thomas Styward's *Pathwaie to Martiall Discipline* of 1582 which included a set of Elizabethan articles; if it is true that the stain on the book is his blood, he may have valued it enough to carry it into battle. The papers of the earl of Essex, parliament's future lord general and an experienced European soldier, included a set of Count Mansfeld's army regulations that addressed practicalities such as camp hygiene as well as standard disciplinary problems.[41] In 1632 Gustavus Adolphus' articles, already circulated in manuscript, appeared in print as *The Swedish Discipline, Religious, Civile, And Military*.[42] In 1631 an English translation of the Dutch ordinances of 1590 had appeared, together with supplementary regulations recently issued at Maastricht, and these were reprinted in full in 1637 in Henry Hexham's account of the principles of the military art.[43]

---

[37] *Lawes and Ordinances... Leycester*, 1.

[38] They provided the model for the earl of Essex's *Lawes and Orders of Warre, established for the good conduct of the service in Ireland* ([1599]).

[39] PRO SP 9/208, fos. 259–62, and note fos. 261, 262.

[40] H. Bullock, 'Articles of War—1627', *JSAHR* 5 (1926), 111–15, printed from PRO, SP Dom. Elizabeth, 237, fo. 36.

[41] Derbys. RO, Gell MS, D.3287; BL Add. MS 46,188, fos. 94–94ᵛ, and see n. 36 above.

[42] *The Swedish Discipline, Religious, Civile, And Military. The First Part, In The Formes of Prayer daily used by those of the Swedish Nation, in the Armie... The second Part, in the excellent Orders observed in the Armie; whereof we here present you the Articles, by which the Souldiery is governed* (1632), 39–73; the author noted three manuscript copies known to him, two at least in the hands of Scottish soldiers who had fought with Gustavus, ibid. 69.

[43] *Lawes and Ordinances touching military discipline. Set downe and established the 13. of August. 1590*, trs. I.D. (The Hague, 1631); Hexham, *Principles of the Art Militarie*, appendix, 9–18. Hexham also printed the Dutch-Spanish protocols for quarter and ransom rates (according to rank) for prisoners, ibid. 3–8.

In 1639 war returned to England, and its laws and practice were no longer a matter of comfortably remote interest in events elsewhere. In 1639 the earl of Arundel, Charles I's general against the Scots, issued at Newcastle a remarkable and innovative set of articles. His *Lawes and Ordinances Of Warre, For the better Government of His Maiesties Army Royall* evolved between 1639 and 1642 to become the basis of the military law of the Interregnum and later of the Restoration, and hence the lineal ancestor of modern British military law.[44] They revealed familiarity with the translation of the Dutch articles of 1590, but were formulated in terms of an English monarchy and of carefully analysed practical military problems. Arundel's greatest innovation, however, was to develop a clear and effective format. The introduction of the categorical heading, trivial as it sounds, presumably greatly improved memorability, comprehensibility, and, therefore, potential effectiveness for literate and illiterate alike when the laws of the army were read aloud to the troops. The sixty consecutively numbered paragraphs of 1627 were replaced by eighty-nine articles under six topical headings. The first group addressed 'Religion: and breach of *Morall* du[t]ies', a comprehensive category that covered blasphemy, sacrilege, church attendance, prayer before battle, gambling, drunkenness, 'whoredome' ('*suspitious* and *common women*' found in the army a second time were to be 'soundly whipped like common *strumpets*'), murder, and rape and other sexual offences, whether against women and children or '*unnaturall abuses*'. Then came a section on 'the safety of the *Armie Royall*, and of the *Kingdome*', which addressed conspiracy, communication with the enemy, mutiny, acceptable conditions for surrender, the dire crime of sleeping on watch, and 'Disparaging . . . Commanders'. Next came 'Captains and Souldiers duties in particular', a long section of twenty-nine practical paragraphs covering everything from pawning arms to silence on the march and from intra-army quarrels to understanding the instructions conveyed by 'the distinct and different *sounds* of *Drums, Fifes,* and *Trumpets*'. Further sections addressed 'the *Campe*, or *Garrison*', which covered order, place, labour, and cleanliness in camp, and 'lawfull *Spoiles* and *Prizes*', which endeavoured to prevent unlawful pillage, to assert central control over what was lawful (anything over the value of 10s. must be reported to the chief commander for sale in the camp), and to prevent private dealings in prisoners. It also sought to protect churches, schools, hospitals, and colleges from destruction, and churchmen, scholars, women, children, and the poor from abuse. Finally a section on 'the administration of *Justice*' set out the powers and procedures of councils of war, courts martial, and provost marshals. In case anything had been forgotten it ended with 'the devil's article', which ensured that the authorities would rarely be at a loss if they needed an offence

---

[44] *Lawes and Ordinances Of Warre, For the better Government of His Maiesties Army Royall, in the present Expedition for the Northern parts, and safety of the Kingdome. Under the Conduct of his Excellence, The . . . Earl of Arundel and Surrey, Earl Marshall of England* (Newcastle, 1639).

with which to charge a soldier: where 'no special order [was] set downe . . . the ancient course of Marshall *discipline* shall be observed'.[45]

The persistence and incorporation of many of the precepts of natural law and military custom is evident. If groupings sometimes seem arbitrary and sections overloaded, there was nonetheless a memorizable logic to Arundel's formulation. The next year the earl of Northumberland, as lord general of the army, refined the system further, increasing the number of heads to twelve, reducing the number of articles in each section, and clarifying categories.[46] In 1641, however, the earl of Holland, the king's next lord general in the 'Northern parts', abandoned the practice of his predecessors, for although his articles largely followed Northumberland's, albeit somewhat shortened, he removed the headings and reverted to an undifferentiated numbering from one to seventy-four.[47] In September 1642 the earl of Essex returned to the model of Arundel and Northumberland, with its clear categorical divisions and headings, for the parliamentary army, but the royalists continued to follow Holland's more retrograde example. It is tempting to see in this parting of the ways a forerunner of the military and administrative habits of both armies, and an omen of their respective success. For parliamentarians principles that already aided sermon memorization had been transferred to military law, so that it was easier for parliament's soldiers to hold its precepts in their minds if not necessarily to observe them in practice. Royalists, on the other hand, already showed an unwillingness to abandon tradition for modernization.

The articles that governed the armies of the English civil war were thus the products of a long evolution. They exist in multiple printings, although for items printed so often and so widely distributed the number of copies that has survived is remarkably small.[48] Substantively they differed little from those promulgated in the 1630s and the articles of the two sides largely covered the same ground; the deviations, however, are instructive. In theory at least there was no excuse for a soldier of either side to be unaware of the content of his army's articles of war, for they were to be read aloud each week so that 'none may be ignorant of the Lawes and Duties required'.[49] They addressed such basic and enduring military requirements as subordination, order, prevention of desertion, and protection of

---

[45] Ibid. 25 and *passim*.

[46] *Lawes and Ordinances of Warre, Established for the better conduct of the Service in the Northern parts. By . . . The Earle of Northumberland* (1640).

[47] *Lawes and Ordinances of Warre, Established for the better government of the Armie in the Northern parts. By . . . The Earle of Holland* (1641).

[48] Many presumably simply wore out from frequent use. Others may well have been disposed of after the war as no longer needed, or perhaps because the owners wanted to put their army experience behind them for personal or political reasons.

[49] *Lawes and Ordinances of Warre, Established for the better Conduct of the Army by His Excellency The Earle of Essex* (1642), 31, 'Of Administration of Justice'; *Military Orders and Articles, Established by His Maiestie, for the better Ordering and Governement of his Maiesties Armie* (Oxford, [1643]), title-page (this is a more elaborate reprinting of the 1642 royalist articles, with an equestrian portrait of Charles I facing the title-page).

supplies, and they also perpetuated old religious and moral rules. On the other hand, they also revealed the new relationship between sovereign power and army and between profit and service, while their details reflected the practices of modern war: a soldier was now forbidden to 'fling away his Powder out of his Bandiliers' in order to speed his exit from the battlefield. Their reach extended beyond specifically military actions and procedures to army administration; four parliamentary articles regulated the rolls by which muster-masters were supposed to prevent fraud by officers claiming pay for phantom soldiers, while royalist articles minutely defined the duties of army chaplains.[50] From time to time supplementary orders were issued to meet special circumstances, and the war years saw a few significant changes, but the essential core of articles remained stable.[51] We shall return to the changes, but a preliminary survey of the earl of Essex's articles of 1642, which remained the basic legal text of the parliamentary army, demonstrates the kind of regulations that tried to control the conduct of the armies of both sides. Nor did the formation of the New Model in 1645 change the legal code of parliament's army. Instead Essex's articles, as revised in 1643, were reissued for Fairfax's army.[52]

The offences that Essex's articles (and their royalist counterparts) legislated against and the punishments they mandated will crop up again and again in later chapters.[53] While they illustrate timeless problems, they also reveal the particular difficulties of early modern English armies whose systems of oversight, administration, and coordination with the civil power were still unsettled, and whose soldiers were often raw, flighty, and quarrelsome. Following the examples set by Arundel and Northumberland, Essex's ninety-five articles were divided into twelve general categories, each devoted to 'duties' of a certain kind. They began with duties to God, and forbade blasphemy, cursing, and neglect of divine worship. Then they turned to fundamental matters of military security, hierarchy, and discipline. These 'general' duties restricted dealings with the enemy to authorized persons; they forbade the surrender of strongholds except 'upon extremity'; and they prohibited the violation of 'safeguards', the passes that provided formal protection for messengers and travellers but that were also intended to restrict communication between enemies to that sanctioned by senior officers. The next section, on duties to 'Superiors and Commanders', asserted duties of obedience and subordination. It was a capital offence to 'use any words tending to the death of the Lord Generall' or to strike an officer (although death for the latter was discretionary rather than mandatory); and it was forbidden to

[50] *Lawes and Ordinances of Warre . . . Essex* (1642), 18, 25–6, 'Of Duties in Action', no. 7, 'Of the dutie of the Muster masters', nos. 2–5.
[51] For supplementary orders for specific circumstances, see e.g. *Orders Established The 14th of this present January, By His Excellency Sir Thomas Fairfax, For Regulating the Army* (1646 [1647]), 3–10.
[52] C. H. Firth, *Cromwell's Army* (4th edn. 1962), 280, 400–12; and see Firth and Rait, 1. 843, for an ordinance of 3 Apr. 1646 on 'the present Articles of War' published 'by the Earl of Essex, and now used in the Army under the command of Sir Tho: Fairfax'.
[53] For the following account, see *Lawes and Ordinances of Warre . . . Essex* (1642), *passim*.

quarrel with or resist officers or provost marshals. Mutiny, seditious words, and failure to report such words were prohibited. Officers' authority was bolstered by orders requiring troops to keep silence so that their commands could be heard; and their soldiers were forbidden to take themselves off to a regiment they liked better. Only after establishing these provisions for fundamental army security, integrity, and discipline did the articles return to moral duties in a catalogue of prohibited vices: drunkenness, 'Unnaturall abuses' (including 'Rapes and ravishments', which merited a mandatory death sentence), adultery and fornication, theft, inciting quarrels, seizing dead men's goods, and murder.

Next followed four sections designed to achieve professional competence. They detailed in turn soldiers' responsibilities in care for their arms, on the march, in camp and garrison, and in action. Here concerns were strictly practical. Arms must be well maintained, and they must not be lost, lent, pawned, or sold; horses must not be lost or gambled away. Duties on the march addressed both military and civilian needs. Soldiers must keep their places and not straggle (less serious than desertion, but an endemic problem). They must also observe the rights of civilians. They must not destroy goods or extort money or victuals, they must not take horses from the husbandman's plough, they must not cut down fruit-trees or 'walkes of trees'. Seventeen articles on duties in camp and garrison followed, directed towards keeping soldiers quiet, orderly, peaceful, dutiful, and inside the camp. So there were to be no unauthorized departures, and equally no unauthorized presences of unenrolled soldiers, no outstaying of passes, no private assaults, no complaints about quarters, no failures to appear for watches or rendezvous. One of the army's unforgivable offences appeared in this section: a sentinel found asleep or drunk or who abandoned his post earned death 'without mercy', for this was a sin that could endanger a whole army. Officers too had their camp obligations: they must not leave camp for dinner or stay away overnight without permission, and it was their responsibility to oversee hygiene, to keep the camp 'cleane and sweet'. The fourth of this group of articles, setting out duties in action, was predictably concerned to ensure that soldiers appeared for action when called and did not run away once engaged; hence the pikeman must not throw away his pike nor the musketeer his musket. Property was not to be burnt or destroyed without orders. Premature retreat before coming to 'handy-blowes' merited shaming punishments: delinquent officers were banished from the camp, and delinquent soldiers were subject to decimation (by which in theory every tenth man would be 'punished at discretion') while the rest were reduced to ignominious service as pioneers and scavengers until they redeemed themselves by a 'worthy exployt [that took] off that Blot'. It was this section, too, that regulated booty and prisoners. There was to be no pillage without permission, and no embezzlement of spoils; instead their distribution was to be officially regulated from the top. Disposal of prisoners too was centrally controlled; no enemy who threw down his arms might be killed, no prisoners were to be ransomed or concealed, and all must be promptly reported to the lord general.

The last four groups of articles regulated the men and procedures that made the army work: the officers in charge of the men; the muster-masters who numbered and paid them; the victuallers who supplied them; and the justice system that tried and punished them. Officers' duties, as set out in the first of these groups, included supervision of their men on the one hand and themselves refraining from forbidden activities on the other. They must ensure their soldiers' attendance at sermons and prayers and also be aware of their discontents so that they could warn the lord general of dangerous unrest, and they were to prevent duels and quarrels. They were also charged with careful training of their troops, a requirement that reflected the emphasis that the new military 'science' placed on drill as a preparation for effective action. These were positive duties. The negative prohibitions revealingly addressed the weaknesses expected in the officer corps. Officers must not be drunk on duty, they must not quarrel, they must not defraud soldiers of their pay or embezzle supplies, they must not fiddle muster lists for their own profit, they must not be absentees. We will encounter all of these offences in the chapters that follow.

The articles finally turned to the auxiliary groups that were not directly engaged in combat: muster-masters, victuallers, and agents of military law. Money and supplies, the sinews of war that could never be divorced from the fighting part of the army, required regulation. So muster-masters were subject to bureaucratic checks that, it was hoped, would make fraud and profit from inflated troop numbers impossible and that would provide at least a rough estimate of available manpower. They were also designed to ensure that camps did not contain a floating population of unaffiliated, unregulated soldiers who moved from one regimental muster to another to pump up numbers and pay. Regulation of victuallers was intended to ensure that the food they provided was neither 'unsound, unsavoury, or unwholesome' nor overpriced, and also that their lodgings did not become centres of disorderly after-hours conviviality. In both cases the interests of honest administration overlapped with the need to control the conduct of camp populations. Last, the articles addressed the administration of justice and the enforcement of the laws previously set out, and the agents of the law. They dealt with the powers of the council of war and the respect due to it, the duties of the provost marshal as the army's chief law enforcement official, and relations between civilians and the army and between military and civilian jurisdictions. Comprehensive as these regulations appear their framers, aware that they could not legislate for every eventuality, retained the compendious 'devil's article' that asserted the right to regulate and punish the unforeseen. Like Arundel's, Essex's 'devil's article' claimed the residual authority of 'the generall Customes and laws of Warre'.[54] Detailed written law coexisted with the power of custom and hence the authority of professional expertise.

---

[54] *Lawes and Ordinances . . . Arundel*, 25, 'Concerning the administration of *Justice*', no. 14.

The substantive changes to parliamentary articles in the years after 1642 responded to deficiencies revealed by actual experience in war. So in the second half of 1643 Essex issued articles that revised the provisions relating to the administration of justice in ways that strongly suggest a response to venality and abuses of power by the army's law enforcers, and a belief that they too should be subject to the law. The article dealing with runaways from the enemy was also revised so that unregistered defectors could henceforth be hanged as spies. Another addition recognized that soldiers' predatory violence must be controlled if the civilian population was not to be alienated. So a new article forbade the soldier to 'abuse, beat, [or] fright his Landlord, or any Person else in the Family, or [to] extort Mony or Victuals, by violence from them'. It vividly brings home the intrusion of war into private lives, but legislation hardly solved one of the enduring problems of a war on home ground; it reflected rather an equally enduring anxiety over the relations between soldiers and the civilians among whom they lived.[55]

More significant than these changes, however, was one that arose from a bitter question that early in the war confronted both sides. Under what conditions could surrender of a stronghold be acceptable? In a war characterized by innumerable sieges many officers faced the problem and the consequences, for surrender could have disastrous effects on lives and careers; it is not surprising that those who surrendered were anxious to proclaim that their action was consensual and that responsibility was shared. The relevant article in Essex's 1642 formulation, which comprehended not only towns and forts but also magazines, food, arms, and ammunition, merely stipulated (like earlier articles) that they must only be yielded 'upon extremity', and that initiatives to surrender must be handled officially through the military governor and his council of war. The practical difficulties of deciding what constituted 'extremity' soon emerged, and were complicated by the fact that what might appear acceptable military extremity to soldiers might appear premature, cowardly, or treacherous submission to less pragmatic, less professional civilians. One of the most notorious early cases of this kind was Nathaniel Fiennes's surrender of Bristol at the end of July 1643, for which he was condemned to death. Although he was later reprieved his reputation did not recover until Prince Rupert too was forced to surrender the city in 1645 (and encountered similar suspicion and damage to his reputation).

---

[55] *Laws and Ordinances of Warre, Established for the better Conduct of the Army, By . . . the Earl of Essex* (1643), B[v], C2[v], D3, [D4], 'Of Duties in generall', no. 8; 'Of Duties in the Camp and Garrison', no. 19; 'Of Administration of Justice', nos. 2, 3, 10. This set of articles, authorized by Essex on 25 Nov. 1643 and printed by Luke Fawne, was stated to be 'of late inlarged by my Command' [D4[v]]. Firth was apparently unaware of this revised Essexian version. He plausibly attributed another, undated, set of articles printed by John Wright, to Fairfax's army (*Lawes and Ordinances of Warre, Established for the better Conduct of the Army* [n.d.]), which in fact exactly repeated Essex's expanded version of 1643, but mistakenly noted that this 'Fairfax' version contained additions that either 'differ[ed] considerably' from or were '[n]ot in the *Lawes and Ordinances* issued by Essex'. Firth, *Cromwell's Army*, 401, 407, 411.

It is not clear whether the amendment of Essex's articles was a response to the Fiennes case or represented a more general recognition of the problem, but by November 1643 one short article had grown to three long ones.[56] The new protocols continued to mandate death for the governor of a stronghold who surrendered 'without the utmost necessity', but they now acknowledged that necessity was not a simple concept. Now a governor forced to surrender under duress from his own officers and men was to be acquitted, but the penalty for the responsible officers was death while for the men involved it was decimation—'they must cast lots for the hanging of the tenth man amongst them'. Another article addressed the tricky question of the 'extremity' that might make a surrender 'blamelesse'. It 'expressly signified' three criteria: 'extremity of want' such that 'no eatable provision' was left; no hope of aid or relief; and expectation of imminent capture so that men and arms 'must of necessity' shortly fall into the enemy's hands.[57] If it could be proved before a court martial that these criteria had been met the accused could be acquitted; if not, death and decimation followed.[58] Later parliamentary articles retained these clarifications.

If parliament's articles changed little in the course of the war except for these few responses to need and experience, and increased in total number only from ninety-five to one hundred and two, the royalists' changed markedly in ways that, we may speculate, revealed the engagement of the king himself. The first set of royalist ordinances, authorized in August 1642 and issued again in 1643, contained eighty-two consecutively numbered and reasonably pithy articles.[59] Later in 1643, however, a revised version appeared, and the preamble noted that the orders regulating 'successfully governed' foreign armies had now been 'advisedly considered', as had 'Our own observations' and the advice of the lord lieutenant-general and the council of war in Oxford. They now consisted of a hundred and fifty-three articles, still consecutively numbered, densely printed,

---

[56] *Laws and Ordinances of Warre . . . Essex* (1643), [A^v]–B^v, 'Of Duties in generall', nos. 3–5. Thomason noted on his copy, 'These are different from the former Impression, By these Colonel Nath. Fiennes was tried at St. Albans & condemned.' This can mean either that the articles were in existence before the surrender of Bristol, or that they were revised in response to the surrender but before the trial. Cf. Firth's belief (see n. 55) that the change came after the formation of the New Model army in 1645. Firth, *Cromwell's Army*, 280, 302, 401.

[57] An unspoken consideration behind this last criterion was that something could probably be salvaged by a negotiated surrender, in particular men and arms. For earlier attempts to define conditions that excused surrender see articles published in 1619 by Edward Davies, who had served in Flanders under the Spanish. These accepted that a soldier might be 'a man of valour' and yet 'constrained' to surrender, but they also set out the conditions that precluded honourable surrender: so long as the commander had victuals, men, munitions, hope of succour, and a defensible position he must not do so. Edward Davies, *The Art of War, and Englands Traynings* (1619), 66–7, 130. The book was dedicated to Prince Charles. I am grateful to Linda Levy Peck for drawing my attention to Davies.

[58] It appears that this was not an either/or situation but that all three criteria must be met for acquittal. *Laws and Ordinances of Warre, . . . Essex* (1643), [A1^v]–B, 'Of Duties in generall', nos. 3–4.

[59] *Military Orders and Articles Established by His Majesty* (1642).

and without either divisional headings or marginal guides to content. Despite the appeal to foreign example, observation, and professional expertise, the general impression is one of complicated micro-management.[60]

Although the military basics remained common to the regulations of both sides, there were differences that went beyond the royalists' overburdened pages or their predictable insistence on the king's sacrosanct dignity and the duty of loyalty. On the one hand, the revised royalist articles added a limited right to ransom. Prisoners 'of note and quality' were to be delivered to the king, but those 'of meane ranke' could be kept by the takers, although they could only be ransomed with the permission of king or general. The practical effect appears to have been slight.[61] On the other hand, early royalist articles ignored the issue of surrender, although it had been addressed in pre-war ordinances, and the revised articles continued to shy away from examination of concepts of extremity and necessity, despite the fact that royalists too had their share of problematic surrenders. Instead, in their revised form, three new short articles forbade communication with the enemy, mandated death or decimation for those who undertook it and reward for those who resisted it, and absolved the governors of strongholds who were 'compelled' by their fellows to surrender.[62]

Two areas in particular reveal more significant variations between the articles of the two sides. The first is religion, and here, contrary to expectations, the royalists outdid the parliamentarians, at least in the quantity of legislation. Parliament's religious articles did not change in the course of the war. They retained their original three articles governing 'Duties to God' and the fourth, in the section on officers' duties, requiring attendance at sermons and prayers. The royalists too devoted their introductory articles to religion, in words virtually identical to parliament's. Both parties began with a prohibition of blasphemy against a trinitarian God and 'the known Articles of Christian Faith', and both specified the same punishment of boring through the tongue with a red-hot iron.[63] The next articles prohibited cursing and absence from sermons and public prayers. Parliament folded respect for places of public worship into the latter article, but

---

[60] *Military Orders And Articles Established by His Maiesty, For the better Ordering and Government of His Maiesties Army* (Oxford, 1643), 1–2, and *passim*.

[61] Ibid. 19, no. 136.

[62] Ibid. 17, nos. 121–3. Articles issued for the earl of Newcastle's northern army in 1642 had retained the 'necessity' criterion for surrender. These ordinances were distinctive in several ways. Not only were they concise (only fifty-one articles), but the first two clauses declared that every soldier, officers and men alike, must take the Oath of Supremacy, and that 'No Papist of what degree or quality soever shall be admitted to serve in our Army'—a provision missing from other royalist articles. They also, uniquely, provided for a lifetime pension for any soldier who was 'maimed, or los[t] any limbe' in the service. *Orders and Institutions of War, Made and ordained by His Maiesty, And by Him delivered to His Generall His Excellence The Earle of Newcastle* (1642), 3, 5, 7, nos. 1, 2, 32, 46. Despite the claim of the king's involvement, they appear to have been the work of a different hand from that responsible for the articles issued in Oxford.

[63] See e.g. *Military Orders and Articles Established by His Majesty* (1642), 2, no. 1; *Lawes and Ordinances of Warre . . . Essex* (1643), [A], 'Of Duties to God', no. 1.

the royalists included a separate prohibition of sacrilege against religious 'Places, and Utensils, or Ornaments' and harm to God's ministers.[64] In 1643 they added prohibitions of damage to churches and hospitals. They also inserted a further seven articles that have no parliamentary counterpart. These minutely regulated the duties of army chaplains and the means of disciplining them and, for good measure, forbade the sale of beer and other commodities when religious exercises were under way.[65]

The royalist emphasis on sacrilege, on offences against holy objects as well as holy places, is not unexpected, and contrasts with the parliamentarians' spare prohibition of harm to buildings, which was in any case subject to discretionary interpretation dependent not only on military needs but on perceptions of good or evil iconoclasm. The expanded royalist articles, however, with their added lawyerly definitions of offences and penalties, are symptomatic of the fussiness previously noted and may have been counterproductive: it is difficult not to suspect that these eleven introductory religious articles deadened hearers' attention even as they spelt out every eventuality that came to the framers' minds. Article 5, for example, specified in laborious detail the duties of regimental chaplains, while Article 6 spelt out the escalating rate at which their pay was to be docked for failure to perform those duties. The regulations serve as a salutary reminder that royalists too were concerned with godliness, but when they were followed by a further unbroken one hundred and forty-two articles soldiers' attention may have wandered.

The second major divergence is socially as well as administratively significant. All early modern European armies were afflicted with quarrelling soldiers who sought resolution to their disputes in duels and affrays. Parliament's armies were not immune, and their articles of war reflected the fact as they attempted by legislation to cool quarrels and prevent duels. From the beginning of the war, however, royalist ordinances devoted greater attention to the problem. When, in a later section, we look at the officers of civil war armies and observe the debilitating effect of habits of trigger-happy quarrelling on royalist unity, we shall see why. Legislation could not end a culture of violence, but their military ordinances suggest that, while it was widely deplored on both sides, it was more resistant to cure among royalists than parliamentarians.

Both armies tried to suppress the quarrels and disturbances inevitable among unruly soldiers. Parliament's officers were ordered to be vigilant for signs of unrest or mutiny, and soldiers were bound to obey their officers. The punishment for a soldier who drew his sword against an officer could be death, but officers too needed regulation. Those who came on duty drunk or who quarrelled and created disorders were to be 'cashiered without mercy' and replaced by a subordinate.

---

[64] Ibid. [A–A^v], 'Of Duties to God', nos. 1–3; *Military Orders and Articles Established by His Majesty* (1642), 2, nos. 1–4.

[65] *Military Orders And Articles Established by His Maiesty* (1643), 3–4, 18, nos. 5–11, 133–4.

They were forbidden to quarrel with a superior officer or to draw a sword in camp in a private quarrel and, like their men, they must not offer 'provocation' by word or act. In the understanding of the time a 'provocation' was commonly the first step to a duel or a fight, and indeed in Arundel's articles this offence had appeared in its traditional insulting form of *'giv[ing]* the *lye'*.[66] Private satisfaction for injury was prohibited, and those who ignored the prohibition faced imprisonment or worse, while the injured were urged to forgive but might also expect official and 'ample' reparation. Officers of the watch were forbidden to allow a soldier 'to go forth to a Duel, or private fight', and quarrels were to be settled by reference to a council of war rather than by fighting. Parliamentary regulations thus comprehensively covered quarrels and duels between soldiers, between officers, and between officers and soldiers. Similar provisions were to be found in royalist articles. Notably, however, only one parliamentary article specifically addressed the problem of duels, while two others did so indirectly, and none explicitly invoked considerations of honour.[67]

With royalists the case was otherwise. In 1642 the clause that forbade an officer of the watch to allow potential duellers to leave the camp was only the first of five related provisions. The second declared that it was no stain on a soldier's honour to refuse a challenge, and that indeed it was his duty to do so, while the challenger was to be punished by court martial and to make reparation. However the next article indicated the difficulties of this stand, for it was necessary to mandate severe punishment for 'upbraiding' a man who refused a challenge and instead sought satisfaction through a court martial. The fourth article imposed a death penalty 'without mercy' for challenging an officer to a duel or single combat. Finally, for those who actually fought and for their seconds (who were to be 'taken for Principalls'), the penalties, though severe, were less harsh: for officers, loss of place and permanent disqualification from army service (unless a kindly court martial could be persuaded otherwise), and for men a period on the wooden horse.[68]

These provisions were repeated in the revised royalist articles, but there were some revealing additions. One addressed the case of a superior who 'offer[ed] any personall injury to any inferiour Officer, such as with their honour they cannot put up'. Clearly the inferior was forbidden by other articles from revenge or resistance to his superior, but the wrong to his honour could not be ignored. He was offered the redress of appeal to the army's great council of war which, if

---

[66] I am indebted to Andrew Hopper for letting me see his transcripts of cases in Charles I's High Court of Chivalry, in which charges frequently took the form of 'provocation' or 'giving the lie'. See also *Lawes and Ordinances of. . .Arundel* (1639), C, 'Concerning Captains and Souldiers duties in particular', no. 18.

[67] *Lawes and Ordinances of Warre. . .Essex* (1642), 22, 'Of the duties of Commanders and Officers in particular', no. 4. Other articles addressed 'provocation' and internecine fights and affrays.

[68] *Military Orders and Articles Established by His Majesty* (1642), 6–7, nos. 47–51.

appropriate, would censure the offender however high his rank. A second article offered similar redress to private soldiers wronged by officers. More dramatically, any man who drew his sword in anger against a fellow soldier while his colours were flying either in battle or on the march was to be 'shot to death', while the same offence in any stronghold led to loss of a hand and expulsion from 'the Quarter'.[69] The revisions suggest that an army whose officials were already concerned to legislate discipline for a touchy, quarrelsome corps of officers and men had found by experience that the demands of honour could threaten hierarchical military discipline, and that habits of instant satisfaction could lead to violence against friend as easily as enemy. Royalist articles of war provide a guide to important weaknesses in the royalist war effort.

If legislation alone could do it, civil war armies would have been well-trained, steadfast, and orderly, united in friendship to their fellows, courageous in battle, respectful of civilians and their property, humane to prisoners, and willing to sublimate greed for the welfare of state and army. Unfortunately, as is often the case, legislation was more revealing of the failures of the system than of its successes. Those who drew up the legal codes for civil war armies assumed that soldiers were by their nature disorderly, corruptible, predatory, and prone to flee. The articles of war set out desiderata of conduct and provided a machinery of punishment for failure to observe the rules. The unwritten laws of war lacked such formal machinery but called on the forces of social, professional, and moral pressure and the equally powerful constraints of self-interest and reciprocity. Before we examine their success in enforcing the rules, however, we must consider the extent to which the rules themselves were made porous by exceptions.

---

[69] *Military Orders And Articles Established by His Maiesty* (1643), 5–7, nos. 23, 24, 30, 31.

9

Theory and Practice

EXCEPTIONS TO THE RULES

The rather amorphous 'system' of moral law, professional custom, and army legislation discussed so far proves to be one in which rules incorporated exceptions or, less formally, could be bent to suit circumstances. There were occasions when the protections for children, trees, or churches were rescinded, just as there were occasions when delinquent soldiers escaped punishment. When soldiers who had been cold, hungry, and unpaid for weeks refused to obey orders, for example, it was neither fair nor prudent to invoke the full severity of the articles relating to mutiny, while troops who, contrary to orders, ran amok in hot blood after a hard siege and storm were less likely to be punished harshly than those who killed in cold blood. The assignment of blame and hence the penalties of the law were subject to extenuating circumstances, from youth and inexperience to drunkenness and grief, but on other occasions the full rigour of the law was summoned up as a form of exemplary deterrence. There were also 'others' who were outside the law.

Military necessity and the demands of discipline could transcend both the protections and the regulations described so far but it did not deny the initial precepts. This dualism was demonstrated in the rules covering surrender on the field of battle. It was a fundamental rule that the life of the soldier who threw down his arms and asked for quarter should be spared, and that as a prisoner he should not be killed or ill-treated. To kill prisoners was 'savage cruelty' and 'contrary to the nature of faire warres'.[1] These protections, however, did not apply to certain classes of prisoners, in particular turncoats and promise-breakers. As a royalist commander said of a prisoner named Paty whom he proposed to hang, 'Paty shall die, deservedly by the law of armes; for having quitted the King's service, . . . and turning rebell.' His fate was no more than 'justice'.[2] It was also accepted that prisoners could be killed in reprisal or if

---

[1] Sutcliffe, *Practice, Proceedings, and Lawes of armes*, 338.
[2] Bayley, *Civil War in Dorset 1642–1660*, 245; the parliamentary commander to whom these threats were addressed implied that, as Paty had served 'only as a scribe', he was not subject to the law of arms, quite apart from the extenuating circumstance that he had only 'turned rebel', because the royalists plundered him.

they posed a threat, and it will be recalled that Shakespeare offered both of these reasons for Henry V's killing of the French prisoners.[3] In practice, as the case of Lilburne and the 'declaration of *lex talionis*' indicated, pragmatic anxiety about possible retaliation limited the use of such loopholes. In Paty's case, his parliamentarian colonel threatened reprisal: 'Patie you may hang, but will not be able to bury him; which may occasion a great mortality among you.' Paty's hanging had itself been intended as reprisal for the threatened hanging of Fabian Hodder, a royalist held by parliament and guilty of 'treachery', and both sides threatened further reprisals for reprisals. Presumably they thought better of it, as both Paty and Hodder survived.[4] Yet although prudence, common sense, even compassion, might moderate the rigour of the law, at other times, as Fluellen observed, offenders must be 'put . . . to execution; for discipline ought to be used'.[5] If some potential victims, like Paty and Hodder, were lucky, other renegades, from humble soldiers to Sir John Hotham and Colonel Poyer, found no mercy.[6]

Sieges, two of which will later be examined in detail, offered many examples of the fluctuating balance between rule and exception. Refusal to surrender was enough to cancel conventional protections, and while the outcome of a negotiated surrender was normally quarter to the defeated soldiers there were less generous options, and protections were not universally applicable. Nor were the weak and harmless infallibly immune from harm either during or after a siege. A besieging commander was under no obligation to moderate his artillery barrage to save the lives of women and children, nor was he obliged to allow them to leave even when they faced starvation. The primary duty to obtain victory then as now overrode the duty to protect the innocent, and victors evaded moral responsibility by blaming the victim.[7] Guilt was transferred to obdurate defenders, and when obstinacy forced besiegers to storm a stronghold virtually all restraints could legitimately be abandoned. What was legal, as was often pointed out, was not necessarily just, but as Sir Thomas Fairfax—generally regarded as a fair and courteous enemy—observed, there were some 'whose hearts God . . . harden[ed] to their own destruction'. In such cases, though with 'some regret', he would proceed

---

[3] Shakespeare, *Henry V*, 4. 6–7; Meron, *Henry's Wars and Shakespeare's Laws*, 155; Bernard, *Bible-Battells*, 249–51.

[4] Bayley, *Civil War in Dorset*, 244–6, 313, 315.   [5] *Henry V*, 3. 6. 55.

[6] Hotham was executed in 1645 and Poyer was shot in Covent Garden in 1649; both were parliamentarians who turned royalist. See also e.g. the three royalist prisoners hanged by parliamentarians at Plymouth as turncoats, BL Add. MS 35,297, fo. 61.

[7] Compare US General Orders, No. 100, 1863, nos. 18, 19 (Lieber's Code): 'When a commander of a besieged place expels the non-combatants, in order to lessen the number of those who consume his stock of provisions, it is lawful, though an extreme measure, to drive them back, so as to hasten the surrender . . . Commanders, whenever admissible, inform the enemy of their intention to bombard a place, so that the non-combatants, and especially the women and children, may be removed before the bombardment commences. But it is no infraction of the common law of war to omit thus to inform the enemy. Surprise may be a necessity.' Hartigan, *Lieber's Code*, 49.

with destruction 'with cheerfulness and rejoicing at the righteous judgment of God'.[8]

Even when there were no formal exceptions to the protections offered by the laws of war, it was recognized that in real life these protections must often, regrettably, be waived. One such case was the prohibition of sacrilege, which was subject to severe strains in practice. The laws of God and man required protection of the fabric and content of churches, an injunction with a long history. Both sides agreed that churches should be treated with respect, and each deplored the other's failure to do so.[9] For most royalists the buildings and the symbols of faith retained both spiritual and aesthetic value. They deplored the destruction of the cross in Abingdon's market-place on both grounds, for it was '[t]he greatest Ornament of that place, and a goodly Piece for Beauty and Antiquity. An Act so barbarous, no People that ever served a God . . . would ever have done; . . . while they pretend to avoid Idolatry, [they] commit all the Sacrilege, Murther, and Impiety that can be imagined'.[10] On the parliamentary side the issue was complicated by the difficulty of distinguishing between godly iconoclasm and dangerously 'tumultuous' destruction. Parliamentary authorities appear to have been tolerant (so long as discipline was not threatened) of anti-royalist, anti-ritualist sacrilege of the kind allegedly committed in the church at Lostwithiel, where 'in contempt of Christianity, Religion, and the Church', soldiers brought a horse to the font and christened it 'by the name of Charles, in contempt of his sacred Majesty'.[11] For many parliamentarians there could be no wrongdoing in attacking manifestations of the whore of Babylon by 'throwing down of Organs, silencing of Cathedrall Roarers, and Squeakers, battering of images, defacing the Popish paint, and gaudery of Churches'.[12]

Both sides in fact turned churches to military use for obvious reasons, and indeed the practice predated the war. They were sturdy buildings and as such the sites of courageous last stands, as at Alton in Hampshire in 1643; and they were large structures, a category in short supply, which could be used to shelter

[8] Rushworth, 6. 105. Cf. Gouge on some of the more uncomfortable passages from the Old Testament (e.g. Deut. 20: 13, 16) concerning the mass killing of enemies, Gouge, *Churches Conquest*, 295–6.

[9] For a comparable modern response, see e.g. Robert Block, 'The Tragedy of Rwanda', *New York Review of Books* (20 Oct. 1994), 7: 'Even Rwanda's churches were bloodied by the violence, both figuratively and literally . . . [T]he sanctity of God's house was not respected by those bent on killing. The largest of the massacres took place in church buildings or church compounds.'

[10] Walker, *Historical Discourses*, 17.

[11] Symonds, *Diary*, 67; and see Ram, *Souldiers Catechisme* (7th edn.), 20–2; Ram's tone in discussing sacrilege was defensive, but he argued that so long as nothing was done 'in a tumultuous manner . . . seeing God hath put the Sword of Reformation into the Souldiers hand, I think it is not amiss that they should cancel and demolish those Monuments of Superstition and Idolatry'. '[V]ery likely' God had 'stirred up the spirits of some honest Souldiers to be his instruments'.

[12] *One Argument More Against the Cavaliers; Taken from their Violation of Churches* ([1643]), 2. On the problem of soldiers' iconoclasm, see Julie Spraggon, *Puritan Iconoclasm during the English Civil War* (Woodbridge, Suffolk, 2003), 200–13.

soldiers, prisoners and horses; they served as storehouses; and they had towers that were useful for observation, sharpshooters, and even artillery, as churches in innumerable towns and villages proved. Parliamentarians did not fail to point to the sins of the royalists, who had 'not only made prisons, but by the inhuman restraint of their Prisoners, Jakes; and in *Devonshire*, and *Cornwall* stables of Gods houses'. Royalists for their part sceptically noted the ease with which godly sacrilege, theft, and disorder merged, as in the case of the soldiers who took their horses into the church at Newton St Cyres in Devon and made off with the communion cup worth £5 and the proceeds, all 8s. 2d., of the poorbox, before moving on to nearby Whitestone where they plundered a black velvet funeral pall valued at £10.[13] Nevertheless it remained the rule that soldiers should not damage or pillage churches. Parliamentary articles mandated 'severe Censure' for violation of 'Places of publike Worship'; the royalists set fines for 'every Souldier who shall abuse or prophane any the places of Gods Worship'.[14] When the rules failed the response was regret, as in a royalist's comment on his own side's taking of Leicester in 1645: 'the Town [was] miserably sackt without regard to Church or Hospital'. As with other protections it was recognized that there were practical exceptions, and in the case of churches and hospitals the rules did not apply when the enemy 'd[id] harme from thence' or soldiers were commanded by their officers to ignore them.[15]

Admirable precept succumbed to military need and unhappy circumstance at many levels. The approach to the natural world and its fruits offers a particularly clear example of the mixture of utilitarianism and altruism, of rule and exception. The Thirty Years' War had familiarized Englishmen with the 'universal desolation' that followed when crops, food, and livelihoods were destroyed.[16] Both sides paid lip service to the biblical injunction that trees, and specifically fruit-trees, should not be destroyed, and agreed that the populace should not be reduced to hunger by loss of crops and livestock. God, according to Deuteronomy, had 'by a special Law' forbidden 'forcing an axe against trees', and parliament's articles of war threatened 'severe punishment' for soldiers who did so.[17] In 1643 Charles ordered that his soldiers treat 'all Our good people

---

[13] For pre-war use of church spaces, note the recommendation in Sept. 1642 that the town magazine of Bury be returned to the 'convenient place in a vault in the church where it formerly lay which is very safe & fitting', Bodl. MS Tanner 63, fo. 146; *One Argument More Against the Cavaliers*, 2; Symonds, *Diary*, 41. For royalist use of churches for storage of gunpowder, ammunition, and supplies, and of church towers as a site for artillery, see Carte, *Original Letters and Papers*, 1. 114; *The Latest Remarkable Truths, (Not before Printed) From Chester, Worcester, Devon, Somerset, Yorke and Lancaster Counties* (1642), [4, 6]; HMC, *Manuscripts of the Marquess of Bath*, 1 (1904), 23, 25; Bulstrode, *Memoirs and Reflections*, 73.

[14] *Laws and Ordinances of Warre . . . Essex* (1643), [A^v], 'Of Duties to God', no. 3; *Military Orders and Articles established by His Maiesty* (1643), 2–3, no. 3.

[15] Ward, *Anima'dversions*, 48; Walker, *Historical Discourses*, 128.

[16] [Vincent], *Lamentations of Germany*, 33–4; Donagan, 'Halcyon Days', *PP* 147 (1995), 75–6.

[17] *Mercurius Rusticus: or, The Countries Complaint* (n.pl., 1646), 45 (citing Deut. 20: 19, 20); Grose, *Antiquities of England and Wales*, 1. 35–6; *Laws and Ordinances of Warre . . . Essex* (1643),

with Brotherly humanity, and that none of them waste or spoyle any Corne, Hay, or other provisions'. Parliamentary articles of war followed tradition in ordering that horses must not feed on sown ground and that husbandmen must not be 'endamage[d]'.[18] This sounds both humane and, to modern ears, environmentally responsible, and indeed the latter consideration was not altogether absent. A royalist declared that the enemy 'plunder[ed] posterity' by destroying fish nurseries as they laid waste everything 'either in the Aire or Water' after the surrender of Wardour castle, and his dismay at destruction was not only economic: 'they cut down all the Trees about the House and Grounds, Oakes and Elmes, such as few places could boast the like, whose goodly bushy advanced heads drew the eyes of the Traveller on the Plaines to gaze on them'. The cutting down of the 'Woods and Groves' of Cambridge colleges and the 'Walks and Orchards' of the town were similarly resented, while parliament noted 'the barbarous destroying of . . . fruit trees' by the Cornish in the west.[19] Yet an earlier military journalist had drawn attention to the tension between humane ideal and military needs when he admitted that it was sometimes 'policy. . . .to procure famine'.[20] Civilians suffered destruction of their crops and woods as well as loss of their goods and houses, and the prolonged presence of troops could denude a countryside. Practice did not consistently follow precept.

It was recognized that in war even more than in peace strict observance of law and custom could neither be expected nor enforced. More important, however, were the caveats embedded in the precepts themselves that explicitly acknowledged the necessities of war. Charles I's proclamation exhorting protection of natural resources carried the proviso 'as much as may be'. God's prohibition against cutting down trees was explained by their food value and incorporated permission to destroy those *'which thou knowest . . . be not trees for meat'*. Churches and hospitals should not be pillaged 'except leave be first given'. And parliament's article forbidding both the burning of houses and barns and the wilful destruction of corn, hay, and straw did so provisionally: there was to be no destruction of anything that could 'serve for the provision of the Army without

C, 'Of Duty in Marching', no. 4; and compare the royalist article of 1643: 'No Souldier shall presume in his Marching or lodging, to cut downe any fruit-Trees, or to deface any walks of Trees, Parkes, Warrens, Fishponds, Houses or Gardens, or to spoyle any standing Corne in the eare or in grasse, upon paine of severe punishment', *Military Orders And Articles Established by His Maiesty* (1643), 11, no. 71.

[18] *C.R. By the King. To Our trusty and wellbeloved Our Colonells . . . and all other Our Officers of Our Army* (20 Jan. 1642–43, broadside), and see Larkin (ed.), *Stuart Royal Proclamations*, ii. 849, for another version of this proclamation; *Laws and Ordinances of Warre . . . Essex* (1643), C2ᵛ, 'Of Duties in Camp and Garrison', no. 18.

[19] *Mercurius Rusticus*, 44–5; *Querela Cantabrigiensis* (Oxford, 1646), 13; *Articles of Agreement Betweene his Excellency Prince Maurice, And the Earle of Stamford, Upon the delivery of the City of Excester* (1643), 4.

[20] Tho[mas] Gainsford, 'Observations of State, and military affairs, for the most Part collected out of Cornelius Tacitus', HEH, EL 6857 (35/c/2) (FAC), p. 62. Sherman's march through Georgia familiarized later generations with the principle.

order'.²¹ The military imperatives of supply for one's own army, of discipline and order within it, and of 'policy' took precedence in times of stress over humanity and the environment.

The protections due to humans proved to have similar reservations, although cruelties committed against women, children, the old, and the clergy remained propaganda staples of both sides throughout the war. The duty to protect them had been regularly asserted in earlier English articles of war, but that blanket protection had been eroded to accommodate military interest. The case of children illustrates the ambivalences of protection of the innocent. Under Henry V's rules the only children under 14 who could be taken prisoner were those who provided military leverage, namely the sons of lords, 'worshipfull gentlemen', and commanders, but by Henry VIII's reign the commercial incentive of ransom had extended the category to include the sons of rich men.²² With the decline of ransom children ceased to be the object of specific military legislation and rejoined the general ranks of the harmless to whom protection was due. Throughout the civil war stories of cruelty to children—some true, some probably apocryphal—were reported with the confidence that they were outrageous departures from the norms of war and humane conduct. When a small boy was seized with his young attendant on his way to his father in Oxford and stripped and robbed by parliamentary troops, the incident was characterized as 'barbarisme to a poore Child farre from his friends, almost distracted with feare'. Equally 'barbarous' and more unequivocally 'atrocious' were stories like that of the husbandman's son half-hanged and 'pricked' with swords to see if he was still alive during an attempt to extract information.²³ Other cases marked a return to the use of children as military pawns, as in that of the gentlemen's sons taken prisoner in retaliation for royalist seizure of adults, or the use of Lord Inchiquin's son to blackmail his father into an exchange of prisoners. More notorious was the case of Lord Capel's son at Colchester, seized and paraded round the siege works in an attempt to coerce his father into surrender. And indeed, as we shall see, the starving infants of Colchester were pawns of both sides, to whom their welfare was irrelevant.²⁴

In one sense such children merely represent the vulnerability to everyday cruelty and disorder that war brought to the civilian population as a whole.

---

²¹ *Military Orders And Articles Established by His Maiesty* (1643), 18, no. 133; *Mercurius Rusticus*, 45; *Laws and Ordinances of Warre . . . Essex* (1643), C3, 'Of Duties in Action', no. 4.

²² Grose, *Antiquities of England and Wales*, 1. 42; *Hereafter Ensue certayne Statuts* (1513), C3, [no. 37], 'For children within the age of 14 year'; *Statutes and ordynances for the warre* (1544), [Bvi].

²³ *Mercurius Rusticus*, 97–8, 113; Thomas Edwards, *Gangraena: Or A Catalogue and Discovery of many of the Errours, Heresies, Blasphemies and pernicious Practices of the Sectaries of this time* (2nd edn., enlarged, 1646), 3. 173.

²⁴ Hutchinson, *Memoirs of . . . Colonel Hutchinson*, 98; Rushworth, 7. 1284. One of these cases also revealed the honourable and generous side of conduct: having given his parole, the boy prisoner refused an easy opportunity to escape, 'which handsome behaviour so tooke the Governor that he freely gave him his liberty without exchange'. Hutchinson, *Memoirs*, 98.

Yet they, like the other harmless innocents, also reveal a sense in military and civilian society that there were bounds to decent conduct, and that to cross them signalled the way to the 'barbarisme' that Sir John Conyers had condemned in Scotland in 1640: to 'kill young infants in their mothers' armes with stones . . . these are indeed inhumane and barbarous things'.[25] This sense that killing the traditionally harmless goes beyond the bounds of acceptable violence and approaches a frightening moral chaos remains familiar, and the litany of 'innocents'—women, children, the old—is unchanged.[26] Both protagonists and victims in the 1640s knew that the unutterable 'calamities and miseries of warrs' included crimes against the innocent and protected: 'children have been dashed to peeces, . . . women ravished, and crueltie committed without pittie'.[27] If such sins could not be eradicated they could, it was hoped, be limited by exhortation, military discipline and punishment, and appeal to the integrity of the Christian and moral self.

Nevertheless women, the old, the clergy, and even children could disqualify themselves from protection. To merit it they must remain innocent and harmless; it was not applicable to persons who moved from non-combatant to combatant status. Royalist soldiers were forbidden to 'tyrannise over any Church-men, aged men, or Women, or maids, or Children, unlesse they first take Armes against them'.[28] Taking up arms immediately cancelled a woman's special status as by definition weak and harmless. We shall see this proviso most extensively exploited in justifications for killing Irish women, and it extended to quasi-military activities. It had long been accepted that women who aided and abetted the enemy faced the same penalties as men, and women spies, like men, risked hanging. Even women who, termagant-like, provoked soldiers to anger, were held to have asked for what they got.[29]

The playing out of rule and exception, then, did not follow a neat and consistent pattern. Distinctions between the legal and the admirable, between the morally desirable and the militarily necessary, between actions in hot and cold blood, all affected the judgement of actions. As one reporter said temperately of the royalist storm of Leicester in 1645, an action famous for its ferocity, the 'hurts' done were 'not any thing to speak of more then what was done in heate',

---

[25] *Ruthven Correspondence*, p. xxvi.

[26] Dismay at offences against the traditionally protected continues to colour modern narratives; in Algeria, we read, 'old men and babies, pregnant women and children [were] ruthlessly slain with no discernible pattern or motive'. It was echoed in the reasoning of the 'Mexican Mafia' in Los Angeles who campaigned to restrain drive-by shootings: 'We're killing our kids and our grandparents.' *Los Angeles Times*, 'Nighttime Terror Wakes Algerians to Bloody Fates' (2 Nov. 1997); *Los Angeles Times*, 'Mexican Mafia Tells Gangs to Halt Drive-Bys' (26 Sept. 1993). In a possibly idealized recent past Los Angeles gang wars recognized 'rules' similar to those of the 17th cent.: 'You don't shoot little children or somebody's mother, let alone fire on a cemetery, hospital or church.' *Los Angeles Times*, 'An Ethic Dies With Gang Chief' (14 Apr. 1992).

[27] Bernard, *Bible-battells*, 52.

[28] *Military Orders And Articles Established by His Maiesty* (1643), 18, no. 134.

[29] *Hereafter Ensue certayne Statuts* (1513), A3; Ward, *Anima'dversions*, 48.

while the killing of women 'was casuall rather then on purpose'.[30] Partisanship too coloured judgement. One side was likely to emphasize the legality of a harsh action, the other its cruelty. Nonetheless recognition, sometimes grudging, persisted that an action, although unpalatable, might yet not be an offence. The massacre of parliamentarian soldiers who surrendered at Hopton castle was notorious, but the men had surrendered to mercy, not to quarter. They had counted on precedents in which such a surrender was generously interpreted, and were tragically wrong. But the royalist commander responsible for their deaths had acted, strictly speaking, within the law; he was called a 'bloody butcher' but he was not penalized when he himself later surrendered to the parliamentarians.[31] Generosity, charity, and humanity in interpretation of the laws of war continued to be admired, but they rarely interfered with the pursuit of military objectives.

Public sentiment, in fact, sometimes outstripped theorists and the law in its humanity. The influential minister William Gouge had not unequivocally condemned torture: it had its uses, notably in extracting information, a view not unfamiliar today. The royalist soldiers' catechism of 1645 agreed.[32] Yet reports of torture in the civil war occasioned horrified revulsion: torture was an atrocity, and as such became a tool in propaganda warfare against a barbarous enemy. So was rape, despite the disagreement among international writers as to its criminality when committed by soldiers in the heat of victory, an ambivalence that persisted long past the seventeenth century.[33] Although all agreed that rape was one of the natural hazards of war, it was condemned by moralists, army disciplinarians, and polemicists who were confident of its power to arouse public dismay and anger, and the articles of both armies forbade it, as they had for generations.[34] Accusations were cast in tones of outrage, as at Birmingham in 1643: '[The royalists] beastly assaulted many women's chastity, and impudently made their brags of it afterwards, how many they had ravished; glorying in their shame, especially the *French* among them were outragiously lascivious

---

[30] *The Moderate Intelligencer*, no. 15 (5–12 June 1645), 114.

[31] Donagan, 'Atrocity, War Crime, and Treason', *AHR* 99 (1994), 1152, 1154.

[32] Gouge, *Churches Conquest*, 296; see also S[wadlin], *Soldiers Catechisme*, 11, which ruled that 'Torments' were permissible in interrogation, for breach of faith, as retaliation ('like for like'), and as response to 'insupportable wrongs'.

[33] Meron comments that 'Under modern international law . . . the protection of women's rights to physical and mental integrity does not appear to have been a priority'; he also notes that rape was not unequivocally prohibited until the fourth Geneva Convention of 1949, and that only with the atrocities in Bosnia did 'reluctance to recognize that rape can be a war crime or a grave breach [of the Convention] beg[i]n to crumble'. Meron, *Henry's Wars and Shakespeare's Laws*, 111–13.

[34] Bernard, *Bible-Battells*, 135. Compare the laws set out for the Virginia colony in 1612, which explicitly prohibited rape of Indian as well as white women. These laws (which combined military and civil jurisdiction) made rape, sodomy, and adultery punishable by death, and fornication by whipping and, after the third offence, a public request for forgiveness. *For the Colony in Virginea Britannia. Lawes Divine, Morall and Martiall, etc.*, compiled by William Strachey, ed. David Flaherty (Charlottesville, Va., 1969), 12–13, 86.

and lecherous.'[35] The French were not always available to extenuate English guilt by demonstrating that others could be worse, but condemnation was a constant.[36]

THE MEANS OF ENFORCEMENT

The laws of war described above were mixed in nature, form, and purpose, but they presented a comprehensive and impressive body of moral, legal, and professional rules. There was, however, no expectation of perfect observance. We have seen so far that the requirements of 'morality, the nature of law, humanity, and sheer necessity' were not always compatible; that the needs of war might legitimately override laws and liberties; and that conventional restraints might fall victim to the hot blood of action, individual pathology, religious zeal, or general disorder, while necessity, then as now, was a matter of debatable and frequently scholastic interpretation. Furthermore, the justice meted out to offenders often varied according to the occasion or the zeal of commanders. The rules and their enforcement made a patchwork rather than a neat system. As the parliamentarian Joshua Sprigge observed, 'Justice is not all of one colour, all purple'.[37] It is surprising that this 'system' worked as well as it did. Despite the acknowledged flexibility of interpretation and enforcement, the protagonists continued to recognize the authority of the core norms and laws of war, to respect its unwritten laws and, on the whole, to enforce written army law, to expect reciprocal observance, and to deplore failures.

The 'embarrassment' posited by the 'social norms' approach had practical consequences and was a powerful force behind the observance of the unwritten laws of war. Sir Edmund Verney's 'civill and honourable' custom between soldiers, and criteria of reason, right, and justice, and even of 'Christian compassion', persisted with enough strength to provide the framework of relations between enemies despite the clamour of charges of breaches of the codes of war.[38] Although such charges were often manifestations of the virulent war of words

---

[35] *Prince Rupert's Burning Love to England Discovered in Birmingham's Flames*, reprinted in J[ay] (ed.), *Four Tracts relative to The Battle of Birmingham*, 31–2; compare Henry V's 'Ordinances of warre', in Grose, *Antiquities of England and Wales*, 1. 34. and e.g. *Lawes and Ordinances of Warre, Established for the better Conduct of the Army* (n.d.), [B3], 'Of Duties Morall', no. 2: 'Rapes, Ravishments, unnatural abuses, shall be punished with death.' In the Bodleian Library's copy of this set of parliamentary articles (printed for John Wright for Fairfax's army) the next article, covering 'Adultery', is one of the few marked with an 'x' in the margin.

[36] See e.g. *The Parliaments Post*, no. 6 (10–17 June 1645), 4, on reported rapes by royalist troops at Uttoxeter, 'some at the very market Crosse, an horrible thing to be spoken'. See also the report of 'barbarous usage' of 'honest women', including at least one rape, in Yorkshire in 1643 by some of Newcastle's forces, 'of which many were French'. A *Miraculous Victory Obtained by the Right Honorable, Ferdinando Lord Fairfax . . . at Wakefield* (1643), 8–9.

[37] Quoted in Round, 'The Case of Lucas and Lisle', *TRHS* NS 8 (1894), 177.

[38] Ibid. 169.

that accompanied the war of action, they reveal a bipartisan recognition that exposure of breaches of the norms could not only lose support for the offending enemy but, as 'perfidious' offences against 'the law of arms, yea against all principles of humanity and the law of nature', might even shame him into reform.[39] Despite imperfect observance, appeals to the normative customs of war continued to justify problematic actions at every level, for their authority was not confined to great events and major actors in the struggle. At the siege of Worcester in 1646, for example, they decided whether a spade could legitimately be used to make new approaches to the town during a 'cessation' or truce. The issue was resolved by appeal to a knowledgeable old soldier, who 'confessed he knew [it] never to be done or granted', and so it was decided that 'the Rules of war' supported 'a Total Cessation'.[40]

Conscientious officers did their best to enforce the conventions of war. When Fairfax was informed that his men had killed a royalist soldier in cold blood after surrender, he said, 'I much mislike it, being against my disposition and contrary to the law of arms', and he promised an inquiry and suitable punishment if the charge was proved.[41] Officers beat their own troops in efforts to force them to observe the terms of treaties of surrender. Senior officers persuaded members of parliament and reminded fellow soldiers that by the laws of war victors were not released from engagements previously entered into, and that promises made to a now defeated enemy should be kept. Parliament indeed set up a Committee of Complaints for Breach of Articles, and Fairfax argued that it 'much concern[ed] the parliament and [him]self to make good [the] engagement for the performance of. . . articles', for 'the Parliament's and Army's Honour. . . [could] not in any Thing suffer more than in the Violation of that Public Faith' engaged in 'Capitulations'.[42] We can see the conjunction of motives that sustained the power of these laws of war. On the one hand each side recognized the utility of reciprocal observance that worked in the interest of both; on the other, honour and faithfulness in keeping promises sustained the soldier's internal sense of professional and personal integrity and his external reputation. In 1645 Rupert acknowledged this conjunction of moral integrity and social benefit in adhering to the laws of war when he appealed to Essex and parliament not to instigate a descent into mutual killing of prisoners. Morally he deplored cruelty and the loss of charity and compassion. Practically he pointed to social consequences and the potential 'degeneration' of the struggle into an animosity

---

[39] For examples, see *Mercurius Belgicus* (n.pl., 1646), E2ᵛ, 18 June 1645; Bodl. MS Tanner 62/1B, fos. 168–169ᵛ; *CSPDom. 1648–49*, 112; BL Add. MS 11,331, fo. 6; *The Round-heads Remembrancer: or, A true and particular Relation of the great defeat given to the Rebels by . . . Sr Ralph Hopton* (n.pl., 1643), 5.

[40] Townshend, *Diary*, 1. 154.   [41] East Sussex RO, Danny MS 58.

[42] Firth (ed.), *Clarke Papers*, 2. 196–7; Derbys. RO, Gell MSS D3287, C/PARL/P/1c–d; *CJ* 5. 59, 419. See also *Clarke Papers*,1. 297 (Ireton on the 'scandall of neglecting Engagements'); Blair Worden, *The Rump Parliament* (Cambridge, 1977), 284; *The Kingdomes Weekly Intelligencer*, 310, 313, 314 (1–8, 22–9 May, 29 May–5 June 1649), 1351, 1374–5, 1378–9.

that would forget that enemies were also 'brethren' and fellow members of 'the English nation'.[43]

I shall return to the role of honour in military conduct when I examine the characteristics of officers and men and their behaviour on and off the field, but we may note here that it comprised more than the flamboyance of dashing gestures, courage, and touchiness to affronts to which much attention has been paid. It also manifested itself in more sober military virtues—in prudence as well as pointless risk-taking, in civility as well as the quick draw—but its bedrock was the sanctity of keeping promises. The given word, once given, should be inviolable, and the ability to depend on the enemy's word was clearly crucial to the whole system of relations between opponents. In a military, as in a civilian, society in which infrastructure and sanctions were inadequate to meet the need to regulate, police, and enforce, parties must be able to rely on promises made, explicitly or implicitly, whether in matters of trade and credit or in paroles, safe conducts, surrenders, and treaties, as well as in conventions of civility and humanity such as those governing retrieval of the dead. The obligation to keep faith was part of a wider moral world, but it was also a powerful agent in the enforcement of the rules of war.

Later chapters will reveal the remarkable successes of this moral and pragmatic approach in ordering the conduct of enemies, but they will also reveal its perennial fragility, its striking failures, and the imperfections of its practitioners. Neither officers nor men were universal paragons of military legality. When, early in the war, parliamentarians complained that the royalists had ignored the king's promise to the mayor of Banbury that he would not harm the town, cavaliers reportedly brushed aside the question of any stain on the king's honour and instead argued that the king 'did not know the condition and state of War'.[44] A royalist complaint that thievish parliamentary soldiers ignored a safe conduct issued by their own commander met an even franker response: '*Puh, say they, we care not for your Passe, you are some Papist, or other Malignant, and you may thanke Heaven . . . that you are fallen into the hands of Gentlemen*'; being gentlemen, they would not strip their victim but would settle for money. When the victim replied that true gentlemen would observe the laws of war and allow both man and goods to pass unmolested, he got short shrift: '*What care we for Articles of Warre? Mony we want, and mony we must, and will have.*'[45] Neither story will bear too close examination, but they are symptomatic of the difficulties in persuading soldiers to pay the serious attention that commanders or theorists might have wished to either the written or unwritten laws of war. As the civil war progressed its

---

[43] BL Add. MS 11,331, fos. 75ᵛ–76ᵛ. Rupert's letter was addressed to Essex (still nominally lord general); it was a reply to parliament's response to his own hanging of parliamentary prisoners (itself an act of reprisal) after he took Shrewsbury.

[44] Andrewes, *Perfect Declaration of The Barbarous and Cruell practises committed by Prince Robert*, [A6ᵛ].

[45] *Mercurius Academicus* (n.pl., 1646), 23–8 Feb. 1646, 98–9.

soldiers became more familiar with the demands of discipline and the usefulness of military custom, but on occasion even the godliest regiments still fled or plundered without regard to laws, and in enforcing rules officers had to preserve a difficult balance between excessive severity with its consequent desertion and mutiny, and excessive forbearance that resulted in an army that was both unfit for action and an intolerable burden on civilians.

The written articles of war set out the basic framework for enforcement of their regulations. Both sides, as we have seen, sought to ensure publicity for their articles. 'Books' were provided to officers for the weekly readings and these, announced by drum or trumpet, were to be plain and distinct so that 'none may be ignorant of the Lawes and Duties required'. At least in theory soldiers were aware of the nature and quality of their acts and of their consequences.[46] Publicity, however, was hardly enough to discipline an army, and the traditional machinery of military justice operated in the armies of the civil war. Each army had, on its general staff, an advocate general and a provost marshal general. The first was the commander-in-chief's legal expert, the second was responsible for the execution of justice. Each regiment in turn had a provost marshal, whose varied duties included apprehension and disposition of offenders, and he in turn had assistants. Both parties to the war, recognizing the opportunities for abuse, placed limits on the powers of the marshals. They did their best to prevent extortion or bribery, so the articles required that marshals must act only on specific charges for which, in serious cases, the approval of the advocate general was required, and that in the absence of such a charge the prisoner must be released. Nor might marshals free prisoners on their own authority or allow them to escape.[47]

All officers and soldiers had a responsibility to 'detect, apprehend, and bring [offenders] to punishment', and they themselves became offenders if they were 'slack' in their duty. This was clearly a council of perfection, and there was much variation in the discipline officers either chose or were able to exercise. The ideal, however, remained swift justice after brief restraint, followed by speedy and visible punishment calibrated according to the seriousness of the crime and to the circumstances. Some offences earned a mandatory death sentence, while for others the choice of life or death was at the discretion of the court. The language of the articles made the distinctions clear. While some articles were couched in terms of 'shall die without mercy' or 'shall be punished with death', others offered a discretionary death penalty or 'severe' or 'arbitrary correction'. There was a crucial distinction between the mandatory 'shall' and the conditional 'may' or 'upon pain of death'. 'Murther', said the parliamentary articles, 'shall be expiated with the death of the Murtherer', but stragglers offended 'upon pain of

<hr>

[46] *Military Orders . . . Established by His Maiesty* (1643), 8, no. 46; *Lawes and Ordinances . . . Essex* (Sept. 1642), 31.

[47] *Military Orders . . . established by His Maiesty* (1643), 15–16, nos. 111–14; *Laws and Ordinances of Warre . . . Essex* (1643), D3–[D4], 'Of Administration of Justice', nos. 2–3, 10.

death'—they might die for their offence, but the court was free to choose from a range of options.[48] For lesser offences there was a wide range of punishments short of death.

Courts martial carefully discriminated between categories of offences and punished accordingly. Parliament's articles of 1642 and 1643 demonstrated the gradations of crimes and their punishments, and their roster of mandatory capital offences reflected both the moral distinctions according to which crimes were judged and the degree of threat they represented to army security. Predictably, these applied to universally recognized moral crimes, to crimes that endangered the army or subverted loyalty to its commander, and to those that sowed dissension between soldiers. Thus, as in civilian law, murder, rape, and 'unnatural abuses' earned a mandatory death penalty, although other sexual offences were matters for discretionary and variable punishment. Theft and robbery above the value of 12d. also fell into the mandatory category of death 'without mercy', as did a group of offences directly related to army security, notably intelligence with the enemy, revealing the watchword, and drunkenness or sleeping on sentinel duty. Another 'mandatory' group identified mortal sins in action, including premature surrender and flinging away arms and powder in order to flee in battle. Order and hierarchy were addressed in the capital penalty for words tending to the death of the lord general. Some mandatory capital offences had a less immediately obvious rationale, but they reflect the customs and anxieties of mid-seventeenth-century armies. Violation of a safeguard, that is, a document officially issued by a commander that promised protection to the persons or goods of travelling civilians, messengers, and prisoners on parole, threatened the whole structure of trust that governed exchanges between enemies. It also defied the general's authority, and the breach of promise reflected on his honour. The death penalty for the officer who drew his sword on a brother officer who was attempting to part quarrelling soldiers suggests anxiety to prevent the formation of officer-led factions in an army, and to ensure that the solidarity of officers against men did not lapse into the heterogeneity of rival bands and their leaders. The death penalty for 'interlopers' who brought roving bands to inflate muster figures reflects a similar anxiety to exclude rogue groups outside the formal command structure—as well, of course, as to prevent financial fraud.

Other serious offences, however, came under the 'discretionary' rubric, allowing useful flexibility to courts martial. Mutiny, for example, fell in the 'on pain of death' category, which meant that the court could take into account different kinds and degrees of mutiny, extent of involvement, and mitigating circumstances, or alternatively the urgency of the need to terrify restive soldiers

---

[48] *Laws and Ordinances of Warre . . . Essex* (1643), [B2ᵛ], B3–[B3ᵛ, Cᵛ], D, [D4]: 'Of Duties Morall', no. 7, 'Of a Souldiers Duty touching his Arms', nos. 1, 2, 6, 'Of Duties towards Superiours and Commanders', nos. 1–9, 'Of Administration of Justice', no. 9, 'Of Duties in the Camp and Garrison', no. 9.

into obedience. Other distinctions prove similarly sensible: although flinging away arms and powder in order to flee earned a mandatory death sentence, flight in battle *per se* did not. Flight was so common that armies could hardly afford to kill or even decimate all who ran; guilt and punishment, again, depended on circumstances. Although threatening the death of the lord general was a mandatory capital crime, striking an officer was a discretionary one. The large and varied class of offences for which the death penalty might be imposed at discretion ranged from uttering seditious words to resisting arrest by the provost marshal, from unauthorized taking of a husbandman's horse from the plough to selling the army's ammunition, from discharging a weapon at night to unlicensed pillaging after battle or unauthorized departure from the camp. These potentially capital offences were heavily weighted towards order and discipline, and towards keeping soldiers where they should be, on duty when they should be, and as effective as possible in action. Many similar but lesser offences merited varying forms of 'severe' retribution. Soldiers who were not fully armed when they came on the watch or to drill risked 'severe correction', while officers who outstayed their leave were to be punished at the general's discretion. Quarrelling with a superior officer or pumping up muster lists with the names fictitious soldiers led to cashiering, a punishment that was both dishonourable and, as it led to loss of position and pay, costly.[49] Given the number and variety of regulations it is not surprising to find some surviving copies of articles of war dotted with marginal lines and pointing fingers.

Royalist articles, like parliament's, distinguished 'according to the importance and quality of the fact' between mandatory and discretionary death penalties and other punishments. Both sides shared the menu of punishments, although royal articles were more likely than parliament's to link specific offences to specific penalties: they required, for example, that a soldier who failed to repair to his colours when called was to be 'clapt in Irons'.[50] Nominally at least royalist articles appear to have offered less room for professional discretion than did parliament's.

The most striking difference between the penalties prescribed by the two parties lay in the distribution of capital punishment. Of the offences in the royalists' one hundred and fifty-three articles, fifty-four (35 per cent) merited death; of these the penalty was mandatory for thirty and discretionary for twenty-four. In parliament's one hundred and two articles, forty-eight offences (47 per cent) merited death but the penalty was mandatory for only fourteen and discretionary for thirty-four. The royalists' lower percentage of articles offering the death penalty reflects their larger total number of articles (including those covering chaplains' duties and other minutiae), but their percentage of mandatory death penalties is significantly higher (20 per cent to parliament's 14 per cent), while the actual number of mandatory death penalties was twice as

---

[49] *Laws and Ordinances of Warre . . . Essex* (1643), 'Of the Duty of Muster-Masters', no. 4.
[50] *Military Orders And Articles Established by his Maiesty* (1643), 2, 6, 9, nos. 1, 29, 60.

high (thirty against parliament's fourteen). We can only speculate on the reasons for and consequences of this difference, and in the absence of systematic royalist court martial records we cannot know to what extent justice was tempered by mercy. Given the common pre-war background of many leading soldiers it is difficult to attribute the difference to continental influence. Some instances may reflect particular unhappy experiences, such as the royalists' mandatory death penalties for victuallers who provided 'unsound' food 'whereby sicknesse may grow in the Army', and for negligent scouts who slept, drank, or idled away their time, offences for which parliament legislated respectively 'Imprisonment, and further Arbitrary Punishment' and punishment 'at discretion'.[51] It is tempting but speculative to see again a royal predilection for micro-management at work.

EXECUTING JUSTICE

It is now time to turn to the execution of justice. Although both sides promptly issued articles of war after the beginning of hostilities, they were not universally and immediately adopted. This seems to have been partly a consequence of administrative uncertainty and inertia and partly the result of constitutional anxiety over potential conflict between military and civilian jurisdiction. The latter point leads to one of the potential pitfalls in discussion of these formally legislated laws of war, namely the sense of the term 'martial law'. Contemporaries referred to the articles of war indiscriminately as martial law or military law, but 'martial law' comprehended both the law of the articles and its modern sense of replacement of civilian government by military power, with accompanying loss of the protections of civilian law. Claims of a right to try and punish soldiers by military law and to exclude civilian law from the process confronted the fear that civilians could be placed under military authority and thereby lose their rights under the old and true law of England. Memories of the Petition of Right of 1628 had hindered execution of Northumberland's articles of war in 1640, when legal experts had opined that 'Martial law' could only be executed in England 'when an enemy is really near at hand', and that Northumberland and his lieutenant-general Viscount Conway therefore needed a pardon for executing a soldier for mutiny. If this were known, observed Conway, 'there [would] be no obedience', for 'who shall compel the soldier?'[52] Jurisdictional problems nevertheless persisted. In June 1641, after a captain was hacked to pieces by his

---

[51] *Military Orders And Articles Established by his Maiesty* (1643), 15, 16, nos. 107, 117; *Laws and Ordinances of Warre . . . Essex* (1643), D2ᵛ, Bᵛ, 'Of Duties in Generall', no. 6, 'Of Victuallers', no. 1.

[52] Quoted in Charles M. Clode, *The Administration of Justice under Military and Martial Law, as Applicable to The Army, Navy, Marines, and Auxiliary Forces* (1874), 7–8; and see William S. Holdsworth, 'Martial Law Historically Considered', in id., *Essays in Law and History*, ed. A. L. Goodhart and H. G. Hanbury (Oxford, 1946), 8–18.

mutinous soldiers, his colonel Sir Thomas Glemham, a professional soldier and soon to be a distinguished royalist, 'sent up to the Parlmt. for to have the exercise of Martiall Law, wch before was inhibited by order of Parlt, & all misdemeanors in the Army referred to the Justices & Constables'.[53] In later years the king's secretary Sir Edward Walker was to comment bitterly that 'the clashing of the Civil and Military Powers amongst us, and . . . the fond Opinion that no Law must be broken, but War and Rebellion suppressed and managed by the Power of Justice of Peace, and Constable, has mainly contributed to our ruin'.[54]

On both sides the restraints on the use of 'martial law' in the modern sense were powerful. Nevertheless it was sometimes imposed to meet particular crises. In August 1644 parliament's anxieties about security and order in London resulted in the grant of martial law powers, in their modern sense, to a commission made up of soldiers and members of parliament for use against soldiers or civilians accused of communicating and plotting with the enemy. Its duration, however, was limited to four months and the House of Lords prevented an extension. It was not until April 1646 that another ordinance setting up a court martial in London passed, but its duration too was short—a scant three months—while its jurisdiction was strictly military, being confined to troops then stationed in the city.[55] Similar reservations over granting powers of martial law were evident in Kent in 1645, when 'secret practices, . . . Uproars, . . . Seditions', warlike assemblies, and designs to seize Dover castle led to the establishment of a council of war empowered to punish all cases that came under 'Military cognizance' according to 'the course and customs of Wars and Laws of the Land'. This extension of military powers to the civilian population was regarded as exceptional and unfortunate. A contemporary commented, 'I am sorry that *County* requires so severe a *Course*, that the *Parliament* is forced as it were to fence them in, from running at their own ruine'.[56] Parliament was also, however, prepared to reinforce military law when necessary by granting a kind of hybrid jurisdiction that gave civilian bodies limited supplementary powers of enforcement, but both the powers and their duration were circumscribed. In June 1645, for example, faced with a flood of runaway conscripts from the New Model army, it granted county committees six months' power to try and punish them in accordance with the articles of war (including the power to impose the death penalty).[57] In all such cases, in the spirit of the Petition of Right, the ultimate authority to extend special 'martial' powers was jealously retained in the

---

[53] Cambridge University Library, MS, Mm, 45. 1,33. I am indebted to David Cressy for this citation.

[54] Walker, *Historical Discourses*, 239–40. The argument remains familiar.

[55] Firth and Rait, 1. 487–8, 715–16, 842–5; Gardiner, *Civil War*, 2. 105.

[56] *Mercurius Britannicus* (9–16 June 1645), 783; Firth and Rait, 1. 674–5, 692–4. The first martial law ordinance for Kent was passed on 23 Apr. 1645, and replaced by the second on 7 June which added civilians to the commissioners appointed to the court. Each was valid for six months only.

[57] Ibid. 1. 715–16.

hands of parliament, and indeed was sometimes a bone of contention between its two houses; they were granted exceptionally and for strictly limited periods of time.

The royalists too suffered from conflicts between military and civilian interests for, as Walker indicated, appeals to the rule of true, English, civilian law complicated the lives of those running the war on both sides. In 1644 and 1645 the royalists in Worcester were forced to accept the presence, and the voting rights, of civilians in court martial cases other than those narrowly concerned with military discipline, but even this did not satisfy civilian demands. In 1645 the king was presented with propositions from the associated western counties that would not only have created a virtually autonomous force but one not subject to military jurisdiction, in which all offences were to be tried by commissions of oyer and terminer and of the peace. Further propositions would have effectively removed soldiers' protections under military law and have substituted trial at common law—'every subject's Inheritance'—in all cases involving civilians.[58]

Both sides, in fact, suffered from unresolved conflicts of jurisdiction between 'Civil and Military Powers' and from the divide, still familiar, between those for whom the demands of perceived security overrode the right to legal protections, and those who were reluctant to impose martial law in its modern sense. In practice, it seems clear that soldiers and politicians knew which kind of martial law they were talking about at a given time, although the well-known dictum that martial law could not be imposed while the courts were open in London offered little guidance in a civil war. It is important to remember that in the war years 'martial law' was more likely to bear the neutral meaning of military law than the constitutionally loaded modern sense.

Soldiers remained convinced that civilians and their law were hostile to them and fears persisted that they would suffer from judges 'not practiced in our profession'.[59] Civilians equally distrusted military law to protect their rights, persons, and property. Yet as Conway knew, armies could neither fight efficiently nor protect vulnerable civilians without reasonably effective execution of military law. As one captain wrote in a bad poem, 'An Army without rule a tumult is', but at first some members of parliament had been reluctant to authorize a distinct military code. Essex, however, successfully argued that if he had 'no Commission of Martial Law, he could not be answerable for what mischief might happen or disorder that might ensue'. On 29 August 1642—a day after the promulgation of the king's articles—parliament discussed a list of military crimes and appropriate punishments, and in September Essex's first set of *Lawes*

---

[58] Townshend, *Diary*, 2. 167, 196–201, 211. The official response to these proposals allowed for proceedings by commission of oyer and terminer but also promised punishment 'according to the strictest discipline of war', ibid. 2. 199.

[59] Memorial of army officers, 1641, quoted in Conrad Russell, 'The First Army Plot of 1641', *TRHS* 5th ser. 38 (1988), 89; BL Add. MS 11,332, fo. 11.

and Ordinances of Warre was issued.[60] It owed little to parliament beyond authorization; it was, as we have seen, a direct descendant of Northumberland's pre-war articles.

Even after official authorization, the articles were apparently slow to take hold. In November 1642 parliament complained of the 'great Inconveniences' resulting from lack of 'strict and severe Discipline' and failure to put Essex's articles in 'due execution', and declared that henceforth soldiers could expect no further 'Forbearance' and must be punished 'according to their demerits'.[61] Unfortunately the problem of army discipline could not be solved by parliamentary fiat. Furthermore, problems also arose over extending the rule of military law to forces not directly under central command, and parliamentary authority was invoked to allow wider enforcement. In January 1643, when troops were being raised in Lincolnshire, members permitted Essex to appoint a deputy general with power to 'use Martial Law to compel Obedience'. Yet Fairfax later recalled that at the end of June 1643 he was still unable to punish soldiers in Yorkshire who, in the midst of battle, stripped and plundered the body of one of their own officers for, he said, '[W]e had not yet martial law among us.' Fortunately on that occasion God intervened and a shot from a royalist cannon killed two of the offenders and wounded the rest; Fairfax was quick to assure his men that 'God would punish when man wanted power to do it.' Man's law, however, was a more reliable deterrent, and a few weeks later we find parliament mandating the use of Essex's articles to govern newly raised Sussex forces.[62] The dissemination of articles of war was thus sometimes piecemeal, and loose ends and circumstances needing special solutions persisted, but by 1644 the records of Sir William Waller's courts martial show that orderly and routine procedures had become both familiar and the norm.

There could still be questions as to how far a court martial's writ ran, and the records indicate that officers were careful about this. Even in the bitter and nervous period of the second civil war they debated the extent of their powers, and when two men were accused in 1648 of plotting to betray Pendennis to the royalists a court martial condemned one to death but raised 'some scruples' about trying the other, he 'being a Country man and no Souldier . . . The Articles of War relating to Souldiers only'. Again, in 1651, when one disbanded soldier killed another, the Dundee court martial concluded that, as neither man at the time of the killing was a member of the army, it must consult a higher authority

---

[60] Clode, *Administration of Justice*, 84; Elton, *Compleat Body of the Art Militarie*, prefatory poem by Captain William Clark; *Perfect Diurnall of the Passages in Parliament From the 29. of August to the 5. of Sept. 1642* (2nd ser. 12, [1642]).
[61] Firth and Rait, 1. 37, and see *LJ* 5. 442; *CJ* 2. 850.
[62] *LJ* 5. 538; Bodl. MS Fairfax, 36, 'A Short Memorial of the Northern Actions during the war there, from the year 1642 till the year 1644', p. 10ᵛ.

before proceeding.[63] Similar legal fastidiousness will be apparent in the actual conduct of cases before courts martial.

When we turn to the administration of the written law the records prove to be more informative for the parliamentarians than the royalists, for we have two sets of reports covering extended periods of their court martial proceedings in 1644 and 1651. As yet, there appears to be nothing comparable for the royalists. The practice they reveal, however, is confirmed by other scattered reports from both sides, often attached to some newsworthy event. Strictly speaking, the 1651 records reflect a time and a situation outside the main focus of this book, but they are invaluable for the detailed insight they provide into processes and argument that were usually referred to briefly or taken for granted. Together the two sets reveal much about the kinds of cases the courts dealt with, their procedures and punishments, the attendance patterns and the reasoning of the officer-judges, and the impact of an army's presence on civilian society.

The articles of both parties legislated the organizational framework for the 'Administration of Justice'. Parliament's set out the bare bones of the system, while the royalists' helpfully elaborated its detail. Courts were to be treated with the full respect due to the law. Mockery or menace on the part of soldiers—perhaps friends of the accused—was punishable by death, while a Scot who put on his hat before a royalist court martial and declared his equality with its members was committed for the offence.[64] Formal records, kept by a secretary or clerk, further asserted the courts' legal authority. Justice was to be speedy. The articles prescribed 'Summary proceedings' for 'All controversies between Souldiers and their Captains', and all but the weightiest and most difficult cases were to be quickly settled by the council of war sitting as a court. As already noted, the soldier was protected from arbitrary imprisonment and trial, and he must be accused of a specific crime. The provost marshal had only a short time—it varied from twenty-four hours to three days—in which to obtain the advocate general's approval of a charge, and without it the prisoner must be released. The soldier was also protected from the clutches of civilian justice for, except in capital cases, a magistrate required a licence to imprison, while in civil cases of debt or trespass he must first appeal to an offender's captain, who could either adjudicate a settlement or give leave to proceed by 'due course of Law'. As a sop to civilian grievances, it was possible (at least in theory) to appeal to the lord general if the captain failed to act. In practice, as the indemnity cases of the

---

[63] Rushworth, 7. 1306; Worcester College, Clarke MSS, 21, fos. 68–70^v, and see fos. 84–6 for the resolution of the case. For a similarly careful approach to problems of jurisdiction see the painstaking opinion of the civil lawyer Dr Walter Walker on the question of whether a court martial might execute the death sentence imposed on a man who had killed a fellow soldier, once the army was no longer in action. BL Add. MS 4159, fo. 180^v. I owe this example to Cynthia Herrup.

[64] Symonds, *Diary*, 252.

late 1640s demonstrated, the conflict between military and civilian jurisdiction was not to be so easily resolved.

The court system had two levels. Members of the council of war, which acted as the commander's advisory and administrative body, sat as judges when it acted as the 'great Court for the whole army', but there were also lower regimental courts. Royalist articles explained the council of war's overlapping identities. Each of the king's armies, they said, was to have 'a grand Councell of Warre' of at least thirteen members, consisting of the most senior commander and other senior officers (from colonels to majors). Below this 'grand Councell' were the regimental councils of war presided over by the colonel or senior officer, which were to decide on smaller regimental affairs. This regimental council could become a 'Court of Warre' when necessary but its powers were circumscribed, for only the general and his 'great Court of Warre' could sentence to death, mutilation, or cashiering. A court martial was thus a council of war sitting in its legal capacity; the distinction between the two roles was more one of function than of personnel or constitutional definition. The shifting membership and multiple functions of the royalist council of war have been lucidly explored by Ian Roy, while the records of Sir William Waller's council of war in 1644 demonstrate the mingling of trial records with broader disciplinary concerns.[65] Sir Edward Dering's account of the investigation and trial of Colonel Fielding for the surrender of Reading in 1643, with its undecided crossings out of 'council' and 'court' to describe the proceedings, indicates contemporary uncertainties.[66] By 1651, however, the format and content of the Dundee records reveals legal confidence as to the role and powers of courts martial and clearer recognition of a distinction between its advisory and investigative and its trial functions.

Proceedings followed a common pattern. Before the court sat depositions were taken from witnesses. These were read in court, where further witnesses might appear in person, and where the accused made his plea. The court then passed judgment and nominated suitable punishment by the traditional method of hearing the individual opinions of its members, beginning with the most junior officer present and proceeding by rank to the most senior. In Waller's army sittings began at eight or nine in the morning and normally ended by noon. In theory his council of war met three times a week, but from April to December 1644 we have reports of only twenty-one courts martial, of which eight were clustered between 22 April and 31 May and a further six in July. The record is clearly incomplete, but external circumstance must always have affected the regularity with which the courts met. For much of 1644 Waller's

---

[65] Ian Roy, 'The Royalist Council of War, 1642–6', *BIHR* 35 (1962), 150–68; Adair, 'Court Martial Papers of Sir William Waller's Army, 1644', *JSAHR* 44 (1966), 207–9, 215, 219; Worcester College, Oxford, Clarke MSS, 21, repr. (with some omissions) in Godfrey Davies (ed.), 'Dundee Court-Martial Records 1651', *Miscellany of the Scottish History Society*, 2nd ser. 19 (1919), [1]–67.

[66] BL Stowe MS 184, fo. 53ᵛ.

was an army on the move—in sixty-three days from May to July it covered some 500 miles—and by the end of the year it was an army under stress, with an embattled general, and heading for disbandment.[67] In Dundee, however, the records—from 17 September 1651 to 10 January 1652—are those of a stationary army of occupation; reports were fuller and meetings less irregular, although still far from a thrice-weekly ideal.[68]

Verdicts were conscientiously reached, although attendance tended to flag. The records are dotted with reminders to officers of their duty to attend, which were backed up by fines and forfeiture of pay. They also suggest some democratization of military justice, for membership of the court extended below the colonels and majors specified in royalist articles. Of the one hundred and four officers who at some time sat on Waller's courts martial in 1644, the most junior were forty-four captains, but the officers who sat on the court in 1651 included at least thirty-one ensigns and cornets.[69] In 1644 attendance seems commonly to have been between twelve and eighteen, but even the most assiduous officer, Colonel Ralph Weldon, was present at only ten sessions and other senior officers attended irregularly. One conscientious captain was present at six courts, but most of his fellows attended only one or two sessions.[70] When, as in 1644, officers had multiple duties and were in action and on the move, lack of interest or laziness were not the only reasons for absence. In Scotland in 1651 the stable base of the occupying army is reflected in the recurrence of many of the same names on the court, but military demands could still conflict with attendance.[71] Although higher than in 1644 it remained variable—twenty-nine on 15 October but six on 21 October, when a lieutenant-colonel was fined for the failure of any officers from his regiment to appear. Nevertheless it was possible to acquire expertise in military law, and it is notable that the presidency of the Dundee court was, with only a few exceptions, in the hands of two senior officers.[72] The value of formal record-keeping was enhanced by this shifting court membership, for court records supplied continuity when a case was held over for later resolution. When Richard Kiddle was condemned to death on 4 May 1644 for running away from his colours, only one of the officers who

---

67 John Adair, *Roundhead General: The Campaigns of Sir William Waller* (Stroud, 1997), 199.

68 See Firth, *Cromwell's Army*, ch. 12, pp. 276–310, on discipline and the administration of justice. Waller's court martial records had not yet surfaced when Firth wrote, and as noted above, he did not address the changes in parliament's articles of war. Ibid. 280–1, 283, 302, 400 nn. 1, 2. For the frequency of meetings in 1651 see e.g. Worcester College, Clarke MSS 21, fos. [34], 37.

69 Adair, 'Court Martial Papers . . . Waller', 212, 223–6; Worcester College, Clarke MSS, 21, fos. 19ᵛ, [28ᵛ bis], 36.

70 Adair, 'Court Martial Papers . . . Waller', 223–6; Firth, *Cromwell's Army*, 1. xix, 81–5, 176, 179, 2. 451–3.

71 Worcester College, Clarke MSS, 21, fo. 7ᵛ, for a trial postponed until the horse returned from an expedition so that a soldier who had transferred himself from the foot to the cavalry could be tried by officers of the horse (presumably more sympathetic) as well as the foot. His ingenious defence was that he had only been a soldier for seven weeks and thought he could choose any service.

72 Ibid., fos. 19, 28ᵛ (bis), and see also fos. 19ᵛ, 29, 40 for the use of fines to increase attendance.

had originally heard the case on 26 April was present, but the court was able to reach a decision on the basis of the testimony of witnesses as found at 'folio 30'.[73]

The 1644 records reveal the justice of an army in action. While soldiers' relations with civilians were an object of concern, the primary focus of the court was on military crimes and sentences were severe. In 1651 the range of offences was wider and the punishments rarely capital. Taken together, the two courts provide a remarkably comprehensive picture of the disciplinary issues confronting civil war armies. In 1644 Waller's army was restive, discontented, and plagued by desertion, and court proceedings reflected these major problems. Of the fifty-three or fifty-four offenders (Richard and Francis Allen may have been the same man), twenty-four appeared on potentially capital charges; of these fourteen were condemned to die, but in the other cases the sentences were tempered by mercy. Of the condemned men, five were guilty of desertion (the commonest crime), three of mutiny, three of highway robbery of civilians, two of assaulting an officer, and one of an unspecified offence. Two further soldiers died for mutiny—but at the hands of their officers, not the hangman. The officers were later acquitted of murder on the ground that they had killed 'in performance of [their] duty and in the suppressing of . . . dangerous Mutiny'.[74]

Even here, where the court was addressing the urgent problems of an army in the field, we can observe the care taken to proceed in accordance with the articles of war. On 20 May, on the march from Abingdon, Robert Hollifax loitered behind the army drinking. His lieutenant ordered him to rejoin his colours, but Hollifax refused, struck the officer twice, and 'willfully refused' to hand over his arms. The court considered 'examinations and depositions' that established his guilt, and condemned him to death for the breach of two articles, 'the 5th and the 7th concerning the duty of Souldiers towards theire superior officers'. On the same day, however, a soldier who had refused to obey his lieutenant-colonel (but taken no physical action) was condemned to be 'layd neck and heeles together at the Maine Guard' for an unspecified time and fed on bread and water, after which, still neck and heels together, he was to be brought to the head of the regiment to 'make an humble acknowledgement of his fault'. This satisfied the second article under 'duties to Superiours', which mandated 'Arbitrary punishment' for quarrelling with a superior officer. The court, following the articles, distinguished between striking an officer and merely quarrelling with him.[75]

---

[73] Adair, 'Court Martial Papers . . . Waller', 211.

[74] Ibid. 217, 220–1. A third such case should probably be added, 'the Busines concerning Captaine Bruce his killing of one of his Troope'. The Judge Advocate was ordered to prepare the case on 15 July 1644, but there is no record of the resolution. Ibid. 217. A propos the total number of capital cases: fifty-four men are named, but in one instance the same man seems to appear under different Christian names.

[75] Ibid. 214.

The 1644 court also dealt with cases less immediately concerned with keeping an army together and ready to fight. It punished for actions against civilians, not only with death penalties for highway robbery but with less severe punishments for lesser robbery. Two soldiers who plundered a doublet and the 'pattern' for a pair of breeches from a Woodstock tailor were sentenced to a whole day lying neck and heels together on a diet of bread and water, and then set at liberty. Another, who plundered a shirt, an apron, and some 'triviall things' was sentenced to run the gauntlet through the whole regiment and then to be 'ignominiously discharged' from the army. Yet another, who confessed to picking a soldier's pocket of 3s., was to run the gauntlet twice. A drunken soldier who had abused and wounded one of his fellows was sentenced to fifteen minutes of the strappado followed by cashiering, as was a marshal who was a plunderer, a drunkard, and an abuser of prisoners. In a quarrel between a physician and a surgeon, essentially over status, turf, and the treatment of a patient, in which the surgeon confessed to calling the physician 'foole, and asse', the surgeon was charged with disobeying the orders of a superior officer and also, in a reversion to earlier functions of the Earl Marshal's court from which military courts martial descended, with 'scandalous words tending to the dishonour and diffamacon' of the physician. For this he was to be cashiered and imprisoned until the general's pleasure was known.[76] Similar officer sensitivity to reflections on reputation and status appeared in the case of a quarrel between two French officers involving good name and 'scandalous' charges. The court, after hearing 'many witnesses', concluded that these proceeded 'meerly from malice', and the offending lieutenant, Lewis Mareshall, was sentenced to immediate cashiering and a public acknowledgement of his 'grosse . . . and impudent' scandal-mongering, followed by imprisonment for as long as the council of war felt inclined.[77]

In September 1651, when the Dundee records begin, the city had just endured siege, storm, and sack by Lieutenant-General Monck's troops. 'The stubbornness of the enemy', said Monck, 'enforced the soldiers to plunder the town.' Scottish casualties, including civilians, had been high and spoils had been rich.[78] The court therefore met in a context in which an occupying garrison, surrounded by a native population of suspect loyalties, had recently been legitimately loosed from controls in its dealings with civilians. The court's business was not only to enforce normal army discipline, as in 1644, but to reassert control over soldiers and to pacify, by protecting as far as practicable, local civilians. The first recorded hearing took place on 17 September, less than three weeks after the town had fallen, when memories and passions were still fresh. The number of accused persons recorded between September and January 1652 was similar to that

---

[76] Ibid. 210–11, 217, 218.   [77] Ibid. 211–12.

[78] Davies, 'Dundee Court Martial Records', 3–5; Firth, *Cromwell's Army*, 2. 534–6. Davies dismissed claims of a 'general massacre' after the fall of the town, but noted that estimates of the dead ranged from 800 to 1,100, and of the number of women among them from 80 to 200.

in 1644—approximately sixty in 1651, fifty-four in 1644—but the different circumstances produced a very different range of offenders and offences.[79] Waller's court martial had tried soldiers; in 1651 the accused included at least five women and three male civilians, and a high proportion of the cases related to dealings between soldiers and civilians, both male and female. Furthermore, very few offenders were tried on capital charges; in many cases the court explicitly opted to try for misdemeanour rather than felony.

Predictably, the usual offences are to be found in 1651. Soldiers still deserted (though more rarely than when in action), quarrelled with their superiors, and were drunk and disorderly. The commonest crime, however, was now plunder, and there was new attention to moral offences, notably fornication, swearing, and—in one case—attempted rape. The defects of army discipline were apparent in the cases arising from unauthorized forays into the countryside and involving civilians, which brought into concentrated focus the perennial problems of civil war commanders in protecting civilians from soldiers and preventing soldiers from becoming an unruly mob. The disorders culminated in a conjunction of seditious threats and a mutinous brawl in Dundee's shambles that began when a hungry soldier seized a leg of mutton from one of the meat-sellers. Forced by the marshal to return it, he and other soldiers fell on 'the Markett folkes' crying 'Go all, go all, and plunder the butchers' stalls'; driven out once, they returned and plundered the market. Meanwhile other soldiers were promising that, if they were not paid by Christmas it would be 'a bluer day . . . in Dundee than that of the storming of the town', making threats against the lieutenant-general and their officers, terrorizing and abusing women, and threatening to put a 'little child . . . on the spit and roast it' or alternatively to 'boil it, it would make good broth'. In 1644 the outlook for the ringleaders would not have been hopeful; in 1651 the court decided in the case of each of the three men brought to trial that the charge would be misdemeanour rather than felony.[80]

An earlier case had demonstrated the need to rein in soldiers' power over the civilian population, and the court martial's anxiety to provide speedy and visible justice for the aggrieved and equally visible deterrence for other potential offenders. On 19 September 1651 Andrew Tindall and his father-in-law James Terry were held up at pistol-point by two troopers crying 'give mee your siller'. Tindall was robbed and Terry beaten. On 20 September the victims gave information on oath and signed the depositions with their marks. The troopers were imprisoned and on 23 September the case was heard before a court of twenty-eight officers. Henry Briggs, one of the offenders, confessed that he had taken 5s. from Tindall and 'struck the old man several times'. As a theft above the value of 12d., their offence warranted a mandatory death penalty as set out

---

[79] These figures are approximate; they do not allow for gaps in the records or for possible duplications.
[80] Worcester College, Clarke MSS, 21, fos. 73–81.

in 'Of Duties Morall'. The court however debated whether they should be tried 'upon the article of life' or the 'article of misdemeanour', and resolved on the latter. They were found guilty, upon testimony and confession, of plundering and violence against two civilians, and their sentence combined the pain, humiliation, and showmanship characteristic of military punishments. They were to

be brought from the prison, with ropes about their necks, and their faults upon their breasts, to the gallows at the time of the parade, and being tied up by the neck receive 30 stripes a piece upon their bare backs. Afterwards to ask forgiveness upon their knees for the injury done to the poor men and to the army. And after that to be kept with bread and water till they have restored four-fold to the countrymen for what they have taken away.[81]

The case demonstrates the speedy progress from crime to trial, the ways in which identity and guilt were established, and the sense that the honour of the army as a whole was engaged in the conduct of its members. More significantly in the present context, it exemplifies the care with which the nature of the crime and the appropriate punishment were adjudged: the Dundee records made explicit the processes that were usually only implicit in 1644.[82] Yet as these cases show, although the processes of courts martial were much the same in 1644 and 1651, their outcomes were strikingly different. In contrast to the twenty-four capital charges and fourteen death sentences of 1644, 1651 saw only three capital charges and two death sentences. The most plausible explanations for the disparity lie on the one hand in the pressure on an active field army in 1644 to deter by capital example its unruly soldiers from desertion and mutiny, and on the other by a recognition in 1651 that wholesale capital sentences were inappropriate for activities that were all too common among members of a garrison that was bored, inactive, unruly, frequently unpaid, and often hungry and drunk.

Once the nature of the crime had been settled and a verdict reached, the court devoted equal attention to the choice of penalty. We have already encountered most of the punishments meted out to offenders. The chief were hanging or shooting; riding the wooden horse; tying neck and heels together; a variant of the strappado; running the gauntlet; flogging; imprisonment; cashiering; and public advertisement or acknowledgement of fault. Of the capital punishments, hanging was the more common; shooting was generally reserved for the privileged, although it was also often imposed on mutineers; in 1643 Colonel Fielding, unusually, had been sentenced to beheading for unjustified surrender. Armies had their own hangmen and men were assigned the duty of erecting the gibbet and wooden horse and seeing that they were 'fit for execution'; sometimes, however, they had to fall back on civilian talent.[83] Hanging was public, before the offender's regiment and sometimes the local populace as well: Robert Bell,

81 Ibid., fos. 7–7ᵛ (bis), 11–11ᵛ (bis).
82 Adair, 'Court Martial Papers . . . Waller', 208, 220, and see 221.
83 Orrery, *Art of War*, 54.

an egregious offender who had led a gang in robbing and terrorizing civilians and was probably a spy, was sentenced to be hanged in the market-place in Dundee.[84] It was the disgraceful death of common criminals, and a denial of the soldier's last claim to honour. Hence the importance to the victims of the alternative of death by shooting, which was, as a parliamentary captain conceded to the condemned royalist Sir Charles Lucas, 'most proper to soldiers'. It was also proper to gentlemen, offering a quicker death and preserving them from the last indignity of the gibbet: to hang a gentleman was to dishonour and declass him.[85]

The common non-capital punishments were, with the exception of imprisonment, physically painful in varying degrees. Riding the wooden horse involved time on a sharply ridged, elevated wooden sawhorse, usually with muskets weighting the ankles, with the hands tied behind the back, and sometimes with the further refinement of the legs being held wide apart.[86] There was only one case in 1644, for absence from guard duty, but in 1651 it was one of the standard punishments. Its severity varied, from a benevolent sentence of half an hour with no muskets to an unspecified time—at 'discretion'—with a total of up to six muskets. It might also be followed by flogging. Tying neck and heels together, a contortion achieved by using muskets to apply torque, became not only excruciatingly painful but dangerous if prolonged, as profuse bleeding and often ruptures followed. There were four instances in 1644, for plunder and refusal to obey orders, but none in 1651. In the English variant of the strappado the victim was manacled and suspended by his wrists so that he hung on tiptoe; fifteen minutes seems usually to have been regarded as all the victim could bear. In 1644 it was imposed for cases of aggravated drunkenness and plunder, but although proposed on several occasions in 1651 it was never the chosen sentence. Running the gauntlet, a regular punishment in the Swedish army, sent the victim down the line between two ranks of his fellow soldiers, each armed with a wooden switch or cudgel, who beat him as he went. It was imposed in two cases of plunder and robbery in 1644 but in none in 1651, although it had not dropped out of general use.[87] Flogging did not appear among the chosen punishments in 1644, but in 1651 it had become, together with riding the wooden horse, a standard penalty for crimes such as mutiny, abusing an officer, and unauthorized plunder that could at other times have earned a death penalty. In 1651 it had also become a penalty of choice for moral crimes, notably fornication and swearing, which had fallen below the radar of the 1644 courts martial. The heaviest sentences were for sixty 'stripes' (paltry by

---

[84] Worcester College, Clarke MSS, 21, fos. 49–51.

[85] Firth (ed.), *Clarke Papers*, 2. 33; Worcester College, Clarke MSS, 21, fos. 29–29[v]; Orrery, *Art of War*, 54.

[86] Firth, *Cromwell's Army*, 288; Henry Marshall, *Military Miscellany; Comprehending A History of the Recruiting of the Army. Military Punishments, &c.* (1846), 152–3. Firth, rather curiously, accepts the view that this was a relatively light punishment particularly employed for 'minor' offences.

[87] See examples in 1648 and 1649 in Firth, *Cromwell's Army*, 287–8.

eighteenth-century standards, particularly as the cat of nine tails was not yet in use), but some were for a mere ten. Publicly administered, they were often part of a composite penalty that included elements such as public confession, restitution, or imprisonment. Cashiering too was matter of shaming, as the offender was ceremonially expelled from the army before his fellows, usually after a confession of his fault, but it also entailed the practical penalties of loss of income and profession. In Waller's army in 1644 seven men were cashiered and discharged and two cashiered and imprisoned. It was primarily a punishment for officers and non-commissioned officers—including the surgeon who disobeyed and abused his superior officer the physician, and the lieutenant who maliciously libelled his captain. It does not appear in the 1651 records, but it remained a standard army punishment.

Finally there was imprisonment. To modern minds it is the normal penalty for both civilian and military crimes but for seventeenth-century armies, for both practical and theoretical reasons, it could not hold this default position. It is not surprising that there were only three sentences of imprisonment in 1644. The accused was normally held in custody by the provost marshal before trial, but prison space was always in short supply and for an army on the move imprisonment was not viable as a standard long-term punishment. In a garrison it was more practicable, but in 1651 it was nevertheless imposed in only six cases, and in some it was a conditional alternative to, for example, making restitution to a victim. Once incarcerated the prisoner's pain or comfort depended on the prison-keeper, and not all were humane.

Faced with this smorgasbord of punitive choice, courts deliberated carefully and endeavoured to make the punishment fit the crime both in its severity and, when possible, in its picturesque details. In 1651 Richard Wright was accused of stealing an ox. The court agreed to try for misdemeanour rather than felony, found him guilty, and proceeded to sentence. One by one, beginning with the ensigns, the fourteen officers present gave their opinions. The first came from Ensign Everard, who specified that Wright should ride the wooden horse under the gallows for an hour with two muskets at each heel and covered by the ox-hide. Nine of the others, including Major Dorney, the president of the court who gave his opinion last, concurred. The suggestions of the other officers had included the strappado and flogging with from ten to forty lashes, but the verdict of the majority followed Everard's suggestion, only adding a rope about Wright's neck to the ox-hide.[88] Similar attention to the aptness of the penalties appeared in cases of swearing. Major Dorney had himself informed on three offenders, one of whom had already been reproved for sitting up drinking and out of his quarters after the tattoo had been beaten and was later overheard 'swearing in a gross manner... "by god's blood and wounds"'. Then, late at night, Dorney overheard 'much swearing' among a group of soldiers and, looking in a window,

---

[88] Worcester College, Clarke MSS, 21, fos. 31–31ᵛ.

particularly noted his other two victims swearing ' "by God" . . . with other oaths and execrations'. All three were sentenced to be gagged while seated on the wooden horse for an hour, 'with their faults written upon their backs'. John Johnson's crime was worse, for he had threatened and struck his ensign as well as swearing, for which he was to be 'tied to the limbers of a piece of ordnance, and to receive 30 stripes from the Westgate to the Eastgate, and afterwards to stand half an hour under the gallows with a gag in his mouth'.[89]

The interplay of offence and punishment was not confined to formal proceedings and official penalties. Richard Symonds reported, as a piece of conventional wisdom, the power of provost marshals to administer summary justice, apparently without benefit of court martial, for they might hang men 'take[n] in actuall fault'. One wonders if this was the fate of the two 'foot-soldiers hanged on the trees in the hedge-row, for pillaging of the country villages', after which the whole royalist army was marched by the bodies, or of the disgruntled soldier who, failing in his attempt to shoot Sir William Waller, was immediately apprehended, and 'deservedly hanged'.[90] More certainly, there were many informal punishments for lesser offences. Officers quelled incipient disorders with blows or by force of personality, and a host of minor misdeeds were corrected by officers, sergeants, and corporals with canes, sheathed swords, reproofs, and 'light blows'. Sir William Brereton explained the progression, from persuasion of the 'tractable' to blows to 'the last remedy . . . of the most unruly and incorrigible' of trial by court martial, by which he endeavoured to 'hold the reins of discipline'.[91] In Dundee we learn of a sergeant who boxed one offender's ears and of a lieutenant who caned another, but such commonplace corrections were rarely recorded. The play of personality, the daily relations between officers and men, and the effect of environment on conduct were also rarely made explicit. Nevertheless it is hard not to suspect that Major Dorney was particularly zealous in his hunt for swearers, while Dundee apparently offered generous scope for sexual offences, and in both categories the ideology of a nominally godly army encouraged highly visible punishments for sins all armies legislated against.

These two runs of court martial records thus throw light from very different angles on civil war armies' problems of law and order. It may be argued that they reveal in the first case an army that had not yet been reformed, in morals and discipline, by the formation of the New Model, and in the second an army in which the ideals of the New Model had grown stale and for which the cause had lost its clarity. They also naturally ignored royalist practice. Nevertheless they allow us to observe a large degree of consistency in judgements as to the seriousness of offences and the aptness of punishments, and also the effect of the military context in the ways in which the same offence—for example, plunder

---

[89] Worcester College, Clarke MSS, 21, fos. [4ᵛ–5], 45–6.
[90] Symonds, *Diary*, 30, 251; *A Wicked Plot against the Person of Sir William Waller* (1644).
[91] BL Add. MS 11,331, fo. 25ᵛ.

or relatively minor incidents of insubordination—was punished in an army on active service, in which desertion and mutiny were urgent concerns, and one not currently in action. They reveal civilians' vulnerability to predatory and unruly soldiers, but they also remind us of soldiers' 'rights' against civilians under customary military law: one soldier caught making off with property from his landlady's house in Dundee, for example, escaped with only 'a sharp reproof', after the court accepted his defence that 'he knew not that the plunder of the town was done'.[92] The court martial records present a microcosm of the uneasy interaction of soldiers and civilians when forced into close quarters, and they demonstrate the common interest of 'respectable' society and the army command in restraining soldiers' disorders. The tailor who was robbed in 1644 and the owner of the ox stolen in 1651 shared an interest in the prompt apprehension and punishment of the offenders and, if they were lucky, in restitution for their losses. The threat to public order and public business was equally dangerous whether it came from highway robbery by soldiers in 1644 or riot and destruction of market stalls in 1651.

In general the evidence from other armies and other courts martial regarding legal proceedings and punishments confirms that from Waller's army and from Dundee, but the records from 1644 and 1651 also suggest two apparent differences between the concerns of the two sides that would repay further exploration. Although royalist articles legislated against moral and sexual offences there is as yet little to suggest that parliament's energetic prosecutions on moral grounds have a royalist counterpart, and it was only in their revised version that provisions against rape and the presence of whores in the camp were reincorporated into the roster of royalist offences. On the other hand, the use of courts martial to vindicate personal honour was a distinctively royalist practice.[93]

Dundee, as an occupied city, offered opportunities for sexual adventure to underemployed soldiers that resulted in severe execution of the relevant articles. In the absence of comparable records it is hard to tell whether proceedings there were bipartisanly characteristic or even, indeed, whether they were representative of earlier parliamentary practice. Rape and 'unnatural abuses', as we have seen, earned mandatory death sentences but other sexual offences—designated in the articles of war as 'Adultery, Fornication, and other dissolute lascivi-ousnesse'—were to be punished at discretion 'according to the quality of the Offence'. The case of attempted rape in Dundee clearly fell within the terms of military criminality. James Grahame had come to a house at midnight, forced an entrance, 'pulled off his clothes' and, when Elizabeth Michelson rebuffed

[92] Worcester College, Clarke MSS, 21, fo. 5ᵛ.
[93] See Margaret Griffin, *Regulating Religion and Morality in the King's Armies 1639–1646* (Leiden, 2004), *passim*. She points out that Holland's articles had dropped the sexual legislation to be found in Arundel's and Northumberland's, and that the earlier royalist articles did not restore them, ibid. 79. For the restored forms, see *Military Orders . . . Established by His Maiesty* (1643), nos. 128, 129.

him, had beaten her and her child black and blue. He then turned on Margaret Patterson, beat her, and threatened to send in the moss troopers and to burn her house. The evidence was clear and convincing; the court had no trouble in convicting him and the sentence was harsh though not capital, presumably because the rape was unconsummated. Once again Ensign Everard led off, proposing that Grahame be whipped from Bonnett Hill to Westgate with sixty lashes, ducked, and afterwards imprisoned at the general's pleasure. With only two exceptions the rest of the court concurred, although they dropped the ducking from the final sentence. One of the dissenters had favoured hanging, the other suggested forty lashes.[94]

In cases of consensual sex between soldiers and civilians a moralistic need, comparable to that aroused by swearing, was at work and judgements went beyond the straightforward military execution of justice evident in Grahame's trial. The cases of 'illicit' sex that came before the Dundee court martial suggest that many civilian inhabitants shared the army's interest in restraining both delinquent soldiers and their own less respectable fellows, for civilian informers initiated cases and worked in conjunction with military officials. Thomas Baldwin, apparently a civilian, called in the guard in the person of Corporal Potter and together they discovered Peter Thorne and Elizabeth Anderson in one bed and Thomas Robson and Margaret Anderson in another. Only Thorne was a soldier, but this was enough to bring military justice down on all four. Each pair was to be coupled together in irons and whipped from the Westgate to the Eastgate 'at the time of the parade' with forty lashes, after which the women were to be turned out of town until they could give security for 'good or better behaviour'.[95] Marian Gurdon earned a more severe sentence and so did the only one of her soldier partners who had the misfortune to be identified. She had, testified Isabel Alexander who shared a room with her, 'since the army's first entrance into this town entertained into her naked bed' a series of 'distinct men for the most part & most of them English men'. Isabel Rankin, who occupied the room above Marian Gurdon, testified that she saw her lie 'in naked bed' with Thomas Peacock, an Englishman, whereupon she informed the gentleman at arms at Peacock's quarters. He sent a guard to apprehend them and their accomplice Agnes Askin, who 'held the candle for them'. Gurdon and Peacock were sentenced to sixty stripes each at the cart's tail as they were whipped from Westgate to Eastgate; Agnes Askin was led through the town with them, and all three were ducked from the quay. Finally, the women were to be 'boated over

---

[94] Worcester College, Clarke MSS, 21, fos. 32–3 (for shorthand, ibid. 20, fos. 17ʳ⁻ᵛ). Davies preferred to omit this case, giving only the verdict, Davies (ed.), 'Dundee Court Martial Records', 33; Clarke's transcript both censored and expanded slightly on his own original shorthand version. As in all matters connected with the Clarke MSS I am grateful to Frances Henderson for her help and unrivalled expertise, and in this case particularly for her transcription from the original shorthand.

[95] Worcester College, Clarke MSS, 21, fos. 7, 10–10ᵛ [bis].

into Fife'.[96] In all these cases the publicity, pain, and humiliation of the offenders served as a call to moral reformation as much as to obedience to military law, although the final expulsion of the women presumably only served to move sin elsewhere.

If the royalists did not show similar moral enthusiasm, they outdid parliamentarians in their use of courts martial to vindicate or impugn honour. Such concerns were not, of course, unknown among parliamentarians. We have already encountered the condemnation of Lewis Mareshall for scandal-mongering in 1644, while Colonel Sexby's trial in 1651 has the appearance of an attempt to railroad the accused out of political and personal animus, for the court concluded that the charges demonstrated 'more malice than matter' and 'a design rather to ruin him out of passion than out of justice'.[97] For senior royalist officers, however, appeal to courts martial was a recognized if not common recourse in quarrels in which honour and political credit were at stake or in justification of potentially blameworthy actions. The cases are scattered but revealing. In 1644 a Colonel Crow brought charges against the earl of Carbery, with whom he was engaged in a long-running feud, before a council of war presided over by the king. His accusations were found to be 'unjust . . . false . . . and scandal[ous]', and for his pains Crow was committed. Early in 1645 Lord Loughborough demanded a hearing as he sought redress against the accusations of fellow officers with whom he too had long been quarrelling.[98] Colonel Fielding, as we have seen, was accused of unjustified and premature surrender of Reading in 1644, that is, of a standard military offence under the articles of war. When he was brought before a 'select court of war', however, the case in fact turned on conflicting claims as to what military honour required rather than on the degree of 'extremity' the defenders had faced. Fielding claimed that his honour bound him to observe a prior agreement with the enemy, but his accusers argued that circumstances had released him from his bond and the court concluded that he should 'lose his head'.[99]

In other cases the initiative came from putative offenders. The most famous concerned Prince Rupert. After the fall of Bristol in September 1645 the king, angered by the prince's failure in 'constancy', attempted to send him quietly into exile, while Rupert's enemies spread stories of treason. Rupert, however, demanded a trial despite the king's cold warning that if he came to Oxford he must

---

[96] Ibid., fos. 16–16ᵛ.

[97] Firth, *Cromwell's Army*, 2. 562–3. I am again grateful to Frances Henderson for allowing me to see her transcript of the full proceedings of this fascinating court martial before publication. Sexby was exonerated on fifteen of the charges brought against him and convicted, on a technicality, on the sixteenth although he had acted in it 'for the public service'.

[98] BL Harl. MS 6802, fo. 129; Newman, *Royalist Officers*, 179. In these cases the council of war was performing a hybrid function, part court martial, part court of honour.

[99] BL Stowe MS 184, fos. 53–4. Expert legal opinion was canvassed before Fielding was brought to trial, suggesting some doubt as to whether his action actually constituted a military crime, and helping to explain the focus on conflicting claims as to the demands of honour.

expect to be 'used either as an accused person . . . or as acknowledging . . . error'. Either way, the king continued, 'You must look for a far different treatment from what you have ever had; and is that not to be eschewed?' Undeterred, Rupert came without permission to Oxford and 'came straight into the presence, and without any usual ceremony, [told] his Majesty that he was come to render an account of the loss of Bristol'. After two days of hearings the court martial and the king concluded that the prince was 'not guilty of any least want of courage and fidelity'. Rupert was publicly exonerated but he was not restored to the king's favour.[100] Shortly afterwards Viscount Ogle, who had surrendered Winchester castle to the parliamentarians in October, followed Rupert's example and, propelled by reports that some of his fellows were 'unsatisfied' by his performance, dramatically asked the king for a court martial to clear his reputation. On 12 November he got his wish. All the field officers present in Oxford attended, the king's Advocate of the Army presented a formal case against Ogle, witnesses were heard, and the court found in detail that his actions fulfilled all the formal requirements (except hunger) for a 'necessary' surrender, and that 'no stain or touch of any conduct, courage, or fidelity could be fastened upon him'. At Ogle's request the verdict was sent to the king, who assured him that he was 'very well satisfied before' and that he had 'needed not' proof of his loyalty.[101] We shall return to problems arising from the sensitivities of royalist officers to aspersions on their honour.

Ogle's court martial was a charade conducted to satisfy the defendant. Most courts martial however were serious hearings that showed concern for army law as well as army discipline, that considered both victims and offenders, and that sought to serve equity, morality, and order. Yet, as Sexby's case has already suggested, in tense political times they were vulnerable to abuse, and at other times personal factors skewed findings. The cases of Fielding and Windebank (executed after his surrender of Bletchingdon House), for example, reveal that Charles I took some surrenders personally and was unlikely to allow a court to put a generous interpretation on the circumstances, while his acceptance of Rupert's vindication was less than whole-hearted. The corruptions to which courts martial were liable were acknowledged, if not regretted, in the parliamentarian Colonel Hewson's approving comment that a court 'would hang twenty ere the magistrate one'. In 1649 such a court practised politics by other means when Leveller soldier-petitioners were found to have written a letter 'scandalous' to the highest institutions of the state which, it was claimed, tended to breed mutiny in the army, and thus brought them under military jurisdiction.[102] In the show

---

[100] Warburton, *Prince Rupert*, 3. 183–203; Clarendon, *History*, 2. 536; BL Add. MS 31,022, fos. 68–9.

[101] BL Add. MS 27,402, fos. 98ᵛ–101. In a final flourish, Ogle asked the king to reissue the patent for the viscountcy bestowed on him before the fall of Winchester castle, and to date it after the court martial as a sign that he was still 'worthy' of the honour. The much-tried king agreed.

[102] S. R. Gardiner, *History of the Commonwealth and Protectorate 1649–1656*, 4 vols. (Adlestrop, Gloucestershire, 1988), 1. 31–3.

trial that followed, proceedings were full and formal and exchanges grew heated: the marshal told one defendant that 'he had no more breeding than a pig'. The court concluded that they 'in high measure' merited death, but settled out of 'Great mercy' for a sentence that exhibited in equally high measure the humiliation, publicity, shaming, and degradation that were designed to deter others and inhibit further action by the offenders. They were sentenced to ride 'with . . . faces towards the Horse-tails, before the heads of [their] regiments, with [their] faults written upon [their] breasts, and . . . swords broken over [their] heads, and so to be cashiered the Army, as not worthy to ride therein'. Once cashiered, they would be neither soldiers nor gentlemen.[103]

The ways in which military justice could be manipulated are evident in this case of the 'five small [Leveller] Beagles', which demonstrated both selection of victims for ulterior purposes and the satisfactions of deterrence by publicity and humiliation. The other face of court martial proceedings appears in the records of painstaking assessments of the nature of crimes and suitable punishments. In 1644, for example, Waller's court distinguished between three 'notorious offenders' who were to be hanged and five soldiers who, though they 'confessed themselves Guilty of death by severall articles', were dismissed to their regiments for lesser punishment 'through the meere mercy of this Court and hope of theire future amendment, desireing to make some difference between offenders'.[104] A case in 1651 showed even more careful discrimination and demonstrated model conscientiousness in the application of military law. John Dodd, by his own confession and the evidence of witnesses, had stabbed Henry Thompson to death. The court had first to decide whether they had jurisdiction, for although the men were still occupying army quarters they had been disbanded four days before the crime occurred. After hearing the relevant depositions on 20 December, the officers referred the problem to higher authority. Three weeks later, that question resolved, they returned to the case. In the early hours of 17 December Thompson had followed Dodd and one of the witnesses upstairs to the quarters they shared with a third man. There they all 'discoursed' about horses and made bets on a race, left the quarters to run it, returned, quarrelled about the winnings, and 'fell to blowes'. In the ensuing lengthy scuffle Thompson, 'being in drinke', seized a pistol, 'broke John Dodd's head with it', and had 'one hand in [his] hair and the other at his throat'. The two witnesses parted them, but Thompson returned to the attack, seized Dodd by the hair, 'and closed with him which occasioned him to strike at . . . Thompson with a pocket dagger'. In his initial defence, Dodd offered a varied list of extenuating circumstances: he had never seen Thompson before (hence no malice or forethought was involved); the scuffle had gone on for an hour before he struck; he at once pulled his knife out of the wound; he

---

[103] *The Hunting of the Foxes from New-Market and Triploe Heath to Whitehall, By five small Beagles* ([1649]), 20–4.
[104] Adair, 'Court Martial Papers . . . Waller', 212–13.

had to bind up his head with his handkerchief to staunch the blood; he had a wife in Edinburgh; he had served in Ireland and his brother was in the service. At the renewed hearing of the case, he reiterated that he had not known the victim before and that Thompson struck him first 'and made the blood run about his ears'.

It is clear that his judges were unwilling to convict Dodd of murder, but it was necessary to justify an alternative verdict. Colonel Cobbett, the president of the court at both hearings, declared himself satisfied that there was no intent to murder and 'that according to the law of England and to the law of God it is manslaughter', but his single opinion was not enough. The law of God, as expressed in the book of Numbers 35: 22, was 'debated at large by all of the officers' before the question was put whether Dodd should be tried on the 'Article of Murder' or the 'Article of Misdemeanour'. Their verdict followed the Bible word for word. In such a case of death 'suddenly without enmity... The congregation shall deliver the slayer out of the hand of the revenger of blood'; they opted for misdemeanour, but on a second question specified 'high misdemeanour'. This left the issue of punishment, and here too the decision was judicious. Dodd's immediate sentence, relatively light, was two months' imprisonment, but the rights of the victim were not forgotten, and Dodd had either to pay or enter a bond to pay in the future £20 to any putative wife or kindred of Thompson who put in a claim. A practical rider added that if there proved to be no claimant after twelve months the bond became void.[105] The court's deliberation as to crime and punishment had thus combined the varying elements ideally ruling military law—adherence to the articles of war, obedience to the law of God as found in the Bible (and interpreted by debate), recognition of the overarching authority of English law, and flexibility, humanity, and common sense in application.[106]

How well did the system of military justice work? We have seen that it was, on the whole, conscientiously administered, but we have no way of knowing how many soldiers were deterred from desertion by the sight of a hanging or persuaded by leniency to a first offence to reform their ways. Some unrepentant repeat offenders were clearly incorrigible. Some remained defiant. After their punishment the Leveller 'Beagles', rather than being cowed by public humiliation, called for a coach and drove off triumphantly to their friends in London, and two weeks later publicized their case in a provocative pamphlet 'Printed in a Corner of Freedome right opposite to the Council of Warre'.[107] On the other hand, some offenders claimed that the fear and trembling induced by last-minute reprieve had brought conversion and reformation. Mutineers

---

[105] Worcester College, Clarke MSS, 21, fos. 68, 70ᵛ, 84–6; Num. 35: 22, 25.

[106] For a similar appeal to God, the laws of the land and 'martial law' see BL Add. MS 11,331, fo. 264.

[107] Gardiner, *Commonwealth and Protectorate*, 1. 33; *Hunting of the Foxes*, title-page.

at Burford in 1649, confronted first by the prospect of their own deaths and then by the actual deaths of the selected victims, 'melt[ed] into a noble and Christian sorrow', shed copious tears, and confessed 'the odious wickedness' of their ways.[108] Many officers—probably most—believed that terror and shame worked, or at least that there was no viable alternative. Executions, in the king's words, were 'performed to the terror of others, and for the prevention of future disorders'.[109] An account of the case of three 'notorious villains' hanged in Kent in 1643 exemplified common reasoning:

[It] hath produced this good effect. That the rest partly out of fear, partly out of shame are all returned to their colours, with an acknowledgement of their crime, asking pardon and promising to redeem their fault, with their future valour, confessing these . . . were the cause of their mutiny. So that mercy in this case had been cruelty, and this drawing some blood upon mercenary rogues may save much of others better [affected].[110]

Justice, it is clear, must not only be done but also made visible, and an element of performance was central to such deterrent punishment. Military justice offered a theatre of cruelty and ridicule in which onlookers, whether horrified, frightened, or amused, shared in the action. Those who enjoyed the more mocking punishments—of the drunken soldier sentenced to the strappado with a jug around his neck and a notice of his crime on his back, or the swearer sentenced to stand on a stool 'with a cleft stick upon his tongue . . . and . . . a paper fixed on his breast, written in capital letters, signifying his offences'—became through their laughter at least temporarily complicit with the punishing authority.[111] Sometimes the publicity of punishment seems to have been merely for show or perhaps, when inflicted on an enemy, to boost morale, as when the royalists seized a messenger carrying letters from Essex and 'hanged [him] below the rendezvous, that all the army might see him as they marched by'. More commonly, public executions conveyed a public message. Prince Maurice, for example, ordered the hanging of a man who had plundered the house of the parliamentarian Lord Robartes in defiance of a 'protection . . . and . . . strict order' that promised immunity to the property. He died 'with a ticket written on him', as a warning against breaking engagements made by commanders on the army's behalf, even when the beneficiary was an enemy.[112]

So far it appears that, in the administration of this system of 'condign and exemplary punishment', all power lay with the army's commanders, its senior officers, and their juniors who sat on the courts martial, and that sentences were carried out to the letter.[113] In practice, however, constraints and discretion unpredictably modified action. Sometimes commanders gave prior warnings before enforcing the full rigour of the law and thus gave offenders a second

---

108 Gentles, *New Model Army*, 344–5.   109 BL Harl. 6851, fo. 135.

110 Bodl. MS Tanner 62/2A, fos. 468, 488.

111 Firth, *Cromwell's Army*, 289; Adair, 'Court Martial Papers . . . Waller', 207–8, 217, 218.

112 Symonds, *Diary*, 46, 54.   113 BL Add. MS 11,331, fo. 26ᵛ.

chance. In 1644, for example, the royalists issued a proclamation warning stragglers to return to their colours; only their failure to do so would activate a 'paine of death' penalty.[114] One major constraint resulted from commanders' recognition that what soldiers perceived as excessive severity or unfairness would in fact encourage a recurrence of sins they hoped to deter, notably mutiny and desertion. In Cheshire in 1645 Sir William Brereton, faced with 'inflamed' and plundering soldiers, applied the 'severe discipline' that he believed was the only way to maintain order and court-martialled four men. All four were condemned and two were promptly hanged, but he sent the others home to Lancashire for execution, 'to avoid mutiny'. He endeavoured to 'improve [the example] to the terror of all', but the fact remained that within his own army he had found it prudent to make a visible example of only two of the malefactors.[115]

Furthermore, justice should conform to customary practice and appear equitable if it was to be accepted without protest. In 1643 the king authorized Sir William Russell to try by martial law the 'principal authors' of a mutiny and to execute 'so many . . . as hath been usual in like cases'; this was to be 'performed to the terror of others, and for the prevention of future disorders', but it was not intended to go beyond familiar parameters of punishment.[116] Justice should also appear to be fair, its exemplary victims chosen neither arbitrarily nor as objects of vendetta. When it was a matter of selecting victims from among a larger group lots came into their own, and in fact the military appeal to lots was one of the few theologically acceptable occasions for their use, for it was generally held that to appeal to chance implied a denial of God's all-knowing design. Limited use was approved, however, when in the face of equal culpability there was no best or worst to dictate choice. Thus when decimation was mandated in cases of equal guilt—of groups of mutineers or deserters, for example, such as the revolted soldiers for whom Fairfax 'mercifully' ordered it in May 1649—the choice was commonly made by lot, that is, by drawing straws or slips of paper or casting dice.[117] Nevertheless, although decimation was a customary practice some held it to be cruel, and a man could not be forced to be complicit in his own death; not even the general could force him to cast dice for his life. Lots were also used to select a single victim from smaller groups, and the most famous occasion of their use in the civil war occurred in 1649 when three renegade parliamentarian officers who had turned royalist were sentenced to death. Offered the chance to draw lots to choose a single victim they refused 'to draw their own destiny', so a child drew for them. The blank lot fell to Colonel Poyer and he was shot in Covent Garden. The traditional and supernatural character of this method of

---

[114] Symonds, *Diary*, 56.   [115] BL Add. MS 11,331, fos. 20, 25ᵛ.
[116] BL Harl. MS 6851, fo. 135.
[117] *The Kingdomes Weekly Intelligencer*, 312 (15–22 May 1649), 1367.

deciding is evident in the conjunction of the 'purity' of the child and the 'purity' of the choice by chance, but the element of chance only compounded the terror and uncertainty of a death sentence.[118]

The uncertainties of punishment extended to the actual carrying out of sentences, for flexibility and discretion remained part of the system. A death sentence might be commuted or the number of stripes reduced. After the mutiny was suppressed at Burford in 1649, a cornet and two corporals were shot but a second cornet, extravagantly penitent, was pardoned by the general.[119] Nor can we assume that all those condemned to death by the 1644 court martial were actually executed; on the other hand it seems probable that the two condemned in 1651 were, in that they were clearly egregious offenders whose degree of guilt had already been triaged by the court when it opted for capital charges. However when Richard Kiddle, whom we have already encountered, was sentenced to be hanged in 1644 the court added the proviso that the sentence was subject to 'the further will and pleasure of the Generall'. Kiddle may have survived.[120]

Sentences and consequences were not written in stone. Capital sentences might be remitted by dramatic last-minute reprieves at the gallows. Cashiered soldiers reappeared in other regiments.[121] Colonel Fielding did not lose his head; instead, despite tarnished honour, he returned to royal service. Many of the Burford mutineers found their way back into parliament's army. Behind the construction of terror and severity there was always a subtext of possible mercy and reprieve, but its operation was unpredictable. Fielding's friends secured a pardon for him, but the intervention of Colonel Windebank's influential family and friends was ineffectual in the face of the king's anger. Nevertheless the right friends could help. When Captain Syppins was condemned to death in 1644 for trying to betray Guernsey to the royalists, Major-General Skippon intervened on his behalf and he was reprieved. In 1648 when William Clarke, disgruntled at the failure to keep promises made to the army, in protest carried off the colours of the Life Guard—an offence against the general's honour, it was claimed—he was condemned to be shot for breach of the articles 'concerning Mutinies, [and]...for Disobeying Superior Officers'. His fellow gentlemen of the Life Guard, however, petitioned

---

[118] J. C[ruso], *The Complete Captain, or, An Abridgement of Cesars warres* (Cambridge, 1640), 114; Firth, *Cromwell's Army*, 285–6; Symonds, *Diary*, 251; according to Symonds, a general could force men to dice for their lives if he was supported by the authority of his council of war or if a special proclamation had been issued.

[119] *The Kingdomes Weekly Intelligencer*, 312 (15–22 May 1649), 1367; Gentles, *New Model Army*, 344–5; Gardiner, *Commonwealth and Protectorate*, 1. 53–4.

[120] Adair, 'Court Martial Papers...Waller', 211.

[121] Several of the witnesses at Sexby's trial, currently officers in the army, were said to have been previously cashiered for 'divers crimes'. Worcester College, Clarke MSS, Henderson transcript, 10 June 1651.

Fairfax with 'sadness of Heart' and 'as Christians, as Soldiers, as Gentlemen', citing Clarke's good character, his 'comfortable' Christianity, his long, faithful, and courageous service, and their regret at the 'Labyrinth' that they were all 'most rashly and suddenly involved into'. Fairfax pardoned and released him.[122]

The system of military law was clearly imperfect and its results mixed. Records of soldiers' actions in major and minor actions of the war and of their relations with civilians, like those revealed in the indemnity hearings of the late 1640s, reveal its multiple failures and civilian dissatisfaction with military justice. We shall shortly look at the protagonists in the war, both officers and men, and observe the recalcitrant raw material on which the laws of war must be imposed if armies were to be tolerably orderly. Yet despite the many imperfections, the armies of both sides deserve credit for creating a system of military justice from scratch and on home ground that not only continued to recognize the power of civilian law but also conceived of army discipline as subject to its own rule of law, and that managed to impose a modicum of order and efficiency on troops who were often both unruly and unwilling.

Army justice was retributive, hence the frequent painfulness of its punishments, and sometimes reformative (as when penalties were reduced in hopes of amendment), but essentially it was deterrent. Offenders were subjected to pain, death, and humiliation because they had earned such punishment for themselves but also, and more important, because their fates, publicly performed, were designed to deter others from following their example. This exemplary, deterrent justice was based on the hope that punishment inflicted *in terrorem* would frighten fellow soldiers into conformity to military law.[123] As a broadside said of five eminent traitors in 1649:

> . . . they were condemned all to dye
> That others may behold with fear,
>   and learn to mend their lives thereby.[124]

The debate as to the efficacy of this approach was to have a long life. Nineteenth-century military reformers argued that 'terror' was not an effective way to inculcate 'moral discipline' in soldiers, that 'punishments which involve the infliction of pain, when legally imposed imply degradation and disgrace', and that '[d]egradation is unfavourable to improvement'.[125] Admittedly English armies of the mid-seventeenth century had not yet adopted some of the excesses

---

[122] Rushworth, 7. 1009–10.

[123] See e.g. 'the story . . . often repeated, and . . . much relied on, that when a man convicted . . . of horse stealing, complained that it was cruel to hang him for only stealing a horse, the Judge told him that he was not to be hanged for only stealing a horse, but that horses might not be stolen'. Quoted in Marshall, *Military Miscellany*, 201.

[124] 'The fatal Fall of Five Gentlemen', in Rollins (ed.), *Cavalier and Puritan*, 244.

[125] Marshall, *Military Miscellany*, 168–9.

of their eighteenth- and nineteenth-century successors, but given conventional pessimism as to the natural moral character of soldiers and the absence of alternative modes of punishment when, as we have seen, imprisonment was not viable on a large scale and transportation of offenders was in its infancy, they were left with terror, cruelty, and humiliation.

10

Outside the Law?

The French, we have seen, were anathematized as natural sexual predators. It was a common view, complained one French visitor, that the only good thing to come out of France was its wine.[1] Such characterizations raise questions about the distinction between mere dislike of certain groups and outlawry from the codes of war, and between habits of overheated polemic and actual conduct. Parliamentarian publicists might claim that 'French, Irish, Papists' were responsible for the 'plunderings, ravishings, butcherings, murtherings, firing and depopulation' inflicted on the English, but in practice neither religion, ethnicity, nor traditional antipathy was in itself enough to justify abandonment of those laws.[2] The English disliked many people. In this, of course, they were hardly unique. Like other nations they were chauvinist at best and xenophobic at worst, and they enjoyed a range of satisfying stereotypes of citizens of other countries, as of non-English-speaking residents of Britain, that confirmed their own moral and social superiority. The Dutch, though Protestant, were drunken boors and Charles Rich, who fought for them, called them 'Logerheads'. Italians would knife you as soon as look at you—but this did not mean that they were outside the pale of international laws. The English might link the Turks and the Spanish in polemical abuse, but in practice they were forced to allow that the Spanish were part of the European world and to recognize international conventions of conduct in their relations with them. The French might be morally deplorable, on occasion a threat to England, and tarred with popery, but in 1643 their emissary was received in London with standard diplomatic civility and optimistically viewed by some as an agent of peace.[3] The Turks, however, were outside the pale. They were 'like theyre father, the Deville', condemned for their pride, cruelty, and injustice, for their practice of slavery, and for their religion, which was worse than that of the Jews.[4] They served as a benchmark of 'otherness' but, despite the intermittent appeals for funds for the relief of captives in Algiers that continued to mark Interregnum parliaments, Turks did not impinge strongly on national consciousness, and the English did not have to think seriously about how they should behave in response to their evil actions.

---

[1] BL Harl. MS 4551, fo. 14.   [2] *Mercurius Civicus*, 49 (25 Apr.–2 May 1644), 489.
[3] BL Add. MS 46,188, fo. 96; BL Harl. MS 4,551, fos. 167–76.
[4] 'Discours of the Turkes by Sr. Thomas Sherley', ed. E. Denison Ross, *Camden Miscellany*, 16, Royal Historical Society, 52 (1936), 14, and 1–14 *passim*.

If the Turks were a paradigmatic evil 'other', this did not mean that all heathens were dismissed as beyond the protection of Christian moral standards. The first laws promulgated for the Virginia colony, published in 1612, had mandated protections for the Indians. Sir Thomas Fairfax's grandfather condemned the Spanish genocide of the 'naked harmless people' of Hispaniola, in fifty years reduced in number from two million to 'fewer than two thousand'. By 1644 John Vicars believed that in forty years the Spanish had murdered, by 'most hideous & horrible waies and devices of tortures to destruction, not lesse than 15 *millions* of the poor *West-Indians*'.[5] West Indians could be represented as harmless innocents, the victims of cruel, popish Spaniards, a view that served polemical purposes but that also appears to reveal genuine dismay at Spanish genocide. When it came to dealing with the Irish in the 1640s English moral reasoning became more complex.

When war came close to home, rules, protections, charity, and pragmatic restraint confronted long-standing prejudices, confessional passions, and claims to the right of reprisal for injuries. The practical consequences varied according to circumstance and personality, but for only one group were the laws of war formally abandoned. Prejudice against foreigners survived, but it could hardly be allowed to shape policy given the extensive presence of foreigners in both armies, whether it was parliament's 'cannonier (a Spaniard)' at Cirencester, the Polish George Sedascue, the eminent Dutch engineer Colonel Dalbier, or Waller's French Protestant artillery general Sir David Hastevik, or, on the royalist side, the Florentine officers John Davalier and Bernard Gascoyne, Lord Byron's general of horse the vicomte de St Paul, the doggedly loyal Lieutenant-Colonel Jammot, or the obscure 'major *Garneer* a Frenchman' killed at Bristol.[6] Nor was it merely a case of scattered, individual foreigners. The queen's regiment of horse was said to be 'mostly French', and the parliamentarian Hans Behre had his own troop of Dutch mercenaries. A royalist newsletter, attempting to neutralize claims that the king had raised a popish army to suppress the Protestant religion, went so far as to claim that parliament had 'whole Troopes of Papist [Walloons] in their Army'. Surrender treaties frequently addressed the issue of foreign soldiers and civilians, who were sometimes justifiably nervous as to whether they would benefit from the terms negotiated for the English. When Sir Ralph Hopton's

---

[5] Strachey, *For the Colony in Virginea Britannia: Lawes Divine, Morall and Martiall*, 12, 15, 37, 48; BL Add. MS 28,326, fo. 8ᵛ; John Vicars, *Babylons Beautie: or the Romish-Catholicks Sweet-Heart* (1644), 18–19.

[6] *A Particular Relation of the Action before Cyrencester* (1642), in Washbourn, *Bibliotheca Gloucestrensis*, 169; R. K. G. Temple, 'The Original Officer List of the New Model Army', *BIHR* 59 (1986), 68–9; Ricraft, *Englands Champions*, 82–3; *CSPDom. 1655*, 40–1; Newman, *Royalist Officers*, 104, 150, 324; *Correspondence of Sir Edward Nicholas*, 3, Camden Society, NS 57 (1897), 203; *Mercurius Belgicus*, 11 Sept. 1645 (1646), E4; and see Mark Stoyle, *Soldiers and Strangers: An Ethnic History of the English Civil War* (New Haven, Conn., 2005), 213–21, for a useful 'preliminary list' of 105 'outlanders' holding positions of authority (i.e. officers and technical experts) in both armies.

royalist army surrendered in the west in March 1646 foreigners were granted permission to leave the kingdom, which 'suited well with the strangers desires, they being afraid quarter would bee denied them, as indeed most of them do deserve'. [7]

There were other disadvantages to being a foreigner, such as lack of patrons to call on to hasten a prisoner's exchange, to provide support in hard times, or to lobby for payment of money due. When two of Waller's former officers petitioned for their arrears in 1645 they pleaded that 'for want of [their arrears], being strangers here, they suffer much'. [8] Hercules Langrish, once carrier to the queen and later a major under Waller, father to the equally parliamentarian Captain Hercules and Cornet Lucullus (who died in the service), complained of malice and neglect of his claims to arrears and payment for his disbursements for the cause to the tune of £5,000; instead, he languished in a debtor's prison.[9] Foreigners were also readily suspected of popery, a particular danger for French Protestants: Waller's quartermaster John De Levet was accused of popish recusancy in 1644.[10] Foreign-ness in fact was a useful weapon in the propaganda arsenal, ready for use when one wished to intensify the response to evil actions, while even the impeccably Protestant Princes Rupert and Maurice were aware of reservations in their acceptance by the English. When parliament's army was reformed it was largely purified of foreign elements, at least among its senior officers, but over a year later there were still rumours of an impending purge of foreign soldiers.[11] Nevertheless when Dalbier was murdered by parliamentary soldiers it was not because he was foreign but because he had offended against the laws of war: the admired parliamentarian had become a turncoat royalist. In the normal proceedings of war foreign soldiers were accorded the same professional rights and protections as the English.

Popery produced equally mixed responses. It could readily provide an excuse for mob action, as in the attack on Countess Rivers and her property in

---

[7] *The Journal of Thomas Juxon, 1644–1647*, ed. Keith Lindley and David Scott, Camden Society, 5th ser. 13 (1999), 53; Bodl. MS Add. D.114, fo. 113; Firth, *Regimental History*, 1. xv, 127; *Mercurius Aulicus*, 23 July 1643 (Oxford, 1642 [1643]), 394. This edn. of *Mercurius Aulicus* runs from 1 Jan. 1643 to 6 Sept. 1645 and is continuously paginated 1–1736. There is a gap from 7 June to 13 July 1645 (i.e. the period covering Naseby).

[8] *CAM* 1. 45. Both had served under Waller. One of the officers, Lieutenant John Drewint, may have been Dutch.

[9] *CSPDom. 1655*, 40–1. Langrish suffered from both sides; he claimed that he and his six children had been ruined by the loss, at the queen's instigation, of his wife's French estate. In addition to Hercules and Lucullus, a Captain Anthony Langrish was serving in Scotland in 1656. Firth, *Regimental History*, 2. 513.

[10] Adair, 'Court Martial Papers . . . Waller', *JSAHR* 44 (1966), 212.

[11] Temple, 'Original Officer List', 54–77; there were only two obviously foreign names on the list, those of Sedascue and Colonel Vermuyden (who was shortly to return to the Low Countries). Temple suggests that Captain Devereux Gibbon (who signed himself 'Deverx. Guybon') may have been French, but in fact both name and spelling suggest Essexian and Rich connections. Dalbier and Behre retained command of regiments of horse. Firth, *Regimental History*, 1. 127. For the presence of French soldiers in Fairfax's army in November 1646, see BL Harl. MS 4551, fo. 564ᵛ.

Essex in 1642, and conventional anti-Catholic rhetoric flourished. A pamphlet entitled *Lancasters Massacre: or the New Way of advancing the Protestant Religion . . . namely, to Cut the Throats of Protestant men, women, and innocent Children, as lately the Papists did at Lancaster* (1643) summoned up memories of the anti-Catholic atrocity literature of the Thirty Years' War and of Ireland. Some royalists were disturbed by the presence of Catholics in the king's army, and Newcastle's articles of 1642 had tried to prohibit it. Nevertheless considerations of social and economic stability and neighbourhood outweighed the attractions of populist attacks on Catholics. Parliament quickly recognized the dangers of 'turbulent times', admitting that 'the soldiers do sometimes mistake a protestant house for a papist's'. The puritan earl of Warwick's steward was sent to Countess Rivers's aid, and a pamphlet published with a parliamentary imprimatur in August 1642 lamented the pillage and 'strange inhumanities' practised by disorderly troops against papists near London, men who were 'sober, moderate, and charitable-minded' and lived 'in . . . love, and credit' with their neighbours. Such conduct 'amongst Christians against Christians' was a 'scandal' to the Protestant religion: 'nay, were they Jewes or Atheists, it is a staine to the Government of the Kingdom'.[12] This humane and tolerant response largely survived in practice amid the pressures of civil war, despite virulent polemic and periodic outbursts of sectarian violence. It was helped by links of kinship, property, and order. Many good parliamentarians—including Essex and Fairfax—had Catholic kin. Money and property were intertwined across confessional boundaries, and their sanctity came close to the sanctity of Protestantism. Furthermore Protestant and Catholic soldiers shared an international military culture. From prisoner exchanges to rules of surrender, from the sin of flight to the duty to observe official passes, they recognized the same rules of conduct. For the professional and utilitarian reasons already discussed, and despite periodic failures, they did not abandon them to suit confessional demands.

A similar pattern of basic adherence to the same codes despite conventional prejudices is to be seen in the relations between fellow Britons, although old stereotypes lived on. Wales was one of the dark corners of the land, in need of religious reformation and peopled by 'cowards' who were 'seduced . . . ignorant' and 'little less than barbarous'.[13] Old jokes about timorous, drunken Welsh with leeks in their hats were still familiar, while a royalist complained to Prince Rupert of his purported allies, 'If your Highness shall . . . command me to the Turk, or Jew, or Gentile, I will go . . . but from the Welsh, good Lord,

---

[12] Bodl. MS Tanner 63, fos. 125, 146; *A Relation of the Rare Exployts of the London Souldiers, and Gentlemen Prentizes, lately gone out of the Citie for the Designes of the King and Parliament* (1642), printed in [Wharton], 'Letters of a Subaltern Officer', *Archaeologia*, 35 (1853), 311–12.

[13] Lloyd Bowen, 'Representations of Wales and the Welsh during the Civil Wars and Interregnum', *HR* 77 (2004), 367, 371, and *passim*. For an interpretation of English relations with non-English fellow Britons as an 'ethnic history', see Stoyle, *Soldiers and Strangers, passim*.

deliver me!'[14] The principality was strongly, though not exclusively, royalist and suffered accordingly from the parliamentarians. In April 1645 complaints reached London that soldiers in the Welsh borderlands declared that as all Wales was against parliament, they could therefore 'rob and spoil . . . without mercy or distinction . . . and that no rules of war or ordinances of parliament do contradict it'. The Welsh, however, still had a voice in London. John Glynne, for example, protested to parliament's commander Sir William Brereton that such 'inhumane dealing' merely hardened in error 'many an innocent and seduced fool whose eyes might by good use be easily opened'. The Welsh, he said, felt themselves to be 'presented as enemies only and not sought after as persons we desire to reform'. Brereton and his colleagues were quick to admit that unpaid, discontented soldiers had taken too much liberty to 'carve for themselves in Wales' and had committed outrages against persons and property, but they also pointed out that it was hardly a case of ethnic discrimination: similar outrages had been committed in Cheshire. Furthermore, such actions were not officially sanctioned, and the ringleaders had been hanged. In future they would be 'careful to take no more of Wales, than what is necessary to maintain and keep the soldiers alive'. This may have offered limited comfort to the Welsh, but it recognized that, although benighted, they were redeemable, and that there was no national vendetta. The 'rules of war and ordinances of parliament' still operated, and when Chester surrendered early in 1646 the terms included specific and generous provision for the Welsh royalist soldiers.[15]

The case of Scotland was more complicated. The Scots were old enemies and had only recently invaded England. In the course of the civil wars they were by turns enemies and friends to both parties, and their soldiers were to be found in the armies of both. In principle, as we have noted, war against the Scots was treated legally as war against a foreign country, and indeed the trial of the duke of Hamilton in 1649 turned in part on whether he should be tried as an English traitor or granted the protections due to a foreign prisoner of war. The Scots were not popular in England. They were 'whoremastering rogues' and treacherous allies. Even praise could be half-hearted. As one of their English supporters said, they were 'lightly esteemed' and 'poore, dejected, and despised . . . no better than a base and barbarous people', while by the summer of 1645 another parliamentarian distrusted the 'geud Brethren' and their 'patterne for the subordination of the Ciuill power to the Ecclesiasticall'.[16] Sir Arthur Hesilrige found his unfortunate Scottish prisoners—who were dying in their

---

[14] Newman, *Royalist Officers*, 98; and see the comment on royalist foot at Bodmin in 1646: 'most . . . were Welchmen, having Leeks in their Hats, and drunk, and . . . disorderly'. [J.R.], *A Letter Sent To the Honble William Lenthal Esq; . . . Concerning Sir Tho: Fairfax's gallant Proceedings in Cornwal* (1645 [1646]), 6.

[15] BL Harl. MS 2135, fos. 68, 138ᵛ; BL Add. MS 11,331, fos. 19ᵛ–20ᵛ.

[16] Bodl. MS Tanner 63, fos. 83, 125; Will[iam] Meeke, *The Faithfull Scout: Giving an Alarme to Yorkshire . . . and all other places . . . freed from the misery of Warre* (1647), 112; 'The Letters of

hundreds from dysentery—'unruly, sluttish, and nasty, . . . rather like beasts than men' and 'exceeding cruel one towards another'.[17]

Nevertheless both sides were at different times heavily dependent on Scottish support, and many parliamentarians could not comfortably forget that the Scots had been leaders in religious defiance to the king. Conservative parliamentarians like the minister William Meeke urged that the Solemn League and Covenant bound both English and Scots to a 'firme irrefragable unity', a view that seems partly to explain—along with his wife's presbyterian enthusiasm—Sir Thomas Fairfax's reluctance to lead a pre-emptive invasion of Scotland in 1650. Sir William Waller lamented, after the Scots turned royalist, that their honour had been laid 'strangely in the dust, even to the stupefaction and astonishment of the world', but he hoped that their 'firy trial' would be 'an occasion to refine, not to consume them'. Many godly Englishmen sought comfort in God's 'dark and imperceptible' ways, and interpreted Scottish intervention as divine correction for their own sin and thus as evidence of his care for England. Yet Waller embodied a common ambivalence towards the Scots among their former allies. He could not forget past debt and admiration—'a lion is a lion though his paws be never so much pared'—but faced by a threat from Scotland he recognized that he was English born and bred, and 'no consideration shall ever make me forfeit that interest'.[18] In a crisis, national identity outweighed religious sympathy. For many less reflective and less sympathetic Englishmen, old national antipathies and present enmity could trigger bloody incidents. After the royalists stormed and sacked Leicester in 1645 (shortly before their defeat at Naseby), they killed men, women, and children, but Prince Rupert 'in his mercy put an end to their cruelties, so far as it concerned the English'. The Scots, however, 'were all put to the sword, being 200 in number', slain 'in cold bloud after quarter given to them'. Although it was claimed in extenuation that the atrocity was committed by the Irish and their English papist adherents, the prince's 'mercy' had not sufficed to protect the Scots, who had not yet become royalist allies.[19] In less lethal circumstances than those at Leicester, however, Scots could expect similar treatment to that meted out to their English friends and enemies. Hesilrige went to great pains to provide a healing diet for his 'nasty', 'cruel', disease-ridden prisoners.

Among English subjects one group was for a time in danger of exclusion from this moral and military commonwealth. Richard Symonds' account of

Sir Cheney Culpeper (1641–1657)', ed. M. J. Braddick and M. Greengrass, in *Seventeenth-Century Political and Financial Papers*, Camden Miscellany, 33, Camden Society, 5th ser. 7 (1996), 230.

[17] 'A Letter from Sir Arthur Hesilrige . . . concerning the Scots Prisoners' (1650), printed in Slingsby, *Original Memoirs*, 342–3; Highlanders survived better than other Scots, Hesilrige suggested, because they were 'hardier than the rest'. Ibid. 345.

[18] Meeke, *Faithfull Scout*, 107, 109; Ludlow, *Memoirs*, 242–4; Gardiner, *History of the Commonwealth and Protectorate*, 1. 257–65; Hutchinson, *Life of Colonel Hutchinson*, 168, 195; Waller, *Vindication*, 216–18.

[19] *A Perfect Relation of the taking of Leicester: with the severall marches of the Kings Army since the taking thereof* (1645), 5; Luke, *Letter Books*, 298.

the royalists' crossing into Cornwall in 1644 suggests that he saw the Tamar as more than a county border. While English, the county was also foreign. It was geographically remote and had unique administrative and legal characteristics, for it was a royal duchy and its stannaries jurisdiction often conflicted with common law. The Cornish retained distinctive characteristics and, despite considerable assimilation to English ways, racial difference and a tradition of independence remained. If use of the Cornish language was in decline, it was still, as Symonds noted, spoken by 'all beyond Truro', while 'at Land's-end they speake no English'.[20]

For royalists like Symonds Cornish strangeness was benign, for Cornwall was powerfully loyal to the king. For parliamentarians, strangeness translated to 'barbarism'. The Cornish were 'a crooked People'; they were 'perfidious and atheisticall'; they enthusiastically supplied the royalists with men and intelligence; and in 1644 the 'Country People', including the women, were so 'incensed' against the parliamentarians that they took prisoners and delivered them as 'daily Presents' to the king, while soldiers who rashly 'straggle[d] out of their Quarters . . . were presently either slain or taken'.[21] The Cornish campaigns had begun in January 1643 with an incident of unusual ferocity, when royalist success at Braddock Down was followed by a pursuit in which the victors 'had the full execution of [the parliamentarians] as far as they would pursue'. Clarendon declared that thereafter royalist conduct in Cornwall was 'more sparing' and that soldiers were known to have resisted the urgings of 'fiercer' officers for further 'execution' on the grounds that 'they could not find it in their hearts' to harm unarmed men. If so, it did little to change parliamentary representations of the Cornish, whose notoriety reached its peak after the overwhelming royalist victory at Lostwithiel in 1644. Royalist troops and country people, men and women alike, plundered and harassed the humiliated, broken parliamentarians as they marched away towards Poole and Southampton. The articles of surrender negotiated between the two armies were ignored, despite the efforts of the king and his officers to beat soldiers into observance and despite the summary hanging of seven plunderers on royal orders, and the escort appointed to protect the defeated on their march proved, according to the victims, only an ineffectual and 'base convoy'.[22] The royalists themselves deplored the conduct of their troops, but blamed the Cornish more: 'both Men and Women had no Compassion'. To a parliamentarian, the Cornish 'expressed the greatest inhumanity that could

---

[20] Symonds, *Diary*, 47, 74 (Symonds was interested enough to collect a glossary of Cornish words and phrases); Coate, *Cornwall*, 1–33 *passim*; M. J. Stoyle, ' "Pagans or Paragons?" Images of the Cornish during the English Civil War', *EHR* 111 (1996), 299–302.

[21] *LJ* 7. 623; Vicars, *Burning Bush*, 18; Walker, *Historical Discourses*, 50–1, 72–3; Symonds, *Diary*, 48.

[22] Clarendon, *History*, 2. 102; Walker, *Historical Discourses*, 79; Symonds, *Diary*, 66–7. In defence of the royalist convoy, we may note the claim that when they parted the parliamentary commander, Philip Skippon, gave the officer in charge 'a large Testimonial of his Civility and Care'. Walker, *Historical Discourses*, 80.

be put in execution; for they stripped our soldiers stark naked from head to foot, and left them nothing to comfort themselves in this distress'. The weather was wet and stormy, the men were hungry from lack of provisions on the hastily organized march, the Cornish refused to relieve them, and the remnant that survived to reach Poole was 'in no very good Condition'.[23] The disaster was widely reported to the general public, confirming perceptions of Cornish barbarity, and the survivors were filled with a desire for revenge. In October, less than two months later, they were buoyed up on a difficult march towards battle by 'hopes to fight with their Cornish enemyes whose barbarisme will never be pardoned till some proporcionable requitall'.[24] They found requital at Newbury where, as a parliamentarian reported, many cavaliers ran away, 'crying out, *Devils, Devils, they fight like devils*; for, ours gave no Quarter to any whom they knew to bee of the *Cornish*'.[25]

It is not surprising, after this 'great slaughter', that as the victorious parliamentarians advanced into Cornwall in early 1646 they 'found the people possest with an opinion, *That there would be no mercy shown unto the Cornish*'.[26] Yet in the event it proved otherwise. This was partly thanks to the 'civil carriage' enforced on the army, but the orderliness and absence of plunder that led the country people willingly to bring in supplies was not enough to explain their change of heart. It owed much to the character of Fairfax and Lord Hopton, the opposing commanders, who conducted negotiations for the royalist surrender with great civility and correctness, and something to judiciously circulated rumours of a possible Irish invasion, which brought 'the Country People' to the aid of parliament. Above all, it had been brought about by Cornish experience of the ravages of Lord Goring's unbridled royalist soldiers. A parliamentary reporter observed that 'there cannot be a greater advantage to us, then to drive *Gorings* Horse before us; for there carriages are so barbarous, that they make every mans hand against them where they come'.[27]

The Cornish had, in parliamentary eyes, offered many grounds for legal and moral ostracism, and their cruelties were not forgotten. Parliamentarians, congratulating themselves on their Christian usage of prisoners after victory at Naseby, contrasted it with the 'Atheisticall' and 'cruell usage of our Forces

---

[23] Ibid. 79; Vicars, *Burning Bush*, 20; Robert Codrington, 'The Life and Death of the Illustrious Robert, Earl of Essex', *The Harleian Miscellany*, 12 vols. (1808–11), 6. 34; *The Kingdomes Weekly Intelligencer*, 17 (10–17 Sept. 1644), 576–7.

[24] *The Weekly Account*, 55 (11–18 Sept. 1644), 435; *The Parliament Scout*, 65 (12–19 Sept. 1644), 519; HMC, *Portland MSS*, 1. 188–9.

[25] Vicars, *Burning Bush*, 59.

[26] [J.R.], *A Letter Sent To the Honble William Lenthal Esq; . . . Concerning Sir Tho: Fairfax's gallant Proceedings in Cornwal* (1645 [1646]), 4.

[27] Ibid.; and see Bodl. MS Clarendon, 30, fo. 103, for the effect on the Cornish of parliament's 'strait discipline' and prompt payment for goods received. See Stoyle, *Soldiers and Strangers*, 184–91, on the parliamentary tactics of rapprochement and the divisions between English and Cornish royalists that preceded the surrender in Mar. 1646.

in *Cornwall* (though upon Articles & Conditions)'.[28] Even royalists could be aroused to anger against the Cornish despite their loyalty: by November 1644 it was reported that royalists at Oxford 'exclaim against Cornwall as much as [Essex's] forces do'.[29]

At Lostwithiel the laws of war had proved an ineffectual protection not only against uncontrollable troops, but also against what was represented as an uncivilized civilian population whose barbarity was only made more manifest by the part women played in their cruelties. Many of the conditions, from cultural and racial foreign-ness to lawlessness and atrocity, were thus present for relegation of the Cornish to a condition of 'otherness', but it did not happen. In part this was because, as the war wound down from late 1645 to the final parliamentary takeover of Cornwall in early 1646, the benefits of conciliation outweighed the pleasures of rhetoric and punishment, while the late transfer of Cornish loyalties provided some atonement for past sins. Furthermore, there had always been a scattering of eminent Cornish parliamentarians like the preacher Hugh Peter and Lord Robartes, as well as humbler 'exiles' who deserved charity for their sufferings and who could now return home. It became convenient to focus on particular scapegoats and to assign the worst evils to 'the *French* and I*rish*, who, like ravenous Wolves, . . . worried' the godly in Cornwall.[30]

Parliament's claimed Christian treatment of prisoners after Naseby did not extend to the Irish. We have already noted the English proclivity for assigning moral evils to the French, but French soldiers were scattered through English armies; they did not make up a coherent group, and the withdrawal of conventional protections was not institutionalized or given formal legitimation. The Irish, however, were consistently demonized by parliamentarians and were hardly loved by most royalists. They made up, at various times, a significant proportion of royalist troop numbers—exaggerated by parliamentarians—and fears of Irish invasion could, as in Cornwall, reliably produce panic and anti-popish reaction to the detriment of the royalist cause. English antipathy to the Irish had a long history, and even English and Irish soldiers who fought side by side for the Spanish in the 1630s 'love[d] not one another'. To most English men and women the Irish were uncivilized, barbaric, and Catholic, and in 1639 their novice soldiers were dismissed by the future royalist commander Henry Gage as 'not serviceable' (unlike their English counterparts) and even when well trained as no better than 'reasonable'. Nevertheless the Irish had refused to be easily conquered despite the best English efforts, and Ireland had been the grave of generations of English soldiers and of many reputations. It was the Irish rebellion of 1641, however, that now ignited English passions, for the flood of pamphlets that poured from the presses presented both a Catholic massacre of Protestants and atrocities that brought close to home the horrors that had been so vividly

---

[28] *The Kingdomes Weekly Intelligencer*, 105 (17–24 June 1645), 841; Vicars, *Burning Bush*, 174.
[29] Luke, *Letter Books*, 71.   [30] *LJ* 7. 623.

pictured in the Thirty Years' War.[31] The atrocities were undoubtedly magnified for propaganda effect and some reports have a suspiciously formulaic character, but much was nonetheless real. In a private letter the earl of Cork wrote from Youghal to his kinsman by marriage the earl of Warwick, of the ferocity of the rebels:

they . . . are so far embrued in English blood as they grow desperate, and do all the spoil and damage to us they can, both to our bodies & goods, with fire and sword, and no longer ago than yesterday, they took eight of my tenants and hanged them up, and bound an English woman's hands behind her, and buried her alive. The cruelties they extend unto the English protestants are so many and unchristianlike [that they] are unexpressible.[32]

As often happens, atrocity bred atrocity, and Cork's letter explained the process:

now we have begun to blood ourselves upon them. I hope God will so bless his Majesty's forces here, as when I now write but of the killing of 100, I shall shortly certify you of the killing of thousands for their unexampled cruelty hath bred such desire for revenge in us as every man hath laid aside all compassion and is as bloody in his designs against the Papists, as they have been in their execution against the Protestants.[33]

He hoped to see 'the popish party of the natives' rooted out and the kingdom planted with English Protestants who would 'settle . . . in the lands of them they shall kill or otherwise destroy'.[34]

This was the legacy on which parliamentary Anglo-Irish perceptions were based in the 1640s. The prospect of the incursion of an Irish army into England produced rumours and panic fears, to which the western regions were particularly vulnerable. The cry that 'we are all as good as dead men, for the Irish Rebels are coming' spread terror as far as Bradford in 1641, and the fear of these 'Incarnate Devils' and 'Cut-throats' did not diminish.[35] By the end of 1642 there were reports of 'a great number of the Irish rebels' in the king's army and of the 'cruell and mercilesse' women who accompanied them. Wandering Irish soldiers frightened householders in Cumberland in 1643 with threats of Irish treatment and new incursions from Ireland. From London Simonds D'Ewes rather charmingly foresaw that 'these bloody murderers are like [to come] upon us like a swarm of caterpillars'.[36] The Cessation negotiated in Ireland in 1643 freed much of the royal army there for service in England and thereby reinforced the royalists in some crucial areas such as Chester, while it fuelled parliamentarian fears of an influx of 'great forces'. Even royalists were apprehensive of the 'unruliness' of Irish troops who were 'so wicked . . . and given to spoil and ruin'.

---

[31] Keith J. Lindley, 'The Impact of the 1641 Rebellion upon England and Wales, 1641–5', *Irish Historical Studies*, 18 (1972–3), 143–76; Bodl. MS Clarendon, 15, fos. 86ᵛ, 128ᵛ, 173.
[32] BL Egerton MS 80, fo. 31.   [33] Ibid., fo. 31ᵛ.   [34] Ibid., fos. 33–33ᵛ.
[35] Lister, *Autobiography*, 7–8.
[36] Andrewes, *Perfect Declaration of . . . Barbarous and Cruell practices*, A2; Bodl. MS Tanner, 62/2A, fo. 439a; Tanner 64, fo. 97.

In 1644 and 1645 there were constant reports of the actual or imminent arrival of Irish soldiers in bodies ranging in size from 2,000 to 30,000 men.[37] Many of the first wave of troops were in fact returning English soldiers who arrived, 'faint and weary', in November 1643 and in desperate need of the clothing that kindly citizens of Chester supplied. Both parties admitted a distinction between 'Native *Irish Rebels*' and 'English Irish', but it made little difference to parliamentarian practice. Even when old acquaintance was acknowledged, 'English Irish' and 'absolute Irish' were treated alike. Pathetically, it was only when their fellows were killed that returning soldiers could 'believe that Englishmen would fight with any Englishmen but Papists'.[38]

The first years of the war were marked by reciprocal but unsystematic atrocities. Irish pirates 'spoiled and tortured' their victims; the English bound Irish prisoners and threw them overboard. Ashore parliamentarians killed Irish prisoners of war and the royalists responded in kind.[39] At first these actions were ad hoc and at the discretion of the commanders involved, although they did not lack official blessing. In July 1644 Essex had written of six Irish prisoners taken in Devonshire that if they 'prove to be absolute Irish, you may cause them to be executed, for I would not have quarter allowed to those', and when a house nearby was stormed in the same month, 'the Defenders cry'd for Quarter, which was granted to all but *Irish* rebels'.[40] On 24 October 1644 parliament added its formal imprimatur and passed an ordinance requiring that 'no Quarter shall be given hereafter to any Irishmen, nor to any Papists whatsoever born in Ireland, which shall be taken in Hostility against the Parliament' by land or sea. They were to be excluded from 'capitulations' (negotiated surrender terms), and when captured they were to be 'forthwith put . . . to death'. All care was to be taken that the ordinance was duly executed, and officers who were found negligent were to be regarded as 'favorer[s] of that bloody Rebellion of Ireland' and punished accordingly.[41]

Parliament had thus legislated to override the laws of war on ethnic grounds in a matter crucial to relations between enemies. The consequences appear to have been mixed. Less than three weeks after passage of the ordinance Liverpool fell to the parliamentarians, its capture aided by the mutiny of royalist Irish soldiers against their commanders who had obstinately refused to surrender, and whom the Irish imprisoned and delivered over to the victors. They hoped that thereby 'they might themselves receive quarter'. Their hope was justified, and the

[37] BL Harl. MS 2125, fo. 135ᵛ; Harl. MS 6802, fo. 169; Luke, *Letter Books*, 633–5, 640–1, 645, 648, 650, 695; Bodl. MS Nalson 3, fo. 241; Townshend, *Diary*, 1. 128.

[38] BL Harl. MS 2125, fo. 135ᵛ; Carte, *Original Letters and Papers*, 1. 30; for conflation of Irish and English Irish see e.g. *Mercurius Aulicus* (7 May 1645), 1579; and see Stoyle, *Soldiers and Strangers*, 57–61 and 209–10 for his estimate of 9,150 men shipped from Ireland to England 1643–6, of whom only 1,970 were native Irish.

[39] Bodl. MS Tanner 62/1B, fo. 162; Tanner 62/2A, fos. 439, 442–3; Clarendon, *History*, 2. 478.

[40] BL Add. MS 29,319, fo. 11; Rushworth, 5. 690; Brereton, *Letter Books*, 1. 228–9.

[41] Firth and Rait, *Acts and Ordinances*, 1. 554–5.

surrender terms specified, contrary to the ordinance, that the Irish should be transported to Ireland after taking an oath 'never to molest England any more'.[42] A similar sense of obligation for military services rendered, combined with recognition of the practical dangers of parliament's policy, was at work in April 1645, when a local commander received an order from Sir William Brereton to execute prisoners who had deserted from the royalists. He might regret that quarter had initially been granted, wrote Major Croxton in reply, 'but having quarter given them I know of no order or ordinance that authoriseth the taking away of their lives'. He would obey a warrant from Brereton, but he pointed out that their own men, now prisoners of the royalists, 'must expect no more mercy than we intend to them'.[43]

In the latter case the ethnicity of the intended victims was not specified, but it came at a time and place in which the royalists employed Irish troops, and Brereton's order was linked to the most notorious sequence of responses to parliament's '*Golden Ordinance*, for giving no quarter to the Irish' (so described by one puritan preacher). It demonstrated all too clearly the destructive momentum of a policy of tit-for-tat reprisal. After Shrewsbury fell to the parliamentarians in February 1645 they killed thirteen Irish prisoners. Rupert, in response, hanged thirteen parliamentary prisoners. In parliamentary eyes the actions were not equivalent. In a letter sent in Essex's name but drafted by the House of Commons, they argued not only that it was absurd to give equal value to English and Irish lives but also that the Irish died 'according to an ordinance of parliament', while the 'Protestants who had quarter given them . . . were notwithstanding murdered upon cool Blood'. Legal execution and cold-blooded murder were not comparable. There could be no 'equality in Exchange with the English nation' for those who had committed such crimes (recited at length) as the Irish had.[44] For Rupert, however, the English prisoners who suffered on his orders had been 'butchered' by parliament's ordinance and by an 'unheard-of . . . Act of Injustice'; these were 'contrary to the Laws of Nature and Nations, contrary to the Rules and Customs of War, in any

---

[42] Luke, *Letter Books*, 377. The royalists felt keenly the 'disloyalty and treachery' of the Irish at Liverpool 'because they were all natives of *Ireland*, and therefore the more trusted here, as not so apt to be seduced as the people of this country'. Lord Byron ordered that any captured Irish 'may be made examples of'. He had already 'done justice' on those few who had come to hand. Carte, *Original Letters and Papers*, 1. 70–1.

[43] Brereton, *Letter Books*, 1. 29, 199–200; Dore suggests that Croxton's 'weighty arguments . . . prevailed'. See also Townshend, *Diary*, 1. 129–31, 133, 173, for an Irish prisoner saved from execution in accordance with the ordinance after a royalist officer threatened reciprocity.

[44] Edmund Staunton, *Phinehas's Zeal in Execution of Iudgement. Or, A Divine Remedy for Englands Misery* (1645), 5, 13; Bodl. MS Add. D.114, fos. 148–9 (badly damaged) and see also BL Add. MS 11,331, fos. 75ᵛ–76ᵛ; *LJ* 7. 304–6; *CJ* 4. 97 Initial reports gave the number of victims on each side as seventeen. Rupert implied that some of the victims were English Irish. *LJ* 7. 329. Essex was still nominally parliament's lord general at this time; he finally delivered up his commission on 2 Apr. Ian Gentles, *The New Model Army in England, Ireland, and Scotland, 1645–1653* (Oxford, 1992), 22–3.

parts of the Christian World'.[45] We have already noted his warning of the consequences, for the conduct of the war and the fabric of society, of a descent into a war of reprisal, animosity, and cruelty and of the extinction of 'Brotherly Affection'.[46]

The ordinance remained on the books, but it seems that both prudence and a sense of professional custom and honour reined in its universal application. Even in Ireland, notorious as English conduct there became, there were to be cases of English officers punished for failure to keep promises of quarter to Irish prisoners.[47] Nevertheless there were still incidents of brutal killing of Irish prisoners either as a considered application of the law or in the hot blood of mass action. After Naseby Fairfax reported to parliament, 'Some Irish are among the prisoners as I am informed . . . I desire they may be proceeded against above, according to the Ordinance of Parliament'. When the town of Scarborough fell in September 1648 Walloon soldiers in the royalist garrison were taken for Irish and killed with less legal nicety; by then parliament's decisive victories in the second civil war had effectively removed fear of reprisal as a deterrent.[48]

It was not only Irish soldiers who fell outside the protections of the laws of war. The Irish women who accompanied them were also endangered. We have seen that women who actively engaged in the conflict lost the protections nominally due to the weak and harmless, so claims that Irish women carried skeans, or knives, are not surprising. By late 1642 there were already reports of savage, pillaging Irish women who 'cruelly cut [the] throats with great Knives' of parliamentarians who lay wounded on the battlefield. When Nantwich fell to Fairfax in January 1644 the royalist prisoners included 'bloudy women' and the dead included 'an hundred and twenty *Irish Women* with long Knives'.[49] Such women, it could be claimed, had clearly disqualified themselves from protection. Some of the accounts of the women killed after Naseby suggested that Irishness in itself constituted a sufficient crime, although the incident was in fact variously reported and some accounts preferred to ignore it. Others acknowledged the presence of women and noted—as did Clarendon—that the wives 'of Officers of Quality' were among those killed or captured in the disorderly pursuit of the defeated royalists.[50]

---

[45] Bodl. MS Add. D.114, fos. 155–54 (*sic*); and see BL Add. MS 11,331, fos. 76–76ᵛ.

[46] Ibid., fo. 76ᵛ.

[47] Firth, *Cromwell's Army*, 2. 628–9; *Severall Proceedings in Parliament*, 97 (31 July–7 Aug. 1651), 1486. I owe the latter citation to Paul Hardacre. For instances of killing Irish prisoners in accordance with the ordinance see Stoyle, *Soldiers and Strangers*, 135–6.

[48] *Three Letters, From the Right Honourable Sir Thomas Fairfax, Lieut. Gen. Crumwell and the Committee residing in the Army* (1645), 2; Robert Ashton, *Counter-Revolution: The Second Civil War and its Origins, 1646–8* (New Haven, Conn., 1994), 404.

[49] Andrewes, *Perfect Declaration of . . . Barbarous and Cruell practices*, A2; BL Harl. MS 2125, fo. 142; [Bulstrode] Whitelocke, *Memorials of the English Affairs* (new edn. 1732), 81.

[50] Clarendon, *History*, 2. 509; *Three Letters, From . . . Fairfax*, 4; Walker, *Historical Discourses*, 115 [131].

Some parliamentary newsletters recorded neutrally that 'in the pursuit three hundred or 400 Women killed' or 'above a Hundred slain', but a royalist newsletter declared that it was done under the pretence that they were Irish women.[51] For others, moral desert legitimated their fate: '100 of your Harlots with golden Tresses killed upon the place', said one.[52] Another, attributing the victory to God, noted that 'three or four hundred whores were killed'. The killings acquired the reputation, however, of a massacre of Irish women, and at their most virulent parliamentary reports combined the sins of Irishness and whoredom to justify their fate. One, recalling earlier accusations, declared that Rupert

had brought into the field many *Irish* women, inhuman Whores, with Skeans or long *Irish* knives about them to cut the throats of our wounded men, and such prisoners as they pleased, . . . to whom our Souldiers would grant no quarter, about a 100 of them were slain on the ground.[53]

Many of the women who escaped alive were mutilated, and again sexual crime justified violence: 'Most of the whores and Camp-sluts that attended that wicked [royalist] Army, were marked in their faces and noses with slashes and cuts, and some cut off: just rewards for such wicked strumpets.'[54] The conjunction of sex, race, and sadism is striking in these accounts. The emphasis on the sinfulness of the victims may indicate a desire on the part of some reporters to validate killings that could still shock, but for others triumphalist vengeance—on female deviance and Irish barbarity—predominated. Military treatment of sexual offenders was hardly benign at best, but no other incident elicited apologia that conflated ethnicity and depravity comparable to those following Naseby.

The Irish could be represented as justifiably outside the law on moral and statutory grounds. They performed, for the English, the useful role that the 'Croats' or 'Crabbats' (in fact a kind of villainous Foreign Legion) played in the literature of the Thirty Years' War, that of scapegoats and bogeymen to whom the worst actions could be attributed.

Yet in spite of the genuine fear and indeed hysteria that the Irish threat could arouse, and prejudice that did not die with the Interregnum, reality was not

---

[51] *Mercurius Belgicus* (14 June 1645); C. V. Wedgwood speculated that the victims were defenceless Welsh women taken for Irish because they 'cried out in a strange language'. There were some Welsh troops at Naseby, but there seems to be no other supporting evidence for this theory. C. V. Wedgwood, *The King's War, 1641–1647* (1958), 455, 670. n. 59.

[52] *Parliaments Post*, 6 (10–17 June 1645), 8; *Kingdomes Weekly Intelligencer*, 104 (10–17 June 1645), 837; *Exchange Intelligencer*, 5 (11–18 June 1645), [33].

[53] Vicars, *Burning Bush*, 163–4.

[54] Ibid.; [G. Bishop], *A more Particular and Exact Relation of the Victory obtained by the Parliaments Forces under the Command of Sir Thomas Fairfax* (1645), 4: 'many [women] taken, which are every one wounded'; *An Ordinance of the Lords and Commons Assembled in Parliament For . . . a day of Thanksgiving . . . for the great Victory Obtained against the Kings Forces, nere Knasby* (1645), 4.

always as melodramatic as propaganda suggested. At Naseby Irish courage won admiration when 'they stood to it, till the last man'. The earl of Essex looked after the interests of his Catholic Irish half-brother the earl of Clanricarde. A few months after their acrimonious exchange about the killing of Irish prisoners, he acceded to Rupert's courteous request for a pass for the duke of Richmond in a reply that was couched in equally traditional and courteous terms. An Irish community survived in London, and in 1647 Barbary Osborn, an English wife, could collect the £2 due to her Irish husband James who, in one of the ironies of war, had made Essex's coffin.[55]

The norms of war extended beyond the conduct of soldiers to each other to comprehend their conduct within a larger community. Any war affects civilian society, but a civil war, and particularly one that ranged widely over the kingdom, must do so with particular intensity. When soldiers and civilians were so intermingled, the extent to which soldiers observed not only the written articles of war but also the laws of God, nature, and nations and the laws of arms mattered to the lives, property, welfare, and dignity of civilians. So did the degree of latitude they were granted to take advantage of exceptions to the rules.

We have noted the basic utilitarian and moral considerations—the force of the reciprocity argument and the power of a validating sense of professional and personal integrity—that lay behind maintenance of the rules. It did not pay to breach laws that benefited both sides. It was unwise to ignore the rule that the life of a surrendering prisoner of war should be saved when you or one of your men might be the next victim in a tit-for-tat reprisal. The prisoner out on parole to seek an exchange did not break his promise to return to his captors without endangering a practice that benefited both sides. Breach of the negotiated terms of surrender after a siege undercut the value of all agreements between enemies. In such a calculus, individual cases could not be dismissed as mere isolated aberrations, for each was a reminder that the system as a whole, dependent as it was on voluntary observance, would lose its normative power if lapses were tolerated and grew in number. A system that revealed what has been called 'the strength of weak ties' could not afford to allow its ties to unravel. Yet neither self-interest nor honour nor morality could secure perfect observance of the laws of war. Both sides in the English civil war recognized the disutility of abandoning rules directed to the cohesion of an orderly army and the preservation of a civil society, but they could not

---

[55] *An Ordinance of the Lords and Commons Assembled in Parliament*, 2; BL Add. MS 46,188, fos. 161–2; Add. MS 46,189, fos. 141–2; Add. MS 5460, fos. 421–2; Kathleen M. Noonan, '"The cruell pressure of an enraged, barbarous people": Irish and English Identity in Seventeenth Century Propaganda and Policy', *HJ* 41 (1998), 151–77, and id., '"Martyrs in Flames": Sir John Temple and the Conception of the Irish in English Martyrologies', *Albion*, 36 (2004), 223–55.

consistently control the conduct of either soldiers or civilians. The extent to which they succeeded or failed had consequences for the nature of post-war society and politics. In the next sections I shall look at the men who fought the war and the ways in which the rules played out in the crucible of siege warfare.

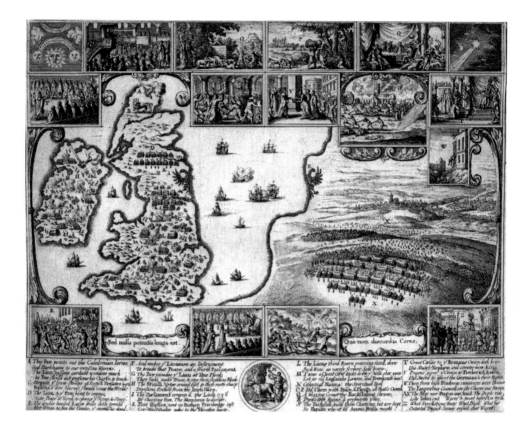

FIG. 1 (*above*) Many Englishmen saw a clear progression from the wars of embattled Protestantism in continental Europe to those that, in 1642, engulfed the British Isles. Wenceslaus Hollar's engraving linked the defenestration of Prague in 1618 and the defeat of the Bohemians at the Battle of White Mountain in 1620 (on the right) to the Scottish wars, Irish rebellion, and early events of the English civil war (on the left), when the three kingdoms were peopled by armies

FIG. 2 (*above right*) Protestant heroes of the Thirty Years' War. This double portrait of Gustavus Adolphus of Sweden and his ally John George, elector of Saxony, the victors of Breitenfeld, was sold in London

FIG. 3 (*below left*) Atrocities of the Irish rebellion of 1641, as represented to the British public. Such illustrations recalled the barbarities of the Thirty Years' War made familiar by the prints and narratives of the 1630s

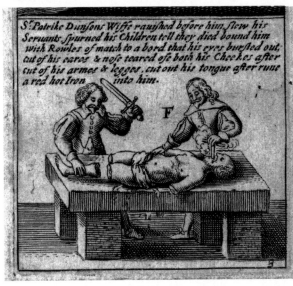

Sr Patrike Dunsons Wiffe rauished before him, slew his
Seruants spurned his Children till they died bound him
with Rowles of match to a bord that his eyes bursted out,
cut of his eares & nose teared ofe both his Cheekes after
cut of his armes & legges, cut out his tongue after ronne
a red hot Iron   into him.

F

The Souldiers in their passage to York turn unto reformers pull down Popish pictures, break down rayles, turn altars into Tables

The rising of Prentises and Sea-men on South-wark side to assault the Arch-bishops of Canter-burys House at Lambeth.

FIG. 4 The disorders that preceded the civil war, whether by unruly reforming soldiers on their way to fight the Scots or by riotous London apprentices and seamen demonstrating against Archbishop Laud in 1640, reinforced fears of the dangers that war would bring to persons, property, and civil society

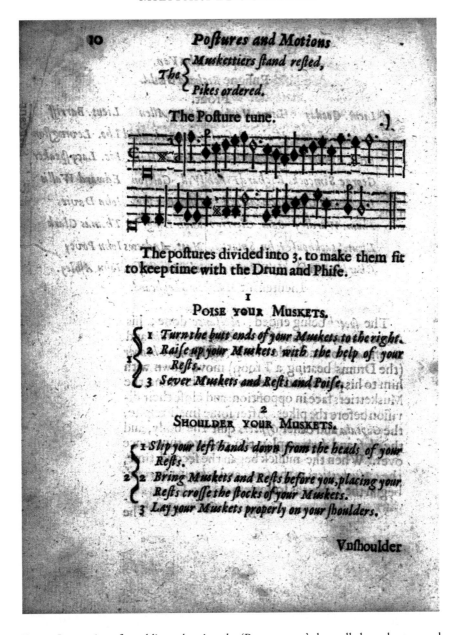

10

Poſtures and Motions

The { *Muſketiers ſtand reſted,*

Pikes ordered.

The Poſture tune.

The poſtures divided into 3. to make them fit to keep time with the Drum and Phife.

1

POISE YOUR MUSKETS.

{ 1 *Turn the butt ends of your Muskets to the right.*

2 *Raiſe up your Muskets with the help of your Reſts.*

3 *Sever Muskets and Reſts and Poiſe.*

2

SHOULDER YOUR MUSKETS.

{ 1 *Slip your left hands down from the heads of your Reſts.*

2 *Bring Muskets and Reſts before you, placing your Reſts croſſe the ſtocks of your Muskets.*

3 *Lay your Muskets properly on your ſhoulders.*

Vnſhoulder

FIG. 5 Instructions for soldiers, showing the 'Posture tune' that called musketeers and pikemen to prepare their weapons for action, and describing the first seven steps for musketeers, out of a total of twenty-four involved in the process. From William Barriffe's *Mars, his Triumph* (1639), an account of a mock battle between Saracens and Christians enacted in the Merchant Tailors' Hall by members of the London Artillery Company in 1638

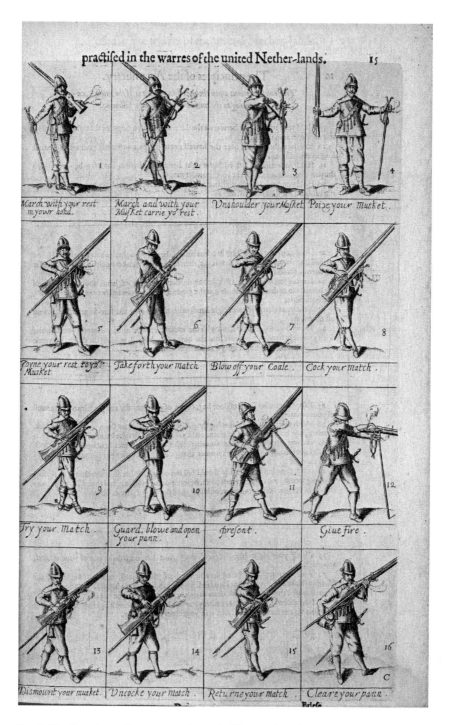

FIG. 6 The first sixteen frames, out of a total of forty-eight, of Henry Hexham's directions for musketeers on how to handle their muskets 'as practiced in the warres of the united Netherlands' (in *The Principles of the Art Militarie*, 1637)

of wood, and the mouth againſt the part of
the door or gate, but if the place be unaccef-
ſible, then make a little Cart with two, or
four wheels, and ſo ſupport the recoyle of
the Petard, ſhooting off: The Petard muſt
be made faſt to a long beams end, that muſt
go a-croſſe the ditch or moat, the reſt of the
beam or heavieſt part thereof reſting upon
the Wheels, able to counterpoize the other
part

FIG. 7 'How to make and prepare a Petard' (from Nathaniel Nye's *The Art of Gunnery*
of 1647, reissued in 1648). The petardier's was a dangerous calling; here he follows the
advice of all the experts, namely to run away fast as soon as the fuse was lit

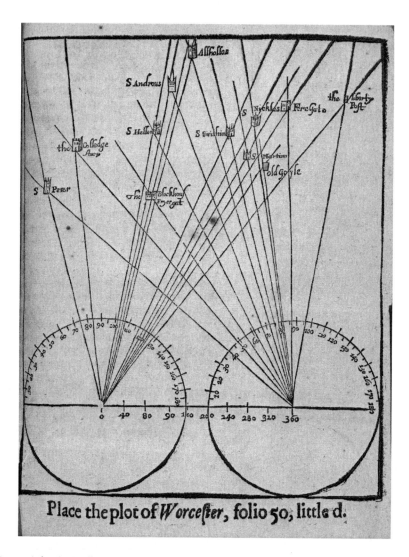

Place the plot of *Worcester*, folio 50, little d.

FIG. 8 (*above*) Artillery targets at the siege of Worcester, as recorded by the enthusiastic young artillery expert Nathaniel Nye, who had planned the barrage. Nye optimistically believed that war was a science as well as an art

FIG. 9 (*right*) This late Elizabethan plan of Chester illustrates the militarily useful detail available to civil war soldiers in pre-war maps. Royalist Chester, intermittently under attack or siege throughout the war, was seriously blockaded from late 1645 until its surrender in 1646. The map shows the city's internal layout, and demonstrates the importance of control of the southern bridge over the Dee and the vulnerability of Handbridge, the suburb across the river that was repeatedly devastated by both sides

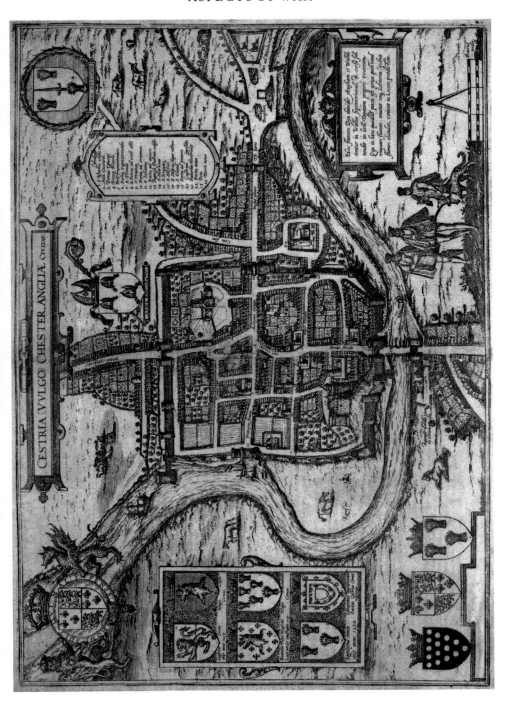

THE SIEGE OF BAZINGE HOVSE

A. THE OLDE HOVSE . B. THE NEW . C. THE TOWER THAT IS HALFE BATTERED DOVNE . D. THE KINGES BREAST WORKS . E. THE PARLIAMENTS BREAST WORKS .

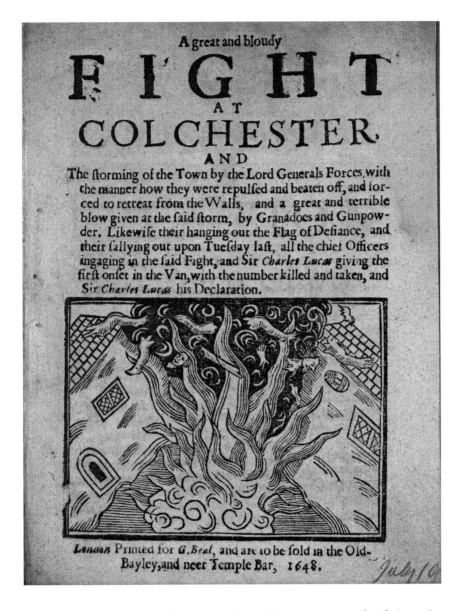

A great and bloudy

FIGHT

AT

COLCHESTER,

AND

The ſtorming of the Town by the Lord Generals Forces,with the manner how they were repulſed and beaten off, and forced to retreat from the Walls, and a great and terrible blow given at the ſaid ſtorm, by Granadoes and Gunpowder, Likewiſe their hanging out the Flag of Defiance, and their ſallying out upon Tueſday laſt, all the chief Officers ingaging in the ſaid Fight, and Sir *Charles Lucas* giving the firſt onſet in the Van,with the number killed and taken, and Sir *Charles Lucas* his Declaration.

London Printed for *G.Beal*, and are to be ſold in the Old-Bayley,and neer Temple Bar, 1648.

July 16

FIG. 10 (*left*) The marquess of Winchester's Basing House, an extensive fortified complex of old and new buildings, was held by the royalists from 1642. It finally fell to Cromwell in October 1645. Here we can see how close the lines of defenders and besiegers were; such intimacy facilitated exchanges of abuse and information between soldiers of opposing sides

FIG. 11 (*above*) During the parliamentarian attack on the Gatehouse at Colchester in 1648 a grenade fell in the royalist magazine. In the subsequent 'great and terrible blow' some sixty soldiers were killed. Such explosions, the results of chance or negligence, were one of the unpredictable hazards of war

The high and Mighty Monarch CHARLES by the
Grace of GOD King of Great Brittaine
France and Ireland. Defender of the Faith etc
1643.   Are to be sould by R: Peake

FIG. 12 Charles I (1600–49). The frontispiece to an edition of royalist *Military Orders and Articles* printed in Oxford in 1643. The background, however, is not Oxford but London, a reassertion of the king's sovereignty over the whole country. Other versions of the royalist articles of war provided different backgrounds for the king and his horse—a generic army camp or Oxford, for example—or omitted the royal portrait

ROBERT DEVEREVX EARLE OF ESSEX HIS EXCEL
lency & Generall of y'e Army

FIG. 13 Robert Devereux, third earl of Essex (1591–1646), an engraving by Wenceslaus Hollar of 1644. A competent soldier with continental experience and the ability to inspire affection in his followers, Essex nevertheless lacked the necessary political skill and tactical imagination to prosper as a commander of parliament's early divided armies. After the passage of the Self-Denying Ordinance in April 1645 he played no further military role in the civil war

Fig. 14 Sir Thomas Fairfax (1612–71) was 'Captain-General' of the New Model Army from 1645; he succeeded his father Ferdinando as third Lord Fairfax of Cameron in 1648. The scion of a military family, his own pre-war experience was limited to a short period in the Netherlands and to service against the Scots in 1640, but he proved an able general who was prepared to judge and act independently of his council of war. Most representations of Fairfax emphasized his long face and black hair—the royalists called him 'Black Tom'—but in this bust of *c.* 1650, the unknown sculptor also caught the power of the successful general

Fig. 15 Oliver Cromwell (1599–1658), a portrait by Robert Walker, *c.* 1649. The artist presented Cromwell in a conventional pose for a military hero, with a commander's baton in his hand and a page adjusting his sash. A portrait of the royalist Colonel George Goring adopts the same formula of commander and attendant page

FIG. 16 Prince Rupert (1619–82), shown here shortly before he became one of the king's senior commanders at the age of 23. A son of the Winter Queen, Elizabeth of Bohemia (sister of Charles I), he was already an experienced soldier. An able cavalry commander and a thoughtful strategist, he could also be excessively rash. He lost the king's favour when he surrendered Bristol in 1645, but later served Charles II at sea in the second civil war

FIG. 17 Sir Henry Gage (1597–1645). A professional soldier and a Catholic, Gage returned from Spanish service early in 1644 to become one of King Charles's most able and admired commanders. He relieved Basing House in 1644 and was made governor of Oxford. Mortally wounded by a 'straggling bullet', he died in January 1645

FIG. 18 Philip Skippon (d. 1660) served in the Low Countries in the 1620s and became a captain in the Dutch armies. Appointed by Charles I to command the London Artillery Company in 1639, he nevertheless led the London trained bands in defence of the city against the king in 1642. He was Sergeant Major General of foot in the New Model Army, and was a highly successful trainer of infantry. Admired as a courageous and dependable commander, he remained a trusted servant of the state through all the upheavals of the Interregnum

Sʳ Wᵐ Waller.

FIG. 19 Sir William Waller (1597/8–1668), *c.* 1648. As a young man Waller served in the armies of Venice and the Palatinate and was present at the battle of White Mountain in 1620 before returning to the life of a country gentleman. After 1642 early successes earned him the title of 'William the Conqueror', but shortages of men and money and quarrels with the earl of Essex led to a string of defeats. He remained a committed parliamentarian but was suspect and sometimes imprisoned under Cromwell, and supported the restoration of Charles II

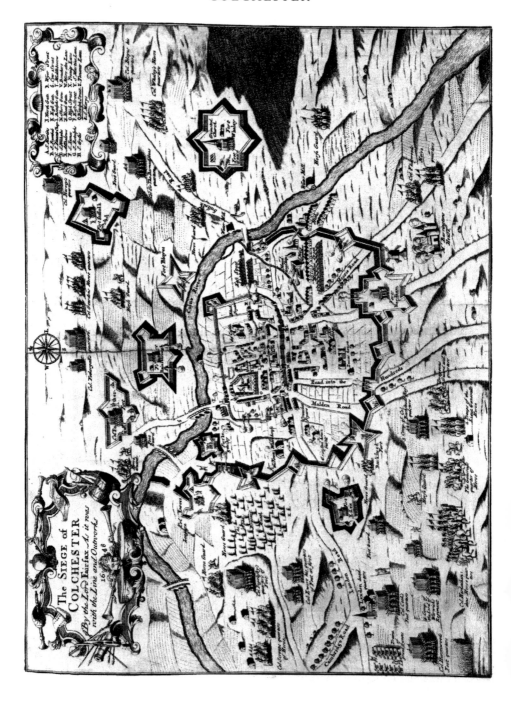

Fig. 20 (*left*) The siege of Colchester, 1648, after Fairfax had closed the ring around the city. This eighteenth-century reworking of a 1648 plan of the siege reveals the strength and textbook deployment of the besieging forces; it also suggests the hold the siege retained on civic memory

Fig. 21 (*above*), The execution of Sir Charles Lucas and Sir George Lisle, 'both shot to death at *Colchester*, Five houres after the Surrender'. They became instant royalist martyrs. The frontispiece to *The Loyall Sacrifice* (1648)

FIG. 22 Arthur Capel (1604–49), first Baron Capel of Hadham, in a miniature of 1647, probably after John Hoskins. Initially a critic of royal policies in the Long Parliament, Capel became an active royalist and was admired for his honour and judgement. One of the royalist commanders at the siege of Colchester, he was executed by parliament in 1649

THE PROTAGONISTS

11

Armies

The armies of the civil war were not large by modern standards, nor were the numbers of men engaged in individual battles large when compared with some of the actions of the Thirty Years' War. By contemporary English standards, however, the overall numbers were big. In 1628 it had been estimated that 24,000 men were necessary for an offensive war, the same number as that raised for defence against the Armada. In 1626 20,000 to 30,000 men had been accounted a great army, and 50,000 'a royall Army'. In the 1640s the numbers of men in arms greatly exceeded these earlier figures, but the totals are and will remain elusive. C. H. Firth suggested that in the civil war the 'men whom each party raised and armed . . . amount[ed] it is probable to 60,000 or 70,000 on each side', but if this was intended to represent a cumulative total for the war years it seems unduly conservative, particularly in view of the volatility of army numbers. Precise conclusions are virtually impossible. Ian Gentles notes that in little over a year, from April 1645 to the summer of 1646, well over 30,000 men served in the New Model army alone, but to this figure he adds perhaps another 10,000 who were recruited but ran away before seeing service. He comments that '[tw]o were pressed for every one who eventually arrived at the front', while even for the foot who actually served, 'membership in the army was no more than a revolving door through which they exited almost as quickly as they entered'. An estimate in June 1644 that set the four parliamentarian armies at 62,000 men (with an additional 22,000 Scots) was almost certainly inflated, but figures for individual engagements combined with the evidence of turnover and replacement of the kind described by Gentles suggest widespread, if often fleeting, army service.[1]

All contemporary figures were of course statements of hope and belief, for needs were variable, establishments rarely filled, and attrition constant. Nevertheless

---

[1] HEH HA Military Box 1 (22); Gouge, *Dignitie of Chivalry*, 427; Firth, *Cromwell's Army*, 22; Gentles, *New Model Army*, 40; BL Add. MS 35,297, fo. 30 (this estimate, the source of the generous 62,000 figure, assigned 40,000 men to the armies of Waller, Manchester, and the Fairfaxes and 22,000 to Essex's army in June 1644, whereas the ordinance of March 1644 had provided for only 10,500, plus reformados and regular officers, in Essex's army); Firth and Rait, *Acts and Ordinances*, 1. 398. In 1593 Matthew Sutcliffe had clearly felt he was putting an extreme case when he urged on the second earl of Essex, father of the civil war general, the feasibility of an army of 30,000, or even 30,000–40,000 if maintained abroad. Sutcliffe, *Practice . . . and Lawes of Armes*, B3.

it seems that demographically speaking the military presence in England in the 1640s, although of shorter duration, was comparable to that in the Germany of the Thirty Years' War and was spread over a much smaller geographical area. Two armies of 60,000 in England—accepting Firth's conservative estimate—would in any single year have accounted for roughly 2.4 per cent of a total population of some 5,100,000; even if the estimate is slashed by half they still account for 1.2 per cent.[2] In the Holy Roman Empire the gross figures greatly exceed those for England and were drawn from a vastly larger population—one estimate suggests that it was fought over by a million troops in the course of thirty years, but also that in 1648 alone the armies of both sides numbered some 210,000 men—but soldiers appear to have accounted for well under 2 per cent of the population.[3] England was highly mobilized, although suggestions that one in five of the adult male population served as a soldier probably exaggerate the extent of active military participation.[4] The degree of mobilization placed heavy burdens on civilian society and fuelled the fears associated with a widely dispersed military presence.

Estimates of total army numbers must thus remain speculative. Those for individual campaigns or notable actions, while still variable, are more useful. By later standards they do not represent huge armies. At Marston Moor in 1644 the confrontation was massive by civil war standards, when perhaps 18,000 royalists faced 28,000 parliamentarians and Scots. At Naseby in 1645, however, there were probably just over 9,000 royalists and between 14,000 and 17,000 parliamentarians (although the estimated totals

[2] See E. A. Wrigley and R. S. Schofield, *The Population History of England 1541–1871* (Cambridge, Mass., 1981), 532, table A3.3. Estimates of total population for selected years are: 1642, 5,112,000; 1645, 5,130,000; 1648, 5,226,000; 1651, 5,228,000.

[3] In the course of thirty years the population of the Holy Roman Empire may have declined from twenty to sixteen or seventeen million. Parker, *Thirty Years' War*, 191, 208, 211. If one takes the lowest population figure of sixteen million and accepts the figure of 210,000 men in arms in 1648, soldiers would have accounted in that year for just over 1.3% of total population. Imperialist strength was admittedly low in 1648, but if one takes the higher figure of 250,000 suggested for the years 1625–35 (ibid. 208) (which is in fact a cumulated number of soldiers over a decade and hence exaggerates the proportion of soldiers in any single year) soldiers would still account for only about 1.6% of a total population of sixteen million or under 1.3% of a population of twenty million. These percentages will obviously not stand close statistical examination, and provide only the roughest of comparisons. Nor do they suggest a demographic penalty in England similar to that paid by Germany or Sweden, but they do suggest that, if the concentration of troops in Germany can be described as 'unprecedented' for the 17th cent., that for England was at least comparable. Ibid. 191, 193.

[4] J. S. Morrill and J. D. Walter, 'Order and Disorder in the English Revolution', in Anthony Fletcher and John Stevenson (eds.), *Order and Disorder in Early Modern England* (Cambridge, 1985), 164. I am grateful to Keith Wrightson for a calculation, based on Wrigley and Schofield's figures for 1641 broken down by sex and age (p. 528), that of a total population of 5,091,725, males aged 15 to 59 would have accounted for 1,512,751; thus an estimate of one in five would mean that nearly 303,000 served as soldiers. Although total population rose between 1642 and 1648 (see n. 2 above), and the one-in-five calculation is based on the whole period of the war, it still seems high. There is, of course, an important distinction between being drafted and serving.

vary they remain relatively modest). Marston Moor thus outdid Lützen in 1632, where each side fielded 19,000 troops, but was outshone by Breitenfeld's 72,000 combatants in 1631. Nor did England match Germany's sustained and repeated engagement of large armies in the 1630s. A few months after Breitenfeld 59,000 men met at Rain; in 1634 58,000 were engaged at Nördlingen.[5]

Contemporary estimates, if not always accurate, nevertheless indicate the scale of operations of English armies and the ways in which forces were dispersed. They reveal the disparity between the nominal number of soldiers in an army and the number available for any given action, and the factors that hindered troop concentration. Armies naturally tended to decline in size, partly by normal attrition in each campaigning season through casualties, capture, sickness, and desertion and, over time, by difficulty in replenishing recruits. In the first year after its formation in the spring of 1645 the size of the New Model ranged from 24,800 to 13,400 men, and a striking drop from 20,000 before to 13,800 not long after victory at Naseby in June had little to do with battle casualties.[6] The concentration of forces demanded by such a major battle was difficult when armies were dispersed over wide geographical areas and innumerable garrisons had to be manned, and was further complicated by divided commands. Parliament had four in 1644, but reorganization into the New Model army did not mean a single, consolidated parliamentary army with a clear vertical command structure. To take only one example, while Fairfax and Cromwell moved to clear the south and west after Naseby, Brereton was fully occupied with operations around Chester and into Wales. Fairfax, who was appointed lord general in February 1645, was not given unified command of all parliamentary forces in England and Wales until July 1647. The royalists too suffered from weakness of central control. Until mid-1644 the king's armies were nominally divided into northern and southern branches, the latter centred on Oxford and under the command of the king himself, but at all times there were also

---

[5] Woolrych, *Britain in Revolution*, 286, 316; Firth, *Cromwell's Army*, 22–3; Parker, *Thirty Years' War*, 126, 129, 131, 140–41. Battle numbers, like most other civil war statistics, are often more estimate than fact, but there is a rough consensus on Marston Moor and Naseby: e.g. Peter Young, *Marston Moor 1644: The Campaign and the Battle* (Kineton, 1970), 60, 68 (between 45,000 and 47,000 troops at Marston Moor); Smurthwaite, *Battlefields of Britain*, 158 (28,000 in the 'Allied' army of English and Scots, 14,000 royalists in Rupert's army, supplemented by an uncertain number from the York garrison, i.e. a total of something above 42,000). For Naseby Smurthwaite posits 13,500 parliamentarians to 9,000 royalists, ibid. 166, 168. Cf. Glenn Foard, *Naseby: The Decisive Campaign* (Whitstable, 1995), 207, who suggests a significantly larger figure: 12,500 royalists, nearly 17,000 parliamentarians, and ibid. 197–209, for a valuable discussion of the bases and methods of assessing troop numbers.

[6] The attrition in parliamentary numbers had begun before the battle. Gentles, *New Model Army*, 37, 39, and see ibid. 31–40, for a discussion of recruitment and retention figures in the New Model army. Despite the 'constant haemorrhaging of . . . numbers' common to the armies of both sides, Gentles suggests that the New Model tended to increase in numbers after 1646, when membership of a victorious, non-fighting army was more attractive. Ibid. 33, and private communication.

refractory local commanders—Ronald Hutton's 'grandees' and 'warlords'—who operated, when they chose, virtually autonomously, like Goring in Cornwall and Langdale and his Northern Horse.[7] The incidence of sieges further hindered the deployment of unified, concentrated armies. Many involved quite small numbers of men, but for others large groups had to be detached from parent armies. In October 1642 an eye-witness had put the king's army at 10,500, including 6,000 foot—but Charles was prepared to detach 4,000 of them to besiege Banbury. The travails of Boarstall and Colchester that will be described in later chapters exemplify the extremes of scale in England's siege warfare: if Colchester was a major undertaking Boarstall, like many other minor sieges, engaged few men and resources. Furthermore, not only was the size of individual armies often quite modest—in 1643 the marquess of Hertford's western army was estimated at 6,000, and in 1644 royal forces of 12,000 at Alresford still merited the description of 'a great Army'—but local detachments were frequently small, heterogeneous and inadequate. In 1645 the parliamentarian defenders of strategically important Leicester numbered 240 horse plus their officers and under 500 foot, the balance of the defenders being 900 enlisted and civilian townsmen.[8] Thus although civil war armies were cumulatively, for England, unprecedentedly large, we should think of them as not only mobile but also, usually, as diffuse and only rarely as heavily concentrated for major battles. Many battles or sieges involved hundreds or thousands of combatants, but few involved tens of thousands. The burden of the armies on the civilian population may have been lighter than that of the 'contributions' levied in Germany, but the combination of mobility and the high incidence of relatively small units meant that it was widely spread.[9]

These armies were raised in a number of ways. At the beginning of the war, both sides relied primarily on the trained bands, whether raised under parliament's Militia Ordinance through the traditional agency of county lords lieutenant and their deputies or by commissions of array issued by the king to county sheriffs. Conflicts had already arisen in the summer of 1642, before the war was formally embarked on. In Leicester, for example, each side sent a peer to seize control of the militia, which led to 'desperate Combats' between their followers.[10] Some trained bands, particularly those from London, were serious military forces; others, in spite of sporadically conscientious efforts in previous decades by local officials, remained a fit subject for the kind of ridicule directed

---

[7] Wilson, *Fairfax*, 116–17; Hutton, *Royalist War Effort*, parts 2, 4, 5, *passim*.

[8] *A Continuation of The late proceedings of His Majesties Army at Shrewsbury, Bridge-North, and Manchester* (12 Oct. 1642), 3, 6; *A Relation of the Battaile lately fought between Keynton and Edgehill* (Oxford, 1642), 1; Robert Derham, *A Manuell or Brief treatise of some particular Rights and Priviledges* (1647), 71; *A True Relation of The late Attempt made upon the Town of Ciceter* (1642); [E.A.], *A Fuller Relation Of the Great Victory obtained (through Gods Providence) at Alsford* (1644), [6]; *Narration of the Siege and taking of the Town of Leicester*, 5.

[9] See Parker, *Thirty Years' War*, 212–15, on the economic effects of the Thirty Years' War.

[10] [Adam Jones], *Horrible Newes from Leicester* (1642), A3.

against them in Newcastle's 1649 comedy, *The Country Captaine*.[11] In 1639 even a sympathetic observer had commented that many trained bands dared not shoot a bullet for lack of practice, while few knew how to calculate the proportion of powder necessary for a charge.[12] Their inexperience, lack of discipline, and reluctance to move far from home exacerbated the disorder and disorganization of the early stages of the war. They were soon replaced as the backbone of the armies by volunteer regiments, many of which retained a strong regional character that often derived from the local influence of their commanders. Their conduct and skill, like the degree of freedom in their voluntarism, were variable and as the war settled down impressment became the norm. If the cavalry of both armies were more willing, steadfast, and principled than the foot, attributes that reflected higher initial social standing and greater economic opportunities (in both pay and booty), many of the conscripted infantry continued bipartisanly to be dismissed as 'scum'. There were of course exceptions, and scum can be resolute and skilful, an idea that survived in romantic myths of the Foreign Legion, but even the New Model had to fight with largely unwilling foot soldiers with a high rate of desertion. 'Conscripting infantry in 1645–6', Gentles has observed, 'was like ladling water into a leaky bucket.'[13] Scattered among these initially raw, unskilled, and reluctant men, however, were the experts already described, whose knowledge came from continental experience or from the more serious kinds of pre-war training at home in companies such as those in the Artillery Gardens or Sir Ralph Bosvile's 'Select Company of Foot' in Kent. By 1642, as we have seen, England had a substantial reservoir of military knowledge and experience.[14] These experts were crucial, as commissioned and non-commissioned officers, in turning unpromising raw material into tolerable soldiers.

As might be expected, soldiers raised in these ways differed in talent and commitment. Some, especially in the war's initial stages, were enthusiastic to join the army, if not to stay with it. Some were very young. Some were foreigners. Some were professionals, some unwilling amateurs. Yet despite the strength of neutralism, the resistance to recruitment, and the disenchantment that often followed actual military experience, we should not forget that a soldier's life had its attractions. Aside from the obvious ones of subsistence for the poor and hopes

---

[11] See Joan Kent, *The Village Constable* (Oxford, 1986), 39–42, 175–80; [Newcastle?], *The Country Captaine*, 3–7, 50. For a survey of 'The Nature of Armies', see Peter Newman, *Atlas of the English Civil War* (1985), 9–14.

[12] Barriffe, *Military Discipline* (2nd edn.), 313. This comment appears as a marginal note in Barriffe's enlarged edn. of his 1635 work.

[13] Gentles, *New Model Army*, 33.

[14] Barriffe, *Military Discipline*, dedications to Sir Ralph Bosvile and 'To all the Worthy Captaines of the Citty'; Elton, *The Compleat Body of the Art Militarie* (2nd edn.), 67–8; Markham, *Souldiers Exercise*, Part III, *The Second Part of the Souldiers Grammar*, 45, on 'old' and 'new' soldiers: 'those of olde and solide experience, and those of late and more quaint practise; The first having nothing but what the warre itselfe formeth, the other the helpe of Garden, Yarde, City, Home and Countrie trialls.'

of profit for all, adventure, travel, friendship, local loyalty, and enthusiasm for
the cause all played their parts. For some war offered change and excitement, as
it had done in the past. In the 1620s a sortie to the Low Countries had done
wonders for the temper of irascible old Sir Thomas Fairfax, the grandfather of
the New Model's general.[15] In the 1630s Monro had pointed out that 'Souldiers
have not always so hard a life, as the common opinion is'. His march along
the Main to Frankfurt, he said, was as 'profitable as it was pleasant to the
eye . . .; for sometimes [soldiers] have variety of pleasure in marching softly,
without feare or danger, through fertill soyles and pleasant countries'. The 'fat
land' of Franconia, even in war, may have impressed a tourist from Scotland
with particular force, but Richard Symonds's marches with the royal army, with
his records of monuments, houses, and local speech and habits, and Nehemiah
Wharton's detour to view that famous Warwick 'antiquity' Sir Guy's cave,
with its chapel, rocky stables, gardens, and the wells Sir Guy drank from 'as is
reported', revealed a similar tourist pleasure in new sights and places. There were
pleasures for the less reflective as well, such as hunting other men's game and
release from civilian prohibitions against destruction, violence, and predation.[16]

We can only guess at the age profile of civil war armies. The official and
traditional age range for liability to military service was from 16 to 60, but there
was considerable variation in practice. In Berkshire in the spring of 1643, for
example, Essex complained that parliament had been sluggish in its recruiting:
the royalists had raised the county's men 'from *16 to 60*' but parliament had
not done likewise, to the detriment of his own army.[17] When the war began
there were many youthful recruits, probably impelled by novelty and adventure
as much as ideology. In October 1642 it was reported that 'many young
boyes [came] in daily' to the king's army, while parliament actively encouraged
recruitment of apprentices by protecting them against possible financial penalties
for breaking their bonds, and by requiring their masters to reinstate them after
service.[18] Some politicians recognized the danger of uprooting the young—the
'Silly yonguelings' fitter for 'the shop or the schoole' than the field who were
traditionally attracted by the glamour of an army—and in October 1641 Pym
had been anxious to persuade young soldiers to return home after the Scottish

[15] BL Add. MS 30,305, fos. 29–29ᵛ. Old Sir Thomas's son, commenting on his father's
improved disposition, reported that he had 'grown forty years younger'.

[16] Monro, *Expedition*, 2. 89; Symonds, *Diary, passim*; Wharton, 'Letters from a Subaltern
Officer', *Archaeologia*, 35 (1853), 2. 325; Bayley, *Dorset*, 283: on one occasion Fairfax's men shot
one of their number instead of a deer, barely missing Fairfax himself.

[17] Bodl. Tanner MS 62/1A, fo. 76.

[18] *Continuation of The late proceedings . . . at Shrewsbury*, 6; *Three Ordinances of the Lords and
Commons Assembled in Parliament . . . for the Incouragement of all such Apprentices as have or shall
voluntarily list themselves in the Service of King and Parliament* (1644), 6; parliament's ordinance
of 1 Nov. 1642 was reprinted in 1644. Firth and Rait, *Acts and Ordinances*, 1. 37. See Bodl. MS
Tanner 62/1B, fos. 211–12, for disorders in Stepney in Aug.–Dec. 1643 arising from the efforts
of parliamentarian recruiters to enrol servants and apprentices who 'had their masters' consent'.

campaign. His desire to get them out of London and back to the restraints of a familiar and stable social context was partly on behalf of the young soldiers, and partly on behalf of the rest of society threatened by the presence of a volatile, youthful group to whom 'great misdemeanours' had already been attributed. London's later apprentice riots confirmed such anxieties.[19]

The experience of war quickly turned many naive young volunteers into hardy young veterans. In parliament's successful defence of Plymouth against Prince Maurice in October 1643 an observer reported of Colonel Gould's youthful regiment, 'the businesse was done by those poore little boyes (for the most part of them are such)'.[20] Nehemiah Wharton's letters reflect the education of one young soldier as he experienced the realities of war between August and October 1642.[21] As in most wars, furthermore, it was possible to rise fast. The civil war brought new opportunities for Prince Rupert and his brother Prince Maurice, aged 23 and 22 and already old soldiers when the war began. John Lambert was a 23-year-old neophyte when he enlisted in 1642 under Lord Fairfax but rapidly made a distinguished military career. Sir Thomas Fairfax had just turned 33 when he was appointed lord general of the New Model army in 1645 and was 38 when he left it in 1650. At a more modest level, Jonathan Trelawny claimed that he had raised a company of foot at 17 and a troop of horse at 18; he was a colonel when he surrendered, aged 23, in 1646.[22] In general, however, the age profile for both officers and men was mixed, and neither army appears to have been strikingly youthful. The requests for aid for the families of the dead and wounded show that many soldiers were married with children, although both armies also contained 'boys', some in traditional servant and factotum capacities, some as combatants like the 'little boys [who] strived which should first carry torches and faggots to fire [the] works' of the besieging parliamentarians at Hereford in 1645, and did so 'to some purpose'.[23] They also had their veterans with years of continental experience behind them. Patrick Ruthven, earl of Forth, was close to

---

[19] Barnes, *Vox Belli*, 24; *The Heads Of severall Petitions delivered by many of the Troopers against the Lord General And some other Officers of the Army. With the Answer which Mr. Pym Made . . . before the Committee on Tuesday, October 5. 1641* (1641), 4. Pym said, '[F]or those that have friends we shall earnestly intreat them to go into the Country to their Parents or Kinsfolkes . . . I would not willingly have you abide about this Towne for feare of scandall, there are many and great misdemeanours lately committed here in this Country, and all is layd upon your backs.' He diplomatically accepted the view that the true miscreants, already in custody, 'went in your habits'. See HEH EL MS 7765, for disorder and iconoclasm in Marshworth, Bucks on 16 Aug. 1642 by 'a certain number of soldiers calling themselves by the name of London prentices'.

[20] *A Letter from Plymouth Concerning the late Occurrances and affaires of that place* (1643), 4.

[21] Wharton, 'Letters from a Subaltern Officer', 2. 310–34 *passim*.

[22] *Trelawny Papers*, ed. W. D. Cooper, *Camden Miscellany*, 2 (1853), 10; Newman, *Royalist Officers*, 376.

[23] Duncumb, *Collections towards the History . . . of Hereford*, 1. 277–8: the besieged royalists 'imployed our boyes by day and night to steale out and fire their workes, securing their retreat under the protection of our musketiers upon the wall'. See DRO Seymour of Berry Pomeroy MSS 1392 M/L 1643/8, 1643/41, for 'one poor boy' among the sick at Dartmouth in Nov. 1643, and a shroud for a boy (perhaps the same one?) in Dec.; BL Add. MSS 11,333, fo. 12ᵛ, for an outpost

70 when he became the king's commander in chief in 1642, while his opposite number the earl of Essex, parliament's first lord general, at 51 years old, had long been a respected if intermittent soldier. In the middling age range both sides had their professionals, from Sir Charles Lucas, 35 at his death in 1648, who had served in the Netherlands and Scotland, to parliament's beloved Philip Skippon, who returned to England in 1639 after some twenty years of European service and shortly afterwards—ironically, at the king's behest—took command of the London Artillery Company. A heterogeneous age profile is predictable in any long war, and the enthusiastic flow of young volunteers appears to have slowed as the realities of war hit home.

Privilege, utility, or compassion exempted many from military service. Early in 1645, for example, when Fairfax was empowered to impress troops, the exemptions included men of very modest property (£5 in goods or £3 in land); students at Oxford, Cambridge, and the Inns of Court; esquires and their sons; servants of members of parliament; tax officials; watermen, mariners, and fishermen; and sons of widows.[24] Once in the army, sickness or incapacity was a legitimate way of leaving it, for soldiers were discharged for 'unfitness to the service'. From the army's point of view this was only practical, and those discharged as unfit normally had a pass to protect them against future attempts to impress or 'trouble' them. At least one soldier received a discharge in 1644 for incorrigible 'disaffection . . . & his perverseness to all religious exercises'. Customary exemptions could be overruled by need, as in April 1644 when the royalists ordered Oxford students to serve, albeit only locally and in segregated companies, in an auxiliary regiment for the city's defence.[25] On the other hand the claims of compassion, especially for those with connections, could overcome the pressure to recruit. One mother's plea that her son was the only hope of the house was sufficient to procure exemption for the boy. The exemption, in February 1645, was accompanied by the admission not only that the young gentleman's disinclination equalled his mother's, but that Devon had 'grown very barren of gentlemen of quality' who were anxious to serve the king.[26]

As that comment indicates, the pressures that had earlier secured enlistment met with greater resistance as the war went on, but from the beginning the responses had been mixed. The royalists had more difficulty in raising men than they expected in 1642: 'there was not such mighty or hasty confluence [to the king's standard] as was expected'.[27] Yet some volunteers flocked to

---

at Chester manned only by countrymen and boys; for wives and children, see e.g. PRO SP 28/18, fos. 112, 130, 131; SP 28/26, fos. 32, 390.

[24] Gentles, *New Model Army*, 31.

[25] *Mercurius Civicus*, 107 (5–12 June 1645), 956; BL Harl. MS 6802, fo. 99; BL Egerton MS 787, fos. 94–94ᵛ; Larkin (ed.), *Stuart Royal Proclamations*, 2. 1030–1.

[26] Devonshire RO, Seymour of Berry Pomeroy MS 1392 M/L 1645/3.

[27] *Considerations upon The present state of the Affairs of this Kingdome* (1642), 4; Joyce L. Malcolm, 'A King in Search of Soldiers: Charles I in 1642', *HJ* 21 (1978), 258–65.

join him, although their initial value was doubtful when, as one observer claimed, 'not one of ten [could] give fire'.[28] A characteristically mixed response appeared in a report of troops being raised early in the war for the earl of Northampton. 'Not many gone off here about', it began. Some, indeed, were 'stirring', but their difficulties were reflected in the comment that one gentleman 'would have furnished a good number of horses could he have got riders'.[29] Some places threw themselves enthusiastically into the war, at least initially. St Albans was only one of the towns seeking permission from parliament to form volunteer companies in August 1642, and in Manchester many members of the town militia became 'very expert musketeers, and active and able pikemen', while the 'country people . . . assembled themselves together in one large body, and marched immediately into the town, and joined the militia and the townsmen'.[30] The national or local reputations of some commanders, such as Essex, Manchester, and Brereton, brought them willing followers, but others recognized the need to prime enthusiasm by incentives. Sir George Booth did so successfully by promising tenants who enlisted recompense for harm if they survived or preferential leases for their families if they died. Others enlisted unwilling men with predictable consequences. The earl of Stamford's failure in the west and his surrender of Exeter in September 1643 were excused on grounds of local neutralism which forced him to 'fight with hands that would treat'.[31] In 1645 the defenders of Leicester had little success when they tried to call up men from the surrounding country to help them: only 150 answered the call, and their enthusiasm was doubtful. Neutralism, sympathy with the other side, and simple antipathy to violence or army life all limited willingness to serve or to fight whole-heartedly once in the army. It was only prudent that the men employed to 'conduct' recruits to regiments should be well paid for the task, but once delivered the recruits remained unpredictable. At Leicester, 'many came, that meant not to fight', and other forms of pressure—such as semi-starvation of a prisoner to force enlistment—produced equally unreliable troops.[32] Even willing volunteers were not necessarily ideal. The traditional suspicion that, unless carefully screened, a

---

[28] *Continuation of The late proceedings . . . at Shrewsbury*, 6.

[29] HEH STT Military Box 1 (25), undated, but apparently late 1642.

[30] 'A Genuine account of the Famous Siege of Manchester . . . 1642', in Fairfax, *Memoirs*, 92–4; *CJ* 2. 712, 714, 717.

[31] *Articles of Agreement Between his Excellency Prince Maurice, And the Earle of Stamford* (1643), 4; Ricraft, *Englands Champions*, 2, 17, 41–2, 76; *Narration of the Siege and Taking of . . . Leicester*, 5. See also Malcolm, 'King in Search of Soldiers', 269; *CJ* 2. 712, 714, 717, for examples of enthusiasm to serve.

[32] PRO SP 28/25 fos. 147, 148, for payments of £3 and £5 for conducting troops to Reading in Oct. 1644; *Narration of the Siege and Taking of . . . Leicester*, 5; HMC, *Seventh Report, Part I*, Appendix, 'Manuscripts of the House of Lords' (1647/8–1665), 2; and see BL Add. MS 11,333, fo. 35ᵛ for the case of Guiles Hurst, forced to serve as a foot soldier 'by compulsion', who 'came over the walls' of Chester in Dec. 1645; and Ludlow, *Memoirs*, 1. 66, for 'a souldier, whom the enemy had pressed to serve them; whose heart being with us' agreed to relay intelligence to the parliamentarians. Conducting troops could be dangerous. See Mark Stoyle, ' "Memories of the

volunteer army would contain too many of society's dregs still flourished, but it was equally clear that little had changed since Falstaff's day and that localities gladly used impressment to rid themselves of undesirables. Brereton complained to the Committee of Both Kingdoms in April 1645: 'It is my unhappiness to have an army composed of forces from several parts who often do most willingly send abroad those whom they find most discontented at home'.[33] The soldiers who had previously been sent overseas 'pro purgamento rei publica' now stayed in England.

The management of these heterogeneously composed and motivated armies fell to officers who, however diverse in enthusiasm, ideology, and background, differed surprisingly little in military practice. Both sides had officers at all levels of competence and incompetence, of commitment to their cause, and of social rank. In spite of some differences in the degree of tolerance for certain kinds of conduct, notably duelling, drunkenness, and swearing (which neither army succeeded in eliminating), the professional ideal of the soldier and gentleman was common to both. This shared code was crucial in their dealings with each other, while royalist and parliamentarian officers alike shared the problem of limiting the excesses of their often disorderly troops. Shared professional ideals, frequently reinforced by connections of family and friendship, gave form and force to agreements that moderated conduct in victory and defeat; they underpinned trust that promises would be kept and outrage when they were not. The differences of conduct and belief that separated the godly roundhead from the loyal cavalier have been intensively studied. We will see their effects in the following chapters on the officers and men of both parties, but we should also remember that these soldiers had much in common, that they faced the same problems, and acknowledged the same professional standards, and that to civilians their presence was often indistinguishable.

Maimed": The Testimony of Charles I's Former Soldiers, 1660–1730', *History*, 88 (2003), 218, for an unwilling recruit who 'struck down his man' with a stone and deserted into the woods.

[33] BL Add. MS 11,331, fo. 37ᵛ.

12

Officers

THE MAKING OF AN OFFICER

There were two necessities if soldiers were to fight well: good officers and money. Of the two, money presented the greater problem, but the deficiencies of officers continued to contribute to flight, defeat, and discontent even after the pool of experienced officers expanded as the war went on. The qualities that made a good officer, however, were well-known and traditional, and they were both technical and moral. He was professionally competent and morally admirable. He 'lived honourable as a Souldier, and dyed . . . happie as a good Christian', said the pious professional Robert Monro.[1] He was strenuous in action and generous and merciful in victory, but he was neither imprudent nor over-trusting. He was not cruel or bloodthirsty. He was a man of his word and courteous to enemies. He was not avaricious, although he deserved a worthy reward. He cared for honour, fame, and reputation, but he was not vainglorious. He was courageous but not rash, particularly when rashness put his men at risk. He cared for the welfare of his soldiers, and did not make impossible demands on them. He was friendly but maintained a distance. He was not afraid to discipline harshly, but only for just cause. He applied his mind to his trade and was good at it, whether drilling a company or directing an army. And ideally, especially if he was a general, he was lucky.[2] There was much practical advice to help this paragon. In his daily dealings with his men, for example, prudence as well as equity dictated a judicious mixture of humanity and justice, for while he must enforce discipline he must also think of his own safety. The enemy was not the only source of danger, and an officer should not be 'too rigid, and harsh, caning and beating them without cause, lest he incurre their hatred, who secretly, or in time of *battail*, will seek to be revenged of him, endaeavouring to kill him, before their enemy'.[3] The ideal

---

[1] Monro, *Expedition*, 2. 180.

[2] Ibid. 2. 152, 166–7, 170, 180, 196, 199; J. C[ruso], *The Complete Captain, or, An Abridgement of Cesars warres . . . Together With . . . a particular Treatise of modern war: Written By the late great Generall the Duke of Rohan* (Cambridge, 1640), 116–18, 189; Ricraft, *Englands Champions*, 4, 6, 25; and compare Sir John Suckling, 'A Letter written to the Lower House of Parliament' [1628], in *Somers Tracts*, 4. 111: 'there are five things necessary in a general, to wit, knowledge, valour, prevention, authority, and fortune'.

[3] Elton, *Compleat Body of the Art Military*, 184.

was a combination of courtesy and kindness that avoided the familiarity that would breed contempt.

A good officer also maintained 'civilities' in his relations with his enemies, which entailed both courtesy in observing formalities in, for example, negotiations for exchange or surrender, and sociable exchanges with acquaintances when appropriate. In a domestic and civil war, however, in which enemies were often kin or former colleagues and friends this entailed special and tricky problems, and civilians did not always appreciate soldierly conventions. When preliminary negotiations for the surrender of Worcester began in 1646, the royalist governor met one of the parliamentary colonels outside the Foregate 'to talk together, being fellow soldiers in the Low Countries'. They were joined by a hundred others for a bibulous five hours of sociability, but the 'Gentry and discreeter sort of Citizens' resented it.[4] In such matters practical and down-to-earth advice was again helpful. In September 1642, after the earl of Bedford had retired from a half-hearted siege of Sherborne undertaken on the earl of Manchester's orders, the earl of Warwick sent a letter to his son-in-law Manchester that combined recognition of the continuation of family bonds with brisk advice on avoiding their pitfalls:

It was ill advice given to send him to take or beat down his brother-in-law's castle; you had been better to have chosen another . . . I pray, stand well upon your guard, both military and politic, . . . and loose not your business with civilities and compliments. Give the Cavaliers an inch, they will take an ell.[5]

Civilities and compliments had their place, but when a conflict could not be avoided military needs must take precedence over social connection and habit. A sensible commander would try to evade such conflicts, but civilities between enemies remained seductive and persistent. They were the bane and the blessing of this intimate civil war.

As the quotations above suggest, the good officer had to negotiate his way through a diverse range of difficulties. Some were common to many wars, some specific to civil wars; some concerned relations with the enemy, some relations with his own men and colleagues. Stories of officers who met their ends at the hands of their own men are not unknown in modern wars, but the dangers of fraternization with old friends only appear acute and widespread in civil wars. The protagonists of the English civil war had to learn to act according to the traditional laws of war as well as the army's specific rules of discipline in the difficult circumstances of a war within their own society and of armies that were miscellaneous in quality and enthusiasm. Commanders, faced by confusing and often conflicting demands, picked their way between flexibility and severity. A

---

[4] Townshend, *Diary*, 1. 149–50. The incident led to '[e]xtreme murmuring' among gentlemen who feared that 'their persons and estates [were] sacrificed to the will and pleasure of soldiers of Fortune'.

[5] HMC, *Eighth Report, Appendix II* (1881), 'Manchester MSS', 59.

good officer owed it to his sense of himself as soldier and gentleman to maintain war's civilities, but equally he owed it to himself to act quickly, professionally, and if necessary ruthlessly, and not to give rise to suspicion that his efforts were rendered half-hearted by ties of friendship, family, or interest. Suspicion of backsliding, never far below the surface, was easily aroused. Nevertheless the professionalism of officers in the civil war ensured that it was fought hard but that, at least until the second war of 1648–9, it was fought without irreparably breaking the rules of war acknowledged by both sides—as had, it seemed, happened in the Germany of the Thirty Years' War—and without terminally endangering the links of kinship and neighbourhood that would enable a return to a recognizable and stable society. We shall later see the beneficial effects of these links of civility in the microcosm of the siege of Boarstall. Their risks were apparent in virtually every aspect of the civil war.

In the next sections I shall consider the question of what made a good or bad officer in practice. First, however, I shall look in more detail at the prescriptive virtues that shaped his concept of himself and at the assimilation, often partial, of a professional ideal of conduct to armies made up of many initially novice citizen officers and many reluctant soldiers. Royalists and parliamentarians shared both the ideals and the problems, and this common ground enhanced understanding between enemies despite the significant differences in ideology and conduct that remained.

The most important element in an officer's perception of himself as a good and professional soldier was his honour. The term is slippery and elusive, but there was a rough consensus about its nature and, as we have seen, it was a major factor in the enforcement of the war's codes of conduct.[6] For officers, it took two forms: the other-regarding honour of external fame and reputation, and the self-regarding honour of personal integrity, of living up to the standards set by one's sense of oneself as gentleman and soldier. External honour of the first kind, it was recognized, could be false or true. False honour was a matter of vulgar fame, celebrity, and glory, and old jokes about honour's counterfeit forms lived on. This was a fine time to gain honour, wrote a pamphleteer in 1644, 'for honour is dog-cheap now, and preferment hangs on every hedge; and if a man can but swear, and swager, and cry God damne me, but I am for the King, he is in the road-way to be knighted'.[7] True honour, on the other hand, while it did not disdain fame, reputation, and reward, was not showy but won 'the ample approbation of the better sort', although these might be few in number.[8] Fairfax epitomized the modest style of true honour for, said his son-in-law (and former royalist) the duke of Buckingham,

---

[6] B. Donagan, 'The Web of Honour: Soldiers, Christians, and Gentlemen in the English Civil War', *HJ* 44 (2001), 365–89.

[7] *The Souldiers Language. Or, A Discourse between two Souldiers* (1644), A3ᵛ.

[8] Robert Ashley, *Of Honour*, ed. Virgil B. Heltzel (San Marino, Calif., 1947), 36.

He ne're seemed Impudent but in the Field, a place
Where Impudence it self dares seldom shew its face.
Had any stranger spy'd him in a room
With some of those whom he had overcome,
And had not heard their talk, but only seen
Their Gesture, and their Mien,
They would have sworn he had the Vanquisht been:
For as they bragg'd, and dreadful would appear,
Whilst their own ill luck repeated,
His Modesty still made him blush to hear
How often he had them defeated.[9]

Concern for fame and profit were not illegitimate, however. Essex's sense of noblesse oblige to his men did not prevent him from promptly claiming and immediately receiving the £140 due to him for fourteen days' pay after he decamped from his army at Lostwithiel, nor does this appear to have harmed him in the eyes of his soldiers. Yet if such motives were too pronounced and self-interest too visible, they were suspect as smacking of continental military entrepreneurship. To be called a soldier of fortune or a 'meere mercinarie souldier' was an insult.[10] In 1644 the condemnation was clear in the report that officers hanged for treachery had 'confessed at their death that they did not fight for the cause, but for honour & gain, & so to lengthen out the war'.[11] Yet although true honour was not vainglorious, quarrelsome, or greedy, the less desirable aspects of honour survived, to the dismay of moralists and often with unfortunate consequences for military performance. We will return to the resulting debilitating squabbles between officers of the same side.

The internalized honour that derived from uncompromised personal integrity was difficult to capture in defining precepts, but it played a crucial part in shaping the conduct of enemies to each other and in justifying conduct against critics of one's own side. For the soldier, its two essential attributes were courage and fidelity. At Chester in 1645 the opposing commanders, Lord Byron and Sir William Brereton, invoked the reciprocity of 'civil and soldierly proceedings' and the reliability of 'the word of a gentleman and a soldier'. Fairfax addressed his royalist opponent Sir Ralph Hopton, as 'an honest Man, a Soldier and a Christian' whose courage was undaunted and whose actions revealed 'Principles of Honour and Conscience'.[12] This honour did not exist in an idealistic vacuum, however, but had practical consequences, for it was linked to such matters as adherence to the precise terms for exchange of prisoners or surrender of towns,

---

[9] *Short Memorials of Thomas Lord Fairfax* (1699), K–K2ᵛ.

[10] *The Clarke Papers*, ed. C. H. Firth, 2 vols. in 1 (1992), 1. 323; Townshend, *Diary*, 1. 150, on distrust of 'the will and pleasure of soldiers of Fortune'.

[11] BL Add. MS 35,297, fo. 56; PRO SP 28/18, fo. 23. See also the suspicion of 'Souldiers of Fortune, [who] would make the best of their trade, by lengthening out the Warre', W.G., *A Just Apologie for An Abused Armie* (1646), 10.

[12] BL Add. MS 11,331, fos. 22, 64ᵛ; Rushworth, 6. 105.

while penalties provided sensible hedges against failures of honour and faith. At its heart was the sanctity of the given word; the honourable soldier was not only brave and steadfast, he kept his promises. Failure to adhere to standards of courage and good faith damaged an officer's standing in the eyes of others and hence his external reputation but also, presumptively, his ideal sense of himself. He was motivated by 'feare of shame' as well as 'a certeine desire of excellencie'. To deny honour, an Elizabethan apologist had observed, was to court 'shame, reproche, and infamie', and the ideals of conduct had not changed.[13] Some officers, like Colonel Goring in the west, appeared to subordinate the demands of honour to harsh military imperatives in ways that recalled Germany and discomfited their colleagues, but the admired models were men like Colonel St George, the conscientious prisoner whose honour forced him to offer to return to custody because of delay in fulfilling all the terms of his release from imprisonment, or loyal Sir Edmund Verney, whose principles led him to fight for a king whose policies he opposed and who died resolutely defending the royal standard at Edgehill, or the second earl of Lindsey who obstinately and hopelessly defended Woodstock 'as a person of honour [was] bound to do'.[14]

When external honour seemed to be tarnished, for example by removal from command or after military failure, the victims attempted to assert their unbroken personal integrity as a means of re-establishing professional standing and public reputation. When the first earl of Lindsey was demoted in 1642 to make way for Prince Rupert, he observed with wounded dignity that 'since His Majesty thought him not fit to perform the office of Commander-in-Chief, he would serve him as a colonel', and he died leading his regiment at Edgehill.[15] After Hereford fell to parliament in 1643 Fitzwilliam Conyngsby declared that he 'should yield [his] reputation a lost thing' if he did not defend himself against the 'viperous tongues' of his fellow royalists. 'Except I mean to leave the brand of treachery and villainy upon my house and posterity', he wrote, 'I . . . ought not to be so senselessly lost to all honour and honesty as not to dare to vindicate my fame', and his consciousness of unstained integrity demanded the acknowledgement by others of his unbroken honour.[16] We have seen that when Rupert and Maurice fell from favour in 1645 they anxiously sought to establish their personal honour and faithfulness.[17] The honour of a good officer was thus not intrinsically flamboyant. Instead it operated as a general control on conduct that did not

[13] Ashley, *Of Honour*, 43.

[14] Nathan Drake, 'Journal of the First and Second Sieges of Pontefract Castle, 1644–1645', *Miscellanea*, 1.2, Surtees Society (1861), 2; Newman, *Royalist Officers*, 26; *Relation of the Battaile . . . between Keynton and Edgehill*, 3.

[15] Cited in Woolrych, *Britain in Revolution*, 229, 239; Newman, *Royalist Officers*, 27.

[16] Bodl. MS Tanner 303, fo. 125ᵛ.

[17] *A Declaration of His Highnesse Prince Rupert. With A Narrative of the . . . City and Garrison of Bristoll* (1645), 33–4; Rushworth, 6. 281; *The Humble Desires of Prince Rupert, Prince Maurice and others their Adherents, To the Kings most Excellent Majestie* (30 Dec. 1645), 4–5. This incident is a reminder that Rupert was not solely (as suggested by parliamentarian propagandists) a royal though

necessarily express itself in sensitivity to insults and in the quarrelling and duelling sometimes represented as typical of 'cavalier' behaviour. Sensitivity to insults and the need to obtain speedy public redress were indeed pervasive characteristics of the royalist armies, but they were not unknown among parliamentarians. When combined with faction or ideological fissures they made for a volatile officer corps.

If some aspects of honour were divisive, others could foster solidarity. A good officer had a keen sense of noblesse oblige to his men; a good commander felt it equally to his junior officers. Rupert, negotiating the surrender of Bristol in 1645, demanded provisions for the 'care of the Noblemen, Commanders, and Souldiers that are under my protection, of whom I am bound to have equall care with my selfe'. When he put prisoners to death early in 1645, he defended himself on grounds of obligation to his own men killed by the parliamentarians. His action was both a deterrent to protect the living and satisfaction of the duty he owed the dead.[18] When Waller pressed parliament for aid he was 'driven by the necessity of those poor men that are engaged with me in your service'.[19] Such links between officers and men were an aspect of officers' honour just as faithful service was of the men's, and they had practical military value. When his men performed well, as at the 'very tedious siege' of Beeston castle in 1645, a good commander should try to secure reward for them; when they performed less well, he should defend them as far as possible.[20] An officer should also preserve the institutional solidarity of regiment or company, which provided both community and protection, and he should care for the wounded and for the families of the dead.[21] He should also attempt to provide for his men's welfare when units were dissolved, as Essex did for the 'broken troops' that were reorganized or disbanded when the New Model was created. Indeed, one of the anxieties preceding that reorganization was not only that displaced officers would prove troublesome, but that the men would be unwilling to 'leave . . . their old, and accept . . . of new colonels'. It went off better than expected, but a strong bond was being broken: one officer declared that 'he had rather parted with his wife than his company'.[22] One of the virtues of victory at Naseby, another claimed, was that it 'seasonably' forged a bond between the officers and men of the New Model army comparable to that which the 'new moulded' soldiers

---

foreign general. He was also a young professional international soldier, for whom aspersions on his honour might dim future employment prospects.

[18] *Declaration of His Highnesse Prince Rupert. With A Narrative of. . . Bristoll*, 27; BL Add. MS 11,331, fos. 75ᵛ–76ᵛ.

[19] Bodl. MS Tanner 62/2A, fo. 410.   [20] BL Add. MS 11,331, fos. 36ᵛ–37; 11,332, fo. 92.

[21] e.g. Manchester's order for 10s. for care of 'one of my soldiers' in 1644, and Essex's order for pay for a lieutenant of his own regiment who, after 'good service', had lost everything at Lostwithiel. PRO SP 28/19, fo. 315; 28/25, fo. 362. See also the recommendation, probably from Cromwell, to the committee at Cambridge in Jan. 1645, for payment to 'This soldier of mine (Mr. Tracie) . . . a man who upon my knowledge hath very faithfully served you, his arrears are great, and his sickness much, and long'. PRO SP 28/26, fo. 225.

[22] BL Harl. MS 252, fo.33; Egerton MS 787, fo. 52.

had previously felt with their old commanders.[23] When Colonel Edgecumbe transfered his allegiance to parliament in January 1646, his prior negotiations ensured that his officers and his regiment stayed with him and shared his favorable terms.[24]

If some officers quarrelled incorrigibly, others formed strong bonds. Edgecumbe's care demonstrated the obligation of senior to junior officers. Two dozen of Colonel Henry Gage's 'old and good officers', fellow veterans of Spanish service, accompanied him to Oxford to seek employment in 1644.[25] Such incidents reflected in part a conventional patronage relationship, in which self-interest and duty joined, but the obligation to act on behalf of dependants took particular forms of soldierly solidarity. Seniors exerted such pressure as they could to secure the release of their juniors when taken prisoner or to obtain new posts for them when regiments were disbanded. Sir Samuel Luke's efforts on behalf of his officers when the Self-Denying Ordinance deprived him of his command epitomized the complex of moral, social, and professional considerations at work. He recommended all of his officers for future employment on the grounds of their 'fidelity, abilities & courage', but he made particular efforts to install his lieutenant-colonel Richard Cokayn as his successor as governor of Newport Pagnell. On 17 May 1645 Cokayn was able to write to Luke, 'Sir, Through your favour & my friends I am this day elected governor of Newport.' Pre-war systems of social obligation survived in war, and Cokayn owed gratitude to an interlocking network of parliamentary, county, family, patronal, and military connections, but it was Luke, his commander, who had been the prime mover on his behalf.[26]

One of Luke's arguments had been that Cokayn had the men's affection and that his replacement would lead to outrage and desertions. None doubted the importance of the links between officers and men in moderating soldiers' tendencies to flight, mutiny, and excesses against fellow soldiers and civilians. The loyalty that officers often exhibited in defending their men against charges by outsiders did not, however, prevent anger and anguish in their dealings with them. Soldiers' failings led to military inefficiency, but to many officers they were also a blot on their own honour. In April 1645 the depredations and embezzlements of his plundering troops were a 'shame and reproach' to Sir William Brereton as well as a political embarrassment. When his threats of severe exemplary punishment were ineffectual he wrote of the guilty soldiers, 'I have

23 Edward Wogan, 'The Proceedings of the New-moulded army from the time they were brought together in 1645, till the King's going to the Isle of Wight in 1647', in Carte, *Original Letters and Papers*, 1. 131. Compare the 200 'lusty soldiers' who offered to share their future fortune with John Gwyn after surrender. BL Add. MS 11,810, fos. 31–2.

24 Newman, *Royalist Officers*, 119; *CSPDom. 1645–1647*, 317–18, 367.

25 BL Add. MS 18,981, fos. 86–86ᵛ.

26 BL Egerton MS 787, fos. 19ᵛ, 28, 30–33ᵛ, 48ᵛ, 56. Cokayn's letter of thanks to Luke enumerated the 'very good friends' and 'countrymen' who had supported him, ibid. fo. 46ᵛ. Unfortunately Cokayn's tenure was not secure and was quickly challenged. See Luke, *Letter Books*, 616–17, 621.

no heart to come amongst them.'[27] A Captain Sandford saw his own honour threatened when his troops breached the terms of articles of surrender and he responded by trying to beat them into more honourable conduct.[28]

Honour alone was not enough. A good soldier should be competent as well as honourable. In 1645, when Rupert was under attack by fellow-royalists, his defence was that he had 'not served [the king] unadvisedly, but like a souldier, as well as a man of honour'. Officers prided themselves on their professional judgement, their 'advised' and rational expertise, and on its efficient application.[29] Before the war, as we have seen, they had acquired this expertise in several ways, of which the most notable was foreign service, and these experienced men formed a professional nucleus whose skills could be turned to domestic circumstances; a list of two hundred 'officers & gentlemen that have served in foreign parts and . . . now elected for his Majesty's service' against the Scots contained many names that were to become familiar in the 1640s.[30] As the civil war went on, however, the number who learned on the job became proportionally greater. Newman has estimated that half of the royalists of the rank of major and above whom he was able to identify were already experienced officers by 1642 (a number swelled by those with recent service in the Scottish wars), but the incidence of prior experience among junior officers must have been significantly lower.[31] The conventional view has been that parliamentary armies started at a disadvantage because they had few trained officers, while godly parliamentarians liked to see the emergence of a capable officer corps from an unmilitary population as further evidence of divine support for their cause. In the words of that great trumpet of the lord, Stephen Marshall,

God . . . can easily raise up instruments to do his worke, from whom wee would never expect it; . . . In the beginning of our publique troubles . . . Wee demanded, where shall wee finde Captaines and Commanders for a warre in a Nation where all men have been bred in ease and peace? God hath found them, and tooke Gentlemen from following their Hawkes and Dogs, and tradesmen from their shops, and Husbandmen from their ploughs, to be able to cope with the most expert Commanders in the world.[32]

---

[27] BL Add. MS 11,331, fos. 26^v, 63^v. Brereton warned that such conduct would 'bring the judgement and curse of God upon the whole army'. See also Denbigh's fretful rejection of responsibility for actions of his officers and soldiers, Bodl. MS Tanner 62/2A, fos. 420^v–421, and see fo. 381^v on 'dishonour' to the commander from his troops' ill conduct. Sir Francis Gamull was 'much troubled' by the 'carelessness' of his soldiers, BL Harl. MS 2135, fo. 46.

[28] Carte, *Original Letters and Papers*, 1. 32.

[29] *Declaration of His Highnesse Prince Rupert. With A Narrative of . . . Bristoll*, 4; Monro, *Expedition*, 2. 152; and note Fitzwilliam Conyngsby's initial favorable impression of Sir Richard Cave (before they fell out), 'the gentleman being charactered to me for a man of honour, courage, & long experience of martial affairs'. Bodl. MS Tanner 303, fo. 115^v.

[30] National Library of Wales, Chirk MS F 7442. These men, it seems, were already at home in England. Others were called home from the continent for service against the Scots.

[31] Newman, *Royalist Officers*, pp. vii–viii.

[32] Stephen Marshall, *The Right Understanding of the Times: Opened In a Sermon preached to the Honorable House of Commons, December 30. 1646. at Margaret Westminster* (1647), 5.

Gratifying as this view was to parliamentarians, the 'gentleman . . . bred up in the warres abroad' was in fact a familiar figure in the armies of both sides, for all contained significant numbers of men with professional experience who returned to arms after a period of civilian life or came home to fight. As the armies shook down in late 1642, the dangers of the loyal but unskilled enthusiast became apparent, and an incident in Essex indicates how parliament too drew on European veterans, even at the cost of affronting local pride. The earl of Warwick replied to one objector:

> If your Essex soldiers be offended at the election of other captains let them consider that the present occasion doth require men bred in warre, and experienced in these affairs. In Holland they have hazarded their lives, and spent some blood to gain a perfect knowledge of all warlike discipline . . . [L]et [Essex soldiers] not think it any dishonour in point of war to suffer the Commonwealth to be served by others as well as themselves.[33]

We have already noted the numbers of English soldiers who had pre-war continental experience; those who fought in England were of all ranks and of varying capability and degree of commitment to the cause. They ranged from the first earl of Lindsey, who had seen action in Denmark, Holland, La Rochelle, and Berwick before his death at Edgehill, to the honest, able sergeant, a veteran of the German wars, sent to help Lady Brilliana Harley in the defence of Brampton Bryan; from Scottish royalists like the Catholic earl of Crawford, who fought for Spain before and after his service in England, and the able but ageing Protestant earl of Forth, who had served Gustavus Adolphus, to the underrated parliamentarian earl of Essex who had served in Germany and Holland.[34] Five members of the royalist Byron family had fought on the continent and in Ireland; Andrew Potley, an 'old soldier', received rewards and pensions on leaving the Swedish army to enter parliament's service; Edward Massey learnt his trade as a military engineer in Holland and Scotland before serving parliament and then the king; Captain Browne Bushell fought in turn for Spain, parliament, and the king; and Sydenham Poyntz served under Protestant, Catholic, and Turkish banners before his return to England.[35] Not all such veterans were at the cutting edge of military expertise: the marquess of Newcastle could satirize the 'old limping decayed Seriant . . . that taught the boyes' and was now elevated to 'dry nurse' to Captain Underwit.[36]

[33] Quoted in Alfred Kingston, *East Anglia and the Great Civil War* (1897), 74.

[34] Newman, *Royalist Officers*, 27, 233–4; Monro, *Expedition*, 2. 108–9; Vernon F. Snow, *Essex the Rebel: The Life of Robert Devereux, the Third Earl of Essex 1591–1646* (Lincoln, Neb., 1970), 94–8, 112–14; *Letters of the Lady Brilliana Harley*, ed. T. T. Lewis, Camden Society, 58 (1854), 202, 205–6.

[35] Newman, *Royalist Officers*, 53–6; [Washbourn], *Bibliotheca Gloucestrensis*, p. clxxxix; White-lock, *Memorials*, 72; *Relation of Sydnam Poyntz*, 45, 124–6, 145, and *passim*; Sir John Maclean, *Historical and Genealogical Memoir of the Family of Poyntz* (Exeter, 1886), 161, and see pp. 181–2 for Poyntz's complaint from Amsterdam in 1648 of parliament's bad faith in its failure to pay him the 'great rewards' formerly promised.

[36] [Newcastle], *Country Captaine*, 6–7.

Not all of these returning professionals were unambiguously committed to their parties. Massey only entered parliament's service after attempts to secure attractive terms from the king failed, and later left it. Such unstable allegiance was not rare. The parliamentarian colonel Thomas Ballard, 'bred up in the warres abroad', owed his education to local gentry. When an attack on Newark under his command failed, Mrs Hutchinson attributed his 'slowth and untoward carriage' to his unwillingness to 'ruine his old benefactors', and she strongly suggested treachery. It is not altogether surprising that he later defected to the royalists.[37] Neither the admirable royalist Gage nor the parliamentarian Poyntz rushed to engage himself, postponing their returns from the continent until the war had been under way for over a year, and in 1648 Poyntz turned royalist. Even Prince Maurice could distance himself from the royal cause, perhaps partly from pique, after he laid down his command in late 1645.[38] The loyalty of professionals was often regarded as unreliable, and they were also open to the suspicion of prefering short-term military benefit to long-term social cohesion. So when the old Scottish professional Forth complained that Lord Herbert of Raglan's prompt payments to civilians for goods and services, 'all upon the penny', set a bad example, Herbert defended himself:

I yielded to his Excellencie to be a better soldier, but still to be a soldier of fortune, here today and God knows where tomorrow, and therefore needed not care for the love of the people, but though I were killed myselfe I should leave my posteritie behind me, towards whom I would not leave a grudge in the people.[39]

The expertise of English and Scottish officers who had served abroad was reinforced by foreign professionals. Their number is uncertain, but they were dispersed through both armies. Rupert and Maurice counted as the most visible on the royalist side, for despite their heroically Protestant British mother, they suffered from the xenophobia of 'the *English Nation* (who are naturally prone to hate Strangers)'.[40] Many other foreign royalists suffered the further stigma of Catholicism, and even the French Protestant officers in Waller's army in 1644 were subject to suspicions of popery; the Dutch and German professionals on both sides, however, were presumed to be acceptably Protestant.[41] Many of these foreigners were specialists, like Monsieur St Roche, the 'fire-works' expert

---

[37] Hutchinson, *Memoirs*, 76–7; Newman, *Royalist Officers*, 248; Gardiner, *History of the Great Civil War*, 4. 196, 275. Gardiner suspected that Massey had already made approaches to the royalists in 1643, ibid. 1. 198.

[38] Ibid. 4. 196—like Massey, Poyntz was a disappointed presbyterian; and see BL Add. MS 11,333, fo. 12ᵛ: in Dec. 1645, when a messenger told Maurice at Worcester that she had no letters for him, he 'said it was no great matter to him he had nothing to do for he had laid down his commission'.

[39] HMC, *Twelfth Report*, 'Beaufort MSS', 60.

[40] *The Declaration of his Highnesse Prince Rupert, Lord High Admirall of all the navy Royall* (n.pl., 1649), 3.

[41] Adair, 'Court Martial Papers', 212.

in Oxford in 1644 or the French artillerist Rupert sent to Reading, or his surgeon Anthony Choquix, and both sides used foreign engineers. Others, like the Florentines Bernard Gascoyne and John Davalier, the French Lieutenant-Colonel Jammot, and the Swedish Lieutenant-Colonel Gam, all royalists, and the Anglo-Dutch parliamentarian Vermuyden were simply professional soldiers.[42]

As Rupert's complaint indicated, foreigners, whether enemies or allies, were treated with a reserve that was chauvinist as much as anti-Catholic. It was satisfying that it was a Dutch officer, Captain Fransway, who fled prematurely at Langport, and the appreciation of Colonel Dalbier's good service to parliament was somewhat grudging: '[A]lthough he bee not an English-man, yet (I hope) none will bee so ungrateful, but acknowledge he hath done England good service.' Mrs Hutchinson disapproved of the caution of 'an old dull headed Dutchman' and of Major Mollanus, probably German, another 'ould souldier'. Both were too risk-averse for her taste. The citizens of Manchester, however, had no such reservations in praising Captain Roseworm, 'their faithful and valiant German engineer', for his contribution to their defence.[43] On occasion foreign-ness could even be useful; it was to save the Italian Gascoyne from a firing-squad in 1648.[44] It was also sometimes an uncertain quantity; the royalist artilleryman Major Carew, born in Holland of English parents, had become Dutch in popular perception.[45] Men like Vermuyden and Carew illustrate the long-standing intermingling of continental and English military experience which facilitated integration of international standards of competence and honour into English practice.

Professional soldiers were aware of their own worth, an awareness increased by the bipartisan efforts to recruit them. When Captain Jordan, who had returned from abroad and expended his own money to serve the king, petitioned for payment of arrears to relieve the poverty of himself, his wife, and five children, he strengthened his case by pointing out that he had—so far—loyally resisted the tempting offers made to him by parliament. On the other hand, Captain Simon Finch, an Irish veteran, was successfully recruited to parliament while a prisoner.[46] Many of course were resolutely loyal and committed. Lieutenant-Colonel Whitbroke, who had been recruited from Holland for parliament's

---

[42] Newman, *Royalist Officers*, 104, 148, 150, 209; William Salt Library, Salt MSS 477.

[43] *Exact and Perfect Relation of the Proceedings of the Army . . . near Langport*, (i2); *The Coppie of A Letter From Sir Thomas Fairfax his Quarters* [1645], i2; Ricraft, *Champions*, 82–3; Hutchinson, *Memoirs*, 98, 100; 'A Genuine Account of The Famous Siege of Manchester', in Fairfax, *Memoirs*, 93–4, 99, 126. See also the praise for a Dutch trooper who took over from a dead cannoneer at Leicester until he was himself 'thrust through' by a pike. *A more Exact Relation of The Siege laid to the Town of Leicester* (1645), 7.

[44] Clarendon, *History*, 3. 137–38.

[45] Firth and Davies, *Regimental History*, 1. 200; Sprigge, *Anglia Rediviva*, 28–9; a regiment refered to as 'Vermodeus' was present at Langport in July. *Coppie of a Letter from Sir Thomas Fairfax his Quarters*, 2; *Narration of the Siege . . . of Leicester*, 4; *Rider of the White Horse*, in Lister, *Autobiography*, 65, 69.

[46] BL Harl. MSS 6804, fo. 99; 2135, fos. 79, 81. Finch's brothers remained royalist and were granted his goods.

service, worked resolutely for the defence of Leicester in 1645, with the aid of a captain who was also a 'Low-country Souldier' and 'another old Souldier, that had been above 30 years in forrain service'.[47] The king's efforts to turn 'the honest English captain' and veteran of the Dutch wars Philip Skippon met with no success, while Colonel Stephen Hawkins's disgruntlement at failure to receive the preferential treatment he believed he deserved for foreign, Scottish, and English service never led him to waver in his loyalty to the king.[48]

The war produced new professionals to swell the ranks of pre-war veterans, men who did not revert to civilian life when fighting ceased but continued their military careers in Ireland, Scotland, and on the continent. Former royalists were to join former parliamentarians in fighting Irish and Scots. Some re-enlistments were hardly voluntary, like those after Naseby and the second civil war, but experienced officers were also tempted by incentives such as the field command against the Scots offered in 1646 to the royalist John Gwyn (which he in fact refused), he 'being well known' to the parliamentarians.[49] Knowledgeable old soldiers retained their value. In 1658 Henry Cromwell recommended a Captain Staples: 'He is a person . . . of a very clear reputation, and generally known to the officers of the army, having always served among us from the beginning of the warr, and well experienced in foot service.' In the same year a Captain Nicholas advertised for recruits for Dunkirk: 'The Captain himself, being an old soldier, chuseth rather to accept of such in the service; therefore any that are old soldiers, or gentlemen, if they repair to the Bell Inn in Kingstreet Westminster, or to the sign of the Pelican in Spinnamland at Newbury may be entertained into the said troop.'[50] The emergence of a body of experienced soldiers, coherent and continuous enough to be seen as the nucleus of the armies of the later seventeenth century and hence of a standing professional English army, can be traced back to the forces of the 1640s. Even when they served on different sides in continental wars, many old officers retained a certain bipartisan professional solidarity. Years later, when they met on opposite sides at Dunkirk, national and professional ties combined as 'old English officers' ate and drank together, exchanged courtesies, and admitted certain unchanging verities of military life: 'they all knew very well what it was to run away from their colours'.[51] Then, as in England in the 1640s, shared ideals of civil and soldierly behaviour moderated the conduct of officers towards each other, while a shared professional culture that admired competence but also acknowledged the realities

---

[47] *Narration of the Siege . . . of Leicester*, 5–6, 11.

[48] [Washbourn], *Bibliotheca Gloucestrensis*, cxxxix; BL Harl. MS 6852, fo. 253.

[49] BL Add. MS 11,810, fo. 31ᵛ. Gwyn served under the earl of Holland in the second civil war, and fought with the Scots at Dunkirk. Ibid., *passim*.

[50] Quoted in Firth and Davies, *Regimental History*, 2. 669, 672; see also 2, chs. 7–13 *passim*, for personnel and careers in English regiments in Ireland, Flanders and the West Indies to 1660, and see 1. xx–xxxvi for the constitution of English armies 1648–60.

[51] BL Add. MS 11,810, fos. 58ᵛ–61ᵛ. For the heterogeneous nature of English officers in the 1650s and into the 1660s, see Firth and Davies, *Regimental History*, 2. 674–5, 695–8.

of human responses, both good and bad, to battle, wounds, chaos, cold, hunger, and fatigue, continued to form another link between enemies. It explains, as in other wars, the difference in tone between soldiers' and propagandists' accounts of events.

Pre-war professionalism and commitment to a military career were not the only ways to effective officer formation. Cromwell, Fairfax, Waller, and even King Charles, exemplify self-made commanders of talent. Both Colonel Edward Harley and his mother lady Brilliana demonstrated the successful application of intelligence, energy, persistence, and force of character to military problems; so, for that matter, did Lady Bankes at Corfe Castle and the countess of Derby at Lathom House. It was not necessary to be a professional soldier or to travel abroad to acquire pre-war knowledge that could quickly form a valuable wartime officer. As we have seen, the art of war was far from forgotten at home even in England's halcyon days of peace and even by civilians. The trained bands, for all their deficiencies, nurtured some serious and enthusiastic civil war officers, men like the royalist colonel Henry Lingen who, as a trained band captain, had mustered his forces by May of 1642, and went on to an active and capable career through the first and second wars.[52] The pre-war skills of London's citizen soldiers enriched the armies of both sides, while serious reading of the flood of technical military publication and of European news in the 1620s and 1630s had helped to prepare many for domestic war. Even in specialist fields innovative talent did not need pre-war combat or travel to flower. James Wemyss, a Scot who became a self-taught artillery expert in London, a patentee and inventor who rose to be Charles's master-gunner with a pension of £300 a year, threw in his lot with parliament in 1642. His reputation was such that the royalists tried to rerecruit him and the parliamentarians exerted themselves to retain him.[53] Even more striking, of course, is Cromwell's self-created military talent. Indeed, there were advantages to self-creation. Fairfax's military education came in part from his brief foreign experience when young, in part from the strong military tradition of his family, but much derived from the light of reason freshly applied to military problems. It was one of his virtues, said his panegyrist, that he was not hidebound by conventional military wisdom: 'His successe hath run through a line crosse to that of old Souldiery, of long Sieges and slow Approaches; and he hath done all so soon, because he was ever doing.'[54] Accounts of Fairfax's decision-making show the process in action; he listened to the opinions of his

---

[52] Newman, *Royalist Officers*, 234; Bodl. MS Tanner 303, fo. 114; HMC, *Bath MSS*, 1. 8, 11, 16, 22 (for Lingen's part in the siege of Brampton Bryan); Hutton, *Royalist War Effort*, 112–15, 136, 199.

[53] Walker, *Historical Discourses*, 32; *DNB*, 'James Wemyss'; in 1648 Wemyss returned to Scotland, fought at Dunbar and Worcester, and was captured and imprisoned in Windsor castle. Charles II reinstated him as master-gunner of England.

[54] Sprigge, *Anglia Rediviva*, 321–2. This was written before Fairfax's slow (but militarily rational) siege of Colchester.

officers but issued his orders in accordance with his own judgement, which sometimes ran counter to theirs.

From such diverse sources, and increasingly from field experience in England, officer corps emerged whose members were judged by their peers for adherence to professional standards of competence and honour, and by their men in more complex, more pragmatic, and less explicit ways.

GOOD AND BAD OFFICERS

The test of good officers lay in what they could get out of their soldiers: in how intelligently they deployed them, in what they successfully demanded of them, and in how well they controlled them. Some commanders drew recruits for reasons of family, region, reputation, and religion, but they kept them partly by force of character, partly by fulfilling hopes of reward, and partly by care for their welfare that sometimes led to affection such as that which Essex seems genuinely to have won from his troops. Civilians in turn benefited from good officers who enforced discipline and kept their men reasonably contented. Yet even the best of officers could be defeated by conditions beyond their control, of which the most prevalent was lack of money to pay their men, while officers whose vices outweighed their virtues (in the view of their peers) might win the loyalty of their soldiers. The following account of the ideal and the actual character of civil war officers is interspersed with narratives of real officers in action that demonstrate a sometimes uncomfortable juxtaposition of qualities: charisma and ruthlessness, courage and stupidity, skill and luck. There were a few paragons, many enigmas, and some outright villains leading the troops in the 1640s.

A good officer cared for his men's physical welfare and was aware of the limits of fatigue, hunger, cold, and morale beyond which it was unreasonable to push them, but he could not be soft in his demands for action or for discipline. As we have seen, he was advised to keep a discreet distance while still behaving 'lovingly' to his troops and, in the words of a parliamentarian catechist, remembering that they were men, not bears. The royalist citizen-colonel Sir Francis Gamull observed that 'where a gentle hand cannot prevail, a violent course must force and command', but in practice the power to lead and to discipline proved inseparable from the power to pay. In 1640 one commander had written, 'I know not any enemy so terrible as want of money', and in the civil war the problems were compounded.[55] Gamull, like other officers, recognized that decent conditions in general and regular pay in particular led to 'greater alacrity' on the part of troops ('money best stoppeth all discontented men's mouths', he said), and also made it feasible to exact better service by 'stricter commands'.[56]

55 *CSPDom. 1640*, 526.   56 BL Harl. MS 2135, fo. 46.

Officers were constantly aware of the state of their troops' pay, for mutiny sent frequent seismic tremors through civil war armies even if full-scale, major eruptions were rare, and money, or its absence, was the most frequent cause. Short of open mutiny, without money troops disbanded, fought half-heartedly, melted away, or increased their unofficial demands on the civilian population. The earl of Denbigh, defending his errant soldiers in 1643, declared they were 'made desperate... for want of pay'.[57] Officers lobbied higher officers and central governments for pay for their men from a combination of self-interest and obligation. They also acted as lenders who advanced money from their own pockets against future reimbursement. Lieutenant-Colonel Thomas Gell's expenditures in 1643 included 'money lent and paid... to keep his soldiers from mutiny when they had no pay'.[58] Waller and Hesilrige sent an impassioned plea to London in June 1643 when they had the royalists at a disadvantage but were unable to take action:

We must not hazard your trust like fools. Neither can we stay here and starve. We have long and often supplicated you for money; [find us] but a way to live without it or else we humbly beg a present supply if not this horse will certainly disband which thought makes our hearts to bleed.[59]

Official pay was not the only incentive offered to soldiers. Officers used the hope of plunder and booty as a stimulus to action; on other occasions they offered rewards for refraining from plunder, or for undertaking particularly risky tasks. In 1643 Essex offered to pay each soldier 12s. in lieu of the storm, sack, and plunder of Reading which generous articles of surrender had plucked from their eager hands.[60] A free hand at extortion was an even more certain way to win soldiers' support, although it alienated civilians. The freedom Colonel Goring allowed his troops in Cornwall dismayed royalist headquarters and turned the county against the king, but it won his men's loyalty.[61]

Money was not an officer's only way to his soldiers' hearts. The sense that officers imaginatively entered into their hardships and did their best to mitigate them helped to forge strong bonds. Brereton, as we have seen, found excuses for the discontent and intermittent mutinies among his unpaid troops around

[57] Bodl. MS Tanner 62/2A, fo. 420ᵛ. See BL Add. MS 11,331, fo. 157ᵛ, for a combination of 'grand mutiny', departure, and dumb insolence in May 1645. Many soldiers had 'broken their muskets and sworn they [would] never serve in this county again' unless they were paid.

[58] Derbys. RO, Gell MSS, D258, 31/30 (aa).

[59] Bodl. MS Tanner 62/1A, fo. 128. For lobbying, see also BL Harl. MS 2135, fo. 46; BL Add. MS 11,332, fo. 40. For advances by officers, see PRO SP 28/25, fo. 3, for the account of Colonel Pickering, 11 June–15 July 1644, which included £ 4 19s. 0d. for money lent to eleven men, 'some dead and run away'; the account was paid in full, i.e. loans were accepted as standard expenses, and see SP 28/25, fo. 69 ('for money lent to men, some dead—11–0'); SP 28/26, fos. 5, 26.

[60] Bodl. MS Tanner 62/1A, fos. 76, 85. The offer proved ineffectual in either protecting Reading or maintaining discipline.

[61] HMC, *Thirteenth Report. Appendix 1. Portland MSS*, 1 (1891), 227–8; Newman, *Royalist Officers*, 162.

Chester in the 'extreme and violent, cold and wet' November of 1645.[62] Some commanders deployed dramatic gestures to proclaim their identity with their men. In December 1642, after the royalist repulse from Tadcaster, the earl of Newcastle 'in a galantry . . . lay with his men in the fields all that night'.[63] The king, we are told, never took to his coach to escape bad weather but patiently endured it, 'how foul soever', like the rest of his army. At Colchester the royalist commanders 'hutted upon the line, where they fedd, and lodged' with their hungry, weary soldiers. Hence the awkwardness of justifying Essex's escape from Fowey in 1644, leaving his men to defeat and misery.[64] Still, sharing did not require equality of suffering, nor equal valuation of sufferers. Reports of casualties constantly made clear that officers' lives were worth more than soldiers'. Nor were all soldiers equal; the foot, as 'least regarded', might be left to the hardship of open fields while better lodgings were found for the cavalry. When officers suffered, it was safe to assume that their men suffered more: 'I dare well say that in 48. hours not a Commander eate a bit, much less a Common Souldier', ran an officer's account of a Yorkshire action at the end of 1642, 'some Sacke we had, but that was not for the poore Souldiers'.[65]

Nevertheless, moral responsibility for one's men and military common sense demanded that officers care for 'the poore Souldiers', and recognize their limits. So a change in the weather caused a council of war to rescind previous orders because the cold would be too much for the troops; the fatigue of '8 days' duty & long watching' provided a reasonable excuse for a retreat; and officers who surrendered a weary, reduced, demoralized, and unrelieved garrison to a force of 'fresh & victorious' men might escape severe censure. Commanders of both sides adapted their plans to provide respite for the 'extream weariness' of men 'tired out with perpetual Duty, and continual Fight'; for men so 'overmarched' and exhausted that they could not be asked to renew engagements; or for armies disabled by 'want of Provision and too great Duty'. In such circumstances, officers who could do so withdrew to 'recreate', regroup, rest, and refresh their soldiers. In 1645 Fairfax delayed pursuit of the royalists into Cornwall, 'fearing to overmarch his men'.[66] Such care, together with attention to shelter, food, clothing, and sanitation, was part of the traditional prescription for the

[62] BL Add. MS 11,332, fo. 77ᵛ.

[63] Sir Henry Foulis, *An Exact and True Relation of a Bloody Fight, Performed against the Earl of Newcastle . . . before Tadcaster and Selby* (1642), 6; see also Clive Holmes, *The Eastern Association in the English Civil War* (Cambridge 1974), 197, on Manchester, who marched with his men on the muddy road from Selby to York.

[64] HMC, *Twelfth Report*, 'Beaufort MSS', 28; Rushworth, 5. 701–4; Ricraft, *Englands Champions*, 57; Slingsby, *Diary*, 145–6, likening Langdale to Caesar, who taught his men 'to endure hardships, by his own example, lighting from his horse & leading ym on foot many times with his head bare, whether the sun did shine, or ye clouds did pour down rain'.

[65] Foulis, *Exact and True Relation*, 6, 42; *Exact and Perfect Relation . . . Langport*, 7.

[66] BL Add. MSS 11,333, fo. 63ᵛ; 35,297, fos. 4–4ᵛ; Rushworth, 5. 708–9; Bailey, *Annals of Nottinghamshire*, 2. 720; Walker, *Historical Discourses*, 35; Carte, *Letters*, 1. 142 (properly 143).

conscientious officer. It united the hearts of soldiers and superior officers, said a pre-war military authority, adding pragmatically that its absence led to double losses, from sickness and from the enemy, to which he might have added the loss of soldiers who voted with their feet by absenting themselves.[67]

A final desirable attribute in a commander was unwillingness to hazard lives unnecessarily. Manchester instructed his officers that they should not do so, while the caution that weakened Essex's performance as a commander derived in part from care for his troops. It delayed his capture of Reading in 1643 for, he explained, 'I am very loath to venture the soldiers upon such works being probable that many may be lost in the storming.' Fairfax was to make a similar calculation at Colchester.[68] Other commanders were less solicitous, while the distinction between the value of the lives of officers and of common soldiers was reasserted in Sir John Gell's explanation of his unwillingness to send his men into action in 1644. For the common soldiers the reasons were purely pragmatic; for the officers they derived from their right as serious moral actors like himself to share in decisions over their own fate:

> our soldiers do expect monies, which if they have not I cannot expect further service from them, one other thing is that I . . . do desire to confer with those captains and officers that should go upon the service before I order them upon service it concerns their lives, and the truth is I am very tender of those brave and valiant friends that have been so faithful in our service.[69]

Not all officers were honourable, competent, zealous, or loved by their men, and many civil war complaints were variations on traditional themes. The pamphleteer of 1644 who complained of captains who 'behave . . . womanish', and who were to be identified '[b]y their Scarfs, not by their scars, skill, or courage' only echoed Elizabethan comparisons between 'silken, golden, embroydered delicate Captaines' and their 'plaine leather, well armed, sober, painefull, valiant' brethren. The latter were clearly forerunners of Cromwell's plain, russet-coated men. Cowardice, greed, drunkenness, absenteeism, quarrelling, and negligence were equally traditional complaints that persisted in the civil war.[70] Even the New Model contained 'deboist Officers' whose drunken habits were restrained with difficulty.[71] Among the royalists, we are told, Colonel Goring 'strangely

---

[67] Robert Ward, *Anima'dversions of Warre: or, A Militarie Magazine of the truest Rules, and Ablest Instructions, for the Managing of War . . . In two Bookes* (1639), 2. 31–2; see also Cruso, *Complete Captain*, 116–17.

[68] Bodl. MS Tanner 62/1A, fo. 76. At Reading the men's gratitude for Essex's solicitude was offset by frustration at the loss of the profits of a storm; see n. 60 above.

[69] Derbys. RO, Sanders MSS 1232 M/08.

[70] *Souldiers Language*, A3; Thomas and Dudly Digges, *Four Paradoxes, or politique Discourses* (1604), 11, and see also 3–5, 16–17, 23–5, 50, 68.

[71] W.G., *Just Apologie for An Abused Armie*, 11: 'I have been glad to heare a deboist Officer saying to his Comrades, when they have been drinking, We must take heed we exceed not our bounds, the Councel of War will reckon with us.'

loved the Bottle, was much given to his Pleasures, and a great Debauchee'. He was cleverer and braver than his rival Lord Wilmot, another heavy drinker, but '*Wilmot* always shut Debauchery out of his Business, and so rarely miscarried in it . . . *Wilmot* never drank, when he was within Distance of an Enemy, and *Goring* seldom or never refused it.' Ultimately, encouraged by two deplorable cronies, Goring's 'Wantonness' turned to 'Riot, and his Riot into Madness'.[72] Admittedly the witness in this case was not impartial, but Goring was not the only royalist officer whose violence was pathological, and it seems probable that the incidence of heavy drinking contributed to the incidence of quarrels in the king's officer corps.

Dramatic instances of cowardice, the great military sin, were rare on either side, although prudent but unpopular withdrawals, as at Saltash in 1644, were likely to lead to accusations of faintheartedness if not outright treachery.[73] Yet even the Falstaffian Captain Bedel, who 'cast . . . himself amongst the dead bodies (as if kill'd)', was only trying to elude capture, and even the major who barely escaped court martial for refusing to march at Preston, only to be shamed by his sergeant's courage, could plausibly argue that he was waiting for reinforcements.[74] Surrender of strongpoints was always a delicate matter but mere flight, given the mobility and volatility of military actions, was hardly distinctive enough to qualify as cowardice.

Unlike cowardice, absenteeism was a chronic problem in all armies. The war had barely begun when parliament blamed the disorders committed by its soldiers on officers' failure to accompany their men on their marches. Attempts to enforce officers' presence by restricting pay to 'such as duly attend their charge' met with limited success.[75] Less than six weeks after Naseby the House of Commons sent for some of Fairfax's officers who had been observed in Westminster Hall and the City, to discover the reason for their 'stay here in Towne in this time of such great action abroad'. The previous year, with the campaigning season well under way, Waller had recalled absentee officers from London 'upon payne of Death' for non-compliance.[76] For the royalists, Oxford had a similar attraction, and they too were troubled by 'officers and souldiers who . . . wander abroad & neglect theire duties and commands'.[77]

---

[72] Bulstrode, *Memoirs and Reflections*, 115–16, 134.

[73] The colonel in charge 'through cowardice quitted Saltash'. BL Add. MS 35,297, fo. 46; a fort was lost at Plymouth by an ensign's 'treachery or cowardize', *A True Narration Of the most observable Passages, in and at the late Seige of Plymouth . . . 1643* (1644), 3.

[74] *Bamfeild's Apologie*, 9; 'Memoirs of Captain John Hodgson', in *Original Memoirs, . . . being the Life of Sir Henry Slingsby, and Memoirs of Capt. Hodgson*, 118.

[75] *Orders of the Lords and Commons . . . For the Regulating of those Souldiers . . . under the Command of his Excellency, Robert Earle of Essex* (19 Aug. 1642); see also Firth and Rait, 1. 403 (ordinance of 26 Mar. 1644).

[76] *A Perfect Diurnall* (1648), no. 104 (21–8 July 1645), 825; *CJ* 4. 215; Adair, 'Court Martial Papers', 209–10; see also *All the severall Ordinances of the Lords and Commons . . . For the speedy establishing of a Court Martiall* (19 Aug. [*sic*] 1644), 8, for a similar proclamation of 16 Sept. 1644.

[77] Larkin, *Stuart Royal Proclamations*, 2. 906–7, 931–2, 936–7, 945. Among royalists especially, war weariness and discouragement may have increased absenteeism. When the king precipitately left

Some officers became more permanent absentees from their original colours by changing sides. Each party tried to attract the other's officers, and a significant number succumbed to a variety of lures. The ease of such defections in a civil war increased readiness to suspect colleagues when quarrels heightened tension or the cause was going badly, and notorious defections such as that of Sir Richard Grenvile, 'that runnagado', inflamed suspicions.[78] Reasons ranged from promises of advancement by the tempter-enemy to disillusion with one's own side (especially among parliamentarians, as their cause seemed to change) to prudence (especially among royalists, as their cause seemed lost).[79] One royalist turned parliamentarian because he feared retribution for speaking out against papists. One parliamentarian turned royalist at least in part because he became enmeshed in the complex plottings of royalist cousins. He paid a high price, and was executed for treason in 1651.[80] The risks were high for a recaptured renegade. Major Brookband, a royalist prisoner taken by Skippon in 1643, 'having formerly deserted the Parliaments Service, was Tried for the same by a Council of War, Condemned, and Shot to Death'.[81] Some renegades were acquisitions of dubious value, like the improvident captain whose defection was impelled by his financial problems; having spent his advance in London, he left debts and unpaid soldiers behind him and went over to the royalists. They often—like that captain—sowed distrust on both sides, spreading unease among former colleagues and uncertainty among new allies.[82] Some indeed were plants, like young Captain Grenvile, Sir Richard's kinsman, who 'came in' to Plymouth 'as if he had departed from the king's party and would serve the parliament'. Promptly made a captain by his new masters, within a week he was attempting to procure a counter-defection by offering a colonel preferment and £300 to join the royalists. The colonel revealed all and Grenvile was summarily tried and hanged 'as a traitor to the state'.[83] Loyalty and treachery became increasingly complex issues, rendered more difficult by the oaths that were broken (in the view of parliamentarians) by royalists who engaged in the second civil war, by the problem of identifying with certainty the sovereign power to which one was traitor, by genuine changes of heart or disillusion, and even by the economic

Oxford in Aug. 1645, many 'gentlemen' stayed behind, 'tired with the Tediousness and Misfortune of the Summer'. Walker, *Historical Discourses*, 136.

[78] BL Add. MS 35,297, fo. 26; and see PRO SP 28/260, fo. 8 (for apparently unjustified suspicion of intent to defect). Newman has estimated that '[s]ome twenty-four of the King's colonels changed sides between 1642 and 1646'; of these, fifteen went over to parliament and nine left parliament for the king. Five more were suspected of harbouring intentions to change sides. P. R. Newman, *The Old Service: Royalist Regimental Colonels and the Civil War, 1642–46* (Manchester, 1993), 119.

[79] BL Harl. MSS 2135, fo. 79; 6802, fo. 258; BL Add. MSS 11,810, fo. 31ᵛ; 35,297, fo. 30ᵛ.

[80] BL Add. MS 11,331, fo. 157; Binns, 'Browne Bushell', 92–7, 104. Renegades were normally tried by court martial. The decision to try Bushell, captured five years after his defection, for treason in a civil court reflected the changed political context after the second civil war.

[81] Rushworth, 5. 297. Other turncoats, although equally undeserving—like Colonel Farr at Colchester (see below)—survived and throve through good luck or the right connections.

[82] BL Add. MS 35,297, fo. 34ᵛ.   [83] Ibid., fo. 47ᵛ.

need to continue professional employment. Residual distrust of the side-changer remained, in spite of a distinguished roster that included such names as Anthony Ashley Cooper, Edward Massey, and James Wemyss. The loyal royalist John Gwyn, who had resisted parliament's bait, retained an 'antipathy against a runaway cavalier' that added zest to attacking renegades in their new service. Sir Richard Bulstrode's animus against his fellow-royalist Colonel Goring stemmed in part from Goring's early change of allegiance; even though it had brought him to the king's side, Bulstrode still smelled untrustworthiness and opportunism.[84]

Some officers, though loyal, were incompetent, making unrealistically severe demands on troops, overriding advice from capable but socially inferior fellow officers, and neglecting obvious preparations. Fitzwilliam Conyngsby bitterly levelled all of these charges at his fellow-royalist Sir Richard Cave after the loss of Hereford.[85] Others, particularly early in the war, were too inexperienced to be efficient, as Warwick had observed to his offended Essex officers. In 1643 Sir Thomas Aston complained that the combination of 'raw men with unready officers' was an infallible recipe for defeat, while a parliamentarian officer anxiously sought a transfer to Nathaniel Fiennes's command because, he said, in his present regiment only two captains 'doth know anything'.[86] In 1644 Waller's council of war, in an effort to improve the performance of cavalry officers, revealingly prescribed punishments for officers who were tardy in bringing their regiments to the army's rendezvous; who were careless in seeking and carrying out orders; who absented themselves from guard duty; and who were negligent in curbing mutinies.[87]

Royalist officers appear to have been particularly prone to certain professional failings. Goring and Wilmot were not unique either in their quarrels or their drunkenness. The ferocious Captain Hodgkins, alias Wicked Will and so famous 'for his desperateness and valour' that he was 'terrible to the Enemy', undertook one foray 'in a medley humour of drink' and was 'so loaded with drink and top heavy that he fell twice by the way, and was carried over Severn in a boat half asleep'.[88] Collectively, there were instances of curious inertia and frivolity. After Tewkesbury was recaptured by parliament in 1643 a royalist lamented, 'those

[84] BL Add. MS 11,810, fos. 29ᵛ–30ᵛ; Bulstrode, *Memoirs and Reflections*, 103; and see Whitelocke's unflattering comment in his *Memoirs*, 81, on Colonel Monck, a royalist in 1643, 'who afterwards served the Parliament, and this was his first turn'—a later 'turn' ensured the restoration of Charles II.

[85] Bodl. MS Tanner 303, fos.115ᵛ, 121, 124: Cave kept men 'in arms 72 hours together and then without refreshment commanded [them] to march to Hereford 12 miles from Monmouth, after 3 of the clock in the afternoon, in which dead march were lost both men & arms to a great proportion'. The good advice of one officer was dismissed because 'his calling was not liable to command'.

[86] BL Harl. MS 2135, fo. 103ᵛ; Bodl. MS Clarendon 22, fo. 75. For precipitate induction to the battlefield, see the case of Isaac Bennet of London, who presented himself at Reading in 1643, was enrolled as a lieutenant, and was in action three days later. *Good and true Intelligence from Reading* (1643), A2–[A3].

[87] Adair, 'Court Martial Papers', 215–16.   [88] Townshend, *Diary*, 1. 126, 167.

that were slain were killed at their ease & in bed, so ever fatal hath security & love of clean sheets been to the king's army'. Another deplored the ambition, laziness, indiscipline, luxury, and dilettantism of the king's officer corps. After Naseby, when the king retired to Raglan castle for three weeks, his faithful secretary regretted, '[W]e were all lulled asleep with Sports and Entertainments, as if no Crown had been at Stake or in danger to be lost.' John Gwyn's refrain in his account of the second civil war was of lost opportunities that could have been exploited if the royalists had 'acted any thing like soldiers'.[89] More endemic and divisive, however, was the royalist tendency to quarrel. We have already noted that their articles of war devoted more attention to quarrels and duels than the parliamentarians'. Quarrels between higher officers over military policy, allocation of resources, office, and prestige shaded into personal quarrels at all levels that arose from causes ranging from slights to honour to irascible bloody-mindedness. Simmering quarrels between senior officers, like those between Sir William Vavasour and Lord Herbert, between Lord Wilmot and Prince Rupert, and indeed between Rupert and assorted royalists from the king down, weakened them militarily and imparted an instability to the command structure surpassing that arising from even the best-known parliamentarian feuds, such as those between Manchester and Cromwell or Waller and Essex, or from ill-feeling following exclusion after the formation of the New Model army.[90]

On both sides, tensions between officers competing for precedence or for men and money, or objecting to depredations by colleagues that hampered their own interests, or disagreeing over policy, or resenting ouster from office, or merely disliking each other, were common, and often broke through the restraints of civility and shared allegiance.[91] Such quarrels pre-dated the civil war. In 1639 quarrels between English officers in Spanish service were 'so high and irreconcilable' that they 'undervalued' the reputation of English forces in Flanders. In 1640, on home ground, viscount Conway wrote to his general, the earl of Northumberland, of the 'many differences' between his officers.[92] Nor

---

[89] Walker, *Historical Discourses*, 116 [132]; BL Add. MS 11,810, fo. 34; HMC, *Twelfth Report*, 'Beaufort MSS', 27.

[90] See Hutton, *Royalist War Effort*, 118, 131, 134–5; 'Journal of Prince Rupert's Marches', *EHR* 13 (1898), 738; Walker, *Historical Discourses*, 125–6; Devonshire RO, Seymour of Berry Pomeroy MS 1392 M/L 1644/44; BL Add. MS 11,333, fo. 24; 18,981, fo. 86; BL Harl. MS 6802, fos. 264, 348–348ᵛ, 15 [2] (on Wilmot's disgrace and attempted exculpation in 1644); Newman, *Royalist Officers*, 416. See also the interlocking quarrels and fluctuating favour of the senior royalist officers William Ashburnham, Sir John Berkeley, Lord Digby, and Lord Mohun, ibid. 8, 25, 109, 257. On presbyterian resentment over exclusion from the New Model, see Thomas Edwards, *The third Part of Gangraena* (1646), 273, and the response of W.G., *Just Apologie for An Abused Armie, passim*.

[91] See BL Add. MS 11,331, fos. 14ᵛ–15, 34ᵛ–37, 56ᵛ; Devonshire RO, Seymour of Berry Pomeroy MSS 1392 M/L 1644/25, 26, 1645/8, 12, 17, 20; J. S. Morrill, *Cheshire 1630–1660* (Oxford, 1974), 148–51, on the deterioration of relations between Brereton and Sir Thomas Myddelton and other commanders. For other parliamentary examples, see HMC, *Portland Manuscripts, Thirteenth Report*, 1. 310; *Fourteenth Report*, 3. 119, 120.

[92] Bodl. MS Clarendon, 15, fos. 86–87ᵛ, 105; *CSPDom. 1640*, 526.

were parliamentary armies immune from officer quarrels that disrupted military efforts and public order. Colonel Hutchinson's troubles with his colleagues were bitterly recorded by his wife. Derby was riven by the quarrels swirling around Sir John Gell.[93] Late in 1644 'there was such difference among the officers at Plymouth', caused by Lord Robartes's punishment of four of their number for swearing, that it spilled over into a violent quarrel between a ship's captain who held that 'there was no commander but must and would swear at times' and the aggravatingly reformist chaplain John Syms, a quarrel that culminated in the captain's lying in wait for the minister and beating him on the dark streets of the town.[94] The incident is a reminder that parliament too had its 'traditional' unreformed officers with a short fuse and a predilection for resolving differences by violence. Sometimes the form was ritualized, as in the case of the parliamentary major who objected to advice at a council of war and later, in the street, gave a provocative blow to the advice-giver, whereupon they drew their swords and the major was killed.[95] Other quarrels found a resolution within the bounds of military law, as when Brereton secured trials, and in one case cashiering, of officers who uttered 'ill and unbecoming words' against him, or when Waller's feuding officers were brought before a court martial. In 1645 only the 'moderation' of a parliamentary colonel prevented a duel after a quarrel in Westminster Hall itself. Other complaints, like Denbigh's of his officers' disobedience and 'private disputes', were less satisfactorily settled. In one case referred to Essex for settlement he could only recommend resignation by one of the quarrelling officers, in the hope of 'avoid[ing] contention'. In another case Luke reported that one party to a dispute was so discontented that he was said to be contemplating defection to Oxford.[96]

Nevertheless although it would be a mistake to idealize parliament's armies for peaceable unity in their godly cause, to a considerable extent the personal passions that produced such destructive fissures among royalists were subsumed in the

[93] Hutchinson, *Memoir*, 111–12, 117, 128–46 *passim*, and note Mrs Hutchinson's complaints, 129, of 'sloth and muttering . . . humor and faction' among officers; see also Derbys. RO, Sanders MS 1232 M, fos. 108 ff., and see Gell and Sanders MSS *passim*, for the complex quarrels in Derby in which military, political, religious, and personal motives mingled; they involved soldiers and civilians, officers and parliamentary candidates, and festered for years.

[94] BL Add. MS 35,297, fos. 53ᵛ–56, 62. Syms's attempts to obtain redress foundered on professional solidarity. The commissioners at the ensuing inquiry 'being captains were all for [the offender]'. Ibid., fo. 57ᵛ.

[95] Bodl. MS Tanner 61, fo. 106; *CJ* 3. 712; [Washbourn], *Bibliotheca Gloucestrensis*, 100, 109; Major Robert Hammond was tried for the murder of Major Gray and was acquitted on grounds of self-defence. See Tanner 62/2A, fos. 420ᵛ–421 for a less lethal quarrel between officers in Dec. 1643 'about the sounding of a trumpet in the night', which ultimately reached the attention of parliament.

[96] BL Add. MS 11,331, fos. 41, 56ᵛ; Bodl. MS Tanner 62/2A, fos. 420, 421; BL Egerton MS 787, fos. 27ᵛ, 73; Adair, 'Court Martial Papers', 212, and see 210–11 for the quarrel between an army physician and an army surgeon also resolved by cashiering after court martial. See also BL Add. MS 18,981, fo. 294.

political and religious divisions among parliamentarians. These, like personal quarrels, sometimes led to violence, but while the violence of the language of sermons and pamphlets rules out claims to conceptual moderation as a defining parliamentary characteristic, military violence was on the whole directed against the enemy. Despite the frequent bitterness of their differences, and the survival of 'deboist' and quarrelsome officers who conformed to traditional stereotypes, parliamentary armies did not suffer to anything like the same degree from the endemic, uncontrollable, disabling, and sometimes lethal outbursts that characterized some royalist officers imbued with melodramatic habits of honour and the fast draw.

Duels were the formal expression of these habits, but they also erupted in random bully-boy aggression. One of the more spectacular manifestations of problems peculiar to the royalist officer corps occurred in Worcester in January 1643. It reveals again the interpenetration of military and civilian society in ways that were not immediately related to conflict between enemies. It also reveals the difficulties of enforcing norms of conduct when an offender remained impervious and unrepentant and when his services were needed, and it demonstrates fault lines within the royalist alliance that impaired planning and action. At Worcester, in the course of a day-long rampage, Lieutenant-Colonel David Hyde beat bystanders in the street and injured, threatened, and frightened women, from a widow whom he pursued into her shop, beating her and dislocating her arm, to the mayor's wife. At dinner with the mayor, furious at finding no New Year's gift under his plate, he threatened to throw his trencher at him, and did his best to extort 'burning money' by promising to fire the suburbs (and the mayor's house with them) unless given pay for his soldiers. The other officers involved, from the governor of the town, Sir William Russell, to the captains charged with restraining Hyde, first tried to turn off his performance as a joke, then to pacify him, then to restrain him, and finally to keep the affair as quiet as possible. They had no help from Hyde, who broke out of confinement and tried to seize command, claiming better authority from the king than Russell's. Thwarted by the notable tact and firmness of a junior officer who persuaded him into the next tavern, promising 'fair respect' if he 'behaved [him]self like a gentleman', he was ultimately returned to custody in his lodgings and disarmed. In the course of these exploits Hyde had not only attempted to subvert the governor's authority but offered violence with sword, cane, pistols, and knife. His particular and persistent venom was directed against Russell and Colonel Sir James Hamilton, both of whom he threatened to 'pistol'. Multiple witnesses testified that he repeatedly called Russell a coward and the son of a bitch; Hamilton's crimes were to be a Scot and a Catholic. In his 'wild passages' Hyde declared he would 'cudgel . . . Hamilton . . . first and then put a brace of bullets into his head'. Then, in the course of a quarrel with a junior officer 'concerning some service at Bergen op Zoom . . . [he] offered rudely to draw him downstairs by the scarf about his neck', after which only timely intervention prevented him from resorting to pistols and sword.[97]

Hyde was clearly fighting drunk, and his performance dismayed on many levels: as an abuse of hospitality, as an offensive display of foul language, as conduct unbecoming an officer and a gentleman, as mutinous, as an attempt to subvert fellow officers, and as bad public relations. From the mayor and his wife to the beaten widow to the threatened bystanders, civilians had been embroiled in military violence that owed nothing to an enemy presence. Nor did the incident help to maintain officer authority over soldiers. No voice was raised in Hyde's favour, and his kinsman Colonel Sir Francis Wortley declared himself 'sorry to hear from the mouth of a kinsman & an officer' such mutinous and dangerous speeches and such reflections on the honour of fellow officers.[98] Order was finally restored, but Hyde got away with a great deal, probably in part because of leniency to a drunk, but also because of the awkwardness of disciplining a senior officer and publicizing rifts within the ranks. Hence the attempts to paper over the cracks and keep things quiet. His attacks on Russell's family and character were classic occasions for quarrels of honour, but his insults to Hamilton were a radical attack on the royalist coalition: 'in a furious way [he] said that he would kill . . . Sir James Hamilton and said that he was a protestant and no papist, and that he was an Englishman & no Scot'.[99] Royalists were not alone in their dislike of Scots but Hyde's aggressive Protestantism, with its echoes of Bergen-op-Zoom, gave expression to a persistent source of tension in royalist armies, in which Catholic officers mingled with veterans of Europe's Protestant wars and domestic anti-Catholics.

The aftermath of the incident indicates that it was not merely an uncharacteristic aberration or an episode of individual alcoholic pathology. Hyde admittedly passed some months as a prisoner in Oxford, but in May a court martial dismissed his case for want of evidence.[100] Meanwhile in March Russell had again faced 'mutinous and seditious carriage' from officers in the regiment of Colonel Samuel Sandys. Two years later the same words were used to describe the same regiment's proceedings against Sir James Hamilton. In 1645 Hyde killed a fellow royalist, Sir John Scudamore, in a duel at Bristol, but six months later he was still in Rupert's entourage.[101] On the one hand the episode reveals what were to

---

[97] BL Harl. MS 6851, fos. 72, 79, 81, 83–94 *passim*, 108–9.

[98] Ibid., fo. 79; cf. Newman, *Royalist Officers*, 208, who suggests that Wortley championed Hyde.

[99] BL Harl. MS 6851, fo. 89ᵛ.

[100] Russell had brought suit against Hyde but failed to appear (he was serving in the west). After examination of Hyde's witnesses the court concluded that there was no case against him. BL Harl. MSS 6804, fo. 88; 6852, fo. 70.

[101] BL Harl. MS 6802, fo. 32(2); 6851, fo. 135; Bodl. MS top. Oxon. C.378, p. 234; *Letters of the Lady Brilliana Harley*, Camden Society, 58 (1854), 253; *CSPDom. 1645–1647*, 190; in Oct. 1645 one of Hyde's companions as he left Oxford was his old enemy Sir James Hamilton. See also Townshend, *Diary*, 1. 152.

be continuing local and sectarian divisions within royalist ranks; on the other, neither Hyde's character nor his actions had disabled him from royal service or forestalled the future elimination of a fellow royalist officer.

Few cases were as egregious as Hyde's, although Richard Symonds's diary of his marches with the king's army in 1644 and 1645 is dotted with references to affrays and duels; his tone suggests that they were worthy of notice but hardly remarkable.[102] Even if most quarrels did not culminate in violence, the febrile climate that surrounded much royalist military decision-making and action—court faction transfered to the conduct of war—cannot but have been a drain on the time, energy, and judgement of senior commanders. For years Rupert had to cope with long-running feuds between Colonel Leveson (another Catholic), Colonel Bagot, and Lord Loughborough, all of whom turned to him for satisfaction. Sir Richard Bulstrode's account of the endless strife and machinations among the officers surrounding Charles I fills one with sympathy for the king. On one occasion accusations and counter-accusations flew so thickly that 'The King was so much surprized at these extravagant and insolent Discourses, that he rose from Dinner in great Disorder.' When one of the participants came close to demanding satisfaction from the king himself his 'Indignation' was so great that he dismissed them all from his presence, but although 'confounded' and 'ashamed' their habits did not change. Another set of quarrels that began when Colonel Samuel Tuke was passed over for appointment as Goring's lieutenant general of horse in favour of the incompetent George Porter, son of the courtier Endymion and one of Goring's cronies, forced Goring himself to intervene to prevent a duel, but the lengthy deliberations and prohibition of a council of war and the attention of senior officers could not restore peace, and both Tuke and Porter continued to agitate for the satisfaction of their honour. The bitter quarrels between Goring and Sir Richard Grenvile destroyed the last royalist hopes in Cornwall, and demonstrated the impotence of the higher command in the face of intransigent, feuding subordinates.[103]

Although particularly damaging to royalists, this tendency to internecine feud and violence intermittently destabilized both sides and reduced the effectiveness of their planning and discipline. It affected the soldiers below the squabbling officers, for they might take sides in the quarrel: the soldiers of the parliamentarian major killed in the hasty street duel fell into 'high discontent' after his death and were pacified with difficulty. They could also exploit the divisions of their betters in their own disputes.[104] Further, duels and affrays on their streets both alienated and terrified civilians, presenting another aspect of war's upheavals

---

[102] e.g. Symonds, *Diary*, 30, 36, 250, 261, 276.
[103] William Salt MSS 481, 502, 550/22; Bulstrode, *Memoirs and Reflections*, 128–30, 142–7. For Colonel Thomas Leveson's quarrels with fellow royalists in Staffordshire and Warwickshire over money, men, supplies, and authority, see 'Some Letters of the Civil War', *Collections for a History of Staffordshire*, Staffordshire Record Society (1941), 142–4, 146.
[104] Bodl. MS Tanner 61, fo. 106.

and depredations, and signalling the intrusion of violence distinct from that of siege and battle into their lives and their powerlessness to circumscribe it. At Worcester in 1646 the quarrels of the hot-tempered, heavy-drinking royalist governor Henry Washington and his officers expanded to include beatings of the town's citizens. At Chichester it was parliament's Captain Higgins who not only angered local citizens by his 'oppressions' but also issued 'a desperate challenge to a worthy gentleman' of the parliamentary committee that had ventured to complain of his conduct.[105]

THE POWER TO COMMAND

The catalogue of officer deficiencies, from avarice to cruelty, from embezzlement to side-changing, could be much expanded. Yet faults, fools, and bad apples notwithstanding, officer leadership could be powerfully effective and its loss devastating. When Sir Bevil Grenvile was killed in 1643 his men followed his young son into action 'with their swords drawn and with tears in their eyes. They did say they would kill a rebel for every hair of Sir Bevil's beard.'[106] At Plymouth in December 1643 the parliamentarian Captain Wanfry was killed in a charge, 'which made our horse to give ground, & both horse and foot after to an absolute rout for 3 fields together', although the same men rallied when 'encouraged' and reinforced.[107] Officers were not simply interchangeable, however, and replacement of the known, trusted, and sometimes loved by the unknown provoked sorrow and unrest. Early in the war one company of London volunteers, while in Derby, lost the captain 'for the love of whom next unto God & the cause [they had] ventured [their] lives'. Without him, they threatened to leave, and only the tact of Sir John Gell kept this band of 'resolute' and 'hopeful young men' in arms: 'to [his] words unanimously they all condescended, and so continued under him as his company, as long as he did bear command'.[108]

'Unready' officers produced unsoldierly performance, but capable officers could do wonders with unpromising material. Through 'special interest'—of local ties, established trust, religious or political sympathy or, if these failed, by 'severe discipline'—they could lead and control. They were not always successful, but even when they could not prevent them they frequently managed to defuse mutinies and outrages, just as in the field they could retrieve disaster. Their death or disablement in action could dishearten and demoralize.[109] A débâcle

---

[105] Townshend, *Diary*, 1. 151–2 (Washington too railed against Hamilton as a papist); Bodl. MS Tanner 62/2A, fo. 461.
[106] John Stucley, *Sir Bevill Grenvile and his Times, 1596–1643* (Chichester, 1983), 148.
[107] BL Add. MS 35,297, fo. 7ᵛ.
[108] Derbys. RO, Gell MSS, D258, 56/28 (i), 60/16.
[109] Officers' efforts often met with a disheartening lack of success. BL Harl. MSS 6804, fo. 182; 2135, fo. 103ᵛ; Add. MS 11,331, fo. 157ᵛ; Bodl. MSS Tanner 61, fo. 106; Carte, *Original Letters*,

at Middlewich in March 1643 demonstrated, in both its success and failure, the importance of an effective officer presence when soldiers were reluctant. Sir Thomas Aston managed to drive his men into position by riding among them and beating them with his sword, but once there they fired into the air, 'no one foot officer being by them to rank or order them'.[110]

The rhetoric of the bond between commander and soldier needs to be taken with many grains of salt, but it also contains truth. It revealed the assumption that, ideally, soldiers should 'love' their commanders and be prepared to hazard their lives for the sake of that personal commitment. It also revealed the mutuality of obligation. Commanders could legitimately make powerful demands on soldiers because they themselves were obliged to share the same risks as well as to care for their military and social welfare. As Sir Marmaduke Langdale told his men, 'I will not have you goe any where, but where I shall lead you my selfe.'[111] This appeal to a personal bond between commander and soldiers recurs in the rather suspect genre of 'battle speeches', of which many reports invite scepticism on stylistic and practical grounds. The insidious echoes of the battle speeches of the admired Gustavus Adolphus suggest that reporters often added a conventional literary burnish to the words of their heroes. Further, the effectiveness or indeed even the delivery of set-pieces as inspiration to troops should be treated with reserve. As that experienced soldier the earl of Orrery observed,

The making a Speech by a General to a whole Army before a Battel, is often read of in our best Histories, as well as romances; but ought, in my belief, to be only found in the latter: since 'tis impossible for any General to speak audibly, in an open Field, to above a Regiment at once.[112]

Nevertheless, Orrery regarded messages of courage and 'Unanimity' transmitted by officers to smaller numbers as both 'very practicable, and highly useful'.[113] Certain unromantic themes persisted amidst the declamatory heroics. So at Marston Moor the Scot, General Leslie, echoing his old master Gustavus, urged, 'Although you run from your Enemies, yet leave not your Generall; though you fly from them, yet forsake not me'. The invocation of the bond between officer and men often worked. When the parliamentarian Captain Booth exhorted his men before storming Preston, ' "Follow me, or give me up for ever," [the] words so animated the soldiers that they became fearless, and forgetting every danger, resolutely followed their brave leader'.[114] Skippon infused his traditional rhetoric with religion:

1. 32; 'The Battle of Hopton Heath, 1643', *Collections for a History of Staffordshire*, Staffordshire Record Society (1936), 183.

[110] BL Harl. MS 2135, fo.102ᵛ.

[111] *A Great Victory Obtained By Generall Poyntz and Col. Copley...at Sherborn in Yorkshire* (1645), 8; and see Keen, *Laws of War*, 151, on the 'idea of reciprocal obligation... deep-rooted in medieval social thought' in the relation between medieval captains and soldiers.

[112] Orrery, *Art of War*, 185.   [113] Ibid. 185–8.

[114] Vicars, *Gods Arke*, in Vicars, *Magnalia Dei Anglicana*, 273; Fairfax, *Memoirs*, 117. Compare Gustavus Adolphus before Lützen, Monro, *Expedition*, 163: to his German troops he said, '[R]unne

Come, my Boys, my brave Boys, let us pray heartily and fight heartily, I will run the same Fortunes and Hazards with you, remember the Cause is for God, and for the Defence of your selves, your Wives, and Children: Come my honest brave Boys, pray heartily and fight heartily, and God will bless us.[115]

As a practical soldier Skippon eschewed an inaudible mass harangue but, like Henry V, went among his men, 'talking to them, sometimes to one Company, and sometimes to another; and the Soldiers seemed to be more taken with it, then with a set, formal Oration'.[116] He was certainly a commander beloved and trusted alike by soldiers, parliament, and public, who agonized jointly over his dangerous wound at Naseby. If these speeches appear suspect, as romanticized and formulaic, they nevertheless reflect an ideal of relations between officers and men. When it was realized, it not only made it easier to elicit competent battlefield performance but also to exert controls over soldiers in their dealings with civilians.

The case of the earl of Essex, who retained public affection after his military eclipse, illustrated the strength of the bonds between commander and men. In them, some 'feudal' elements survived alongside newer professional and ideological ones. When Londoners flocked to him before the war, crying 'We will live and die with you my Lord', he replied, 'And I by the help of God am ready to do the like with you.'[117] Failure and flight at Lostwithiel did not dim his popularity with his soldiers, despite the disillusionment of his more activist fellow officers. Its elements were hereditary, religious, and personal. A mantle of popularity and Protestantism had descended from his father.[118] He was personally courageous, and careful of his soldiers' lives and welfare; he was, an unusual item of praise, merciful to beast as well as man; he was not covetous; he was easy-going. There are elements of standard panegyric in this list of virtues, but in fact even the royalists could not really dislike him, which did not prevent a stream of jokes against 'the great Cuckold'. He was, said the king's secretary Edward Walker, 'of a stout but easie disposition', and would have been incapable of the ultimate wickedness of killing the king.[119] Essex clearly possessed a quality,

---

not away, and I shall hazard my body and bloud with you for your best, if you stand with me.' To his own Swedes, however, he promised that valour would bring God's mercy, the world's honour, and the king's reward, but that cowardice would bring his vengeance: 'I sweare unto you, that your bones shall never come in *Sweden* again.'

[115] Whitelock, *Memorials*, 65.   [116] Ibid.

[117] Ricraft, *Englands Champions*, 2; Whitelock, *Memorials*, 65.

[118] See Gouge, *Dignitie of Chivalry*, 423, for the process by which Elizabeth's Essex was gathered into the fold of godly soldiers; see also Sir Henry Wotton, 'Some Observations by Way of Parallel of Robert Devereux, Earle of Essex, and George Villiers, Duke of Buckingham, in the Time of their Estates of Favour', *Somers Tracts*, 4. 160–1; Walker, *Historical Discourses*, 343, noted that Essex 'affected Popularity (which he had on his Father's score)'.

[119] Ricraft, *Englands Champions*, 4, 75; Walker, *Historical Discourses*, 343; Bodl. MS Tanner 62/1A, fo. 76; HEH STG Box 11(4); for further examples of royalist jokes at Essex's expense, see Devonshire RO, Seymour of Berry Pomeroy MSS 1392 M/L 1644/24 and 1644/51: 'I hope his horns as yet are not long, it being but the spring', and '[L]et the Ephesian beast look to his horns'.

accessible to his soldiers and his friends, of the kind that must always escape the historians' measuring-glass, that of lovability and the ability to inspire loyalty. In 1628, when he was out of favour with the king and out of command, Sir Jacob Astley, future royalist and experienced professional soldier, wrote from the Low Countries, 'I hope to live . . . to see your Lordship the chief director and head of an army in some brave employment . . . & look . . . to follow you to the world's end'.[120] In 1640 the king was told that he was 'a popular man' and that it would give 'extraordinary satisfaction to all sorts of people to see him in employment again'. At Turnham Green in 1642, when he rode from regiment to regiment to encourage his troops, 'the Soldiers would throw up their Caps, and shout, crying, *Hey for old Robin*'. His collapse at Lostwithiel may give us a glimpse of war psychosis that is otherwise virtually invisible in the civil war. A royalist pamphleteer suggested alcoholism, reporting that 'a world of empty Bottles' was found in his quarters. His secretary reported that afterwards he was sick in body and mind. A month later, however, he was actively engaged in re-equipping his army.[121] After his fall his 'noble worth' was still acknowledged by the supporters of the New Model, for whom he became Moses to Fairfax's Joshua.[122]

Essex was clearly an imperfect commander and, although professionally capable, one unsuited to the highest command in a war that demanded quick and agile responses to rapidly changing circumstances and skill in political infighting. Nevertheless he understood the mutual dependence of commander and soldiers, and in a speech in September 1642 he set out their ideal relationship. He made promises (such as regular pay) that he was unable to keep, but he also made explicit a commander's view of the implied contract between himself and his soldiers, and effectively deployed a robust, unpretentious, paternalistic but demanding strain of exhortation. 'Gentlemen and soldiers,' he began, 'I shall desire you to take notice what I, that am your general, shall, by my honour, promise to performe toward you, and what I shall be forced to expect that you shall performe toward me.' He undertook to share their dangers; he declared, falsely as it proved, 'I will . . . either bring you off with honour, or . . . fall with you'; and he promised to adjudicate equitably between 'the poorest of [his] souldiers, though against the chiefest of [his] officers'. Officers, he said, should instil willing obedience and good training, which did not, however, mean parade ground spit and polish, 'the ceremonious formes of military discipline'. In return, the men's obligations included obedience, soldierly competence, preparedness,

---

[120] BL Add. MS 46,188, fo. 110, and see the letters of Sir Charles Rich, another professional soldier, fos. 95–8; for the king's 'displeasure' see fos. 102, 107.

[121] Whitelock, *Memorials*, 1. 65; *Mercurius Aulicus* (Oxford, 1642–5), 1154; Robert Codrington, 'The Life and Death of the Illustrious Robert, Earl of Essex', in *Harleian Miscellany*, 6.34; Bodl. MS Clarendon 18, fo. 271ᵛ.

[122] W.G., *Just Apologie for An Abused Armie*, 7. The author adopted the Moses/Joshua comparison from 'two Reverend Divines'; the desire to preserve the face of parliamentary unity and to retain Essexian good will led to the attribution of Essex's displacement to God not parliament: 'the Lord was pleased to lay [Essex] aside, and gave the Army to Sir *Thomas Fairfax*'.

conscientiousness, abstention from hate-inducing depredations against civilians, care of their horses, sobriety, and sabbath observance. 'Lastly,' Essex concluded, 'that you avoid cruelty; for it is my desire rather to save the life of thousands than to kill one, so that it may be done without prejudice.'[123] The balance between clemency and prejudice to the cause proved in the event to be difficult to maintain, but the implied contract between commander, officers, and men, in which each had obligations to the others, and which was couched in familiar, affectionate, yet unmistakably hierarchical and disciplinary terms, provided the framework for effective relations between officers and men. The splendour of Essex's funeral in 1646 was largely stage-managed for political purposes, but it also suggests that in his case the bond, though strained, did not break.[124]

Essex's account of the relationship between commanders and soldiers represented an ideal, and his hold on a large body of public affection derived from a fusion of partisan commitment and personal charisma. An account of a minor operation led by an admired professional demonstrated the success that more commonplace elements such as planning, management, and leadership could bring to a careful officer and his imperfect troops, and the way in which a series of small foresights based on experience and intelligence could prevail over unpromising circumstances. In September 1644 a relief expedition set out from Oxford to resupply beleaguered Basing House in Hampshire with food, arms, ammunition, and troops. The operation was small in scale but it was characteristic of the many minor, mobile actions that formed the background to the civil war's more famous battles and sieges. It was led by Colonel Henry Gage, a professional soldier, a Catholic, and 'a very brave man', who had been in Spanish service for a dozen years before he arrived in Oxford in March 1644 with his clutch of junior officers.[125] On 9 September he set out for Basing House and after a night march arrived by five in the morning of the eleventh, having disguised his men as parliamentarians by supplying them with orange-tawny scarves—although one of his junior officers, too foolish to keep up the pretence, revealed their presence.[126] It was a hard march, and to ease his weary foot Gage had the cavalry take them up behind or alight to let them ride. To encourage his men further he held out hopes of great pillage and promised money on

---

[123] 'A Worthy Speech, spoken by his Excellence the Earle of Essex, in the Head of his Armie, . . . The 24th of September, 1642', in *Somers Tracts*, 4. 476–7. This speech presumably fell into Orrery's category of 'inaudible beyond a regiment'; however, allowance must always be made for word-of-mouth transmission of what the general *may* have said, and for the effect of publication. In the present case, audibility or inaudibility does not affect its value as a statement of the ideal of commander/soldier contractual obligations.

[124] Ian Gentles, 'Political Funerals during the English Revolution', in Stephen Porter (ed.), *London and the Civil War* (1996), 210–17; Gardiner, *History*, 3. 148–9.

[125] BL Add. MS 18,981, fos. 86–86ᵛ; [Walsingham (ed.),] *Alter Brittanniae Heros: or the Life of the Most Honourable Knight, Sir Henry Gage, Late Governour of Oxford, Epitomiz'd* (Oxford, 1645), 5–8.

[126] The following account is taken from Walker, *Historical Discourses*, 90–5; *Mercurius Aulicus, a diurnall* (Oxford, 1642–5), 1161; [Walsingham], *Life of Gage*, 12–16.

their return to Oxford. Once arrived at Basing he ranged them in battalions for an assault on the parliamentary besiegers. They wore 'a white Tape, Ribband, or Handkerchief, [tied] upon their right Arm above the Elbow', a prearranged signal designed to prevent confusion on the part of the royalist defenders who sallied out to help them. Before the attack, Gage rode up to each squadron to deliver 'the Word, St. *George*' and 'good Words and Encouragement', but he reported with satisfaction that the men were already 'well resolved of themselves'. Despite heavy flanking musket fire and a mist so thick that they 'could not discerne one the other', they succeeded in entering Basing House, where they left ammunition and reinforcements before marching to Basingstoke. There all available horses and carts were pressed into service to resupply the house with wheat, malt, salt, oats, bacon, cheese, and butter, together with powder, muskets, two parliamentarian cannon, fifty cattle, and a hundred sheep.

By now men and horses were tired and hungry. When parliamentarian troops confronted them Gage ordered a retreat to Basing House, for he noted that his numbers were growing thin, 'many Mean [sic] stealing privately out of their ranks', and the horse 'slincking away by reason of the extreame fatigue and fasting'.[127] Prudently, he did not allow his troops to spend the night in the town for, he observed, 'I feared our Men would quit their Guards and betake themselves to the Houses, drinking and committing disorders in the Night.' The next day was spent in bringing in more provisions for the garrison, but meanwhile Gage sent out spies and on the basis of their reports decided secretly and unilaterally, without the advice of his council of officers, on an abrupt departure. In preparation for this he initiated a campaign of misdirection, sending out warrants 'which [he] knew would fall into the Enemies Hands' and orchestrating troop movements that would lead the parliamentarians to believe that he was settled at Basing House for at least another day. Then, at eleven at night and with the aid of good local guides, his soldiers marched silently away. His scouts were instructed that, should they encounter any of the enemy, they were to say that they were parliamentarians sent to waylay royalist relief forces. Gage and his weary men returned safely to Oxford, having lost eleven dead and some fifty wounded, none seriously, and taken a hundred prisoners.

The operation demonstrated problems of identification and interchangeability of troops, of finding one's way, and of unreliable soldiers that were typical of many civil war actions, but it also demonstrated the kind of rational, pragmatic planning and effective execution that should ideally characterize a capable officer. In this small and well-planned exercise Gage handled multiple demands, paying attention to its military goal, the resupply of Basing House; to the enemy, through intelligence and misdirection; to civilians, by protecting them from disorderly soldiers; and to his men in many ways: by care for their welfare in attempting to lessen fatigue and recognizing when they had reached limits of exhaustion and

---

[127] Ibid. 14.

hunger, and by care for morale through exhortation, example, and sharing of their hardships. He had, for example, marched three miles on foot so that a weary foot soldier could ride and later, 'himselfe giving the first example', encouraged his officers to take foot soldiers up behind them, but he had also acknowledged and circumvented their deficiencies, such as their tendency to disorder, or to melt away when they had had enough. Gage was, indeed, a professional paragon: 'as his judgement and prudence was excelling, so his Successe was equall'. He was, said a fellow-royalist, a 'man of singular Humanity and temper'. When he was killed marching at the head of his men in January 1645 he was 'much lament'd, being a compleat Souldier & a wise man'.[128]

There were, it is clear, many sides to the good officer, as to the bad, and few managed to incorporate all of his desirable attributes in their conduct. Nor were all of those professional virtues morally benign in other contexts. Fairfax was admired as an energetic, demanding, and 'untraditional' commander, and he also won praise for his courage, the modesty of his personal style, and his clemency 'which . . . kept his Army less stained in the Blood of his Enemy: but not less Victorious'.[129] As we shall see at Colchester, however, this did not preclude iron determination and implacable rigour. Less elevated virtues such as wiliness and ingenuity were also much admired, as in Waller's bluff that mimicked preparations for a full-scale attack on Malmesbury and led to its surrender, or Colonel Bampfield's planning of a dark and silent surprise attack at Exeter.[130] Spectacular courage, like that shown by Fairfax at Naseby as he rode bareheaded into the thickest fighting and spread confidence through the army, had an exemplary effect. Phlegmatic courage that refused to panic even in defeat won admiration, like that of gouty old Ruthven as he perforce sat out the battle at Alresford, passing the time with a deck of cards until, after his horse were routed, he struggled onto the field.[131] Yet foolhardy courage that risked the hero or his men for no rational military end elicited an ambivalent response in which admiration was tempered by regret, while the victims of foolhardy risks got limited sympathy. When Captain Flemming was shot in the belly at Boarstall House the wound was 'probably mortall', but the reporter's response was cool: 'he adventured further then his Commission, and the unrulinesse of his Horse brought him among the enemy unawares'.[132] Rupert's brilliance and professional competence were acknowledged, but his rashness was deplored—he was, said one critic, better at taking than keeping advantage, and his impetuous pursuit

[128] [Walsingham], *Life of Gage*, 12, 16; Walker, *Historical Discourses*, 121; *Mercurius Belgicus* (n.pl., 1646), D2–D2ᵛ, 11 Jan. 1644/5; Slingsby, *Diary*, 139; Newman, *Royalist Officers*, 146–7.

[129] Sprigge, *Anglia Rediviva*, 322; Fairfax, *Short Memorials*, K–K2ᵛ.

[130] *A Letter From Sir William Waller, A Member of the House of Commons, To the . . . Earl of Essex* (1643), 6–7; *Bamfeild's Apologie*, 6.

[131] [E.A.], *A Fuller Relation Of the Great Victory obtained . . . at Alsford*, [6]; Woolrych, *Battles of the English Civil War* (1966), 131–2.

[132] *The Copy of A Letter from An Eminent Commander in Sir Thomas Fairfax Army* (1645), 5.

of the fleeing enemy at Naseby left his foot 'naked' and the army dependent on courage when 'Conduct failed'.[133]

The example of officers in battle had a powerful influence on their men. Hence the praise for Ruthven's nonchalance, and for Skippon and Luke who never turned their backs on the enemy.[134] Yet expectations remained realistic. Every officer could not match Colonel Gage or even be truly expert, but he could be conscientious and dutiful. An epitaph on two parliamentarian officers killed at Taunton distinguished between the colonel, 'a Gallant . . . Religious experienced Souldier', and his less expert (and perhaps less godly) lieutenant colonel, who was only 'a stout honest man'. As a poem in praise of Skippon noted,

> More things to make a souldier compleat,
> Are required than a valiant heart;
> Time, travaile, art, experience great,
> And scars, make up the whole of every part
> Of warlike worth.

It also helped if, like Skippon, the officer had 'piety good store'.[135]

A perfect combination of personal and professional talents was probably unattainable by any single officer in the real world, yet for all the failures, whether through incompetence or half-heartedness or through cruelty and violence (as in the cases of men like Hyde or Sir Richard Grenvile or Sir Francis Doddington), Gage remains an exemplar who showed that it was possible to come very close to the ideal. It is now time to turn to the soldiers with whom, by direction and example, these good and bad officers had to seek victory and impose order.

---

[133] Bulstrode, *Memoirs*, 81–2, 125–6.   [134] Ricraft, *Englands Champions*, 59, 78.
[135] *Exact and Perfect Relation . . . Langport*, 4; Ricraft, *Englands Champions*, 55.

13

Men

Expectations were lower for ordinary soldiers than for officers. They were naturally prone to actions of positive badness, from drunkenness to mutiny, from flight to pillage. And as common men they could not be expected to understand or respond to the higher demands of honour. Such, at least, were the assumptions that shaped the traditional view of the soldiery and that recurred in the comments of their betters in the civil war. Their courage was sometimes greeted with patronizing surprise, as in the case of a messenger condemned to death on dubious grounds who 'dy[ed] with another kind of Courage than could be expected from a Man of such condition and education'.[1] The ideology of a godly New Model army raised expectations and altered rhetoric, but even its supporters confessed that its troops could behave in thoroughly traditional ways, while enemies merely added sanctimonious hypocrisy to their charges.

Yet soldiers constantly behaved better than unflattering convention predicted. Even raw troops could win praise for dogged resolution in adversity, like the royalists who, in withdrawing from the outskirts of London late in 1642, 'made one of the most resolute, if not the most souldierly Retreats hath been heard of in our Age'. Ordinary soldiers could show exemplary enthusiasm, like the parliamentarians at Plymouth in 1643 who, after a successful attack, had to be dissuaded by their officers from pushing on in a risky attempt to penetrate enemy defences and seize their guns, and like Cromwell's men in the final attack on Basing House who 'fell on withe great Resolution and cheerfulness' and refused to hear of a parley.[2] Courage, offensive and defensive, soldierly competence and solidarity, and recognition of moral obligation were bipartisan phenomena. It was, however, the obverse of the medal that received most attention from officers and politicians as they struggled to field effective armies, and from the partisan writers who kept soldiers and civilians informed. On the one hand, commanders were all too aware that 'the common people . . . for the most part judge our cause by the demeanour of our army' and that it was possible to 'gain . . . their hearts' by good usage, particularly when the enemy's was worse.[3] On the other, they were not

---

[1] Clarendon, *History*, 2. 314.

[2] *Considerations upon The present state of the Affairs of this Kingdome*, 5; BL Add. MS 35,297, fos. 9^v–10; BL Stowe MS 184, fos. 112–112^v.

[3] BL Add. MS 11,331, fo. 25^v.

averse to exploiting the threat of soldiers' violence and uncontrollability to secure concessions from enemies or civilian authorities. Shakespeare's 'enraged soldiers in their spoil' lived on in the rhetoric of 'fury' and 'rage' that would be unleashed against those who provoked them. The early months of the war, in which soldiers often appeared to be no better than an armed rabble, heightened civilian fears, and even after organization and discipline improved, Leicester, Reading, and Naseby, to name only a few examples, showed that such threats were not idle. Furthermore, 'the reins of discipline' were under constant strain from routine grievances such as hardship and lack of pay as well as from the heat of battle.[4]

Both sides complained endlessly about the conduct of their soldiers. A survey of some of their salient characteristics will inevitably be heavily weighted towards their failings, which attracted vocal attention from disappointed officers, anxious civilians, and publicists—including those of their own side. As in many wars, contemporary accounts were schizophrenic; soldiers were represented as heroes or as brutes according to circumstances. Either way, the presence of disorderly bodies of men, armed and with official standing, was deeply disturbing to a nation that at the best of times was anxious about the fragility of social order. To provide arms to recruits of 'meane condition' raised the question of whether they were 'fitt . . . to be trusted with them'.[5] The civilian response to their presence, however, could be equally threatening to social order, for hostility found expression not only in large-scale confrontations between clubmen and soldiers but in random acts of violence. In 1645 Brereton complained of 'the cruelty of the country by snapping and killing our men' as they foraged in Wales. In London in 1648, when a soldier 'accidentally got among' unruly petitioners, the civilians quickly turned nasty and 'fell upon [him] with their swords and clubs, [he] was run through and conceived dead'.[6] Indeed, civilian 'hub-bub' could be as threatening as the enemy. Royalist northern troops asked to be 'guarded [out of Wales] to their own country, . . . securely from the enemy & the tumult'.[7]

In 1628 Sir John Suckling had warned of the dangers to persons and polity from the presence of troops in England:

Innovations in all states are dangerous, especially where there is diminution of the laws, or a fear to execute justice, through too much liberty given to soldiers; no country but hath more hurt by their garrisons, than by their enemies; enemies only rob the frontier, the other the whole country; the enemy may be resisted, the other not spoken against; the enemy giveth a sudden attempt, and returneth; the others do every day rob and spoil; the enemy surpriseth with fear; the others have neither fear nor shame.[8]

---

[4] Ibid.; BL Add. MS 11,332, fos. 93–93ᵛ; Walker, *Historical Discourses*, 239.

[5] William Salt Library, Salt MSS 545.

[6] BL Add. MS 11,331, fo. 29ᵛ; Worcester College, Clarke MSS 114, fo. 16. Dore suggests that 'snapping' meant 'taking by surprise', *Brereton Letter Books*, 1. 306.

[7] BL Add. MS 18,981, fo. 294.

[8] Sir John Suckling, 'A Letter written to the Lower House of Parliament', in *Somers Tracts*, 4. 111.

In the 1640s Suckling's dire prediction of the effects of the presence of resident, domestic armies appeared to materialize before English eyes. The rampages of disorderly soldiers, like the riots of civilians, that marked the early months of the war combined with demands for money and supplies from garrisons and field armies to link the presence of soldiers with threats to society and property. The memory was to cast a long shadow over English politics.

THE CHARACTER OF A SOLDIER

In describing the good and bad attributes of officers we have already touched on many of the characteristics of their men. The ideal of the good soldier, loyal, brave, and competent, was not dependent on rank, but in real life the low expectations of the common soldier were enough to demolish hopes that a war fought in part for religion would be any better than other wars. In January 1643 a neutralist observed,

If Religion be the principall reason: how few hopes have we to see it rectified by War which is the nurse of barbarisme. The Souldier the instrument of this kind of reformation . . . we shall scarce ever finde devoted to anything of Religion besides the pretence and noyse of it, in their talke, only to set a glosse upon their quarrell: from them we must looke for little else, but prophanation and sacriledge. And suppose these men of War prove more civill and pious then all other Souldiers before them what religion shall we expect to be exercised during this War, which will be a continuing Holy-day to all licentiousnesse?[9]

For public consumption, each side officially denied the barbarism and licentiousness of its own soldiers while asserting those of the enemy's, but each unofficially recognized that truth was otherwise. Parliament's soldiers were 'admired by the Enemy for their gallantry and Conduct', declared their indefatigable publicist Hugh Peter in 1646, for not only were they habitually modest, but their depredations were inconsiderable. 'Feare not that Army', he urged, 'whose Commanders . . . can aske any County or Towne where they have been whose Oxe or Asse they have taken? never fewer complaints, nor many men of such quality.'[10] The cavaliers, by contrast, were 'infamous Livers, Atheists, Epicures, Swearers, Blasphemers, Drunkards, Murderers, and Ravishers, and (at the least) Papists'.[11] Their royalist defender, while 'vindicat[ing] the Major part' of these 'scandalous aspersions', admitted 'I cannot excuse all of our Party', but he added 'no more than you can all of yours'. Even Peter gave a significant part of his case away when he urged a foreign war (should Ireland not suffice) for, he said, 'It is

---

[9] *The Moderator expecting Sudden Peace, or Certaine Ruine* (1642), 7.
[10] *Mr Peters Last Report of the English Wars* (1646), 5.
[11] *The Cavaliers Catechisme, and Confession of his Faith* (1647), 2.

one of the great interests of this state to keepe warre at distance.'[12] By 1646 the attractions of such a policy were clear if as yet unattainable.

The prescriptive rules for soldiers, like those for their officers, were simple and combined the abstractly moral with the severely practical. The articles of war regulated with varying success specific offences from larceny to mutiny, from cowardice to rape, but there were also more general exhortations designed to shape the good soldier. Both kinds of prescriptions embodied traditional hopes and fears, and employed a mixture of flattery and threat. In 1626 William Gouge had assured his Artillery Garden audience that courage was a sign of righteousness as timorousness was of sin; in the same vein *The Souldiers Pocket Bible* of 1643 began, 'A Souldier must not doe wickedly', for soldiers who disobeyed God could not expect to withstand their enemies. Yet although this parliamentarian handbook of energizing texts emphasized the divine role in the soldier's life and fortunes, it also reflected more immediate problems. '[D]oe violence to no man, neither accuse any falsely, and be content with your wages', it adomonished, quoting St Luke's gospel.[13] The New Model recognized that godliness was not enough to ensure an orderly and victorious army, and the armies of both sides, in their efforts to maintain order, did not wait for divine judgement. As a military manual of 1639 advised, justice must be 'seen to bee put in execution; for if Justice do not govern in an Army, all things goe to ruine'. Unruly, pilfering, pillaging soldiers who disrupted their own supplies, alienated local populations, and quarrelled among themselves, endangered the armies to which they belonged.[14]

Attitudes to soldiers thus varied according to occasion, one day praised for their courage and religion, the next deplored as the dregs of the country. In practice they proved a volatile aggregation drawn—particularly the foot—from those ranks of society that men of substance regarded warily at the best of times as only uneasily constrained by hierarchy, deference, and order. It was the constant and difficult business of officers and the army's legal, punitive, and ideological machinery to shape recalcitrant human material into effective fighting forces that were disciplined but neither brutalized nor mutinous, that were motivated by ideology but also by material incentives, and that satisfied both motivations without taking such vengeance on enemies or such booty from civilians as to render present war and future peace more difficult.[15]

The raw material of both armies ranged from the committed and capable to the pathetic, reluctant, and criminal. An assessment of men raised for

---

[12] Ibid. 3; *Mr Peters Last Report*, 5; foreign wars, Peter claimed, would disseminate English benefits abroad, for they would 'teach Peasants to understand liberty'.

[13] Gouge, *Dignitie of Chivalry*, 422–4; *The Souldiers Pocket Bible* (1643), 2–3. I am grateful to Ian Green for directing me to this work.

[14] Ward, *Anima'dversions*, 32; Monro, *Expedition*, 2. 197.

[15] Ibid. 2. 166: 'the best way of Command is, to keepe men in awe of dutie, not so much with crueltie (as many base Generalls doe) as with a moderate severenesse'.

the Scottish war in 1639 looks back to Falstaff's recruits and forward to complaints by civil war officers. There were seven possibles from Ashridge, Hertfordshire. Four were 'given to drink: but not . . . drunk . . . nor insufferably debauched'; another was a yeoman kept short of money by his father and father-in-law, whose wife was willing that he should go: the sixth was a reformed drunkard; only the seventh, a farrier, was judged 'a sober honest man', with a useful skill to boot.[16] Clearly, compromises were necessary in filling the ranks. Yet individually such men do not sound particularly frightening. It was the transformation of individuals of whom little could be expected into collective bodies authorized to use violence, provided with the means to do so, and placed in situations where communal frenzy, fear, greed, blood-lust, or need overcame weak personal controls, that aroused fear in civilians and usually—although not always—anxiety in officers. '[T]he Violence of the Souldier' that would have exposed London to 'Fire, Plunder and Ruin' was King Charles's ostensible reason for not attacking the city. That violence could also, however, be a useful threat. In the cold December of 1648, when Fairfax was trying to extract bedding for his soldiers and unpaid assessments of £40,000 from the city, he noted with polite regret the 'trouble & inconvenience to the inhabitants' that would ensue from the 'discontent or differences' of unsatisfied soldiers. There was no need to make explicit the violent subtext.[17] Parliamentary soldiers who inflicted damage indiscriminately on civilian enemies and friends in the Thames valley in 1644 were seen as behaving stereotypically: 'such insolencies and mischiefs must be expected from this brood of Men or rather brutish Soldiers, who know no difference between Freinds and Foes, but all is Plunder that they can fasten their hands upon'.[18] The moral categories of man and soldier had become distinct.

In the years immediately before 1642 the nation had been regaled with reports of murder of officers, of troops who, if they did not run, were too dangerous to arm, of plunder, of gang rape, of an English army incapable of withstanding the Scots, and of the costs of maintaining their own men and paying off the victors.[19] The Scots had in some ways appeared frighteningly disciplined—the sober march of their army, with its phalanx of ministers massed around the Bible and soldiers trailing pikes adorned with mourning ribbons, aroused wonder and respect—but the civil population suffered alike from disciplined Scottish

---

[16] HEH EL MS 6602 (FAC). Compare the comment from London in 1625: 'The late presses of soldiers have ridded the City of a great many unprofitable persons.' *Proceedings in Parliament 1625,* ed. Maija Jansson and William B. Bidwell (New Haven, Conn., 1987), 669.

[17] Walker, *Historical Discourses,* 239; *A Declaration Of His Excellency the Lord Generall Fairfax, Concerning the Supply of Bedding Required from the City of London* (1648), *passim; A Letter Of His Excellency Thomas Lord Fairfax, To the Right Honorable, The Lord Mayor of the City of London, For the better preserving a right Understanding between the City and Army* (1648), *passim.*

[18] Whitelock, *Memorials,* 114.

[19] Mark Charles Fissel, *The Bishops' Wars. Charles I's Campaigns against Scotland, 1638–1640* (Cambridge, 1994), ch. 7, pp. 264–86.

enemies and undisciplined English friends.[20] Some of the offences of these and later soldiers were violent and serious, genuinely subverting military effectiveness and civil society. Others, more venial, outraged civilians but did not greatly disturb experienced commanders. The earl of Warwick could jovially explain one outbreak by soldiers 'much disordered by drink' as the result of a 'barrel of beer and fifty shillings in money' sent by a benefactor, 'of whose kindness it seems they took too much'. He resolved the problem by sending the ringleaders to the house of correction. Many civilians, however, could not share this aristocratic insouciance. Major and minor offences alike seemed to threaten personal danger, property loss, and social breakdown.[21]

Soldiers had ample reasons for many of the faults imputed to them. Initial reluctance to serve or later disillusionment exacerbated tendencies to fear and flight. Pay was low and arrears chronic, and legitimate incentives merged seamlessly with illegitimate crimes. Lodgings, food, and clothing were often bad and insufficient. Rain, cold, mud, and disease regularly accompanied service. Long marches and unrelieved duty brought fatigue; battles produced fear and confusion. The consequences were not surprising. They included unwillingness to fight, flight, desertion, straggling, side-changing, defiance of officers, and on occasion outright mutiny, all of which could in turn affect civilians. Reluctance to fight might be principled, but more often it was self-preservative. Some soldiers could not at first believe that they should harm or would be harmed by Protestant fellow-countrymen, although this illusion died quickly.[22] More significantly, some men had 'no military spirit', as young Joseph Lister frankly avowed of himself, but unlike Lister were not lucky enough to avoid service. Some preferred keeping their heads down to firing at the enemy; others refused to 'come out roundly' in attack because their zeal was 'cooled' by 'the falling of some'; some 'newly raised' men fled before they fought. All represented an unmilitary spirit that officers had to counter as best they could.[23] It is in fact remarkable, particularly in the early days of the war, that 'unexperienced fresh-water men' such as those recruited in Yorkshire in January 1643 only three days before they were thrown into action, or the Bradford men too ignorant to know how 'to keepe ranke or file', fought with such courage.[24] Yet although training could do much to produce good soldiers, nature often remained intractable.

[20] See e.g. the letters, petitions, etc. preserved in the Ellesmere papers, HEH EL MSS 7842, 7844, 7849, 7851–2, 7855, 7857, 7859–60, 7868. The account of the Scottish army on the march is in 7852.

[21] Alfred Kingston, *East Anglia and the Great Civil War* (1897), 25.

[22] Carte, *Original Letters*, 1. 30; Sir Henry Foulis, *An Exact and True Relation of a Bloody Fight* (1642), 4.

[23] Lister, *Autobiography*, 34; BL Harl. MS 2135, fo. 102ᵛ; 'Memoirs of Captain John Hodgson', in Slingsby, *Original Memoirs*, 116; *A Letter From Sir William Waller, A Member of the House of Commons, To the . . . Earl of Essex* (1643), 5; Fairfax, *Memoirs*, 66.

[24] *Rider of the White Horse*, 67; Fairfax, *Memoirs*, 35; see Foulis, *Exact and True Relation*, 3, for preference for volunteers over easily frightened, readily fleeing impressed men.

As a commander wrote in disillusion to Speaker Lenthall, 'A soldier by a long continued practise in warlike actions may supply the defects in his profession but cannot supply the defect of nature, which is to make cowards valiant. So that, to be short, our horse carried themselves valiantly, but a great part of the dragoons most basely.'[25]

HOW SOLDIERS FAILED

Cowardice was not the only reason why soldiers failed, but it remained the most shameful. It brought public infamy and required a 'desperate exploit' in expiation. When frightened men of Essex's guard cried 'faces about' and fled 'in . . . [a] disorderly manner back to the quarters', Colonel Goodwin wrote to his daughter, 'I know you will hear of it.'[26] Yet it was recognized that courage was a fluctuating commodity, and that the conduct of troops was not uniform. Circumstances, as well as morale and training, had much to do with how they performed. Today's mutinous rabble might become tomorrow's stalwart soldiers, today's heroes might be tomorrow's cowards. Writing of a royalist attack on Nottingham, Mrs Hutchinson noted the 'strange ebbe and flow of courage and cowardize in both parties'. First the cavaliers in 'valliant dreadfullnesse' marched over the bodies of their fellows under the cannons' mouth and the parliamentarians fled. A few hours later these 'frighted' men redeemed their flight and returned 'as men that thought nothing too great for them', and it was the royalists' turn to run. Mrs Hutchinson was sure that courage came from God, 'and when he with-holds his influence, the brave turne cowards, . . . and greate men doe those things they blush to thinke on'.[27] Whatever the cause, it was a commonplace that triumphant action could rapidly be followed by ignominious flight. Within days of their successful relief of Gainsborough in 1643 Lord Willoughby was writing, '[T]he hearts of our men have been so deaded, as we have lost most of them by running away', while even the formidable royalist Northern Horse could be so 'discouraged' that there was 'little hope of success' until 'their fears [were] digested'.[28] 'Discouraged' troops whose morale was low were reluctant, sluggish, at a disadvantage in action, and potential deserters.

Of the other causes of failure, the most persistent was lack of pay, and as we have already seen, the complaints of both officers and men were unceasing. '[S]low payment of the soldier lessens our army', said a parliamentarian; 'our men

[25] Bodl. MS Tanner 62/1B, fo. 205.

[26] Bodl. MS Carte 103, fo. 94; Wharton, 'Letters from a Subaltern Officer', *Archaeologia*, 35 (1853), 2. 326, 328.

[27] Hutchinson, *Memoirs*, 114–15. Mrs Hutchinson added: 'The events of this day humbled the pride of many of our stout men, and made them after more carefully seeke God, as well to inspire as to prosper their vallour.'

[28] BL Add. MS 18,981, fo. 270.

are ready to break for want of pay', said the Shropshire committee; and royalists agreed that money was the way to induce 'alacrity' and discipline for if an army was 'orderly paid' it could 'by consequence [be] kept under command'.[29] No one, however, had a good word for the mercenary soldier, whose actions were governed by greed, not principle:

> While money chinks my Captain I'le obey . . .
> Let not the Trumpet shrill, ere rend the ayre,
> Untill it cite us to the place where we
> May heaps of silver for our payment see.
> I came not forth to doe my Countrey good.[30]

Nevertheless where pay, or the lack of it, was concerned even loyal and committed soldiers on both sides eventually ran out of patience and, like their mercenary colleagues, refused to fight. The manifestations of discontent, ranging from dumb insolence and failure to obey orders to permanent or temporary departure and mutiny, could paralyse forces. Yet even when officers faced clear mutiny, it was often prudent not to invoke the punishments mandated for the offence, but instead to work by persuasion and incentive. In 1644 Rupert and Newcastle 'play[ed] . . . the orators to the soldiers in *York*, (being in a raging mutiny in the town for their pay)' in order to get them on to the field at Marston Moor.[31] The ripple effects of want of pay and the varied forms taken by soldierly resistance were demonstrated by parliament's Blue Regiment in Lancashire in May 1645, where 'a grand mutiny' was reported. Many men—'I almost say the most', said their colonel despairingly—marched away, and many of those who remained refused to perform their duties in spite of 'extreme importunities and persuasions'. Only the assurance that they would get a full month's pay had persuaded them to stay for a few more days and their colonel, desperately seeking money, wrote that without it the service would be 'deserted'. Already his men had unanimously refused to advance when marched to the field of battle, and many had 'broken their muskets and sworn they [would] never serve in this county again'.[32] When the arrears of royalist soldiers were cut off early in 1646 they were 'every where discontented, and many of them ready to lay down their arms and make their peace'.[33] The ill effects of lack of pay stretched beyond the army to civilians, for it intensified the foraging, expropriation, and plunder to which they were subject at the best of times.

---

[29] Bodl. MS Tanner 62/1A, fos. 63, 128; BL Harl. MS 2135, fo. 46; 6852, fo. 176; BL Add. MS 11,332, fos. 40, 72ᵛ, 94ᵛ; PRO SP 28/126, fo. 21; Derbys. RO, D258, 31/30 (aa).

[30] 'The Mercenary Souldier', in Rollins (ed.), *Cavalier and Puritan*, 168.

[31] Carte, *Original Letters*, 1. 57.

[32] BL Add. MS 11,331, fo. 157ᵛ. In 1643 Colonel Edward Harley was warned that lack of pay and removal from their quarters would not only lead to departure of his men but would endanger his own life. HMC, *Portland MSS. 14th Report. App. Pt. 2*, 117–18; see J. S. Morrill, 'Mutiny and Discontent in English Provincial Armies 1645–1647', *PP* 56 (1972), 49–74, for widespread disorders in parliamentary armies.

[33] William Salt Library, Salt MS 547.

Money was not the only ground of disaffection. In April 1643 the minister Cornelius Burges reported from Essex, 'I find among the bulk of the common soldiers not only mutterings for want of a surgeon, ammunition, wagons to carry it, and especially of an able preacher, but professed resolutions... that they will not march beyond this county... without those supplies.' Burges was convinced that, if unsatisfied, most would disband.[34] There were even more pressing grievances such as deficiencies of provision, clothing or lodging. When Brereton's men 'r[a]n away very fast from him' in April 1645 a royalist commented, '[H]e needs no greater enemy than hunger.' When he faced mutiny in October the cause was not only two months' arrears of pay but also shortage of basic provisions, especially bread. A 'hunger-bitten' royalist drummer sent out as a messenger from Arundel castle yielded as a prisoner rather than return. When parliamentary soldiers were forced to 'lye upon stalls' in Exeter in 1643, over a hundred ran away, and after Colonel Carr's men were turned out of their quarters all 200 of them 'disbanded and [were] gone'. Soldiers at Newport Pagnell threatened to disband if they did not get coats and other necessaries as well as pay.[35] In addition, soldiers might mutiny or flee when they lost their officers or, alternatively, when they did not like or know them, or when they suspected them of making off with their pay or depriving them of prize money.

Although disgruntled men might be kept together by a trusted officer and fellow 'countryman', the power of leadership could fail. Colonel Harrison, we are told, was 'more forward and bold, then his men'. When one captain 'could not get on his own men' in an assault on Corfe castle, Sir Walter Erle took over but his initial success was short-lived. '[S]ome of them went with me a pretty distance', he recounted, 'but the bullets coming thick about us they fairly ran away and left me alone', and he added, 'the like was done by others... to those that were their leaders (no man having cause to boast)'.[36] Another common problem was soldiers' unwillingness to serve far from home, or to do so for long periods. In 1643 'the old superstition of not going out of the Country' led to the disbandment of royalist local forces when they were ordered to march into Devon, while early in 1644 parliamentarians concluded that it was pointless to raise Lancashire foot to serve in Cheshire, for they 'will not be held together long out of their own country. They are but for present designs, and presently straggle home.' In 1644 Waller complained that he had no hope of retaining his disorderly

---

[34] Bodl. MS Tanner 62/1A, fo. 65. There is a touch of special pleading in Burges's insistence on the demand for an able preacher.

[35] BL Egerton MS 787, fos. 39ᵛ, 72ᵛ; Add MS 11,332, fo. 28; *Articles of Agreement Betweene his Excellency Prince Maurice, And the Earle of Stamford* (1643), 5; Bodl. MS Nalson III, fo. 203; *A Wicked Plot against the Person of Sir William Waller* (1644), A3ᵛ.

[36] Bodl. MS Tanner 62/1B, fo. 219ᵛ; *A Perfect Diurnall of some Passages in Parliament*, 261 (1648), 2098; see also BL Harl. MS 6804, fo. 182; Add. MSS 11,332, fo. 77ᵛ; 11,333, fo. 69; BL Egerton MS 787, fo. 56.

London brigade, they 'being come to their old song of home, home'. Hence the attraction for commanders of an integrated army 'merely your own that you may command', and the value of unitary organization such as the New Model's.[37] Finally, in the armies of both sides the problem of soldiers 'disordered' by drink was endemic and apparently incurable. As the court martial records and articles of war already examined suggest, drink was the soldier's solace when off duty and often when on duty as well, and the only operative distinction was that between drunk and very drunk. Drink and sociability were closely connected, as they were in civilian life. In May 1645 the parliamentarian Sir Samuel Luke complained to his kinsman Colonel Edward Montagu of the two conductors, 'disorderly in drink and language', who had been sent to escort men to the garrison: 'For your own good, our quiet and the credit of the Cause, employ soberer men.'[38] A royalist noted that it was a mistake to hold a meeting at six in the evening, for it was 'a time when soldiers and malcontents be well heated with wine and other liquors'.[39] This partial catalogue of reasons behind soldiers' unsoldierly conduct may conclude with a reminder that it could also arise from principles beyond the military world. The army's grievances at Bury St Edmund's in 1647 and the mutiny at Burford in 1649 at least in part looked beyond day-to-day hardships and discontents to political principles shared with some parts of the civilian population.

There was nothing new in the difficulty of fielding a full complement of soldiers. In 1639 Gervase Markham had instructed his readers that war was 'a knowne enemy' to keeping companies at full strength:

sicknesse, mortality, slaughter, ill diet and lodging, hunger, cold and surfeits doe so attend upon Armies, that by them companies are exceedingly weakened and made less, so that he which mustreth one hundred men if he bring threescore and ten able men into the field to fight, is oft held for a strong company.[40]

One parliamentary colonel described an 'army of sick and runaway men', and a lieutenant characterized the absentees from his own company as 'wounded, sick, runaway & dead'.[41] Parliamentary losses near Oxford in 1644 amounted to 'slain, wounded and run away in four Days near 500 men'. In 1645 the royalist defenders of Chester claimed that after one attack parliamentary losses were 500 dead and wounded and an equal number run away.[42]

[37] Clarendon, *History*, 2. 103; *CSPDom. 1644*, 301; BL Harl. MS 6804, fo. 182; Derbys. RO Gell MSS D258 31/33 (1); William Salt Library, Salt MS 551/1; Walker, *Historical Discourses*, 7, 67.
[38] Luke, *Letter Books*, 289.   [39] Townshend, *Diary*, 1. 146.
[40] M[arkham], *The Second Part of the Souldiers Grammar*, 47–8. See Parker, *Military Revolution*, 53–8, on attrition rates in early modern armies.
[41] Bodl. MS Carte 103, fo. 86; PRO SP 28/26, fo. 5, and see fos. 26, 482, 527, 670, for the difficulties of officers who had advanced money to absentees. Some absences were temporary (e.g the 'drunkards' to whom Captain William Pell had disbursed 12s.), but others were simply characterized as 'men that are run away owing ... money'. Ibid., fos. 482, 527.
[42] Walker, *Historical Discourses*, 18; *Mercurius Belgicus*, in *Mercurius Rusticus* (1646); BL Add. MS 11,332, fo. 81ᵛ.

It is impossible to quantify the reduction of military strength by absenteeism. Estimates were impressionistic, situations fluid, and some at least of those who fled or loitered or got drunk or took a vacation returned, like the man reported as absent from the muster of his company but now 'come again'.[43] Nevertheless it could have a devastating effect on military strength, as two examples, from the beginning and the end of the war reveal. In 1642 a raw parliamentary regiment of 500 was rapidly reduced: at the enemy's first alarm, 'they all ran away save 200, and those are now run to 80'. In 1648 the earl of Norwich's royalist army in Kent numbered 8,000 but after the battle of Maidstone, in which he lost 300 killed and 1,300 taken prisoners, only 3,000 remained. Losses by attrition were therefore some 3,400 men, and it was reported that the royalists had become so discouraged that 'the greatest part of their Army left them, and were dispersed, and a great number of Officers and Gentlemen . . . fled to shift for themselves'.[44] These, perhaps, represent extremes of initial inexperience and ultimate discouragement, but other instances, if less dramatic, were equally crippling. By July 1644 Waller's army had fallen to less than half its original strength of eight or nine thousand, not merely through losses at Cropredy Bridge but through desertions as his men melted into the countryside or returned to London. His desperate efforts to recruit fresh troops in London made slow progress and, together with the inadequate supplies granted to him, fuelled his bitterness against his rival the earl of Essex and explained, in his own eyes, his military failures.[45] Troop attrition had to be factored into military plans, although sometimes with happier results than in Waller's case. When the king and Prince Maurice joined forces at Crediton in July 1644, the king's foot numbered over 4,000 and Maurice's some 4,500. Less than two months later the king's were 'much diminished' and Maurice's had been reduced by more than half. The decision to try for a 'speedy Issue' which led to success at Lostwithiel arose from the consideration that their army was already so reduced that it would be wise to move quickly before it shrank further.[46]

Absenteeism, less dramatic and more pervasive than mutiny, recurs monotonously in officers' reports on their men. While some was involuntary, the result of sickness, capture, or death, much was voluntary. As we have seen, the articles of war of both sides tried, with only limited success, to prevent it by legislation, and they distinguished between its various manifestations—flight, desertion, straggling, side-changing—and degrees of culpability. Application of the laws was prudently discretionary, for when there was no immediate threat from the

[43] PRO SP 28/26, fo. 527.

[44] Foulis, *Exact and True Relation of a Bloody Fight*, 3; [Sir Thomas Fairfax], *The Lord General's Letter To . . . the Honorable William Lenthal Esq. . . . Wherein is fully related, The Particulars of the Fight at Maidstone* (1648), 5–6.

[45] Walker, *Historical Discourses*, 7, 35, 40, Walker claimed that it was nothing for Waller 'to wear out two Armys in a Year', ibid. 64.

[46] Ibid. 67, 87–8.

enemy sensible officers did not inflict excessively severe punishments on useful soldiers who were absent merely because they were sleeping off a heavy night's drinking or had stopped along the way to socialize with old friends.

Flight from the scene of action was the most basic and visible form of absenteeism, but there was a distinction between acceptable if undesirable flight and unjustified flight that could be imputed to cowardice or treachery. Defeat and retreat, often accompanied by disorderly flight from one's colours, were recognized as a normal part of war, regrettable but not incompatible with courage and loyalty. Flight indeed was a constant problem in even the best of armies, and one that was little alleviated by bracing exhortations to valour and steadfastness:

> Soldier...
> ... let me tell thee if thy heels prove light
> What ere thy Colours be, thy Livers white,
> Therefore be stedfast, Though the giddy rout
> Wear windmills in their heads and wheel about.[47]

It was no secret that even the Swedes at Nördlingen, like the New Model at Naseby, suffered episodes of flight, but in good armies these did not become total routs and, with luck, the troops could be reformed. At Naseby both armies experienced flight and reformation, just as both contained units whose steadfastness was disciplined and indomitable and others whose flight was irreversible.[48] Military theory might argue that rigorous punishment would prevent cowardice and imprint a belief that flight merely exchanged a glorious for an infamous death, but in practice commanders lived with flight as a fact of military life. They could hope to reduce its incidence—by training, luck, ideology, and example—but hardly to eradicate it.[49]

Soldiers who actively tried to avoid combat, whether by unjustifiable flight in battle, desertion, or more devious means, faced the harsh penalties legislated by their army's articles of war. Royalist soldiers who 'retire[d] before the retreat sounded, or . . . thr[e]w away [their] Arms' and fled, or who refused to obey orders to go into action 'for feare of Danger', merited death without mercy. Some royalist articles went further and, in imitation of those of Gustavus Adolphus, promised indemnity for killing a soldier who took to his heels in battle.[50] In parliament's armies such offences were punishable by death at discretion, while

---

[47] Samuel Kem, *Orders given out; the Word, Stand Fast* (1647), prefatory verse by M.D.

[48] Some of the parliamentarian left wing fled as far as Northampton; some of Ireton's horse were lost for the day but others reformed; the same was true of Langdale's royalist horse; some of the royalist foot surrendered, others chose flight. See Woolrych, *Battles of the English Civil War*, 129–33.

[49] See C[ruso], *Complete Captain*, 114, on the Roman practice of decimation to prevent flight.

[50] *Military Orders, and Articles Established by His Maiestie* (Oxford, [1643]), B[v], no. 52; for the indemnity provision, see *Military Orders . . . Established by His Maiesty* (1643), 10, no. 64, and *Orders and Institutions of War, Made . . . by . . . The Earle of Newcastle* (n.pl., 1642), 5, nos. 27, 28; 'The Second Part of the Swedish Discipline', 51, nos. 60, 64, in *The Swedish Intelligencer* (1632).

a trooper who 'spoiled' his horse 'willingly of purpose to be rid of the service' earned reduction to pioneer and forfeited the horse. As we have seen, the articles also provided for collective punishment, with discretionary penalties for every tenth man and reduction to 'Pioners and Scavengers' for the rest. In 1643 Waller publicly cashiered a whole troop who had deserted their colonel in action.[51] Both avoidance of action and unjustified flight could therefore earn harsh penalties, although for obvious reasons practice did not always follow the letter of the law. Allowance was made, for example, for the recognized phenomenon of panic flight. As that experienced officer Monro had earlier observed, 'Panicke feare without cause doth betray many brave men, and divers good enterprizes.'[52] At Marston Moor many thousands 'post[ed] away being amazed with Panick feares'.[53]

Desertion, however, was another matter. Its multiple causes have already been noted. Forced enlistment, sickness, hunger, defeat, low morale, hardship, boredom, unwillingness to leave familiar for alien surroundings, all played their part, although excuses often elicited a sceptical response. As one captain wrote to Sir Samuel Luke in 1644, 'In the last letter I received from you I understood the soldiers that ran away from their colours are sick. They were well enough when they left their colours.'[54] Desertion in fact proved ineradicable in the armies of both sides, and it presented officers with unsettling doubts and uncertainties that undermined the bonds of trust and mutual dependence that, in theory, should exist between them and their men. After some of his men had run away over the walls of Edinburgh in 1640 old Patrick Ruthven had written, '[N]ow I dare not trust any of them.' Their desertion, he said, was more troubling 'than the falling downe of the walls, or any such disaster'.[55] Deterrence may have curtailed desertion, but it could not prevent it. When Waller's court martial condemned three 'notorious' deserters to death, two were repeat offenders and the third had ignored the deterrent message of 'a fresh example of justice for the same offence'. A multiple deserter was unanimously condemned to death for running away from not one but 'several Captaines'. Yet when Richard Kiddle was condemned to die his ultimate fate was left to the general, perhaps because although he left

---

[51] *Lawes and Ordinances of Warre...Essex* (1642), [14], 19–21, 'Of Duties in Action', nos. 1–3, 7, 11, 'Of a Souldiers Duty touching his Armes', no. 5; John Adair, *Cheriton 1644: The Campaign and the Battle* (Kineton, 1973), 176. Nehemiah Wharton noted the need for 'some desperate exploit' to wipe away the 'blot' from an 'overmuch timorous' troop that had fled in disorder, but they appear to have escaped formal punishment. Wharton, 'Letters from a Subaltern Officer', 2. 326.

[52] Monro, *Expedition*, 2. 152. The best defence against panic, Monro believed, was officers too 'wise and stout' to succumb to rumour and infectious fear.

[53] Vicars, *Gods Ark Overtopping the Worlds Waves*, 275; see also BL Add. MS 11,810, fo. 12, for panic flight following a major explosion.

[54] *CSPDom. 1645–1647*, 519; Foulis, *Exact and True Relation*, 7; Luke, *Letterbooks*, 355; BL Add. MS 11,333, fo. 35ᵛ (for combined excuses of compulsion and hunger).

[55] *Ruthven Correspondence*, 61. See Parker, *Military Revolution*, 55–8, on desertion as a chronic problem of early modern armies.

voluntarily and was heading for the royalists at Basing House, he acted 'through the persuacons' of others. Mutual support, encouragement, and group persuasion explained many collective departures.[56]

Desertion was infectious, but although it merited severe punishment it was clearly impractical, as the number of offenders increased, to impose the severest penalties in all cases. 'Notorious offenders' fared worst, but mere followers might have another chance. Furthermore, armies hoped that some deserters would be retrieved. So in December 1644 the royalists ordered all of the many officers and men who had deserted in the past two years to return to their commands; only if they failed to do so would they become liable to the death penalty. After formation of the New Model, parliament gave deserters six days' grace in which to return to their colours before they were liable to 'pain of death to be inflicted without mercy'.[57] Not all returnees could expect to be benevolently received, however. As a parliamentary officer wrote with meaning: 'Command them all to come to their colours and then I shall take a course with them that shall please you.'[58]

In this war between countrymen deserters, even those far from home, could hope to fade into the general population to a degree impossible in continental Europe, or even in Scotland or Ireland. When soldiers served close to home it was relatively easy for them to melt into the community, while even soldiers who were initially outsiders but who had spent any time in a locality had the benefits of familiarity if they chose to desert.[59] Hence legislation designed to deter civilian complicity in a military offence. The measures promulgated to counter deserters' safe disappearance into civilian society provide further evidence of the intermingling of military and civilian experience in the 1640s. Articles of war prohibited aid to runaway soldiers, but as time passed stronger measures were needed. In Essex in 1644 Manchester imposed a fine of £20 'upon every town where any runaway soldiers shall be found and forty shillings upon every person harbouring any such'. Parish constables were to be 'very painful and diligent' in apprehending soldiers, 'all excuses set apart', and to send them back for punishment and future service. Yet after a few months the county committee complained of failure to execute warrants to bring in runaway soldiers, and a year later, addressing the problem of Fairfax's men who had 'come home without licence', constables were ordered to 'let . . . the general inhabitants know' that if they harboured or gave work to these soldiers they would be fined 40s., which would be levied or distrained on goods or chattels.[60] The royalists imposed a fine

---

[56] Adair, 'Court Martial Papers', 206–8, 211–12.

[57] BL Harl. MSS 6802, fos. 267, 317; Harl. 6804, fo. 92; Larkin, *Stuart Royal Proclamations*, 2. 1053; Firth and Rait, *Acts and Ordinances*, 1. 676.

[58] Luke, *Lettter Books*, 355.

[59] BL Harl. 6802, fo. 122; Add. MS 11,043, fo. 39, on the 'great failing in the number of the foot' and the failure to recover runaway soldiers raised in Herefordshire for local service. See also Walker, *Historical Discourses*, 40.

[60] BL Stowe MS 189, fos. 21, 29, 37.

of £5 on any person aiding or harbouring deserters, £1 of which was earmarked for their 'discoverer', while reading of the proclamation in a four-county area deprived civilians of the excuse of ignorance and publicized their risk. Parliament followed the establishment of the New Model with an ordinance 'for punishing Souldiers Imprested and forsaking their Colours' that levied a fine of £2 on the concealer of a deserter, and a further £10 to be paid by his town or parish. Each party thus added incentives to inform in an effort to undercut solidarity with the runaway and his protector.[61] Local sensibilities could be offended by the resulting military demands. In 1644 Rupert, seeking the return of deserters, had to placate the aldermen of Chester who suspected him of infringing city privilege that exempted inhabitants from impressment, and he hastened to assure them that he sought only 'such loose persons, as are fled [to Chester] from other quarters and live out of command'.[62] Armies were in fact heavily dependent on the cooperation of local constables, communities, and informers to retrieve their deserters.

Punishment of deserters was, like many other aspects of the law, limited by an enforcement system dependent on fallible means of identification as well as by the discretion of local enforcers. If local troops could count on familiarity and, presumably, kin and friends for protection unless conscience, cash, or fear prevailed to betray them, strangers on the other hand, had some advantages in their anonymity, for who was to identify them? So in the summer of 1645, when the order went out to punish those who 'ran from Sir *Thomas Fairfax* Army', the response was: 'the question is, how shall they be known, for few men were imprest but straglers who had no dwelling, who will never returne to the place whence they came'.[63] Still, there were some absentees whom neither familiarity nor anonymity protected. The more foreign the deserter the more difficult his disappearance into civil society, whether he was French or Irish in England or English in Scotland. This was probably one factor behind the virtual absence of desertion among offences tried by the English court martial in Dundee in 1651, which contrasts with its incidence in Waller's court martial records of 1644, although the incentive to desert also naturally declined when the army was not in action.[64]

Desertion was intended to be permanent, but more informal and temporary kinds of absenteeism also undercut firm estimates of army strength available at any given time. The methods of quartering troops often made it hard to keep

---

[61] *Lawes and Ordinances . . . Essex* (1642), 29–30, 'Of Administration of Justice', no. 7; Larkin, *Stuart Royal Proclamations*, 2. 1053; Firth and Rait, *Acts and Ordinances*, 1. 676; BL Harl. MS 6802, fos. 317–317ᵛ.

[62] BL Harl. MS 2135, fo. 35.

[63] *The Moderate Intelligencer*, 18 (26 June–3 July 1645), 139.

[64] Davies (ed.), 'Dundee Court-Martial Records', 9–66. One trooper, 'examined about his going into Fife', claimed that he went to see about a horse, admittedly without leave, but that he 'thought to come presently back againe'. Ibid. 20.

track of men's whereabouts, while soldiers incurably strayed from their allotted places. Civil war armies, whether on the move or in winter quarters or garrisons, had a variety of lodgings, from churches, stables, private houses, and inns to the tents that appear ranged with unlikely neatness as the background to portraits of commanders, where they make visible a rarely realized ideal of hierarchy and order. The smaller the groups of men in their ad hoc lodgings, the more difficult it was to coordinate and control their actions. Even in camp, regulations to prevent frequenting victuallers' tents at 'unseasonable hours' of the night, like those prohibiting officers from casual absences for dinner or overnight, reflect the constant struggle against straying personnel and habits of sociability, and the consequent difficulty of ensuring that a commander knew where all his men were or could call them effectively into action. Officially, they were kept track of by quartermasters who assigned lodgings and muster-masters who kept a weekly account of the presence or absence of men and arms, but the persistent need to regulate against fraud and substitution in musters reveals the intractability of the problem.[65] Much depended on the zeal and efficiency of non-commissioned officers and of the troop and company commanders overseeing their own small bodies of men.

This dispersal and informality of lodgings facilitated straggling and other casual forms of absence. Unlike deserters, stragglers usually intended to rejoin their units after a pause to drink or rest or catch rabbits or pass a convivial evening. It was an old and familiar problem, but although it was less criminal than desertion it still seriously hampered armies. It rendered discipline and operations more difficult, because soldiers were neither in their appointed places, nor within disciplinary range of their superiors, nor reliably available for action. In 1586 Leicester had ordered that soldiers must not 'goe a foraging' on their own, or hang behind with the carriages 'to ride or ease themselves', and civil war armies were still trying to force their men to keep rank and file on the march and not to stray far from their camps. Parliament's articles ordered that no soldier should 'presume in marching to straggle from his Troope or Companie, or to march out of his rank upon paine of death'.[66] Once in camp he was not to leave

---

[65] All articles of war devoted extensive attention to prevention of fraud in musters. See *CJ* 3. 653, for an attempt to prevent unofficial movement of soldiers between armies of the same side, and acknowledgement that officers knowingly accepted them. The incentive to muster a full complement of men, whether of real or fictitious bodies, was strong when the amount of pay to be distributed depended on numbers mustered and its distribution was in the hands of commanders, some of whom had been known to skim.

[66] *Lawes and Ordinances... Essex* (1642), [15], 'Of Duty in marching', no. 3, and see also [16], 'Of Duties in the Camp and Garrison', no. 1, which coincides word for word with *Military Orders... by His Maiestie* (1643), [6], no. 30: 'No man shall depart a mile out of the Army, or Camp, without Licence, upon paine of death'. See also *Lawes and Ordinances, set downe by Robert Earle of Leycester... in the Lowe Countries* ([1586]), repr. in Cruickshank, *Elizabeth's Army*, 301, nos. 36, 37. Leicester's further requirement that men were not to 'make any shout or crie' when 'any Hare, or any other beast' was put up as they marched by, suggests that breaking ranks to hunt game was (and probably continued to be) a common problem. Ibid. 302, no. 48.

it by any but 'ordinarie' ways nor to move more than a mile beyond its radius without licence.[67] These were ideal prescriptions only, however, in view of the uninstitutionalized nature of army food supplies and lodging, the attractions of what a soldier could pick up for himself, and the difficulty of keeping track of him when he was lodged, officially or otherwise, away from the body of his fellows.

The ebb and flow of troops close to their home regiments was compounded by straggling at greater distances. As the Dundee trials indicated, it was not normally a capital offence. Some was strictly informal in its origins, some began as an official task that turned unofficial in duration and execution.[68] The 'official' origin of some straggling lay in the use of foraging parties, legitimately dispatched on quartermasters' orders to seek provisions for man and beast, which offered opportunities for more extended absenteeism. In an attempt to cut the link between foraging, straggling, and plunder, articles of war provided for the presence of assistants to the provost marshal on these expeditions in order to punish wanderers and stragglers and also to protect the civilian population.[69] The passage from legitimate to illegitimate expropriation was murky at best, however, and civilian well-being once again depended on effective military limitation of extortion and terrorization. Unfortunately control of plunder remained imperfect. In 1645 Brereton in Cheshire regretted the absence of the horse who could have restrained their fellows in the foot and thus 'have been a great preservation to the country by snatching up and restraining stragglers and small parties from plundering and driving away cattle and the like'. Meanwhile the royalist army in Derbyshire was accompanied by 'straggling troops which plundered the country', and parliamentarian 'straggling scouts' were carrying off 'coales, corn and all manner of plunder' from the environs of Hawarden.[70]

In practice, none of the war's armies was able to cure the problem of straggling or of associated disorder and extortion. In the 1640s Waller's proclamation against any 'souldier [who] upon any pretence whatsoever shall dare to stay behind or straggle from his Colours' was matched by royalist provisions against stragglers who had plundered and oppressed local inhabitants.[71] We have seen that in 1651 straggling still plagued the parliamentary army in Scotland, where the court martial records reveal its casual and refractory persistence. Absenteeism was compounded by extortion, drunkenness, and terrorization of civilians, and

---

[67] *Lawes and Ordinances . . . Essex* (1642), [16], 'Of Duties in the Campe, and Garrison', nos. 1–2; see also the articles, probably of 1625, regulating an army on home territory and prohibiting departure of more than a mile from garrison or lodging, and unlicensed absence. PRO SP 9/208, fo. 260.

[68] Adair, 'Court Martial Papers', 222; Davies, 'Dundee Court-Martial Records', 20–1, 42.

[69] Elton, *Compleat Body of the Art Military*, 179–80.

[70] BL Add. MS 11,331, fos. 18ᵛ, 146, 149; BL Harl. 6802, fo. 308; Larkin, *Stuart Royal Proclamations*, 2. 1050.

[71] Adair, 'Court Martial Papers', 222; Larkin, *Stuart Royal Proclamations*, 2. 1050; BL Harl. MS 6802, fo. 308.

the five soldiers who, in a two-day marauding foray while absent without leave, killed sheep, stole a cloak, damaged property, and menaced and struck a woman with a sword, earned a harsh and well-publicized punishment. They were to 'bee led from the prison with ropes about their neckes round about the parade, and to receive ten stripes there, and then to be tide uppe to the gallowes and receive 20 stripes a peece. Somethinge of their faults to bee written and sett uppe uppon the gallowes.'[72] The penalty was directed against crime against property and persons as well as the purely military offence of absenteeism. From the point of view of both army and civilians, however, the two kinds of crime were powerfully linked, whether in England or in Scotland. If armies were to be effectively kept together, and to operate in an environment in which civilians were as little hostile as possible and resources were reserved for designated military purposes rather than subject to random private depredations, then both unauthorized movement and 'displacements' within the army, as well as major absenteeism by stragglers who too easily became marauders and predators, should be controlled. Civil war armies had only limited success in their attempts to do so.

Finally, stragglers weakened armies because they were easily picked off. The temporary straggler could involuntarily become the long-term prisoner. A parliamentarian complained at Alresford in 1644 that the royalists 'took some few of our men that were straggling from their colours'. Shortly after, it was the royalists' turn to lose men 'who stayed . . . carelessly behind', for the enemy 'took some few stragling Souldiers, who regarded their Drink more than their Safety'.[73] In defeat fleeing soldiers who perforce became stragglers might be captured before they could rejoin their units. Nevertheless when they believed themselves secure from the enemy soldiers were incorrigible. Late in 1645 parliamentarians believed that the surrender of Beeston castle was imminent, but their confidence was suddenly shaken by reports of the approach of relieving royalists. In a panic, officers had to send for reinforcements, for in their mistaken security 'many of [their] men [had] straggled abroad'.[74]

If straggling and lesser absenteeism were endemic contributors to army inefficiency, they nevertheless lacked the moral stigma of desertion or that other great method of inter-army mobility, side-changing. The case of the individual turncoat attracted more opprobrium than did collective switches, for it smacked of voluntary and personal betrayal rather than succumbing to pressure and circumstance. Large-scale side-changing by ordinary soldiers cannot be quantified, but it was a major form of troop attrition and acquisition. The resulting transfers, while superficially gratifying to the acquirers as evidence of the attraction and virtue of their cause, nonetheless often remained volatile. They

---

[72] Davies, 'Dundee Court-Martial Records', 9–10, 12; in addition, the offenders were to pay 2s. each to the owners of the sheep, who were 'poore folkes' and 'country people', ibid. 19, 21.

[73] [E.A.], *Fuller Relation Of the Great Victory obtained . . . at Alsford*, [2]; Walker, *Historical Discourses*, 43.

[74] BL Add. MS 11,332, fos. 100ᵛ–101.

added a further element of uncertainty to military plans, and caused widespread anxiety that oaths would be devalued and hence a vital guarantor of social stability weakened, as soldiers formerly sworn to one cause were resworn to its opposite. In July 1645 a parliamentarian reported that royalists who had formerly been parliamentarians until captured and 'entertained' by the king's forces had now run back to Fairfax. He warned of the potential risks if they were allowed to rejoin Fairfax's army, even if they took the Covenant, 'the frequency of oaths having brought them to a formality, and Perjury being now grown familiar', and he predicted shrewdly that '[m]any of the prisoners taken at *Naseby* we shall be constrained to fight with once again'.[75]

We know far more about individual officers who changed sides than about individual common soldiers, but condemnation of the practice had little to do with rank. The king himself declared that 'a *Turncoat* Souldier *can hardly prove an honest Man*'.[76] Parliamentary soldiers at Plymouth imprisoned their own commander when they suspected him of changing allegiance, while a parliamentarian publicist admitted, 'One constant *Royalist* (though bad's the best) is worth more than 2... *rotten-hearted Turn-coats*', and decried 'the *Apostacy* of... *tergiversatious Bats*' of the kind contemptuously dismissed by the royalist soldier Richard Symonds: 'first for the Parliament, then for the King, then theirs, then taken prisoner by us, and [with] much adoe gott his pardon, and now pro *Rege*, God wott'.[77] Such condemnations nevertheless did not prevent the wooing of turncoats with promises of rewards in the form of employment, favour, and money.[78]

Changing sides entailed risk for men and officers alike, and animus gave a fillip to action by former allies. When the twelve parliamentarian prisoners who had formerly served the king were 'hanged... all on one crab tree' by Rupert in 1645, their status as renegades enhanced the legitimacy of the action.[79] The scale of side-changing, however, precluded universally draconian punishment at the hands of erstwhile friends, and both armies remained willing to swell their

---

[75] *Exact and Perfect Relation... Langport*, 8.

[76] Walker, *Historical Discourses*, 104. The king himself here emended Walker's much blander original comment on Colonel John Urry, a man of multiple defections. Christ Church, Oxford, MS 164, fo. 124.

[77] *Mercurius Civicus, Londons Intelligencer*, 15 (1643–[1644]), 118; Vicars, *Gods Arke Overtopping the Worlds Waves*, in *Magnalia Dei Anglicana*, 261–2 (extending condemnation to civilian turncoats); Symonds, *Diary*, 196.

[78] In 1649 Rupert offered any mariners, watermen, and soldiers who came over to him a reward according to 'their Qualities, and... imployment befitting them. Likewise any *Gentleman*, or other of inferior Ranke, who are willing to serve their *King*, if they will repayre to us, shall be entertained with much respect, tho they have beene our Enemies, yet wee will procure an *Act of Indemnity* for them'. *The Declaration of his Highnesse Prince Rupert. Lord High Admirall*, 8. Incentives for turncoats could cause resentment among steady loyalists who felt themselves under-rewarded; see e.g. BL Add. MS 35,297, fos. 34–34ᵛ.

[79] BL Add. MS 11,331, fo. 141ᵛ, and compare the royalist John Gwyn's 'antipathy against a runaway cavalier', Add. MS 11,810, fos. 29–30.

numbers with former enemies. Some side-changing represented genuine change of heart; some was a matter of necessity; some was stimulated by defeat. Much was only notionally voluntary, for prisoners, not surprisingly, re-enlisted in large numbers with their former enemies when offered the chance. This method of handling the prisoner problem was traditional, international, and bipartisan.[80] Even without the threat of captivity one army's success could encourage the soldiers of another to join it, as when the 'prosperous proceedings' of the parliamentarians in Lancashire in 1643 stimulated many royalist defectors to 'chearfully offer... their service'. A few months later, at the other end of the country, 150 royalist dragoons 'came in... profering their aid and assistance' after a successful parliamentary assault on Tonbridge.[81] In 1646, as the royalist cause foundered, 120 fully armed foot deserted their fellows in Pendennis castle and volunteered to serve under Fairfax 'and with him continue'. In doing so, they asserted a measure of control over their own fate, rather than waiting to become passive counters in the surrender terms that were negotiated between commanders five months later.[82] At other times, soldiers followed their officers to the other side, like the men who accompanied Major-General Chudleigh when he joined the royalists in 1643, or the Cornishmen who followed their lieutenant to parliamentary service the same year, or the men whom Colonel Edgecumbe took with him in 1646.[83] It was a contagious practice, but unfortunately such recruits were apt to remain flighty. Two troops who came in from Waller when his fortunes were at a low ebb in October 1644 'were enterteyned by Lord Bernard [Stuart],... and the next night ran away agen'.[84] Nonetheless the recognized dangers of volatility and questionable loyalty were not enough to end the practice of 'entertaining' former enemies. In 1648 Cromwell was still arranging for officers to command a troop of horse, 'the greatest part whereof came from the enemy to us'.[85]

There was thus an ameliorating and reconciling element in side-changing that appears at first to run counter to detestation of renegades and anxiety over multiple oath-takers and breakers. Formulations that reduced guilt, together with the ease of persuasive communications between opposing soldiers, help to explain the apparent contradiction. At Lostwithiel, for example, the king offered either to 'entertain' soldiers or to grant passes for a safe return home because,

---

[80] After taking Leipzig Gustavus Adolphus 'entertain[ed] most of the garrison and [swore] the rest not to bear arms against him'. BL Add. MS 46,189, fo. 28.

[81] Fairfax, *Memoirs*, 131; *A True and Exact Relation Of the whole proceedings of the Parliaments Forces, that went... into Kent* (1643), 3.

[82] [J.R.], *Sir Ralph Hopton and All his Forces comming in to the Parliament* (1646), 8.

[83] *Articles of Agreement Betweene his Excellency Prince Maurice, And the Earle of Stamford* (1643), 4; BL Add. MS 35,297, fo. 30ᵛ; *CSPDom. 1645–1647*, 317–18, 367; and note the 200 men who offered in 1646 to follow John Gwyn wherever he went. BL Add. MS 11,810, fo. 31ᵛ.

[84] Symonds, *Diary*, 127.

[85] Wilbur Cortez Abbott, *The Writings and Speeches of Oliver Cromwell*, 4 vols. (Cambridge, Mass., 1937–47), 1. 619.

he said, 'many of his good subjects [had] been seduced & others enforced to take up arms'.[86] If enlistment or re-enlistment was not voluntary but forced, or if it was misguided action by the ignorant, culpability was reduced. The ease of communication between opposing soldiers also encouraged voluntary movement between armies by reducing the sense of difference between them, for fraternization was a recognized means of 'inviting' soldiers to change sides. One side could argue that the side-changing enemy had seen the light; the other might accept the defence, if the side-changer was recaptured, that he had had no choice. In surrender negotiations the defeated—as at Lostwithiel—tried to prevent solicitation or forced enlistment with the victor, but they were rarely able to secure terms that prohibited voluntary side-changing.[87] In practice, what emerged was a bipartisan recognition that side-changing among common soldiers was a fact of war, and that fraternization and attractive incentives to change were methods of indicating benevolent and conciliatory intentions.[88]

The fluidity and volatility of personnel described above forms an essential part of any discussion of civil war armies. It had effects beyond military misfortunes and frustrations arising from plans miscarried through flight and desertion, and beyond the imperfect benefits of a ready source of recruits. It also affected the experience of war of the larger community. Deserters and stragglers were not foreigners but countrymen who were loosed into civilian society, whether as predators or as fugitives seeking shelter. The mobility of armies and the wide areas of the country that experienced their presence meant that a large part of the population had some experience of this unofficial, as of the official, face of opposing armies, and often again found little to choose between their representatives. Some forms of army absenteeism depended on the integration of civil and military society and on the interchangeability of men who could so readily shed the external marks that identified them as soldiers or as parliamentarian or royalist. Side-changing itself further emphasized that interchangeability, for it was a continuing reminder of common roots and ties off the battlefield.

ENCOURAGING PERFORMANCE

If side-changing and even desertion and straggling had some benign effects in that they made the divisions of civil war less absolute, they nonetheless exacerbated the multiple problems that commanders faced in managing their men. In their efforts to overcome them, to counteract deficiencies of pay, training, and morale,

---

[86] BL Harl. MS 6802, fo. 258.
[87] Walker, *Historical Discourses*, 77, 79; BL Harl. MS 2135, fo. 138ᵛ.
[88] [J.R.], *Sir Ralph Hoptons and All his Forces*, 7; *Declaration of his Highnesse Prince Rupert. Lord High Admirall*, 8.

and to inculcate soldierly performance and reliable allegiance, officers drew on a traditional and international range of incentives and deterrents. When incentive, exhortation, example, and inspiration failed they turned to threats and punitive violence.

A minor incident from the early months of 1643 provides a case study of the difficulties commanders faced when confronted by the pervasive, unmilitary, and ingenious reluctance of soldiers to be heroic or even soldierly. We have already seen Sir Thomas Aston's frustrated attempt to make his men fire at the enemy. That, however, was only the beginning of an ignominious episode. Some of his musketeers, having fired one round, 'fell down, and crept away leaving their arms'. The rest of the foot would have fled if the cavalry, drawn up behind, had not prevented them, but when the horse belatedly advanced the foot took the chance to turn and run. The horse in turn then 'wheeled back' but, said Aston, 'I stayed them perforce, standing fully exposed to shot.' With the help of Colonel Ellis, a professional with Swedish service behind him, he got most of the artillery away, but the pikemen and musketeers intended to cover its withdrawal 'quit their trenches having never exchanged a shot, or never seen the enemy or cause of fear, but their fellows flying'. The remaining foot who should have prepared for a last stand in the church were instead piled 'like billets in a woodpile, no man at his arms'. When Aston tried to deploy the remaining artillery for a final defence he found quarrelling cannoneers and infantry who refused to help them move the pieces; 'nor', he concluded, 'could I draw out ten musketeers out of the church, would it have saved the world'. Ultimately no one was left but Aston and a handful of his men.[89] Admittedly this case dates from early in the war and Aston, although loyal and conscientious, was an unremarkable commander. In time training and discipline strengthened officer control over men in action, but neither Aston's methods nor his limited success were unique. Of a later incident Lord Byron would remark, '[T]he officers did as much as [they] could but were deserted by their soldiers.'[90] Aston's humiliating experience is indicative of much of the raw material from which effective armies had to be built.

Raw English soldiers had their defenders, at least compared with the raw soldiers of other nations, and in 1639 a letter from Brussels had claimed that 'if the commander be resolute the English will fall on bravely how raw so ever he be'.[91] In the long haul, however, something more than resolution, brio, and leadership were needed. Officers drew on well-tried methods, from drill and discipline to shaming punishment to morale-raising indoctrination, in their efforts to militarize unmilitary recruits. One way to counter soldiers' deplorable tendencies, for example, was to inculcate a warlike spirit. Even raw

---

[89] BL Harl MS 2135, fos. 102ᵛ–103; Newman, *Royalist Officers*, 10–11, 121–2. Compare the 'newly raised' royalists at Preston who 'shot at the skies', 'Memoirs of Captain John Hodgson', in Slingsby, *Original Memoirs*, 116.
[90] William Salt Library, Salt MS 486.   [91] Bodl. MS Clarendon, 15, fo. 173.

troops could be transported above themselves if their morale was high. There were recognized methods of enhancing it which went beyond exhortations by officers and sermons by chaplains, and even beyond pay and plunder. They ranged from prayer to drink to song. On the march to Dunbar Captain Hodgson was so buoyed up by hearing 'so much of God' from a cornet who prayed aloud as he rode that he could then encourage his own 'poor weak soldiers, which did much affect them'.[92] Other methods were more secular. At Chester in 1645, in order 'to possess [them] with more than ordinary spirits', attackers were primed with 'aqua vitae & gunpowder. . . to drink'. We have already noted the enlivening benefits not only of parliamentarian psalm-singing but also of 'brisk lively tunes' and '*Shouting to* the Battel' which, like the rebel yell of a later civil war, had its intended effect on the shouters as well as the enemy.[93] Ingenious commanders diverted and cheered their men with military tricks and jokes. The beleaguered royalists at Hereford in 1645 sent out 'dogs, cats, and outworne horses, having light matches tyed about them' that so distracted the parliamentarian besiegers that 'sometimes they charged one another. . . and one morning, instead of beating *reveillie*, we had a cry of hounds in pursuit after the train of a fox about the walles of the citty'. These 'recreations' contributed to the notable 'valour of our common souldiers and townsmen'.[94] Unfortunately such methods of encouragement had ephemeral results unless they built on a foundation of discipline and training.

If warlike spirit failed commanders resorted to more forceful means. We have seen their readiness to beat their troops into action or, in the words of one officer, 'to keep the men at the Works with our swords'.[95] Another practice, employed by Aston and many others in their efforts to force reluctant soldiers into action, had an ancient history: the use of an army's horse against its own foot as well as against the enemy. Charles Martel was reported to have placed troops of horse in the rear with orders to kill all who ran from the Saracens, but by the time the royalists resorted to the practice at Leicester in 1645, it had acquired unchristian overtones. '[A]fter the manner of the *Turks*, the Horse forced on the Foot to fight', noted one parliamentary reporter. Another confirmed that in the ebb and flow of attack the royalist foot were 'driven on by as many horse as oft as they were driven to retreat'. When the same reporter acknowledged a similar practice by his own side, however, he invested it with a different moral aura: the

[92] 'Memoirs of Captain John Hodgson', in Slingsby, *Original Memoirs*, 146.

[93] BL Harl. MS 2155, fo. 114ᵛ; Add. MS 11,810, fo. 28; Walker, *Historical Discourses*, 113; Orrery, *Art of War*, 186; Firth, *Cromwell's Army*, 330–1. Compare the parliamentary soldiers who, after reverses at Appleby in 1648, were 'with shouting. . . most of them drawne out of the Towne to line the Hedges'. *A Perfect Diurnall . . . From . . . the 24 of July till . . . the 31 of July 1648*, 261 (1648), 2098. See Sprigge, *Anglia Rediviva*, 70, for a series of sermons 'to encourage the soldiers to go on'.

[94] Duncumb, *Collections Towards the History . . . of Hereford*, 1. 279.

[95] *Major Gen: Poyntz's Letter to The Honorable William Lenthal Esq: . . . Or, A true Relation of the Storming . . . of Belvoyr-Castle* (1645), 5.

parliamentary horse, he said, 'backed our foot, and kept them to their duty'.[96] It is not surprising that horse and foot were sometimes uneasy allies. Troopers not only enjoyed a physically commanding position over foot soldiers, besides being better fed and paid three times as much, but their greater mobility enabled them to escape more easily in defeat, to find better pickings in victory, and sometimes to prey on their own fellows. Early in the war Nehemiah Wharton complained that there was 'great desention betweene our troopers and foot companies, for the footmen are much abused and sometimes pillaged and wounded'.[97] The foot were also quick to suspect that the horse would desert them, as they did at Lostwithiel. This suspicion of the horse, who were employed off the battlefield as well as on it as auxiliary 'enforcers' against fleeing or plundering infantry, serves as a reminder that all soldiers, even those in the same army, were not treated alike nor did they all have common interests.[98] The resulting tensions presented yet another complex of difficulties to commanders.

Beyond the moral and physical methods of encouragement so far described lay a whole range of economic incentives to military efficiency, for profit famously joined honour in motivating soldiers, 'profit being one of the ends why men undertake the Military profession, and honour not the onely (though the chiefest) of their aims'.[99] Plunder, the most satisfying source of profit, was endemic and often existed in a legally grey zone between legitimate takings and illegitimate pillage; lenient officers who were not fussy about strict legality won gratitude from their men but might find them busy with plunder when it was time for action. War also had direct money value. Pay or the lack of it, as we have seen, was the greatest single issue affecting the state of armies. Rates of pay varied with time and circumstance but the variations occurred within a narrow range, while for obvious reasons neither army could afford a significant spread between its rates and those of the enemy.[100] Those of the parliamentary army in 1645 were typical, when a foot soldier received 8d. a day, a trooper 2s., and a dragoon 1s. 6d., out of which they fed and, usually, clothed themselves and, in the case of

---

[96] Sprigge, *Anglia Rediviva*, 24; *A Perfect Relation of the taking of Leicester: With the severall marches of the Kings Army* (1645), 2.

[97] Wharton, 'Letters from a Subaltern Officer', 2. 321. Wharton himself was pillaged, and organized 'revenge upon the base troopers'. Ibid. 321–2.

[98] For grounds for distrust of the horse by the foot, see Bodl. MS Tanner 62/1A, fo. 75; *A Diary of the Siege of Colchester by the Forces under the Command of his Excellency the Lord Generall Fairfax* (1648), 15, 18 July; BL Add. MS 11,331, fo. 146; Vicars, *Burning-Bush*, 34, in *Magnalia Dei Anglicana*. For disparities of reward and conditions: *CSPDom. 1644–1645*, 232; BL Stowe MS 842, fo. 4. Regional differences were also a potential source of division. See Adair, 'Court Martial Papers', 215, for 'scandalous and reproachful language' directed against a London regiment.

[99] [T.R.], *Souldiers Accompt*, A3.

[100] Ibid. This handy ready reckoner listed pay for every rank above common soldiers and troopers, in horse, foot, and artillery, and provided tables by which the soldier 'not expert with his pen' could reckon what was due to him for service of 1–28 days and 2–13 months. A pay month equalled 28 days, therefore a year contained 13 pay months. By checking these tabulations a general or a cornet or a corporal could ascertain what was due to him for e.g. 19 days' or 5 months' service.

troopers and dragoons, fed their horses. In 1649 Lambert's troopers were allowed 4d. per meal but the foot only 2 1/2d., while troopers who had to march on foot because of shortage of horses still received their higher rate of pay. The gulf between men and officers was of course even greater than that between horse and foot, for at the higher ranges a colonel might receive as much as 30s. a day and his commanding general £10. Officers' horses, it may be noted, were rated at the same 2s. a day as were troopers.[101]

The soldier retained his public character as 'Mercenary', and an unsympathetic observer could still say in 1653, 'Hey boyes, its poecuniae that makes the souldiers merry.'[102] Money nevertheless played an accepted part in securing loyalty, and when pay was withheld from Sir William Waller and his men he pointedly remarked that they 'had nothing to keep [them] faithful to the cause but [their] affection to it'.[103] Affection alone often proved a tenuous support, and it was a truism not only that 'high-minded souldiers . . . desire to make a fortune' but that some were 'so covetous, as there is nothing which they will not undertake for money'.[104] The hope of profit indeed did wonders for soldierly performance, and rewards ranged from officially distributed danger money to unofficially liberated plate, shirts, and iron pots. Soldiers also had customary rights beyond their pay, such as shares, calculated according to recognized formulae, in the prize after a successful siege, and delays in sharing it out could make them restive. After the fall of Lathom House in December 1645 Brereton found his horse would not obey his orders to move on until he promised 'effectual' action to preserve 'their proportion of the prize', and after the 'very tedious siege' at Beeston castle he took particular care that the prize was distributed equally among the soldiers.[105] When sieges were ended by storm, soldiers enjoyed a legitimate free-for-all. This was a powerful incentive, although not infallibly effective. It took drink as well as promises of booty to persuade parliamentary soldiers to attack that formidable stronghold Corfe castle in 1643. Old terrors of drunken, looting soldiery survived with reason. The parliamentarian troops who stormed the suburbs of Chester in 1645 with 'loud shouts crying a Town, a Town', had been fuelled by more than 'aqua vitae & gunpowder'; they had also reportedly been promised that 'the lives & fortunes of the destined citizens [would be] freely left to their disposal'.[106]

Other incentives addressed particular military needs and were a recognized way of securing performance of dangerous, specialized, or unpopular tasks and of rewarding success. So sentries, cannoneers, or front line troops, for example,

---

[101] *CSPDom. 1644–1645*, 232; *CJ*, 16; Derbys. RO, Gell MS D258, 31/10 (ia); BL Stowe MS 842, fo. 4. See Gentles, *New Model Army*, 47–52, on withholding a proportion of officers' and troopers' pay 'upon the public faith' for later payment, and Firth, *Cromwell's Army*, 184–7, on variations in later pay rates.

[102] *Moderate Intelligencer* (27 June–4 July 1653), 66; 'The Mercenary Souldier' in Rollins, *Cavalier and Puritan*, 167–70.

[103] Ludlow, *Memoirs*, 1. 97.   [104] Cruso, *Art of Warre*, 60–1.

[105] BL Add. MS 11,332, fo. 92; 11,333, fo. 69.

[106] BL Harl. MS 2155, fos. 113, 114ᵛ; *Mercurius Rusticus* (Oxford, 1646), 107.

might get extra payments. When Leicester was under siege in 1645, the town's committee 'distribut[ed] Money unto souldiers that stood at the line, for their better incouragement'.[107] Storming strongholds was a particularly dangerous business for those in the vanguard, so commanders offered cash incentives. As Fairfax prepared to storm Bristol in 1645 he ordered that the men carrying the storming ladders were to receive 5s. apiece, while the sergeants in charge were to have 20s. each, and there were further rewards for the musketeers and sergeants who backed them up. When it came to the storm itself, 'the Generall to incourage and animate the Souldiers, saw the Commissioners pay to each of them six shillings, which they accepted very thankfully'.[108] Three years later, when he decided to storm the gatehouse of St John's abbey close to the walls of Colchester, six soldiers were paid 3s. apiece to toss in grenades and another twenty were paid half a crown each to carry ladders.[109] When the parliamentary foot were so 'banged' in their attack on Donnington castle that they lost their zeal to continue, troopers were 'hired' to lead them with a promise—according to a royalist newsletter—of the remarkable sum of £300 in payment.[110] We have already noted that soldiers were paid on a piece-work basis for the risky endeavour of retrieving spent bullets for recycling, as at Sherborne, where soldiers 'deservedly' got their rewards of 6d. or 4d. for each bullet retrieved from under the walls.[111]

Soldiers were also rewarded for success. After Fairfax took Bridgewater in 1645, 'as a reward upon the common souldiers for their good services in the storming of the place', each man received 5s., raised on the sale of royalist goods that had been brought in to the town for safety.[112] An incident at the surrender of Hawksley House to Rupert in 1644 indicates that defenders' attempts to buy off victors in order to save property provided another source of profit. When the governor decided that further resistance was hopeless he came out to Rupert with a purse containing £200 which the prince then, according to his custom, distributed among his men before they entered the house. In 1648, when loyalties had become more complex, political reliability earned a reward; parliament ordered that a 'Gratuity' of £1,000 be paid to officers and soldiers 'for suppressing the late Insurrection in the City of *London*'.[113]

There were also non-cash perquisites that served as incentives. Although not rights many had become customary and, like plunder, they could obstruct military plans. Soldiers stripped the dead on the battlefield if they got to them before local civilians, and if their expectations were thwarted by counter-orders, as at Naseby, they grew disgruntled. Recognized conventions governed these practices. For example, the royalist garrison at Donnington castle claimed the right to strip

---

[107] *Narration of the Siege and taking of . . . Leicester*, 7; Derbys. RO, Gell MSS D258, 31/30 (aa).
[108] S. Sheppard, *The Yeare of Jubile* (1646), 30; *CSPDom. 1644–1645*, 232. After all their trouble the ladders proved too short.
[109] *Diary of the Siege of Colchester*, 15 July. [110] *Mercurius Aulicus*, 1180, 27 Sept. 1644.
[111] *A True Relation of The taking of Sherborn-Castle, With Six hundred Prisoners* ([1645]), 5.
[112] Sprigge, *Anglia Rediviva*, 73. [113] *LJ* 10. 194.

parliamentarian dead who had 'fallen within pistoll shot of the Castle' before they were delivered naked for burial. Parliamentarian soldiers and surgeons claimed the diamond ring and bracelet of one of their own dead officers as 'their due', until their commander threatened 'to deal with them, as with enemies, if they did not deliver the same to be sent to his lady'.[114] In the often complex question of claims to battlefield property, appeal was made to the customary 'old law of warr'.[115] Yet as a reminder, finally, that men did not fight for economic motives alone, we should note that soldiers would sometimes forgo the 10s. reward paid for captured enemy colours, preferring to cut them up and wear the pieces as trophies.[116]

Another means of preventing non-performance by troops—its role was hardly more positive—was an appearance of equity in dealing with them. The administration of military law as a means of enforcing discipline and extracting desirable military behaviour has already been discussed; but the law imposed on soldiers, like the demands made on them for action, had to appear equitable if it was not to become a further ground for discontent. This did not mean that either the law or the demands were necessarily 'fair' in any abstract sense. War, like life, was intrinsically unfair: at the simplest level, why should Joseph Lister escape service and Thomas Slie die of wounds received at Sheffield, leaving his widow only the consolation of £2. 12s. 0d. in back pay?[117] From a practical military standpoint, however, it was desirable that punishments, rewards, and demands should not appear to reflect personal favouritism or caprice. Courts martial not only laboured conscientiously to discriminate between degrees of culpability and to impose penalties accordingly, they also used the paper so often placed on the offender to publicize their reasons for differential penalties: it served to inform as well as to humiliate. Punishment could be summary but it should not appear arbitrary. The use of lots in assigning soldiers to dangerous or unpopular duties was similarly designed to support an appearance of impartiality. At Bridgewater, when the parliamentarians decided on the difficult storm, '[l]ots were drawn for every one to take their posts, some to storm, some to be reserves, others to alarm'.[118] The procedure was routine, as in the case of Nehemiah Wharton's company in which watches were regularly assigned 'by lot'. Men selected in this way were hardly volunteers, but the choice could be seen as random, impartial, and equitable.[119] Lots also had their part in pre-battle incentives: 'They had cast lots for the spoil of us', a parliamentarian reported of the royalists at Preston in 1648.[120]

---

[114] Carte, *Letters and Papers*, 1. 129; Mastin, *History and Antiquities of Naseby*, 117; *Mercurius Aulicus*, 1173 [properly 1181], 27 Sept. 1644; Vicars, *Burning-Bush*, 34, in *Magnalia Dei Anglicana*; Woolrych, *Battles of the English Civil War*, 78.

[115] Symonds, *Diary*, 245.   [116] Woolrych, *Battles of the English Civil War*, 78.

[117] Lister, *Autobiography*, 34; PRO SP 28/25, fo. 139; Ellen Slie at least succeeded in collecting her £2. 12s. 0d. promptly.

[118] Sprigge, *Anglia Rediviva*, 69.

[119] Wharton, 'Letters from a Subaltern Officer', 2. 322, 324, 326; *Journal of Sir Samuel Luke*, 1. 1; Elton, *Compleat Body of the Art Military*, 184, 187; Lithgow, *Siege of Newcastle*, 24.

[120] 'Memoirs of Captain John Hodgson', in Slingsby, *Original Memoirs*, 119.

Finally, the struggle to produce effective armies and troops with a basic level of competence was tied to their organizational structure and to hierarchies of command and division of labour. Much depended on the control, example, and exhortation of regimental colonels and majors and the junior officers who commanded troops of horse and companies of foot. They in turn depended on their non-commissioned officers whose duty it was to turn raw recruits into soldiers who could understand and obey orders, handle and care for their weapons, act in unison, and stand fast in action. The hierarchy of organization was designed to convert the plans of the general—usually formulated after debate within a council of his senior officers—into action by common soldiers, by way of colonels, majors, captains, lieutenants, sergeants, corporals, lance-corporals ('Lanspassadoes'), veteran soldiers (who could be given greater responsibility and whose status was signalled by their placement in formations), and so ultimately down to the common or garden rank and file. Elton, an old soldier, explained the specific responsibilities of each rank in this hierarchy, and although they inevitably overlapped in practice they revealed the articulation of a system that, through its descending roster of duties, covered the operations of the army from general to new recruit.

At the head of the regimental structure was the colonel. He had overall responsibility for his regiment, overseeing its officers, exercising certain judicial and investigative powers, advising the field commander and executing his plans. As in the case of Colonel Gage, he could imprint a character on his regiment's general conduct and on its conduct of particular operations. His primary assistant was the 'Serjeant Major', whose place was one of 'great pains and toile', for it was he who prepared a regiment for action, disposing companies and captains, checking terrain and quarters, deciding on the placement of guards, and on occasion exercising the whole regiment.[121] Next came the captains and lieutenants responsible for the regiment's individual companies or troops. A captain of foot, for example, organized the drawing up of his company and should be 'a good *Posture-man* himselfe', so that he could correct men who handled their arms 'in an undecent and slovenly' manner, while evidence of his expertise was said to improve the cheerfulness and confidence of his troops. More generally, he was to administer petty justice and 'to have a fatherly care of his Souldiers', which included not only caring for the sick and wounded but also not skimming his men's pay. Finally and hopefully, 'he ought to be very religious, temperate, and discreet, faithfull in his trust, valiant in the field against the face of his Enemy'.[122] In real life, however, captains might be decorative or gentlemanly figureheads who left the hands-on management of their companies to their lieutenants, many of whom were old military professionals. It was the lieutenants, as their captains' deputies, who had the most immediate and regular role in producing soldiers who knew what to do in battle, for it

[121] Elton, *Compleat Body of the Art Military*, 183–5.   [122] Ibid. 184.

was they who exercised their companies 'in *Military Motions, Skirmishings,* and *False-firings* in *the pan*', and who supervised the non-commissioned officers, oversaw exercises, and monitored the men's military skills.[123] Majors and lieutenants in fact provided the professional backbone to the officer corps in its relations with non-commissioned officers and men. Armies depended on them, as the depositories and disseminators of professional knowledge, to act as partners to experienced senior officers and to counterbalance the consequences of inexperienced gentlemen colonels and of green or lazy captains who commanded troops and companies.[124]

The influence of sergeants and corporals on the rank and file was even more immediate than that of lieutenants, and a survey of their duties reveals the importance of the diaspora of veterans of European wars and artillery garden training who could transmit their skills to the expanded forces of the civil war, and train a new generation of non-commissioned officers to remedy the ignorance of 'freshwater' soldiers.[125] Sergeants were the aides and agents of their captains and superior officers; to them, as skilled practitioners of their trade, the practical, day-to-day running of a military unit could be entrusted. They corrected the faults of those who mishandled their arms and, in exercises, drew the men up in the files appointed by their captains and placed chosen soldiers in positions of honour (as file-leaders, for example). On the march the sergeant's place was not at the head of his particular group or 'division' of men but on the flanks where he could make sure that the whole company kept rank and order. If a man was out of order the sergeant was advised to 'cast in his *Halbert* between their ranks, to cause him to march even a brest with his right and left-hand men'.[126] In skirmishes it was his duty to see that musketeers kept evenly abreast, their muskets at the ready, and that they fired in unison; he was also to teach them how to 'fall off' and then rally, a practical skill given the incidence of flight. He had other duties: to convey offenders to prison or to the provost marshal; to fetch the company's ammunition, powder, and match; to obtain the 'word' for the watch each evening and transmit it to those authorized to receive it; to direct his corporals in setting sentries, to make frequent rounds and, if he found one asleep, 'to commit him to the hand of justice'.[127] He was, effectively, the

---

[123] Elton, *Compleat Body of the Art Military*, 181.

[124] See the requirements set out for Scottish regiments in 1639: captains and ensigns might be 'noblemen or gentlemen', but colonels, lieutenant-colonels, and sergeant-majors (the 'prime officers') 'should be men of skill, and must be sent for out of Germany and Holland', as should lieutenants and sergeants. *CSPDom. 1638–1639*, 409.

[125] See Parker on the success and failure of such 'old souldiers' in transmitting continental professionalism to raw recruits. Parker, *Military Revolution*, 175–6.

[126] Elton, *Compleat Body of the Art Military*, 180. This suggests that there was at least an ideal of orderly marching and, taken with the presence of drummers on the march, that armies sometimes—depending on road and other conditions—achieved the 'cadenced step' the existence of which in 17th-cent. armies has recently been questioned.

[127] Ibid.

company's site manager, responsible for its preparation for battle and its conduct in battle and camp.

With corporals we move to the hands-on micro-management of 'squadrons' within each company. A corporal's duties included teaching his men the use of pike and musket; keeping a roll of his squadron, notifying his sergeant when a soldier's name was deleted, and then training his replacement; distributing victuals, powder, bullet, and match, and providing wood, coal, and candles when the squadron was on guard. He was also particularly charged with setting out guards and sentinels, safeguarding the 'word', making sure that his men were vigilant and prepared for action, and enforcing silence around guard posts. As the authority figure in closest touch with the men he was to note and make the best use of his experienced soldiers and, more generally, to 'have an eye to . . . lives and manners'. He should protect the interests of the sick and wounded, taking care of their baggage and money, and be a model to his men, 'sober, wise and discreet, for the avoiding of ill example unto others'.[128]

These were clearly councils of perfection, although based on a realistic map of military division of labour, and Elton regretted that some through sloth failed to learn their proper attributes.[129] Nevertheless this organizational map, with its gradations of responsibility, duties, and command, reveals the ways in which, through that division of labour, the plans and precepts of high command could be translated into something like the intended action, and it places the innumerable small actions of the war within a larger pattern. It also reveals the vital role of the non-commissioned officers in fielding an army. Sergeants served as the liaison between officers and men and were general overseers of company skills and discipline, while corporals provided the small-scale training, care, and oversight that endeavoured to make the best of the armies' imperfect raw material.

The professional soldier Robert Monro had recognized that even the best of plans and organizations still confronted problems of chronic inattentiveness and unsoldierly habits, and he offered practical, common-sense remedies: give commands from the front; capture attention by a prologue and secure eye-contact; require silence (otherwise the men would be 'babling one to another'); enforce exact obedience to commands; ensure silent movement in regular ranks with no rattling of arms.[130] Civil war officers and their sergeants and corporals attempted by similar means to produce effective armies. The best instructors were characterized by expertise that bestowed authority and by the clarity and accessibility of their instructions as they drilled their men. As Elton explained,

He that intends to exercise a Body of men, must truly know what he shall command, and so to give his directions unto the Souldiers, as they may aptly make ready execution of

---

[128] Ibid. 178–9.   [129] Ibid. 181.   [130] Monro, *Expedition*, 187.

the same. He must at such times above all the rest, assume unto himself the confidence & presence (as near as he is able) of a complete Souldier.[131]

Ideally the instructions given to the troops should be specific and understandable, as in the following directions by which a body of men could change the direction in which it faced while remaining in the same place. They demonstrate the care with which actions were deconstructed, but also the complexities involved in training 'freshwater soldiers':

The left foot is always to be kept fixed like the *hinge* of a door, and unto what hand or part they shall be commanded to face, every particular Souldier is immediately to turn his body upon the *ball* or *center* of his left foot by *wheeling*, until he hath brought his *Aspect* unto the place commanded.[132]

Officers who could give such commands and men who could follow them were on the way to becoming 'complete Souldiers'. With time the armies of both sides contained increasing numbers of such men, but both armies also still contained men—including 'complete Souldiers'—who on many occasions were the despair of their officers.

ROUNDHEADS AND CAVALIERS

These soldiers, restive, dilatory, spurred on by threat, incentive, and occasional inspiration, do not sound very like the godly, disciplined New Model army of legend, but nor do they on aggregate sound like Goring's uncontrolled ravagers of the west country. They continued to be forgetful, negligent, destructive, wasteful, and riotous, but with luck and effort these attributes could be kept within limits and the damage they inflicted on army efficiency and civilian welfare controlled. As the war went on, more troops became better trained and 'soldierly' as commanders laboured to impose professional standards on their recruits. As early as the end of August 1642, for example, an order had already come down to the troops at Coventry that 'all soildiers should attend their colors every morne by six of the clock to march into the feilde to practise'.[133]

Attention to drill and basic tactics produced more reliable and cohesive troops and more effective deployment. So soldiers learnt to follow a standard set of orders, to hold their fire and to maintain it at a regular rate, and to march or trot at a steady pace. Cromwell and his Ironsides are the best-known of

---

[131] Elton, *Compleat Body of the Art Military*, 21.

[132] Ibid. 22. *The Grounds of Military Discipline*, a verse broadside detailing the motions that a good soldier should master, may have daunted rather than enlightened the reader, as it explained at length how to 'Open, close, face, double, countermarch, wheel, charge, retire: Invert, Convert, Reduce, Trope, March, Make readie, Fire.' It is reproduced in James Scott Wheeler, *The Making of a World Power* (Stroud, 1999), following p. 152.

[133] Wharton, 'Letters from a Subaltern Officer', 2. 317.

the courageous, resolute, and disciplined bodies that emerged, but although they reached their height in the New Model army these characteristics were not confined to parliamentary troops.[134] Nor should we forget that although the godly soldier may have believed that he was God's instrument doing God's work, faith was not a substitute for professional competence. Despite the rhetoric of its clerical supporters, the New Model was a professional army, not a missionary organization. Oliver Cromwell's letters to Fairfax on military affairs were strikingly secular, and references to God's mercies and assistance were occasional if heartfelt. Instead they were concerned with the business of war, with troop movements and tactical priorities and estimates of enemy strength.[135]

In spite of heroic efforts by officers and non-commissioned officers that led to notable improvements over time, however, casual, low-level, almost homely deficiencies continued to accompany more dramatic offences like flight and desertion. A 'Drawbridge . . . accidentally left down', for example, enabled a royalist party to capture an important prisoner; a corporal drunk at the wrong time wrecked plans for a surprise attack. Even on their critical marches after Naseby royalist 'neglect of guarding' led to the surprise of a large body of cavalry by parliamentarians who 'found all their horses at grass, and some of the men asleep, some a swimming, and the rest carelessly resting in the fields'. Shortly afterwards, on a misty morning, negligent parliamentarians were in turn surprised.[136] At times there was good-tempered bipartisan recognition of a universal problem. In June 1645 the royalists were able to capture Hougham House in Lincolnshire because the defenders, ignorant of their approach, were asleep; so they manacled their prisoners' hands, tied their feet, and laid them on the ground beyond the moat 'to take another nappe if they could'. There they were found by the parliamentary relief, who 'first laughed heartily at [them], and then instantly unbound them', after which they retook the house.[137]

Even in the New Model old military deficiencies were not exorcised, if they were better controlled, and civilians still suffered in traditional ways from the presence of soldiers. In both armies the moral and pious still deplored what they could not control. After the Restoration an old royalist, a 'Loyal Indigent Officer', regretted the character of many of his fellows:

Some hold themselves no Souldiers, till they can Gracelessly . . . thunder out Bloody Oaths; Common Swearing maketh one apt to forswear himself, which is a fearfull sin . . . . 'Tis a horrid Sin, . . . some out of Passion, and some out of Custom, makes nothing of it in their Drinking: Which Sin made us odious in the sight of God and Man.

[134] For accounts of civil war practice, and for directions for drill, see Firth, *Cromwell's Army*, 93–5, 130–4, 137–41, 383–5.
[135] Abbott, *Writings and Speeches of Oliver Cromwell*, 1. 336–7, 341–2, 346–7, 368–9.
[136] Rushworth, 5. 622; Carte, *Letters and Papers*, 1. 131, 133; Bodl. MSS Clarendon, 34, fo. 25.
[137] Vicars, *Burning-Bush*, in *Magnalia Dei Anglicana*, 157–8.

'Tis that which has been cast upon the Kings Party formerly, though hated by many Officers, and as strictly reprooved and punisht by them in their Souldiers.[138]

His royalist 'God dammees' had much in common with the parliamentarians whom Denbigh tried unsuccessfully to reform late in 1643. They were, he pointed out, 'employed in a service that tends to God's glory, [and] . . . carrying on a work of reformation'. They should therefore refrain from 'swearing [and] excessive drinking' and 'be of a good demeanour & inoffensive, . . . otherwise . . . they shall . . . scandalise the cause'. But the 'ill deportment of . . . officers and soldiers' continued unabated.[139] The formation of the New Model indeed brought improvement to the parliamentary armies, despite ever shriller royalist accusations of drunkenness, whoring, blasphemy, plunder, stealing, rapine, villainy, and the impressment of the 'scum' of local society to fill its ranks.[140] Even the defenders of 'the new Nodellers' who, it was said, were 'able by an eye of Faith to behold . . . the King of Saints, walking in the midst of them, and continually furnishing them . . . with wisdome, innocency, strength and courage', did not claim perfection.[141] In the New Model, one apologist declared, soldiers were now respected according to their piety and godliness, whereas in the past they could scarcely keep 'unspotted from riot and excesse'. Then, soldiers who would not join in drinking healths, profane speech, roaring and swearing had been 'accounted plain Roundheads, . . . men of low and poore spirits, scarce fit for an Army'. Now, civility and godliness reigned. Nevertheless he implicitly conceded that the basic character of the soldier 'fit for an Army' had not changed quite as dramatically as rhetoric suggested and that reasons for the apparent transformation were external as much as internal, for it owed much to the exemplary justice meted out by commanders who embodied the 'very spiritual essence of Magistracy'. Furthermore, he admitted, there was still drunkenness and swearing in the army, but 'for the most part to be found amongst inferiour Officers, and private Souldiers'.[142]

These admissions by a committed friend of the New Model are revealing. Joshua Sprigge's famous paean contains similar muted caveats. Sprigge's army was religious: 'men conquer better as they are Saints, then Souldiers; and in the countries where they came, they left something of God as well as Caesar behind them, something of piety as well as pay'. Its soldiers were orderly 'both respectively to it selfe, and the country', and they were not mercenary: 'they . . . had more

---

[138] Charles Hammond, *The Loyal Indigent Officer. Being A Brief Description of the Truly Loyal Commissioned Officers, which hath faithfully served his late Majesty* [*c*.1675], 16–17.

[139] Bodl. MS Tanner 62/2A, fos. 381ᵛ, 420.

[140] 'Cat will to kind, like to like', said the royalist Thomas Swadlin of the 'scum' who had been impressed by local officials anxious to get rid of them. See [Swadlin], *The Soldiers Catechisme*, 8th edn. [*sic*] (1645), 19, 28–30, 40 (this is the royalist parody of Ram's parliamentary catechism).

[141] Samuel Kem, *The King of Kings His Privie Marks* (1646), 31 (a sermon preached on 28 Feb. 1646); W.G., *A Just Apologie for An Abused Armie* (1646), 2.

[142] Ibid. 10–12.

civility then money'. They were obedient to superiors, and pious, sober, and moral: 'many of those fought by principle as well as pay, and that made the work goe better on, where it was not made so much a matter of merchandize as of conscience'. Yet this praise acknowledged the continued presence of those who fought for pay more than principle, while Sprigge too conceded the importance of punishment, of 'Justice upon Offenders', to secure a reformation that he admitted was incomplete: 'Armies are too great Bodies to be sound in all parts at once.'[143] The court martial records of 1644 and 1651, like the records of other aspects of military life, reveal the continuity of a patchwork of admirable and appalling conduct by soldiers of armies of both sides, including the godly New Model.

I have given little attention to the more abstract attributes of civil war soldiers, to the ideology and religion that bolstered loyalty or fostered disaffection and that coexisted with the conduct, good and bad, that engaged the attention not only of the army command but also of civilians. On the whole the evidence on these matters is less explicit for the royalists, although the power of loyalty and personal affection is apparent in, for example, the response of Sir Bevil Grenvile's soldiers to his death and, at a further remove, in response to the king's claims to authority and allegiance. It is more explicit on parliament's side, and the role of godly and disciplined soldiers was trumpeted abroad by their publicists and has since been widely explored. Such soldiers could lapse into many of the military sins already described, but their officers recognized that they had also 'faithfully co-operated with us in the kingdom's service'.[144] In the extraordinary efflorescence of political radicalism that followed the first civil war their claims were notable not only for their constitutional force but also for the sense of professional dignity and self-worth expressed in petitions over more mundane matters such as pay, indemnity and terms for Irish enlistment. They were deserving because they had been a 'gallant & faithful army . . . instrumental for the public good'.[145] Years earlier Cromwell had written of his men, 'I have a lovely company, you would respect them did you know them.'[146] 'Respect' was a word rarely used in connection with civil war soldiers but it deserved, along with more familiar terms of abuse and dismay, to be added to the vocabulary applicable to this heterogeneous and volatile body of men.

This account of soldiers has been largely external. Their own voices as they fought, suffered, and offended are rarely heard directly—even court martial records are few—whereas narratives, letters, and memoranda from officers, chaplains, and politicians abound. The men can be heard more directly as, later, they petitioned for aid, redress, and indemnity. For the present, we may conclude

---

[143] Sprigge, *Anglia Rediviva*, 323–4.   [144] Worcester College, Clarke MSS, 110, fo. 54.

[145] See e.g. ibid. fos. 16–16ᵛ, 17ᵛ, 55.

[146] BL Stowe MS 184, fo. 55. Cromwell distinguished his men from the earl of Manchester's, who were bad, mutinous, and unreliable—a condemnation that may owe something to his notorious quarrel with Manchester.

with more views from above, which confirm the infinite variety of civil war soldiers and the conjunction of military virtue and vice. The mixture appears in the royalist Sir John Digby's sharp distinction, after the fall of Grafton House, between his troopers 'who behaved themselves so gallantly', and his mutinous foot 'who shrunk and failed me in my greatest need'.[147] In October 1644 little was to be expected of the parliamentary foot, shattered and demoralized after their recent disaster at Lostwithiel, but as they marched towards Newbury they were praised for 'diligence' and cheerfulness despite wet weather, bad roads, 'penurious' lodgings, and inadequate provisions. Admittedly they were in part sustained by hopes of revenge against the barbarous Cornish.[148] Captain John Hodgson summed up the paradoxes of noble cause and ignoble agents, of soldiers both brave and deplorable, when he praised the courage of one of the parliamentary regiments at Preston in 1648: 'Such valiant acts were done by contemptible instruments!... The Lancashire foot were as stout men as were in the world, and as brave firemen. I have often told them, they were as good fighters, and as great plunderers, as ever went to a field.'[149]

It is time now to turn from generalized description of these bipolar armies with their combinations of courageous fortitude and ignominious flight, of discipline and disorder, and of the conditions that put the best-laid military plans at risk, to the conduct of soldiers and their interaction with civilians in specific wartime situations.

---

[147] 'Life of Sir John Digby (1605–1645)', *Camden Miscellany*, 12, Camden Society, NS 18 (1910), 96–7.

[148] HMC, *Portland MSS. 13th Rept. App. 1*, 1. 188–9.

[149] 'Memoirs of Captain John Hodgson', in *Original Memoirs . . . of Sir Henry Slingsby*, 119.

CASE HISTORIES: TWO SIEGES

The major battles of the civil war have been extensively studied, and their place in its political and religious as well as its military history is widely recognized. Sieges have on the whole had less intensive attention; they have often been placed in a local rather than a national context, or seen as instances of personal heroism in which the fortitude of defenders like Lady Derby and Lady Harley is lauded. Sometimes, as in the misfortunes first of Nathaniel Fiennes and later of Prince Rupert at Bristol, their impact on matters at the centre forces attention, but despite the tactical importance of many sieges, their untidy on-again-off-again character and the absence of a compelling dramatic shape have sent them to historians' sidelines.

The two sieges described here demonstrate the interaction of rules and conditions, of habits of peace and imperatives of war, in specific episodes of the English civil war. In a long siege, unlike a battle, we can observe phenomena over time. We can see soldiers consciously operating—with successes and failures—within a framework of accepted codes of conduct, and the conditions of daily life that affected their proceedings. We can also, in ways only rarely and briefly possible in battles, observe the effects of war on civilian populations and the tension between military and civilian institutions. The first of these exemplary cases was a relatively minor affair, but it serves as a prelude and a foil to the second which, to contemporaries, was as significant as the battle of Preston in determining the outcome of the second civil war.

We have already seen some of the rules that in theory covered the conduct of besieged and besieger. The sieges of Boarstall and Colchester exemplify the playing out of the rules of the game in specific circumstances. Both ended with surrender, not storm, and thus escaped the bloodiest of conclusions such as those that befell Leicester in June 1645 or Basing House in the following October. Acknowledged conventions formally ruled conduct to the very end, yet the strains to which those conventions were subject, the ways in which they were observed, and the relations between enemies differed markedly. In both cases the besieged were royalist, the besiegers parliamentarian, but the affiliation of the party inside the walls made little significant difference.

Both sieges occurred in periods of distinctive stress, when fears and irritants might endanger a vulnerable system. The first, that of Boarstall House, was a small-scale military event but it dragged on to the middle of 1646; by then the defenders' obstinate refusal to admit that their party had been defeated and that further resistance was futile frustrated and irritated the parliamentarian enemy. The second, that of Colchester, was a focus of national attention when war was renewed in the spring and summer of 1648. It was nasty, long, and a major military operation, and it exposed parliamentarian shock, anger, and sense of betrayal, and royalist desperation. Yet although both sieges were shaped by exceptional stresses, the first shows the relatively untroubled if sometimes testy survival of rules, conventions, and social emollients; the second reveals a system of military conduct close to breaking point on crucial issues and an incipient crisis in the balance of civil and military power in the state.

14

Boarstall House 1645–1646

Boarstall's is a straggling, shapeless story, with an ending but no climax. During most of the royalist tenure of the house it was a garrison and base for skirmishes and collection of supplies and money; intermittently it was a besieged stronghold. It offers a case study in the tension between idealized loyalty and the practicalities of war and defeat, in the survival of friendship between enemies and its constraints, and in the interaction of personal honour, forms of civility, and military calculation.

Boarstall House was a fortified medieval manor house some ten miles north-east of Oxford which became part of the screen of nearly twenty minor strongholds that protected Oxford and its access routes. 'It is', said one observer, 'an old house moated round, and every way fit for a strong garrison. At the north end is a tower much like to a small castle.' Its owner, Lady Penelope Dynham, was a parliamentary sympathizer.[1] For the first year of the war troops of both sides ebbed and flowed through the village. Then, late in 1643, the royalists seized the house to cover Oxford and put in a small garrison, only to evacuate it in May 1644, believing that after the fall of Reading it served no useful purpose. They realized their error when parliament promptly installed a garrison that harassed the approaches to Oxford and disrupted communications and supplies.[2] In June a well-equipped royalist force under Colonel Gage seized the church and the outbuildings and turned their artillery on the house. The battered parliamentarians resisted briefly before seeking a parley, and 'surrendered on very easy Conditions'. Gage was generous because, like Fairfax later, he weighed the 'hazard' of taking Boarstall against easy conditions and plumped for the latter.[3]

Shocked, parliament ordered its recapture and also the prevention of depredations by its defenders on the surrounding countryside. As Clarendon pointed out, the garrison not only effectively defended Oxford but 'did very near support

---

[1] George Lipscomb, *The History and Antiquities and of the County of Buckingham*, 4 vols. (1847), 1. 87.

[2] *Journal of Sir Samuel Luke, Scoutmaster General to the Earl of Essex 1643–4*, ed. I. G. Philip, vol. 3, *Oxfordshire Record Society*, 33 (1952–3), 218, 258, 265, 270–1; Walker, *Historical Discourses*, 26; Stephen Porter, 'The Civil War Destruction of Boarstall', *Records of Buckinghamshire*, 26 (1984), 86.

[3] Clarendon, *History*, 2. 381–2; *CSPDom. 1644*, 216, 320; Roy, *Royalist Ordnance Papers*, 1. 139, 2. 455; Walker, *Historical Discourses*, 26.

it self by the Contribution it drew from *Buckingham-shire*, besides the prey it took from the neighbourhood of *Aylesbury*'. Nothing came of the orders for recapture. After one vain attempt under Waller it was recognized that a siege would require a strong mixed force and, for a storm, strong artillery support. The parliamentary officers who had occupied it confirmed that so long as it was well-supplied with food and ammunition it could sustain a long siege. Parliament settled instead to a watching brief, and until 1646 it remained a thorn in their side, a 'very ill . . . neighbour' to their forces, and a base for both military raids and demands on civilians for money, horses, and supplies.[4]

The only serious threat to Boarstall in that period came in the late spring of 1645, when Fairfax and Skippon mounted an attack during their abortive siege of Oxford. Hopes of success were high, but their 1,200 men sustained heavy losses in their unsuccessful assault 'and that night they raised the siege'.[5] By 5 June Fairfax was ordered to join Cromwell for a sterner confrontation at Naseby. The experience, however, reinforced the general wisdom as to the difficulty of taking the place, and gave Fairfax a healthy respect for the strength of its moated site and the courage of its defenders. He later admitted that the memory of this 'forcibl[e] but ineffectual' earlier attempt affected the terms on which he was prepared to settle for surrender in 1646.[6]

The governor of Boarstall was Colonel Sir William Campion of Combwell, Kent. He had been granted full powers in October 1644 but his formal commission was delayed until December and was issued by Prince Rupert. Even after Rupert's dismissal late in 1645 he remained loyal to the prince as well as to the king.[7] Despite his impeccably royalist career Campion had entered the king's service only after months of prayer, reflection, and advice confirmed his judgement. 'I did not rashly nor unadvisedly put my life upon this service', he said, but once the decision was made his loyalty was unshakable: 'I am bound to assist by my oath of allegiance, but rather than fail, I had rather die a beggar, than wittingly to violate my conscience towards my God and King.'[8] His scrupulous conscience shaped his actions in 1645 and 1646, and his intransigent loyalism was as distinctive a quality among many royalists as intransigent faith in their role as divine instruments was among many parliamentarians. A neglected theme of the civil war is the accommodation of such ideological absolutism to the disappointments of real life. Boarstall, like other sieges, offers an opportunity to observe the progression from loyal defiance to grudging surrender. There the character of the progression owed much to the strength of Campion's principles

[4] *CSPDom. 1644*, 325–7, 334, 341, 362–3, 394–6; Clarendon, *History*, 2. 382; Luke, *Letter Books*, 37, 50, 101, 253, 294.

[5] Ibid. 299–300; Symonds, *Diary*, 188, 190.

[6] *CSPDom. 1644–1645*, 565–7; East Sussex RO, Danny MS 110; Luke, *Letter Books*, 303.

[7] Ibid. 50, 71; East Sussex RO, Danny MSS 38, 40, 41, 55, 67, 68, 108.

[8] Ibid., Danny MS 64; Combwell, near Goudhurst, is close to the Sussex border, hence Campion's social and familial Sussex connections.

and, one must suspect, the force of personality that enabled him to override the faction and doubts that commonly set in among the besieged. Nor was his scrupulosity confined to the larger cause: his antennae for the punctilios of honour were acutely sensitive. His very virtues were to inspire both exasperation and admiration among his friends as well as his enemies as they prolonged Boarstall's hopeless defence. Ultimately, however, he was forced to recognize circumstances in which the externals of honour became 'needless ceremony'.[9]

Until mid-1645 the siege of Boarstall was a relaxed affair, interrupted only by the brief periods of investiture by Waller and Fairfax. The garrison's freedom of movement was little restricted and Campion won praise for the moderation with which he treated the surrounding inhabitants. After Naseby, however, the demands to supply men and money for the king grew heavier and aroused increasing civilian opposition, while the noose around the house itself gradually tightened.[10] Still, much of Campion's activity continued to be the routine stuff of garrison life. He secured men, money, and supplies from the countryside, issued safe conducts, led sorties, and punctiliously negotiated prisoner exchanges.[11] He was guided by conventions of civility, honour, and professionalism, and any suggestion of lapses from 'the honour of a soldier' led to touchy self-justification.[12]

The Boarstall garrison was typical in its mingling of military and civilian inhabitants. Besides the soldiers and their officers there was, it seems, a significant population of prisoners, for Campion had plenty to bargain with, and their presence suggests that food supplies were not seriously straitened.[13] Campion's wife Grace, her children, and her servants were all at Boarstall, as were wives of other officers; Lady Dynham seems to have been there in 1644 at least, and her son-in-law came and went from East Anglia to collect rents from his wife's jointure lands near Brill.[14] Considerations of danger and health, not of hunger, led to attempts to arrange Lady Campion's departure from Boarstall. In June 1645 Fairfax had refused a request to allow her to leave because it would be 'prejudicial' to his plans, but by early August, after his departure and his army's triumphs at Naseby and elsewhere, Campion's old parliamentarian friend Herbert Morley urged him to send his wife out to be cared for by her friends, fearing that the garrison would soon be blocked up. By then it was too late; his pregnant wife was so near her time, wrote Campion, that she had fits every night. By March 1646, however, he was anxious for her to have some respite and to 'enjoy the country air' away from Boarstall. She was allowed to leave, but she

---

[9] Ibid., Danny MS 108.   [10] Ibid., Danny MSS 69–70, 74–6, 79–81, 84, 91.

[11] Ibid., Danny MSS 37, 48–50, 53–4, 58, 71, 86; *CSPDom. 1645–1647*, 147, 151–2; Luke, *Letter Books*, 225, 233, 255, 286–8, 291–2, 473, 504, 521, 545. For frequent minor actions emanating from Boarstall see *The Life and Times of Anthony Wood, Antiquary, of Oxford*, ed. Andrew Clark, 2 vols. (Oxford, 1891–2), 1. 117–18, 123.

[12] Luke, *Letter Books*, 617; East Sussex RO, Danny MS 71.   [13] Luke, *Letter Books*, 97, 101.

[14] East Sussex RO, Danny MSS 86–8; *CSPDom. 1645–1647*, 69–70 (Boarstall is mistakenly identified as 'Boston, in Bucks').

was soon recalled through a change of policy that embarrassed the parliamentary officer who had to relay the message.[15] It heralded new rigour and the beginning of the end for the garrison. The incident also reminds us that, although Boarstall's situation was more benign than Colchester's a few years later, the hardships of siege life were not confined to soldiers.

In one way the siege of Boarstall was unusual. Razing the environs of a stronghold was a standard practice to give a clear field of fire and remove cover for a surprise attack. Buildings that offered vantage points for sharpshooters and protection for troops were among the first to go and churches, with their useful towers, steeples and sheltering walls went with the rest, without regard to ancient protections, royalist attachment to the church, or the claims of both sides to respect holy places. So in 1644 the king ordered Campion to pull down the church and adjoining houses 'for the better fortifying of Boarstall House'.[16] Destruction was nevertheless limited until the fright of Fairfax's first investment in 1645 forced more radical action. Within days the royalists burned the village, and by the end of July the church was demolished, its bells sent to Oxford to make ordnance, and 'all the trees, gardens, and other places of pleasure were cut down and demolished'.[17] The consequence was a village not merely deserted but destroyed. It never revived, but the destruction left a fortified, strengthened site, able to hold out for nearly a year as the royalist cause grew more desperate, and at the last to survive a ten-week siege in good enough condition to extract reasonably generous conditions from the victors.

Thus when the siege entered its long last stages, a pragmatic parliamentarian commander, who was prepared to make a cost-benefit analysis of concessions that would enable him to achieve his end as cheaply as possible, faced a royalist governor for whom allegiance and obligation outweighed other considerations and were an intrinsic component of his personal and professional integrity and honour. Their forces confronted each other in a site that had been cleared and stripped for defence and where triple lines of palisadoes further strengthened walls and moat.[18] For a time the severity of the siege was moderated by the higher priority of campaigns elsewhere and by social habits and connections as well as by 'the law of armes, which every soldier is to keep inviolate'.[19] In the spring of 1646, however, with only a few royalist strongholds still holding out, the king abandoned Oxford, leaving the governor, Sir Thomas Glemham, to negotiate the best terms he could. The siege and surrender of Boarstall were linked to

---

[15] East Sussex RO, Danny MSS 59, 63, 64, 86–8.   [16] Ibid., Danny MS 42.

[17] Luke, *Letter Books*, 687–8, 691; East Sussex RO, Danny MS 61; Wood, *Life and Times*, 2. 135; and see generally Porter, 'Civil War Destruction of Boarstall', 87–9. Porter suggests that the delay in wholesale destruction may have been due to the need to use nearby buildings to quarter men and horses and reluctance to alienate the civilian population.

[18] Symonds, *Diary*, 231. Symonds described the defences in Aug. 1645: 'A pallazado or rather a stockado without the graffe [moat]; a deep graffe and wide, full of water; a palizado above the false bray [slope or hill] and another six or seven foot above that, neare the top of the curten.'

[19] East Sussex RO, Danny MS 86.

the fate of Oxford and were part of the mopping up operations that effectively ended the first civil war with the surrenders of Raglan and Pendennis in August 1646.

The last crisis for Boarstall began slowly. The evolution of relations between besiegers and besieged merits attention, for they reveal the persistence of personal ties in conjunction with unyielding commitment to a cause of a kind that shaped much in the civil war. They do indeed offer, as an earlier writer said, 'a pleasing picture of the kindly feeling of old friends who found themselves on opposite sides' but, beyond sentimentality, they also offer another picture that demonstrates the limits that principle and military necessity imposed on friendship.[20] Although Fairfax was the controlling presence, he remained largely off-stage; day-to-day dialogue took place between his subordinates and Campion, for whom the king was increasingly an absent and unreachable figure. Although his loyalty never wavered, it was the disgraced Prince Rupert who, he hoped, could understand his difficulties and his actions.[21] The exchanges between Campion and his parliamentarian opponents—Herbert Morley, Thomas Bulstrode, and Thomas Shilborne—between July 1645 and June 1646, reveal familiar patterns: they demonstrate the coexistence of convivial friendship between enemies with readiness to suspect disloyalty on one's own side, and the survival of social civility and adherence to the laws of war joined with adamant severity if the cause required it. One constant theme is insistence on 'civility' in conduct as an external measure of internal honour and integrity.

The nature of the personal ties between Campion and his three well-wishers differed. Colonel Morley of Glynde Place, Sussex, was a zealous, influential, and often implacable parliamentarian; although no longer a member of the army, he remained a member of the House of Commons, a justice of the peace, and a Sussex committeeman. He and Campion had already faced each other at Basing House in 1644, Morley as a commander of the besiegers and Campion as a member of Gage's relieving force.[22] In his commitment to the parliamentary cause Morley does not seem to have shared what has been called the predilection of most Sussex gentry 'to put personal ties and class solidarity before single-minded effort towards the defeat of Charles I'. Yet in his dealings with Campion he demonstrated the same 'desire for reconciliation and a return to harmony' as his less zealous peers. His links with the Kentish Campion came through Campion's wife, the daughter of a Sussex neighbour.[23] Nor were these links merely conventional and formal: Morley's letters breathe affection and concern, and a willingness to risk indiscreet and possibly dangerous action. In return, Campion treated Morley as a friend to whom honesty, plain dealing, and

[20] Charles Thomas-Stanford, *Sussex in the Great Civil War and the Interregnum 1642–1660* (1910), 191, 193.

[21] East Sussex RO, Danny MS 108.   [22] Thomas-Stanford, *Sussex*, 159–60.

[23] Anthony Fletcher, *A County Community in Peace and War: Sussex 1600–1660* (1975), 46–7, 264–6, 289, 290.

serious explanation of motive were due. Enemies could continue to be friends, and Morley made it clear that in Campion's case others shared his feelings. Yet neither budged an inch on principles.

Their exchange dates from late July and early August 1645, when the king's prospects were already gloomy and when a close siege already loomed in Boarstall's future. Morley's first letter began: 'Old acquaintance needs no apology; all your Sussex friends [are] in health, & continue their wonted affections towards you: equally valuing your welfare with their own.' When he came to consider where Campion's welfare lay, however, caution took over: 'I could impart more but letters are subject to miscarriage.' Instead he suggested that Campion send a 'character' so that he could communicate in cipher what he was 'unwilling to delineate'. Even better would be a conference, and to this end he promised a pass if Campion would send his wife to meet him. Campion replied in kind, grateful for the news of Sussex friends and expressing confidence in Morley 'by reason of our former acquaintance'. Unfortunately his wife's pregnancy made a meeting impossible, and he had no 'character' that could be deciphered without inordinate trouble (once again the laboriousness of cipher communication conflicted with the desire for security). Campion realized that there was something Morley wanted to say, however, so he proposed either that Morley himself offer a 'character' or that he send a confidential messenger, to whom he promised a pass and safe return. 'There is none', he concluded, 'that shall be more glad to find a way to serve you than your true friend and servant Will. Campion.'[24] 'I hope I may love you without offence although at Boarstall', responded Morley, as he repeated his urging to send Lady Campion away. At the same time he added a delicate reminder that 'reputation' bound Campion to use kindly the bearer of the letter, 'an honest man whom your friends have persuaded to be this messenger to convey their respects to you'. His purpose was to persuade Campion to surrender on terms that would be as favourable as his friends could contrive. Here Morley realized that he was moving to dangerous ground and—vainly—he asked Campion to burn his letter, lest the friendship it professed should become grounds for suspecting his own loyalty.[25]

Campion replied with a confession of political faith that answered not what Morley had written but the message brought in by word of mouth. He could, he said, have prolonged negotiation to investigate the deal offered him, but as it came from 'my friends and old acquaintance I scorn it'; true friendship demanded frankness, not manipulation. He explained the process of serious prayer and reflection that led to his taking up arms for the king and, significantly for his present and future actions, made clear that apparent defeat was no ground for abandoning his course, whatever the costs to individuals along the way. Indeed, like his parliamentary opponents, he saw reverses as providential—'God oweth a judgment to this land and is now paying of it for our sins.' Despite the king's

---

[24] East Sussex RO, Danny MS 62.   [25] Ibid., Danny MS 63.

present sad condition, he said, 'I am as confident as I am alive that the king or his posterity at length will be restored, which I am bound to assist by my oath of allegiance.' Yet if his loyalty to the king was unshakable, his political and religious creed was moderate; he abhorred popery and hoped for the preservation of the Protestant religion as settled in Queen Elizabeth's day, and he supported both the just prerogatives of the king and the privileges of parliament.[26]

What is just is of course a slippery concept, but such adaptable, unextreme formulae help to explain how, in the face of perceived social and political threats, erstwhile royalists who shared Campion's views and an erstwhile republican fellow-traveller like Morley could come together on a political resolution at the Restoration. So does the maintenance of courtesy and amity. Campion rejected Morley's efforts to save him from himself, but he concluded, 'I heartily thank you for your desire of the preservation of me and mine and if ever it lie in my power to do any courtesy for you, it shall not be wanting in your faithful friend and servant.'[27] Friendship was nurtured and preserved, but it was expressed through the conventions of honourable war, as in the issue of passes, and through honesty that refused to exploit that friendship, while at the same time it had cautiously to negotiate the dangers incurred from one's own side by communication between enemies. Campion's dealings with Morley help us to understand the coexistence of the softening qualities of personal friendship and observance of honourable codes of war with obstinate insistence on fighting past any point of common sense. Many commanders and councils of war made rational professional judgements that led to surrender, or held back only because of the dangers accompanying 'premature' surrender, but Campion was not alone in the stubborn, quixotic, and principled resistance he was shortly to offer.

Thomas Bulstrode, unlike Morley, does not seem to have known Campion before the war, although they had acquaintances in common; their relationship was brief and shaped by their military situation.[28] He came from an ancient Buckinghamshire family, was a member of the county committee, and by the end of 1644 had risen to the rank of lieutenant-colonel. He was rejected for service in the New Model army, but in November 1645 the House of Commons appointed him governor of Aylesbury.[29] His exchanges with Campion hinged on the sensitive topics of the reception due to deserters, the obligations of prisoner exchange, and the privileges to be granted to women. They insisted on civility but at times grew acrimonious, and they ended in embarrassment.

---

[26] Ibid., Danny MS 64.

[27] Ibid., and see Fletcher, *County Community*, 318–21, on Morley's response to the Restoration; Jason Peacey, 'Morley, Harbert', *ODNB*.

[28] East Sussex RO, Danny MS 86.

[29] *The Victoria History of the County of Buckingham*, 3, ed. William Page (1925), 283, 315–16; Lipscomb, *History . . . of Buckingham*, 2. 22, 4. 502–3, 572, 574–5; Luke, *Letter Books*, 341; Firth, *Regimental History*, 1. 336; *CSPDom. 1644*, 377; *CSPDom. 1644–1645*, 349.

We have only Bulstrode's side of their correspondence, the first letters dating from 12 March 1646 in response to letters from Campion. Oxford still held out, but the war was effectively over. Boarstall was not yet closely invested, but its situation as a satellite to Oxford was growing more precarious. The exchange began over two men and a boy who had come to Aylesbury from Boarstall 'to abjure hostility against the parliament'; desertion, always a problem, increased as prospects dimmed. Bulstrode 'gave them the oath', took away their horses, let them keep the money they brought with them, and allowed them to set off for home. Campion wanted them back, indicating that they were not the guiltless runaways that they claimed to be and that the money was not rightfully theirs. He was too late. The offenders had gone, for Bulstrode did not believe in trusting traitors or letting them linger where they might do harm. 'This garrison is not suffered to be a receptacle for your fugitives, to continue long therein', he wrote, 'for I . . . confide not in their service.' Had he known of Campion's accusations in time he would have acted differently, but in any case the royalists themselves were hardly blameless, and he cited the case of a murderer whom they had refused to deliver 'though I demanded him to satisfy for the blood'. Then Bulstrode came to the real insult, the suggestion that he himself had profited by seizing as prize the money the men had brought. Stiffly, he wrote, 'I have not yet learned to be so complete a soldier, as to thrive by my sword: I never took my share of any prize, but leave it wholly to the soldiers, that most want it.' He concluded, equally stiffly, 'I hope you will, as to any incivility in this matter, hold guiltless, Sir, your servant Tho. Bulstrode.'[30] As this minor incident shows, Campion too could be intemperate, and reflections on an opponent's honour put a severe strain on civility. It also demonstrates the nervousness felt about the reliability of side-changers and deserters. At the same time, however, it reveals an assumption that what was a serious crime under the laws of England and God remained a bipartisan concern, punishable under the jurisdiction in which the crime was committed—even when it meant returning the offender to the enemy.

In a second letter on the same day Bulstrode was for the most part carefully civil. In response to Campion's request for a pass for his wife to allow her a respite from Boarstall he loftily replied 'that none under my command shall offer the least incivility to any of her sex, without condign punishment. It's the law of arms, which every soldier is to keep inviolate.'[31] Besides, they both knew the inconveniences of 'taking ladies prisoners'. He promised a pass, and in return, as an 'exchange of courtesy', he asked for a pass for the wife of the high sheriff of the county. Then, however, he turned to the more strictly military matter of exchange of prisoners, a subject that raised issues of

---

[30] East Sussex RO, Danny MS 85. Bulstrode did not deny the legitimacy of a 'share' of the prize, but said that it was contrary to his own sense of honour to take it. He prevaricated on the question of whether the fugitives had succeeded in keeping the money they came with from other marauding hands, only saying, 'they carried [it] with them, for aught I know to the contrary'.

[31] Ibid., Danny MS 86.

honour, good faith, and civility. He justified cases in which he had refused parole, for he had merely acted reciprocally in response to similar severity by Campion. If he had failed to observe the rules of 'civility' the fault was originally Campion's: 'Unless enforced I use not rigour.' In proof of his own civility he sent two prisoners to Boarstall and assured Campion that '[I]n all points of honour & civility. . . none shall be more studious to serve you, so far as may be justified' than himself.[32] Courtesies had been exchanged in the relatively cost-free matter of the women, a favour had been done by the return of two desirable prisoners, and anger contained over reciprocal 'incivilities'. As the letters reveal, limited movement in and out of Boarstall remained relatively free, subject to no more constraints than were normal for a loosely encircled garrison.

A little over three weeks later the situation began to change radically. As Fairfax blocked up the garrison the strain on patterns of sociability increased. On 4 April Bulstrode abruptly sent back the pass for the high sheriff's wife and asked in return for that granted to Lady Campion, 'which I may no longer continue'. If she did not return within two days, 'I must be excused, if any inconvenience follow'. There is little doubt that he was acting under orders to increase pressure, for Fairfax did not believe in helping beleaguered garrisons by relieving them of useless female mouths to feed, whether in the relatively relaxed circumstances of Boarstall or the harsher ones of Colchester. Nevertheless Bulstrode was uncomfortable and apologized for reneging on his undertaking and withdrawing a conventional courtesy. 'Sir,' he wrote, 'It's not usual with me to retract a civility, wherefore resent it not, as any incivility', and the next day he reiterated his creed of conduct between enemies: 'Could I justify the continuance of. . . the protections any longer, I should not have in the least point retracted, none being more studious of civility.'[33]

Urgency had not yet prevailed over all forms of civility and sociability, however, although they were exercised with due caution, and surprising social amenities persisted. Boarstall's supply of sack was running low, so Campion wrote to the parliamentarian Major Shilborne at nearby Brill to ask for a cask. On 14 April Shilborne replied, regretting that there was 'none in this town worth presenting to so gallant an enemy'. Instead they had sent to London for a cask of the best available, and meanwhile a few bottles of the best Brill had to offer were sent to Boarstall. Yet Shilborne was not an old friend like Morley or a social equal like Bulstrode, or even the senior officer at Brill. He had risen in the service, but in 1645 one of his own side had dismissed him as 'now a captain of horse, and heretofore a pasture-keeper to his father, and one of the meaner rank of men'. He and Campion do not appear to have been acquainted before the siege, although Shilborne acknowledged past 'civilities'; he was shortly to emerge as an intermediary trusted by both sides. For the present, even as he invited Campion

---

[32] Ibid., and Danny MS 71.   [33] Ibid., Danny MSS 87, 88.

to 'drink a bottle or two of wine' he added the proviso, 'if it is not beneath your condition to honour me with so high a favour'.[34] Only prudence, not sensitivity to social status, prevented the meeting, for Campion feared that it would feed rumours about suspect loyalty. He promised to drink Shilborne's health, but at present such a meeting 'would not be consonant with mine honour' for he feared that 'villains' would 'ill construe' it. Scandalous reports had been spread about him and although the king had rejected them as frivolous Campion remained uneasy.[35] His anxiety was not unreasonable, for in August 1645 his brother Edward was reported to be in London negotiating with an intimate of Lord Saye, while in September 1645 Campion had himself made a direct appeal to London. The appeal was intended only to secure an exchange for the deplorable Colonel Richard Thornhill, formerly one of the Kentish cavaliers with him at Boarstall—'a lewde, . . . dishonest, wicked man', said one observer, 'the veriest beast there ever was', said another, but like Campion a royalist whom misfortune never deterred. The approach was brusquely dismissed, and his brother's mission bore no fruit, but Campion feared lingering suspicion.[36]

As the sands ran out for Boarstall Shilborne, now in the lines around the house, continued to be an intermediary between the principals, Campion and Fairfax. In the sterner days of late May and early June 1646, however, his freedom to act with spontaneous sociability had gone and the tone of his letters became correct and reflected his general's impatience. He hammered home the collapse of royalist hopes and the fragility of Campion's bargaining position. On 31 May he told him that if he persisted in resistance the chance for good conditions would be lost: men were 'much set against you because you are so obstinate'.[37] His letters breathed frustration and exasperation at his failure to persuade despite compelling arguments, allied to anxiety to save Campion from himself: 'I write this not only so much for the sparing of more blood, as for that I desire you would look upon your present conditions, and if in any thing I may be serviceable to bring this to a speedy end, I shall think my endeavour well bestowed.'[38] Yet he could be no more than a correct if well-wishing go-between, for the exchange that mattered was that between the commanders. Fairfax preserved the politeness due between enemies, but with barely veiled irritation at pointless delay and bloodshed. Campion, aware of the inevitable outcome of 'present conditions', clung to the 'niceties' of honour and observance that validated his commitment to the king.

[34] Luke, *Letter Books*, 291: Luke was not alone in disliking Shilborne, ibid. 240, 279, 421, 530, 539; East Sussex RO, Danny MS 92. Campion wrote in reply to this letter, 'I shall let slip no opportunity of meeting you', ibid. For Shilborne's taste in wine, especially that seized from those suspected of disaffection, see PRO, SP 28/126, fo.163.
[35] East Sussex RO, Danny MSS 89, 92.
[36] *CSPDom. 1645–1647*, 99, 151–2; Everitt, *Community of Kent*, 119, 213–14, 244, 278–9, 281, 283–4. The Committee of Both Kingdoms told Campion that they did not 'meddle' with exchanges and referred him to Fairfax.
[37] East Sussex RO, Danny MSS 94, 98.   [38] Ibid., Danny MS 98.

There is an air of unreality about the last days of the siege. The king had left Oxford in disguise on 27 April, and on 5 May he delivered himself to the Scottish army investing Newark. There he ordered its royalist garrison to surrender, and within days was on his way to Newcastle in the custody of the Scots. Already in March the prince of Wales and his advisers had left for the Scillies, while the remains of the royalist field army had been destroyed after defeats at Torrington and Stow on the Wold, and Lord Hopton and Lord Astley had surrendered the remnants of their forces. Chester fell in February; Exeter followed in April. Oxford had not yet surrendered and minor garrisons remained, but their outlook was bleak. Yet Boarstall's quixotic course was not unique. The slow process of negotiation, the observance of professional convention, the insistence on niceties of law, custom, and honour, the exasperation of the victors-to-be and the defiance of the already defeated, can all find parallels at Worcester, Pendennis, and Raglan. The ultimate quixotry was that of the garrison of Harlech castle, which did not surrender until March 1647; by then they were 'forgotten men, defending a forgotten cause'.[39] What impelled these courageous and foolish men at the last was an amalgam of professional pride, a sense of the conduct necessary to sustain faith in one's own integrity, and loyalty and allegiance. Yet they did not deny reality. In Campion and his fellow defenders we can trace all of these elements.

Campion above all insisted that things must be done right, but form was related to substance and to personal honour. As Fairfax strengthened his forces around Boarstall, Campion explained the principles that guided his conduct. If the king was in any condition to relieve the garrison then he would hold the place as long as he was able for, he said, 'I had rather die than live with an ignominious brand upon me of betraying trust.' If it was true that the king was in parliament's power, however, 'and our differences are drawing to a period, I should be glad if we might close without the shedding of more blood'. He had served the king's cause

with that faithfulness and integrity, that his majesty may be very willing that I may make my best conditions, when he shall be in a condition to be served no longer by me, and I formerly promised him not to part with the place as long as in my power but by his consent and knowledge.[40]

There lay the rub, for while Campion recognized the professional criteria that could justify surrender, he also believed that release from a promise made to the king must come from the king himself, although if no word came from him professional honour might be satisfied by positive proof that there was no possible hope of relief. The king's position could not be taken on trust, however, and the word of an enemy did not suffice; the information must be authenticated by friend, not foe. 'I am confident you will desire nothing prejudicial to my honour,

---

[39] John Kenyon, *The Civil Wars of England* (1988), 157.
[40] East Sussex RO, Danny MS 94.

that shall not injure your cause and glory', he wrote to Fairfax, but he clearly now hoped for 'an end to these unhappy divisions'. He wanted two things: a formal summons from Fairfax, and the right to send to the king to know his pleasure, which 'will confirm him in his good opinion of me in performing my trust'.[41] Provisions formulated for a very practical reason—to prevent premature surrender—had become a punctilio of honour when both the possibility of capital sanctions (as in the case of Colonel Windebank) and any military point to resistance had vanished.

Fairfax obliged on 12 May with a formal summons to surrender but he demanded an answer the same day. He refused Campion's request for permission to send to the king, or at least to his commissioners at Oxford where the governor, Sir Thomas Glemham, was also trapped by the king's failure to authorize surrender. Fruitless parleys followed until finally on 26 May, in a desperate attempt to discover the king's will, Campion sent him a clandestine letter. He reminded the king that they had now been blocked up for eight weeks, but reasserted the garrison's determination to serve him and resist to the end. There is however a pathetic plea implicit in his declaration, 'I doubt not of your majesty's care of us.'[42] In any case, nothing came of it. Three days later he turned to Shilborne, who replied on 31 May that Fairfax was adamant in refusing permission for a message to the king, and with the news that Glemham had been summoned to surrender Oxford. With the fall of Oxford imminently expected and with no hope of relief, Shilborne wrote, Campion's obstinacy made the chances of good terms slimmer by the day.[43]

Campion replied with gratitude to his 'fair and noble enemy'. He did not doubt the truth of Shilborne's news, but he explained what motivated a resistance that though vain was not meaningless. It was not a matter of 'vain niceties' but of integrity, 'nothing being more precious to us than our honour, which now is all in effect that is left to us'. Nevertheless, if no word came from the king he would be satisfied by an answer from Glemham confirming the impossibility of relief. After that, 'I shall soon strike up this business.'[44] He wanted a way to yield, but it must be one that preserved honour through observance of proper forms.

This was precisely what Fairfax refused, for he was governed by his own scrupulous sense of his duty to parliament. What Campion wanted went beyond military relations between commanders. Fairfax's rationale appears to have been that an appeal to the king trespassed into the area where competing claims to national sovereignty collided. He explicitly distinguished his power as a soldier from the power of the state; the power of parliament overrode that of the army and apparent conflicts should be reconciled by recognition of that superiority. This did not mean that professional obligation and honour could be abandoned,

[41] East Sussex RO, Danny MS 94; this is a copy of Campion's letter; no recipient is designated, but it was clearly intended for Fairfax.
[42] Ibid., Danny MS 97.   [43] Ibid., Danny MS 98.   [44] Ibid., Danny MS 99.

but the general's autonomy was only military and professional. The issue was peripheral at Boarstall; it reappeared in more difficult conditions at Colchester.

Fairfax has often been represented as a moderate, gentlemanly foil to Cromwell, but where his principles as parliamentarian and soldier were concerned he was an iron man. Now, although Shilborne sought him out in person to present Campion's case, he was adamant:

I should be as willing to do any civility for Sir William Campion as any man, but must not neglect the duty of that trust I owe to the parliament. I do wonder he should stand upon such niceties, as his desire to send a letter to the governor of Oxon. about the surrendering of the garrison of Boarstall. I know it is not fit for me to permit such a thing . . . I wonder men should think themselves engaged in honour to defend places of so little consequence to them they serve, especially considering to what their affairs are reduced.[45]

Fairfax too adhered to a code of honour and his sense of obligation to the parliament matched Campion's to the king, but the impatience of the successful general in the face of a pointless but costly military gesture is also obvious. Nevertheless he still sought a compromise, and he now sent Shilborne a copy of a letter from Glemham—its authenticity attested by Edward Campion and another officer—that discussed Oxford's negotiations, and he still offered good terms if only Campion would cease to be 'obstinate'. Shilborne, whose manner was now stiffer and more cautious, observed, in a letter of 2 June, not altogether hopefully, '[I]t may be I may say something to you that may give you some satisfaction.'[46]

In fact, however, the defenders of Boarstall seized on Glemham's letter as evidence that there was no possibility of relief. An honourable path to surrender was at last open to them, and Campion and his council of war agreed that 'it was fit there be a treaty'. The next day commissioners from both sides, including Shilborne and Campion's brother Edward, were appointed to negotiate. By 6 June twenty-seven of the garrison wrote to Campion supporting the terms that had been hammered out. Responsibility was thus shared and diffused (and Campion prudently retained a copy for the record) while at the same time the officers justified their position: '[H]aving seriously considered all intelligences, & circumstances, [we] do verily believe the king is not in a condition to relieve us.' Honour was further satisfied by their insistence 'that we may not be disenabled for his majesty's service hereafter'. The question of the circumstances in which the defeated might return to arms was to resurface in the second civil war and became acute at Colchester.[47]

Agreement was reached on 6 June to take effect on 10 June, and hostages were exchanged to guarantee its execution. The terms demonstrated the meticulous

---

[45] Ibid., Danny MS 100.   [46] Ibid., Danny MSS 100–2.

[47] Ibid., Danny MSS 103–5, 108. For unexplained reasons two of the signatories on 2 June did not sign the document of 6 June.

attention to detail characteristic of surrender treaties, and in the circumstances they were generous. Arms, ordnance, ammunition, provisions and 'furniture of war' were to be delivered, carefully inventoried, to Fairfax for parliament's use, but the governor, commissioned officers, and gentlemen could march out with horses, arms, and their own goods. Common soldiers and all others within the garrison could, if they wished, march away with their goods and horses to their own homes, and once there they had the general's protection to live unmolested as long as they submitted to all the ordinances of parliament. Those who wished to make composition with parliament had Fairfax's 'effectual recommendation' that their fines should not exceed two years' revenue for real estate and a proportional rate for personal estate. The terms included a retroactive amnesty for anything said or done 'in prosecution of their commissions'—that is, for legitimate professional actions as soldiers—since the beginning of the Long Parliament. Those who wished to go overseas would have a pass from Fairfax, but they and all others were granted two months' freedom from molestation while they settled personal business. The sick and wounded in the garrison were to be cared for until cured, after which they too would benefit from the provisions and passes of the articles.[48] Thus enough of the outward signs of honourable surrender were preserved to avoid humiliation. Strong hope was offered that financial penalties, although severe, would be limited. Retroactive vengeance for the 'normal' events of war was ruled out, and life was made easier for the sick, the wounded, and those with affairs to settle. Fairfax, faced by criticism, justified his preference for this negotiated and moderate settlement over further expense of 'time and blood' to achieve total victory. Defending the article designed to limit composition to two years' revenue, he wrote drily to the House of Commons that he would rather save their friends' blood than take their enemies' money.[49]

Campion too felt a need to justify himself. On 6 July he wrote to Prince Rupert as his 'most true admirer' and as one who needed to prove that he had 'done handsomely'—a need that he believed Rupert would understand: 'Your highness by sad experience knows, that innocency itself is not now free from detraction.' He defended Boarstall's articles as, with only one significant exception, no more severe than those granted to Oxford. That exception related to the ceremony of surrender. At Oxford the defeated had been granted the full panoply of honourable surrender, with the right to march out with colours flying, drums beating, trumpets sounding, fully armed, and prepared to fire their weapons—for fifteen miles, after which they too surrendered all but personal arms, horses and baggage. 'That punctilio in carrying their arms 15 miles, . . . I had offered me', said Campion, 'but rejected it as a needless ceremony.' That stickler for the niceties of honour was concerned with those that embodied personal integrity, not those that made an external show, yet a residue of discomfort remained

---

[48] East Sussex RO, Danny MSS 106–7 (107 is a faulty copy of 106).
[49] Ibid., Danny MS 110.

and he reiterated the substantive reason for surrender and the importance of Glemham's letter, the unanimity of the garrison's desire to treat, and above all the fear that if they did not take advantage of present terms and held out beyond Oxford's surrender they 'would . . . all be disenabled to serve his majesty hereafter, if occasion should be offered'.[50]

Insistence on ability to serve the king in some more hopeful future points directly to events to be discussed in the next chapter. In the short term the major protagonists turned to more immediate concerns, while the minor players withdrew from urgent preoccupation with Campion's affairs. Morley continued to be a convinced and influential Sussex parliamentarian; Bulstrode returned to the sidelines; Shilborne stayed with his Buckinghamshire horse, later helping to suppress the Leveller mutiny at Burford, and dying in Ireland, colonel of his own regiment, 'of a flux' in 1651.[51] Meanwhile in the days immediately after Boarstall fell, Fairfax oversaw the final surrender and occupation of Oxford, mopped up remaining strongholds, and retired briefly to Bath with his wife to recuperate from his ailments before returning to cope with the political and religious tensions of an underemployed army.[52] From Bath he interceded on behalf of Campion and his fellows, reminding the House of Commons of his 'effectual recommendation' of limits to fines on their real estate. The matter fell within parliament's jurisdiction but Fairfax reminded members of the mutual obligations that the 'civilities of war' imposed on victor and defeated alike. He faced criticism of the surrender terms and defended their relative leniency, adding that Campion had been 'a very fair enemy', who had often protected the local people from 'plunder and violence'. On the same day, 3 August, he granted an extension of time for royalist officers to make their composition with parliament and issued a safe conduct for Campion and his household to go overseas.[53]

Campion had first to deal with some of the penalties that loyalty had incurred, although his financial troubles could not all be blamed on the war. His seat was in Kent but he also held valuable Essex properties, and in 1640 and 1642 he had raised £2,600 by alienation of three of them. For Campion, as for many others, war and defeat exacerbated pre-existing difficulties. When he compounded on the Boarstall articles his fine was set at £1,354, and in addition there were problems over who should receive the rents of lands that had been sequestered and about the financial liabilities of leaseholders for his royalist sins. Nevertheless by 26 January 1647 he had managed to pay the fine, and thereafter he was allowed to receive arrears of rents; in April 1647 furthermore he was granted a special

[50] Ibid., Danny MS 108; Rushworth, 6. 281.

[51] Fletcher, *County Community*, 294–5, 300–1, 311–12; Firth, *Regimental History*, 112, 596–7, 609.

[52] Aside from his chronic gout, Fairfax had suffered acutely from the stone; his wife had been 'very ill in her head'. Wilson, *Fairfax*, 93–4.

[53] East Sussex RO, Danny MSS 110, 112, 113.

pardon.[54] The financial respite was brief, however, for in August 1646 he had also been ordered to pay an assessment of £800, and on 5 May 1647 an order went out to seize his Essex estate for non-payment.[55] The Campion family survived at Combwell, but the immediate effect of royalism was to weaken a financial situation already under strain. At his death his debts were fairly modest—he owed his mother £763 and there were also outstanding debts to shopkeepers which she meticulously recorded—but wartime disposal of landed property led to reduction in income with which to handle both debts and regular expenses.[56]

Campion's misfortunes were unremarkable among defeated royalists, but one outcome of the siege of Boarstall was unusual: the survival of the house, but the permanent obliteration of the village. Sieges had consequences that extended beyond soldiers and outlasted hostilities. So completely was the village eradicated that inhabitants could not even enter a formal claim for redress, 'by reason', said one, 'our houses with writings have been consumed with fyer [and] we dispersed soe that we are altogether in a confusion'.[57] Yet because surrender had come so late in the war there was little point in slighting the house itself, and within months the Buckinghamshire committee granted Lady Dynham £240 towards removing the earthworks. After the Restoration she rebuilt the church, albeit on a more modest scale, and by the time she died in 1672 the grounds had been restored. A print of 1695 shows the house again surrounded by formal gardens and ranks of well-grown trees, its prospect now uncluttered by a village huddled at its walls.[58]

The story of Boarstall was not only one of honour, rhetoric, courage, the rules of war, and hard military bargaining. Much remains opaque, from the siege life of the women caught up in it, and even their numbers, to the character of the garrison, although among the officers we can identify Kentish cavaliers who presumably came with Campion and members of old Buckinghamshire families, and we also catch a tantalizing glimpse of Captain Pudding, formerly Jack Pudding the rope-dancer.[59] Yet we know little of the garrison's casualties and virtually nothing of their day-to-day life except for the glimpses of sociability offered by a cask of sack and bottles of wine.[60] The homely, domestic side of the

---

[54] East Sussex RO, Danny MSS 116–17; *CCC*, 1450–51; at least one of the 1642 alienations occurred in May 1642, before the outbreak of war. Campion may have sold the Essex properties outright (instead of leasing them) in order to pay his fine. The complicated disposition of the Essex properties still engaged the Committee for Compounding in 1652.

[55] *CCAM* 2. 717–18.

[56] Ibid. 2. 718; the debt to the dowager Lady Campion may have been arrears of her jointure, or a consequence of the complicated sale of Lamborne Hall, Essex.

[57] Quoted in Porter, *Destruction in the English Civil War*, 1.

[58] Ibid. 90–1; Wood, *Life and Times*, 2. 252; Lipscomb, *History ... of ... Buckingham*, facing p. 76.

[59] East Sussex RO, Danny MSS 88, 103, 105; Everitt, *Community of Kent*, 213; *CCC*, 2. 1422–3, 1452–3; Luke, *Letter Books*, 97.

[60] Ibid. 56–7. Compare Luke's concern over the supply of wine, plovers, and rabbits, which rubbed shoulders with concern over the supply of ordnance.

civil war was never far from its grander military events, and military and civilian society could rarely be wholly separated.

Boarstall's fortunes were a matter of civilian as well as military interest, and its surrender was a public happening. Interest was enhanced by its being a late survivor of a defeated cause. Its surrender was history made visible. Years later Anthony Wood remembered that his schoolmaster in nearby Thame gave the boys 'free libertie' for the day so that they could go to Boarstall to observe this rite of passage. There they joined hundreds of others who had come to view the ceremony of defeat. Its public character reveals how the concern for the presence or absence of symbols of honour gained part of its force from the fact that surrender was not a private military event but was enacted on a public stage with an audience that might include friends and neighbours. Siege and surrender were not only dramas of blood and fighting; of fear, depredation, and disorder; of the rhetoric of courtesy and honour and adherence to codes of personal integrity; and of the symbolic expressions of courage and mutual respect. They also provided a stage for the homely, the undignified, the anticlimactic. Perhaps the last words on Boarstall should be Anthony Wood's. He could not get into the garrison (where he had been warned to touch no food or drink lest it be poisoned—distrust died hard). Instead

he. . . stood, as hundreds did, without the works, where he saw the governor, Sir William Campion, a little man, who upon some occasion or other laid flat on the ground on his belly to write a letter, or bill, or the form of a pass, or some such thing.[61]

At Boarstall, as in other sieges, the heroic and the prosaic met.

[61] Wood, *Life and Times*, 1. 128.

15

Colchester 1648: 'The Mournfull City'

How sad a spectacle it is to see goodly buildings, well furnished houses, and whole streets, to be nothing but ruinous heaps of ashes, and both poor and rich now brought almost to the same wofull state, to see such people scarce able to stand upon their legges, and women some presently upon their delivery, some ready to be delivered. Infants in their mothers lappes and some hanging on their mother's breasts, all turned out of harbour and left helplesse to lie on the cold ground, to see poor and rich men, late of good quality, now equal to the meanest, toyling and sweating in carrying some mean bed or other away, or some inconsiderable household stuffs out of the burning, all of them with wailing weeping gastly countenances and meager thin faces, shifting and flying in distraction of mind they scarce no whither, to heare the lamentable cries of people comming from the Towne, old and young women, children poor and rich, lying before and crying unto the Generalls guards to passe . . .

The Lord make their hands sensible of that smart whose hands are so fild with cruelty to others.[1]

This passage did not describe a German city. It reported 'the wofull state of distressed Colchester', for in the summer of 1648 'the sad face of a New Warr threatn[ed] to bury in her own Ashes that woful Town'.[2] Physically and morally we have entered a different world from Boarstall's, although the rules acknowledged by both sides remained unchanged. After the courteous longueurs of Boarstall, Colchester's story illustrates the harsh face of acute siege, exacerbated by the sense of betrayal and desperation that characterized the second civil war. Civility and friendship had little place in a struggle marked by severity, bitterness, and desire for retributive justice. The siege demonstrated, furthermore, the impossibility of separating the military and civilian spheres of

---

[1] *Colchesters Teares: Affecting and Afflicting City & Country* (1648), in *The Clarendon Historical Society's Reprints* (Series 1, Edinburgh, 1882–84), 492–3. For the siege and its context see M. C[arter], *A Most True And exact Relation of That as Honourable as unfortunate Expedition of Kent, Essex, and Colchester* (n.pl., 1650); Brian Lyndon, 'Essex and the King's Cause in 1648', *HJ* 29 (1986), 17–39, and 'The Parliament's Army in Essex, 1648: A Military Community's Association with County Society during the Second Civil War', *JSAHR* 59 (1981), 140–60, 229–42.

[2] *Colchesters Teares*, 483, [477].

war. The ruthlessness with which civilian interests were subordinated to military necessity frighteningly conjured up the practices of the Thirty Years' War and seemed to foretell their naturalization in England. It also demonstrated the strains imposed on adherence to the codes of war when war seemed to change its character. On one side accusations of betrayal and treason resounded, on the other claims that loyalty to the king and the laws of nature and nations superseded oaths and obligations to the present state. If Boarstall revealed a society anxious, in the end, not to tear itself apart, Colchester presented in microcosm all the dangers of civil war.

The account of Colchester above, from a self-styled 'moderate man', resolutely attributed blame for that 'mournfull citty's' sufferings to the royalists who held the town and had precipitated a new war, and to the townspeople who had weakly granted them entry.[3] Yet the writer could not withhold pity and horror. His was a common response to the mingling of the civilian and the military and to the consequences when civilians were at the mercy of military decisions. Another parliamentarian who rode into Colchester after its surrender found it 'a very strange place': it was 'a sad spectacle to see many fair houses burnt to ashes & so many inhabitants made feeble and weak with living upon horseflesh & dogs, many glad to eat the very draught & graines for preservation of life'.[4] Echoes of La Rochelle are obvious; the descriptions that had circulated twenty years earlier of the horrors of prolonged siege now came home to England. Nor did the royalists, despite the brave face they assumed to hearten supporters, pretend otherwise.[5] Instead they blamed the parliamentarians, accused them of cruelty, of abandoning protective conventions, and above all of setting a new and dangerous precedent by the notorious executions that followed surrender.

Boarstall was a marginal operation, but Colchester was a central event of the second civil war and a focus of national attention in private letters and public print. It had a literary life that extended beyond newsletters and factual narratives such as that by Matthew Carter, the earl of Norwich's young quartermaster-general, whose *Most True And exact Relation of That as Honourable as unfortunate Expedition of Kent, Essex, and Colchester* contains the most famous account of the siege. It also lived in works like the anonymous *Famous Tragedie of King Charles I* and Bishop Henry King's 'Elegy on Sir Charles Lucas, and Sir George Lisle', and in more popular genres such as ballads and published dying speeches. The controversial executions of Sir Charles Lucas, Sir George Lisle, and Lord Capel provided the inspiration for many of these literary effusions, but they also

---

[3] Ibid. 492.

[4] Worcester College, Clarke MSS 114, fo. 72^v; 'draught & graines' were the residue left from making beer.

[5] See e.g. the two issues of the royalist *Colchester Spie* (n.pl., 1648), both dated 10–17 Aug. 1648, i.e. very close to final surrender.

addressed the judicial, military, and constitutional issues involved, set the siege in a national context, and exploited its picturesque and pathetic aspects.[6]

Boarstall was a leisurely affair, but events at Colchester moved relentlessly to their harsh climax. The eleven weeks that elapsed between investment and formal surrender were filled with military action, defiance, and negotiation, and the mounting sufferings of civilians and soldiers. Relations between opponents were rarely ameliorated by the links of society and region, and the laws of war were no longer a vehicle for demonstration of civility, courtesy, and, implicitly, fundamental social solidarity. Instead they were interpreted at best with cold punctilio, at worst—in the view of victims and their friends—abandoned before the claims of reason of state. At Colchester the laws of war that protected women and children, that regulated prisoners and parole, that provided the framework for surrender negotiations, and that legislated treatment of the defeated, were applied with a severity that sought out permissible exceptions to rules. And sometimes—as on other occasions in the second civil war—accusations of treason or 'war crime' replaced appeals to the laws of war.[7] The personalities of the principal actors contributed to this outcome, but the chief cause was the nature of the war. It was an ill-planned throw by the royalists, based as so often on misreading of information and inflated hopes. To parliamentarians it unjustifiably plunged the kingdom again into war and blood and entailed massive breach of faith. Although with hindsight the royalist effort appears doomed to failure, the conjunction of cavaliers again at the head of troops, an actively disgruntled populace, naval revolt, and Scottish incursion seemed to threaten real danger to a fragile state.

The sense of that fragility lay behind the outbreak of the second civil war and shaped response to it. The end of the first war had brought neither tranquillity nor settlement. Parliamentarians fell out and, without the pressure imposed by an armed enemy, ceased to paper over the fissures.[8] In 1648 deep political divisions remained, while in the provinces sporadic riots, even serious risings, erupted against an array of grievances. There was, as Robert Ashton has said, no peace dividend. The army itself grew divided, anxious over pay, disbandment, and indemnity for past actions, while the high command, divided in its sympathies, struggled to contain the rise of political radicalism. Meanwhile the captive king played off faction against faction, and royalists reintegrated themselves into social, economic, and judicial aspects of society at a rate that made many of their former

---

[6] *The Famous Tragedie of King Charles I. Basely Butchered...In which is included, The several Combinations and machinations that brought that incomparable Prince to the Block* (n.pl., 1649; I owe this citation to Steven Zwicker); *The Poems of Henry King*, ed. Margaret Crum (Oxford, 1965), 101–10; Rollins, *Cavalier and Puritan*; *The Several Speeches of Duke Hamilton...Henry Earl of Holland, and Arthur Lord Capel, Upon the Scaffold Immediately before their Execution* (1649).

[7] Donagan, 'Atrocity, War Crime, and Treason', *AHR* 99 (1994), 1137–66.

[8] See Ian Gentles, 'The Struggle for London in the Second Civil War', *HJ* 26 (1983), 277–305; Robert Ashton, *Counter-Revolution: The Second Civil War and its Origins, 1646–8* (New Haven, Conn., 1994), *passim*.

enemies both resentful and nervous. Petitions from all over the country spelled out grievances and demanded a treaty with the king.[9] The defeated king now grew confident that he had the support of the army, and sought a settlement in which he made few concessions.[10] In January 1648 parliament responded to his manœuvres by passing a Vote of No Addresses which made treasonable any further attempt at negotiations: he had double-crossed them once too often, they believed, in signing an Engagement with the Scots.[11] One of the ironies of the second war was the coexistence of increased anti-royalist bitterness with renewed pressure in parliament and in London to reach agreement with the king; only days before Colchester fell the Vote of No Addresses was formally repealed. For some, however, Colchester's surrender proved how mistaken compromise would be; it constituted 'a warning to *London* how they imbrace those whom God fights against'.[12] Parliamentarians thus fought this second war against a background of unresolved political and religious strife. Not enough of them were sufficiently disenchanted to affect its outcome by changing sides but the war did not erase divisions, which erupted again as soon as victory was clearly in hand.

THE RETURN TO WAR

The spring of 1648 was an apprehensive time. 'I fear', wrote one Englishwoman, 'the evils coming . . . upon this poor land.'[13] The winter and spring had seen serious riots in Canterbury, Bury, Norwich, and a scattering of other towns. In Canterbury at Christmas royalists had declared themselves 'For God, King Charles, and Kent', and nearly a thousand of the town's 'honest Christians', deprived simultaneously of 'Cheare and devotion', rioted in favour of 'Pies and Plum-pottage'. More dangerously, they challenged order and hierarchy, attacking even the venerable mayor, whom they 'esteemed . . . lesse rationall than his Horse'. In May a mutiny in Bury erupted in 'a *great Combustion . . . about setting up of a* May-pole', with six or seven hundred men in arms crying 'For God and King Charles' as they attacked soldiers quartered in the town. It had taken a serious military effort to crush the outbreak. Reports of 'misery',

---

[9] Bodl. MS Fairfax 36, fos. 4ᵛ–5ᵛ; see Ashton, *Counter-Revolution*, ch. 2, and ch. 4, pp. 117–58, on 'petitions and politics'; and Clive Holmes, *Seventeenth-Century Lincolnshire* (Lincoln, 1980), 92, on perception of the county committees as 'a wartime excrescence which threatened the traditional pattern of local administration and the social order'.

[10] Fairfax noted that the king told him, ' "I have as great an interest in the army as you." By which I plainly saw the broken reed he leaned on.' Bodl. MS Fairfax 36, fo. 5ᵛ.

[11] See Ashton, *Counter-Revolution*, chs. 2, 3, 10, and *passim*; for local responses see e.g. Everitt, *Community of Kent*, 219–40; Holmes, *Seventeenth-Century Lincolnshire*, 190–3, 200–3; R. W. Ketton-Cremer, *Norfolk in the Civil War: A Portrait of a Society in Conflict* (1969), 331–49.

[12] *A True and Exact Relation Of the taking of Colchester, Sent in a Letter From an Officer of the Army. (who was present during the siege . . .) to a Member of the House of Commons* (1648), 4.

[13] Bodl. MS Add. A.119, fo. 27ᵛ.

declining trade, dear provisions, and tumults in London, put the blame on the army, and mingled with reports of mutinous officers in the west.[14] In the spring south Wales erupted in full-scale revolt; shortly afterwards Scots and royalists occupied Berwick and Carlisle, while a larger Scottish army prepared for invasion; at the end of May the fleet in the Downs mutinied and ten ships joined the royalists; in May Kent rose, and in June Pontefract in Yorkshire was betrayed into royalist hands. Parliament's forces, reduced by disbandment, were stretched thin although, unlike their royalist adversaries, they were largely seasoned veterans. To the anxious government in London and the army leaders the whole country seemed ready to burst into flames, but in fact the major outbreaks of the second war were geographically dispersed and episodic; it was less a planned and coordinated war than, as John Kenyon has said, a 'series of scattered uprisings'.[15] Its main theatres were Wales, Kent, the north, East Anglia and, in a bumbling operation led by the earl of Holland and the young duke of Buckingham, a corridor from Kingston-on-Thames to final débâcle at St Neots. Nor were motivations uniform. In Wales one of the major catalysts was a disgruntled parliamentarian officer convinced that the services done by him and his soldiers in the time of 'greatest necessities' were now forgotten; in Kent, on the other hand, localist feeling seems to have fuelled the rising.[16] There were also royalist plotters who ignited and fanned the flames of revolt, and committed royalists on whose services they could rely.[17] In the face of renewed threats from fellow Englishmen and from the Scots, and of domestic war on multiple fronts, parliament had to re-equip and recharge its depleted war machine while coping with half-hearted supporters and a volatile public that was often hostile to its soldiers.[18]

The royalists' best serious hope of success lay in control of the fleet and of London, the two factors that, we have seen, were strategically crucial to parliament's victory in the first civil war. But their seizure of the fleet was only partial, and the earl of Warwick, parliament's old Lord Admiral, was brought back to conciliate and reassert command over the remainder. If he was reluctant to put the loyalty of his mariners to the test by a major engagement he was

[14] Everitt, *Kent*, 231–4; *Mercurius Dogmaticus*, 1 (n.pl., n.d.), 4–5; Rushworth, 7. 1119; BL, Stowe MS 189, fos. 39–39ᵛ.

[15] Kenyon, *Civil Wars*, 179, and see pp. 176–96 for a lucid account of the diffuse progress of the second civil war; cf. Lyndon, 'Essex', 18–19, who argues that in 1648 'full civil war [was] renewed as a coherent, nationally orchestrated royalist programme'. See also J. R. Powell and E. K. Timings (eds.), *Documents Relating to the Civil War 1642–1648*, Navy Records Society, 105 (1963), 302–6; Gardiner, *History of the Great Civil War*, 4, chs. 60–5, *passim*.

[16] Worcester College, Clarke MSS, 114, fo. 8ᵛ. Although the Christmas riot in Canterbury was suppressed, the county continued to simmer with unrest. Everitt, *Kent*, 231–4, and see ch. 7, 'The Community in Revolt, 1647–8', 231–70; Ashton, *Counter-Revolution*, 359–61.

[17] See Magdelene College, Cambridge, Pepys MS 2504, fo. 641, for Colonel Thomas Blague's 'encouragement'—authorized by Prince Charles—of the gentlemen of Norfolk and Suffolk in the spring of 1648.

[18] See e.g. Worcester College, Clarke MSS, 114, fos. 9–10, 16, 21, 23ᵛ–24ᵛ.

nonetheless able to prevent royalist control of the seas and, most importantly, of seaborne access to London, and his ships played their part in the blockade of Colchester. Nor, in spite of high hopes and considerable support inside the city, were the royalists able to seize London.

In Kent the affable but unmilitary earl of Norwich led a mixed body of troops, countrymen in arms, 'cavaliers, citizens, seamen and watermen'.[19] He intended to rendezvous at Blackheath, where he confidently expected an influx of volunteers and support from London, to be shortly followed by occupation of the city. Instead Fairfax dispersed a thousand men gathered at Blackheath on 30 May, and on 1 June, on a night of pouring rain, he decisively defeated the royalists at Maidstone. Royalist losses were heavy and much of Norwich's force melted away. He escaped with some 3,000 men and headed for Blackheath and London, but the expected support failed to materialize. Confronted by the city's militia under the loyal and redoubtable Philip Skippon, he abandoned his London plan and ferried his men across the Thames from Greenwich, the foot in boats, the horse swimming alongside. Once in Essex his numbers swelled again with infusions of London apprentices and old royalist officers, among them Sir Charles Lucas and Sir George Lisle. Shadowed by a parliamentarian force of horse and foot under Colonel Whalley the royalists moved towards Chelmsford, where 'a rabble of Mutineers' led by Colonel Farr, a former parliamentarian, had seized the members of the county committee as they deliberated.[20]

Recruits and supplies poured into Chelmsford, but Norwich's force was ill-disciplined and ill-armed. His experienced officers—including Lord Capel and Lord Loughborough and several ex-parliamentarian colonels—made some progress in bringing order to the 'confusion . . . which . . . rendered . . . numbers ineffectual', while the classic motivation for recruitment was also at work: 'a good number of the poor Bay Weavers, and such like People wanting employment, listed', and Farr's influence prevailed to bring many members of his trained bands into royalist ranks.[21] Among the experienced officers was Sir William Campion, commanding a regiment of foot.

On 10 June the army marched out of Chelmsford, carrying with them the captive county committee. On 12 June, with Whalley nipping at their rear, they reached Colchester. The city's ordeal was about to begin, but it was in a sense accidental. Norwich had intended to move towards Norfolk and Suffolk, where he expected gentry support and seaborne supplies from the continent

---

[19] Quoted in Kenyon, *Civil Wars*, 183. The parliamentarians referred to Norwich as Lord Goring, refusing to recognize the earldom conferred on him by the king in 1644.

[20] Bodl. MSS Clarendon, 31, fos. 109–109ᵛ (reporting parliamentary losses of 600–800 men at Maidstone, although 'they confessed to but 30'); Worcester College, Clarke MSS, 114, fo. 35; HMC, *Fourteenth Report. Appendix. Part IX* (1895), 'Round MSS', 281; HMC, *Twelfth Report. Appendix. Part IX* (1891), 'Beaufort MSS', 21; *A Letter From His Excellency the Lord Fairfax to the House of Peers, upon Munday being the fifth of June, 1648. concerning all the proceedings in Kent* (1648), 2–3; Gardiner, *Great Civil War*, 4. 138–48; Everitt, *Kent*, 261–5.

[21] HMC, *Fourteenth Report*, 'Round MSS', 281–2; HMC, *Twelfth Report*, 'Beaufort MSS', 21.

but he was persuaded to detour by way of Colchester in the expectation that Lucas's influence in his home town would secure more recruits. With Kent now safe for parliament, however, Fairfax was free to pursue the enemy into Essex, and Norwich had not allowed for the speed with which he would move his troops northwards. He was already close on the royalists' heels. On 11 June he crossed the Thames at Gravesend (thus taking a route considerably shorter than Norwich's via Greenwich), and by the evening of 12 June Fairfax was at Lexden, 'two small miles' west of Colchester, at the head of a thousand horse. The next day the rest of his army arrived. Norwich, instead of moving on, was forced to make a stand.[22]

The size of the opposing forces that now confronted each other is uncertain. One royalist account declared that Norwich had brought '4000 undisciplined men', incompletely armed, to Colchester, where they faced a parliamentarian army totalling 7,500. Other estimates put the royalist strength variously at between 5,000 and 6,000, although one observer noted that they were 'new-raised men, and not well acquainted one with another'. Another noted the presence of 'French and Walloons that could speak no English', but some of them may at least have been professionals. Fairfax's initial strength seems in fact to have been well below the 7,500 suggested above; according to one report he had just over 3,000 of his own seasoned troops, supplemented by five troops of Essex horse and dragoons and two regiments of auxiliaries and train bands. As late as 10 July Capel estimated Fairfax's forces at no more than 3,500 foot and 1,200 horse. Commissary-General Ireton, Cromwell's son-in-law, likened Colchester at the beginning of the siege 'to a great bee-hive, and [parliament's] army to a small swarm of bees sticking on one side of it'. Fairfax could however draw on county forces of Essex and Suffolk to block access by river and road and to cover his rear. And unlike the royalists', his forces could grow; within a week six companies arrived from Wales, while on 24 June the Suffolk men crossed the Stour and 'advanced out of their owne County', having rejected royalist overtures and abandoned the pretence that they were merely defending their county. Led by Sir Thomas Barnardiston and other Suffolk colonels, they blocked the north-east approaches to Colchester; at the same time the 'well-affected' of Essex, Norfolk, and Cambridge dispatched more troops.[23] As the two sides prepared to fight on 13 June, however, Fairfax's strength was, in numbers at least, less than the royalists'.

---

[22] Worcester College, Clarke MSS, 114, fos. 42–3; HMC, *Fourteenth Report*, 'Round MSS', 282.

[23] Gardiner, *Great Civil War*, 4. 150; HMC, *Twelfth Report*, 'Beaufort MSS', 22, 26; Lyndon, 'Essex', 29; I. C. Gould, 'The Siege of Colchester', *Trans. Essex Archaeological Society*, NS 8 (1903), 377 (letter from Capel of 10 July); HMC, *Thirteenth Report. Appendix. Part I. The Manuscripts of . . . the Duke of Portland*, 1 (1891), 459; *Exact Narrative*, 5; HMC, *Fourteenth Report*, 'Round MSS', 282–4; *A Diary of the Siege of Colchester by the forces under the Command of his Excellency the Lord Generall Fairfax* (1648; broadsheet); Ludlow, *Memoirs*, 1. 197. One contemporary estimate put the initial number of Parliament's regular troops at only 1,500, supported by two regiments of Essex trained bands, against 5,000–6,000 royalists. *True and Exact Relation*, 4–5.

It has taken a long time to reach Colchester, but the prologue merits attention, for it helped to shape both the conditions and the anxieties behind the well-known events of the siege itself and the responses to victory. Much of the general context of the siege, however, was commonplace enough, from bad weather to the general's ill-health. The rain at Maidstone proved to be the forerunner of a miserably wet summer; on 23 July John Clopton of nearby Little Wratting in Suffolk wrote that as much rain 'had fallen at this season of the year as ever was remembered', and for the rest of the summer he recorded rain, 'extreme flood', consequent damage to crops, and scarcity. Soldiers were often 'wet to their Skins', while the weather only added to the troubles of the besieged and of the many rendered homeless. 'God seems', said a royalist, 'to have bent his Bow in the Clouds . . . to destroy us.'[24] This was a sodden siege, in which rain exacerbated the discomforts of besieged and besiegers alike. Meanwhile Fairfax's task was made more difficult by gout and stone, but although his letters from Colchester reveal again the iron in his character, they show no sign of gout-ridden passion. Norwich's derisive offer to cure him of his disease only infuriated parliament's soldiers.[25]

Other, more divisive elements accompanied the siege. Old fears and hatreds were recalled, amidst suspicion of royalist resurgence and betrayal by former allies. A previously unpublished manuscript account of the first duke of Buckingham's conduct at the Isle of Ré in 1627 had recently appeared in print, for example, reminding the public that the cowardice, pride, and incompetence of the present duke's father had there betrayed his fellow Englishmen to slaughter; now the son followed his own dangerous path.[26] The theme of treachery and distrust was more common in this second war than in the first. Turncoats like Colonel Poyer in Wales, Colonel Morris at Pontefract, and 'Colonel Farre (the Apostate)' were joined by others; in Essex, for example, Colonel Sayers 'had formerly served the Parliament, but being undeceived was come to make atonement for his fault'.[27] Fortunately for parliament such recruits sometimes proved to be more talk than action or to be readily distracted by quibbles and jealousies.[28] Nevertheless old fears took on a new nervous intensity. 'We were', wrote one colonel, 'all upon the

[24] ERO, D/DQ s18, fos. 46ᵛ, 49ᵛ–51ᵛ; *True and Exact Relation*, 1; Rushworth, 7. 1164; Lionel Gatford, *Englands Complaint: Or, A sharp Reproof to the Inhabitants thereof* (1648), 51–2.

[25] Rushworth, 7. 1155. Fairfax's health was a matter of perpetual family concern, e.g. a letter from one of his sisters to another in May 1647: 'My brother Fairfax is much better in his health since his physic but full of troubles.' Bodl. MS Add. A.119, fo. 17ᵛ.

[26] [W. Fleetwood], *An Unhappy View of the Whole behaviour of my Lord Duke of Buckingham, at the French Island, called the Isle of Rhee* (1648). For a manuscript version, see Magdelene College, Pepys MSS 2099, fos. 26–36ᵛ. The account seems to have circulated widely in manuscript after the Ré disaster.

[27] HMC, *Twelfth Report*, 'Beaufort MSS', 22; Lyndon, 'Essex', 27. Although there were notorious defectors and turncoats in the first civil war, the sense of potential wholesale treachery was not pervasive as it was in the second.

[28] Bodl. MSS Clarendon, 31, fo. 258. One side-changing colonel who had expressed 'great desire and readiness' to serve the king was later dismissed as a man of 'much talk . . . no action'. Newman, *Royalist Officers*, 37.

pit's brink.'[29] Nor was it only turncoats who fostered an embittering sense of the decay of honour. The return to arms of many who had surrendered on terms that precluded further action against parliament represented both individual breach of faith and subversion of the structure of trust, obligation, and the sanctity of the oath on which society depended in so many ways, and by which relations between military enemies were largely governed. It was to be an issue on which royalists were defensive and parliamentarians unforgiving.

The climate of uncertainty, suspicion, and anxiety that had prevailed in the spring continued after revolt flared openly. London's multiple and conflicting responses to the crisis 'will require some Logique to tell you', wrote one puzzled reporter at the beginning of June, while another concluded 'that a man cannot tell what to believe'.[30] Fortunes were volatile; initial royalist euphoria was soon dispelled by the 'tediousness' of bad news, but parliament could feel little security as new eruptions strained manpower and reminded that no part of the country could safely be depended upon. Even as Colchester's position became—with hindsight—hopeless, reports of relief by seaborne forces under the prince of Wales or the duke of York heartened royalists and fed parliamentary fears. Through it all London remained divided, and in August there was a threat in the House of Lords to rescind Fairfax's commission.[31] Meanwhile, although the Welsh rising had collapsed, Cromwell was 'still in Wales entangled in a[n] ill favoured engagement with those mountaineers'. Only after Pembroke surrendered on 11 July was he able to move north to support John Lambert's New Model regiments against native royalists and Scottish invaders, but this brought little help to Fairfax.[32] At the local level, John Clopton's diary gives us the flavour of life in East Anglia in this wet, unstable, anxious spring and summer of 1648. It is filled with news of 'mutiny [that] waxt greater' in Bury, of the 'great rising in Kent', of 'mutinies & new distractions'. On 9 June his household sat up at night waiting for news, and he sent his children away for safety; two days later some of the ladies rode off to seek refuge elsewhere, although his pregnant wife could not join them. At last, just before midnight on 13 June, he heard that Norwich was in Colchester.[33]

EMBATTLED COLCHESTER

Colchester was not the royalists' favorite city. Like Essex as a whole, it had 'beene long possest with the spirit of disobedience', but now some at least of

[29] HMC, *Thirteenth Report. Portland MSS*, 1. 476.
[30] Bodl. MSS Clarendon, 31, fos. 110, 127, 157.
[31] HMC, *Twelfth Report*, 'Beaufort MSS', 27; Bodl. MSS Clarendon, 31, fo. 127; *A great and bloudy Fight at Colchester* (1648), 6; *A Great Fight at Colchester Upon Tuesday night last* (1648), 1–2; *Perfect Diurnall*, 261 (24–31 July 1648), 3001–2; Worcester College, Clarke MSS, 114, fo. 56.
[32] Bodl. MSS Clarendon, 31, fo. 110.   [33] ERO, D/DQ s18, fos. 36–41.

its citizens had become 'most zealous Royalists' who 'r[o]se in armes in great numbers' to join Norwich, and his army was 'mett by neere a thousand of the townesmen who . . . welcome[d it] as their deliverers'.[34] A body of horse from the town offered some ineffectual opposition but Sir Charles Lucas, fearing that innocent fellow townsmen might suffer 'in equall danger with the guiltie by the indistinguishing souldier', sent two Essex colonels, 'their countreymen', to persuade the townspeople to surrender. They were promised indemnity for lives and fortunes, a promise kept 'as farr as our necessities would comporte', said the royalists, which proved to be not far at all. Only the disaffected horsemen who had offered resistance were excepted from indemnity; they were left at liberty but stripped of arms and horses, and their lives and fortunes remained at the mercy—in the technical sense—of Lucas. Later, royalists were quick to point out the bitter irony of his benign interpretation of his power. For the present, however, the town once 'furiously mad' against the king received his army with 'showts & acclamations of joy'.[35]

Weak though the resistance to royalist entry had been, it nevertheless indicated that not all in Colchester regarded Norwich's army as their deliverers. The 'disaffected' were clothiers, an 'officious race of traytors', for 'clothiers through the whole kingdome were rebells by their trade'. Colchester's continued to be 'volunteers in rebellion' and some escaped to join the besiegers. The community they left behind was not united in support of Norwich and the king, however, while the large Dutch community compounded the town's diversity. Nevertheless 'riotous & tumultuous' demonstrations of 'rude & evil disposed people' had worried the parliamentarian city authorities, and recent mayoral elections had indeed shown a strong anti-parliamentarian faction.[36] These discontents stemmed less from enthusiastic commitment to the royalist cause than from disillusionment with parliament, its local agents and its army, from the continued decay of trade, and from fear of the forces of disorder that now appeared increasingly threatening. Norwich in his turn was to suffer from the vocal discontents of the disgruntled, suffering men and women of Colchester, who had a foretaste of what was to come on the very night that their royalist deliverers arrived when the troops, refusing to stay in their encampment outside the walls, mutinied and marched into the town in search of food.[37]

Neither Norwich nor Fairfax had planned a siege at Colchester. Once his army came up, Fairfax intended a quick, clean defeat of Norwich's forces. So on 13 June he sent waves of horse and foot against the royalist camp in the south-west suburbs of the town. Characteristically, Norwich had declined his

---

[34] HMC, *Twelfth Report*, 'Beaufort MSS', 22; HMC, *Thirteenth Report. Portland MSS*, 1. 458; *Colchester Spie*, no. 1, A2.

[35] HMC, *Twelfth Report*, 'Beaufort MSS', 22–3; *Colchesters Teares*, 12–13.

[36] *Colchesters Teares*, 12–13; BL Stowe MSS 842, fos. 14–14ᵛ; HMC, *Twelfth Report*, 'Beaufort MSS', 22–3.

[37] HMC, *Twelfth Report*, 'Beaufort MSS', 23–4; *Colchester Spie*, no. 1, A2–A2ᵛ.

engineers' offer to entrench, overnight, a line around the camp, 'and now there was no time', while his scouts failed to warn of the imminent action by the parliamentarians. He had, however, placed cannon in St Mary's churchyard, which commanded fields and suburbs to the south and west from a corner of the city walls, lined the hedges with musketeers, and kept a reserve in the suburbs. His cannon inflicted heavy casualties on Fairfax's advancing troops before they were forced to desist as the men of the two sides mingled in close combat. At last, in the face of parliamentary 'fury, and . . . Gallantry', royalist 'gallant Resistance' turned to 'Pel-mel' flight into the town, saved from rout only by the stand of Lord Capel, on foot with a pike and seconded by Lucas and Lisle, who 'like Horatius Cocles—opposed themselves to the furie of the enemie, whilst under the cover of their courage, the remains of our men saved themselves within the porte'.[38] A parliamentary regiment, the Tower Guards, followed them in, but they were driven back, cut down by waiting musketeers, artillery, and cavalry; 'most of them that had so rashly entered were cut in Peices'. Three more times Fairfax's men attempted to storm and were driven back with heavy losses, while the guns in St Mary's churchyard played lethally on the reserves. Fairfax was in the thick of it, and 'never . . . in so great danger in these warres as in this charge'. Finally at midnight they withdrew, leaving behind cannon and many dead and having fought, so royalists said, with courage and ferocity worthy of a better cause: 'This madness amongst the vulgar is more admired than true valour', wrote one grudgingly. Among the royalist dead was 'that worthy gentleman Sir William Campion'.[39]

Both sides now settled in to a siege. The royalists could not march away because the open, unhedged 'champion' country close to Colchester would leave their inexperienced foot at the mercy of the strong enemy horse. So, with 'active and cheerful diligence', they began to repair the town walls, 'like the Jewes in Jerusalem,—with [their] swords in one hand and [their] trowels in the other'. Fairfax abandoned thought of a further storm, calculating that it would require more troops than he had at his disposal. Instead 'he resolved to turn his Siege into a Blockade, and reduce them by Hunger'. It might be slow but it was 'better then to cast away such gallant men against walls and bulwarks'. So he set up headquarters at Lexden, barring the way for possible aid to the royalists from London, and placed strong guards on the Cambridge road to prevent escape in that direction. At the same time he began the process of fortification and encirclement for a blockade, and was immensely aided by the receipt of forty heavy cannon from the Tower of London.[40]

---

[38] *Colchester Spie*, no. 1, A2–A2ᵛ; HMC, *Thirteenth Report. Portland MSS*, 1. 458; HMC, *Fourteenth Report*, 'Round MSS', 282–3; *Diary of the Siege of Colchester*.

[39] HMC, *Twelfth Report*, 'Beaufort MSS', 24–5; HMC, *Thirteenth Report. Portland MSS*, 1. 459.

[40] HMC, *Thirteenth Report. Portland MSS*, 1. 459; HMC, *Fourteenth Report*, 'Round MSS', 284–5; *Two Sallies Forth by the Lord Goring and Sir Charles Lucas at Coulchester* (1648), [A2]; Carter, *Most True And exact Relation*, 139; Bodl. MSS Fairfax, 36, fo. 6. The processes of siege and

Colchester had some natural advantages as a stronghold. Set in an angle of the Colne, the river protected it to the north and east. Walls and gates still encircled the town proper although the castle, set on a high point at the north-east corner, was militarily outmoded and largely irrelevant to the siege. To the south and west, beyond its walls, the town lay open to the country, with roads leading to London, Maldon, and Mersea. On the north the river ran close to the walls, while within its wider north-eastern angle walls and earthworks protected the approach to the castle; elsewhere, between walls and open country or the river, lay the suburbs and, to the east, Colchester's port access at the Hythe. Fairfax surrounded the suburbs by his lines of circumvallation and forts and gradually tightened his control until finally the royalists were confined within the old town walls. These, though newly strengthened, provided only an old-fashioned defence. When the royalists arrived in Colchester they had found it 'a *Naked* Towne . . . void of all *Fortification*' and, except for a full magazine of grain, ill supplied with victuals. To 'the judicious eye of an experienced soldier' it was an unsuitable place for a garrison.[41] The advantages of its site and the determination of its defenders nevertheless made it a tough nut to crack.

Over the first three weeks of the siege Fairfax closed off the western approaches from the river Colne in the north to the Maldon road in the south-west, whence he moved east to meet the Colne again after it turned south towards the sea. He thus controlled the left and bottom sides of the square that was walled Colchester. The river protected the town to the north and east, but a series of parliamentary forts thrown up beyond the water inhibited access by bridge and ford. By the beginning of July 'the whole town was entirely shut in' except for the opening to the east across the river at the Hythe. A formidable line of earthworks extended around three sides and linked sconces that served as artillery platforms; these were backed by major forts. It was a massive and expensive effort, involving civilian as well as military labour as men dug their way around Colchester and were paid by the rod (usually at about 6s. per rod dug). One set of accounts largely devoted to costs of 'the works' totalled £1,695. The enterprise is a reminder of how much deeper the parliamentary pocket was in money and men than the royalist, despite the multiple claims imposed by this second war. The result was probably the most sophisticated set of siege lines of either civil war, planned on the best modern principles. Even Capel granted that the enterprise was 'not unsouldyerly'.[42] By mid-July the only remaining approach—from the east by

blockade are now normally seen as coterminous but in the 17th cent., although siege often involved blockade it did not necessarily do so; hence the number of loosely invested strongholds and the leisurely interludes in many sieges, whether minor ones like Boarstall or major like Chester.

[41] Carter, *Most True And exact Relation*, 139.

[42] *True and Exact Relation*, 5; 'Some Civil War Accounts, 1647–1650', ed. Ethel Kitson and E. K. Clark, in Publications of the Thoresby Society, 11(1902), 203–35 (the 'Accounts of the works before Colchester, June 18, 1648, to Aug. 27, 1648' also included payments for maimed soldiers, coals, horses, cleaning, etc.); *Clarke Papers*, ed. Firth, 2. 29.

way of the port at the Hythe and the East Bridge—was threatened, for on 1 July Colonel Whalley had captured the church facing the bridge, fortified the position, and set up a battery.

Meanwhile much was the usual stuff of sieges. There were quiet days: 'Nothing of importance' ran one diary entry, and another recorded, 'Nothing of importance happened, but three of Captain *Canons* men killed with a Canon Bullet', probably the same lucky shot from the 'great Guns' in St Mary's churchyard that 'killed three Horsemen'. Artillery took its toll of the unimportant of both sides. This was indeed a siege in which artillery played a major, if hardly decisive, part. The royalists appear to have been outgunned but their artillery was skilfully managed, particularly from its commanding position in St Mary's.[43] There were also royalist sallies out the town that sometimes turned into costly skirmishes. Fairfax meanwhile sent a force to Mersea Island at the mouth of the Colne to prevent the ships that had revolted from parliament's fleet from coming up the river to relieve the town. The pattern of destruction that marked the siege began with the initial assault when royalists pulled down houses on the walls and parliamentarians tried to burn others huddled beneath them; arson, as we shall see, was to be a bipartisan tactic that prompted both recrimination and defensiveness. News and messages continued to move, clandestinely and with some difficulty, in and out of the town, like the intelligence of Holland's expedition brought in by a man 'comming from the Bell in *Gratious*-street, [who] stole into the Town', or the message from Capel reputedly thrown over the town wall concealed in a hollow bone. More formal communication followed the conventions of war, from the messengers who carried letters between principals to the 'Trumpeter [who] went in with the Lady *Campions* Servant, with a Letter to her Husband, for she did not beleeve that he was slaine'.[44]

The royalist response to Fairfax's relentless investiture of the town was remarkably passive, as some acknowledged. Norwich was constrained by weaknesses of men and matériel and by his determination to use what he had to buy time for the king's cause elsewhere. '[A] disaster here', Capel observed, 'would let [Fairfax] loose'; hence 'we hazard not more than needs must stand with our duty and honour'.[45] Nevertheless Norwich managed to strengthen the lines at strategic places such as the east and north bridges, to bring in cannon from ships lying in the Colne, to raise volunteers and to arm and discipline his raw men. At the same time, ever optimistic, the royalists believed that 4,000 Suffolk men were ready to march at an hour's notice to their relief, and when they did

---

[43] *Diary of the Siege of Colchester*, 16 and 25 June; HMC, *Fourteenth Report*, 'Round MSS', 285; HMC, *Twelfth Report*, 'Beaufort MSS', 29; *A great and bloudy Fight at Colchester* (1648), 2–3.

[44] *Diary of the Siege of Colchester, passim*; HMC, *Fourteenth Report*, 'Round MSS', 284–5; HMC, *Twelfth Report*, 'Beaufort MSS', 24–5; *An exact Narrative of Every dayes Proceedings Since the Insurrection in Essex . . . till the 18 of June* (1648), 5; Gould, 'Siege of Colchester', 377: the story of the letter in the bone appears to be based on its size (7″ × 2″) and local myth.

[45] Worcester College, Clarke MSS, 114, fo. 52 (10 July).

not come attributed it to the machinations of presbyterians mistakenly trusted by the prince of Wales. Their hopes flared again at the beginning of July with news of Holland's 'hopefull engagement' but these were snuffed out within days, 'like an erring light [that] misleade some well affected gentlemen and then vanish'd'.[46]

'He that will picture War, must first begin with the belly', said a popular maxim.[47] The most important royalist achievement of these early stages was to augment their supplies of food and arms, a doubtful benefit for the townspeople perhaps, for without these efforts the siege could never have lasted eleven weeks. The town itself yielded match and seventy barrels of powder in the magazine and a thousand arms in private houses. Outside the town the strong royalist horse, once they broke through parliamentary lines, could scour relatively wide areas for provisions. Within days of the beginning of the siege large parties of horse were dispatched towards Harwich and the sea and returned with 'a very great quantity of provisions, and abundance of sheep and Black-cattle'. Closer to home, at the Hythe, the royalists found supplies of rye, salt, and wine. A sally across the East Bridge brought in fifty-six bullocks and some cows. Another expedition towards the Isle of Mersea garnered cattle and five waggonloads of corn. Earlier, before access by sea to Mersea was closed off, two ships had brought in corn, provisions, and men from Kent. They were unloaded overnight and most of the corn sent in hoys up the river to the Hythe, just ahead of parliamentary ships from Harwich that seized the two frigates and their twenty-one guns, and henceforth blocked access from the sea. Royalists claimed that Fairfax's greatest mistake, indeed 'an unpardonable error', was not to close off access to the Hythe at the beginning of the siege, for without it they 'could not have subsisted five days'. The 'error' was probably related to Fairfax's straitened supply of men in those early days, while the royalist quest for supplies was conducted with unusual effectiveness, for which much of the credit went to Lord Loughborough. Through control of the Hythe, forays into the country, and a few old soldiers' tricks, the royalists 'fedd seven thousand mouthes, souldiers, and inhabitants for eleven weekes'.[48]

---

[46] Bodl. MSS Clarendon, 31, fo. 127; HMC, *Twelfth Report*, 'Beaufort MSS', 26–7.

[47] Carter, *Most True And exact Relation*, 140.

[48] HMC, *Fourteenth Report*, 'Round MSS', 284–5; HMC, *Twelfth Report*, 'Beaufort MSS', 28; *Diary of the Siege of Colchester*, 17–18 June. According to *The Colchester Spie*, a resolutely upbeat royalist newsletter, Fairfax sent a hundred head of cattle under the town walls as bait, intending to ambush and cut to pieces the hungry besieged who came out to retrieve them. But '*it is not easie to catch old birds with chaffe*, or to surprize old Souldiers with weak stratagems'. So that wily veteran Lucas turned the tables: inside the gate 'he caused a Bull to be fastned to a stake with cords, pepper in his nostrills, and a hot iron stuck in his flesh, who no sooner fell a roaring, but the whole heard [*sic*] of cattell under the walls came running in a main'. Ibid., no.2, A2ᵛ. Other versions of the story make the purpose less practical. In one the bull was encased in lead covered with flax, tar, and pitch, set on fire, and sent out 'to make a Sport of War yet so as to terrify the Rebells', in which he gratifyingly succeeded while also serving as a cover for a sally that netted prisoners and booty. *Mercurius Anglicus. Numb. 1. Communicating Intelligence from all parts of the Kingdome* (27 July–3

From the outset royalist leaders recognized the danger of a long siege and the end of the time of plenty, when hungry troops would abandon discipline.[49] Their attempt to regain control over the East Bridge and thus restore access for supplies failed, and on 14 July Fairfax moved decisively to close the ring.[50] To the east one party took the Hythe and the suburbs between it and the town walls. To the south another forced the royalists from their suburban stronghold in the Lucas family house, which lay between Fairfax's lines and the walls and commanded the southern approaches and suburbs. Its defenders were driven into the gatehouse of St John's abbey, and the next day Fairfax decided to storm it. The incentive rates for grenadiers (3s. apiece) and ladder carriers (half a crown each) were a tribute to its strength, but the money proved well spent. A lucky hand grenade fell among four barrels of powder in the magazine, blew up the gatehouse, and buried most of the defenders. The parliamentarians spent the rest of the evening 'digginge and pullinge the dead bodyes of the enemy: findinge here and there a legg and an arme by itself'. They estimated that of 140 royalist defenders only some 60 survived, although the royalists admitted to only four or five killed and claimed—more plausibly—that it was an expensive success for the enemy, who lost many experienced soldiers under the gatehouse walls.[51] Carnage aside, Norwich and his men were henceforth 'cooped up in the high Town' inside the walls, and Colchester was closely blockaded on all sides.[52]

The siege had entered its infamous long last stage. The actions of 14 and 15 July were accompanied by the most notorious of the fires that destroyed the suburbs. Hunger soon afflicted soldiers and civilians alike, but horses suffered before humans. Cut off from forage, and without a supply of hay and oats, they ate thatch and the boughs of trees, while their masters made risky expeditions outside the walls to collect grass.[53] They became a liability (or so it seemed at first) for they now had little military use except as a means to escape. So on 15 July the horse, led by Lucas and Lisle, attempted to force their way out towards Suffolk, with the intention of preserving cavalry for the king's service elsewhere; another incentive, it was suggested, was the precarious position of these officers if the town yielded, in view of accusations of breach of parole. The effort in any case came to nothing; deserted both by their local guides and the pioneers who were to dig a way open for them, they were driven back. More attempts, equally

Aug. 1648), [A3ᵛ]; *Mercurius Melancholicus. Or News from Westminster, and the Head Quarters* (n.pl., 1648), 8.

⁴⁹ On 10 July Capel wrote: 'it is to be doubted when we are driven to strait[en] the provisions our men will not be kept well satisfied'. Worcester College, Clarke MSS, 114, fo. 52.

⁵⁰ HMC, *Fourteenth Report*, 'Round MSS', 286, and see HMC, *Twelfth Report*, 'Beaufort MSS', 27; *Diary of the Siege of Colchester*, 5 July, for variant estimates of casualties and prisoners.

⁵¹ Ibid., 14 and 15 July; HMC, *Fourteenth Report*, 'Round MSS', 287; HMC, *Thirteenth Report. Portland MSS*, 1. 483; Rushworth, 7. 1192; Carter, *Most True And exact Relation*, 163–4.

⁵² *Colchesters Teares*, 13.   ⁵³ Carter, *Most True And exact Relation*, 159–60 (bis).

unsuccessful, followed but were finally abandoned as the foot, suspecting that they were being forsaken, grew mutinous.

Unity inside the walls of Colchester was already cracking, but the senior officers remained stalwart in defiance. As news of other royalist reverses seeped in and hunger bit more sharply the strain grew greater. Desertion became routine. On 10 July a parliamentarian reporter noted that 'Severall of the Enemy came away to us', but within weeks the tide swelled and a royalist lamented that 'the Souldiers deserted every Day in great numbers'. They continued to 'r[u]n from the Enemy' to Fairfax's lines until the end of the siege. While 'the numbers [of the parliamentarians] were continually supplied, . . . the Besieged diminish'd'.[54] Unfortunately Norwich was unable to diminish the number of the useless besieged, the women and children who consumed too much of his vanishing supply of food and added yet another strand of disruption and disunity inside the walls, for by now many of those who had welcomed, or at least accepted, his arrival had grown 'very uneasy'. Even the town's chief minister, who had reviled parliament's army as heretics and schismatics, and townsmen who had once abused its soldiers, now longed for deliverance by those they once despised. Yet all this while, as hunger, sickness, and destruction brought memories of Europe's great sieges to home ground (Colchester was likened to Ravenna and Breda), the conventions of war survived even if exchanges were edgy and provocative, unlike the 'civil' and 'courteous' manners so painfully preserved at Boarstall.[55] Trumpets carried messages of summons and defiance between commanders, proposals for prisoner exchanges were discussed, and each side assessed the conduct of the other in terms of what was 'souldierlike' and honourable.

We shall return to these exchanges and to the nature of Colchester's sufferings. For the present we can pass briefly over the last stages of the siege. Fairfax, who had now moved his headquarters to the Hythe, knew what the end must be and was prepared to wait, while the royalists, neglected by those in whose cause they suffered and by their fellows in the field, were too short of ammunition—and probably energy and manpower, given the inroads of hunger, disease, and desertion—to indulge in any very active defence.[56] Yet if this last phase was partly marked by return to inaction, by days on which 'nothing of concernment hapned', it was also to become notorious for hunger and the shifts to which it drove the inhabitants, for burning, for sickness, and for ruthless subordination of civilian to military needs by the commanders of both sides. The picture of Colchester in the extract at the beginning of this section is drawn from these

[54] *Diary of the Siege of Colchester, passim*; HMC, *Fourteenth Report*, 'Round MSS', 287–8; Thomas Cromwell, *History and Description of the Ancient Town and Borough of Colchester, in Essex*, 2 vols. (1825), 1. 134.

[55] HMC, *Fourteenth Report*, 'Round MSS', 287. *True and Exact Relation*, 4. 'Never was there towne, that hath held out so gallantly as this, no, not Breda, or Ravenna', wrote the *Colchester Spie*, no. 1, in Aug.

[56] HMC, *Twelfth Report*, 'Beaufort MSS', 29.

last weeks and their aftermath. Meanwhile news from other fronts heartened the parliamentarians and vengeance was gratifyingly wreaked on turncoats. In July the earl of Essex's admired Dutch quartermaster general of the first civil war, who had now become 'Colonel *Dalbeer*, the Runnegadoe', was 'hewed in pieces' by 'Parliament's souldiers, to express their detestation of [his] treachery'; and in August John Lilburne's brother Henry, who had 'trecherously betrayed' Tynemouth castle met his reward when it was retaken and 'his own souldiers (most justly) cut off his head'.[57] Through it all, efforts to obtain the release of the captive Essex committeemen, and especially of Sir William Masham, continued. Fairfax still summoned the garrison to surrender, and the terms were delivered to the high command by the traditional etiquette of trumpeter-messengers, but he also spread the news of generous terms and parliamentary victories to the rank and file inside the walls by means of 'Arrowes, (with papers of advertisement)' and paper kites.[58]

The end came slowly nonetheless. Norwich continued defiantly to reject all approaches, in part, it was said, because he expected a treaty between the king and parliament in which the Colchester garrison would be included. When at last hunger and military and civilian unrest made his position untenable, he still asked for a delay of twenty days in which to send to the king's forces; then, if no relief came, he would treat. We recall Campion's scrupulosity in seeking honourable grounds for surrender, and also his attempts to use delaying tactics. As at Boarstall Fairfax denied the request, observing that he 'hoped in much lesse time than twenty dayes, to have the Town without Treaty'. Then came news of Cromwell's 'routing the *Scotch* army' at Preston on 17 August, news that was promptly sent in to Colchester: a kite hovered over the town for long enough to attract attention, then dropped its cargo of bad news. Its psychological effect was enhanced by the celebratory volleys that shortly followed in the parliamentary camp. Capel, Lucas, Lisle, Gascoigne, and other leading officers, finding Fairfax's terms 'incompatible with [their] honour', resolved to try to cut their way out at the head of 800 chosen men. The resolution was never put into practice, but the unchosen knew of the intention to desert them; it was the final blow to discipline and unity. Stories of approaching relief and of parliamentary disasters elsewhere, promises of new clothes and even that soldiers 'should all be gentlemen', had no effect; only when Norwich disbursed money were they 'pacified', but the remission was temporary. By now Norwich had only twenty-six pieces of ordnance, and many of the soldiers' weapons were broken. Faced internally by mutinous troops, unruly townspeople and starvation, and externally by a defeated cause and no hope of succour, Norwich negotiated a

[57] *Diary of the Siege of Colchester*, 11 July, 17 July–16 Aug, *passim*; Ludlow, *Memoirs*, 1. 198; Gardiner, *Civil War*, 4. 179–80. For royalist attempts to put an optimistic spin on events—notably Lambert's reverses—see *Mercurius Melancholicus*, 5–6.
[58] *Diary of the Siege of Colchester*, 25 July, 20, 22 Aug.; *True and Exact Relation*, 1–2.

surrender. Hopeless as his situation was, the process was not without haggling, which achieved little beyond clarification of Fairfax's definition of the vital terms 'mercy' and 'quarter', a definition that was to prove fatal to some of the defeated. Ten days passed between the first request for a treaty of surrender and the signing of the articles at 9 a.m. on 28 August. The next day, for once, was fair, but then the rain returned. The weather foretold more tears for Colchester, for its troubles and those of the surrendering royalists were not over.[59]

[59] *Diary of the Siege of Colchester, passim; True and Exact Relation,* 2; Ludlow, *Memoirs,* 1. 205; Carter, *Most True And exact Relation,* 184–5; Worcester College, Clarke MSS, 114, fos. 60ᵛ, 73ᵛ; ERO, D/DQ s18, fo. 51ᵛ.

16

Colchesters Teares: Fire, Hunger, and Atrocity

The siege of Colchester was uncommonly harsh in the suffering it brought to soldiers and civilians, and no other siege evoked such acute need to justify actions taken or ended with comparable mutual recrimination. Much in the military management and the treatment accorded civilians at Colchester was nonetheless the ordinary stuff of sieges, but much was also exceptional and was seen to be so by contemporaries. Some claimed not only that European levels of starvation and destruction had been introduced into England, but that the codes of war had been abandoned. Each side accused the other of being the instigator of civilian suffering and at the same time legalistically justified its draconian interpretation of the laws of war.

FIRE

Like any besieged town, Colchester suffered destruction from multiple causes. Artillery damaged houses and churches and soldiers were notorious vandals, but what set Colchester apart in popular imagination was fire. 'Flames and desolation' and unbridled 'burn[ing] and ruin [of] houses and persons' that brought to mind 'a Limbeck set up in sad Colchester' not only assimilated an English siege to European experience but prompted the question from supporters of both parties, '[W]hat good can be in these cruelties or desolations?'[1] Most of the burning at Colchester occurred in the suburbs and had a tactical purpose. Each side attempted to present its own recourse to fire as being within 'correct' and justifiable limits, and each accused the enemy of burning merely for reprisal or malice or to excess, and thus of actions for which there was no acceptable excuse. In the public imagination, moreover, Colchester evoked a visceral reaction to wilful infliction of a harm that all town-dwellers feared and many were all too familiar with, for fire was a constant urban danger. It was the dramatic scenes of burning and destruction conjured up by virtually all reporters, with their echoes

---

[1] *Colchesters Teares*, 17–18; and see Porter, *Destruction in the English Civil Wars*, 68, 120, and *passim*.

of the Europe of the Thirty Years' War, that focused contemporary attention, rather than legalistic squabbles over the justifiability of the actions.

The first accusation of intentional military arson arose from parliament's initial assault on 13 June and was directed against Fairfax. Houses in the suburbs 'blinded' the approach to the town gate so that parliamentary cannon brought up to batter it were forced to move in dangerously close, thus enabling royalist musketeers to pick off carriage horses and soldiers and to force abandonment of the guns. Fairfax, according to the royalists, was 'highly enraged', and ordered that houses adjoining the walls be burnt. Only 'greate industry' and God's providence—in the form of wet weather—saved the town itself.[2] A lull followed, but on 29 June the royalists burnt Sir Harbottle Grimston's house in the south-west suburbs. It had been used by the royalists to fire on a parliamentarian fort under construction nearby until Fairfax turned his artillery on the house, forcing the royalists to abandon it, and they fired it as they went. It could be argued that the case fell into the 'legitimate' category of removing bases for enemy action, as did destruction to clear a field of fire or to aid observation and prevent surprise, but parliamentarians saw it as an act of 'rage' and retaliation. If Grimston's house was arguably a site of military value and had in any case been partly destroyed by his friends before his enemies finished the job, no such case could be made for a second great house south of the town that burnt that day: 'at night [the royalists] fired Mr. *Barringtons* house, out of meer malice, (it being of no advantage to either side)'.[3] Although there was nothing new in the actions at Colchester or the reasons for them—in the siege of Chester, for example, the suburb of Handbridge was repeatedly destroyed—there was nevertheless a clear sense of outrage at conduct that was felt to be excessive or gratuitous: to burn the whole town, the intention imputed to Fairfax, or to act out of 'meer malice', both exceeded the bounds of the militarily excusable.

The events that followed on 15 July merited censure on both grounds. They set a pattern for the rest of the siege, although no future fire equalled them in scale, and they seized popular imagination. They came after the royalists in their turn were 'enraged' by the fall of the gatehouse and their failed attempt to break out of the town, or so parliamentarians claimed. Royalist accounts denied malice or revenge. Both agreed however that the royalists had fired the suburbs 'in six or seven places, which burnt in a most dreadful manner all night long, [so] that the Town might be seen almost as well by night as by day, so great was the flame'.[4]

---

[2] HMC, *Twelfth Report*, 'Beaufort MSS', 24–5. John Clopton reported from Suffolk on 13 June, 'It rained often this day'. ERO, D/DQ s18, fo. 41.

[3] *Diary of the Siege of Colchester*, 29 June; Cromwell, *History and Description of . . . Colchester*, 1. 119; Grimston's house 'was never fit for a gentleman's mansion subsequently to the Siege', and in the 18th cent. became the town's workhouse. Ibid. 1. 188.

[4] HMC, *Thirteenth Report. Portland MSS*, 1. 483; *Diary of the Siege of Colchester*, 15 July; *Mercurius Pragmaticus*, 17 (18–25 July 1648), [R3ᵛ]; *A great and bloudy Fight at Colchester*, 3, reported that Lucas 'fired all the Suburbs' by means of granadoes shot from the town.

An eye-witness insisted on the nightmarish, almost apocalyptic, quality of the scene:

[P]resently began that fearful sight and woeful spectacles of firing all round the walls, the streets on both sides being by my Lord Gorings party set on fire, and from the time of taking the Gate-house all that night for about a mile in length continued burning and flaming, that some of us being a little distance had light almost to read a letter so far, and a terrible red duskye bloody cloud seamed to hang over the Town all night, and so furious was the fire by reason such stately and goodly buildings were burnt thereby, that many times the flashes mounted aloft far above house, church, or any buildings, and continued with such horror, cracklings heard a mile or two from the town, and with such lamentable outcries of men women and children, that to moderate men standing by . . . it was more than merciless crueltie to act.[5]

As cool an observer as John Rushworth reported to parliament 'the saddest spectacle to bee seene that hath fallen out in this age, there beeing now burneing in a grate plaine houses above a mile in length, and with that violence as it is a wonder to behold it'. So 'desperately' were the royalists bent that it was believed that they might burn the town itself as well as the suburbs.[6] Hundreds of houses burned and whole streets were reduced to ashes. The ensuing personal losses were vividly represented as rich and poor, equal in disaster, 'toyl[ed] and sweat[ed] in carrying some mean bed or other away, or some inconsiderable household stuffs out of the burning'.[7] Indeed, one of the unsettling qualities of fire, in an age before insurance, was that it was a social leveller: material goods and the wealth they embodied, once lost to fire, were gone for good and men, women and children were 'turned . . . a begging to the wide world'.[8]

Royalist response to the fire was righteous but uncomfortable. They first attributed a second, lesser round of fires the next day to the parliamentarians, urging the townspeople 'to come out of their houses to see what barbarous acts they did'.[9] Next they claimed that, fearing a surprise attack, they had been forced to fire houses in the suburbs to prevent the enemy from coming within pistol shot of the walls, and that 'any considering souldier' would accuse them of excessive moderation for their 'respect' for inhabitants had endangered their own safety. Another apologist went further. Not only did he point out that Norwich's decision to fire the suburbs was reached with the advice of his council of war, thus asserting adherence to professional practice, but the royalist leaders were so principled that they promised compensation: recognizing that fire was likely to 'deject' the townsmen, Norwich, Capel, Loughborough, and Lucas bound themselves by indenture 'to make all good again'. As evidence of good faith, the *Colchester Spie* printed verbatim the instrument by which they and their heirs

---

[5] *Mercurius Elencticus*, 34 (12–19 July 1648), 268; *Colchesters Teares*, 13–14.
[6] HMC, *Thirteenth Report. Portland MSS*, 1. 483.
[7] *Colchesters Teares*, 16; Rushworth, 7. 1193.　　　　[8] *Colchesters Teares*, 14.
[9] *Diary of the Seige of Colchester*, 15 July.

were bound to pay the town's magistrates £ 1,000 a year for six years and to 'make good with [their] estates' the damages caused by 'this necessitated fire'.[10] Their public relations venture was never put to the test, but it revealed the felt need to justify and mitigate resort to fire, and fire's power to alienate 'dejected' townsmen.

Lesser fires spotted the last month of the siege. On 11 August, for example, parliament's diarist observed, 'Nothing of note. The enemy that night burnt 30 houses.'[11] Yet if fires had become unremarkable, cumulatively they fostered a discourse that explicitly recalled the horrors of Germany. Royalists, for example, were accused of extracting 'burning money', *Brandschatzung*, from residents of the suburbs: 'they have entered covenant with severall in *East Street* not to fire, and taken money some say £14 some £15 and some £40 into their hands and then presently have fired the same houses themselves and lay the fault upon the round heads'.[12] Not only were they held to be morally guilty of breach of promise as well as cruel destruction, but the whole moral question of whether, even for his own defence, 'a man may burn at all' was raised. To burn in self-defence, it could be argued, did not merit 'the evill of punishment', but to burn 'needlessly' and without serious consideration was 'the eville of sinne'.[13] We can catch a hint of the dismay and revulsion aroused by this sense of burning as a routine weapon of war now imported into England in royalist satisfaction at the fate of parliamentarians who tried to burn a cornmill on the Colne. They approached by water and were cut down by Norwich's 'scythe Souldiers'—his 'shavers', as he jovially called them. The *Colchester Spie* called up memories of a Websterian world when it reported with satisfaction that 'the Fishermen caught nothing, but an everlasting cold being drowned in the attempt'.[14]

The total number of houses burnt or destroyed by other means must remain uncertain. A list drawn from six of the town's twelve parishes gives a total of 186 houses destroyed, of which 136 were burnt and ruined, 45 merely burnt, and 5 pulled down. Most of these parishes were close to the walls—both inside and outside them—and therefore particularly vulnerable. It seems safely conservative to suggest that, in all twelve parishes, somewhere over 300 houses were destroyed, overwhelmingly by fire, but such an estimate takes no account of damage, which was often extensive.[15] Yet the figure seems anticlimactic after the

[10] HMC, *Twelfth Report*, 'Beaufort MSS', 29; *Colchester Spie*, no. 1, [A2(2)ᵛ]; *Mercurius Pragmaticus*, 17 (18–25 July), [R 3ᵛ].

[11] *Diary of the Siege of Colchester*, 11 Aug.   [12] *Colchesters Teares*, 14–15.

[13] Ibid. 14, 18.

[14] Cf. John Webster, *The White Devil*, 5. 6: 'I have caught / An everlasting cold; I have lost my voice / Most irrecoverably'; *Colchester Spie*, no. 1, [A2(2)ᵛ]. The 'scythe Souldiers', former cavalrymen whose horses had been killed for food, owed their makeshift weapons to royalist shortage of conventional arms. Their straightened scythes, fastened to handles, were about 6 feet long and, although unwieldy and as great a threat to friends as to the enemy, were much feared by parliamentarian troops. HMC, *Twelfth Report*, 'Beaufort MSS', 28.

[15] Philip Morant, *The History and Antiquities Of the County of Essex*, 2 vols. (Colchester, 1768), 1. 68; Cromwell, *History of . . . Colchester*, 1. 160; Porter, *Destruction in the English Civil Wars*, 68,

rhetoric, even allowing for the long economic shadow cast by such destruction. Contemporaries, however, believed that 'many hundred Houses' burned in the first great July fire, to be followed by yet more the next night, by thirty more on 11 August, and by unnumbered others in the initial assault and on other scattered occasions. This cruel burning, said one observer, rendered the royalists, and Norwich in particular, 'very odious' to many who were previously their friends. More than 600 families were 'undone and disinhabited' in the suburbs, claimed another, besides 'many thousands . . . dis-inabled' there and in the surrounding country.[16] For the present, it is these contemporary perceptions that matter. For the town's inhabitants, for both armies, and for spectators all over England, Colchester's flames offered light by which to see war's 'grizly face of woful desolation'.[17]

HUNGER

Fire and sword were not the only aspects of woeful desolation at Colchester. Hunger and disease also took their toll, and were not unrelated. Colchester's hunger, as recounted in virtually all narratives of the siege, became a dramatically familiar part of its sufferings. Hunger became an instrument of policy, and its consequences in relations between commanders and in the plight of civilians caught between the claims of military need and humane obligation tell us much about interpretation of the codes of war and the limitations on civilians' control over their own lives.

The royalists had started the siege with serviceable supplies for themselves and the town's inhabitants and, thanks to Loughborough's efforts, supplemented them by judicious raids in the countryside. As the noose around the town tightened these local sources became inaccessible. In any case the demands of two armies, compounded by bad weather, were rapidly exhausting them, and the 'faire-promising, chearefully flourishing Corne-fields' of East Anglia now promised little replenishment in this summer of almost unprecedented rain. The parliamentarians themselves complained of scarcity of local supplies; before the end of June one of their colonels wrote, 'Our country begins to be so exhausted of provisions that it may well be doubted that the poor will be compelled to rise for want of bread.'[18] By the middle of July some royalists at least were admitting the urgent need for food and ammunition, but they cheered themselves with

---

takes the figure of 168 destroyed by all means in six parishes as representing the total of all houses destroyed by fire in the whole town.

[16] Rushworth, 7. 1193; *Diary of the Siege of Colchester*, 11 Aug.; BL Harl. MS 7001, fo. 186ᵛ; *Colchesters Teares*, 15.

[17] Ibid. 14.

[18] Gatford, *Englands Complaint*, 52; HMC, *Thirteenth Report. Portland MSS*, 1. 467.

hopes of a relieving expedition by the prince of Wales who surely would 'hazard much, rather than Colchester suffer'. Such illusory hopes kept up some royalist spirits almost to the end.[19] Meanwhile Fairfax's army had London and the rest of the country to draw on for supplies of all kinds. Norwich had to make do with what he had.

Early in July royalist reports still claimed that the town's situation was comfortable and cited low prices as evidence of plenty. Others, however, reported that butter was already selling for 5 shillings a pound and cheese for nearly as much, while townsmen grew short of bread as parliamentary soldiers destroyed cornmills and royalist soldiers seized meal from the remaining mills and bread from the bakers. Within weeks there was a dramatic change for the worse as the once 'infinite store of Wheat, Rie, Barley, Peas, and . . . all sorts of graine' dwindled. Meanwhile fodder for the horses grew short, and by 21 July news was spreading that Colchester 'was straitened much for provision, feeding on horse-flesh'.[20] Some royalists claimed that the earlier failure of the horse to break out was providential, ensuring future food; others that the soldiers, 'like prudent warriors', merely ate horse-flesh once a week to accustom themselves in case of future need, while yet others lauded the tasty dishes that horse-flesh provided. Some continued to assert royalist plenty. In mid-August one reporter claimed that the defenders had 'fish [especially sturgeon] raisins, wine, & strong bear rie and barly more then enough', and he ridiculed the story that the dwindling cheese supply must be preserved to catch 'the poor *well-affected Animals* called *Rats* and *Mice*'. In bombastic verse the *Colchester Spie* declared, 'Yet Colchester bears bravely up, / They eat and drink apace', but the reality was different.[21]

The picturesque characteristics of Colchester's hunger are well-known, as the defenders denuded the town of horses, cats, and dogs. Reluctance to eat horse meat was overcome by necessity and helped by festivity: the authorities had a horse 'roasted . . . neer the North bridge to make the souldiers merry at the entrance into such Diet', but reservations remained. Troopers did not want their horses killed, for economic as well as sentimental reasons, but animals were culled

[19] Ibid. 469; Magdelene College, Pepys MSS 2504, fos. 203–4; *Mercurius Melancholicus*, 5–6. For persistent royalist optimism, at least for public consumption, see *Mercurius Elencticus*, 32 (28 June–5 July 1648), 252; 40 (23–9 Aug. 1648), 327, 333–4; *Mercurius Pragmaticus*, 15 (4–11 July 1648), [P4]; 21 (15–22 Aug. 1648), Bb; *Mercurius Aulicus*, 3 ([21 Aug. 1648?]), 23.

[20] *From the Leaguer at Colchester . . . 6 Julii, 1648* (1648), 5; *Two Sallies Forth by the Lord Goring and Sir Charles Lucas*, [2]; Worcester College, Clarke MSS, 114, fos. 44ᵛ, 52; Rushworth, 7. 1181; ERO, D/DQ s18, fo. 46ᵛ; *Colchester Spie*, no. 1, A2; BL Harl. MS 7001, fo. 186ᵛ; *Mercurius Elencticus*, 32, (28 June–5 July 1648), 252. After destruction of the windmills, millstones found at the Hythe were brought into the town and set up as horse-mills. Morant, *Essex*, 1 61.

[21] HMC, *Twelfth Report*, 'Beaufort MSS', 28; *Colchester Spie*, no. 2, [A1], A2ᵛ; *Mercurius Aulicus*, 3 ([c.20 Aug. 1648]), 23; *Mercurius Elencticus*, 35. (19–26 July 1648), 276; *Mercurius Pragmaticus*, 21 (15–22 Aug. 1648), Bb; see also *Mercurius Anglicus*, 1 (27 July–3 Aug. 1648), [A3ᵛ]: 'the Towne is in very good condition, and abounds with plenty of all sorts of provisions (the truth whereof) let no man doubt'.

from each troop until few were left of the 700 odd mustered at the castle on 19 July. Some were eaten fresh, some salted or 'powdered'. The problems of slaughter and disposal in the confined spaces of a besieged town in themselves appal and suggest public health hazards; according to royalist estimates over 800 horses were killed in the last month of the siege. One butcher gained anonymous fame because he could not bring himself to do it, while the flow of deserters increased as they ran away to the parliamentarians 'much complaining of their Diet in horse-flesh'.[22] Even officers' stabled horses were not safe, although their fate was less official, for as the royalist quartermaster general complained, '[E]very morning one Stable or other was rob'd, and our Horses knock'd o' th' head, and sold in the Shambles by the pound.' Most horses, he concluded, changed the stable for the slaughterhouse.[23] Colchester was not the first siege in which the hungry were driven to horsemeat, but the scale on which it happened there and the desperate condition it revealed combined with the siege's length and bitterness to catch and shock public imagination.[24]

The deficiencies of siege diet arose from more than disrelish of horse-flesh. To supplement their diet agile soldiers trapped cats and dogs, until by the end of the siege there was 'not so much as a *Dog* or *Cat* left' in Colchester. They rifled civilians' houses for hoarded supplies, but the plight of most civilians was worse than their own while that of the poor, unable to afford the inflated prices of what little food was available, was worst of all. The 300 quarters of corn released from the general store to feed the poor at the urging of Sir Charles Lucas, who 'commiserat[ed] with them as his own Towns-born people', was soon depleted. Well before the height of the crisis their daily bread allowance was reduced to a coarse threepenny loaf per family. Meanwhile 'Souldiers deserted every Day in great numbers not being able to bear the want of food, as being almost starved with Hunger', while their fellows who stayed behind had their daily ration reduced to a 20 ounce loaf of bread each, eked out by twenty leaves of tobacco between forty-seven men, and whatever horseflesh they could steal. Two or three days a week they missed the tobacco, which helped to deaden the pangs of hunger, and ultimately the daily ration fell to 7 ounces of 'unwholesome', unpalatable bread, and they were so 'wasted with *Hunger*, that their *Backs* and *Bellies* met'. They were still better off than the poor, 'reduced to that extremity that they eate soape and candle'. The most fortunate were the imprisoned members of the Essex committee, for although Norwich declared that, since the king's servants had been reduced to eating horseflesh, 'the Prisoners should feed as they fed',

---

[22] *Diary of the Siege of Colchester* (19–23 July); Carter, *True And exact Relation*, 165–151 (bis, misnumbered), 175–6; BL Harl. MS 7001, fo. 186ᵛ; *Perfect Diurnall*, 261 (24–31 July 1648), 3001: the troopers objected to the killing of their horses, 'altogether unserviceable' though they were, 'not knowing how to get others'.

[23] Carter, *Most True And exact Relation*, 161 (bis), 166.

[24] See e.g. Bodl. MSS Tanner 62/1A, fo. 75: at the siege of Reading in 1643, after only a week of siege, some townsmen were reduced to killing and eating a horse.

he nonetheless allowed them to receive provisions and money sent in by their solicitous friends.[25]

This black picture masks some of the complexities of siege suffering. Even at Colchester, some were less hungry than others. One of the factors that forced Norwich to make his first overture of surrender to Fairfax, in mid-August, was a review of the remaining provisions not only in the army's magazine but also in the hands of private families. If stocks were desperately low and would not last much longer, nonetheless at that stage some still existed. On 21 August Norwich could confine his order for civilians to leave the town to those who lacked twenty days' provisions for themselves and their families; this may have been a notional criterion, however, for a house-to-house search for provisions was said to have left each family with only one peck of corn. He, Capel, and Lucas won praise because in this time of crisis 'they fedd and lodged with their souldiers' on the line, and according to one story Norwich and senior officers dined on 'a boil'd quarter of a Dog and six carrots', but we do not hear that they went hungry.[26] Even reports from deserters that emphasized hardship suggested the uneven distribution of acute hunger, for they revealed the existence of a market for those with money to pay, although the food it yielded—cats, dogs, starch, bran, grains—was hardly nutritious. Hasty puddings were made from a pound of starch costing 4d. mixed with a pennyworth each of sugar and currants; a pound of starch could also be made into a pancake fried with oil and combined with two carrots at a penny and a penny parsnip. Yet when William Osborne entered the town on 28 August, although he noted 'a scarcity of all things', he also reported that he and others 'found a table well spread with varietys, had [their] shares, and gave an alarum of it to others, that were in a hungry condition'.[27] Clearly not everyone was threatened by starvation with the same immediacy, and hungry soldiers who searched and rifled private houses sometimes had good reason to do so. Colchester confirmed the experience of other sieges that the poor who had no reserves and no money suffered most; on this occasion they were probably joined by victims of fire who would once not have expected to find themselves in this company. The better-off, with stores in hand and money to buy more in an inflated market, were able to postpone and then moderate the worst effects of siege. Nevertheless, all caveats allowed, by August conditions in Colchester were dreadful for all: 'both poor and rich [were] now brought almost to the same wofull state'.[28]

[25] *Mercurius Elencticus*, 41 (30 Aug.–6 Sept. 1648), 331; HMC, *Fourteenth Report*, 'Round MSS', 287–9; HMC, *Twelfth Report*, 'Beaufort MSS', 29; *Colchesters Teares*, 15; Carter, *Most True And exact Relation*, 158–9; Worcester College, Clarke MSS, 114, fos. 53ᵛ, 60ᵛ.

[26] HMC, *Twelfth Report*, 'Beaufort MSS', 28–9; Worcester College, Clarke MSS, 114, fo. 61; *Mercurius Pragmaticus*, 21 (15–22 Aug. 1648), Bb.

[27] Worcester College, Clarke MSS, 114, fo. 60ᵛ; Carter, *Most True And exact Relation*, 178; *True and Exact Relation*, 4; BL Harl. MS 7001, fo. 189ᵛ.

[28] *Colchesters Teares*, 16.

Malnutrition must have been almost universal; starch hardly brought strength even if enlivened by currants and carrots. It is not surprising that at the end of the siege 'people [were] scarce able to stand upon their legges'.[29] Most immediately damaging to the defenders' health was the quality of what food and drink they had. By the end of July the parliamentarians had cut off all water pipes, not only gaining a handy store of lead for bullets but also reducing those in the town to water that was either muddy 'or annoyed with dead horses'. Royalists claimed it did not matter as they had plenty of sack and strong beer, but by 21 August they had run out of malt for beer or bread.[30] The salt supply ran low and was finally exhausted so the slaughtered horses, already 'lean as carrion', were inadequately preserved and often inedible. Horseflesh, soldiers complained, 'was attended with Gentlewomen in white Gownes and blackhoods [meaning Maggots]' who bred in 'whole regiments'.[31] The bread issue, on the other hand, had too much salt, for it was 'made of maulte oates and rye which had taken salte water' and was so unpleasant that soldiers often prefered to eat their horse and dog meat without it. If the bread was 'unwholesome' the ill-salted horsemeat produced 'wens' and dysentery; soldiers grew 'sickley, and many Died of Fluxes'. In August the *Colchester Spie* proclaimed that the well-fed defenders were in excellent health, and denied that 'evill diet' had brought raging bloody flux to the town, but royalist bravado rang hollow in the face of diet that was unhealthy, 'uncouth', and 'distastefull' and reduced soldiers and townspeople alike to a 'miserable' and 'deplorable' condition.[32]

We do not know how many died of flux and other siege-induced illnesses, nor how army and town coped with nursing and burial, although we are told that surgeons' neglect killed wounded soldiers.[33] Once again the besiegers, with their access to medical supplies and their freedom of movement in the environs and to London, were better able to provide care for their sick and wounded (although their surgeons too were accused of lethal neglect), just as better diet and lesser exposure to effects of insanitary overcrowding acted as preventives against malnutrition and disease of the kind suffered inside the walls. There, it is clear, hunger, disease, and fire-induced homelessness joined with bombardment, the confinement of a close siege, and wet weather, to reduce both military and civilian inhabitants of Colchester to a pitiable condition.

---

[29] *Colchesters Teares*, 16.

[30] *Perfect Diurnall*, 261 (24–31 July 1648), 3001; *Mercurius Anglicus*, 1 (27 July–3 Aug. 1648), [A3ᵛ]; Worcester College, Clarke MSS, 114, fo. 60ᵛ.

[31] HMC, *Fourteenth Report*, 'Round MSS', 289; Worcester College, Clarke MSS, 114, fo. 60ᵛ; *Diary of the Siege of Colchester*, 2 Aug.; BL Harl. MS 7001, fo. 186ᵛ; *Mercurius Pragmaticus*, 20 ([counterfeit?], 8–15 Aug. 1648), Z.

[32] HMC, *Twelfth Report*, 'Beaufort MSS', 29; HMC, *Fourteenth Report*, 'Round MSS', 289; *Colchester Spie*, no. 2, A2ᵛ; *Mercurius Pragmaticus*, 21 (15–22 Aug. 1648), Bb. The 'wens' were probably bacterial infections such as boils, resulting from lowered resistance due to dietary deficiencies.

[33] Carter, *Most True And exact Relation*, 154; Worcester College, Clarke MSS, 114, fos. 61–2.

It was hunger that proved the catalyst for the protests that, together with mutiny, forced Norwich's hand in the inevitable move toward surrender. '[T]heir Bellies sound[ed] alarums to their Mouths', wrote one royalist of the town's vociferous poor.[34] In the ensuing exchanges between commanders pity was often invoked but rarely governed practice. Everyone agreed that women and children merited special protection, but a notorious incident demonstrated that, even when faced by starvation, they remained pawns to the military imperative. Both Fairfax and Norwich tried to use their sad condition as a bargaining counter, Fairfax to obtain exchange of the Essex committeemen, Norwich to secure a twenty-day grace period to delay negotiations, and each side blamed the other's intransigence for the continued suffering of the victims.[35]

As the citizens grew desperate and unruly, the mayor and aldermen, with Norwich's permission, asked Fairfax to allow all civilians to leave the town. Fairfax refused. 'The Rabble' then clamoured for surrender, assembling nightly 'in a vast Crowd' before Norwich's quarters, but the general obdurately denied them. The men were beaten off by soldiers, but the women and children they brought with them 'lay howling and Crying on the ground for Bread [and] . . . would not stir, bidding the Soldiers kill them, saying they had rather be shot than be starved'.[36] The men of the town set the women on, it was said, and some of the soldiers sympathized. As in other sieges, the powerless, if they could not control events, could sometimes influence them or at least compound the difficulties of those in charge. Norwich on this occasion made things worse by his jovially rough and ready tongue for—so it was reported—he told protesters that 'they must eat their children'. The women replied in fury that they would pull his eyes out rather than starve, and the spectre of cannibalism of the innocent once raised did not go away. Another report claimed that a soldier responded to a woman pleading on behalf of herself and her child only with the great cavalier oath, '*God damn me*' and the addendum, 'that child would make a great deal of good meat wellboyld'.[37]

Real 'cruelties', more prosaically, had a conventional military rationale. When, for example, a woman with five children, one at her breast, fell down before the parliamentary guards to beseech passage out of the town for herself and her children, she was turned back on the ground that if she were allowed to pass hundreds more would follow and 'much prejudice the Service'. When Norwich offered surrender out of 'compassion' for the townspeople and to save the 'effusion of Blood' that a storm would entail, he demanded 'Hon[oura]ble Terms' in return; his proposal to send out many of the townspeople to preserve them from suffering had the primary purpose of husbanding his meagre food

---

[34] Carter, *Most True And exact Relation*, 158.
[35] Worcester College, Clarke MSS, 114, fos. 56–56ʳ, 59–59ʳ.
[36] HMC, *Fourteenth Report*, 'Round MSS', 289.
[37] Rushworth, 7. 1233; *Diary of the Siege of Colchester*, 15 Aug.; *Colchesters Teares*, 15.

supplies and also, incidentally, of relieving him of their unruly complaints. Fairfax was equally adamant, and would only allow the townspeople to leave in exchange for release of the imprisoned Essex committee, and even this offer explicitly excluded the wives and children of townsmen who had taken arms with the royalists. Blame for civilian sufferings was once again thrown back into the court of the besieged who refused to surrender: Norwich's refusal of the offered terms strengthened Fairfax's resolve to keep the civilians in, 'to let them take part of the miseries of the town & so to force surrender', and he ordered his troops to be watchful to prevent escapes.[38] Delay, the parliamentarians recognized, increased the pressures on Norwich and was 'now the best part of our Game'. Requests on behalf of 'famished' poor people ran a poor second to 'Policy'.[39] Hunger was an agent of policy, and the fate of its victims, including women and children, was unfortunate but irrelevant.

Norwich's response was to turn 500 women and children out of the town. They marched confidently towards the quarters of Colonel Rainsborough, who tried to warn them off with a harmless cannon shot. They were undeterred. Next he ordered musketeers to fire blanks, but 'that daunt[ed] them not'. Only when he sent soldiers to strip them, and after four had actually been stripped, did the women run. Fairfax had refused to receive them, but Norwich refused to have them back. Their 'condition was most lamentable for they could neither go backwards nor forwards, nor remain where they were but die suddenly'. Fairfax accused Norwich of taking advantage of 'a necessity of their own creating upon the miserable inhabitants' to force a treaty on his own terms, and ultimately Norwich readmitted the women. The only advantage the royalists gained from this attempt to free themselves of useless mouths came from a parliamentary horse killed between the lines, for the next day townspeople braved parliamentary fire to cut pieces off the stinking carcase.[40]

The rhetoric of protection thus coexisted with harsh application of the laws of war. For each side, this incident of relegation of women and children to a no man's land between the lines served as a vehicle of moral blame, of evidence of the inhumanity of the enemy. It shocked because it overtly contravened the atavistic belief, still familiar today, that cruelty to women and children was worse than cruelty to adult men and was a sign of the dehumanization of the perpetrators. The parliamentarians were unwilling to kill, but they felt in no sense obliged to try to save women and children whose interests conflicted with

[38] HMC, *Fourteenth Report*, 'Round MSS', 289; Rushworth, 7. 1232, 1235; Worcester College, Clarke MSS, 114, fos. 59–59ᵛ.

[39] Rushworth, 7. 1234; Carter, *Most True And exact Relation*, 171.

[40] Rushworth, 7. 1236–7; Worcester College, Clarke MSS, 114, fo. 60. According to a royalist account, those sent out were 'the People' generally, not women and children only; it also claimed that when they reached Fairfax's camp the guards were ordered to fire on them. HMC, *Fourteenth Report*, 'Round MSS', 289. Another royalist account claimed that the parliamentarians 'shott many women and children' who attempted 'to passe out of the towne'. HMC, *Twelfth Report*, 'Beaufort MSS', 29.

military needs. Fairfax's confidence that God would assist him to bring the siege to a fortunate conclusion was not impaired. Yet if the prospect of starving women and children suspended in a limbo, rejected by two armies of their countrymen, dismayed Englishmen, it did not constitute an atrocity. Indeed, Fairfax acted strictly within the codes of war, and according to a rule that has had a long life after the seventeenth century. Lieber's 'code for the government of armies of the United States in the field', issued in 1863 as General Orders No. 100 and later the basis of provisions in the Hague and Geneva Conventions, included the following provision: 'When a commander of a besieged place expels the non-combatants, in order to lessen the number of those who consume his stock of provisions, it is lawful, though an extreme measure, to drive them back, so as to hasten on the surrender.'[41]

ATROCIOUS ACTS?

If the treatment of starving women and children was 'lawful, though . . . extreme', other incidents were seen as outside the laws of war. Some were atrocities by any standards, some offended against particular aspects of professional codes, and some seem to have been regarded as unsporting. Occasionally we can discern the mitigating influence of social links and standards that crossed the lines of hostility; at others we are presented with stories of cruelty that remain depressingly familiar in their details, formulaic in their use of broken taboos to arouse revulsion, and crudely propagandist in intention.

The professional offences are the easiest to deal with. Some, more unsporting or unmannerly than atrocious, were nonetheless represented as breaches of conventions mutually observed between enemies. Late in July, for example, a troop of Norwich's 'shavers' sallied out, took some soldiers working on the line, and miserably wounded a county soldier, not one of Fairfax's main army, who was moreover 'but a Spectator'. This seems to have been regarded as unfair.[42] Bad professional manners were also condemned. Norwich's defiant response to Fairfax's initial summons to surrender was 'not becoming a Gentleman'. To a later summons he, Capel, and Lucas jointly replied with a threat to hang any trumpeter who in future came bearing such a message. There was of course a convention of rhetorical bombast in replies to summons to surrender, but Norwich seems to have gone beyond acceptable limits and thereby 'much enraged the Soldiers'. Parliamentarians complained that royalist leaders at Colchester acted with 'scorn and reproach' and manifested a 'wilfull obstinacie, and hautinesse of spirit, that lost them the opportunity to obtain honourable Terms'.[43] The 'bold and

[41] Hartigan, *Lieber's Code and the Law of War*, 1, 49, no. 18.
[42] *Diary of the Siege of Colchester*, 27 July.
[43] Ibid., 13 June, 16 July; Worcester College, Clarke MSS, 114, fo. 50; *True and Exact Relation*, 1; Rushworth, 7. 1155.

scornful' language of the royalists may in part have been a reflection of Norwich's bluff personality, but it also reflected the embitterment of relations between enemies.[44] The contrast with the courtesies of Boarstall is striking.

The use of chewed or poisoned bullets was of more practical concern and a more unequivocal breach of accepted professional practice. The two offences were often lumped together, although their effects differed. On 20 June a prisoner deposed that he had heard Norwich order soldiers to 'chew their bullets & square their slugs & cut notches in them', and on 28 June royalist soldiers taken with allegedly chewed and poisoned bullets declared that they were distributed by Norwich's 'speciall Command'. Fairfax sent the information in to Norwich with a message that his men should expect no quarter if they used such bullets. Norwich denied giving either orders or consent, and royalist leaders claimed that the affadavits came from perjured deserters and that they 'disown'd the Practice'. Rough-cast slugs however must be excused, they added, for they were inevitable given the circumstances of manufacture. We have already noted that home-made bullets produced under pressure lacked fine technical finish and were more likely to have the tumbling, tearing motion that made chewed bullets outlawed weapons.[45]

No such innocent explanation could be given for poisoned bullets, and the parliamentarians seem genuinely to have believed that the royalists sometimes used them. When a Lieutenant-Colonel Shambrooke was wounded the bullet was found to be poisoned, 'boiled in Coprice' (vitriol). He died a day later, and parliamentarians unhesitatingly attributed his death to the poisoned bullet. On 15 July John Rushworth sent news to the House of Commons that the royalists 'still persiste[d] in theire venemous disposicion to shoote such things as may bee sure to ranker and poyson the flesh', and sent evidence to prove it. Stories of the use of poisoned bullets already circulated among the troops, who were in a mood to take their own revenge, and after one action in which between eighty and a hundred royalist prisoners were taken 'most of them [were] miserably wounded; the Soldiers giving them a Payment for their poison'd Bullets'. Of these 'sore cut' prisoners twenty died the next day of wounds inflicted 'meerly for their using poisoned Bullets, who otherwise had received fair Quarter', and Fairfax's soldiers hoped for more revenge at their next engagement.[46] Meanwhile the royalists, not to be outdone, claimed that they had removed 'chawd' bullets from their

[44] Rushworth, 7. 1193.

[45] Worcester College, Clarke MSS, 114, fo. 46ᵛ; *Diary of the Siege of Colchester*, 28 June; HMC, *Fourteenth Report*, 'Round MSS', 288; Morant, *Essex*, 1. 59 (bis).

[46] *Diary of the Siege of Colchester*, 5 July; HMC, *Thirteenth Report. Portland MSS*, 1. 483; Rushworth, 7. 1179, 1181. Rushworth noted with apparent satisfaction that of the royalist dead 'most [were] Gentlemen, their good Apparel and white Skins speak no less'. Alternative explanations—such as surgeons' neglect or severe weather—of the high parliamentary death rate after the engagement of 5 July did not shake the belief of Fairfax's soldiers that the deaths were caused by poisoned bullets. Morant, *Essex*, 1. 60 (bis).

wounded men and from the muskets of prisoners.[47] The issues seem to have subsided, and the episodes were minor in themselves, but the parliamentarian response revealed grass-roots rough justice at work in reprisal for a perceived breach of the rules of war, a reprisal that took the form of a countervailing breach, in this case abuse of the rules of quarter by killing or wounding surrendering soldiers. The events suggest heightened readiness at Colchester to see atrocity and to place blame for it in high places.

The siege also produced standard atrocity propaganda in titillating stories of offences against the classically protected: women, children, the weak, and the dead. Most, more or less circumstantial, must count as not proven, and they recall the taboos invoked by prohibitions found in the earliest articles of war. So the horrors of homelessness and vulnerability to bullets were illustrated by the fate of women with child and newly brought to bed, and royalist barbarity and immorality were confirmed by tales of rape, actual, or attempted. '[M]uch filthinesse might be named of women, attempted sometimes, forced others, shreeking, crying, flying', claimed one pamphleteer. It is remarkable, however, that in all the instances he cited the women appear to have escaped unscathed and indomitable, notably the 'gentlewoman who if she did not yeeld had a pistoll set to her breast, yes, saies shee, I shall cheerfully imbrace your pistoll and my death, but not you'. Nor did commanders escape accusation: Lucas 'insnared' an intended victim for his evil purposes, and only when Norwich intervened to send him about his military business did she escape to flee over the wall and spread her story.[48] Some narratives are suspiciously familiar. *Colchesters Teares* tells us of royalist cruelty to the maidservant who, for defending her mistress, 'had her fingers tyed, light matches put to them and burnt her fingers to the stumps'. The royalist *Colchester Spie* recounted the story of 'the pretty stripling of fourteen years of age', sent out as a messenger and captured and interrogated by parliamentarians who, in the first of a catalogue of 'barbarous and horrid' tortures, 'caused lighted matches to be tied to his fingers, and burnt them almost to the bones'. This form of torture already had a long history in the propaganda literature of the civil war, and while accounts may have been true, particularly as methods and means were simple, homely, and accessible, repetitions of the formula invite some doubt.[49] Other stories were less dramatic and intrinsically more persuasive but, relatively, anti-climactic: frail Mr Hughes, for example was terrorized and plundered by royalist marauders from Colchester, but he refused

---

[47] Henry Ellis, *Original Letters Illustrative of English History*, 1st ser., 3 vols. (London, 1825), 305.

[48] *Colchesters Teares*, 15–16.

[49] Ibid. 16; *Colchester Spie*, no. 1, [A2(2)ᵛ–3]; cf. *Mercurius Rusticus*, 3, 9. According to the *Colchester Spie* the boy was also half hanged, burnt 'so that he was black all over like an Ethiope, crying out with horrible yells . . . and in all probability they have murdered him'. In another version the last torture came by water and he was nearly drowned before being pulled out; his ultimate fate remained uncertain. *Mercurius Elencticus*, 36 (26 July–2 Aug. 1648), 281–2.

although 'trembling [and] troubled' to take a sacrilegious oath. When a soldier drew his sword, 'Mr Hughes went mad thereupon'.[50] Even this vignette appealed to ancient horrors of sacrilege and madness.

The overheated narration of many of these stories leads us, perhaps unjustly, to suspend belief, but they are nonetheless evidence of the bitter hold the siege of Colchester took on imagination. Others, equally traditional in their evocation of horror at overturned norms of conduct, have stronger evidence to support them. One famous incident flouted the respect due to the bodies and resting places of the dead. Lord Lucas's house in the suburbs had already been gutted by the 'Colchester Plunderers' in August 1642; when it was taken in 1648 Fairfax's soldiers, disappointed in their hopes of richer pickings, ravaged the family vault beneath the chapel. They broke open the family tombs, including those of the mother and sister of Lord Lucas and Sir Charles, who 'were so lately buried, that their sinues and haire were unconsumed', scattered the bones, cut off their hair and wore it as trophies in their hats. Deeply felt taboos were transgressed, but the incident reminds us of earlier iconoclastic orgies and the widespread belief that Lord Lucas was a papist, and of the ferocity and bloodiness of the preceding fight for the gatehouse.[51] The royalists made much of this atrocity while parliamentarians largely ignored it, but the accounts are persuasive.

The siege also produced its stories of offences against children. In one humble incident a weaver was interrupted as he worked at his loom by parliamentary troops demanding money. When he said that all he had was taken by the last party of soldiers they refused to believe him and, it was laconically reported, in frustration they shot him dead and 'cut . . . and . . . cruelly wounded his son'.[52] The case of Lord Capel's son, which we have already encountered, received more attention and revealed the fragility under pressure of the protections nominally due to children, for in it a child was intentionally endangered and became both an instrument and a victim of policy. Royalist condemnation was unequivocal, and royalist publicists manipulated the story to make monsters of their enemies.

The trigger to events in the Capel case was the deep anxiety felt by the House of Commons about the fate of the captive Essex committee and especially about that of their fellow members. In their attempts to strengthen Fairfax's hand in negotiating for the committee's release, the House on 26 June had added Lord Capel's son and heir to the list of prisoners offered in exchange for the committee.[53] The ploy was unsuccessful. Capel refused to be blackmailed and instead took the high moral ground, deploring the seizure of one so young and in such pathetic circumstances, and impugning Fairfax's honour: 'How inhuman an act it is to bear away the boy from his mother at this time of her weakness

---

[50] *Colchesters Teares*, 15.

[51] John Walter, *Understanding Popular Violence in the English Revolution. The Colchester Plunderers* (Cambridge, 1999), 32–7; HMC, *Twelfth Report*, 'Beaufort MSS', 28; Carter, *Most True And exact Relation*, 164–5; Newman, *Royalist Officers*, 241.

[52] Carter, *Most True And exact Relation*, 137–8.   [53] Rushworth, 7. 1165.

and lying in, and he of so tender an age that he is not capable of bringing inconvenience to the affairs either of the house or army I leave to the censure of all men of honour.' In a ringing assertion of his own honour and loyalty he spurned any exchange for his son, declaring that it was a joy to see any of his family by their suffering 'pay that duty they owe to the king & to the laws of the kingdom'.[54] Capel's defiance was a gift to royalist mythology and was embellished in the telling: in one version he declared to Fairfax that he 'might Murder his son if he pleased', in another that 'if his wife and all his children were there he would doe his duty'. In the most extreme variant 16-year-old Arthur Capel became 'an infant of tender yeares . . . ravisht from his mother's armes', and the author regretted parliamentary squeamishness in preserving his life and thus evading instant divine retribution:

> I wish that in that feirce and cruell moode,
> You had gone on, and quafft the Infants blood.[55]

Behind the extravagances lay a certainty that seizing the boy as yet another means of bringing pressure on his father, and doing so as his mother was lying in offended against the protections due to children and to women in childbed.[56] The case was made worse by the treatment of the captive. Young Capel was sickly, sheltered, 'and had scarce rid ever on horseback, or been out of the family'. Now he was forced to take the long ride to Colchester, lodged in primitive conditions, and 'every day [he] was carried round the works' as an incentive to his father to surrender. The *Colchester Spie* placed 'the Innocent Child' in front of the royalist cannon's mouth 'so in case any shot was made [he] might first lead the dance of death'.[57]

The story of Arthur Capel provides a further demonstration that protection for the weak was less a right than a favour dependent on military needs, but it also shows how denial of protection could be exploited to vilify the enemy. Yet the use of prisoners as pawns in sieges was not confined to Colchester, nor was the use of family members as hostages to induce good behaviour unique, while the manipulation of young Capel's age was a flagrant bid for sympathetic outrage, particularly in view of the fact that many youths had begun their military careers by 16.[58] Nevertheless it seems that parliamentarians were not entirely comfortable with the situation. Arthur Capel's trials were short, and after 'much sollicitation', he was allowed to return home. He was fortunate in his

---

[54] Worcester College, Clarke MSS, 114, fo. 48[v].

[55] HMC, *Fourteenth Report*, 'Round MSS', 288 (in this account Capel's defiance is misdated to 22 July); HMC, *Twelfth Report*, 'Beaufort MSS', 45–6; *Colchester Spie*, no. 1, A2[v].

[56] HMC, *Twelfth Report*, 'Beaufort MSS', 15.   [57] Ibid. 45; *Colchester Spie*, no. 1, A2[v].

[58] See the imprisonment of Lord Inchiquin's son as punishment for his father's actions and his use as a pawn for exchange of English prisoners in Ireland; Ashton, *Counter Revolution: The Second Civil War*, 290; *CJ* 5. 529; Rushworth, 7. 1284.

connections, for much of the solicitation was orchestrated by the marchioness of Hertford, whose son Lord Beauchamp had married his sister Mary. Through her agents she made sure that the House of Lords in London was aware of a threat to their privileges and 'sencible of the injury done to the Peers by such an order and acte, hee being a Peere's eldest sonne'. She also persuaded Lady Fairfax to write to her husband, 'to have him civily used and exposed to no danger'.[59] In Arthur Capel's case it proved possible to mobilize influence and ultimately secure his release. The channel from royalists with old parliamentarian connections (Hertford had once been regarded as a 'country' sympathizer against the court, and his wife was the earl of Essex's sister) to parliament's politically moderate if militarily draconian general by way of his independent-minded wife, was still open. A residue of the moderating social links observed at Boarstall still lingered at Colchester.

[59] HMC, *Twelfth Report*, 'Beaufort MSS', 15, 46.

17

Reciprocity, Negotiation, and Surrender

Mobilization of influence across party lines was not the only way in which earlier habits of war persisted. The case of Arthur Capel was minor and isolated; for Fairfax it was clearly a failed stratagem, and one moreover with negative effects on public opinion. It cost him little to abandon it. It was more important to preserve practices of war that had clear utility, that offered reciprocal benefits, and that each side could hope to manipulate for its own profit. At Colchester treatment of prisoners, methods of negotiation, and conceptions of honour retained their traditional character despite the strains the siege placed on conventional observance and despite the animosities that had replaced the civilities of Boarstall. When the siege ended, however, a new severity seemed to threaten the bonds not only of civility but also of honour and professionalism that had hitherto, with difficulty and despite lapses, moderated relations between enemies.

THE ESSEX COMMITTEE AND OTHER PRISONERS

Two major problems arose over prisoners: their treatment and their exchange. Despite Norwich's 'enraging' reply to Fairfax's initial summons to surrender, conventional courtesies persisted in the handling of prisoners and, grievances and accusations notwithstanding, the basic mutual rules for prisoners survived. The situation was complicated, however, by the fact that the most valuable and sensitive group of prisoners, the Essex committeemen held by the royalists, was not military but civilian and political. Fairfax's efforts on their behalf were subjected to anxious scrutiny and interference from parliament.

Early reports that the committee was ill-used prompted Fairfax to write to Capel asking that a messenger be allowed to inspect their condition and discover 'what Necessaries they want'.[1] His intervention worked, and thereafter the prisoners were conscientiously supplied by their friends, while the royalists boasted of the 'civility' that allowed them 'to receive any provisions of fresh and hot meats, as Venison Pasties and the like . . . whilst the Lords and Gentlemen

---

[1] *CJ* 5. 589; Rushworth, 7. 1155.

themselves fed generally on Horse flesh'.[2] The prisoners admitted that they had been 'used civilly', while even the minister who preached a triumphal sermon celebrating their final release had to allow that they had been permitted to '*eat the fat* and *drink the sweet*, when many of [their captors] starved, and others suffered very much, by their more unwholesome provision'.[3] The royalists nevertheless got little credit, the parliamentarians claiming that their actions were either directed by self-interest or were the result of God's direct intervention. To the accusation that the committee members had been deliberately housed 'upon the Line' to be killed 'by the Impartiall shot of their Friends'—an echo of treatment inflicted on parliamentarians at Crowland—royalists replied that they had merely been housed in the 'best and most convenient Inne' available. Nevertheless the danger of their situation could not be denied, for the top of their house was several times 'shot through with great shot' by parliament's artillery, which must 'either forsake advantage, or at every shot endanger the lives of those worthy persons'. This, said the royalists robustly, was no more than any house in the town might expect, and besides Fairfax could have honoured their request not to shoot in their direction.[4] The vulnerability of their position told on the prisoners and increased their nervous anxiety for exchange, but although imprisonment reduced some to psychological frailty their troubles ended with surrender. For royalist prisoners the real problems only began then.

Fairfax also addressed the simpler business of equivalent exchanges, and here old practices survived. At the beginning he held some 500 royalist prisoners, and wrote, '[I]f you have any of my Soldiers Prisoners, I desire to know the Number and Quality of them, and I shall send you as many in Exchange.' Norwich, Capel, and Lucas replied in kind, requesting a list of the names of those held, promising to send a comparable list, and asking that those in Fairfax's hands be reassured that everything possible was being done to gain their release. Fairfax instantly replied with a list of officer prisoners and information about common soldiers. These courtesies were sustained in the midst of the 'hourly Motion and Action' of 15 June.[5]

The combination of special pressure on behalf of the Essex committee and normal professional practice continued. Calibrated exchanges of the conventional kind occurred throughout the siege. At the end of July, for example, Norwich wrote to Fairfax about one agreed exchange of a parliamentary ensign and a corporal for six royalist soldiers which was delayed because only three of

---

[2] Worcester College, Clarke MSS, 114, fo. 53ᵛ; HMC, *Fourteenth Report*, 'Round MSS', 288; Carter, *Most True And exact Relation*, 158–9 (bis).

[3] BL Harl. MS 7001, fo. 186ᵛ; Samuel Fairclough, *The Prisoners Praises for their Deliverance* (1650), 29.

[4] Carter, *Most True And exact Relation*, 158–9 (bis). HMC, *Thirteenth Report. Portland MSS*, 1. 470, 480.

[5] *CJ* 5. 589; Rushworth, 7. 1155.

the six had yet been sent; he suggested negotiations about the exchange of another corporal, and noted that Fairfax's list for another proposed exchange of thirty-three men was still two short. Such routine negotiations continued to the eve of royalist surrender, although progress was sometimes bumpy, and Fairfax refused to deal with Lucas, citing a point of honour, a matter to which we shall return.[6]

The problem of the Essex committee, however, remained unresolved. Parliament's efforts on their behalf, and particularly on behalf of Sir William Masham, one of the county members for Essex and recently appointed to the powerful Derby House committee, continued unabated from the time of their capture at Chelmsford, but their efforts were unavailing.[7] From Colchester the prisoners themselves added their voice. Less than a week after the siege began Masham and his fellow prisoners—committeemen and others—sent a plea for 'a Treaty for Peace'. Fairfax discounted it, rightly suspecting that it had been written under duress, but parliament and the Derby House committee, intent on looking after their own, kept up the pressure on their general.[8] Time and again Norwich, who knew the value of his goods, refused point blank to negotiate, or negotiations foundered on a technicality or drifted to inconclusion. In July parliament added John Ashburnham, the king's devoted servant captured at St Neots, to the equation as an attractive counterweight to Masham, but the double offer of Capel's son and Ashburnham for Masham and another parliamentarian was rejected. Later that month near-agreement collapsed because the parties could not agree on the terms of the passes to be granted to the prisoners.[9] At last at the beginning of August Masham and Ashburnham were exchanged. The hopes of the rest of the committee cautiously rose and Fairfax and parliament continued their efforts, but none of the ingenious formulae they offered worked.[10] Finally on 20 August Fairfax offered a deal by which the civilian population of Colchester would be allowed to leave the town so long as the committee came out with the first batch.[11] This proposal too was rejected. When Norwich was at last forced to negotiate surrender his emissaries included royalist officers and also two of the imprisoned gentlemen, who had first to give their parole to return. They carried a letter from the prisoners declaring that they feared for their lives if no

---

[6] Worcester College, Clarke MSS, 114, fos. 53ᵛ, 68; *Colchester Spie*, no. 2, [A2(2)]; Rushworth, 7. 1234; HMC, *Fourteenth Report*, 'Round MSS', 284.

[7] *CJ* 5. 579, 589, 601, 609, 611, 612.   [8] HMC, *Fourteenth Report*, 'Round MSS', 284.

[9] *Diary of the Siege of Colchester*, 30 June; *CJ* 5. 615; HMC, *Fourteenth Report*, 'Round MSS', 286, 288; Rushworth, 7. 1204; *Perfect Diurnall*, 261 (24–31 July 1648), 3001: the royalists demanded a pass for Ashburnham that would allow him to go where he pleased, while only promising Masham a pass that would allow him 'to go all England over'. A pass that would allow Ashburnham to leave the country had obvious value in 1648, whereas the terms proposed for Masham's pass were in fact restrictive.

[10] BL Harl. MS 7001, fo. 186ᵛ; *Colchester Spie*, no. 2, A2ᵛ; *CJ* 5. 668; Worcester College, Clarke MSS, 114, fos. 55–55ᵛ.

[11] Ibid. 114, fo. 56ᵛ. The offer did not extend, however, to the wives and children of those that 'abide in arms'.

agreement were reached and begging Fairfax to listen to 'Mr Barnardiston, one of the Committee . . . sent out to use his rhetoric'. The writers implicitly recognized that the strain of siege and imprisonment could undermine honourable standards, for their anxiety that Fairfax ensure Barnardiston's punctual return suggests a fear that he might be tempted to break his parole and stay safely in the parliamentary camp, leaving the remaining prisoners open to reprisal. Their concern may have been justified, for when Barnardiston talked to Fairfax and his officers he 'discovered much of self, much fear, which carried him on to speak that for which afterwards he made an apology'. The council of war—which included his kinsman Lieutenant-Colonel Barnardiston—was unmoved and voted 'Nemine contradicente' to ignore his plea.[12]

The committeemen's ordeal and parliament's anxiety only ended with the surrender of Colchester. Their saga focuses attention on the unusual extent to which political considerations and military judgement mingled there. It also illuminates the psychological strains imposed by the siege. The urgent efforts of Masham and Barnardiston to achieve truce or release suggest more than the usual humiliation and restriction of the prisoner's lot. Prisoners' expectations as to what would happen to them grew more uncertain in this more bitter war, and the morale-breaking stress of weeks of bombardment and exposure to danger took their toll. Barnardiston's breakdown may offer a rare window through which we can gain some understanding of the psychological state of those other passive sufferers, the civilian population in Colchester and in many other sieges.

FROM STALEMATE TO SURRENDER

The approaches to surrender, like the handling of prisoners, followed conventional paths. These did not exclude a certain amount of abuse and ridicule or claims that the enemy was ignorant of proper professional behaviour. At the beginning of the siege Fairfax, like Norwich, was accused of offering a 'rude' and 'most unsouldierlike affront'. He had urged surrender to prevent the spilling of 'much Blood' and the plunder and ruin of the town, and ended with a conventional transference of guilt for future suffering: 'The Evil must lie upon you if you refuse.'[13] Norwich's provocative reply descended to personal insult and in turn elicited an angry response from parliament's soldiers, who were enraged by mockery of 'Lame Tom's' physical frailties.[14]

---

[12] HMC, *Fourteenth Report*, 'Round MSS', 289–90; BL Harl. MS 7001, fo. 189; Worcester College, Clarke MSS, 114, fos. 64ᵛ–65ᵛ.

[13] HMC, *Fourteenth Report*, 'Round MSS', 285; HMC, *Twelfth Report*, 'Beaufort MSS', 24, 27; Rushworth, 7. 1155.

[14] Ibid.; *Mercurius Elencticus*, 39 (16–23 Aug. 1648), 334.

The exchange set the ill-tempered tone that characterized many exchanges at Colchester.

A more measured exchange a few days later raised what were to be crucial issues in all future negotiations. One was the conditions to be granted to the defeated, and here terms were never to be so generous again, for Fairfax offered liberty to 'Gentlemen and Officers to go beyond sea, and the souldiers to go home, without prejudice'. Another issue that was to grow in importance now made its first appearance, that of the constraints on Fairfax's power imposed by his duty to parliament; for the present he merely noted that neither general nor army had the power to make decisions of national policy: 'if a general peace was intended, . . . then it was proper for the parliament to determine of that'.[15]

Norwich for his part tried to divide his enemies by exploiting regional differences. On 22 June he offered a separate peace and generous terms to the Suffolk forces, who were at first reluctant to cross their county boundary into Essex. It was a less than compelling offer given the military circumstances, explicable only by a hopeful belief that Suffolk was ready to rise in the king's cause, but it demonstrated the royalist propensity to misplaced optimism and was an attempt to play to the localist neutralism that had marked phases of the first civil war.[16] The 'commons of Suffolk' may have been infused with 'loyall heate' but if so it was easily cooled, and the Suffolk troops played a valuable part in Fairfax's siege campaign.[17] Royalist efforts in the second civil war appear as a series of ill-coordinated local ventures, but local discontents only rarely proved sufficient to provoke a return to arms in the king's cause. The parliamentarian response was organized on a national scale, and in 1648 the Suffolk forces were assimilated to the efforts of a national army whose leaders explicitly served a sovereign parliament.

After the predictable failure of these early gestures towards an agreement, both sides settled to the business of unnegotiated siege, although Fairfax reiterated the generous terms available for soldiers who deserted Colchester and presented themselves 'peaceably' to his guards, and from time to time he made sure that the 'poor, deceived, and deluded souldiers' inside the walls knew what they were missing by sending the message in by arrows. His twofold intention was to encourage desertion and to sow dissension between commanders and the soldiers they were 'deceiving'. Some royalists claimed that these attempts to 'corrupt' their resolute men were not only unsuccessful but the actions 'rather [of] serpents than souldiers'. Others, more frankly, admitted that Fairfax's offer was 'a great loss to the Royalists, for now the men, foreseeing

---

[15] HMC, *Fourteenth Report*, 'Round MSS', 285; *Diary of the Siege of Colchester*, 19–20 June; *Severall Papers and Letters Betwixt his Excellency the Lord Fairfax The Earle of Norwich, Lord Capell, Sir Charles Lucas, about the surrender of Colchester* (27 June 1648), [3]–5.

[16] Rushworth, 7. 1163–4; HMC, *Twelfth Report*, 'Beaufort MSS', 26.

[17] Ibid. 26–7; HMC, *Fourteenth Report*, 'Round MSS', 285.

the great Hardships they were like to suffer, began to slip away'. Norwich forbade desertion on pain of death and instituted constant horse patrols to apprehend deserters, 'notwithstanding which many of them got away'.[18] Norwich's counter-offer of back pay and hope of indemnity to any parliamentary soldier deserting into Colchester, cast as an appeal to 'the duty of good Christians, and Loyall Subjects', was presumably neither unsoldierly nor serpent-like but, as royalist bad news mounted, it was one that parliament's soldiers felt able to refuse.[19]

Thus although there was a hiatus in formal negotiation after the first days of the siege, incentives to private peace remained in place. They obviously worked most strongly on those inside the walls, but it is impossible to quantify the royalist haemorrhage. An estimate of 300 who fled to surrender in response to Fairfax's invitation seems low, and in any case to have been greatly exceeded by less formal desertions. Unofficial departures in this integrated war were facilitated by the ease with which unofficial runaways could hope to melt back into society, while 'official' deserters were explicitly promised the right to go back unpenalized to where they came from. Beneath the level of formal exchanges between commanders and of large-scale surrender, and beneath the claims of the steadfastness and incorruptibility of one's own soldiers, there was informal, fluid, personal abandonment of the siege of Colchester. Integration and physical intimacy fostered both friendly exchanges between enemies and unofficial, independent action by ordinary soldiers, increasingly so as the end grew visibly inevitable and royalist discipline and organization unravelled in the siege's last days. Then, while leaders haggled, the troops of both sides alternately threw stones and talked, with 'no fire given on either side', without waiting for a formal truce.[20]

Formally, however, nearly a month passed after Fairfax's early summons before he tried again. In mid-July the time seemed propitious. Pembroke castle had fallen and the rising of Holland and Buckingham had collapsed. At Colchester the gatehouse had fallen bloodily, the blockade was tight, and the city endured its worst night of fires. The next day Fairfax sent in a trumpeter with a summons to surrender. The terms had become harsher. While common soldiers and lesser officers were to have liberty and passes to go home, for others the more ominous proviso of 'submitting to the Authority of Parliament' appeared. The royalists dismissed the message as 'a very confident *Flim Flam*' and Norwich's reply was 'bold and scornful', while in a flourish bizarrely reminiscent of the sprinkling of romantic challenges in the first civil war, he called upon Fairfax for a kind of military show-and-tell in which officers of each side would inspect troops, arms, and victuals to demonstrate which had the greater remaining strength

---

[18] Rushworth, 7. 1163; *True and Exact Relation Of the taking of Colchester*, 1; HMC, *Twelfth Report*, 'Beaufort MSS', 29; HMC, *Fourteenth Report*, 'Round MSS', 285.
[19] Carter, *Most True And exact Relation*, 159–60.   [20] Ibid. 189.

and would evaluate past achievements.[21] Fairfax did not rise to the bait, and henceforth all negotiation occurred under pressure of extreme royalist necessity. For parliamentarians, obstinate rejection of three summons had forfeited the opportunity for honourable terms.[22]

The last month of the siege was quiet. Fairfax made ostentatious preparations for a storm, although it is doubtful if he in fact intended any such unnecessarily costly operation. Indeed, members of his army grew defensive as London civilians wondered why the enemy was allowed 'to enjoy so much peace'. The council of war, however, had several reasons for preferring 'rather to starve than storm'. Since an army must be maintained in the south, it was better to employ it at Colchester than to keep it 'lying still', for the dangers of an inactive army were already well-known. Furthermore, as a deterrent to future trouble they were not averse to making the county feel 'what a sore scourge war is'.[23] Meanwhile inside the walls hunger increased, ammunition ran low, and vague hopes for relief tenuously supported morale. On 17 August, faced by 'Captain *Storm* without, and Captain *Hunger* within', an angry citizenry, a breach in the walls by parliament's cannon, and uncertain news of royalist fortunes elsewhere, Norwich, Capel, and Lucas approached Fairfax with a proposal for a twenty-day truce while they sought news of Sir Marmaduke Langdale's fortunes in the north; if there proved to be no hope of relief, they would treat for surrender. Fairfax summarily rejected this well-worn delaying tactic. The ploy would in any case have been fruitless, for the proposal came on the same day as Cromwell's victory over the king's northern forces at Preston. Courtesy was by now strained and 'tart Messages and Answers were exchanged on this Occasion'.[24]

Fairfax continued to intimidate by highly visible preparations for a storm. Norwich still breathed defiance and demanded 'Hon[oura]ble Terms', but his position was desperate, his food and ammunition virtually exhausted. At the end he had only a barrel and a half of powder left. His council of war decided they must treat and on 19 August, under colour of a humanitarian plea on behalf of the starving poor of Colchester, Norwich wrote to Fairfax, '[W]e have resolved to . . . treat about the condition of this town.'[25] Fairfax was in no hurry. His siege had been long, but no longer than 'soldiership & discretion' required, and 'Delay [was] now the best part of [his] Game'. He left Norwich to face

---

[21] *Diary of the Siege of Colchester*, 16 July; *Mercurius Pragmaticus*, 17 (18–25 July 1648), [R3ᵛ]; Rushworth, 7. 1193; Worcester College, Clarke MSS, 114, fo. 50.

[22] *True and Exact Relation Of the taking of Colchester*, 1.   [23] BL Harl. MS 7001, fo. 186ᵛ.

[24] Worcester College, Clarke MSS, 114, fo. 59; *True and Exact Relation of the taking of Colchester*, 1; Carter, *Most True And exact Relation*, 168–9; *Diary of the Siege of Colchester*, 17 August; HMC, *Fourteenth Report*, 'Round MSS', 289. In the latter version the royalist leaders also sought permission to send a message to the prince of Wales, who was with a royalist fleet at the mouth of the Thames.

[25] Ibid.; *Diary of the Siege of Colchester*, 19–20 Aug.; Carter, *True And exact Relation*, 172, 190; Worcester College, Clarke MSS, 114, fo. 56. According to Carter, royalist stores were calculated to contain only 'two dayes provision of bread' and the magazine enough for only 'two hours fight'.

the pressure of restive populace and soldiers for another night until he and his officers could discuss the matter the next day. The delay was nearly fatal to him, for that evening royalist case-shot came close enough to scatter him with dirt. A royalist soldier killed by parliamentarians as he looked over the wall was less lucky. The elaborate rituals of surrender among his betters had human costs.[26]

Fairfax was not disposed to be lenient. On 20 August he told the royalists that they had held out for so long and denied his summons so obdurately that this would be his last answer and their last chance of mercy. He offered junior officers below the rank of captain (other than turncoats from parliament's service) passes to return home unmolested once they had engaged not to bear arms again against parliament.[27] The fundamental elements of the final surrender were taking shape, including 'exception' from generous terms for turncoats and mercy, in its technical, discretionary, and not necessarily merciful sense for senior officers and their associated gentlemen; however the benign terms offered at this time to common soldiers and junior officers were to be a casualty of the siege's last days. The royalists, in any case, rejected Fairfax's offer, which so little acknowledged 'the Honour of [their] actions, that [they were] thought unhonourable to be accepted'.[28] There followed royalist defiance and desultory aggression carried out with the help of home-made powder and match; more threatening preparations that seemed to foretell a parliamentary storm; royalist counter-measures such as the cauldrons of boiling pitch kept on the ramparts for use against attackers; exchange of self-justifying rhetoric as women and children stood exposed between the armies; and multiplying troubles for Norwich as importunate civilians protested and soldiers grew increasingly receptive to the offers of good terms sent in by arrows and kites, offers which also tempted them with incentives to turn on their officers. On 21 August Fairfax repeated his terms, and Norwich and the mayor dispatched an intermediary, the physician Dr Glissen. At last, too, they received news of the disaster at Preston, sent in by a trumpeter who carried a printed account of Cromwell's victory. Initial refusal to believe it gave way to sad understanding: '[W]e had done our utmost . . . and now at last [were] destitute of any hopes remaining of a possible relief.'[29]

There was still no plain sailing. Despite petitions from the townsmen and from the imprisoned committee, Fairfax did not budge in his refusal to let civilians leave. Nor would he moderate surrender terms. In Colchester the council of war again balked at terms by which 'our libertyes may be infringed, and our Honours blemisht'. They engaged not to desert one another or the foot, who

---

[26] Worcester College, Clarke MSS, 114, fo. 59; Rushworth, 7. 1234.

[27] Ibid. 7. 1235–6; HMC, *Fourteenth Report*, 'Round MSS', 289.

[28] Worcester College, Clarke MSS, 114, fo. 59ᵛ; Carter, *Most True and exact Relation*, 173.

[29] HMC, *Twelfth Report*, 'Beaufort MSS', 30; Carter, *Most True And exact Relation*, 172, 175, 180; Worcester College, Clarke MSS, 114, fos. 61–61ᵛ, 68ᵛ.

were already suspicious that their leaders would abandon them; the abortive plan for a break-out by a party led by Lucas and Lisle further compounded Norwich's troubles and provoked open mutiny. Royalist claims that their troops were undaunted, courageous, and above all obedient collapsed. Taking a leaf out of the book of the Agitators (the regimental representatives who had challenged the high command of the parliamentary army in 1647), Norwich's soldiers now sent some thirty representatives to the council of war with an ultimatum: if the council did not make conditions on their behalf, 'they would Article for themselves over the Line, and leave their Officers to shift for themselves as they understood their Officers would have done by them'. Norwich managed to pacify them temporarily, but the last fiction, that of a reliably loyal soldiery, had gone.[30]

The royalists knew that they faced 'unavoidable ruine': they could no longer 'protract time' and could only hope for 'an honourable conclusion'.[31] Nevertheless, obstinate, consistent, pathetic in their adherence to 'what became [their] Honour and fidelity', the royalist council refused to surrender on terms that promised only 'mercy' to senior officers and demanded 'termes of honour befitting their qualities'. On 24 August they sent Fairfax the 'lowest conditions' that they would accept, some of which would have been generous in the best of circumstances. They included a proviso that commanders, officers, gentlemen, and soldiers were to march a mile out of the town with their horses and arms before surrendering them, after which the four chief commanders were to be allowed to march away with all their horses, arms, and equipment, and senior officers and all cavalry officers were to be allowed a horse and a servant each and their arms as well as more servants to carry their swords and baggage; other officers might keep their swords, and all might have passes to go home unmolested and, if they wished, passes to go overseas with a promise not to serve again against parliament. Private soldiers were to have free lodgings on the way home.[32] The appearances of honour, thus given painstaking hierarchical expression, would be preserved and the ritual of such a surrender would allow the defeated to tell themselves that their unsullied personal honour had received public recognition.

It is hard to believe the royalists seriously thought that Fairfax would accept their terms, and the refusal was prompt and uncompromising. Fairfax argued, as both threat and statement of the laws of war, that rejection of earlier, more generous terms 'disengaged' the offerer from any obligation to repeat them; he was free to impose a harsher peace. There was a sense of imminent crisis and relentless judgement. At noon on the 24th time ran out on previous offers of good conditions for soldiers and junior officers. Meanwhile Fairfax kept up the pressure on the town's battered inhabitants. In one morning his artillery

---

[30] Ibid. 114, fos. 66–66ᵛ; HMC, *Fourteenth Report*, 'Round MSS', 289; Carter, *Most True And exact Relation*, 176–87.

[31] Ibid. 175–6.

[32] Worcester College, Clarke MSS, 114, fos. 63–63ᵛ; *Mercurius Pragmaticus*, 22 (22–9 Aug. 1648), Ddᵛ.

pounded a section of the walls with 140 'great shot', doing little material damage but adding three more victims to the list of dead, and presumably adding to the strain and terror of already overstrained civilians, while the fears of the imprisoned committeemen that the royalists would cut their throats intensified. To heighten suffering, 'extraordinary' wet weather continued: swollen rivers made travel hazardous and flood threatened besieged and besiegers alike. Through it all Fairfax remained unyielding and his soldiers angry and vengeful. The royalists' demand for 'honourable terms' only concentrated the anger aroused by the second civil war:

(after they have spilt so much blood, burned, & ruined a town, impoverished a country by so long a siege) [their offer] will in no kind be hearkened unto, & therefore you may expect these men will taste of the fury of an exasperated soldiery & have but little quarter, for justice must be done on such exemplary offenders who have embroiled the kingdom in a 2nd bloody war.[33]

The warning was timely.

The news of Preston joined mutiny to make both defiance and temporizing pointless. For the first time there are hints of 'disaffection' among members of the council of war, while *suggested whisperings* bred a most dangerous *Mutiny*. Sack and claret, raisins and prunes (miraculously conjured up in starving Colchester), new clothes and good words, could not persuade mutinous soldiers to support officers they no longer trusted. Instead they barred the gates and threatened to 'kill that officer that offered to stir out' and to seize those who would not treat. Private soldiers parleyed across the lines and a parliamentarian observed with satisfaction that mutiny rendered the once obstinate enemy 'as humble as a lamb'.[34] On 26 August the royalists again sent out Barnardiston and their own Colonel Samuel Tuke to accept Fairfax's previous terms, but also to ask for clarifications. Fairfax called a council of war, which agreed that soldiers and junior officers might have 'fair quarter' but no more, for they had 'slipt their opportunity' for better terms. Turncoats were again excepted, and 'the lords, general officers & captains [must be] surrendered to mercy'.[35]

By now the royalists had run out of options. They now urgently wanted a settlement, recognizing that it was increasingly hard for parliamentary officers to control their men who 'could not without much difficulty & slashing be kept, from falling upon them, so greedy they were of new clothes and of the spoils

[33] Worcester College, Clarke MSS, 114, fos. 64–5, 69; BL Harl. MS 7001, fo. 186; Carter, *Most True And exact Relation*, 182; *True and Exact Relation of the taking of Colchester*, 2.

[34] *The Loyall Sacrifice: Presented In the Lives and Deaths of those two Eminent-Heroick Patternes, For Valour, Discipline, and Fidelity: The generally beloved and bemoaned, Sir Charles Lucas, And Sir George Lisle* (n.pl., 1648), 70–2; Worcester College, Clarke MSS, 114, fos. 66–66ᵛ; BL Harl. MS 7001, fo. 189; Carter, *Most True And exact Relation*, 189. The availability of sack, claret, raisins, and prunes as emergency 'sweeteners' is further evidence that starvation did not bite equally; the higher command still had reserves at its disposal.

[35] Worcester College, Clarke MSS, 114, fos. 66, 69ᵛ.

of their enemies'.[36] The royalist council of war appointed commissioners with full power to reach agreement, but even now bargaining had not ended.[37] The commissioners asked for clarification of Fairfax's terms, especially and critically the meanings of 'fair quarter' and 'mercy'. Other issues, concerning for example the clothes and horses of those rendered to mercy, may appear minor but they concerned not only the comfort and property of the prisoners but the appearance they would present to the world. Fairfax however would promise no more than that they might keep the clothes on their backs. He insisted that all horses and arms must be delivered up, but he granted that the general and officers would have horses fitting 'to their qualities'. They would not be humiliated by appearing before the world on broken-down nags when they rode away from Colchester. Even in royalist defeat, Fairfax implicitly conceded, some of the appearances of hierarchy were to be maintained.[38]

SURRENDER

Royalists had little time for Fairfax—a 'pernicious treacherous foole', said one. He now became in their eyes the tool of his council of war, in particular of the intransigent Ireton and Rainsborough, respectively Cromwell's socially conservative son-in-law and the radical champion at the Putney debates. Despite their differences in the autumn of 1647 they were now united in a relentless demand for retribution, but they were no harsher than Fairfax himself on the central issue of the severity due to senior royalists. His statements on the treatment of the defeated reveal considered positions on the military and political principles according to which he and parliament should act, and belief in the correctness of the ruthless justice that was about to be meted out. His replies to questions about quarter and mercy reflected the bitterness of the second civil war and a consequent unforgiving military legalism in treatment of enemies.[39]

On 27 August his commissioners explained the meaning of the crucial terms. Officially, 'fair quarter' meant 'quarter for their lives', freedom from wounding or beating, warm clothes, and suitable food while men remained prisoners. Unofficially, interpretation was less generous: soldiers could expect 'to have their skins whole, though stripped of all their outward apparel'. 'Mercy' was a still harsher matter. It meant surrender to the lord general or his deputy 'without certain assurance of quarter so as the Lord General may be free to put some immediately to the sword if he see cause'. Fairfax's intention, so the commissioners reported, was to render most of the senior royalist officers to 'the mercy of parliament & General'. They cited his past 'civility' to prisoners but

---

[36] BL Harl. MS 7001, fo. 189.   [37] Carter, *Most True And exact Relation*, 188.
[38] Worcester College, Clarke MSS, 114, fos. 70–70ᵛ.
[39] *Colchester Spie*, no. 1, A2; Carter, *Most True And exact Relation*, 188.

ominously pointed out that he was 'not engaged thereto' in the case of those who had surrendered to mercy. There was little the royalist commissioners could do, but they succeeded in modifying the provision as to whose mercy they were rendered to. They rejected formulations that specified surrender to lord general and parliament or 'to the Lord General who intended to deliver them up to the Parliament', and finally agreed to surrender to the mercy of the lord general alone. This was no mere quibble. It kept the prisoners who had surrendered to mercy, so royalists were later to argue, under a military jurisdiction and protected them from civilian charges that parliament might choose to bring.[40]

There remained only agreement on the technicalities of surrender, on the details of takeover and on times and places for delivery of men, arms, and the surviving horses. For Fairfax too agreement was becoming urgent as his soldiers 'talk[ed] and parley[ed]' with enemy soldiers and townsmen and 'great confusion' threatened.[41] Finally, at ten o'clock on the night of 27 August the commissioners of both sides signed the articles. The definitions of free quarter and mercy already described were annexed to the treaty, thus gaining formal standing, and the nine articles themselves were precise and practical, revealing the professional planning involved in a comprehensive dismantling of enemy power. Times were staggered, places varied, loopholes closed. A 'cessation' of all hostilities went into immediate effect, but all other provisions awaited the next day. At eight o'clock on the morning of 28 August all royalist guards were to be withdrawn and their places taken by Fairfax's men. At nine o'clock horses must be delivered to the churchyard of St Mary's, whence Norwich's artillery had played on the parliamentarians, and saddles and bridles taken in to the church. At ten o'clock arms, colours, and drums must be brought into St James's, another large church; there was to be no honourable ritual of marching out with colours and drums on this occasion. At the same time all ammunition and all military waggons were to be delivered to the comptroller of Fairfax's artillery train. By ten o'clock too all soldiers and junior officers, with their clothes and baggage, were to be drawn up near the East Gate to surrender themselves into custody, with a promise of fair quarter as defined by the commissioners. By nine o'clock Fairfax was to have a list of all general and field officers, and by eleven o'clock 'the Lords, and all Captains, and superiour Officers, and Gentlemen of Quality' were to be drawn up at the King's Head, with their clothes and baggage, to surrender to the mercy of the lord general. Meanwhile all ordnance was to be left in place 'without wilful spoil'—the articles were anxious to prevent last-minute pilfering or damage by the defeated—and transferred to parliamentary guards. On a more humanitarian note, the articles also included the usual provision for care of the sick and wounded, who were to be provided with suitable accommodation and cared for by surgeons until they were sufficiently recovered to move 'without prejudice

---

[40] Worcester College, Clarke MSS, 114, fos. 69–70[v]; HMC, *Twelfth Report*, 'Beaufort MSS', 30.
[41] Worcester College, Clarke MSS, 114, fo. 71.

to their Healths'.[42] These then were the military provisions of settlement that demolished royalist forces in Colchester and effectively, despite lingering pockets of resistance not finally eradicated until 1649, ended the second civil war.

The town's civilian inhabitants were not included in this military treaty. The provisions of their separate settlement made no allowances for their sufferings, for Fairfax and his council of war insisted that they shared responsibility for 'the long tedious siege . . . in so wet a season' in which parliament's soldiers had 'undergone so hard a duty'. If the soldiers were to be deprived of the right to plunder—a right which, Fairfax argued, the military settlement did not abrogate—then the townsmen must pay. A fine of £14,000, later abated to £12,000, was imposed on the town; in return it would be 'preserved from Plunder'. Fairfax's separation of military and civilian settlements, which effectively withdrew the protection that a negotiated surrender was supposed to provide against sack by victorious soldiers, seems to have been based on pragmatic recognition that the nature of the siege had made it impossible to prevent uncontrolled plunder by his men unless they were promised a substantial pay-off.[43] His fears proved justified. The burdens on Colchester's civilians did not end with peace.

The immediate consequences of surrender were worse than the royalists feared: they ranged from captivity and plunder to death. The ritual dance of negotiation, from Norwich's first approach to Fairfax on 17 August, had taken ten days which saw the sufferings of civilians and soldiers alike grow more acute, women and children used as pawns by both commanders, and more casual deaths. In that time Fairfax had operated according to military calculation and righteous conviction. For the royalists, as for their predecessors at Boarstall, there was little but honour left and they sought to preserve it. On 27 August the captive members of the parliamentary committee were released amid 'great acclamations of joy' and on 28 August it was all over. In the morning Fairfax's agents entered the town and the process of surrender began; in the afternoon Rainsborough's regiment and others rode in to the 'sad spectacle' of the 'very strange place' that was Colchester.[44] There were over 3,500 prisoners: 281 officers and associated gentlemen, from Norwich down to ensigns and cornets, 183 sergeants, 3,067 private soldiers, and uncounted servants. On 31 August a letter from Fairfax setting out the details of victory was read in the House of Lords and promptly printed. Meanwhile his soldiers had demonstrated the fragility of paper protections by flocking into Colchester through breaches in the walls before the gates were opened, contrary to

[42] Rushworth, 7. 1242, 1244(*sic*)–7. Carter's account of the surrender, written after the event, differs in some details (e.g. times) from that in immediately contemporary documents. Carter, *Most True And exact Relation*, 190. The surviving horses seem to have been officers' mounts. According to Carter, there were 'not many' left; a plan for every officer (except the general and major-general) 'to pistol his own horse' before the troops, thus showing that they did not intend to abandon them, was not put into execution, hence the survivors on 27–8 Aug. Ibid. 175–6, 181–2.

[43] Rushworth., 7. 1242 (bis); Worcester College, Clarke MSS, 114, fos. 66, 69ᵛ; BL Stowe MS 842, fo. 34; Morant, *Essex*, 1. 69.

[44] Rushworth, 7. 1242, 1242 (bis), 1247; Worcester College, Clarke MSS, 114, fos. 71ᵛ–72ᵛ.

the articles, seizing surviving horses from stables, and plundering everything they could lay hands on. The afternoon of 28 August saw the first dire consequence of surrender to mercy and one of the most notorious incidents of either civil war. The lord general had retained the right 'to put some immediately to the Sword, if he [saw] Cause'. The cause he saw was exemplary justice, and the subsequent execution, after a summary court martial, of the two 'Persons pitched upon for this Example' became a celebrated royalist martyrdom.[45]

HONOUR AND DEFEAT

In the account of negotiations to end the siege of Colchester one concept has been inescapable, one term has persistently recurred: 'honour'. Before turning to the final act of the siege it is worth considering its role at Colchester, for the language of honour pervaded exchanges between enemies and increasingly, as failure grew manifestly inevitable, reaffirmed for defeated men their authentic selves as soldiers and loyal subjects. The external protocols of honour and the cultivation of an internal sense of adherence to what was demanded of the soldier undoubtedly lengthened the siege and killed more victims. It was part of the vocabulary of both sides, but was used most persistently and flamboyantly by the royalists. The worse their condition became the more anxious they were to proclaim and preserve their honour and to appeal to it as a touchstone of conduct. It was a sticking-point in negotiations, and after surrender royalists perceived massive failures of honour among parliamentarians, who in turn defended their own honour and good faith.

We have already seen professional, moral, and social components of honour. Ridicule and demeaning actions could offend against it, as could failure to extend the privileges and courtesies that convention demanded between men and soldiers of like honour. Hence royalist revulsion at refusal to grant 'honourable' surrender terms to men who had done 'nothing but what became our Honours and fidelity'. The 'Honour of [their] actions' long made it 'unhonourable' to accept Fairfax's treaty. Nevertheless when the conditions that legitimated surrender were met, suicidal last-ditch resistance was not required, and would in any case have been difficult in the midst of their own mutinous troops. In such circumstances, honour did not preclude hard bargaining.[46] When it came to

---

[45] Rushworth, 7. 1243–4, 1247; Carter, *Most True And exact Relation*, 190; HMC, *Fourteenth Report*, 'Round MSS', 290. Rushworth's account of these events, as of the surrender articles, follows with only minor variations the pamphlet version of Fairfax's dispatch to the House of Lords, *A Letter From his Excellency the Lord Fairfax Generall of the Parliament's Forces: Concerning the surrender of Colchester, The Ground and Reasons of putting to death Sir Charles Lucas and Sir George Lysle; . . . Together with a List of all the prisoners taken* (1648); it was read in the House of Lords, 31 Aug. 1648. As was usual with civil war statistics, estimates of numbers of prisoners varied, but on this occasion the variations were minor.

[46] Carter, *Most True And exact Relation*, 172, 173, 177, 179.

bargaining, however, Fairfax denied that the honour of the enemy's proceedings entitled them to generous terms, and cited both practical military grounds and their larger breach of faith.

In the course of the siege the whole gamut of possible senses of this elusive quality found expression. Its manifestations ranged from the romantically chivalric to the rational, from the bombastic to the modest. It was invoked both in claims of honour and assertions of dishonour, and justified strident challenges whose purpose was to insult and dishonour the enemy. There were extravagant stories of edifying loyalty and willing sacrifice that deserved 'never dying fame', while less elevated and more defiant declarations of honour aggressively strengthened morale in difficult situations.[47] Nor was honour confined to officers and gentlemen; it was sought and sometimes found among common soldiers. Officers' defiance should be expressed in terms 'becomming a Gentleman', but the rough honour of ordinary soldiers could take a more demotic form. The royalists claimed that until traduced into final mutiny, their soldiers had never acted dishonourably, rejecting all the 'alluring charms' sent in by arrow to induce them to desert the king's service. The terms of their rejection might not become a gentleman, but they raised morale even as they defied the enemy: 'they . . . took some of their own Arrowes annointing them with a T. and wrapping the same in paper fastned it to the heads of the Arrowes, and writ on the paper this superscription, *An Answer from Colchester August the* 11th. 1648, *as you may smell*'. This exercise, it was said, animated and enlivened the troops.[48]

These are examples of the rhetoric of honour. Its practice was more important. The siege of Colchester demonstrated the familiar honour of high and noble actions but also a military honour that found expression in more mundane military virtues. Carter, for example, admired the sang-froid of troops under heavy fire who showed no more concern than 'if it had been but a sporting skirmish amongst tame soldiers at a general muster'.[49] Royalist officers descended to 'the meanest undertakings' to serve the public good and shared hardships with their soldiers. Significantly, their professional application and industry was contrasted with earlier failings of the royalist officer corps, and their willingness to undertake 'mean' tasks was praised as 'an honorable striving of gentlemen for their birthrights—I meane their proprieties limited and protected by the lawes—against needy and barbarous murders'.[50] The noble end transformed lowly means.

The rash and furious courage more conventionally associated with military honour played its part at Colchester, but its cooler manifestations were also acknowledged. Capel, on foot and armed only with a pike, repelling parliamentary

---

[47] See Carter, *Most True And exact Relation*, 156–7 (bis), for the story of the nameless ensign who died lamenting that his friends would not know that '*I really loved my* KING, *and that I liv'd, and cheerfully dyed in His, and My Countryes service*'.

[48] Ibid. 165–6 (bis), 186.

[49] HMC, *Twelfth Report*, 'Beaufort MSS', 22; Carter, *Most True And exact Relation*, 150.

[50] HMC, *Twelfth Report*, 'Beaufort MSS', 26, 28–9.

fury at the Head Gate on 13 June revealed his 'incomparable honour and presence of judgment in the greatest dangers', an honour that was compounded of manifest courage and a judicious eye for military opportunity and that served a 'worthy cause'. Honour, courage, and prudence were allied: it was not necessary to invite 'imprudent hazards' to gain 'a reputation of valiant'.[51] The death of Sir William Campion elicited the tributes to 'incomparable and unblemisht honour' due to a soldier who was admired professionally and morally and whose courage was joined to reason and discretion. Praise for such qualities was a far cry from the propagandist excesses of carefully constructed stories of individual acts of martyrdom or heroism. Campion, more soberly, 'fell with honour, a public loss for the public'.[52]

Fairfax's sticking-point, when he considered the honour of royalist enemies at Colchester, was breach of faith, for this could never be honourable. Campion's re-engagement in war and blood in the second civil war did not impugn his honour as an offence against the laws of war: it will be remembered with what care the royalists at Boarstall insisted that the terms of surrender should leave them free to serve the king again. Many officers at Colchester, however, were vulnerable at surrender to the severest penalties for failure to observe an oath not to take up arms again against the parliament.[53] In Lucas's case there was the further complication of accusations of breach of parole, and Fairfax's refusal to deal with him over exchange of prisoners in the first week of the siege boded ill for his future prospects. '[H]e wou'd not treat with Sr Charles', declared Fairfax, 'for that he, Sr Charles, being his prisoner upon his Parole of Honour, and having appear'd in Arms Contrary to the Rules of War, had forfeited his Honour and faith, and was not capable of command or trust in Martial affairs.'[54] To Fairfax Lucas, who became his prisoner in March 1646 and was paroled, was still on parole and had manifestly broken its conditions. Lucas, on the other hand, although he provocatively acknowledged an 'inclination and duty' to his present service, was at pains to explain why he no longer considered himself Fairfax's prisoner and therefore could not be accused of dishonourably breaking parole. Even a fellow royalist, however, described his response as an 'excuse for his breech [*sic*] of his Parole'. It was clear that from the beginning of the siege Fairfax was convinced that one of his enemies by his breach of 'the Rules of War', had forfeited his Honour and faith', and was thereby unfitted for command and undeserving of trust.[55]

[51] HMC, *Twelfth Report*, 'Beaufort MSS', 24–5.

[52] Carter, *Most True And exact Relation*, 135; East Sussex RO, Danny MS 119; Worcester College, Clarke MSS, 114, fo. 47; HMC, *Twelfth Report*, 'Beaufort MSS', 24.

[53] HMC, *Fourteenth Report*, 'Round MSS', 284.

[54] Ibid.; Worcester College, Clarke MSS, 114, fo. 46; *CCC*, 1. 95–6, 3. 1821–2; *ODNB*, 'Sir Charles Lucas'; Gardiner, *History of the Great Civil War*, 4. 205–6 n. 1. Lucas argued that he had purchased his freedom and estate by large payments into Goldsmiths' Hall and had written to Fairfax's secretary informing him that he had fulfilled his 'engagements'. He claimed that the secretary's noncommittal reply confirmed his disengaged status.

[55] Rushworth, 7. 1244.

Arguments about the honour of surrender may seem rarefied and extravagant, a means by which officers satisfied social and psychological needs while their men were randomly picked off on the walls. They were also, however, an aspect of a professional ideology that enabled enemies to understand and, within limits, trust each other, and to operate within a world of known elements of conduct rather than one in which actions were random and uncontrolled. Honour as a matter of conduct that merited internal self-respect and external reputation among friends and enemies alike animated soldiers on both sides. At Colchester we can observe its role not only as a moral abstraction or a component of personal worth or a shaper of battlefield conduct, but as a factor that influenced a wider political and military world. There can be no doubt that royalist perceptions of honour lengthened the siege, which in turn affected the later fate both of soldiers and the town's civilians, nor that parliamentarian perceptions of royalist dishonour contributed to justification of the notorious retribution visited on their eminent prisoners. For Lucas his putative failure to observe its requirements led him to the firing squad. For Fairfax, a difficult debate about honour and legality was just beginning.

THE MARTYRS

At eight in the morning of 28 August royalist guards around the town were replaced by Fairfax's men. Weapons were collected and officers and men gathered in the places assigned in the surrender treaty. At two in the afternoon Fairfax rode into Colchester. He viewed the royalist lines and 'shew[ed] himselfe in triumph' to the defeated soldiers. Then he repaired to his quarters and called a council of war.[56] What followed became the stuff of royalist legend.

A colonel was dispatched from the council to the captive officers at the King's Head. They expected a visit of courtesy, but instead he 'brought a message of death in his heart': Sir Charles Lucas, Sir George Lisle, Sir Bernard Gascoigne, and Colonel Farr were to return with him to the council. Lucas, suspecting what was to come, took solemn leave of his fellow prisoners, and he, Lisle, and Gascoigne left them. Farr had escaped. Soon a message came to the King's Head asking for a chaplain, 'which strook a dead sorrow in to the hearts of all'. The three officers were to be summarily executed. Fairfax and his council had condemned them in absentia. They had 'past their doom without ever calling the convicted to the Court, or Bar. A new unheard of way, of condemning men in our Nation.'[57] The royalist quartermaster Matthew Carter, one of the prisoners, left a record of what went on at the King's Head in

---

[56] C[arter], *Most True And exact Relation*, 191–2. [57] Ibid. 192, 194–5.

which the themes of martyrdom and of unprecedented illegality are already in place.

The court martial had also condemned Norwich, Capel, and Loughborough. Loughborough too had escaped, if only temporarily, but Fairfax reserved Norwich and Capel for the judgement of parliament. It was more suitable to try them by civil jurisdiction, he said, because they were 'considerable for estates and family', unlike Lucas and Lisle who were 'mere soldiers of fortune & falling into our hands by the chance of war'.[58] He may well not have wished to offend the members of parliament's residual House of Lords by the execution of two peers. The reasons for the selection of Lucas are clear enough. He was, said Henry Ireton, 'one of the heads of a great party', as well as commander of the horse and one of the inner royalist command group; he was held responsible for the royalist presence in Colchester; and, as we have seen, Fairfax believed that he had broken his parole. Once the decision had been made to kill him other justifications could readily be discovered, such as accusations of harshness to the people of Colchester and earlier killing in cold blood. Lisle, a commander of foot and another European veteran, was Lucas's 'constant Loyall' and 'dearest friend'. He too was accused of breach of parole and of being 'a great cause' of burning the town's houses. He and Gascoigne, however, belonged to the second level of command, unlike Lucas, Norwich, and Capel. It was in fact clear from the outset that Lucas, Lisle, and Gascoigne were to be exemplary victims. They were the 'Persons pitched upon for this Example', said Fairfax; they were 'examples of Justice', said a newsletter.[59]

The three were hurried from the council of war to the castle, where Commissary-General Ireton told them to prepare to die. Lucas demanded to know 'by what Law they were to dye, or whether by an Ordinance of Parliament, by the Councell of Warre, or by command of the Generall?' Like other Englishmen in the civil war, he clung to legal distinctions and appearances of legality, and in doing so raised the issue of parliamentary jurisdiction as opposed to military law or a commander's arbitrary choice. Ireton evaded the issue, citing the authority both of the council of war and of a parliamentary order of 20 June that all found in arms were to be proceeded against as traitors.[60] The understanding reached in the first civil war that captured enemies would not be executed as traitors was now set aside.

Lucas asked unavailingly for a respite until the next morning, to settle his affairs in this world and prepare for the next, 'that I might not be thrown out

---

[58] Bodl. MS Fairfax, 36, fos. 6–6ᵛ. Given the military history of Fairfax's own family, this dismissal of the claims of Lucas and Lisle is curious.

[59] *Clarke Papers*, ed. Firth, 2. 35; *Loyall Sacrifice*, 74–5; Rushworth, 7. 1243; *True and Exact Relation Of the taking of Colchester*, 2–3.

[60] C[arter], *Most True And exact Relation*, 195; Worcester College, Clarke MSS, 114, fos. 89–89ᵛ; *Clarke Papers*, ed. Firth, 2. xii–xiv, 34–5.

of this world with all my sins about me'. Lisle too asked for 'a little respite' to write to his father and mother, which was also denied. They were at least granted the comfort of Capel's chaplain. Ireton left them, and they prayed and received the sacrament. Lucas's prayers, according to Carter, were leavened by 'zealous expressions and heavenly ejaculations'. The Florentine Gascoigne asked to make his confession, but this led to 'much Expostulation and Discourse' for the chaplain objected to auricular confession. At last he was accommodated by conversation with another chaplain, and all three prepared for death.[61]

From the time of their arrival in the castle yard we have an extraordinary eye- and ear-witness account of events recorded by young William Clarke, secretary of the General Council of the Army. Sober, unvarnished, and detailed, it provides a verismo counterpoint to the more florid heroics of Carter and his fellow royalists. The constant in both is the courage and dignity of the victims. Lucas declared himself guiltless of wrongdoing, but he lamented the shortness of the time granted for repentance, 'for the best of us all hath not liv'd such a life but he does deserve a longer time of repentance then I have now'. The three victims talked together of sin and repentance in the face of death, of comfort to family and friends, of duty and love to the king, and of comradeship, affection, and support for one another. 'Come, my heart,' said Lucas to Gascoigne, 'I need not cheer you up, I know your chearfulnesse by my owne.' There were flashes of reflection on their own natures. 'I do not professe my self a rhetorician att all', said Lucas, as he tried to express his loyalty and piety. Lisle comforted himself that it was God's will, '[t]hough I don't believe in predestination'. They acknowledged sinfulness but unshakenly defended both the righteousness and the legality of the actions that led to their deaths. 'I am a true subject to my King' and 'the lawes of the Kingdome', said Lucas. At the core of their royalism were service, allegiance, and love. Lucas sent his 'duty' to his 'Prince and Master' and Lisle 'bes[ought] God to send all happinesse which is due to so just, so good a man'.[62]

When Lucas asked by what authority they were to die, Ireton replied that it was dual: they were condemned as traitors by parliament, but in the context of Colchester and their exception from quarter, the authority was military. In their lengthy exchange Lucas first appealed to military law which mandated a trial before condemnation for a capital crime, a claim Ireton dismissed by citing the meaning of surrender to mercy. Lucas then appealed to the law of the kingdom, which rendered it impossible for a man who acted in accordance with a commission from the king to be a traitor; Ireton reiterated the superior

61 Ibid. 2. 32–4; C[arter], *Most True And exact Relation*, 196–7; *Loyall Sacrifice*, 76; Rushworth, 7. 1242 (bis).

62 *Clarke Papers*, ed. Firth, 2. 31–6; Clarendon, *History*, 3. 137. Clarke's account begins at the point of their 'first coming into the Castle yard', ibid. 2. 31, but some of his passages are very close to speeches that Carter places earlier. Carter may have manipulated the order of speeches in the interest of his drama, but the substance of both reports, the ideas expressed, and often the language, remain very close.

legitimacy of parliamentary law although at one point he conceded that it was 'a certaine rule, that among armes the lawes are silent'. Lisle's appeal to the consciences of the members of the court martial—they should 'consider what it is to take a way a man's life in this kind'—and soldiers' interventions adverting to royalist killings in cold blood and denial of quarter, were swept aside in the flood of Ireton's rebuttals to Lucas's pleas and arguments. The exchanges—on the relative spheres of military and civilian law, and on the relation of justice and mercy—continued. Ireton at last admitted that he was not an expert on the laws of arms, and discussion of the relative spheres of military and civilian law reached a dead end with irreconcilable assertions of legal treason and legal loyalty.[63]

Lucas, resigned to his own fate, asked that his life might 'satisfy' for those of Lisle and Gascoigne. Lisle intervened on his own behalf. 'I have given many hundred men quarter', he said, but the argument had no weight. The friends prayed and embraced, and Lucas prepared to die 'like a soldier'. He remembered his friends, asked forgiveness where it was due, begged for decent burial with his ancestors, and—recalling recent orgies of destruction and desecration in the family vault in St Giles—that they might 'from henceforth lye in quiet'. He prayed that vengeance would not fall on his killers, and made his last request, 'When I shall [fall] lay me downe decently . . . Oh Father, Son, and Holy Ghost, receive my soule.' He knelt to pray, then rose with a 'cheerful countenance', opened his doublet and showed his breast, put his hands at his sides, and called, 'See I am ready for you, now Rebells do your worst.' The six dragoons allotted to the task fired and 'he was suddenly dead'.[64]

Lisle's death followed immediately. Clarke gave it half a sentence, but others celebrated the 'heroick . . . untroubled, undaunted' end that smote 'his Enemies . . . with horror, though not with compassion'. He had been taken aside so that he should not see his friend fall. Now he was brought to the place and saw his body 'dead and bleeding on the ground'. He knelt and kissed it, Carter recounted, 'sobbing forth a funeral Elegie in many sweet Characters of his peerlesse and unspotted honour'. He stood up, took five pieces of gold from his pocket (all he had) and gave one to the executioners and the rest to a gentleman nearby as a last legacy for friends in London. He spoke of father, mother, and friends, and then addressed the spectators: 'Oh! how many of your lives here have I saved in hot blood, and must now my self be most barbarously murdered in cold? . . . I dedicate my last prayers to Heaven, and now Trayters do your worst.' He urged the musketeers to stand closer. When one replied, ' "I'le warrant you, Sir, Wee'll hit you": he Answer'd smiling, "Friends, I have been nearer you, when you have miss'd me." ' Thereupon they all fired upon him, and did their

<hr/>

[63] *Clarke Papers*, ed. Firth, 2. 36–8.
[64] *Clarke Papers*, ed. Firth, 2. 36–8; Carter, *Most True And exact Relation*, 198; *Mercurius Pragmaticus*, 23 (29 Aug.–Sept. 1648), [Ee3ᵛ]; HMC, *Twelfth Report*, 'Beaufort MSS', 27–8; Walter, *Understanding Popular Violence*, 349–50.

work home, so that he fell down dead of many wounds without speaking word.'
Thus fell, concluded one chronicler, 'these matchlesse twins of valour, and payre
of glorious Martyrs'.[65] Charles I is said to have wept at the news of their deaths.
It is not surprising that they became the instant stuff of legend.

The Italian Gascoigne, a professional soldier with a record of distinguished
service to the king, now prepared to share his friends' fate. As he stood ready with
'his doublet off', he was suddenly reprieved. Carter noted that he 'was reprieved
out of the consideration that he was a stranger to the Kingdome', and this seems
to have been the generally accepted explanation; it was said that when Fairfax
learned that he was Italian he was reprieved lest his countrymen be tempted to
take vengeance against English travellers in Italy. Another explanation offered
was that his 'faire' conduct in the past towards parliamentarians now won him
mercy.[66] Later that evening, after the executions, Fairfax sent a message to the
apprehensive royalists at the King's Head that he now assured them of 'faire
quarter as Prisoners of warre'.[67]

From the deaths of Lucas and Lisle royalists created a history of martyrdom to
which the actual characters of the victims were irrelevant. Lisle, indeed, seems to
have been widely admired for his personal as well as his professional attributes.
His was 'belov'd of all', including his soldiers, said Clarendon: 'no Man was
ever better followed'.[68] Lucas was a more difficult character. Clarendon did not
care for him, finding him rough, proud, abrasive, and taciturn, but he conceded
that he was 'as good a Commander of Horse . . . as the Nation had' and that
his men willingly followed him into battle; although he was no 'rhetorician',
on the way to Colchester his eloquence had won the support of doubtful Essex
countrymen for the royalist cause.[69] In fact, however, the past characters of the
victims had little to do with the myth of their martyrdom, which depended on
the commitment to the king's cause that they shared with their panegyrists, the
wickedness ascribed to the villains, and their unflinching and principled courage.

The themes of royalist outrage varied little over the years.[70] They were
unconcerned with such legalistic details as the distinction between mercy and
quarter as they condemned Fairfax and his fellow perpetrators for illegality,
bad faith, cruelty, and murder. Fairfax, for his part, although defensive about
his actions, never changed his mind about their legitimacy. In his 'Short
Memorials' he noted that the terms at Colchester were not exceptional. Not
only did Colchester's articles conform to the recognized laws of war but the

---

[65] *Mercurius Pragmaticus*, 23 (properly 24) (5–12 Sept. 1648), F3; C[arter], *Most True And exact Relation*, 198–9, 201; Clarendon, *History*, 3. 137; *Mercurius Elencticus*, 41 (30 Aug.–6 Sept. 1648), 332; *Loyall Sacrifice*, 84.

[66] Clarendon, *History*, 3. 137; Worcester College, Clarke MSS, 114, fo. 73ᵛ; *True and Exact Relation Of the taking of Colchester*, 4; Carter, *Most True And exact Relation*, 197.

[67] Ibid. 201–2.   [68] Clarendon, *History*, 3. 138.

[69] Ibid.; HMC, *Twelfth Report*, 'Beaufort MSS', 21.

[70] See B. Donagan, 'Myth, Memory and Martyrdom: Colchester 1648', *Essex Archaeology and History*, 34 (2004), 177–8, and below.

meaning given to their terms was conventional: 'delivering upon mercy is to be understood, that some are to suffer the rest to go free'. He had acted according to his commission, and the 'trust imposed in me'. Significantly, when his nephew published the 'Short Memorials' in 1699 this defence of the 'justice' of his proceedings was omitted.[71]

Fairfax had in fact to walk a tricky path in 1648, for he had on one hand to explain to members of parliament the military conventions governing surrender, and on the other to reassure them that the army was not attempting to usurp parliament's power. He distinguished between 'military Justice' and the 'publick Justice' of parliament or other 'civil Judgment', and he attempted to balance claims for army autonomy in military matters, including jurisdiction over prisoners, against acknowledgement of the sovereignty of parliament.[72] The problem of the proper relations between army and parliament was to loom large in the near future. It was new to England, and it had broad constitutional and legal significance, but it did not interest royalist polemicists. Nor, except accidentally and indirectly, did questions that engaged then and still engage theorists of the laws of war, whether unwritten as in the seventeenth century or internationally codified (for what that is worth) as in our own day. What are the rights of the prisoner of war and the obligations of his captors? How are claims to 'human rights' to be captured in legal language and process? And, indeed, what is a war crime? Then as now, the answers are not always benign.

---

[71] BL Harl. MS 2315, fos. 11–12.

[72] Worcester College, Clarke MSS, 114, fo. 89ᵛ; Rushworth, 7. 1243, 1303–4. *Clarke Papers*, ed. Firth, 2. xiii–xiv, gives a variant reading of the last sentence of the relevant passage.

18

Colchester: The Aftermath

In the summer and autumn of 1648, as in other times of historical crisis, the quotidian and ordinary coexisted with high drama and extraordinary ideas and actions. National and personal attention was not exclusively focused on Colchester or even on the wider struggle. John Clopton recorded the events of the siege together with other national news, but they shared his attention with the weather and its effects on the hay harvest and with the birth of his daughter Jane on yet another rainy night, when his wife's sudden labour sent him 'running through the stone yard in [his] shirt' in search of the midwife. He reported the deaths of Lucas and Lisle, but by 1 September the sense of crisis had receded and he placidly recorded that he had won a little money playing slidegroat. That summer John Evelyn, on a visit from France, had glanced at the events of the war, but his personal affairs took more of his attention. He spent £3,300 on a manor, had his portrait painted, went hunting, attended his brother's wedding, and on the fateful 28 August went to London to see Bartholomew Fair. In Fairfax's own family, the summer and autumn saw routine attention to the routine expenses—for a hat, for the barber, for a study table—of Sir Thomas's cousin Bryan at Cambridge. Cases continued to grind their way through courts and committees. Norwich's son Lord Goring did not interrupt his service with the Spanish army in the Low Countries.[1] Such continuities are hardly surprising in this or any war, but they provide a salutary foil to the obsessive concerns of protagonists and propagandists.

Nor had the siege itself been all a matter of high policy, important military heroics, exceptional suffering, and unprecedented severity. Much was common-place, whether it was satisfaction at the lethal skills of one's own side, praise for the courage of an individual hero, or sociability with one's peers. The royalists, for example, celebrated the élan of a lone soldier who charged the besiegers single-handed and, when finally taken prisoner, was offered service in the par-liamentary army as a tribute to his mad courage. Soldiers still ate and drank gregariously when they could. Four officers were cut off by royalist artillery as they were going to 'recreate their ungodly guts with sack and sugar Cakes at a

---

[1] Essex RO, D/DQ s18, fos. 39ᵛ–52; *The Diary of John Evelyn*, ed. E. S. de Beer, 6 vols. (Oxford, 1955), 2. 541–2; Bodl. MSS Fairfax, 32, fos. 167–8; HEH, STT MSS, Parl. Box 2; Bodl. MSS Clarendon, 31, fos. 231–231ᵛ.

Hut'. William Osborne and a friend made a sightseeing expedition to Mersea and on their way home 'had a fish dinner soles, Mayds & oysters, very cheep'. Some of these incidents have a domestic charm: the courageous soldier wanted only to go home, for which a pass was 'freely granted', while Osborne wrote to his wife that her company had been much missed at his fish dinner.[2]

Neither the survival of old habits, civil and military, nor parliament's victory at Colchester led to immediate relaxation and reconstruction. To most parliamentarians, danger and instability still threatened; to some royalists, resistance and new ventures still beckoned. Some contemporaries already perceived a 'dying rebellion' by the end of June, but to most the situation at the end of August was still hazardous. London remained volatile; rumours of foreign intervention and attacks by the prince of Wales persisted; the revolted ships remained in royalist hands; Pontefract and Scarborough still held out; reports of plots, more and less plausible, continued to circulate, including one for the 'private massacre' by 900 royalist infiltrators of members of parliament as they lay in their beds; and recent experience showed the need for more and stronger garrisons in strategically significant towns such as Berwick, Carmarthen, Rye, and Yarmouth.[3]

Success at Colchester did not bring a neat ending. Some of the continuing issues were specific to the town, others merged with the wider consequences in politics and society of the second civil war. For the civilians of Colchester there was no happy return to the status quo of the spring of 1648, while the thousands of prisoners, joining other prisoners of the second war, faced uncertain and varied futures. For one party a hagiographic industry created a mythic memory of the siege and its victims, for the other the vexed questions presented by the execution of Lucas and Lisle had ramifications touching the looming conflict between parliament and army.

One immediate problem was that of what to do with the victorious troops. They had celebrated unofficially by plundering when they entered Colchester on 28 August. On 30 August they received the official tribute due to victors when Fairfax's army held a rendezvous with the Suffolk and Essex auxiliaries. The ceremony was curtailed by more wet weather, but they 'shook hands; great volleys of shot past, and [the auxiliaries] were dismist'. Dismissal was sweetened for these county troops by the promise of £2,000 of the fine imposed on the citizens of Colchester.[4] On 31 August there was a day of thanksgiving. By 4 September, although some troops remained in Colchester and the Committee

---

[2] *Great and bloudy Fight at Colchester*, 2; *Mercurius Melancholicus*, 7–8; BL, Harl. MS 7001, fo. 186ᵛ. 'Mayds' were young skate.

[3] *CSPDom. 1648–1649*, 258–61, 274; *Mercurius Pragmaticus*, 23 (29 Aug.–5 Sept. 1648), Ff 2ᵛ; HMC, *Thirteenth Report. Portland MSS*, 1. 469–70; Rushworth, 7. 1279; Worcester College, Clarke MSS, 114, fos. 97, 99; Magdalene College, Pepys MSS 2504, fos. 203–4, 207–12.

[4] Rushworth, 7. 1250; BL Add. MS 7001, fo. 189ᵛ. The £2,000 seems to have been pay rather than a bonus, and a supplement to other sources of funds; see Essex RO, D/DQ s18, fos. 55ᵛ–56 for the £1,600 paid to the Suffolk forces.

for the Army established itself there, dispersal of Fairfax's forces had begun with the dispatch of several regiments to Yarmouth. For political as well as financial reasons parliament was anxious to reduce the army once their most acute need for it had passed, and by October Fairfax was battling a wary, budget-cutting House of Commons, arguing that he would not disband until pay was settled, and that in view of the increased claims on army manpower its establishment should in fact be increased by 3,000 men.[5] Relations between parliament and army were moving towards a crisis, and some of its elements were already evident in the efforts of the Derby House Committee to control allocation of troops, and in Fairfax's struggle to distinguish between the proper jurisdiction of the army and that of the civil power.[6]

CIVILIANS: 'RUINE AND DESOLATION'[7]

In Colchester a political purge followed within a week of surrender, although the structure of the town's government limited its scope. Nevertheless, on 4 September the undistinguished mayor of the siege period was replaced—although he remained an alderman—by Henry Barrington, a man of more radical sympathies, while thirteen members of the corporation, roughly a third of its membership, were expelled and replaced by new members.[8] A chastened and radicalized body faced the problems of a devastated and demoralized city.

The first of these was the fine imposed by Fairfax as a quid pro quo for an assurance that his men would not pillage the town. Although the soldiers, defying their officers, had flocked in through the broken walls before the gates were opened and seized everything they could lay hands on, the fine remained in place. £2,000 of the initial £14,000 had been abated, but £12,000 had still to be raised. Colchester's government quickly found a way to lighten the burden on 'native' townsmen: £6,000 would be paid by the city's Dutch congregation.[9]

---

[5] Gentles, *New Model Army*, 257; Rushworth, 7. 1250; Worcester College, Clarke MSS, 114, fo. 97.

[6] *CSPDom. 1648–1649*, 240, 258–9, 270–1.

[7] *Mercurius Pragmaticus*, [24] (misnumbered 23) (5–12 Sept. 1648), F3.

[8] In later years, in response to the discontents of electors, the body's more customary conservatism reasserted itself until in 1656, in an attempt to rein in the 'malignant corporation', a new charter was issued that restricted the number of eligible voters. J. H. Round, 'Colchester during the Commonwealth', *EHR* 15 (1900), 645–8, 655–9; David Underdown, *Pride's Purge. Politics in the Puritan Revolution* (Oxford, 1971), 324–5; Walter, *Understanding Popular Violence*, 74–7.

[9] BL Stowe MS 842, fos. 34–5; BL Harl. MS 7001, fo. 189; On the Dutch church in Colchester, see Ole Peter Grell, *Calvinist Exiles in Tudor and Stuart England* (Aldershot, 1996), 53–73 *passim*, especially 64, 67–9. The size of the fine varies in different accounts, from £14,000 (HMC, *Fourteenth Report*, 'Round MSS', 290, and *Mercurius Pragmaticus*, [24] (misnumbered 23) (5–12 Sept. 1648), F3) to £11,000 (BL Harl. MS 7001, fo. 189ᵛ). However the total of £12,000 given here, which is based on the statement of the Dutch community and on their tax assessments to achieve their designated half share of the town's total fine, seems reliable. Of this £12,000 total,

The members of the Dutch community, who had been established in Colchester since 1570 and were by now overwhelmingly native-born, immediately but unavailingly protested. They paid their half of the fine but commented, '[H]ow just it was, we leave God and all sober people to judge.'[10] Two lists of tax payments offer some evidence as to the relative burdens placed on English and Dutch inhabitants. One lists the individual amounts paid by eighty members of the Dutch congregation, the other the payments of fifty-nine 'native' residents of two of the city's wards. The Dutch list accounted for their full £6,000 assessment, that from the two wards for £3,923 of the remaining £6,000 due.[11] It has been suggested that the equal division of the burden between the two communities reflected the wealth of the Dutch, and indeed there were some impressively large Dutch payments, but that division also indicates the value of a resident population of vulnerable 'others' who in the past had enjoyed favoured status and incurred consequent resentment, onto whom an unwelcome burden could be inequitably offloaded.

It seems that to achieve their quota the Dutch had to reach down to poorer levels of their community and also to make heavier demands on the prosperous than did the English. The tight-knit families of this immigrant population paid a high price. Seven members of the Taispill family paid 24 per cent of the total Dutch fine, of which £985, or over 16 per cent, came from only two men, and a further £485 or 8 per cent of the total came from five more kinsmen. Four members of the Fromiteel family contributed £600, and eight Everits contributed £405 in amounts ranging from £5 to £150. Over £4,000, or two-thirds of the fine, came from nine families. There is no comparable degree of family concentration in the English ward list. English taxpayers, moreover, were helped by the burden placed on two men who paid £500 each, or nearly 17 per cent of the total: these appear to have been punitive assessments, for one victim was an expelled alderman while the other shortly emerged as a leading opponent of Barrington's party. In both English and Dutch groups those assessed at the lowest rates of £10 or less—and presumably therefore relatively poor, although not indigent—made up some 16 per cent of the whole, but judging by the size of the assessments the Dutch community had to reach down to a lower economic level to meet its obligation than did the English. For those in the middling ranges, things were easier for the English; five Dutch each paid between £210

£2,000 went to pay the county troops and £2,000 for relief of the poor of Colchester, BL Stowe MS 842, fo. 34; Carter, *True And exact Relation*, 202; Morant, *Essex*, 1. 69.

[10] BL Stowe MS 842, fos. 34–5. There were Dutch in Colchester by the mid-16th cent., but their officially sponsored presence dated from 1570–1. *Victoria History of the County of Essex*, ed. W. Page and J. H. Round, 2 (1907), 387, 390, 392–4. The adjectives 'English' and 'Dutch' in the present context refer to communal status rather than place of birth. By 1616 a survey of the Dutch community found that out of a population of 1,271 only 248 had been born abroad. Morant, *Essex*, 1. 74.

[11] BL Stowe MS 842, fos. 33–33ᵛ, 35ᵛ–37ᵛ.

and £400, for example, but only three English paid as much as £200. Only in the group of those paying between £100 and £200 did the English outnumber the Dutch. The distribution and rate of assessments suggest that, aside from the two punitive cases, the wind was tempered for English contributors at both the top and bottom of the tax range, payments instead clustering around a moderate if still painful middle. For the Dutch they ran more evenly and more severely through the whole community and cast a shadow over its economic recovery.[12]

These comparisons must be treated cautiously, but the fact remains that a minority population paid half of the fine. The Dutch congregation was in fact a double victim. Its members shared the sufferings of their fellow townsmen at the hands of the besiegers; but afterwards those townsmen found them a convenient cash cow that could reduce financial demands on 'real' Colchester men and women. The Dutch petition to the mayor and aldermen not only pointed out the inequity of this allocation of burden, but also warned of its destructive effect as it portrayed the straits to which this formerly prosperous community, the backbone of the town's cloth trade, was reduced. Early in the siege Fairfax had conceded that the bay and say makers (primarily Dutch) should be allowed to offer their goods to outside merchants at market rates, with a promise of post-siege payment, but this does not seem to have helped them materially. Indeed, it is doubtful if the concession ever took effect, and Dutch losses in the siege had been great: '[M]any of us have lost the principal part, and many a great part, of their estates, partly by firing, partly by scattering of their commodities abroad in the country, where their workmen and spinners have made sale of them, and thereby we are extremely damnified'.[13]

To these losses of property and stock a large fine was now added. It is probable that the resulting heavy drain of cash, combined with lowered production through destruction of plant and equipment, greatly reduced the credit and resources available for recovery among a community accustomed to strong intra-family and intra-group support. They feared that they would 'be undone and disenabled for the future', and that they would be unable 'to subsist or to remain a congregation'. Furthermore, they faced the burden of the greatly increased number of their own poor, a problem they shared with the rest of Colchester, but when they asked for relief they received another rebuff. When Fairfax returned £2,000 of the total £12,000 fine to the city for the benefit of the poor and those who had suffered in the siege Dutch hopes rose, only to be disappointed again: '[W]e expected half of it for our Dutch poor. We could, with some trouble, at last, get of the town one hundred pounds.' They had paid

---

[12] The Dutch commmunity appealed for help to the London Dutch church, which collected a contribution of £523. 16s. 0d. Ibid., fos. 33ᵛ–37ᵛ; VCH, *Essex*, 2. 396; Round, 'Colchester during the Commonwealth', 646, 651.

[13] BL Stowe MS 842, fos. 34ᵛ–35.

half the fine but received only 5 per cent of its rebated benefits.[14] The Dutch were not relegated to a position outside the law like the Irish, nor were they objects of vitriolic polemic. Nevertheless this story of displacement of burden to a weaker victim reveals much about English attitudes to outsiders during the civil wars. The sufferings of the Dutch community did not find a place in royalist complaints against the financial oppression of the town's loyal citizens.

The burden of Fairfax's fine made up only one part of Colchester's post-war troubles. We have already seen the impression made by the destruction of buildings and the enfeebled state of its inhabitants on the victors when they entered the town. This experience was not confined to soldiers, for Colchester became a 'sight' that drew visitors. On 8 September, for example, John Clopton in Suffolk recorded a visit from a family party of five who 'had been to see Colchester'.[15] As with the surrender of Boarstall, military events entered the consciousness of civilians who had not themselves been participants but who had viewed the consequences, which were then recounted to friends and neighbours. Colchester did not in fact rival Breda, Ravenna, or Magdeburg in significance or horror, but its fame as a siege of continental scale and effect was disseminated by those who had seen it, whether as tourists like Clopton's kin or officials like John Rushworth, as well as by the vivid and prolific literature that it spawned.

Before 1648 Colchester, unscathed by hostilities, had done well out of war, and the godly were tempted to believe that pride in former prosperity had led 'the Lord [to] humble their hearts' by 'a heavy and dolorous day of affliction'.[16] The effects of that affliction, architectural, economic, and personal, were slow to dissipate. The physical consequences were the most obvious. Houses, churches, and mills had all suffered, and surrender was promptly followed by demolition of more of the town walls. Morant, Colchester's eighteenth-century historian, recorded that after the siege much of the town was 'shattered and demolished'. Recovery was slow. In 1656 John Evelyn found that Colchester, although 'a faire Towne', was still 'wretchedly demolished by the late Siege; espe(c)ialy the suburbs all burnt & then repairing'.[17] By 1722 Daniel Defoe reported that the town was populous, with 'fair and beautiful' streets and abundance of well-built houses but added, 'It still mourns, in the ruins of a civil war.' Shattered walls and ruined churches remained, lines of contravallation were still visible, and the steeple of St Mary's, whence a large culverin had played on parliament's troops, was still 'two thirds batter'd down'. Such sights nurtured memory, and Defoe kept it alive among a wider audience by printing a siege diary kept in the summer of 1648.[18]

---

[14] BL Stowe MS 842, fos. 34–5; VCH, *Essex*, 2. 395–6.

[15] *Mercurius Elencticus*, 44 (20–7 Sept. 1648), 355; Essex RO, D/DQ s18, fo. 52 (misnumbered for 53).

[16] *Colchesters Teares*, 13.   [17] Morant, *Essex*, 1. 69; Evelyn, *Diary*, 3. 176.

[18] Daniel Defoe, *A Tour through the Whole Island of Great Britain* (1974), 16, 18–31; the diary is that printed from the Round MSS in HMC, *Fourteenth Report*, 281–90.

In the wet autumn of 1648 many were homeless, and not only those who had previously been unhoused and poor. Granaries and storehouses were empty and the surrounding countryside depleted of supplies. There was a certain righteous satisfaction in the fact that hunger had no favorites and that those who had once lived well, who had been accustomed to dine on such local delicacies as 'Oysters and RingoRoots', were among its victims.[19] We know little of how the homeless and hungry coped with their situation after surrender, although we can assume that the fortunate were taken in by friends and kin who still had roofs over their heads or, able at last to move beyond the town, took refuge with country families. Food could now be brought in. When parishes began to distribute the relief provided by Fairfax's refunded £2000, some payments were for as little as a few shillings, which probably went to those with urgent needs to sustain life, but food was not the only necessity. Shirts were distributed and payments for clothing noted. Most relief payments fell between £1 and £3, but smaller sums of 3s. or 5s. went to widows, daughters, and soldiers. Some of the more substantial grants went towards restoring livelihoods, essential for civic as well as personal recovery. The Dutch, as we have seen, had lost tools and commodities through fleeing workmen. Troops had shattered looms and ruined mills; bales of wool had been sacrificed to protect town walls against artillery and then borne off as booty by the attackers; burning, plunder, and unfriendly fire had damaged or destroyed real and chattel property. It was as necessary to restore the means of production of this manufacturing and trading town as to feed and clothe its needy. So one weaver was granted £1 for a new loom, and another received £2. 6s. 0d. to replace 'a loom burnt at Wallend'. Even the 5s. for two loads of clay given to widow Randall presumably had an economic purpose.[20]

Fairfax's proclaimed care for 'so eminent a Town' had an ironic ring to its inhabitants. They had suffered both during and after the siege from the severity with which he interpreted the rules of war and the privileges of the victor. Humanitarian and economic pleas on behalf of its weavers and the 'Thousands of poore people in this Towne' who depended on them for their livelihood had elicited little sympathy. Nor had the claim that free trade with London (vital for sales of cloth) was a part of those 'free Trades [which were] the Subjects right and the sinewes of the Common wealth'. Instead, as Fairfax had pointed out during the siege, the town, when under parliament's control, had enjoyed all the benefits of whose loss the inhabitants now complained and their loss resulted from their own choice.[21] The consequences were severe for English and Dutch alike, and clearly Fairfax's £2,000 charitable refund provided little more than a band-aid.

[19] *True and Exact Relation of the taking of Colchester*, 4. 'RingoRoots' (candied sea-holly) were a local specialty, valued in part as an aphrodisiac. Evelyn, *Diary*, 3. 178.

[20] BL Stowe MS 842, fos. 39–53 *passim*, and note fos. 39–43, 50; *Great and bloudy Fight at Colchester*, 3.

[21] *Severall Papers and Letters Betwixt his Excellency the Lord Fairfax The Earle of Norwich . . . about the surrender of Colchester* (1648), [3].

Furthermore, destruction had effects that extended beyond the material and economic. After their houses were destroyed the Lucases and Grimstons did not return, and the town lost useful patronage.[22]

Economically, almost all inhabitants, but most notably the trading part, were brought to 'inexpressible poverty and distress'. Many would never recover from the summer's 'calamities'. Even for the more fortunate the way back was slow. The siege offers another reminder of the importance of chattel property and the meaning of its loss for the lives of the poor and modestly comfortable. Their lost looms, pots and pans, and mattresses were to them as important as the lost tapestries and plate of the prosperous. The attention paid to sequestration, damage, and forced sale of real property has too often obscured the significance of such humble material goods. We are also reminded that, before insurance, material loss was not indemnified unless civilian law could be persuaded to supply redress (hence the importance to soldiers of acts of indemnity or oblivion protecting them from liability for wartime actions), or the state could be prevailed upon to provide some compensating benefit. The petition of John Aylet of Colchester to the Treasury Commissioners in 1660 reveals civilian vulnerability to loss and the chancy, delayed nature of reparation. Now, twelve years after the siege, when the defeated had returned in triumph, Aylet petitioned for the vacant office of Customer of Colchester in recompense for his losses in 1648 and after. He had lost, he claimed, £3,000 through the plunder of his house and malting place, and this had been followed by payment of £150 towards the fine and more heavy taxation.[23] For others the way back came through return of trade, above all restoration of the trade with London. Evelyn's comments in 1656 show that Colchester had re-established itself in the cloth business, while after the Restoration the Dutch were again to win royal favour. Even Morant admitted that although 'the unhappy Siege brought universal distress and Poverty . . . Trade and Riches flourished amongst us again, till towards the end of K. William's reign'. By then the cloth trade had entered on troubled times, but the villains who hastened its decline in Colchester were not Fairfax and his destructive army but foreign wars and loss of Spanish markets, allied to competition from France and from parts of England where labour was cheaper and less demanding and coal was plentiful. Economics prevailed where the siege had not, and the Dutch congregation dissolved itself in 1728.[24]

PRISONERS

Fairfax had entered Colchester at about two in the afternoon of 28 August. Lucas and Lisle were shot at about seven. As the summer night fell the chaplain

---

[22] Morant, *Essex*, 1. 69.   [23] Ibid.; *CSPDom. 1660–61*, 155.
[24] Evelyn, *Diary*, 3. 177; Morant, *Essex*, 1, 'Colchester', 1. 75 and 3. 19; VCH, *Essex*, 2. 396–8; and see Defoe, *Tour*, 17, for the town's continued dependence on 'Colchester bays' in 1722.

returned to the apprehensive prisoners at the King's Head, where they had been crowded into one room. There the humiliations of imprisonment had already begun. They were 'viewed' by victorious parliamentary officers, and if one of them stepped into another room, claimed Carter, he was immediately stripped stark naked. When they heard the chaplain's news they looked at each other 'with clouded faces . . . for the untimely loss of those Gentlemen so untimely by a barbarous mercy murdered', and each feared that his turn might be next.[25] Finally, 'about Candlelighting', their worst fears were allayed by Fairfax's message assuring them of 'faire quarter as Prisoners of Warre'. Privately they may have felt relief, but their public response was defiant. Fairfax would have earned more thanks had he saved the lives of Lucas and Lisle and treated all alike, said Capel. The messengers found their response ungrateful.[26]

The problems of triage and disposal of some 3,500 prisoners had now to be faced. If we accept that at the beginning of the siege Norwich had roughly 5,000 men, by its end he had lost about 30 per cent to battle, disease, and desertion. The remainder still presented a formidable challenge, and the solutions reflected the greater harshness of this second war. The royalists claimed that in Kent, at the very outset of the Colchester campaign, Fairfax and parliament had planned to refuse exchanges and instead to try prisoners by a council of war or to '*transport* and *sell* them beyond *Sea* for *slaves*'. Wiser councils prevailed, they admitted, but within a week of Colchester's investiture rumours of unprecedented measures against prisoners spread, according to which the council of war had resolved on selective killing at rates that ranged from every fifth to every thirteenth man.[27] We hear no more of such super-decimation, however: not only did the royalists hold the trump card of the Essex committee, but the simple utilitarian objections of ordinary soldiers to the spectre of reprisals are obvious. Instead, as we have seen, mutual treatment of prisoners during the siege largely followed conventional lines. Nevertheless, the theme of exceptional severity had been introduced.

By 3 September a plan for the prisoners was drawn up. The lords, each with two attendants, and twelve other officers—'the better class of prisoner', a later writer called them—were to march out with Fairfax's regiment on 5 September and then to Windsor castle. The rest of the officers were to be dispersed to various strongholds, some as distant as Pendennis and Cardiff, others closer at hand, but none were to be sent north of the Trent, which would have brought them dangerously close to the Scots. Common soldiers were to be conveyed

[25] Carter, *True And exact Relation*, 191, 201; BL Harl. MS 7001, fo. 189ᵛ. 'Naked' could merely mean reduced to shirt and breeches, or even unarmed; one should be cautious about concluding that prisoners were stripped to the skin. Compare the 'Naked Valour' of Sir George Lisle, when he charged in 'an Holland Shirt' at Newbury, and the 'naked, harmlesse' petitioners attacked by troops in Surrey in 1648. King, *Poems*, 102; *Mercurius Elencticus*, 41 (30 Aug.–6 Sept. 1648), 329; *Loyall Sacrifice*, 45.

[26] Carter, *Most True And exact Relation*, 201–2.

[27] *Mercurius Elencticus*, 36 (26 July–2 Aug. 1648), 280; *Exact Narrative of Every dayes Proceedings*, 6.

west to Bristol and other ports 'that so they may pass to *America, Venice*, or as they shall be appointed'. In parliamentary eyes they had brought this severity on themselves: 'These men had not come to this sharpe accompt, but that God had hardened their hearts, which were full of bitterness of spirit, against this handfull of men that did besiege them.'[28]

The Colchester prisoners were not the only ones to be disposed of in 1648. Campaigns in the north and west, the Kent uprising, Holland's and Buckingham's fiasco, and Scottish defeat swelled numbers, while fear, shock, sense of betrayal, and size of the problem all prompted severity. Reports of ill-treatment were common, and royalists claimed that the gentlemen sent to Windsor and to 'noysome *Prisons*' in London lacked '*common necessaries*' and were 'ready to starve', while Scottish and Herefordshire prisoners were 'used . . . like Dogs'. Furthermore, given the decisiveness of parliament's victories the restraints of reciprocity between enemies were no longer powerful, and to this was joined reluctance to harbour large numbers of untrustworthy, disaffected former soldiers in England. Nevertheless proposals for handling prisoners were not uniform, and some were mild. English country soldiers who had been 'misled' into royalist service were dismissed with a caution, while an ordinance at the beginning of September that addressed the broad category of those recently engaged in rebellion in Surrey, Sussex, Kent, and Essex provided that they should be admitted to composition at a fourth value of their estates; the penalty, that is, was financial, and sequestration and compounding continued to be widely used. More generally, however, penalties were heavier, with greater resort to transportation and exile, which had previously been employed only to a limited degree. Scots taken at Preston and elsewhere, for example, faced lifelong exile to the plantations or to Venetian service. They were handed over to contractors who were instructed 'to disburthen the Kingdom of their Charge' within fourteen days so that 'none shall ever return'. The Welsh taken in 'great Numbers' at St Fagan's in Glamorganshire, it was claimed, were 'sold for twelve pence a piece to certain Merchants, who bought them for Slaves to their Plantation'. Enslavement was to be a common royalist accusation.[29] The treatment designated for Colchester prisoners was thus at the severe end of a spectrum of punishment and was, in the eyes of the victors, merited by their guilt. What actually happened to them was much less tidy than the plans suggested.

The elite prisoners at Windsor, who were joined by other royalist leaders such as the duke of Hamilton, had to wait to learn their fate. In the course of the ensuing debates issues of army autonomy, jurisdiction, and sovereignty precipitated by the second civil war were extensively explored. For the rest of

---

[28] Rushworth, 7. 1250; Owen Morshead, 'Royalist Prisoners in Windsor Castle', *Berkshire Archaeological Journal*, 56 (1958), 6; *True and Exact Relation*, 3–4.

[29] *Mercurius Pragmaticus*, 22 (22–9 Aug. 1648), Dd; 23 (29 Aug.–5 Sept. 1648), Ff2ᵛ; 31 (24–31 Oct. 1648), [Xx3]; *Mercurius Elencticus*, 42 (6–13 Sept. 1648), 342; 43 (13–20 Sept. 1648), 350; Rushworth, 7. 1249–50, 1273; King, *Poems*, 106.

the officers at Colchester what followed combined humiliation and expense, and marked a new commercialization of military prisoners. The first plan, to disperse them all to strongholds, was modified after Fairfax devised 'a new stratagem' by which he could use prisoners to pay his officers, the common soldiers and county forces having already been provided for by the fine on the town. A certain number of prisoners was now allocated to each regiment 'as slaves to the galleys', said Carter bitterly, after which they might ransom themselves from their keepers.[30] Such official, large-scale, formal ransom of military prisoners was an innovation in the English civil war. Ransom had lingered in dealings with civilians, but before 1648 it had ceased to be a normal part of the protocol by which enemies handled disposal of their prisoners. This is not to say that there were not exceptional and undercover cases, nor can it be denied that composition had some of the characteristics of ransom, although the beneficiaries were the state and its agents rather than the individual soldier. Nevertheless, an official return to the practice of ransom was new.

The manner in which the policy was executed deepened the shame and indignity of the prisoners' position. Carter, who was one of them, wrote that the officers of the regiments to which prisoners had been allocated

came to the Pound (as the manner of grasiers is by their cattell) and called them first out of that into another, and then drove them away for the market, to make the most of them; so most of them afterwards as they were able, and according to the civility of those they were distributed to, bought their liberties, and returned home.[31]

Unfortunately prisoners did not always have the money to buy their freedom, and denial of help could add to the strains that civil war imposed on family solidarity. Clopton recorded that his uncle was very angry at his refusal to send the £20 needed to buy his liberty.[32] Yet even Gascoigne could benefit from the transition from vengeance to profit. From his imprisonment at Windsor he wrote to Lord Colpeper asking for money to secure his release. His request was presumably successful, as in May 1649 an order went out to rearrest him for the trouble he was stirring up in London. Meanwhile, the residue of the prisoners who were not disposed of by the market were dealt with according to the original plan, and were sent to strongholds—according to Carter—as far from their homes as possible. Overall, it is clear that the disposition of officers and persons of influence was more closely supervised after the second war; they were not to be let loose to aggravate the divisions of a volatile state. Sometimes, however—as in Gascoigne's case—the profit motive conflicted with security considerations.[33]

---

[30] Carter, *Most True And exact Relation*, 202. Formal ransom is to be distinguished from the fees due to gaolers and keepers, although these could become a form of extortion.

[31] Ibid. 203.   [32] Essex RO, D/DQ s18, fo. 52ᵛ.

[33] Magdelene College, Pepys MSS 2504, fo. 894; *CSPDom. 1649–1650*, 161, 534; Carter, *Most True And exact Relation*, 204; *CSPDom. 1648–1649*, 283–4.

Common soldiers and inferior officers had been put in churches under guard. There they were left to the mercies of parliamentarian troops who freely pillaged them until they were left with 'hardly shirts'. In this state they were then marched away on yet another day of violent rain. Thereafter their fates were less certain, but according to royalist report they were marched from place to place and lodged in churches and other makeshift shelters until many 'starved', and some who grew too weak to march were 'pistold in the high waies'. Some were sold, like their Scottish allies, to be transported into foreign countries, far from wives and children, but 'no matter so they were once gone'.[34]

Yet despite royalist rhetoric and punitive rulings directing wholesale transportation of prisoners overseas, it seems that the number who actually went may have been relatively small. In the decade after the second civil war exile and some degree of servitude were indeed a newly favoured means of disposing of large numbers of potentially dangerous defeated enemies. They were called into use after the battles of Preston, Dunbar, and Worcester as well as Colchester and in response to plots and to Penruddock's rising in the 1650s. Yet it has been argued that, even for the Scots, to whom the method was more notoriously applied than to the English, 'no more than a small proportion of those at first allotted to the colonies ever reached their destination'—and this not merely because of death or shipwreck. Nor were servitude and forced labour confined to the colonies. In 1650 plans to send thousands of Scottish prisoners from Dunbar to serve in Ireland were frustrated by massive, lethal epidemic, but some of the survivors were set to work in the Northumberland salt-pans of the 'well-affected'.[35] It was, however, transportation to the Caribbean and north America, not labour at home or Irish or even Venetian service, that captured royalist imaginations.

For those dispatched abroad the nature of service varied. Life as a mercenary soldier in a Venetian army was a different matter from transportation to a distant colony, tropical or otherwise; it was closer to home for those who survived their term of service and, like soldiering in Ireland, could be assimilated to the long familiar practice of military service beyond the sea. Even for those sent to the colonies the consequences varied. It was sometimes possible to buy freedom on arrival. Nor, it seems, was the prohibition against return absolute in practice, and some survivors eventually seeped homeward. In 1658 in Herefordshire Sir Thomas Myddelton, out of charity for a namesake, gave 2s. 6d. to 'one Myddelton a highlander Souldier that was returninge to his owne Countrey from

---

[34] Carter, *True And exact Relation*, 203–4.

[35] Abbot Emerson Smith, *Colonists in Bondage. White Servitude and Convict Labor in America 1607–1776* (Chapel Hill, NC, 1947), 155, and see 152–65, on transportation of Scottish, English, and Irish prisoners; Carla Gardina Pestana, *The English Atlantic in an Age of Revolution, 1640–1661* (Cambridge, Mass., 2004), 185–94; 'Letter from Sir Arthur Hesilrige', in Slingsby, *Original Memoirs*, 339–45.

Barbadoes'.[36] Other soldiers never left England and were gradually reabsorbed into civilian life. One such was James Harding, a private soldier who had served under Lucas at Colchester. In December 1650 he petitioned to compound for his estate, and a month later a fine of £1. 13s. 4d.—a modest sum for a run-of-the-mill soldier—wiped his slate clean.[37] Even highly visible royalists might not suffer as harshly as the surrender settlement promised. The earl of Northampton's younger brother, Sir William Compton, was admitted to composition for his property by June 1649, while by the end of September 1648 the House of Lords voted to allow the king's devoted servant Ashburnham, who had previously been exchanged for Masham, to return to England to 'prosecute his Composition'. Even the turncoat Colonel Farr prospered through his connections with the earl of Warwick.[38]

Such shadings did not form part of the royalist picture of treatment of prisoners. Publicists were not interested, for example, in legal or moral distinctions between slavery and indentured service, and the litany of misery and ill-treatment ignored the fact that the sufferings of Colchester's prisoners were not unique: the lot of common soldiers as they were pillaged and marched in rain and hunger in 1648 recalls the fate of other soldiers after other defeats, including that of the parliamentary prisoners after Lostwithiel. Now, however, royalist polemic added a striking rhetoric of enslavement, as in the reports of 'the Captiv'd Welch ... Marketted, like Cattel, by the Head', and 'sold as slaves and for slaves'.[39] Such rhetoric had political resonance, for it presented the king's as the party of Englishmen's freedom and law. It also conjured up visions of Englishmen as slave-masters and slaves, roles normally allotted to the non-Christian, the racially inferior, and the alien. Parliament, wrote Bishop King, now practised 'the Turkish Art, / To Ship your taken Pris'ners for a Mart'. The Saints were no better than Turks. Once they had claimed to set their brethren free, but now they sold or killed them:

> Though luckless Colchester in this out-vies
> Argiers' or Tunis' shamefull Merchandise;
> Where the Starv'd Souldiers (as th'agreement was)
> Might not be suffer'd to their Dwelling pass,
> Till, led about by some insulting Band,
> They first were shew'd in Triumph through the Land;
> In which for lack of Dyet, or of strength
> If any fainted through the Marche's length,

---

[36] Smith, *Colonists in Bondage*, 154–5; *Chirk Castle Accounts, A.D. 1605–1666*, comp. W. M. Myddelton (St Albans, 1908), 77.

[37] *CCC* 4. 2671.

[38] *CCC* 3. 1831; Rushworth, 7. 1247, 1278; *Mercurius Electicus*, 57 (19–26 Dec. 1648), 541–2. Two weeks after the Lords' order, however, Ashburnham's name was on the list of those excluded from pardon. *ODNB*, 'John Asburnham'.

[39] King, *Poems*, 106; Gatford, *Englands Complaint*, 11.

> Void of the Breasts of Men, this Murth'rous Crew
> All those they could drive on no further, Slew.[40]

It was a comprehensive indictment, accusing parliamentarians of failure of Christianity, of breach of faith, of enslavement, of cruel infliction of shame and hunger, and of murder.[41]

There were unmistakably new, harsh, unforgiving elements in the treatment of prisoners after the second civil war. They were not confined to the crisis year of 1648 although, over time, moderation, habit, and inertia largely reasserted themselves. This harshness became part of the royalist canon of parliamentarian cruelty and tyranny. What turned Colchester into the stuff of royalist legend, however, was not fire or the picturesque hunger of its civilians or the courage of its defenders or the 'enslavement' of the defeated, but the 'martyrdom' of Lucas and Lisle.

ANXIETY, MYTH, AND MEMORY

This second war and its aftermath were not simple continuations of the first war and the first parliamentary victory. Much was new, distinctive, and potentially dangerous to the old parliamentary polity and to old social relations. We have noted the anxiety and bitterness that marked 1648. If the royalists were desperate and had embarked on a gamblers' throw, sometimes encouraged by the sense that they had nothing further to lose, parliamentarians fought not only with the conviction that the royalists had broken faith and cast the kingdom again into 'war and blood', but also with a suspicion that many on their own side could no longer be trusted. During the siege soldiers on the front lines wondered, as they contemplated London's unsettled politics, that those whom they had 'lookt upon as friends, & to carry on ye same designe' should now pull in different directions and hazard their own destruction. Victory brought no relief. Internal divisions and distrust between parliamentarians continued to exacerbate political and military insecurities. Veterans like Osborne feared that their efforts would prove to have been in vain and that the villains of the war would 'escape ye sword of justice' as parliament again proved soft for, he wrote, 'of their clemency we have all had sad experience'.[42]

---

[40] King, *Poems*, 106–7.

[41] Ibid. 107. The poet bolstered his case with accusations of killings at Thame and Wheatley, and a marginal note recorded that at St Albans a Captain Grimes, formerly a tinker, had killed four prisoners 'being not able for Faintness to go on'. In 1650 it was reported that officers marching sick and starving Scottish prisoners towards Berwick 'were necessitated to kill above thirty, fearing the loss of them all, for they fell down in great numbers and said they were not able to march', 'Letter from Sir Arthur Hesilrige', in Slingsby, *Original Memoirs*, 341.

[42] BL Harl. MS 7001, fo. 186ᵛ. See the case of Captain Richard Humfrey, who joined the royalists at Colchester in a last desperate response to his escalating economic woes, University of Chicago, Regenstein Library, Bacon MS 4286.

Social and political insecurity and outrage, whether at traitorous royalist adventurism or barbarous parliamentary vengefulness, combined to heighten the nervousness and the polemical stridency that marked the siege and the months that followed. Many parliamentarians could agree with the royalists that restraints on social volatility had been loosed and that disorder and anarchy threatened. The royalists saw themselves as beset by '*a raw promiscuous rude Uncivilized Multitude*'; 'the people have drank *Opium*, and are all mad', said one.[43] Conservative parliamentarians for their part feared radical levellers and an uncontrolled mob, while parliamentarians of all stripes feared soldiers, both their own and the enemy's, many of whom had cast aside military discipline to prey on the populace. During the summer the House of Commons heard complaints of murder, assault, and robbery committed by their own troops upon civilian victims. By September reports of roving royalists, now outlaws as much as soldiers, who set upon civilians and soldiers alike, created an atmosphere of danger and instability in which rumours of massacre and murder flourished. Assassination joined the horrors of war in the polemicists' repertoire, and reports 'from good hands' named Fairfax himself as an intended victim.[44]

This sense of a society on the edge of chaos joined suspicion of baroque and secret negotiations that on the one hand might rob the king of his essential powers, or on the other might give away the cause for which devoted parliamentarians had fought. They coexisted with and were reinforced by vivid reporting of the cruel events and shocking aftermath of an infamous siege. It is a measure of the sense of emergency and of the extreme responses to it that already in the summer and autumn of 1648, the killing of the king had become a commonplace of royalist discourse. In August *Mercurius Aulicus* warned that strange stars and comets presaged the judgment of the gods on '*bloody Regicides*'. By the beginning of December the deposition and death of the king were treated as a foregone conclusion.[45]

Civil war rhetoric and polemic were never marked by coolness and balance, but in 1648 they exhibited a particular desperation. Parliamentarian rhetoric of blood, breach of faith, and individual atrocities (such as accusations of use of poisoned bullets) paled beside the royalist barrage. Royalist writers, masters of spin, ignored, downplayed, or postponed attention to the reverses of their own side, while inflating every minor setback of their enemies. They were adept at having it both ways: Colchester had plenty of food, said *Mercurius Aulicus* in mid-August, but in any case, they would fight 'so long as a horse hoofe [was] left in the Towne'.[46] They were ever optimistic, and saw light at the end of every

---

[43] *Loyall Sacrifice*, 73; *Mercurius Melancholicus*, 3.

[44] BL Harl. MS 7001, fo. 186ᵛ; Rushworth, 7. 1279–80; HMC, *13th Report. Appendix 1. Portland MSS*, 1. 492.

[45] *Mercurius Aulicus*, [no. 2], [9]; *Mercurius Elencticus*, 54 (29 Nov.–6 Dec. 1648), 517; and see *Mercurius Pragmaticus*, 16 (11–18 July), [Q4]; 23 (*sic*, 24) (5–12 Sept.), G.

[46] *Mercurius Aulicus* ([21 Aug., 1648]), 23.

tunnel. When defeat could not be denied, they found new weapons with which to vilify the enemy.

At every stage, the weapons they deployed with most enthusiasm were abuse, scorn, and ridicule. They raised traditional spectres of cannibalism and offences against women and children, including terrorization of women in childbed; they reported torture and death by pressing; they titillated their readers with ad hominem attacks that accused parliamentarians individually and collectively of physical, social, and sexual failings. Their targets ranged from individuals to generalized 'Saints of reputation', from members of parliament to excise men and whores. Many attacks derived from the events of the siege, for Colchester was 'the very center of . . . Loyall thoughts', but the wider national scene was not forgotten. Cromwell was hailed as 'Oliver, oh ever refulgent NOSE', a minister was dismissed as the son of a mustard-maker, the misfortune of a colonel shot in the testicles was celebrated, and the radical member of parliament Miles Corbett was stigmatized as a 'Monster', 'a hideous Creature', and a Jew, who was abused, kicked, and caned (in itself an affront to a gentleman) by cavaliers who encountered him in the street with a whore on his arm. In a similar vein scandals were improvised with relish, including adultery between Cromwell and Lambert's 'Pretty Spouse', while collectively parliament '[fed] hie, / *Lucullus*-like to heighten Luxurie', and 'tumbl[ed] on . . . Yvorie Beds'; there was 'not a member of the House / But is a Couckold maker'.[47]

Throughout the siege the most persistent attacks were directed against Fairfax, only to grow in venom in its aftermath. Indeed, at this time he overshadowed Cromwell in the royalist pantheon of villains; it was Fairfax who loomed as a possible 'King *Tom*'. His standing not only as lord general and commander at Colchester, but also as the personification and leader of army power and a potential contender for supreme rule in the state, prompted repetitive abuse that rang the changes on a few major themes. He was '*Black Tom* of the *North*'; he was 'Sir gouty-foot Thomas' and 'His *Gowty Excellency*'; he was a cuckold, his 'swarthy brow' adorned by horns; he was 'Sir Rebell *Fairfax*' who acted from 'Vindictive spleene' and 'bloudy inclination'; he was unprofessional and cautious to the point of cowardice.[48] Much of this was the standard stuff of polemic,

---

[47] Demophilus Philanactos, *Two Epitaphs, Occasioned by the Death of Sr Charles Lucas, and Sr George Lisle, basely assassinated at Colchester* (1648), A2, 6; Mercurius Elencticus, *The Anatomy of Westminster Iuncto, or A Summary of their Designes agdinst [sic] the King, City, and Kingdom* (n.pl., [1648]), B; Mercurius Melancholicus, 4; Mercurius Pragmaticus, 16 (11–18 July 1648), [Q3]; 23 [24] (5–12 Sept.), G; 25 (12–19 Sept.), K–K; 31 (24–31 Oct.), [Xx3–3]; Mercurius Aulicus, no. 1, 7; Mercurius Anglicus, no. 1 (27 July–3 Aug., 1648), A2–[A3]; Mercurius Elencticus, 42 (6–13 Sept., 1648), 341–2, 45 (27 Sept.–4 Oct. [375]).

[48] Mercurius Aulicus, no. 1, 7, no. 2, 11, 13, no. 3, 21; Mercurius Elencticus, 33 (5–12 July 1648), 256, 40 (23–9 Aug.), 334; 41 (30 Aug.–6 Sept.) 331 (bis); Demophilus Philanactos, *Two Epitaphs*, 5–6; Mercurius Pragmaticus, 23 [24] (5–12 Sept.), F3; Mercurius Anglicus, 1 (27 July–3 Aug. 1648), A1. In defeat royalists comforted themselves by aspersions on the parliamentarians'

now allied to the traditional literature of atrocity and hardship in war. It was spiced with generous pinches of sexual scandal, jokes, and innuendo that aspired to return a sense of power and superiority to the increasingly powerless. The authors' vigour was in part a function of the failure of their cause.

Theirs was not the work of fools, however. Their sources of information were excellent, particularly for events in London and the House of Commons and for the progress of negotiations with the king, and beneath the spin their political and military comments were often shrewd. With the inevitability of surrender had come dignity and pathos. By late August even *Mercurius Pragmaticus* could not deny hardship inside the walls but declared it served as a spur to valour. *Mercurius Elencticus* proclaimed that Colchester's defenders were as 'valiant' and 'couragious' as ever, but by the beginning of September he could no longer jest on 'so sad a *subject*'.[49] After the executions of Lucas and Lisle, royalist publicists adopted the language of moral and legal outrage. For them it was never other than murder in cold blood, for which no excuse or palliation could be offered, and Fairfax became a serious moral villain. Against the perfidy and cruelty of parliamentarians were set the loyalty and spotless valour of the victims, whose fate acquired Christ-like echoes: in one version Lucas was tied to a pillar before being 'cruelly butcher'd', in another Fairfax, like Pontius Pilate, abdicated responsibility to vengeful Ireton and Rainsborough.[50] Royalist publicists created the memory of Colchester as a history of martyrdom.

Their newsletters became the basis of successive narrations, and a stream of '*Elegious Poem[s]*', indifferent in quality but passionate in feeling, embroidered on their themes. The language was that of 'torrents' of 'Loyall Blood', of 'butchering true spotlesse Innocence', of 'wad[ing] in Blood, and div[ing] in Gore', of 'bleeding honour', and of the contrast between the exemplary honour of the undaunted martyrs and the shame of their judges who had 'murther'd [their] own *honors*' and no longer merited 'the Souldier's Name'.[51] It was above all the language of murder, of killing in cold blood men who had surrendered, of mercy promised and withdrawn, of betrayal of the codes of war, and thereby of the soldierly honour of Fairfax and his officers. The accepted military meaning of surrender to mercy played virtually no part in this discourse, which insisted on crime and illegality, and on the barbarity of denial of mercy in its colloquial sense. In a sermon composed—although not delivered—for the obsequies of

---

'unheroic' waiting game at Colchester: 'Resolving now no more to fight, but lurk / Trench'd in their Line or earth'd within a Work. / Where not like Souldiers they, but Watchmen, creep, / Arm'd for no other office but to sleep.' King, *Poems*, 102.

[49] *Mercurius Pragmaticus*, 22 (22–9 Aug. 1648), B2; *Mercurius Elencticus*, 40 (23–9 Aug. 1648), 329; 41 (30 Aug.–6 Sept.), 327 (bis).

[50] *Mercurius Pragmaticus*, 23 [24], F3; *Famous Tragedie of King Charles I*, 25.

[51] John Quarles, *Fons Lachrymarum; or a Fountain of Tears . . . And an Elegy Upon that Son of Valor Sir Charls [sic] Lucas* (1655), 115, 119–21; *An elegie On the Death of that most Noble and Heroick Knight, Sir Charles Lucas* [1648], broadsheet; King, *Poems*, 102–3.

Lucas and Lisle, and printed within weeks of their death, the author conceded that Colchester had surrendered 'upon Tearmes of Mercy', but even such a glancing recognition of treaty and law was exceptional. Instead guilt was assigned without nuance: the victims 'were most barbarously, and cruelly shot to death by the appointment of the Army'.[52] The themes of royalist outrage were to vary little over the years. Most writers were untroubled by legalistic details, and many assumed a false premise of quarter granted and then withdrawn. The standard royalist accusation remained one of tyrannical and arbitrary action that 'contradict[ed] / The Laws of Justice':

> Say *Tyrants*, say, was't not a shameful strife
> To send a *Death*, after a promis'd *Life*?
> If this be *Mercy*, Heav'n protect us all
> From such a *Mercy*, so *tyrannical*.[53]

Thus to 'cruelties immense' were added accusations of tyranny and overturning the 'course and current of the Lawes'. Parliament's claim to stand for liberty and the laws was exposed as a fraud, and the royalists, through the deaths of their martyrs, shown to be the party not only of loyalty but of the rights and protections secured by the law. Fairfax's treaty was 'a Cheat', and his claim to have executed military justice a pretence. Posterity, like the authors, would 'pronounce Crimes to be Crimes'.[54]

In 1656 Evelyn summed up the received wisdom—albeit with a new primary villain—when he visited the town and recalled that Lucas and Lisle 'were barbarously shot to death & murdered by *Ireton* in cold blood & after rendission upon articles'. By 1656, too, Carter's assertion that grass would not grow where the martyrs had fallen was accepted 'as a kind of miracle', and indeed the site was still bare in 1662.[55] With the Restoration martyrdom was officially proclaimed. In 1648 Lucas and Lisle had been privately buried in the north aisle of St Giles's church, long associated with the Lucas family. In June 1661 their funerals were magnificently solemnized with full civic honours and a black marble stone was laid over the vault; it proclaimed that they 'were . . . by the command of Sir Thomas Fairfax, the General of the Parliament army, in cold blood barbarously murdered'. According to tradition and in one of the many ironies of civil war reconciliations and reversals, the duke of Buckingham, once the royalist insurgent of 1648 but now married to Fairfax's daughter, approached

---

[52] *The Triumph of Loyalty: or The Happinesse of a Suffering Subject* (London, 1648), 17 and title-page.

[53] Quarles, *Fons Lachrymarum*, 119.

[54] *Elegie On the Death of* . . . *Sir Charles Lucas*; King, *Poems*, 103, 105; Demophilus Philanactos, *Two Epitaphs*, 6.

[55] Evelyn, *Diary*, 3. 177; by Feb. 1652, at the time of Ireton's funeral, Evelyn already held him responsible for the executions, ibid. 3. 58. By 1660 his memory was shakier and he included Capel among the immediate victims of 'the transaction at *Colchester*' who 'sufferd in cold bloud, after Articles of reddition', ibid. 3. 250.

Charles II to have the epitaph erased. Lord Lucas, Sir Charles's brother, agreed to abide by the king's decision, so long as he could replace the original inscription with one that declared that Lucas and Lisle had been 'barbarously murdered for their Loyalty to K. Charles I. and that his son K. Charles II. ordered this memorial of their loyalty to be erased'. He made his point and on the king's order, so it was said, the original epitaph was carved in as deeply as possible.[56]

In time response to the deaths of Lucas and Lisle came to be less intertwined with the supernatural. By 1722 Defoe drily noted that the story that grass would not grow 'is now dropp'd, and the grass, I suppose, grows there as in other places', while Morant dismissed it as 'vulgar' and explained the previous absence of grass by the 'great resort of people to see the place'.[57] That great resort is, however, revealing of public interest and memory, and later generations still grew passionate over the fate of Lucas and Lisle. Fairfax has had his defenders, including S. R. Gardiner and C. H. Firth, but some modern historians, following the seventeenth-century martyrologists, still see the executions as murder.[58]

The central problem, of course, was not that Fairfax and his council had acted ''gainst all Lawes' but that the rigour with which they had executed them was rare and highly visible; hence, even before the surrender, the outcry against his refusal to allow women and children to leave the town, and after it the shock and outrage at his lack of clemency to the martyrs. Royalists insisted that he had 'Shed . . . the Blood of War in time of Peace', a claim that suggested radical incomprehension of the effect that this second war had on parliamentarians, who saw no reason to be conciliatory to enemies whom they had been forced to defeat for the second time.[59]

A few royalists indeed clung to their view of Fairfax as the moderate face of parliamentarianism and attempted to lessen his responsibility by attributing blame for the fate of Lucas and Lisle to those implacable members of his council of war, Ireton and Rainsborough. In 1649, for example, one martyrologist portrayed Fairfax as protesting that execution would infringe the laws of arms but succumbing to radical blackmail that argued that failure to act would undermine his power by laying him open to suspicion of royalist sympathies. As he handed the victims over he murmured:

> My Soule (I feele) is wondrously perplext,
> Who knowes but mine or your turne may be next?

---

[56] Morant, *Essex*, 1. 68.   [57] Ibid. 1. 67–8.

[58] Round, 'The Case of Lucas and Lisle', *TRHS*, NS 8 (1894), 157, 159, 165, 180; P. R. Newman, 'The King's Servants: Conscience, Principle, and Sacrifice in Armed Royalism', in Morrill, Slack, and Woolf (eds.), *Public Duty and Private Conscience*, 241.

[59] King, *Poems*, 109; Demophilus Philanactos, *Two Epitaphs*, 7.

The anonymous author indeed foresaw the conservative political and social anxieties Fairfax was later to express, but the problem with his half-hearted exoneration was that Fairfax himself took responsibility for and justified the executions in 1648 and to the end of his life. He was on this issue quite as implacable as Ireton and Rainsborough. He had acted according to military law and within his military powers. Having once decided to execute 'examples' before granting quarter to the remaining prisoners who had yielded to mercy, there was no difficulty in producing sufficiently plausible accusations, although by strict interpretation of the rules of mercy none were necessary. For Fairfax, 'military Justice' and vengeance for 'innocent Blood' and for the troubles brought on Colchester and the kingdom demanded satisfaction. His argument that Lucas and Lisle were 'mere soldiers of fortune' and socially inconsiderable relegated them to a category of deracinated professionals and social inferiors rather than that of fellow professionals and fellow Englishmen; they could be judged and punished according to the harshest criteria of military law without consideration either of social links or of the magnanimity to the defeated that was in theory a mark of soldierly honour and true nobility.[60] In contrast to the careful civilities of Boarstall, the implacable outcome at Colchester threatened to open the way to a harsher conflict in which the laws of war became a vehicle and a justification for severities that they had formerly moderated.

---

[60] *The Famous Tragedie of King Charles I, Basely Butchered* (n.pl., 1649), 25; Rushworth, 7. 1243; Bodl. MS Fairfax, 36, fos. 6–6ᵛ.

Conclusion

This book has attempted to uncover some of the ideas that lay behind legitimate engagement in war, to examine its practices and personnel, and to explore some of the legal and social complications added by *civil* war. It has emphasized the intimacy that resulted on the one hand from the weapons with which it was fought and from its physical environment as mobile armies marched through the countryside or garrisoned towns and strongholds, and on the other from the links of family, friendship, or pre-war antipathy that persisted between enemies. It has shown a small society at war within itself and suggested that, while this did not make post-war reconciliation easy, it enhanced the perceived value of getting along with former enemies and a return to a viable if imperfect status quo. It has stressed the role of laws in governing wartime conduct and the pressures that put strains on effective and uniform enforcement, ranging from the necessity not to punish military offences so severely that enforcement itself led to more disorder, desertion, and mutiny, to the temptations to abandon law for reprisal and 'justified' punishment. It has explored the character of officers and men and the challenges of instilling order, professional discipline, and skills in soldiers who were often raw and not strongly committed either to the army or the cause they fought in. It has looked at the incidence of chance and accident, inescapable in this as other wars, and the fallible connection between plan and action, and suggested that for both parties such uncertainties were palliated by a providential faith in God's guiding hand. That faith, however, did not lessen the responsibility of individuals to be as active and competent as they could in God's chosen cause, whether that cause was parliamentarian or royalist.

Despite the hindrances that lay in their way—of technology, personnel, intelligence, and politics—the armies of the civil war constituted a powerful military presence and had remarkable achievements to their credit. Nevertheless they were neither stable nor homogeneous nor, often, united bodies. It is tempting to speak of 'the army', whether royalist or parliamentarian, as an entity to which, *per se*, intentions, actions, and characteristics can be ascribed. This book has tried instead to describe more protean forces that frequently displayed contradictory characteristics of military virtue and military vice, of piety and lawlessness, and that operated in a world in which even more was unknown and unpredictable than is the case in modern wars. The armies that were the instruments of policy for both royalists and parliamentarians were unwieldy bodies, capable of great achievements and of embarrassing disasters; they could not be taken for granted and their management was a matter of constant concern to their masters. The political and religious leaders of both sides could never forget, in their calculations, the nature of their armies.

The nature of the armies was also central to the civilian experience of war, which in turn had powerful political consequences. War as it was experienced by civilians has been treated only peripherally in this book. I hope in a companion volume to explore the impact of the war on the civilian population of England, and to consider some of its social, material, and intellectual consequences. It is already clear that in this intimate, geographically wide-ranging conflict civilian and military experience could not be divorced. Civilians not only suffered in besieged towns, observed battles, counted the dead, and bore the presence of quartering and marching troops. They also paid vastly increased taxes that extended to new and humbler levels of society and to new commodities. Trade was often interrupted and cash money scarce. Rich and poor alike lost household goods to predatory troops and sometimes to opportunistic neighbours. Property and financial relationships were disrupted when land was sequestered or interest and rents became uncollectable. Destructive soldiers and discontented tenants alike trashed records, and the gusto with which 'evidences' were destroyed fed the anxiety of the propertied that the foundations of orderly society were threatened. Old ties were strained and broken as kindred, friends, neighbours, and colleagues found themselves on opposing sides and would-be neutrals found their position untenable.

Yet there were also many who did well in the war. Like other wars, it offered new opportunities and it too had its profiteers. If many suppliers had long waits for payment or, particularly on the royalist side, accumulated unrecoverable debts, others throve by supplying armies' needs. Nehemiah Wallington's more successful brother grew prosperous supplying parliament's armies: by 1651, for example, a single shipment of 4,000 spades and shovels brought him £306.[1] Large-scale entrepreneurs developed profitable putting-out systems that provided laundry or shoes; armament makers were busy, although payment was often slow; more modestly, nurses entered the cash economy in large numbers as they cared for the wounded. Able young men like John Rushworth, William Clarke, and Thomas Clarges served their causes as recorders and administrators and made connections that furthered their later careers. Some men discovered the attractions of an active life of affairs and the opportunities that came with it. William Osborne, for example, had assured his plaintive wife that once the siege of Colchester was over he would not again leave the comforts of home, but within weeks of the surrender he set off on a mission to the Low Countries: 'Let

---

[1] *CSP Dom. 1651*, 587, and 557, 564; Paul S. Seaver, *Wallington's World: A Puritan Artisan in Seventeenth Century London* (Stanford, Calif., 1985), 235 n. 28; see also Ben Coates, *The Impact of the English Civil War on the Economy of London, 1642–1650* (Aldershot, 2004), chs. 3 and 4, on the impact of the war on London's financial and manufacturing economy.

not my absence which may raise me, cast ye down', he wrote to her.[2] Brokers dealt in plundered and commandeered goods, and the eminent did not scruple to buy them: the earl of Manchester bought a set of Lady Bankes's tapestries that had found their way, through the hands of the parliamentary colonel who liberated them, to a London broker.[3] With the expansion of regulation and bureaucracy opportunities, and hence rewards, increased for informers. Skilled operators sought and found ways to exploit the state's punitive legal and financial apparatus to the disadvantage of fellow citizens but to their own benefit. As a crony wrote to Thomas Gell in 1647, 'I have some business of good consequence to impart unto you, wherein I conceive you may much advantage yourself in point of profit, and do good to some of your friends besides.'[4] His business methods included the provision of dinner and 'plentiful drink' for promising witnesses against putative royalists and the lure of payment of £10 for each victim whose delinquency they 'proved'.

During the 1640s England experienced most of the evils of war, sometimes as occasional aberrations but often over protracted periods, and in both minor and major episodes. As we have seen, they did not take the English by surprise. The pre-war rhetoric of justified war had recognized its accompanying evils and the news from contemporary Europe had familiarized them with potential horrors. In 1642 King Charles had temperately noted that 'the residence of an Army is not usually pleasant to any place'. By July 1643 the Speaker of the House of Commons observed, 'Such is the nature of war as to be full of troubles and burdens, even to those for whose good it is undertaken. For various and peremptory necessities of an army . . . must needs produce bitter effects not only to enemies but even to friends.'[5] The transition from theory and news from abroad to immediate and neighbourly experience shocked and dismayed English men and women.

Preceding chapters have tried to convey something of the actuality of this civil war, and the responses of soldiers and civilians to its professional, moral, and material demands. Study of the war reveals, alongside occasional atrocities, frequent cruelties, and vituperative narratives, the attempt to restrain conduct within bounds that would make it possible to preserve a recognizable—and, structurally, a fundamentally unchanged—English society. So on both sides military discipline sought to prevent 'the peremptory necessities' and the disorderly and often violent proclivities of their soldiers from producing incurably 'bitter effects'. Yet this effort had to be balanced against the need for troops who were

---

[2] BL Harl. MS 7001, fos. 186, 189–93.

[3] Kingston Lacy, Bankes MSS, 'Autograph Letters,' I, no foliation: 15 Jan. 1646/7, 'goods sold by Bingham to Stone the broker'. The earl of Manchester paid £150 for a set of tapestries depicting 'the history of Astraea & Celidon' (another list suggested a price of 'two or 300 l.').

[4] Derbys. RO, Gell MSS D258 41/31 (ya), and see 41/31 (za) and (ab).

[5] *The True Copie of a Letter written By Captaine Wingate, now Prisoner in Ludlow, taken by the Malignant Partie* (1642), [6]; Bodl. MS Tanner 62/1B, fo. 168.

both competent and motivated, and was complicated by the fact that much legitimate military motivation, most notably the right to kill and plunder, ran counter to the restraints and protections mandated by other parts of military law and by social prudence and compassion. The conjunction of authorized takings (for example, by regimental foraging parties), customary and legitimate plunder (as after the storm of a town) and undisciplined, free enterprise seizure of private goods (as at the end of the siege of Colchester) was familiar to every level of society in the war years. It is hard not to believe that such familiarity influenced many in their willingness to accept regimes in the 1650s and 1660s that they found less than perfect.

The two sieges described in detail above embodied many of the characteristics of war discussed in earlier chapters. Both revealed the survival of professional rules and customs in relations between enemies, whether benevolently as at Boarstall or irritably and legalistically as at Colchester. We previously saw similar conduct moderating the harshness of war in, for example, the parliamentary soldiers who saved Hopton's troops from the consequences of their premature assumption of a truce in 1646, or the convivial drinking party of old colleagues, now enemies, at Pontefract. Nor was the harshness of defeat at Colchester, although extreme and ultimately controversial, unrelated to earlier experience at Hopton castle or Leicester or Basing House.

Proceedings at Colchester brought new severities and seemed to foretell more to come, but they also revealed military continuities. The soldiers who fought there differed little from those of the first civil war—if, indeed, they were not themselves veterans. On both sides they required careful handling by their officers. Despite royalist claims of notable loyalty in 1648, their men deserted and mutinied just as earlier soldiers had done, while even Fairfax's New Model troops had grown, at the end, so undisciplined that their officers, like their earlier counterparts, slashed at the men in vain attempts to enforce orders. On both sides we can see how the desires and disorders of common soldiers could force amendments to the policies of their betters, but also the importance of officer leadership and discipline—although the comment that royalist officers at Colchester were superior to those of the first civil war is a telling confirmation of earlier failures. It seems in fact possible that the royalist command group at Colchester not only demonstrated competence, personal rapport, and the solidifying pressure of acute crisis, but also benefited from the king's absence from the scene, for it removed the focus for the divisive factional manœuvring that had previously weakened the royalist officer corps.

Conditions at Colchester made it an exceptionally miserable siege, but they were not unique and demonstrate again the vulnerability of armies to factors beyond the control of their commanders. It is indeed remarkable, given the appalling weather and flooded roads and bridges, how little both offensive and defensive actions were diverted from their purposes, but the physical conditions serve as another reminder of what life in armies that are usually collectively represented as biddable agents of higher policy was really like. They confirm the influence of external conditions on morale and on what the soldiers were actually capable of doing, and the consequences that could range unpredictably from desertion and mutiny to heightened enthusiasm. Brereton had recognized that cold and hunger set limits to what he could ask of his soldiers in Cheshire; on the other hand, the miseries endured by Essex's defeated troops as they marched away after Lostwithiel in yet another wet season had brought the later benefit of a morale-enhancing desire for revenge at Newbury. Nor were Colchester's soldiers alone in their sufferings in 1648 or in their responses to them. In June and July, as the parliamentarian Captain Samuel Birch marched his men towards victory at Preston, he noted the 'extreamity of wet and foul weather' that had 'not beene seene in the memory of man'. It was, he said, as 'miserable [a] time for the souldiers as I have seene at any time'.[6] By September he could congratulate himself that his men, unlike those of other officers, had stayed with him, at least until they were paid. Yet his company had an attrition rate of 33 per cent: of 149 officers and men raised between May and September, 49 ran way and 4 were 'turned off'—presumably cashiered—for mutiny or stealing.[7] Furthermore, when in November half of Birch's company were offered the opportunity to go home, 'the greatest part of them' seized it.[8] We are reminded that the problems of a volatile soldiery, often cold, hungry, and unpaid, and subject to the vagaries of English climate, long marches, and local inhabitants who rarely welcomed their presence, were endemic and bedevilled both armies. The soldiers who voted with their feet at Colchester were part of a continuum that stretched from the desertions of the war's early years to the straggling absentees in Scotland in 1651, and that included godly New Modellers as well as ungodly cavaliers.

For all the disorder and unpredictability of the civil war's armies and the desta-bilizing miseries to which they were subject, the heroic efforts of officers—and to a lesser extent of godly ministers—had a remarkable degree of success in turning them into effective agents of their respective causes. In their mixed character they were less different from armies of later ages than we are sometimes tempted to think: Wellington would have recognized much; the First World War had its mutinies; the 'liberated' property of the Second was not unrelated to the plunder of the seventeenth century; participants in other civil wars have faced the conflicting attractions of restraint and retribution.

One characteristic of the English civil war, however, is distinctive but has received little attention: its demonstration of the strength of English legalism and of the English as a people of the law. The claims of both sides to be the upholders of England's law are familiar, and we have already noted the importance of

---

[6] HMC, *Fourteenth Report. Appendix, Part II. Manuscripts of . . . the Duke of Portland*, 3 (1894), 174.

[7] Ibid. 181–6. Of the further fourteen men raised from Oct. to Jan., two ran away for 'knavery' and stealing. A few men also left with permission, e.g. because they were sick.

[8] Ibid. 178.

the issue of sovereignty and that the Militia Ordnance of 1642 forced a choice between the primary duty of obedience to the king's law or to parliament's, a choice that played out in ways that went beyond the initial decision as to whether it was legitimate to bear arms against the king. Even those who initially tried to evade choice still faced decisions as to who had a right to levy taxes or what constituted treason. These were large constitutional questions, but they had local and personal applications. Responses might differ but they persistently revealed English addiction to the authority of law, and to its processes as well as its more abstract claims. To ordinary seventeenth-century English men and women the adjudication of life's smaller conflicts—over money or property or minor violence or trespass—was more immediately the stuff of law than high constitutional argument. Yet reliance on and familiarity with law at this lower level gave added force to larger rhetorical and partisan claims to be acting as the champion of the law that was the Englishman's birthright.

This familiarity with and reliance on orderly, regular legal rules and procedure was evident in the execution of military as well as civilian law. In the military sphere we have seen its force in the observation of unwritten as well as written, codified law. It was evident in adherence to customary processes of negotiation, and in appeals to 'soldierly' usages of very diverse kinds that ranged from licence to strip dead enemies who fell within a specified distance of defenders' walls to immunity for surgeons and their mates on the battlefield. These rules, furthermore, must be observed precisely and specifically, and associated 'rights' could be withdrawn if they were not: rejection of Lucas's claim that his correspondence with Fairfax was sufficient to release him from his obligations as a prisoner contributed to his subsequent vulnerability as a parole-breaker. Practice was less than perfect, but failure to observe conventions could be exploited as evidence that the enemy was an offender against the laws of war.

Adherence to formal legal procedures was strikingly revealed in the application of codified articles of war. What is legal is not, of course, necessarily just or equitable, a fact made abundantly clear by the courts martial already discussed in which the deterrent and exemplary nature of military law and, in its execution, the need to be responsive to current military circumstances, might result in 'unfair' and unequal penalties for similar offences. Nevertheless discretion was exercised within the limits set by an army's written codes of law, and overseen by the judge advocate and senior officers. If a court could choose whether a desertion merited punishment as a capital crime or as a lesser offence, it was nonetheless not free to decide that pawning arms merited death. In both cases its members were bound to act within the limits set by the articles of war. We have seen the care with which these courts distinguished between felonies and lesser offences and weighed degrees of responsibility. We have also seen the care with which the procedures of military law were observed, from the depositions of witnesses to the votes, given in ascending order of seniority so that juniors were not swayed by their superiors, as to guilt and fitting punishment. Military law, then as now, was not notably humane, but in the civil war it was not arbitrary, its workings were familiar, and regular processes of interpretation of law and of decision-making were followed. Rogue courts and court-presidents seem to have been rare. Instead a military legal system operating according to recognized rules and procedures was accepted, if not loved, by the soldiers it regulated. Offenders and their judges acted within a known covenant of military law.

When military law, either customary or codified, intersected with civilian law, difficulties multiplied, and after the second civil war they became more acute, as the cases of its defeated leaders were to reveal. Among ordinary soldiers the prospect of disbandment roused fears that they would be held liable under civilian law for their wartime actions in suits brought by men unsympathetic to the cause they had fought in, and heard by equally unsympathetic courts. One consequence of engagement in such a civil war as theirs was that after it was over participants did not take ship to a distant homeland but resettled in the same country and under the same law as civilians whom they may have hurt or whose property they had destroyed, damaged, or appropriated.

In 1647, in response to the army's anxieties, parliament passed indemnity laws that pardoned soldiers for injuries done to private persons *as* soldiers while in arms and for the service of parliament.[9] The protection was limited, for it did not extend to all actions done *while* soldiers; pardon would not extend, for example, to an unprovoked drunken assault on a civilian, although it would probably protect a soldier who had injured a civilian who obstructed him in performance of his duty. The history of the indemnity cases, of which over 1,100 were heard between 1647 and 1655 by members of the special committee appointed for the purpose, reveals the readiness to appeal to law on the part both of the civilians who originated the cases in local courts and of the soldiers who appealed their findings before the committee. Later historians have seen exoneration of soldiers—by no means a foregone conclusion—as a case of victors' justice practised by a court packed in their favour; soldiers at the time complained that the court was biased against them.[10] In fact the indemnity hearings reveal a remarkably conscientious committee attempting to disentangle cases brought by Englishmen who believed that appeal to law was a normal and proper mode of dispute-resolution and had a reasonable hope of a satisfactory outcome. Some were also wily and knowing enough to attempt to manipulate the law in their favour, as in the case of the civilian who had arranged for a short incarceration so that he could later bring a suit for false

---

[9] Firth and Rait, *Acts and Ordinances*, 1. 936–8, 953–4; Gentles, *New Model Army*, 121–5; B. Donagan, 'The Army, the State and the Soldier in the English Civil War,' in Michael Mendle (ed.), *The Putney Debates of 1647: The Army, the Levellers and the English State* (Cambridge, 2001), 90–5.

[10] *An Humble Representation from his excellencie Sir Thomas Fairfax, and the councel of the armie . . . Decemb. 7. 1647* (1647), 23–4.

imprisonment (it was ultimately dismissed as 'vexatious' molestation), while other defendants grew skilled in obstruction.[11] Hearings were time-consuming and often imposed hardships of time and travel, but they were notable for their procedural correctness and attention to the evidence, for the committee's efforts to ensure that the litigants had proper representation, and for the time (normally three hearings) devoted to each case. The indemnity laws were an outcome of the need to protect ex-soldiers against civilian exploitation of revivified civilian courts, in cases that were sometimes justified and sometimes put-up jobs, by creating a new and temporary appeals court; they worked in part because they operated in a recognizably 'legal' fashion.

English law provided one of the significant continuities in English society in the war years and later, not only through its forms and methods and their adaptation to new purposes but also through the survival of most of its content. There were some significant changes, as in the disappearance of Star Chamber and the Court of Wards, and hopeful programmes for legal reform, but despite the disruptive circumstances of war the basic laws of property, inheritance, tenancy, and contract that perpetuated the structure of relations between families and neighbours survived. Sequestration, fines, and ensuing debt might force sales and arouse enmities through hearings that were retributive and sometimes visibly corrupt, but even they retained a semblance of traditional legal hearings.

For a time, however, in the immediate aftermath of the second war, it seemed that a punitive system of victor's justice was being instituted in the treason trials of its royalist leaders and in those that followed the surrender of Pontefract in 1649. In these cases, unlike that of Lucas and Lisle, the offenders were tried under civilian treason law and in civilian courts. These punitive trials of defeated enemies by civilian law disturbed some soldiers, who feared that surrender to quarter would lose its protective power and that its benefits would become a matter of political and arbitrary choice. One of them, Captain Wingate, offered his own case in the first civil war as a precedent to his fellow members of the House of Commons; given quarter in the field by his royalist captors he was nonetheless later tried but, he said, his life was then 'foreborne'.[12] Soldierly protests were ineffectual, and in 1649 Colonel Morris, a double turncoat who had been unexceptionably excluded from quarter when Pontefract surrendered, was tried at the assizes for the political crime of treason, denied counsel, and subjected as a felon to the accompanying humiliations of manacling at his trial and of hanging. He pleaded that as a 'martial man' he should be tried by a court martial (which could in fact have condemned him to death with perfect military

---

[11] PRO, SP 24/3, fos. 22ᵛ–23, 58–58ᵛ, 63. Gentles argues persuasively that the cases heard by the indemnity committee represent only a part of the 'several thousand judicial prosecutions' brought against soldiers all over the country in the years 1645–55. Gentles, *New Model Army*, 122.
[12] Worcester College, Clarke MSS, 114, fo. 92ᵛ.

propriety as a turncoat), and furthermore that actions in support of the king could not be construed as treason under the then ruling statute of 25 Edward III. Parliament had indeed recognized the problem of defining treason in the new circumstances following execution of the king and abolition of the monarchy, and in May had passed a new treason law that formally established parliament as the institution to which loyalty was due. Morris's arguments were brusquely dismissed by his judges, as was his warning that his case offered a dangerous 'precedent to any soldiers hereafter'.[13] The restraints of *lex talionis* recognized in 1642 for a time gave way to reprisal and the need to assert publicly and visibly the new sovereign power in the state. Fortunately the tide of politically punitive actions against defeated military enemies receded, but it left eminent victims in its wake.

The varied fates of those involved in the second civil war exemplified the mingled strands of moderation and severity that characterized the war years. They provide evidence of the survival of old social links alongside new enmities, but they also reveal a more overt and unforgiving intrusion of unstable politics into what had formerly been a military relationship between enemies. That instability showed itself in fluctuations in power and policy that meant life or death for the royalist leaders of 1648. By the end of September the House of Commons had moved to attaint Norwich and impeach Capel, and sought elucidation from Fairfax as to the meaning of the terms of surrender, in particular his 'leaving them to the further Justice and Mercy of the Parliament'.[14] By mid-November however the prisoners' prospects had improved, and both Houses voted to reduce the penalties to banishment. On 13 December, in yet another reversal, the Commons revoked this decision as 'destructive to the Peace and Quiet of the Kingdom and derogatory to [its] justice'. Pride's Purge had intervened on 7 December and the prisoners faced the less tender mercies of the Rump parliament. The king's trial and execution followed; then came abolition of the House of Lords and the establishment of the High Court of Justice to try Norwich and Capel and three other royalist leaders. All pleaded that they had surrendered to quarter, but the court asserted that a military promise could not bar the action of a civil court. All were condemned to die and the executions of Capel, the earl of Holland, and the duke of

[13] Ibid.; Donagan, 'Atrocity, War Crime, and Treason', 1151–62; Firth and Rait, *Acts and Ordinances*, 2. 120–1, and see pp. 193–4 for the expanded version of 17 July 1649; the latter included protection of the property rights of heirs and wives of offenders, a position foreshadowed in the relief granted to Lady Capel in May.

[14] Parliamentary opinion was divided. Selden and the 'civilians' on the House of Commons argued that, quarter being once granted, lives should be saved. Others believed that Fairfax would be 'very bloody to condemn them when it lies in his power with a word to save them', but that 'should he write anything favourable' those who wanted execution 'would say he is against the doing of justice'. Fairfax was between a rock and a hard place, and the writer thought that the 'purpose [was] to bring the odium of the business upon him'. Worcester College, Clarke MSS, 114, fo. 92.

Hamilton swiftly followed. Norwich was granted a short respite which turned into a reprieve, for on 7 May 1649 he was pardoned and 'forthwith [set] at Liberty'.[15]

The fate of the prisoners thus followed a political trajectory. Parliament's recognition of military opinion as a valid component of decision did not prevent capital charges. The progression from initial agreement on trial for a capital crime, when anger and fear caused by the second war were fresh in members' minds, to the more benevolent penalty of banishment, followed by reinstatement of the death sentence, reflected the divisions and power struggles between moderates and conservatives on the one hand and unforgiving 'radicals' on the other, and the victory of the latter in December. By the time of the trials in March their desire for retributive justice against three of the accused had not cooled, while Norwich escaped by the narrowest of margins. The vote on his stay of execution ended with a tie (24–24), and he was saved by the casting vote of the Speaker, William Lenthall. The reasons offered for Lenthall's vote offer significant pointers to considerations that aided the post-war survival of a civil society. He acknowledged a debt for past favours—a reminder of the 'civilities' so carefully preserved at Boarstall—and Clarendon suggested that he may have been uncomfortable with the nature of the trials. It is also possible that some members of the court were moved by Norwich's 'many' creditors who, hardly disinterestedly, petitioned on his behalf, or by the fact that despite his intransigent royalism and fondness for impolitic jokes, he was a man whom they found it difficult to hate.[16] Taken together the suggested explanations are a reminder of ways in which social—and financial—links survived the war and sometimes softened its consequences, and of persistence of a sense that law should not be so distorted that it became a mere instrument of policy or revenge.

The story is also a reminder of the vagaries of conduct and motivation that make any simple picture of the consequences, both personal and national, of the civil war false to experience. Responses to actions varied not only according to unsettled politics but also according to the beliefs and circumstances of individuals and to changes in what, for want of a better term, can be called the public state of mind. The executions of Capel, Holland, and Hamilton in March 1649 still reflected anger at the treacherous infliction of another war on the country (although Capel was respected and his end regretted). Norwich's pardon in May suggests a softening of anger and perhaps a recollection of his relative harmlessness. It is interesting that on the same day the House made what looks very like a gesture of amends to Lady Capel, when it voted to discharge

---

[15] *CJ* 6. 32, 37, 45, 72, 96, 158–60, 204; *LJ* 10. 483, 590, 596, 598; S. R. Gardiner, *History of the Commonwealth and Protectorate*, 1. 10–11. A fifth prisoner, Sir John Owen, was also reprieved, possibly because he was, unlike the others, a relatively minor figure.

[16] Clarendon, *History*, 3. 207, 210; *CJ* 6. 159; *ODNB*, 'George Goring, first earl of Norwich'.

from sequestration a long list of properties inherited from her father or settled on her at her marriage by Capel's father.[17]

These incidents reveal some of the ways in which war intensified life's difficulties and uncertainties. The practices of law indeed offered continuities with the past, but it was still necessary to cope with new ordinances and new bureaucracies in matters ranging from church observances to tax liability. The methods of dealing with these and other government demands reveal another continuity in English life, for the importance of ties and influence did not wane. Adjustments had to be made as new cadres of influential men emerged, and even when the influence of old patrons survived it faced new constraints. The earl of Warwick, as we have seen, was instrumental in protecting the turncoat Colonel Farr from parliament's vengeance, but his urgent efforts could not save the life of his brother the earl of Holland. Yet 'friends' were as necessary as ever, although neither their influence nor their identity were certain as old patterns shifted. Changes brought anxiety and fears of the breakdown of old networks and community, and often the humiliation of seeking favours of those who had once been inferiors. When the system failed—when 'friends' would not act or lost their way in new corridors of power—supplicants were tempted to suspect betrayal.

Lady Brilliana Harley, reluctantly but capably left in command at Brampton Bryan where she was assailed by her old Herefordshire neighbours and acquaintances, exemplified the bitterness that came when those who had formerly been part of a known and interdependent social network became enemies. Writing to her husband, she complained of the malice and lack of 'common civility' that surrounded her and of her isolation, so that there were now no friends she could turn to for 'justice' in a crisis. She had received 'not one tittle of kindness in this county'; old acquaintanceship had turned sour and occasional courtesies were, she believed, hypocritical. Her husband was no longer respected; tenants withheld their rents; those formerly at odds with each other were now united against her and parliament. 'Herefordshire', she wrote to Sir Robert in London, 'is another county than when you were in it.'[18] When Sir Henry Lingen, a royalist colonel and sheriff of the county, wrote to warn her of the consequences of refusal to surrender, he reminded her of their previous 'relations' which made him and his fellow Herefordshire royalists unwilling to harm her. Lady Harley's reply expressed defiance but also a sense of betrayal of the bonds of friendship and community:

Your relations to me which you are pleased to make mention of might have invited you to another piece of service than this that you are now come upon, in which if you should have your desire it would never crown you with honour before men, nor blessings from God.[19]

---

[17] *CJ* 6. 204.

[18] HMC, *Fourteenth Report . . . Manuscripts of the Duke of Portland*, 3. 90, 92–3, 96, 104, and *passim*.

[19] HMC, *Calendar of the Manuscripts of the Marquis of Bath*, 1, 'The Harley Papers' (1904), 8.

The sentiments were unrealistic in a civil war, but they were symptomatic of the sense of social fragility and of the threat to ties that had formerly helped families to negotiate the way through their world.[20]

The balance between the harsh imperatives of winning a war and maintaining a known form of national society seemed threatened in the 1640s by military demands and failures, as at Colchester, and by political developments, whether the outbreak of army radicalism and its suppression or the execution of the king. The years of the Commonwealth and the Restoration continued to see 'manifold Distractions', but it is striking that neither domestic plots, the Scottish invasion of the 'third civil war' of 1650–1, or risings like Penruddock's in 1655 or Booth's in 1659 managed to achieve a critical mass of popular support or effective military strength. Instead, despite the constitutional changeability of the years after 1648 much of the population settled, adapted, and came to terms with what they may not have liked but were unable to challenge or, at least, preferred to a return to war. Among parliamentarians, conservative revolutionaries like Waller and Fairfax were pushed aside with varying degrees of consideration and honour: Waller endured imprisonment; Fairfax in his retirement was admired and respected; neither ever disavowed the rightness of their original decision to engage in war. Warwick came to terms with the Cromwellian regime. The vicissitudes of the part of the Verney family that had once been parliamentarian are well known. Some royalists, including Norwich, spent a decade largely in continental exile, but others compounded for their estates and sought to rebuild their fortunes after the losses incurred by contributions to the king's cause, by fines and sequestration at the hands of parliament, and by damage to houses, woods, and livestock inflicted by soldiers, tenants, or neighbours.

Such losses were not confined to royalists, although they clearly suffered most acutely, for until 1660 their access to redress was more limited. Men and women on both sides however faced losses, fines, and imprisonment, and their efforts to alleviate their troubles by maintaining or rebuilding old bonds and networks and by seeking access to new ones throw further light on the fissures war had created in society as well as on the familiar processes by which they sought recompense or reconciliation. The war years subjected old bonds to new stresses, and Lady Harley was not alone in finding that she lived in 'another county' from the one she had known. In Dorset the indomitable royalist Lady Bankes defended Corfe castle in two sieges against neighbours and former friends who, after it fell, stripped it of everything, from its luxurious furnishings to timber and barrels of butter; among the predacious victors was Sir Walter Erle, a neighbouring landowner and member of parliament. Edward Pitt of Stratfield Saye in Hampshire, an Exchequer official whose inclinations were

---

[20] HMC, *Calendar of the Manuscripts of the Marquis of Bath*, 1. 13–22. Lady Harley's relations with other neighbouring royalists, notably Sir William Vavasour and Sir John Scudamore (before his death at the hands of David Hyde) were less acerbic, but none of them budged an inch on principle.

royalist but who wished only to be neutral and unnoticed, suffered plunder and imprisonment and the humiliation of becoming a suppliant to former equals and colleagues before he, like his wife and eldest son, died of war-induced disease. Yet while the histories of the Pitts and the Bankes reveal the tectonic shifts to which old relationships might be subjected, they also demonstrate the survival of links across party lines that aided a return to a civil if wounded society. Lady Bankes's co-trustee and staunch ally in her attempts to recover her family's property was Giles Greene, an associate of her husband's before the war and, until Pride's Purge, member of parliament for Corfe castle. The trials of the Pitt family were ameliorated by the influence of Edward Pitt's brother William, a parliamentarian and member of the Hampshire committee, and by the care of William's equally parliamentarian wife Abigail. Nor, despite the hardships of the war years, were the families ruined. In both the heirs prudently spent some time abroad. Later George Pitt made a profitable marriage and at the Restoration was worth £4,000 a year. The Bankes never returned to ruined Corfe castle, but in 1661 Lady Bankes's son Ralph built a handsome new house at Kingston Lacy which remained in the family until the twentieth century.[21] Some partisan feuds indeed lived on after hostilities ended: local legend had it that the Bankes and the Erles in Dorset remained enemies for generations. On the other hand the young duke of Buckingham, Holland's ally in their futile venture in support of the king in 1648, married Fairfax's daughter. The marriage was a disaster, but Buckingham's admiration for Fairfax and his contempt for boastful but defeated fellow royalists when he saw them in the company of the modest victor are convincing. As his comments suggest, in the aftermath of this intimate war it was rarely possible to cleave to a path in which one did not in some measure associate with former enemies.

Friendship and obligation continued to cast long shadows, just as charitable understanding of the realities of war sometimes smoothed difficulties. In the midst of the crises of 1648 and 1649, for example, Fairfax's uncle came to the aid of a suspected royalist with whom he had old connections; another uncle had earlier written in favour of 'one of the most innocent delinquents in all the country' whose actions were 'extorted from him by threats & imprisonment'.[22] These were minor affairs, but they were typical of many in the 1640s and 1650s, and such cases did not end with the Restoration. Memories of the war and of its associated connections, obligations, and grievances had a long life and were not confined to dramatic events like the deaths of Lucas and Lisle. Twenty years after the Restoration a member of the Wynne family sought a place at Christ Church for his son as a delayed

---

[21] For the Pitt family, see BL Add. MS 29974, fos. 358–410; B. B. Woodward, T. C. Wilks, and C. Lockhart, *A General History of Hampshire, or the County of Southampton, including the Isle of Wight*, 3 vols. (n.d.), 276; for the Bankes family, see Kingston Lacy, Bankes MSS, 1, *passim*; *ODNB* 'Mary, Lady Bankes'.

[22] BL Add. MS 30305, fos. 127, 140; Bodl. MS Fairfax, 32, fo. 126.

return for his own service to the king at Denbigh more than thirty years earlier.[23]

Memory was not, of course, always benign. In 1685 the mathematician John Wallis was accused of collaboration during the civil war. He denied it, but more to the point he questioned 'whether it [was] now proper to repeat what was done forty years ago'.[24] In the later years of the Interregnum and in the Restoration Englishmen on the whole preferred to apply memory selectively; most did not want to open the way to a return to armed conflict. Bitter experience of war had not been confined to the affluent, nor physical suffering to soldiers. The troubles of the Harleys, the Pitts, and the Bankes had their counterparts at every level of society: the houses of the poor in Handbridge, a strategic suburb across the river from Chester, were repeatedly destroyed for military purposes; modest landowners and rich grandees alike were unable to collect their rents; humble householders lost their stools and feather beds to soldiers' plunder and vandalism; townspeople died of the war's diseases or from random shots; informers subverted old patterns of community and old affections were strained when allegiance was divided. War, it seemed, had engulfed a once peaceful society, and the attractions of a return to peace outweighed the imperfections of the settlements by which it was achieved. The English had experienced a transition from the days before 1639 when England, if not 'halcyon', was nevertheless unlike continental nations and rarely at war, to a time when there were few years in which the country was not engaged in hostilities at home or abroad. In the 1650s the puritan Nehemiah Wallington felt that England was now adrift: 'these wars I cannot find any warrant for them', he wrote.[25] Actual domestic experience had led to greater scepticism about the virtues of war, however godly, as a means to political or religious ends; the dangers to social stability, to property, and to friendship and connection that accompanied civil war now self-evidently outweighed benefits.

In 1660 the earl of Bristol, as George Digby one of the king's most active if more troublesome officers, explained to the House of Lords his reasons for opposing a policy based on retribution.[26] They were pragmatic rather than charitable or humanitarian. He supported execution of the regicides, and lamented the absence of revenge: 'I find myself set on fire, when I think that the blood of so many vertuous and meritorious . . . persons . . . so cruelly and impiously shed, should cry so loud for vengeance, and not find it from us.' Yet when 'the criminal and the misled . . . [made] up so numerous a part of the nation', failure to provide them with 'the firmest assurances of impunity' would open the way to 'new combustions'. Only 'security from . . . guilty fears' could ensure 'still water' after

---

[23] Kingston Lacy, Bankes MSS, 'Autograph Letters. I', no foliation, letter of Humphrey Wynne, 21 Feb. 1682.

[24] Magdelene College, Cambridge, Pepys MS 2646.

[25] Quoted in Seaver, *Wallington's World*, 179.

[26] For Digby, see Ian Roy, 'George Digby, Royalist Intrigue and the Collapse of the Cause', in Gentles *et al.* (eds.), *Soldiers, Writers and Statesmen*, 68–90.

'past tempests'. It was a 'mischief' to fail to mete out justice, but the alternative was worse: 'better innumerable mischiefs to particular persons and families, than one heavy inconvenience to the public'.[27] Not all Englishmen agreed with him, but after two decades in which each side experienced both victory and defeat, and in which most of the population had felt the effects of the conflict at first hand, whether through battle, plunder, or mere taxation, war was seen as too dangerous a way to solve the country's quarrels. Civil war had loosed the bonds of civil society and precipitated popular disorders of the kind that both sides feared. A degree of compromise, even of injustice, was acceptable to prevent 'new combustions' that might return the kingdom to 'war and blood'.

[27] 'The Earl of Bristol's Speech in the House of Lords, the 20th Day of July, 1660, upon the Bill of Indemnity' [1660], in *Somers Tracts*, 7. 460–1.

Bibliography

The place of publication of printed works is London unless otherwise noted.

MANUSCRIPTS

Bodleian Library

MS Add. A. 119
MS Add. D. 114
MS Carte 7, 74, 103
MS Clarendon, vols. 15, 18, 22–3, 25, 30–2, 34, 36
MS Fairfax, vols. 30–2, 36
MS Firth c. 6
MS Nalson 3
MS Tanner 61, 62/1A, 62/1B, 62/2A, 63–4, 303
MS top. Oxon. c. 378

British Library

Additional MS 4159, 4275, 5207.A, 5460, 11043, 11331–3, 11810, 14294, 18979, 18981, 21935, 28326, 29319, 29974 (1 and 2), 30305, 31022, 35297, 46188–9, 70001, 70109
Egerton MSS 80, 787
Harleian MSS 252, 519, 1944, 2125, 2135, 2155, 2315, 4551, 6802, 6804, 6851–2, 7001
Sloane MS 5247
Stowe MS5 184, 189, 842

Cambridge University Library

MS Mm 45.1.33

Cheshire Record Office

DDX 428 (Brereton MSS)

Christ Church College

Oxford MS 164

Derbyshire Record Office, Matlock

Gell MSS D258, D3287
Sanders MS 1232

Devonshire Record Office, Exeter

Seymour of Berry Pomeroy MS 1392

East Sussex Record Office, Lewes
Danny MSS 58, 119
Frewen MS 4223

Essex Record Office, Chelmsford
MS D/DQ s18

Henry E. Huntington Library, San Marino
Ellesmere MSS 6520–1, 6547, 6571, 6576, 6601–4, 6857, 7842, 7844, 7849, 7851–2, 7855, 7857, 7859–60, 7868
Hastings MSS 45148: F[inancial] 12, nos. 10, 13; 13, no. 46; Military Box 1, nos. 13, 20

Kingston Lacy, Dorset
Bankes MSS, 'Autograph Letters'

Magdelene College, Cambridge
Pepys MSS 2099, 2504, 2646, 2871

National Library of Wales, Aberystwyth
Chirk MS 7442

Public Record Office, Kew
Assize 44/3
State Papers 9/208, 24/3, 28/3, 28/18–19, 28/21–6, 28/126, 28/260, 84/05

University of Chicago, Regenstein Library
Bacon MS 4286

Wadham College, Oxford
'Sir William Waller's Remarks—Experiences'

William Salt Library, Stafford
Salt MSS 477, 481–2, 486, 502, 517–18, 544–7, 550–1, 564, 600

Worcester College, Oxford
Clarke MSS 20–1, 110, 114

ARTICLES OF WAR: MANUSCRIPT AND PRINTED

For articles of Richard II, Henry IV, Henry V, and Henry VI see also Grose, *Antiquities of England and Wales* and *Military Antiquities . . . of the English Army*, and Bentley, *Excerpta Historica*, listed below.

'Charter of Richard, King of England, for the government of those who were about to go by Sea to the Holy Land' (1189), *JSAHR* 5 (1926), 202–3.

Magdelene College, Cambridge, Pepys MS 2871, fos. 158–70, 'Martial Lawes in the King's camp in the time of Henry 6th'.

Huntington Library, 'Huth fragments' (1493).

Hereafter Ensue certayne Statuts and Ordenances of warre made ordeyned & establysshed by the most noble victoryous, and most Christen Prynce our most drade Souveraygne lorde Kynge Henry the viii (1513).

Statutes and ordynances for the warre (1544).

BL Harl. 519, fos. 72ᵛ–80ᵛ, 'The institution and discipline of a soldier' ('temp.Eliz.': general precepts for military conduct, followed by a set of articles).

CSP Foreign 1562, 326–7, 'Orders for the English soldiers in Newhaven'.

Lawes and Ordinances, set down by Robert Earle of Leycester, the Queenes Maiesties Lieutenant and Captayne General of her armie and forces in the Lowe Countries ([1585]).

Lawes and Orders of warre, established for the good conduct of the service in Ireland. Robert Earle of Essex . . . her Maiesties Lieutenant and Governour generall of the kingdome of Ireland, To all Officers of the Armie ([1599]).

Strachey, William (comp.), *For the Colony Virginea Britannia, Lawes Divine, Morall and Martiall, etc.* (1612), ed. David H. Flaherty (Charlottesville, Va., 1969).

PRO, SP 9/208, fos. 259–62, 'Martiall lawes ordained and instituted by his Matie:w[i]th the advice of the Council of War, for the good ordering of the troops in this Kingdom . . . to punish the malicious and wicked, and to defend the innocent, according to the Custom of all well governed Kingdoms' ([1625?]).

'Instructions for the execution of Martial Law in His Majesty's Army', in 'Articles of war—1627', ed. H. Bullock, *JSAHR* 5 (1926), 111–15.

Lawes And Ordinances touching military discipline. Set downe and established the 13. of August. 1590, tr. I.D. (The Hague, 1631) (ordinances of the United Provinces).

'The Second Part of the Swedish Discipline: Containing those Orders and Articles of warre, which have beene commanded by the King of Sweden, to be under their severall Penalties observed in his Majesties Camp, Garrisons or elsewhere', in *The Swedish Intelligencer* (1632).

'The Lawes, Articles and Ordinances touching marshall discipline. Sett downe and established by the Lordes the States (*sic*) the 13 day of August 1580' [*sic*, properly 1590], in Henry Hexham, *Principles of the Art Militarie* (1637), 9–15.

Lawes and Ordinances Of Warre, For the better Government of His Maeisties Army Royall, in the present Expedition for the Northern parts . . . Under the Conduct of Thomas Earl of Arundel and Surrey (1639).

Lawes and Ordinances of Warre, Established for the better conduct of the Service in the Northern parts. By . . . The Earle of Northumberland (1640).

Lawes and Ordinances of Warre, Established for the better government of the Armie in the Northern parts. By . . . The Earle of Holland (1641).

Camp Discipline, or The Souldiers Duty, in certain Articles and Ordinances of Warre, commanded to be observed in the Armie. By his Excellence The Lord Generall of the said Armie (1642) (a reprint of Scottish articles).

Lawes and Ordinances of Warre, Established for the better Conduct of the Army by His Excellency the Earle of Essex (1642).

Laws and Ordinances of Warre, Established for the better Conduct of the Army, By His Excellency the Earl of Essex . . . And now inlarged by the command of His Excellency (1643).

Lawes and Ordinances of Warre, Established for the better Conduct of the Army (n.d., probably for Fairfax's army; follows Essex's 1643 text with minor typographical variations, but Essex's imprimatur is omitted).

Laws and Ordinances of Warre, Established for the better Conduct of the Army: By His Excellency the Earl of Essex, Lord Generall Of the Forces raised by the Authority of the Parliament . . . Together with Orders established By His Excellency the Lord Fairfax, January 14. 1646. for regulating the Army (1646 [1647]).

Orders Established The 14th of this present January, By His Excellency Sir Thomas Fairfax, For Regulating the Army and For Soldiers paying of Quarters, and fair behavior in the Countreys (1646 [1647]; published separately from the above: an example of supplementary orders designed to meet particular circumstances).

Orders and Institutions of War, Made and ordained by His Maiesty, And by Him delivered to His Generall His Excellence The Earle of Newcastle (1642).

Military Orders, and Articles, Established by His Maiestie, For the better Ordering and Government of his Maiesties Armie. With the Oath which every souldier is to take (Oxford, [1643]; 'Re-Printed by His Maiesties Command', and thus a version of an earlier set of articles; they retain a reference to the earl of Lindsey as Lord Lieutenant General, an office that Lindsey ceased to hold in October 1642. 82 articles; roman type).

Military Orders And Articles Established by His Maiesty, For the better Ordering and Government of His Majesties Army (Oxford, 1643; 153 articles; gothic type).

PRINTED SOURCES

Newsletters

The Colchester spie. Truly Informing the Kingdome of the estate of that gallant Town, and the attempts of Fairfax against it (1648).

The Exchange Intelligencer (1645).

The Kingdomes Weekly Intelligencer (1643–9).

The London Post: faithfully communicating his intelligence (1644–5).

Mercurius Academicus (Oxford, 1645–6).

Mercurius Anglicus . . . Communicating Intelligence from all parts of the Kingdome of England. Chiefly from Westminster, London, Colchester (1648).

Mercurius Aulicus, a Diurnall, Communicating the intelligence and affaires of the Court to the rest of the Kingdome (Oxford, 1642[3]–5).

Mercurius Britannicus: communicating the affaires of great Britaine (1643–6).

Mercurius Civicus, Londons Intelligencer (1643–6).

Mercurius Elencticus. Communicating the unparallell'd proceedings at Westminster (1647–9).

Mercurius Melancholicus. Or Newes from Westminster, and the Head Quarters, and other parts of the Kingdome (July 1648; a counterfeit issue).

Mercurius Pragmaticus. Communicating intelligence from all parts (1647–9).

The Moderate Intelligencer: Impartially Communicating Martiall Affaires to the Kingdome of England (1645–9).

The Parliament Scout: Communicating his Intelligence to the Kingdome (1643–5).

The Parliaments Post. Faithfully Communicating To the Kingdome Proceedings of the Armies on both sides (1645).

A Perfect Diurnall of the Passages in Parliament (1642–3).

A Perfect Diurnall of some Passages in Parliament And daily proceedings of the Army under his Excellency the Lord Fairfax . . . Collected for the satisfaction of such as desire to be truly Informed (1643–9).

Severall Proceedings in Parliament (1649–55)

The Weekly Account (1643–8)

General

Adams, Tho[mas], *The Souldiers Honour. Wherein By divers inferences and gradations it is evinced, that the Profession is iust, necessarie, and honourable* (1617).

All the severall Ordinances and Orders of the Lords and Commons Assembled in Parliament: For the speedy establishing of a Court Martiall Within the Cities of London, Westminster, or Lines of Communication . . . 17 August. 1644 (1644).

Andrewes, R., *A perfect Declaration of The Barbarous and Cruell practises committed by Prince Robert, the Cavalliers, and others in his Majesties Army, from the time of the Kings going from his Parliament until this present day* (1642).

The Anti-covenant, or a sad complaint concerning the new oath or covenant (Oxford, 1643).

An Antidote against An Infectious Aire. Or A Short Reply of Wel-wishers unto the Good and Peace of this Kingdome; Unto the Declaration of the 11th of February. 1647 (n.pl., 1647).

Articles of Agreement between his Excellency Prince Maurice, and the Earle of Stamford, Upon the delivery of the City of Excester, The fifth of September, 1643 (1643).

Ashley, Robert, *Of Honour*, ed. Virgil B. Heltzel (San Marino, Calif., 1947).

Bachiler, Samuel, *The Campe Royall, Set forth in briefe Meditations on the words of the Prophet Moses, Deut. 23.9.14 . . . preached in the Army at the Laager* (1629).

Barnard, Francis Pierrepont (ed.), *The Essential Portions of Nicholas Upton's De Studio Militari. Before 1446. Translated by John Blount. Fellow of All Souls (c.1500)* (Oxford, 1931).

Barnes, Tho[mas], *Vox belli, or, An Alarum to Warre* (1626).

Barriffe, William, *Military Discipline: or the Yong Artillery Man. Wherein is discoursed and showne the Postures both of a Musket and Pike: the exactest way, & c. Together with the Motions which are to be used, in the exercising of a Foot-company* (1635); 2nd edn., revised and enlarged (1639); 3rd edn., 'Newly revised and much inlarged', (1643); 4th and 5th edns. (1643, 1647).

——*Mars, his Triumph. Or, the Description of an Exercise performed the XVIII. of October, 1638. in Merchant-Taylors Hall By Certain Gentlemen of the Artillery Garden, London* (1639).

Barrington Family Letters 1628–1632, ed. Arthur Searle, Camden Society, 4th ser. 28 (1983).

'The Battle of Hopton Heath, 1643', *Collections for a History of Staffordshire edited by the Staffordshire Record Society* (1936), 179–84.

B[edell], W[illiam], tr. and preface, *A Free Schoole of Warre, or, A Treatise, whether it be lawfull to beare Armes for the service of a Prince that is of a divers Religion* (1625).

[Bentley, Samuel] (ed.), *Excerpta Historica, or Illustrations of English History* (1833).

Bernard, Richard, *The Bible-Battells. Or the Sacred Art Military* (1629).

Bingham, John, *The Art of Embattailing an Army. Or, the Second Part of Aelians Tacticks. Containing the Practice of the best Generals of all Antiquitie, concerning the formes of Battailes* (1631).

_____ *The Tactiks of Aelian. Or art of embattailing an army after ye Grecian manner Englished & illustrated wth figures throughout* (1616).

Bishop, G., *A More Particular and Exact Relation of The Victory obtained by the Parliaments Forces under the Command of Sir Thomas Fairfax . . . With a true Coppy of a Letter of the regaining of Leicester* (1645).

The Bloody Treatie: or, Proceedings between the King and Prince Rupert (1645).

[Border, Daniel], *A Wicked Plot against the Person of Sir William Waller. Declaring, How one of his Soldiers eyther for hire or malice would desperately have shot him, but (by the providence of God) his Musket not taking fire he immediately was apprehended; and deservedly executed* (1644–5).

[Boteler, William], 'The Civil War Papers of Sir Will. Boteler, 1642–1655', ed. G. Herbert Fowler, *Publications of the Bedfordshire Historical Record Society*, 18 (1936), 1–42.

Boyle, Roger, Earl of Orrery, *A Treatise of the Art of War: Dedicated to the Kings Most Excellent Majesty* (1677).

[Brereton, William], *The Letter Books of Sir William Brereton*, ed R. N. Dore, Record Society of Lancashire and Cheshire, 123, 128 (1984, 1990) (and see BL Add. MSS 11,331–3 and Cheshire Record Office DDX 428).

_____ *Travels in Holland the United Provinces England Scotland and Ireland M.DC. XXXIV–M.DC.XXXV*, ed. Edward Hawkins, Chetham Society, 1 (1844).

[Brinckmair, L.], *The Warnings of Germany. By Wonderfull Signes, and strange Prodigies seene in divers parts of that Countrye between the Years 1618. and 1638. Together with a briefe relation of the miserable Events which ensued* (1638).

Buggs, Samuel, *Miles Mediterraneus. The Mid-land Souldier. A Sermon Preached in the . . . Military Garden in the well governed Citie of Coventry* (1622).

Bulstrode, Richard, *Memoirs and Reflections upon the Reign and Government of King Charles the Ist. And K. Charles the IId . . . Wherein the Character of the Royal Martyr, and of King Charles II. are Vindicated from Fanatical Aspersions* (1721).

[Byron, John], 'John Byron's Account of the Siege of Chester 1645–1646', *The Cheshire Sheaf*, 4th ser. 6 (1971), 1–25.

[Bysshe, Edward], *Nicolai Uptoni De Studio Militari, Libri Quatuor. Johan.de Bado Aureo, Tractatus de Armis. Henrici Spelmanni Aspilogia* (1654).

Calendar of the Proceedings of the Committee for Advance of Money, 1642–1656, ed. Mary Anne Everett Green, 3 vols. (1888).

Calendar of the Proceedings of the Committee for Compounding, & c., 1647–1660, ed. Mary Anne Everett Green, 5 vols. (1889–92).

Carte, Tho[mas], *A Collection of Original Letters and Papers, Concerning the Affairs of England, From the Year 1641 to 1660. Found among the Duke of Ormonde's Papers*, 2 vols. (1739).

C[arter], M[atthew], *A Most True and Exact Relation of That as Honourable as Unfortunatae Expedition of Kent, Essex and Colcheter* (n.pl., 1650).

Caryl, Joseph, *Ioy Out-joyed: or, Joy in overcoming evil spirits and evil men, Overcome by better Joy: Set forth in a Sermon . . . praising God, for reducing the City of Chester by the Forces of Parliament, under the Command of Sir William Brereton* (1646).

[Cashman, Robert], *A Sermon Preached at Plimoth in New England* (1622).

A Catalogue of the Names of the Dukes, Marquesses, Earles and Lords, that have absented themselves from the Parliament, and are now with His Maiesty . . . As also, A List of the Army of his Excellency, Robert Earle of Essex (n.pl., 1642).

The Cavaliers Catechisme, and Confession of his Faith, Consisting in four principall Heads (1647).

[Cavendish, William, Marquess of Newcastle (?)], *The Country Captaine, And the Varietie, Two Comedies, Written by a Person of Honour* (1649).

Certain Observations, Upon the New League or Covenant, As it was explained by a Divine of the New Assembly, in a Congregation at London (Bristol, 1643).

'The Charter of the Company of Gunmakers, London', *JSAHR* 6 (1927), 79–92.

Chirk Castle Accounts, A.D. 1605–1666, comp. W. M. Myddelton (St Albans, 1908).

The Clarendon Historical Society's Reprints, series 1 and 2 (Edinburgh, 1882–4, 1884–6).

Clarke, Sa[muel], *A Generall Martyrologie, containing A Collection Of all the greatest Persecutions which have befallen the Church of Christ From the Creation to our present Times* (1651).

_____ *The Lives Of sundry Eminent Persons in this Later Age* (1683).

The Clarke Papers: Selections from the Papers of William Clarke, ed. C. H. Firth, 2 vols. in 1, Royal Historical Society (1992).

Codrington, Robert, 'The Life and Death of the Illustrious Robert, Earl of Essex, &c.', *Harleian Miscellany*, 6. 5–35.

Colchesters Teares: Affecting and Afflicting City & Country (1648), in *Clarendon Historical Society's Reprints*, 1 (1882–4).

Considerations upon The present state of the Affairs of this Kingdome. In relation to the three severall Petitions which have lately been in agitation in the Honourable City of London. And A Project for a fourth Petition, tending to a speedy Accommodataion of the present unhappy Differences between His Maiesty and the Parliament (1642).

The Coppie of A Letter From Sir Thomas Fairfax his Quarters to the Parliament, concerning the great Battell between Sir Thomas Fairfax and Goring at Langport on Thursday the 10. of July 1645 (n.pl., 1645).

The Copy of A Letter from An Eminent Commander in Sir Thomas Fairfax Army, to severall worthy Members of Parliament of the Honourable House of Commons assembled in Parliament. Dated at Marston, within a mile and little more of Oxford, May 24. 1645 (1645).

'The Court Martial Papers of Sir William Waller's Army, 1644', ed. John Adair, *JSAHR* 44 (1966), 205–26.

C.R. [Charles I], *By the King. To Our truly and wellbeloved Our Colonells, Lieutenant-Colonells, Serjeant-Majors, Captaines, and all other Our Officers of Our Army* (Oxford, 1642–3).

[Cromwell, Oliver], *The Writings and Speeches of Oliver Cromwell with an Introduction, Notes and a Sketch of his Life*, ed. Wilbur Cortez Abbott, 4 vols. (Cambridge, Mass., 1937–47).

Crowne, William, *A True Relation of all the Remarkable Places and Passages Observed in the Travels of the right honourable Thomas Lord Howard, Earle of Arundell and Surrey, Primer Earle, and Earle Marshall of England, Ambassadour Extraordinary to his sacred Majesty Ferdinando the second, Emperour of Germanie, Anno Domini 1636* (1636).

C[ruso], J[ohn], *The Art of Warre, or Militarie discourses . . . by The Lord of Praissac. Englished by I.C.* (Cambridge, 1639 and 1642).

_____ *The Complete Captain, or, An Abridgement of Cesars warres, with observations upon them; Together With a collection of the order of the Militia of the Ancients; and a particular Treatise of modern war: Written By the late great Generall the Duke of Rohan: Englished by J.C.* (Cambridge, 1640).

_____ *Militarie Instructions for the Cavallrie: or Rules and Directions for the Service of Horse, Collected out of Divers Forrain Authors Ancient and Modern, and Rectified and Supplied, According to the Present Practice of the Low-Country Warres* (Cambridge, 1632).

[Culpeper, Cheney], 'The Letters of Sir Cheney Culpeper (1641–1657)', ed. M. J. Braddick and M. Greengrass, *Camden Miscellany XXXIII*, Camden Society, 5th ser., 7 (1996).

Davenport, John, *A Royall Edict for Military Exercises: Published in a Sermon preached to the Captaines, and Gentlemen that exercise Armes in the Artillery Garden at their generall meeting* (1629).

Davies, Edward, *The Art of War, and Englands Traynings* (1619).

A Declaration Of His Excellency the Lord Generall Fairfax. Concerning the Supply of Bedding Required from the City of London For the lodging of the Army in voyd houses to prevent the Quartering of Souldiers upon any Inhabitants (1648).

The Declaration of his Highnesse Prince Rupert, Lord High Admirall of all the navy Royall, belonging to the Kings Majesty Charles the II. Wherein hee cleareth himselfe from many Scandalous Rumours which have bin cast upon his Reputation (n.pl., 1649).

Defoe, Daniel, *A Tour through the Whole Island of Great Britain*, introductions by G. D. H. Cole and D. C. Browning (1974).

Demophilus Philanactos, *Two Epitaphs, Occasioned by the Death of Sr Charles Lucas, and Sr George Lisle, basely assassinated at Colchester* (1648).

Derham, Robert, *A Manuall or Brief Treatise of some particular Rights and Priuileges belonging to the High Court of parliament: Wherein is showed how of late times they have been violated* (1647).

A Dialogue betwixt a Horse of Warre, and a Mill-Horse; Wherein the content and safety of an humble and painfull life is preferred above all the Noyse, the Tumults, and Trophies of the Warre. Full of harmeless Mirth, and variety (1643).

A Diary of the Siege of Colchester by the Forces under the Command of his Excellency the Lord Generall Fairfax (1648).

[Digby, George, earl of Bristol], 'The Earl of Bristol's Speech in the House of Lords, the 20th Day of July, 1660, upon the Bill of Indemnity', *Somers Tracts*, 7. 460–1.

[Digby, John], 'Life of Sir John Digby (1605–1645)', *Camden Miscellany XII*, Camden Society, NS 18 (1910).

Digges, Thomas, and Digges, Dudley, *Four Paradoxes, or politique Discourses. Concerning Militarie Discipline, written long since by Thomas Digges Esquire* (1604).

Documents Relating to the Civil War 1642–1648, ed. J. R. Powell and E. K. Timings, Navy Record Society, 165 (1963).

Drake, Nathan, 'A Journal of the First and Second Sieges of Pontefract Castle, 1644–1645', Surtees Society, *Miscellanea I*, 37 (1860–1).

'Dundee Court Martial Records 1651', ed. Godfrey Davies, *Miscellany of the Scottish History Society III*, Publications of the Scottish History Society, 2nd ser. 19 (1919), 1–67.

[Dyve, Lewis], 'The Tower of London Letter-Book of Sir Lewis Dyve, 1646–7', ed. H. G. Tibbutt, *Publications of the Bedfordshire Historical Record Society*, 38 (1958), 49–86.

[E. A.], *A Fuller Relation Of the Great Victory obtained (through Gods Providence) at Alsford, on Friday the 28. March, 1644. By the Parliaments Forces, under the Command of Sir William Waller* (1644).

The Earle of Strafford's Ghost. Complaining Of the Cruelties of his Countrey-men, in Killing one another. And persuading all great Men to live honestly, that desire to die Honourably (1644).

Edwards, Thomas, *Gangraena: Or, A Catalogue and Discovery of many of the Errors, Heresies, Blasphemies and pernicious Practices of the Sectaries of this time, vented and acted in England in these four last years*, 2nd edn., enlarged (1646).

An Elegie on the Death of that most Noble and Heroick Knight, Sir Charles Lucas (n.pl., [1648]).

Ellis, Henry (ed.), *Original Letters Illustrative of English History; including Numerous Royal Letters*, 1st ser., 3 vols., 2nd edn. (1825).

[Ellis, Thomas], *An Exact and full Relation of the last Fight Between the Kings Forces and Sir William Waller. Sent in a letter from an Officer in the Army to his friend in London. Printed to prevent mis-information* (1644).

Elton, Richard, *The Compleat Body of the Art Military: Exactly Compiled and Gradually Composed for the foot, in the Best Refined Manner, According to the Practice of the Modern Times*, 2nd edn. (1659).

[Evelyn, John], *The Diary of John Evelyn*, ed. E. S. de Beer, 6 vols. (Oxford, 1955).

Everard, John, *The Arriereban: A Sermon preached to the Company of the Military Yarde, At St. Andrewes Church in Holborne on St. James his day last* (1618).

An Exact and Perfect Relation of the Proceedings of the Army under the Command of Sir Thomas Fairfax. From the sixth of the instant July to the eleventh of the same. Wherein is expressed the particulars of the Victory obtained by the parliaments Forces, over Goring, near Langport (1645).

An exact Narrative of Every dayes Proceedings Since the Insurrection in Essex. Together with a more perfect List of what persons are slain and taken by both parties, till the 18 of June present, 1648. Also the Resolution of the Councell of War concerning the manner of punishing the Prisoners they have taken in that County (1648).

Fairclough, Samuel, *The Prisoners Praises for their Deliverance from their long Imprisonment in Colchester. On a day of publique thanksgiving set apart for that purpose . . . Preached at Rumford Septemb. 28. 1648* (1650).

[Fairfax, Thomas], *The Memoirs of General Fairfax: Wherein is contained An Account of all his Sieges and Battles in the North of England . . . Written by Himself; With Improvements, selected from the Noted Historians of those Times. Also, A full and genuine Account of the various Skirmishes before, and at the Taking and Pillaging of Bradford . . . Taken from a Manuscript of Joseph Lister, and Others* (Leeds, 1776).

—— *Short Memorials of Thomas Lord Fairfax. Written by Himself* (1699).

The Famous Tragedie of King Charles I. Basely Butchered . . . In which is included several Combinations and machinations that brought that incomparable Prince to the Block (n.pl., 1649).

Featley, Daniel, *Roma Ruens, Romes Ruine: Being A Succinct Answer To A Popish Challenge, Concerning The antiquity, unity, universality, succession, and perfect visibility of the true Church, even in the most obscure times* (1644).

[Ferne, Henry], *The Camp at Gilgal. Or, A View of the Kings Army, and spirituall provision made for it* (Oxford, 1643).

Firth, C. H., and Rait, R. S. (eds.), *Acts and ordinances of the Interregnum, 1642–1660* (1911).

F[isher], T[homas], *Warlike Directions: or the Souldiers Practice. Set forth for the benefit of all such as are, or will be Scholars of Martiall Discipline. But especially for all Officers as are not yet settled, or rightly grounded in the Art of Warre*, 2nd edn., 'corrected and amended' (1643).

[Fleetwood, George], 'Letter from George Fleetwood to his father giving an account of the battle of Lützen and the death of Gustavus Adolphus', ed. P. de M. Grey Egerton, *Camden Miscellany I*, Camden Society Publications, 39 (1847), 1–12.

[Fleetwood, William], *An Unhappy View of the Whole Behaviour of My Lord Duke Buckingham, at the French Island, called the Isle of Rhee Discovered By Colonell William Fleetwood, an unfortunate Commander in that untoward Service* (1648).

Foster, Henry, *A true and Exact Relation of the Marchings of the Two Regiments of the Trained Bands of the City of London, being the Red and Blew Regiments, as also the three Regiments of the Auxiliary Forces, the Blew, Red, and Orange, who marched forth for the Reliefe of the City of Glocester* (1643), printed in Washbourn, *Bibliotheca Gloucestrensis*, 251–71.

Foulis, Henry, *An Exact and True Relation of a Bloody Fight, Performed against the Earl of Newcastle and his Forces before Todcaster and Selby in Yorkshire: By The Lo: Fairfax . . . With the number of Souldiers that were slain* (1642).

Four Tracts relative to The Battle of Birmingham Anno Domini 1643, ed. Leonard Jay (Birmingham, 1931).

From the Leaguer at Colchester, More certain News of the Fight on Wednesday last; And of their present condition (1648).

Gatford, Lionel, *Englands Complaint: Or, A sharp Reproof for the Inhabitants thereof; against that now raigning Sin of Rebellion. But more especially to the Inhabitants of the County of Suffolk. With a Vindication of those Worthyes now in Colchester* (1648).

Gentili, Alberico, *De Iure Belli Libri Tres*, 2 vols. (Oxford, 1933).

Gerbier, Balthazar, *The First Publique Lecture, read at Sr. Balthazar Gerbier his Academy, Concerning Military Architecture, or Fortifications* (1649).

The German History. The Seventh Part. Wherein is conteyned the principall passages of the last summer. Methodically digested into times, places and actions, and brought down to the present. With the siege and taking of Regenspurg, as also the Siege and Battell of Norlingen, with an exact Mappe thereof (1634).

Gil, A[lexander], *The New Starr of the North, Shining upon the Victorious King of Sweden* (1632).

Gilbert, Eleazer, *The Prelatical Cavalier Catechized, and the Protestant Souldier encouraged. By a Missive sent King Charles in the name of the Protestants beyond Seas* (1645).

Good and true Intelligence from Reading Being A true Relation of the late Fights betweene the Parliaments Forces and the Malignants (1643).

Gouge, William, *Gods Three Arrowes: Plague, Famine, Sword. In three Treatises. I. A Plaister for the Plague. II. Dearths Death. III. The Churches Conquest over the Sword* [2nd edn.] (1631).

Gouge, William, *The Dignitie of Chivalry, Set forth in a Sermon, Preached before the Artillery Company of London, June xiij. 1626*, 2nd edn. (1631).

A great and bloudy Fight at Colchester and The storming of the Town by the Lord Generals Forces with the manner how they were repulsed and beaten off, and forced to retreat from the Walls, and a great and terrible blow given at the said storm, by Granadoes and Gunpowder. Likewise their hanging out the Flag of Defiance, and their sallying out upon Tuesday last . . . Sir Charles Lucas giving the first onset in the Van, with the number killed and taken, and Sir Charles Lucas his Declaration (1648).

A Great Fight at Colchester Upon Tuesday night last, being the 25. of this instant July, and the advancing of General Lucas and his Forces to the very Guards of the Parliamenteers, with the particulars of the Fight, and the numbers that were killed and taken prisoners on both sides, and the springing of a Mine to blow up part of the the Leaguer . . . And a bloudy Fight at Deal Castle in Kent (1648).

A Great Victoy Obtained By Generall Poyntz and Col. Copley, against the Kings Forces Under the command of the Lord Digby, and Sir Marmaduke Langdale, at Sherborn in Yorkshire, the 15. of October, 1645 (1645).

Gutch, John (ed.), *Collectanea Curiosa; or miscellaneous tracts, relating to the history and antiquities of England and Ireland, the Universities of Oxford and Cambridge, and a variety of other subjects*, 2 vols. (Oxford, 1781).

G., W., *A Just Apologie for An Abused Armie. Shewing, The unreasonablenesse of that bad opinion that many are of late falne into, concerning the Parliaments Army, under the command of his Excellency Sir Thomas Fairfax* (1646).

Hammond, Charles, *The Loyal Indigent Officer. Being A Brief Description of the Truly Loyal Commissioned Officers, which hath faithfully served his late Majesty of ever Blessed Memory, and his Majesty that now is. With A Discovery how to be known from the number of the pretended Commission'd Officers* (c.1675).

[Hammond, Lieutenant], 'A Relation of a Short Survey of the Western counties Made by a Lieutenant of the Military Company in Norwich in 1635', ed. L. G. Wickham Legg, *Camden Miscellany XVI*, Camden Society, 3rd ser. 52 (1936).

The Harcourt Papers, ed. Edward William Harcourt, 14 vols. (Oxford, [1880–1905]).

The Harleian Miscellany; or, A Collection of scarce, curious, and entertaining Pamphlets and Tracts, as well in manuscript as in print, found in the late Earl of Oxford's Library, 12 vols. (1808–11).

[Harley, Brilliana], *The Letters of Lady Brilliana Harley*, ed. T. T. Lewis, Camden Society, 58 (1854).

H[arwood], R[ichard], *The loyall Subiect's retiring-roome. Opened in a sermon at St Maries, on the 13th day of Iuly (being Act-Sunday) in the After-noone, A.D. 1645, Before the Honourable Members of both Houses of Parliament, Assembled in Oxford* (Oxford, 1645).

The Heads Of severall Petitions delivered by many of the Troopers against the Lord General And some other Officers of the Army. With the Answer which Mr. Pym Made to the severall Heads or Petitions, before the Committee on Tuesday, October 5. 1641 (1641).

'Henry VIII's preliminary letter of retainer to Colonel Frederick von Reiffenberg for the raising of 1500 men-at-arms: An Explication of a Sixteenth-Century Mercenary Contract', ed. Gilbert J. Millar, *JSAHR* 67 (1989), 220–5.

[Hesilrige, Arthur], 'A Letter from Sir Arthur Hesilrige to the Honourable Committee of the Councel of State for Irish and Scotish [*sic*] Affairs, at Whitehall, concerning the Scots Prisoners', [1650], in Slingsby, *Original Memoirs*.

Hexham, Henry, *The Principles of the Art Militarie: Practised in the Warres of the United Netherlands* (1637).

Historical Manuscripts Commission, *Reports*:

Second Report (1871): Myddelton-Biddulph MSS.

Seventh Report, i (1879): House of Lords MSS, Lowndes MSS.

Eighth Report, ii (1881): Manchester MSS.

Ninth Report, ii (1884): Chandos-Pole-Gell MSS.

Twelfth Report, iii, ix (1889, 1891): Cowper MSS, Coke MSS, Beaufort MSS.

Fourteenth Report, ix (1895): Round MSS.

Fifteenth Report, vii (1898): Somerset MSS.

Bath, i, v (1904, 1980): (i) Harley MSS.

Montagu (1900).

Portland, i, iii (1891, 1894): (iii) Harley MSS.

[Hodgson, John], 'Memoirs of Captain John Hodgson of Coalley-Hall, near Halifax; touching his conduct in the Civil Wars, and his troubles after the Restoration. Written by himself, and now first published from his Manuscript', in Slingsby, *Original Memoirs*.

Holland, Philemon, *A Learned, Elegant and Religious Speech, Delivered unto his Most excellent Maiestie, at his late being at Coventry . . . When as, his royall Maiestie was graciously pleased to grant and command the erecting of a military garden therein: And sithens to enlarge the aforesaid Cities Charter* (1622) (printed with Buggs, *Miles Mediterraneus*).

[Howell, James], *Englands Teares, for the present Wars, which for the nature of the Quarrell, the quality of Strength, the diversity of Battailes, Skirmiges, Encounters, and Sieges, (happened in so short a compass of time), cannot be parallelld by any precedent Age* (1644).

The Humble Desires of Prince Rupert, Prince Maurice, and others their Adherents, To the Kings most Excellent Majestie; To Be tried at a Counsell of War. Together with His Majesties Letter to Colonel Samuel Sands Governour of Worcester, Concerning the Persons aforesaid (1645).

An humble Remonstrance from his Excel. Sir Thomas Fairfax and The Army under his Command concerning the present State of Affaires in relation to themselves and the Kingdome, with their desires and present Resolutions thereupon. Presented to the commissioners at St. Albanes, Iune 23. to be by them humbly presented to the Parliament (1647).

The Hunting of the Foxes from New-Market and Triploe-Heaths to Whitehall, By five small Beagles (late of the Armie) Or the Grandie-Deceivers Unmasked (that you may know them.) Directed to all the Free-People of England (1649).

Hutchinson, Lucy, *Memoirs of the Life of Colonel Hutchinson with the fragment of an autobiography of Mrs. Hutchinson*, ed. James Sutherland (1973).

Hyde, Edward, earl of Clarendon, *The History of the Rebellion and Civil War in England, Begun in the Year 1641*, 3 vols. (Oxford, 1702–4).

Instructions for Musters and Armes, And the use thereof: By order from the Lords of His Maiesties most Honourable Privie Counsaile. Whitehall the 27. of Iuly 1631 (1631).

'Iter Carolinum, being a succinct relation of the necessitated Marches, Retreats, and Sufferings of his Majesty Charles the first, from January 10, 1541 [*sic*], till the time of his Death, 1648: Collected by a daily Attendant upon his sacred Majesty, during all the said time', in Gutch, *Collectanea Curiosa*.

Jackson, Thomas, *Judah must into Captivitie. Six Sermons On Ierem. 7.16. Lately Preached in the Cathedrall Church of Christ in Canterburie, and elsewhere* (1622).

[Jones, Adam], *Horrible News from Leicester* (1642).

'The Journal of Prince Rupert's Marches, 5 Sept. 1642 to 4 July 1646', ed. C. H. Firth, *EHR* 13 (1898), 729–41.

J. R., *A Letter Sent To the Honble William Lenthal Esq; Speaker of the Honorable House of Commons. Concerning Sir Tho: Fairfax's gallant Proceedings in Cornwal, Since his advance from Torrington and Launceston to Bodman* (1645).

_____ *Sir Ralph Hoptons and All his Forces comming in to the Parliament. On Thursday last, according to the Articles and Propositions sent him by Sir Thomas Fairfax* (1646).

[Juxon, Thomas], *The Journal of Thomas Juxon, 1644–1647*, ed. Keith Lindley and David Scott, Camden Society, 5th ser. 13 (1999).

Kem, Samuel, *The King of Kings His Privie Marks for The Kingdoms choyce of new Members: or A Project for the Kingdoms or Cities speedy prosperity; and the beneficent blessing attending A New Model* (1646).

_____ *The Messengers Preparation For an Address to The King For a Well-grounded Peace. As it was delivered in a Sermon, at Oxford, on Sunday, Novemb. 26. 1644. Before the Commissioners of both Kingdomes, the morning before their presenting the Propositions to His Majestie* (1644).

_____ *Orders given out; the Word, Stand Fast* (1647).

[King, Henry], *The Poems of Henry King*, ed. Margaret Crum (Oxford, 1965).

Knowler, William, *The Earl of Strafforde's Letters and Dispatches, With an Essay towards his Life by Sir George Radcliffe*, 2 vols in 1 (1739).

Lacrymae Germaniae: or, The Teares of Germany. Unfolding her woefull Distress by Jerusalems Calamity (1638).

Larkin, James F., and Hughes, Paul L. (eds.), *Stuart Royal Proclamations*, i. *Proclamations of King James I 1603–1625* (Oxford, 1973).

Larkin, James F. (ed.), *Stuart Royal Proclamations*, ii. *Royal Proclamations of King Charles I 1625–1646* (Oxford, 1983).

The Latest Remarkable Truths, (Not before Printed) From Chester, Worcester, Devon, Somerset, Yorke and Lanchester counties, as also from Scotland . . . Together, With a most exact Relation of the Siedge of Manchester (1642).

Leech, I., *The trayne Souldier. A Sermon Preached Before the worthy Societie of the Captaynes and Gentle men that exercise Armes in the Artillery Garden. At Saint Andrew-undershaft in London* (1619).

[Leighton, Alexander], *Speculum Belli sacri: or the Lookingglasse of the Holy War, Wherein is discovered: The Evill of War. The Good of Warr. The Guide of War. In the last of these I give a scantling of the Christian Tackticks, from the levying of the Souldier, to the sounding of the Retrait; . . . I have applied the generall rules warranted by the Word, to the particular necessity of our present times* (1624).

A Letter From his Excellency the Lord Fairfax Generall of the Parliament's Forces: Concerning the surrender of Colchester, The ground and Reasons of putting to death Sir Charles Lucas and Sir George Lysle (1648).

A Letter From His Excellency the Lord Fairfax to the House of Peers, upon Munday being the fifth of June, 1648, concerning all the proceedings in Kent (1648).

A Letter from Plymouth concerning the late Occurrances and affaires of that place (1643).

A Letter Of His Excellency Thomas Lord Fairfax, To the Right Honorable The Lord Mayor of the City of London, For the better preserving a right Understanding between the City and Army (1648).

A Letter From Sir William Waller, A Member of the House of Commons, To the Right Honorable Robert Earl of Essex his Excellencie; Of a Great Victory he obtained at Malmesbury, 23 Martii, in the County of Wilts (1643).

[Lister, Joseph], *The Autobiography of Joseph Lister, of Bradford in Yorkshire, to which is added a Contemporary Account of the Defence of Bradford and Capture of Leeds by the Parliamentarians in 1642*, ed. Thomas Wright (1842).

Lithgow, William, *The Siege of Newcastle* (Newcastle, 1820).

The Lord General's Letter To the Honourable William Lenthal Esq., Speaker of the Honorable House of Commons, Wherein is fully related, The Particulars of the Fight at Maidstone, Where were near Three hundred slain, about One thousand three hundred Prisoners, Five hundred Horse, Three thousand Arms, Nine Foot Colours, and Eight pieces of Ordnance, with great store of Ammunition, taken by the Lord Generals Forces (1648).

The Loyall Sacrifice: Presented In the Lives and Deaths of those two Eminent-Heroick Patterns For Valour, Discipline, and Fidelity . . . Sir Charles Lucas, And Sir George Lisle (n.pl., 1648).

[Ludlow, Edmund], *The Memoirs of Edmund Ludlow Lieutenant-General of Horse in the Army of the Commonwealth of England 1625–1672*, ed. C. H. Firth, 2 vols. (Oxford, 1894).

[Luke, Samuel], *Journal of Sir Samuel Luke: Scoutmaster General to the Earl of Essex*, Oxfordshire Record Society, 29, 31, 33 (1947, 1950, 1953).

———— The *Letter Books of Sir Samuel Luke 1644–45*, ed. H. G. Tibbutt, Publications of the Bedfordshire Historical Record Society, 42 (1963).

Markham, G[ervase], *The Souldiers Exercise: in three Bookes. Containing most necessary and curious rules for the exact mustering both of Horse-troopes, and Foote-bands, with severall formes of Battailes described in Figures* (1639).

Marshall, Stephen, *The Right Understanding of the Times: Opened In a Sermon preached to the Honorable House of Commons, December 30. 1646. at Margaret Westminster* (1647).

Meeke, Will[iam], *The Faithfull Scout: Giving an Alarme to Yorkshire, (especially to the East-Ryding) and all other places at this time freed from the misery of Warre. Or, A Treatise tending to stirre up men from security which possesses them, because (as they think) all danger is past, now that the Seat of Warre is removed from them* (York, 1647).

Mercurius Belgicus: or, A briefe Chronologie of the Battails, Sieges, Conflicts, and other most remarkable passages from the beginning of this Rebellion, to the 25. of March, 1646. Together with A Catalogue of the Persons of Quality slain in both Sides (n.pl., 1646).

Mercurius Elencticus, *The Anatomy of the Westminster Juncto, or A Summary of their Designs against the King, City, and Kingdom* (n.pl., [1648]).

Mercurius Rusticus: or, The Countries Complaint of the barbarous Out-rages Committed by the Sectaries of this late flourishing Kindgome. Together with A briefe Chronologie of the Battails, Sieges, Conflicts, and other most remarkable passges from the beginning of this unnaturall Warre, to the 25. of March, 1646 (n.pl., 1646).

A Miraculous Victory Obtained by the Right Honorable, Ferdinando Lord Fairfax, against the Army under the Command of the Earl of Newcastle at Wakefield (1643).

Monro, Robert, *Monro His Expedition with the Worthy Scots Regiment (called Mac-Keyes Regiment) levied in August 1626 by Sir Donald Mac-Key Lord Rhees, Colonell for his Majesties service in Denmark, and reduced after the Battaile of Nerling to one Company in September 1634 at Wormes in the Paltz* (1637).

A more Exact Relation of The Siege laid to the Town of Leicester: How it was maintained, and how lost, and what Quarter was given by the Kings Forces (1645).

A most true Relation Of divers notable Passages of Divine Providence in the great deliverance and wonderful victory obtained by the Parliaments Forces under the command of the Earle of Stamford, in the county of Devon, against the Army of Cavaliers, raised by Sir Ralph Hopton and his adherents, rebels and traitours, Cornish-men and others: upon Tuesday the 25. of April. 1643 (1643).

A Narration of The great Victory, (Through Gods Providence) Obtained by the Parliaments Forces Under Sir William Waller, At Alton in Surrey the 13. of this instant December, 1643. Against the Cavaliers; where were taken neer a thousand Prisoners, a thousand Arms, two hundred Horse, with divers Officers of great quality ([1643]).

A Narration of the Siege and taking of the Town of Leicester The last of May. 1645. by the Kings Forces: Together With other proceedings of the Committee, and answers to some Aspersion cast upon that Committee (1645).

[Nicholas, Edward], *Correspondence of Sir Edward Nicholas, Secretary of State*, 4 vols., Camden Society, NS 40, 50, 57, and 3rd ser. 31 (1886–1920).

Norden, John, *An Intended Guyde For English Travailers. Shewing in generall how far one Citie, & many Shire-Townes in England are distant from other Together, with the Shires in particular: and the Chiefe Townes in every of them* (1625).

[Norton, Ralph], *A Letter Concerning The Storming and Delivering up of the Castle of the Devises unto Lieutenant Generall Cromwell, For the Service of the Parliament* (1645).

Nye, Nathaniel, *The Art of Gunnery. Wherein is described the true way to make all sorts of Gunpowder, Gun-match, the Art of shooting in great and small Ordnance: Excellent ways to take Heights, Depths, Distances, accessible, or inaccessible, either single or divers distances at one operation: to draw the Map or Plot of any City, Town, Castle, or other fortified place. To make divers sorts of Artificiall Fire-works both for War and Recreation, also to cure all such Wounds that are curable, which may chance to happen by Gunpowder or Fire-works* (1647).

One Argument More Against the Cavaliers; Taken from their Violation of Churches ([1643]).

Orders Established The 14th of this present January, By His Excellency Sir Thomas Fairfax, For Regulating the Army (1646 [1647]).

Orders of the Lords and Commons . . . For Regulating of those Souldiers . . . under the Command of his Excellency, Robert Earle of Essex (1642).

An Ordinance of the Lords and Commons Assembled in Parliament, For Thursday next to be a day of Thanksgiving within the Lines of Communication. And throughout the whole Kingdome the 27 of this instant Iune, for the great Victory. Obtained against the Kings Forces, nere Knasby . . . Together with two exact Relations of the said Victory (1645).

Parival, J[ean], *The History of this Iron Age: Wherein is set down the true state of Europe, as it was in the year 1500. Also, The Original, and Causes of all the Warres, and Commotions, that have happened: Together with A Description of the most memorable Battels, Sieges,*

Actions and Transactions, both in Court and Camp, from that time till the present year 1656, tr. B. Harris, (1656).

A Particular Relation of the Action before Cyrencester (or Cycester) in Gloucestershire. Taken on Candlemas Day, 1642, by part of His Maiesties Army under the Conduct of His Highness Prince Rupert (1642), in Washbourn, *Bibliotheca Gloucestrensis.*

A perfect diurnall of the severall passages in our late journey into Kent ([1642]).

A Perfect Relation of the taking of Leicester; With the severall marches of the Kings Army since the taking thereof. Colonell Hastings being made the Goverour. With the state of the Town at this present. And how they plunder the Country (1645).

[Peter, Hugh], *Mr Peters last Report of the English Wars, Occasioned by the importunity of a Friend Pressing an Answer to Seven Quaeres* (1646).

Pond's Almanack for the yeare of our Lord Christ 1649 (Cambridge, 1649).

[Povey, Thomas], *The Moderator expecting Sudden Peace, or Certaine Ruine. Directed by Reason, Arising out of the consideration of what hath already happened, Our present Condition, and the most likely Consequents of These* (1642).

[Poyntz, Sydenham], *Major Gen: Poyntz's Letter to the Honorable William Lenthall Esq. . . . Or, A true Relation of the Storming . . . of Belvoyr Castle* (1645).

—— *The Relation of Sydnam Poyntz 1624–1636*, ed. A. T. S. Goodrick, Camden Society, 3rd ser. 14 (1908).

Prince Rupert's Burning Love for England Discovered in Birmingham's Flames. Or A more Exact and true Narration of Birmingham's Calamities under the barbarous and inhumane Cruelties of P. Ruperts' forces (1643), in Jay, *Four Tracts relative to . . . Birmingham.*

Proceedings in Parliament 1625, ed. Maija Jansson and William B. Bidwell (New Haven, Conn., 1987).

Quarles, John, *Fons Lachrymarum; or A Fountain of Tears: From whence doth flow England's Complaint, Jeremiah's Lamentations Paraphras'd, with Divine Meditations: And an Elegy Upon that Son of Valor Sir Charles Lucas* (1655).

Querela Cantabrigiensis: Or, A Remonstrance By way of Apologie, For the banished Members of the late flourishing University of Cambridge (Oxford, 1646).

Raikes, G. A. (ed.), *The Ancient Vellum Book of the Honourable Artillery Company, being the Roll of Members from 1611 to 1682* (1890).

Ram, Robert, *The Souldiers Catechisme: Composed for The Parliaments Army: Consisting of two Parts: Wherein are chiefly taught, 1. The Justification, 2. The Qualification, of our Souldiers. Written for the Incouragement, and Instruction of all that have taken up Armes in this Cause of God and his People; especially the common Souldiers*, 7th edn. (1645).

—— (*sic*, properly Thomas Swadlin), *The Souldiers Catechisme*, etc., as above, 8th edn. (1645; a royalist parody version of Ram's *Souldiers Catechisme*).

A Relation Of the Victory obtained by Sr. Thomas Fairfax, Generall of the Parliaments Forces, over the Enemies Forces, neer Harborough, on Saturday, June 14. 1645 Being a Letter brought from the Army by the City Scout, to the . . . Sheriffe of the City of London (1645).

[Reresby, John], *Memoirs of Sir John Reresby: The Complete Text and a Selection from his Letters*, ed. Andrew Browning (Glasgow, 1936).

Ricraft, Joseph, *A Survey of Englands Champions, and Truths faithfull Patriots. Or, A Chronological Recitemnt of the principall proceedings of the most worthy Commanders* of the prosperous Armies . . . With a most exact Relation of the severall Victories, as also the number of Commanders and Souldiers that have been slain on both sides, since these uncivill Wars began (1647).

The Rider of the White Horse And His Army, Their late good Successe in York-shire. Or A true and faithfull Relation of that famous and wonderfull victory at Bradford, obtained by the Club-men there . . . And of The taking of Leeds and Wakefield by the same men under the command of Sir Thomas Fairfax (1643); in Lister, *Autobiography*.

Roberts, John, *The Compleat Cannoniere: or, The Gunners Guide. Wherein are set forth exactly the Chiefe grounds and principals of the whole Art, in a very breife and Compendious forme, never by any set forth in the like nature before. With divers excellent Conclusions, both Arithmeticall and Geometricall belonging thereunto* (1639).

Rogers, Francis, *A Sermon preached on September the 20. 1632. In the Cathedrall Church of Christ at Canterbury, at the Funerall of William Proud, a Lieutenant Colonell, slaine at the last late siege of Mastricke* (1633).

Rollins, Hyder E. (ed.), *Cavalier and Puritan. Ballads and Broadsides Illustrating the Period of the Great Rebellion 1640–1660* (New York, 1923).

The Round-Heads Remembrancer: or, A true and particular Relation of the great defeat given to the Rebels by His Majesties good subjects of the County of Cornwall, under the Command of Sr Ralph Hopton, on Tuesday May 16. 1643 (1643).

Roy, Ian (ed.), *The Royalist Ordnance Papers 1642–1646*, 2 vols., Oxfordshire Record Society, 43, 49 (1963–4, 1971–3).

[Rupert, Prince], *A Speech Spoken by His Excellence Prince Rupert To his Sacred Majesty, and the Lords of his Privie Councell, at his returne from Redding to Oxford: Wherein is freely delivered his opinion concerning the present Warre, With his advise for the erecting of Forts and Garrison Townes in this Kingdom, and calling in the old English regiments out of Holland* (1642).

Rushworth, John, *Historical Collections of private Passages of State. Weighty matters in Law. Remarkable Proceedings*, 8 vols. (1680–1701).

[Ruthven, Patrick, earl of Brentford], *Ruthven Correspondence. Letters and Papers of Patrick Ruthven, Earl of Forth and Brentford, and his Family: A.D. 1615–A.D. 1662. With an Appendix of Papers Relating to Sir John Urry*, ed. William Dunn Macray, Roxburghe Club (1868).

Sedgwick, John, *Englands condition Parallell'd with Jacobs for troubles, salvations, hopes, Laid open in two sermons* (1642).

Severall Papers and Letters Betwixt his Excellency the Lord Fairfax The Earle of Norwich, Lord Capell, Sir Charles Lucas, about the surrender of Colchester. His Excellencies last Summons and Articles offered upon the Surrender thereof With the Answer in reply to the same. Also a Letter from his Excellency the Lord Fairfax To the . . . Inhabitants of the Towne of Colchester in answer to their desires for a free trade and commerce with the City of London during the Seige (1648).

Several Speeches of Duke Hamilton . . . Henry Earl of Holland, and Arthur Lord Capel, Upon the Scaffold Immediately before their Execution (1649).

Sheppard, S[amuel], *The Yeare of Jubile: Or, Englands Releasment, Purchased by Gods immediate assistance, and powerfull aiding of Her renowned Parliament and the Forces raised by them: Under the command of the Right Valiant, Prosperous, and pious Generall, Sir Thomas Fairfax* (1646).

[Sherley, Thomas], 'Discours of the Turkes by Sr. Thomas Sherley', ed. E. Denison Ross, *Camden Miscellany XVI*, Camden Society, 3rd ser. 52 (1936).

[Slingsby, Henry], *The Diary of Sir Henry Slingsby, of Scriven, Bart.*, ed. Daniel Parsons (1836).

____ *Original Memoirs, Written during the Great Civil War; being the Life of Sir Henry Slingsby, and Memoirs of Capt. Hodgson* (Edinburgh, 1806).

'Some Civil War Accounts, 1647–1650', ed. Ethel Kitson and E. K. Clark, *Thoresby Society Miscellanea*, 11/2 (1902), 137–235.

'Some letters of the civil war', *Collections for a History of Staffordshire*, Staffordshire Record Society (1941), 137–47.

[Somers Tracts], *A Collection of Scarce and Valuable Tracts on the most Interesting and Entertaining Subjects: . . . selected from an infinite number in print and manuscript, in . . . libraries; particularly that of the late Lord Somers*, ed. Walter Scott, 2nd edn., 13 vols. (1809–1815).

The Souldiers Language. Or, A Discourse between two Souldiers, the one coming from York, the other from Bristoll, shewing how the Warres go on, and how the Souldiers carrie and demean themselves (1644).

The Souldiers Pocket Bible: Containing the most (if not all) those places contained in holy Scripture, which doe shew the qualifications of his inner man, that is a fit Souldier to fight the Lords Battels . . . And may bee also usefull for any Christian to meditate upon, now in this miserable time of Warre (1643).

Sprigge, Ioshua, *Anglia Rediviva; Englands Recovery: being the History of the Motions, Actions, and Successes of the Army under the Immediate Conduct of His Excellency Sr. Thomas Fairfax, Kt. Captain-General Of all the Parliaments Forces in England* (1647).

Staunton, Edmund, *Phinehas's Zeal in Execution of Iudgement. Or, A Divine Remedy for Englands Misery. A Sermon Preached before the Right Honourable House of Lords in the Abbey at Westminster, at their late Solemne monethly Fast, October 30. 1644* (1645).

[Styward, Thomas], *The Pathwaie to Martiall Discipline, devided into two Bookes, verie necessarie for young Souldiers, or for all such as loveth the profession of Armes: latelie set foorth by Thomas Styward Gentleman* (1581).

____ *The Pathwaie to Martiall Discipline. Now newly Imprinted, and devided into three bookes. Whereunto is added the order and use of the Spaniards in their Martiall affaires: which Copie was lately found in the Fort in Ireland, where the Spaniards and Italians had fortified themselves* (1582); this edition includes *A Compendious Treatise entituled, De re Militari, containing principall orders to be observed in Martiall affaires. Written in the Spanish tongue, by that worthie and famous Captaine, Luis Gutierres de la Vega, Citizen of Medina del Campo*, tr. Nicholas Lichefild (1582).

Suckling, John, 'A Letter written to the lower House of Parliament', *Somers Tracts*, 4. 106–15.

Sutcliffe, Matthew, *The Practice, Proceedings, and Lawes of armes, described out of the doings of most valiant and expert Captaines, and confirmed both by ancient, and moderne examples, and praecedents* (1593).

S[wadlin], T[homas], *The soldiers catechisme, composed for the Kings armie; wherein His 1. Cause is justified, and his enemies condemned. 2. Soldier is instructed, and the Rebell reclaimed. Written for the encouragement and direction of all that have taken up armes in this cause of God, his Church, and his anointed; especially the common soldiers* (Oxford, 1645).

S[wadlin], T[homas], *See also* Robert Ram [*sic*], *Souldiers Catechisme*, 8th edn.

The Swedish Discipline, Religious, Civile, And Military. The First Part, In The Formes of Prayer daily used by those of the Swedish Nation, in the Armie. Together with two severall Prayers, uttered upon severall occasions by the pious King, which God immediately heard and granted him. The second Part, in the excellent Orders observed in the Armie; whereof we here present you the Articles, by which the Souldiery is governed. The third Part, in the Kings Commission for levying of a Regiment: . . . *Last of all, Is the famous Battell of Leipsich, in two fayre Figures also set forth* (1632).

The Swedish Intelligencer. The first part. Wherein, out of the Truest And choicest Informations are the famous Actions of that warlike Prince Historically led along: from his Majesties first entering into the Empire, untill his great Victory over the Generall Tilly, at the Battell of Leipsich, 'Newly Revised, and corrected' (1632; and see the second and third parts, 1632, 1633).

[Symonds, Richard], *Diary of the Marches of the Royal Army during the Great Civil War; kept by Richard Symonds*, ed. C. E. Long, Camden Society, 74 (1859).

—— *Diary of the Marches of the Royal Army* (as above), with supplementary introduction by Ian Roy (Cambridge, 1997).

Taylor, John, *The Carriers Cosmographie. or A Briefe Relation of The Innes, Ordinaries, Hosteries, and other Lodgings in, and neere London, where the Carriers, Waggons, Foote-posts and Higglers doe usually come, from any parts, townes, shires and countries* . . . *With nominations of what daies of the weeke they doe come to London, and on what daies they returne* (1637).

Three Letters, From the Right Honourable Sir Thomas Fairfax, Lieut. Gen. Crumwell and the Committee residing in the Army. Wherein All the Particulars of the Great Victory obtained by our Forces against His Majesties, is fully related, fought the 14 of Iune, 1645 (1645).

Three Ordinances of the Lords and Commons Assembled in Parliament. One Concerning the Trained Bands . . . *Another, That every Captain shall choose a Marshall for his Company, to take notice of Delinquents* . . . *And lastly, for the Incouragement of all such Apprentices as have or shall voluntarily list themselves in the Service of King and Parliament* . . . *under* . . . *the Earle of Essex* (1644).

T. J., *The Christian Souldier. Or, Preparation for Battaile. A Legend containing the Rules for a Souldier, in whom is met at once Religion and Resolution* (1642).

[Townshend, Henry], *Diary of Henry Townshend of Elmley Lovett 1640–1663*, i, ed. J. W. Willis Bund, Worcestershire Historical Society (1920).

T. R., *The Souldiers Accompt. Or, Tables Showing the Personall Allowance of Pay to all Officers and Souldiers belonging to an Army, either Foot or Horse, from a day to a week, from a week to a moneth, from a moneth to thirteen moneths. Also To all Officers and Attendants on a Train of Artillerie, consisting of thirty six Pieces of Ordnance. Together with The Charge of Pay to 40000. Foot, and 10000 Horse, from a day to a year* (1647).

Trelawny Papers, ed. W. D. Cooper, *Camden Miscellany II*, Camden Society, 55 (1853).

The Triumph of Loyalty: or The Happinesse of a Suffering Spirit. Set Forth In a Funerall Sermon, composed for the Obsequies of those two incomparable and noble Warriors, Sir Charles Lucas and Sir George Lisle, Who after the Surrender of Colchester upon Tearmes of Mercy; were most barbarously, and cruelly shot to death by the appointment of the Army: At Colchester, Aug. 27. 1648 (1648).

A True and Exact Relation Of the taking of Colchester, Sent in a Letter From an Officer of the Army, (who was present during the siege in that service,) to a Member of the House of Commons. With a List of the Ordnance, Arms, and of 3076. private souldiers there taken: Also a List of the names of most of the Officers of note, and an account of the Cause of giving no quarter to Sir Charles Lucas, and Sir George Lisle (1648).

A True and Exact Relation Of the whole proceedings of the Parliaments Forces, that went out under the command of Colonel Brown with Colonell Manwaring Forces into Kent. To appease the tumult raised there by the Malignants and ill-affected to the Parliament. Wherein is a true Relation of the taking of the Towne of Tunbridge . . . Related by one that was not only an eye witnesse, but in the whole service (1643).

True, But Sad and Dolefull Newes from Shrewsbury. Expressed in two severall Letters: Wherof, The one was written to a Gentleman of the Inner-Temple: The other, To a friend in London, relating at large the severall Passages of the late skirmish at or near Worcester, between a Party of each Army, viz. Under the Command of Prince Robert on the one side, and of Colonell Sands on the other (1642).

A True Narration Of the most Observable Passages, in and at the late Seige of Plymouth, from the fifteenth day of September 1643, until the twenty fi[r]st of December following. Attested from thence under the hands of the most Credible Persons: Wherein is manifested to the World the handywork of God, and his gracious assistance to the United Forces of that Towne and Garrison. Together with an exact Map and Description of the Town and Fortifications thereof (1644).

A True Relation of The late Attempt made upon the Town of Ciceter in the County of Glouc', the seventh day of January, 1642. By the Lord Marquesse Hartford, Lord Generall of the Cavaliers of the Western parts, assisted by Prince Robert . . . Together with the Answer of Io: Georges, Esq., (an Inhabitant there, and one of the Burgesses of the Parliament) . . . to the severall Messages sent by that Lo: Generall (1642).

A True Relation of The taking of Sherborn-Castle. With Six hundred Prisoners, One thousand Arms, and great store of other Provisions. Sent in two Letters, The one, To the Right Honourable William Lenthall . . . And the other, to Edmund Prideaux and Dennis Bond, Esq.; Members of the said House ([1645]).

Two Sallies Forth by the Lord Goring and Sir Charles Lucas at Colchester, on Monday and Tuesday last; the manner of the severall Fights, and the number that were killed and taken prisoners on both sides. The taking of the Enemies Court of Guard, the setting fire thereof, and burning downe the Wind-Mills (1648).

Venn, Thomas, *Military Observations or Tacticks put into Practice for the Exercise of Horse and Foot; the Original of Ensignes; The Postures of their Colours; with Sir Francis Veres Directions for Officers, And a small treatise of Invasion* (1672).

Vicars, John, *Babylons Beautie; or the Romish-Catholicks Sweet-Heart. Containing a most lively and lovely Description of Romes Cardinall Vertues and rarest Endowments* (1644).

——— *Magnalia Dei Anglicana. Or, Englands Parliamentary Chronicle*, comprising: *Jehovah-Jireh. God in the Mount* (1644); *Gods Arke Overtopping the Worlds Waves* (1646); *The Burning-Bush not Consumed* (1646).

[Vincent, Philip], *The Lamentations of Germany. Wherein, As in a Glass, we may behold her miserable condition, and reade the woefull effects of sinne. Composed by Dr. Vincent Theol. an eyewitnesse thereof, and illustrated by Pictures, the more to affect the Reader* (1638).

Walker, Edward, *Historical Discourses, upon Several Occasions* (1705).

Waller, William, *Recollections*, in *The Poetry of Anna Matilda* (1788).

_____ *Vindication of the Character and Conduct of Sir William Waller, Knight, Commander in Chief of the Parliament Forces in the West* (1793).

[Walsingham, Edward], *Alter Brittanniae Heros: or the Life of the Most Honourable Knight, Sir Henry Gage, Late Governour of Oxford, Epitomiz'd* (Oxford, 1645).

Ward, Robert, *Anima'dversions of Warre; or, A Militarie Magazine of the Truest Rules, and Ablest Instructions, for the Managing of Warre* (1639).

[Washbourn, John] (ed.), *Bibliotheca Gloucestrensis: A Collection of Scarce and Curious Tracts, relating to the County and City of Gloucester; illustrative of, and published during the Civil War; with an Historical Introduction, Notes, and an Appendix* (Gloucester, 1825).

Wentworth Papers 1597–1628, ed. J. P. Cooper, Camden Society, 4th ser. 12 (1973).

[Wharton, Nehemiah], 'Letters from a Subaltern Officer of the Earl of Essex's Army, written in the Summer and Autumn of 1642; detailing the early movements of that portion of the Parliament Forces which was formed by the Volunteers of the Metropolis; and their further movements when amalgamated with the rest of the Earl of Essex's Troops', ed. Henry Ellis, *Archaeologia*, 35 (1853), 2. 310–34.

Whitelock, [Bulstrode], *Memorials of the English Affairs: or, An Historical account of what passed from the Beginning of the Reign of King Charles the First, to King Charles the Second His Happy Restauration*, 'New Edition', (1732).

[Whiteway, William], *William Whiteway of Dorchester. His Diary 1618 to 1635*, introd. David Underdown, Dorset Record Society, 12 (Dorchester, 1991).

A Wicked Plot against the Person of Sir William Waller (1644).

Wills and Inventories from the Registers of the Commissary of Bury St. Edmunds and the Archdeacon of Sudbury, ed. Samuel Tymms, Camden Society, 49 (1850).

[Wilde, George], *A Sermon preached upon Sunday the Third of March In St Maries Oxford, Before The Great Assembly of the Members, of the Honourable House of Commons there Assembled* (Oxford, 1643).

Wilson, Arthur, *The Inconstant Lady, A Play* (Oxford, 1814).

[Wingate, Edward], *The True Copie of a Letter written by Captaine Wingate, now a Prisoner in Ludlow, taken by the Malignant Partie, in the late Battaile fought at Worcester . . . Setting forth The inhumane barbarous and savage Cruelties towards him, and how he was compelled to ride through the Army naked: with his Resolution to die in the Parliaments Cause* (1642).

Wirley, Edward, *The Prisoners Report: Or, A true Relation of the cruell usage of the Prisoners in Oxford. Together with the strange deliverance of about fourtie men out of the Dungeon in Bridewell in Oxford March the 5. and 6.* (1642/3).

Wogan, Edward, 'The Proceedings of the New-moulded army from the time they were brought together in 1645, till the King's going to the Isle of Wight in 1647', in Carte, *Letters*, 1. 126–42.

[Wood Anthony], *The Life and Times of Anthony Wood, antiquary of Oxford, 1632–1695, described by Himself*, ed. Andrew Clark, 2 vols. (Oxford, 1891–2).

A Worthy Speech, spoken by his Excellence the Earle of Essex, in the Head of his Armie, before his Arrivall at Worcester wherein is declared every particular Order and Duty which his Ecellence expects to be performed, both by his Commanders and Souldiers (1642), *Somers Tracts*, 4. 476–7.

Wotton, Henry, *A Parallel betweene Robert late Earle of Essex, and George late Duke of Buckingham* (1641), *Somers Tracts*, 4. 154–65 (with emended title).

Zouche, Richard, *Iuris et Judicii Fecialis, sive, Iuris Inter Gentes, et Quaestionum de Eodem Explicatio*, ed. Thomas Erskine Holland, 2 vols. (Washington, DC, 1911).

PRINTED SECONDARY WORKS

Adair, John, *Cheriton 1644: The Campaign and the Battle* (Kineton, 1973).

——— *Roundhead General. The Campaigns of Sir William Waller* (Stroud, 1997).

Adams, Simon, 'A Puritan Crusade? The Composition of the Earl of Leicester's Expedition to the Netherlands, 1585–1586', in *The Dutch in Crisis, 1585–1588: People and Politics in Leicester's Time* (Leiden, 1988).

Apple, R.W., 'A New Way of War', *New York Times* (20 Apr. 2003).

Ashton, Robert, *Counter-Revolution: The Second Civil War and its Origins, 1646–8* (New Haven, Conn., 1994).

Aylmer, G. E., *The King's Servants. The Civil Service of Charles I 1625–1642* (1961).

Bailey, Thomas, *Annals of Nottinghamshire. History of the County of Nottingham, including the Borough*, 4 vols. ([1853]).

Baker, Anthony, *A Battlefield Atlas of the English Civil War* (1986).

Bayley, A. R., *The Great Civil War in Dorset* (Taunton, 1910).

Beckett, Ian F. W., *The Amateur Military Tradition 1558–1945* (1991).

Beller, E. A., 'The Military Expedition of Sir Charles Morgan to Germany, 1627–9', *EHR* 43 (1928), 528–39.

Binns, Jack, 'Captain Browne Bushell: North Sea Adventurer and Pirate', *Northern History*, 27 (1991), 90–105.

Block, Robert, 'The Tragedy of Rwanda', *New York Times* (20 Oct. 1994).

Box, E. G., 'Kent in Early Road Books of the Seventeenth Century', *Archaeologia Cantiana*, 44 (1932), 1–12.

Bowen, Lloyd, 'Representations of Wales and the Welsh during the Civil Wars and Interregnum', *HR* 77 (2004), 358–76.

Bull, Hedley, 'The Importance of Grotius in the Study of International Relations', in Bull *et al.*, *Hugo Grotius and International Relations*, 65–93.

——— Kingsbury, Benedict, and Roberts, Adam (eds.), *Hugo Grotius and International Relations* (Oxford, 1992).

Burghclere, [Winifred], *Strafford* (1931).

Carman, W. Y., *A History of Firearms From Earliest Times to 1914* (1955).

Chandler, David G., *Atlas of Military Strategy* (New York, 1980).

Clode, Charles M., *The Administration of Justice under Military and Martial Law, as applicable to The Army, Navy, Marines, and Auxiliary Forces*, 2nd edn. (1874).

——— *The Military Forces of the Crown; their Administration and Government*, 2 vols. (1869).

Coate, Mary, *Cornwall in the Great Civil War and Interregnum 1642–1660* (Oxford, 1933).

Coates, Ben, *The Impact of the English Civil War on the Economy of London, 1642–50* (Aldershot, 2004).

Coates, Charles, *The History and Antiquities of Reading* (1802).

Cockle, Maurice J. D., *A Bibliography of English Military Books up to 1642* (1900).

C[okayne], G. E. (ed.), *The Complete Peerage*, revised edn., 13 vols. (1910–59).

Collinson, Patrick, *The Birthpangs of Protestant England: Religious and Cultural Change in the Sixteenth and Seventeenth Centuries* (1988).

Contamine, Philippe (ed.), *War and Competition between States* (Oxford, 2000).

Cromwell, Thomas, *History and Description of the Ancient Town and Borough of Colchester in Essex*, 2 vols. (1825).

Cruickshank, C. G., *Elizabeth's Army*, 2nd edn. (Oxford, 1966).

Cust, Richard, 'News and Politics in Early Seventeenth-Century England', *Past and Present*, 112 (1986), 60–90.

Dalrymple, James, and Sage, Adam, 'The War Crimes the Allies Chose to Forget', *Independent* (27 Mar. 1990).

Dawson, William Harbutt, *Cromwell's Understudy: The Life and Times of General Lambert and the Rise and Fall of the Protectorate* (1938).

Derbridge, G., 'A History of the Drums and Fifes 1650–1700', *JSAHR* 44 (1966), 50–5.

Dobson, Mary J., 'The Last Hiccup of the Old Demographic Regime: Population Stagnation and Decline in Late Seventeenth and Early Eighteenth Century South-East England', *Continuity and Change*, 4 (1989), 395–428.

Donagan, Barbara, 'The Army, the State and the Soldier in the English Civil War', in Mendle (ed.), *The Putney Debates of 1647*, 79–102.

—— 'Atrocity, War Crime and Treason in the English Civil War', *AHR*, 99 (1994), 1137–66.

—— 'Codes and Conduct in the English Civil War', *Past and Present*, 118 (1988), 65–95.

—— 'Halcyon Days and the Literature of War: England's Military Education before 1642', *Past and Present*, 147 (1995), 65–100.

—— 'Myth, Memory and Martyrdom: Colchester 1648', *Essex Archaeology and History*, 34 (2004), 172–80.

—— 'Understanding Providence: The Difficulties of Sir William and Lady Waller', *Journal of Ecclesiastical History*, 39 (1988), 433–44.

—— 'The Web of Honour: Soldiers, Christians, and Gentlemen in the English Civil War', *HJ* 44 (2001), 365–89.

Draper, G. I. A. D., 'Grotius' Place in the Development of Legal Ideas about War', in Bull *et al.* (eds.), *Hugo Grotius and International Relations*, 177–207.

—— 'Wars of National Liberation and War Criminality', in Howard (ed.), *Restraints on War*, 135–62.

Dukes, Paul, 'New Perspectives: Alexander Leslie and the Smolensk War, 1632–4', in Murdoch (ed.), *Scotland and the Thirty Years War*, 173–89.

Dumbauld, Edward, *The Life and Legal Writings of Hugo Grotius* (Norman, Okla., 1969).

Duncumb, John, *Collections towards the History and Antiquities of the County of Hereford*, 3 vols. (Hereford, 1804–82).

Edwards, Peter, *Dealing in Death: The Arms Trade and the British Civil Wars, 1638–52* (Stroud, Glos., 2000).

—— 'Logistics and Supply', in Kenyon and Ohlmeyer (eds.), *Civil Wars*, 234–71.

Everitt, Alan, *The Community of Kent and the Great Rebellion 1640–60* (Leicester, 1986).

Firth, C. H., *Cromwell's Army: A History of the English Soldier during the Civil Wars, the Commonwealth and the Protectorate*, 3rd edn. (1921).

—— *The Regimental History of Cromwell's Army*, 2 vols. (Oxford, 1940).

Fissel, Mark Charles, *The Bishops' Wars: Charles I's Campaigns against Scotland, 1638–1640* (Cambridge, 1994).

Fletcher, Anthony, *A County Community in Peace and War: Sussex 1600–1660* (1975).

——and Stevenson, John (eds.), *Order and Disorder in Early Modern England* (Cambridge, 1985).

Foard, Glenn, *Naseby: The Decisive Campaign* (Whitstable, 1995).

Frank, Joseph, *The Beginnings of the English Newspaper 1620–1660* (Cambridge, Mass., 1961).

Friedrichs, Christopher R., 'The War and German Society', in Parker (ed.), *Thirty Years' War*, 208–15.

Frost, Robert I., 'Scottish Soldiers, Poland-Lithuania and the Thirty Years' War', in Murdoch (ed.), *Scotland and the Thirty Years' War*, 191–213.

Gardiner, S. R., *History of the Commonwealth and Protectorate 1649–1656*, 4 vols. (Adlestrop, Glos., 1988).

——*History of the Great Civil War 1642–1649*, 4 vols. (1987).

Gaunt, Peter, *The Cromwellian Gazetteer: An Illustrated Guide to Britain in the Civil War and Commonwelth* (Gloucester, 1987).

Gentles, Ian, 'The Iconography of Revolution: England 1642–1649', in Gentles, Morrill, and Worden (eds.), *Soldiers, Writers, and Statesmen*, 91–113.

——*The New Model Army in England, Ireland and Scotland, 1645–1653* (Oxford, 1992).

——'Political Funerals during the English Revolution', in Porter (ed.), *London and the Civil War*, 205–24.

——'The Struggle for London in the Second Civil War', *HJ* 26 (1983), 277–305.

——Morrill, John, and Worden, Blair (eds.), *Soldiers, Writers and Statesmen of the English Revolution* (1998).

Gimson, Basil L., and Russell, Percy, *Leicestershire Maps: A Brief Survey* (Leicester, 1947).

Goebel, Julius, Jr., *Felony and Misdemeanor: A Study in the History of English Criminal Procedure*, i (New York, 1937).

Gould, I. C., 'The Siege of Colchester', *Trans. Essex Archaeological Society*, NS 8 (1903), 377.

Gregg, Pauline, *Free-Born John: A Biography of John Lilburne* (1961).

Grell, Ole Peter, *Calvinist Exiles in Tudor and Stuart England* (Aldershot, 1996).

Griffin, Margaret, *Regulating Religion and Morality in the King's Armies 1639–1646* (Brill, 2004).

Grose, Francis, *The Antiquities of England and Wales*, 8 vols. ([1783]–1797).

——*Military Antiquities respecting a History of the English Army, from the Conquest to the Present Time*, 2 vols. (1786–8).

Grosjean, Alexia, 'Scotland: Sweden's Closest Ally?', in Murdoch (ed.), *Scotland and the Thirty Years' War*, 143–71.

Haggenmacher, Peter, 'Grotius and Gentili: A Reassessment of Thomas E. Holland's Inaugural Lecture', in Bull *et al.* (eds.), *Hugo Grotius and International Relations*, 133–76.

Hale, J. R., *Renaissance War Studies* (1983).

Hall, A. R., *Ballistics in the Seventeenth Century* (Cambridge, 1952).

Hardacre, P. H., 'Patronage and Purchase in the Irish Standing Army under Thomas Wentworth, Earl of Strafford, 1632–1640', *JSAHR*, 67 (1989), 40–5, 94–104.

Harley, J. B., 'Meaning and Ambiguity in Tudor Cartography', in Tyacke (ed.), *English Map-Making 1500–1650*, 22–45.

Hart, B. H. Liddell, *Strategy: The Indirect Approach*, 3rd edn. (1954).

Hartigan, Richard Shelly, *Lieber's Code and the Law of War* (Chicago, 1983).

Healy, Thomas, and Sawday, Jonathan (eds.), *Literature and the English Civil War* (Cambridge, 1990).

Helgerson, Richard, 'The Land Speaks: Cartography, Chorography, and Subversion in Renaissance England', *Representations*, 16 (1986), 50–85.

Holdsworth, W. S., *Essays in Law and History*, ed. A. L. Goodhart and H. G. Hanbury (Oxford, 1946).

Hollings, J. F., *The History of Leicester during the Great Civil War* (Leicester, 1840).

Holmes, Clive, *The Eastern Assocation in the English Civil War* (Cambridge, 1974).

——— *Seventeenth-Century Lincolnshire* (Lincoln, 1980).

Howard, Michael (ed.), *Restraints on War: Studies in the Limitation of Armed Conflict* (Oxford, 1979).

Hughes, Ann, *Politics, Society and Civil War in Warwickshire, 1620–1660* (Cambridge, 1987).

Hutton, Ronald, *The Royalist War Effort 1642–1646* (New York, 1984).

——— and Reeves, Wylie, 'Sieges and Fortifications', in Kenyon and Ohlmeyer, *Civil Wars*, 195–233.

Kamen, Henry, 'The Economic and Social Consequences of the Thirty Years' War', *Past and Present*, 39 (1968), 44–61.

Keegan, John, 'If you Don't, we Won't', *TLS* (24 Nov. 1995).

Keen, M. H., *The Laws of War in the Late Middle Ages* (1960).

Kennard, A. Norris, 'A Civil War Hand Grenade', *The Bradford Antiquary*, NS 39/8 (1958), 191–3.

Kent, Joan R., *The English Village Constable 1580–1642: A Social and Administrative Study* (Oxford, 1986).

Kenyon, John, *The Civil Wars of England* (1988).

——— and Ohlmeyer, Jane (eds.), *The Civil Wars: A Military History of England, Scotland, and Ireland 1638–1660* (Oxford, 1998).

Kerling, Nellie J. M., 'A Seventeenth Century Hospital Matron: Margaret Blague (Matron of St. Bartholomew's Hospital, 1643–1675)', *Transactions of the London and Middlesex Archaeological Society*, 22/3 (1970), 30–6.

Kingston, Alfred, *East Anglia and the Great Civil War* (1897).

Lattey, R. T., Parsons, E. J. S., and Philip, I. G., 'A Contemporary Map of the Defences of Oxford in 1644', *Oxoniensia*, 1 (1936), 161–72.

Lee, Ross, *Law and Local Society in the time of Charles I: Bedfordshire and the Civil War*, Bedfordshire Historical Society, 65 (1986).

Lindley, Keith J., 'The Impact of the 1641 Rebellion upon England and Wales, 1641–5', *Irish Historical Studies*, 18 (1972–3), 143–76.

Lipscomb, George, *The History and Antiquities of the County of Buckingham*, 4 vols. (1847).

Luttwak, Edward N., 'Au-dessus de la mêlée', *TLS* (29 Jan. 1994).

Lyndon, Brian, 'Essex and the King's Cause in 1648', *HJ* 29 (1986), 17–39.

——— 'The Parliament's Army in Essex, 1648: A Military Community's Association with County Society during the Second Civil War', *JSAHR* 59 (1981), 140–60, 229–42.

Maclean, John, *Historical and Genealogical Memoirs of the Family of Poyntz* (Exeter, 1886).

Malcolm, Joyce L., 'A King in Search of Soldiers: Charles I in 1642', *HJ* 21 (1978), 251–73.

Markham, Clement R., *'The Fighting Veres': Lives of Sir Francis Vere . . . and of Sir Horace Vere* (1888).

Marshall, Henry, *Miscellany; Comprehending a History of the Recruiting of the Army, Military Punishments, &c.* (1846).

Mastin, John, *The History and Antiquities of Naseby* (Cambridge, 1782).

Mendle, Michael (ed.), *The Putney Debates of 1647: The Army, the Levellers and the English State* (Cambridge, 2001).

Meron, Theodor, *Henry's Wars and Shakespeare's Laws* (Oxford, 1993).

Morant, Philip, *The History and Antiquities Of the County of Essex*, 2 vols. (Colchester, 1768).

Morgan, Victor, 'The Literary Image of Globes and Maps in Early Modern England', in Tyacke (ed.), *English Map-Making*, 46–56.

Morrill, J. S., *Cheshire 1630–1660: County Government and Society during the English Revolution* (Oxford, 1974).

——— 'Mutiny and Discontent in English Provincial Armies, 1645–1647', in Morrill, *The Nature of the English Revolution* (1993), 332–58.

——— and Walter, J. D., 'Order and Disorder in the English Revolution', in Fletcher and Stevenson (eds.), *Order and Disorder in Early Modern England*, 137–65.

——— Slack, Paul, and Woolf, Daniel (eds.), *Public Duty and Private Conscience in Seventeenth-Century England: Essays Presented to G. E. Aylmer* (Oxford, 1993).

Morshead, Owen, 'Royalist Prisoners in Windsor Castle', *Berkshire Archaeological Journal*, 56 (1958), 1–26.

Murdoch, Steve (ed.), *Scotland and the Thirty Years' War 1618–1648* (Leiden, 2001).

Nef, John U., *War and Human Progress: An Essay on the Rise of Industrial Civilization* (Cambridge, Mass., 1952).

Newman, Peter, *Atlas of the English Civil War* (Beckenham, 1985).

——— 'The King's Servants: Conscience, Principle, and Sacrifice in Armed Royalism', in Morrill *et al.* (eds.), *Public Duty and Private Conscience*, 225–41.

——— *The Old Service. Royalist Regimental Colonels and the Civil War, 1642–46* (Manchester, 1993).

——— *Royalist Officers in England and Wales, 1642–1660: A Biographical Dictionary* (New York, 1981).

Noonan, Kathleen M., ' "The cruell pressure of an enraged barbarous people": Irish and English Identity in Seventeenth Century Propaganda and Policy', *HJ* 41 (1998), 151–77.

——— ' "Martyrs in Flames": Sir John Temple and the Conception of the Irish in English Martyrologies', *Albion*, 30 (2004), 223–55.

O'Riordan, Christopher, 'Thomas Ellison, the Hixson estate and the Civil War', *Durham County Local History Society Bulletin*, 39 (1987), 3–11.

Parker, Geoffrey, 'The Etiquette of Atrocity: The More Things Change, the More they Stay the Same', *MHQ: Quarterly Journal of Military History* (1993).

——— *The Military Revolution: Military Innovation and the Rise of the West, 1500–1800* (Cambridge, 1988).

Parker, Geoffrey *et al.*, *The Thirty Years War* (1984).

Parry, Graham, 'A Troubled Arcadia', in Healy and Sawday (eds.), *Literature and the English Civil War*, 38–45.

Pestana, Carla Gardina, *The English Atlantic in an Age of Revolution* (Cambridge, Mass., 2004).

Porter, Stephen, 'The Civil War Destruction of Boarstall', *Records of Buckinghamshire*, 26 (1984), 86–91.

—— *London and the Civil War* (1996).

Prest, Wilfrid (ed.), *The Professions in Early Modern England* (1987).

Raikes, G. A., *The History of the Honourable Artillery Company*, 2 vols. (1878–9).

Raudzens, George, 'Firepower Limitations in Modern Military History', *JSAHR* 67 (1989), 130–53.

Reay, Barry, *The Quakers and the English Revolution* (1985).

Redlich, Fritz, *De Praeda Militari: Looting and Booty 1500–1815*, Vierteljahrschrift für Sozial- und Wirtschaftsgeschichte, 39 (1956).

Redworth, Glyn, 'Of Pimps and Princes: Three Unpublished Letters from James I and the Prince of Wales Relating to the Spanish Match', *HJ*, 37 (1994), 401–9.

Roberts, Keith, 'Citizen Soldiers: The Military Power of the City of London', in Porter (ed.), *London in the Civil War*, 89–116.

Rosen, Jeffrey, 'The Social Police: Following the Law, Because you'd be Too Embarrassed Not to', *New Yorker* (20–7 Oct. 1997).

Round, J. H., 'The Case of Lucas and Lisle', *Trans. RHS* ns 8 (1894), 157–80.

—— 'Colchester during the Commonwealth', *EHR* 15 (1900), 641–64.

Roy, Ian, 'England Turned Germany? The Aftermath of the Civil War in its European Context', *Trans. RHS* 5th ser. 28 (1978), 127–44.

—— 'George Digby, Royalist Intrigue and the Collapse of the Cause', in Gentles, Morrill and Worden (eds.), *Soldiers, Writers and Statesmen*, 68–90.

—— 'The Profession of Arms', in Prest (ed.), *Professions in Early Modern England*, 25–63.

—— 'The Royalist Council of War, 1642–6', *BIHR* 35 (1962), 150–68.

Russell, Conrad, 'The First Army Plot of 1641', *Trans. RHS* 5th ser. 38 (1988), 85–106.

Schubert, H. R., *History of the British Iron and Steel Industry from c.450 B.C. to A.D. 1775* (1957).

Seaver, Paul S., *Wallington's World: A Puritan Artisan in Seventeenth Century London* (Stanford, Calif., 1985).

Sharpe, Kevin, *The Personal Rule of Charles I* (New Haven, Conn., 1992).

Skelton, R. A. (comp.), *County Atlases of the British Isles 1579–1850*, i. *1579–1703* (1970).

—— (comp.), *Saxton's Survey of England and Wales, with a Facsimile of Saxton's Wall Map of 1583* (Amsterdam, 1974).

Skinner, Quentin, *The Foundations of Modern Political Thought*, 2 vols. (Cambridge, 1978).

Smith, A. E., *Colonists in Bondage: White Servitude and Convict Labor in America, 1607–1776* (Chapel Hill, NC, 1947).

Smith, D. L., 'The Fourth Earl of Dorset and the Personal Rule of Charles I', *JBS* 30 (1991), 257–87.

Smith, Victor, and Kelsey, Peter, 'The Lines of Communication: The Civil War Defences of London', in Porter (ed.), *London and the Civil War*, 117–47.

Spraggon, Julie, *Puritan Iconoclasm in the English Civil War* (Woodbridge, Suffolk, 2003).

Smurthwaite, David, *Battlefields of Britain: The Complete Illustrated Guide* (Exeter, 1984).

Stearns, Stephen J., 'Conscription and English Society in the 1620s', *JBS* 11 (1972), 1–23.

Stewart, Richard Winship, *The English Ordnance Office 1585–1625* (Woodbridge, Suffolk, 1996).

Stoyle, M. J., '"Pagans or Paragons?": Images of the Cornish during the English Civil War', *EHR*, 111 (1996), 299–323.

_____ *Soldiers and Strangers: An Ethnic History of the English Civil War* (New Haven, Conn., 2005).

Strong, Roy, *Recreating the Past: British History and the Victorian Painter* (New York, 1978).

Stucley, John, *Sir Bevill Grenvile and his Times 1596–1643* (Chichester, 1983).

Temple, R. K. G. (ed.), 'The Original Officer List of the New Model Army', *BIHR* 59 (1986), 50–77.

Thomas-Stanford, Charles, *Sussex in the Great Civil War and the Interregnum 1642–1660* (1910).

Trevelyan, G. M., *History of England* (New York, 1928).

Tyacke, Sarah (ed.), *English Map-Making 1500–1650* (1983).

Underdown, David, *Pride's Purge: Politics in the Puritan Revolution* (Oxford, 1971).

The Victoria County History of the County of Essex, ii, ed. William Page and J. Horace Round (1907).

The Victoria County History of the County of Buckingham, iii, ed. William Page (1925).

Wallace, John M., *Destiny his Choice: The Loyalism of Andrew Marvell* (Cambridge, 1968).

Walter, John, *Understanding Popular Violence in the English Revolution: The Colchester Plunderers* (Cambridge, 1999).

Warburton, Eliot, *Memoirs of Prince Rupert and the Cavaliers*, 3 vols. (1849).

Wedgwood, C. V., *The King's War, 1641–1647* (1958).

Wheeler, James Scott, *The Making of a World Power* (Stroud, Glos., 1999).

Whetham, Catherine Durning, and Whetham, William Cecil Dampier, *A History of the Life of Colonel Nathaniel Whetham: A Forgotten Soldier of the Civil Wars* (1907).

Wilson, John, *Fairfax: A Life of Thomas, Lord Fairfax, Captain-General of all the Parliament's forces in the Civil War, Creator and Commander of the New Model Army* (New York, 1985).

Woodward, B. B., Wilks, Theodore C., and Lockhart, Charles, *A General History of Hampshire, or the County of Southampton, Including the Isle of Wight*, 3 vols. ([1869]).

Woolrych, Austin, *Battles of the English Civil War* (1961).

_____ *Britain in Revolution 1625–1660* (Oxford, 2002).

Worden, Blair, *The Rump Parliament* (Cambridge, 1977).

Wrigley, E. A., and Schofield, R. S., *The Population History of England 1541–1871* (Cambridge, Mass., 1981).

Young, Peter, *Civil War in England* (1981).

_____ *Marston Moor 1644: The Campaign and the Battle* (Kineton, 1970).

_____ and Emberton, Wilfrid, *Sieges of the Great Civil War 1642–1646* (1978).

Index

Abingdon, Berks., 118, 159
absenteeism, 149, 242, 244, 267–75
Adams, Thomas, 16
advocate general of the army, 168, 175
Agitators, 355
agriculture, protection of, 160–2
Albemarle, George Monck, 1st duke of, 45, 244 n. 84
Alexander the Great, 33
Alford, John, 59
allegiance, 7–10, 21, 130–1, 291, 300–1
Alresford, Hants., 71–2, 88, 89, 120 n. 113, 218, 256
Alton, Hants., 88, 101, 121 n. 120, 159
Ampthill, Beds., 67
Anglo-Scottish wars (1639–40), 4, 25, 51–4, 60–1, 127, 232, 236, 262–3
anti-Catholicism, 20, 24–5, 27–31 passim, 67, 132, 153 n. 63, 197–9, 210, 248
apprentices, 220–1, 317
armaments,
    ammunition, 84–6, 90–2, 120, 160 n. 13, 283, 326, 328, 338, 342–3, 354, 383
    cost, 80, 81, 87–8
    artillery, 74–5, 77–8, 83–90, 237, 322, 324, 331, 348–50
    killing rate vs. firepower, 86–7
    miscellaneous and informal (grenades, scythes, etc.), 36, 75–7, 79, 80, 82, 85, 90–2, 105, 333, 341
    'muscle-powered' (pikes, swords, etc.), 37, 74–6, 78, 80, 90, 351, 361
    negligence and accidents, 65, 91–3, 120–1
    production, quantities and suppliers, 78–82, 84–5
    small arms (muskets, pistols), 74–93 passim
    unstable provenance and variable quality, 63–4, 76–85, 90–1, 93
armies
    age profile, 220–2
    attrition rates, 219, 266–8, 351–2, 356, 392–3,
    command structure, 9, 61, 217–9, 266, 285–7
    confusion in action, 95, 116–8, 120–3, 254–5
    false musters and fraud, 143, 148, 150, 169–70, 273
    foreigners in, 120, 179, 197–8, 204, 234–5, 318, 328, 379

pay and arrears, 110 n. 68, 180, 198, 233 n. 35, 238–9, 264–5, 267 n. 41, 281–3, 326
pre-war formation, 40–61 passim, 198 n. 11, 218–9, 221–2, 228, 233–4
professionalism, 40–54, 232–3, 235–7
recruitment, 18, 59–60, 75, 215, 217–24, 261–3, 268, 278, 317
size of, 217–8
and see desertion; drink; flight and panic fear; intelligence; maps and plans; morale; officers; soldiers; straggling; turncoats
armies, Dutch and Swedish, 39, 145
armouries, 79
articles of war, to 1641, 39, 141–7
articles of war, 1642–49, 148–56, 168
    and see courts martial; punishment and deterrence
articles of war, distinctive characteristics
    parliamentarian, 146–8, 151–3
    royalist, 147, 152–6
Artillery Gardens and private military companies, 38–9, 55–60, 219, 286
Arundel, Thomas Howard, 14th earl of, 29, 51, 52, 146–8, 155, 185 n. 3
Arundel Castle, Sussex, 88, 103, 266
Ashburnham, John, 349, 381
Ashburnham, Col. William, 245 n. 90
Ashton, Robert, 314
Astley, Maj. Gen. Sir Jacob, 1st baron, 40 n. 32, 46, 48, 52, 61, 96, 253, 305
Aston, Maj. Gen. Sir Arthur, 41, 104
Aston, Col. Sir Thomas, 122, 244, 251, 279, 280
atrocities, real and feared, 26–31, 86, 90, 135–6, 162–5, 197, 206, 262, 339–46 passim
Ayala, Balthasar, 131
Aylet, John, 376

Bachiler, Samuel, 18, 40
Bagot, Col. Richard, 108, 249
Ballard, Col. Thomas, 234
Bampfield, Col. Joseph, 92, 104–5, 119 n. 108, 256
Banbury, Oxon., 88, 110 n. 66, 167
Bankes, Sir John, Chief Justice of Common Pleas, 6, 7, 10
Bankes, Lady Mary, 391, 400–1

Bankes, Ralph, 401
Bard, Col. Sir Henry, 78
Barnardiston, Mr., 350, 356
Barnardiston, Lieut. Col. Sir Thomas, 318, 350
Barnes, Thomas, 18–9
Barriffe, William, 36–9 passim, 55–60 passim
Barrington, Henry, 331, 371
Barrington, John, 46, 47 n. 63, 50, 53
Barrington, Sir Thomas, 30 n. 25
Basing House, Hants., 88, 118, 254–6, 258
Basset, Maj. Gen. Thomas, 73 n. 35
Bastwick, Dr. John, 131 n. 16
Baxter, Ralph, 100–1
Baxter, Richard, 71
Beauchamp, Sir Henry, 246
Bedel, Capt., 242
Bedell, William, 21–3, 41–2
Bedford, 67
Bedford, William Russell, 5th earl of, 226
Beeston Castle, Cheshire, 66, 88, 110, 230, 275, 282
Behre, Col. Hans, 197–98
Berkeley, Sir John, 245 n. 90
Bernard, Richard, 17
Berwick-upon-Tweed, Northumb., 96, 316, 370
Bethlen Gabor, king of Hungary, 41
Bingham, John, 39–40
Birch, Capt. Samuel, 393
Birmingham, War., 31, 164–5
Blackheath, London, 317
Black Will, cannoneer, 84
Blague, Col. Thomas, 315 n. 17
blasphemy and swearing, 72, 159, 180, 182–4, 289–90
Bletchingdon House, 66, 188
Boarstall, Bucks., siege of, 295–303, 327, 388
  honour, loyalty, and surrender, 304–7
  social links between enemies, 299–304
  surrender as public performance, 308, 311
  surrender terms, 307–9
Booth, Sir George, 223, 400
Bosvile, Sir Ralph, 55, 219
Braddock Down, Corn., 67, 202
Bradford, Yorks., 76, 79, 84 n. 47, 205
Brampton Bryan, Heref., 72, 87, 92, 108, 233
Breda, Netherlands, siege of, 39, 327, 374
Breitenfeld, Saxony, 89 n. 67
Brentford, earl of, see Forth
Brentford, London, 67
Brereton, Sir William, 8, 52–3, 105–10, 113, 121–2, 174, 184, 192, 200, 207, 217, 224, 231–2, 239–40, 245 n. 91, 246, 259, 282

Brett, Sir Alexander, 26
Bridgnorth, Shrops., 105
Bridgewater, John Egerton, 1st earl of, 8, 78–9
Brinckmair, L., 30
Bristol, 9–10, 66, 81, 90, 151–2, 187–8, 230, 377–8
Bristol, George Digby, 2nd earl of, 245 n. 90, 292, 402
Brookband, Maj., 243
Buckingham, George Villiers, 1st duke of, 50, 57, 319
Buckingham, George Villiers, 2nd duke of, 227–8, 316, 319, 352, 378, 401
Buggs, Samuel, 24 n. 2
Bulstrode, Sir Richard, 244, 249
Bulstrode, Lieut. Col. Thomas, 299, 301–3, 309
Burford, Oxon., 267, 309
Burges, Cornelius, 266
Bury St Edmunds, Suff., 267, 315
Bushell, Capt. Browne, 233, 243 n. 80
Butler (or Boteler), Col. John, 107
Byron, Maj. Gen. John, 1st baron, of Rochdale, 85, 89, 107, 207, 228

Caernavon, Robert Dormer, 1st earl of, Col., 102
Cambridge, 67, 107 n. 47
Campion, Edward, 304, 307
Campion, Lady Grace, 297–303 passim, 324
Campion, Col. Sir William, 296–311 passim, 317, 322, 324, 362
Canterbury, Kent, 315, 316 n. 16, 320
Capel, Arthur, 1st baron, of Hadham, Lieut. Gen., 108, 162, 317–62 passim, 364, 377, 386 n. 55, 397–9
Capel, Arthur (son of above), 344–7
Capel, Lady Mary, 397 n. 14, 398–9
Carbery, Robert Vaughan, 1st earl of, Lieut. Gen., 187
Cardiff, Wales, 377
Carew, Maj., 235
Carlisle, Cumb., 96, 316
Carr, Col. 266
Carter, Matthew, 313, 359 n. 42, 361, 363–7, 379, 386
Caryll, Joseph, 128
Cassington, Oxon., 67
Catholics, English, 41–2, 198–9, 210, 248–9
Cave, Sir Richard, 232, 244
chaplains, military, 148, 154, 280, 363, 365, 376–7, 393
Charles, Prince of Wales (Charles II, 1649), 38, 305, 316 n. 17, 320, 335, 353 n. 24, 387

Charles I, 6, 57, 69, 90, 127, 131, 136, 237, 249, 253, 298, 305, 367, 391, 392, 397
  articles of war of, 152, 173
  and military law, 191–3
  Naseby, 66 n. 6
  and Prince Rupert, 187–8
Chelmsford, Essex, 317, 349
Chester, 66–7, 73, 76 n. 9, 84–5, 89, 105–13 passim, 121, 228, 239–40
children, protections under laws of war, 139, 157, 162–3, 201, 344–5
Cholmley, Col. Sir Hugh, 116 n. 94
Choquix, Anthony, 235
Christianity and war, 15–23, 25, 28, 30–1, 125, 128–9, 135–6, 163, 197, 199
Chudleigh, Maj. James, 277
churches, protection and destruction, 86, 146, 153–4, 157, 159–60, 298
Cicero, 15
civilians
  and the army, 2, 7, 11, 63–71, 89, 92, 99–114 passim, 150–1, 179–81, 185–7, 200, 250, 262–3, 271–3, 297–8, 310–88 passim
  profit and loss, 180, 234, 309–10, 371–6, 390–1, 400–1
  protections of military codes, 146, 149, 151, 158, 162–3, 179–81
  social bonds: kinship, friendship and neighbourhood, 7–8, 11–12, 100–1, 199, 210, 299–304 passim, 390, 399–402
Clanricarde, Ulrick Burke, 1st earl of, later 1st marquess, 210
Clarendon, Edward Hyde, 1st earl of, 5, 24, 27, 33, 202, 295–6, 367, 398
Clark, William, 193–4
Clarke, William, 365–6, 390
clergy, protections under laws of war, 146, 162–3
Clopton, John, 319, 320, 331 n. 2, 369, 374, 379
code, legal, defined, 136 n. 10
codes and ciphers, 109–10
codes of military conduct
  unwritten, *see* laws of God; laws of nature and nations; laws of war
  written, *see* articles of war
Cokayn, Lieut. Col. Richard, 231
Colchester, Essex, siege of, 312–88
  army and parliament, respective powers of, 352, 364, 365, 386–8, 395, 397–8
  atrocities and breaches of laws of war, 32, 333, 339–41, 343–5
  civic divisions, 314–7, 320–1, 344, 371
  Essex committeemen, 328, 340, 347–50, 359, 377

financial penalties and Dutch community, 359, 371–4
  fire and destruction, 312, 324, 330–4, 374
  hunger and disease, 322, 325, 327, 338, 375
  negotiations, progress of, 328, 351–7, 359, 360–3
  prisoners, 327, 348–9, 357–8, 362, 377–82 passim
  surrender terms, 329, 354–68 passim, 377
  weather, 319, 334, 338, 356, 370
'Colchester martyrs', 370, 385–8
  execution of Lucas and Lisle, 363–8
  quarter and mercy defined, 329, 356–8, 365, 367–8
Collinson, Patrick, 19
colours, regimental, 115–6, 140, 284, 308, 358
Commission of Array (royalist), 218
commissions of oyer and terminer, 173
commissions of the peace, 173
Compton, Col. Sir William, 381
conscience, 7, 21–2, *and see also* allegiance
constitutional issues, 8–10, 21–2, 130–2, 173, 351, 364, 368, 371, 393–4, 397–400 passim
Conway, Sir Edward, 1st Viscount, 47
Conway, Edward, 2nd Viscount, 171, 173, 245
Conway, Sir Thomas, 50
Conyers, Sir John, 163
Coyngsby, Col. Fitzwilliam, 84, 229, 232 n. 29, 244
Cooper, Anthony Ashley, 1st earl of Shaftesbury, 244
Copley, Commissary Lionel, 83 n. 41
Corbett, Miles, 384
Cork, Richard Boyle, 1st earl of, 69, 205
Cornwall and Cornish, 63, 73, 201–4
councils of war
  as advisory bodies, 9 n. 15, 95, 104, 106, 108, 151, 176, 244, 353–4
  as courts martial, 169–90 passim, 243, 363–4
county committees, parliamentary, 172, 315, 317, 328, 336–59 passim, 377
courage, 228, 251, 258, 261, 263–4, 269, 361–2, 369
Court of Wards, 396
courts martial, 146, 150, 169–90 passim, 246 n. 96, 272, 291, 343 n. 80, 394–5
cowardice, 236–7, 241, 242, 264, 269, 350
Craven, William, 1st baron of Hampsted Marshall, 48
Crawford, Ludovic Lindsay, 16th earl of, Col., 233
Crediton, Devon, 268
Cripplegate, London, 55, 57
Crispe, Sir Nicholas, 60, 81

Cromwell, Henry, 236
Cromwell, Oliver, 2–3, 11, 16, 69 n. 18,
     88–9, 122, 217, 237, 245, 288–9, 291,
     307, 320, 328, 354, 384
Cropredy Bridge, Oxon., 268
Crow, Col. Henry, 187
Crowland, Lincs., 348
Crowne, William, 52
Croxton, Maj. Thomas, 207
cruelty
     gratuitous, as atrocity, 17, 29–30, 137–8
     permissible, 22
Cruso, John, 34, 36–9 passim, 56

Dalbier, Col. John, 197–8, 235, 328
Davalier, Col. John, 197, 235
Davenant, Sir William, 81
Davies, Sir Edward, 152 n. 57
decimation, *see* punishment and deterrence
Defoe, Daniel, 374, 376 n. 24, 387
De la Roche, Bartholomew, 84, 234–5
De Levet, John, 198
Denbigh, Basil Fielding, 2nd earl of, Maj.
     Gen., 232 n. 27, 239, 246, 266, 290
Derby, 246
Derby, Charlotte Stanley (de la
     Trémouille),countess of, 237
Derby, James Stanley, 7th earl of, 75
Dering, Sir Edward, 176
desertion, 8, 53, 107, 108, 118, 149, 168, 178,
     185, 192, 215, 217, 219, 241, 263–72
     passim, 278, 301–2, 327, 351–2, 393
     and see straggling
D'Ewes, Sir Simonds, 57, 205
disease, 50–1, 121–2, 201, 267, 270, 338
     and see Colchester
Doddington, Col. Sir Francis, 257
Dorney, Maj. Henry, 183–4
Dorset, 102
Dorset, Edward Sackville, 4th earl of, 24 n. 2
Drewint, Lieut. John, 198 n. 8
drink and drunkenness, 280–2
     articles of war, penalties, 146, 149, 150, 154
     and crime and disorder, 178–82, 189,
          241–2, 244, 247–8, 250, 253, 255,
          263, 267, 274–5, 289–90
     and sociability, 183, 236, 267, 303–4, 310,
          369
drums and trumpets, 37–8, 58, 71, 88 n. 65,
     111, 114–6, 140, 146, 168, 324, 354
duels and quarrels, 122, 150, 154–6, 180,
     187, 189–90, 230, 241–2, 244–50, 267,
     275, 289–90
Dunbar, Scotland (1650), 3 n. 2, 380
Dundee, Scotland (1651), courts
     martial, 177–87 passim, 272, 274

Dunkirk, Netherlands, (1658), 236
Dunstable, Beds., 67
Dutch, 145–6, 196–8, 234–5
Dynham, Lady Penelope, 295, 297, 310
Dyve, Sir Lewis, 109–10

Earl Marshal's Court, 179
Edgecumbe, Col. Piers, 231, 277
Edgehill, War., 65, 76 n. 11, 88, 119, 229
Elizabeth, Princess (daughter of James I), wife
     of Elector Palatine, 27, 41, 48 n. 68, 111,
     234
Ellesmere, Shrops., 118
Ellis, Col. Robert, 279
Elton, Lieut. Col. Richard, 40 n. 29, 99–106
     passim,
     115, 285–8
England, pre-civil war
     chauvinism, 196–9
     domestic peace and continental wars, 9, 13,
          24–32, 127, 135, 391
     population, 53, 70–1, 216 n. 4
     preparation for war, 33–61 passim
Erasmus, 15
Erle, Sir Walter, 102, 400–1
Essex, 66–7, 317–78 passim
Essex, Robert Devereux, 2nd earl of, 215 n. 1,
     252
Essex, Robert Devereux, 3rd earl of, Lord
     General, 47 n. 63, 52, 54, 75, 82, 86, 96,
     116–7, 198 n. 11, 199, 215 n. 1, 220,
     228, 246, 264
     articles of war, 147–52, 173–4
     character and popularity, 223, 252–3
     generalship, 101, 109, 117, 204, 230,
          240–1, 245, 253–4, 268
     and Irish prisoners, 166–7, 206–7, 210
Evelyn, John, 369, 374, 376, 386
Everard, Ensign Richard, 183, 186
Exeter, Dev., 305
Exmouth, Dev., 91

Fairfax, Lady Anne (Vere), wife of Sir
     Thomas, 47, 201, 309 n. 52, 346
Fairfax, Bryan, 369
Fairfax, Thomas, 1st Baron Fairfax of
     Cameron, 48, 197, 220
Fairfax, Sir Thomas, 3rd Baron Fairfax, Lord
     General, (1647), 44, 47–8, 50, 76 n. 7,
     102, 110, 118, 220 n. 16, 221, 296–9,
     304–9, 320, 401
     articles of war, 148, 166, 193–4
     character, 203, 227–8, 262, 357, 377,
          383–8, 400
     and constitutional issues, 8, 10, 307, 351,
          364, 368, 371, 397

generalship, 95, 108, 237–8, 256, 307–8,
    321–2, 327–8, 339–41, 344–6, 353,
    355–6, 359
health, 309, 319, 350
and Irish prisoners, 208
and laws of war, 166, 303, 329, 357, 362,
    367–8, 388, 394, 397
and New Model army, 69, 75, 99, 193–4,
    217, 221
and siege of Colchester, 315–88 passim
Fairfax, Col. Sir William, 75
Fane, Col. Sir Francis, 48
Farr, Col. Henry, 243 n. 81, 317, 319, 363,
    381, 399
Ferne, Henry, 18–20
Fielding, Col. Richard, 104, 176, 181, 187,
    188, 193
Fiennes, Nathaniel, 66, 157–2, 244
Finch, Capt. Simon, 235
Firth, C.H., 5, 151 n. 55, 215, 387
Fisher, Thomas, 34, 38, 39, 54
Fiske, William, 96
fleet, parliamentary, 3, 81, 314, 316–7, 320,
    324, 370
Fleetwood, George, 45, 46
Fleming, Capt. Christopher, 256
flight and panic fear, 36, 121, 156, 169–70,
    236, 242, 258–79 passim, 286
Forest of Dean, 81
Forth, Patrick Ruthven, 1st earl of, and 1st earl
    of Brentford, 36, 48, 221–2, 233, 234,
    256, 257, 270
fortifications, 2, 87–8, 295, 298, 322–3
fortune, luck, and chance, 35, 90, 92, 122,
    192–3, 225, 284
France and French, 25–6, 41, 164–5, 196–8
    passim, 204, 235
Fransway, Capt., 235
Frescheville, Peter, 39

Gage, Col. Sir Henry, 41, 42, 50, 204, 254–6,
    257, 285, 295
Gainsborough, Lincs., 264
Gam, Lieut. Col. Laurentz, 235
Gamull, Col. Sir Francis, 232 n. 27, 238
Gardiner, S.R., 5, 387
Garneer, Maj. John, 197
garrisons, 65–7, 71, 217, 295–8
Gascoigne, Col. Sir Bernard, 197, 235, 328,
    363–7, 379
Geere, Capt. William, 55 n. 96, 57 n. 104, 60
Gell, Col. Sir John, 39, 43–4, 46, 79 n. 24,
    99, 107 n. 52, 109, 145, 241, 246, 250
Gell, Lieut. Col. Thomas, 81, 84, 239, 391
Gell, William, 43–4, 46, 53
Geneva Conventions, 131, 164 n. 33, 341

genocide, 197
Gentles, Ian, 212, 217 n. 6, 219, 282 n. 101
Gentili, Alberico, 15, 16, 129, 132 n. 17
Gerard, Col. Gilbert, 108
Gerard, Col. Richard, 42
Gerbier, Sir Balthazar, 16–7, 77
Germany, *see* Thirty Years' War
Gibbon (or Guybon), Capt. Devereux, 198
    n. 11
Glemham, Col. Sir Thomas, 38, 172, 298,
    306, 307, 309
Glissen, Dr. Francis, 354
Gloucester, 70, 118
Glynne, John, 200
Goforth, John, 103
Goodwin, Col. Arthur, 264
Goring, Col. George (Lord Goring, 1644), 45,
    47, 48, 52, 67, 203, 218, 229, 239,
    241–2, 244, 249, 369
Goring, George, 1st Baron and 1st earl of
    Norwich, *see* Norwich
Gosson, Stephen, 16 n. 5
Gouge, William, 16, 22, 35, 56, 57, 83, 164
Gould, Col., 221
Gray, Maj., 246 n. 95
Greene, Giles, 401
Grenvile, Col. Sir Bevil, 250, 291
Grenvile, Lieut. Gen. Sir Richard, 243, 257
Gresley, Sir George, 113
Grey, Col., 72 n. 32
Grimes, Capt. John, 382 n. 41
Grimston, Sir Harbottle, 331
Grose, Francis, 143
Grotius, Hugo, 15, 39 n. 28, 129, 138 n. 17
guides and scouts, 99–102, 171, 255, 326,
    and see intelligence
Gustavus Adolphus, king of Sweden, 34, 35,
    41, 46–51 passim, 87, 233, 251, 277
    n. 80
    articles of war, 145, 269
    as general and protestant hero, 2, 18, 27, 29
Gutierrezde la Vega, Luis, 39 n. 26, 144, n. 36
Gwyn (or Gwynne), John, 90–1, 116–7, 236,
    244, 245, 276 n. 79, 277 n. 83

Habsburg, house of, 20, 27
Haesdonck, John van, 80 n. 26, 81–2
Hague Convention, 135, 341
Hamilton, Col. Sir James, 247–8, 250 n. 105
Hamilton, James, 1st marquess and 1st duke
    of, 200, 378, 397–8
Hammond, Lieut., 56, 59 n. 112
Hammond, Charles, 289–90
Hammond, Maj. Robert, 246 n. 95
Harcourt, Col. Sir Simon, 52, 54
Harding, James, 381

Harley, Lady Brilliana (Conway), (wife of Sir Robert), 47, 48, 92, 233, 237, 399–400
Harley, Col. Edward, 39, 47–8, 237, 265 n. 32
Harley, Sir Robert, 38 n. 32, 399
Harrison, Col. Thomas, 266
Harwood, Richard, 128
Hastevik, Gen. Sir David, 197
Hawkins, Lieut. Col. Stephen, 51
Hawley, Col. Francis, 129 n. 6
Henrietta Maria, Queen, 81, 197
Henry, Prince of Wales (d. 1612), 115
Henry V, articles of war, 142–3, 162
  and see Shakespeare, *Henry V*
Henry VIII, articles of war, 142–3, 162
Hepburn, Col. Sir John, 48 n. 69
Herbert of Raglan, Lord, *see* Worcester, marquess of
Hertford, Frances (Devereux) Seymour, marchioness of, 346
Hertford, William Seymour, 1st marquess of, 218
Hesilrige, Col. Sir Arthur, 85, 200–1, 239, 382 n. 41
Hewson, Col. John, 188
Hexham, Henry, 35–9 passim, 47, 98, 145
Higgins, Capt., 250
Hochstadt, Swabia, 30 n. 24
Hodder, Fabian, 158
Hodgkins, Capt. (alias Wicked Will), 244
Hodgson, Capt. John, 105, 292
Holland, Henry Rich, 1st earl of, 44
  articles of war, 147, 185 n. 3
  second civil war and execution, 316, 324–5, 352, 378, 397–9, 401
Hollar, Wenceslas, 97
honour, 129, 140–1, 155–6, 181–3, 185, 193, 201, 225, 227–33 passim, 248, 258, 347, 366
  and good faith and promises, 166–7, 224, 301, 305–6, 319–20
  and surrender, 304–8, 353–5, 358–63
Hopton, Gen. Sir Ralph, 1st Baron Hopton of Stratton, 12, 86, 91, 101, 103, 122, 129 n. 6, 197–8, 203, 228, 305, 392
Hopton Castle, Shrops., 164
horses, 160–1, 326, 333 n. 14, 335–6, 357–8
hospitals, 146, 160–1
Hotham, Sir John, 44 n. 47, 158
Hougham House, Lincs., 289
Houghton, John Holles, Lord, 44, 50
Humfrey, Capt. Richard, 382 n. 42
Hungary, 41
hunger and starvation, 135, 158 n. 7, 160–1, 266, 322, 326–7, 334–41, 353
Huntingdon, Ferdinando Hastings, 6th earl of, 39, 69

Hutchinson, Col. John, 107 n. 52, 117, 246
Hutchinson, Lucy (wife of Col. John), 78 n. 17, 107 n. 52, 234–5, 264
Hyde, Lieut. Col. David, 247–9, 257, 400 n. 20
Hyde, Sir Thomas, 70

iconoclasm, 154, 159–60, 344
Inchiquin, Murrough O'Brien, 6th Baron, later 1st earl, 345 n. 58
informers, 391
intelligence, 95, 99–114
Ireland and the Irish, 4, 137, 197, 207, 209–10, 260, 380
  atrocities, reciprocal, 22, 25, 28, 31, 132, 163, 199, 204–9
  as pre-war experience for English soldiers, 40, 51–2, 57–8
Ireton, Commissary General Henry, 166 n. 42, 318, 357, 364–6, 386–8
Islip, Oxon., 67
Italians, 186–7, 235, 365–7, 379

Jackson, Thomas, 20
James, duke of York (James II 1685), 104, 320
Jammot, Lieut. Col., 235
Jones, Lieut. Col. Michael, 105
Julius Caesar, 33, 39
jurisdiction, civilian vs.military, 131–2, 171–5, 309, 364–5, 368, 371, 397–8
justices of the peace, 172
just war theory, 4, 16–23, 128–9, 391
Juxon, Capt. Thomas, 59

Kent, 65, 66, 316, 317, 320, 378
Kiddle, Richard, 177, 270–1
Kineton, *see* Edgehill
King, Bishop Henry, 313, 381–2
Kingston-on-Thames, London, 70, 316
Kirk, Sir Lewis, 48

Lambert, Maj. Gen. John, 3 n. 2, 39–40, 221, 282, 320, 328 n. 57, 384
Langdale, Maj. Gen. Sir Marmaduke, 218, 240 n. 64, 251, 353
Langeren, Jacob van, 97, 99 n. 15
Langport, Som., 100 n. 18, 119 n. 107, 121
Langrish, Capt. Anthony, 198 n. 9
Langrish, Maj. Hercules, and sons Capt. Hercules and Cornet Lucullus, 198
language, shared, 71–3, 352, 356
La Rochelle, 20, 25, 26, 28, 32, 50, 313
law, English, 393–7, *and see* jurisdiction
law of God, 125, 129, 136–8, 159, 160–1, 190, 210

law of nature and nations, 18, 20, 125, 129, 136–9, 166, 207, 210, 313
laws of war, customary and international, 3, 11–12, 128–9, 134, 136, 139–41, 157–65, 196–7, 204, 313, 314, 330, 355, 382, 394
  enforcement, 156, 165–7, 210, 394
  minor customary rules, 141, 283–4
  and see articles of war; honour; parole; plunder; prisoners; reciprocity and reprisal
Leech, Jeremy, 20
Leeds, Yorks., 75
Legge, Col. William, 110 n. 65
Leicester, 66 n. 6, 78, 85, 89, 119, 160, 163–4, 201, 218, 223, 236, 259, 283, 293, 392
Leicester, Robert Dudley, 1ˢᵗ earl of, 144–5, 273
Leighton, Alexander, 18 n. 13
Lenthall, William, Speaker of House of Commons, 6, 391, 398
Leslie, Gen. David, 48, 251
Levellers, 6 n. 5, 188–90, 193, 267, 309, 383
Leveson, Col. Thomas, 108, 249
Lexden, Essex, 318, 322
lex talionis, 130–1, 158, 397
  and see reciprocity and reprisal
Lieber's Code (1863), 135, 158 n. 7, 341
Lilburne, Col. Henry, 328
Lilburne, John, 131–2, 158
Lindsey, Montagu Bertie, Col., 15ᵗʰ Lord Willoughby de Eresby and 2ⁿᵈ earl of, 229
Lindsey, Robert Bertie, Lieut. Gen., 14ᵗʰ Lord Willoughby de Eresby and 1ˢᵗ earl of, 229, 233
Lingen, Col. Sir Henry, 237, 399
Lisle, Col. Sir George, 313–4, 317, 322, 326, 328, 355, 363–7, 369–70, 376–7, 382, 385–8, 401
Lister, Joseph, 263
Lithgow, William, 76 n. 10
lodging, soldiers', 69–70, 266, 274, 337
London, 3, 67–8, 71, 79–81, 107, 108, 115, 242, 268, 283, 315–6, 320, 370, 382
Lostwithiel, Corn., 67, 75, 82, 87, 107, 108, 119, 159, 202, 204, 252–3, 268, 277–8, 281, 292, 393
Loughborough, Henry Hastings, 1st Baron, Col., 187, 249, 317, 325, 332–3, 334, 364
Low Countries, *see* Netherlands
Lucas, Gen. Sir Charles, 313, 317, 321–55 passim, 362–4, 369, 370, 376–7, 382, 385–8, 394, 401
Lucas, Col. Sir John, 1ˢᵗ Baron Lucas, 344

Ludlow, Col. Edmund, 72, 131 n. 16
Ludlow, Capt. Robert, 131, n. 16
Luke, Sir Samuel, 80, 82, 101, 110, 112–3, 231, 246, 257, 310 n. 60
Lunsford, Col. Sir Thomas, 41, 45

Machiavelli, Niccolo, 39
Magdeburg, Germany, 29, 31–2, 374
Maidstone, Kent, 268, 317
Mainwaring, Lieut. Philemon, 106, 110–1
Manchester, 76 n. 7, 87
Manchester, Edward Montagu, 2ⁿᵈ earl of, Gen., 116, 215 n. 1, 223, 226, 230 n. 21, 240 n. 63, 241, 245, 271, 391
Manwaring, Lieut. Col. Randolph, 59–60
maps and plans, 95–100
Markham, Gervase, 38, 39, 267
Marshall, Stephen, 232
Marston Moor, Yorks., 2, 68, 88, 118, 123, 216–7, 270
Martel, Charles, 280
martial law, 171–4
Masham, Robert, 48
Masham, Sir William, 328, 349, 350, 381
Massey, Col. Edward, 233, 234, 244
Maurice, count of Nassau, 33
Maurice, Prince (brother of Prince Rupert), 33, 80, 105, 122, 191, 198, 221, 229, 234, 268
Meeke, William, 201
Meese, Sybil, 103 n. 32
mercenaries, 43, 197, 228, 234, 265, 364
Mersea Island, Essex, 324
mercy, surrender to, *see* prisoners; quarter and mercy; surrender
messengers, 102–3, 110–2, 138, 148, 169, 191, 234 n. 38, 258, 324, 343, 347
miles, English, 69 n. 15
Mohun, Warwick, 3ʳᵈ baron of Okehampton, Col., 245 n. 90
Mollanus, Maj., 235
Monck, *see* Albemarle
Monro, Andrew, 36, 51
Monro, John, 51
Monro, Col. Robert, 29, 34, 36, 39, 42, 44, 46, 48 n. 69, 98 n. 11, 53, 69, 220, 225, 270, 287
Montagu, Col. Edward, 267
Montrose, James Graham, 5ᵗʰ earl and 1ˢᵗ marquess of, 10, 49 n. 70
Moore, Samuel, 112–3
morale, 117–8, 121–2, 279–80
Morant, Philip, 374, 376, 387
Morgan, Col. Sir Charles, 47, 53
Morley, Col. Herbert, 297, 299–301, 309
Morris, Col. John, 319, 396–7

muster masters, 148, 150, 169, 273
mutiny, 118, 154, 157, 169, 178, 181, 192, 250, 258, 263, 265–7, 309, 356, 389, 393
and *see* articles of war; courts martial
Myddleton, Sir Thomas, 86, 245 n. 91, 380
Myddelton, Sir William, 117–8

Naseby, Northants., 3, 66 n. 6, 72, 77, 83 n. 40, 88, 108, 119, 203–4, 208, 230–1, 256–7, 259, 276
Irish women, report of massacre, 208–9
number of troops engaged, 216–7
victory parade in London, 71, 115–6
Netherlands, 2, 38, 41–54 passim, 61, 144, 226, 233, 235–6
neuters and neutrality, 4, 7, 16–7, 223
Newcastle, Northumb., 65
Newcastle, William Cavendish, 1st earl of, later marquess and duke, 153 n. 62, 165 n. 36, 199, 219, 233, 240
New Model Army, 5–6, 49, 55, 113, 116, 148, 198, 221, 230–1, 245, 261, 267
army numbers, 60, 122, 172, 184, 215–9
mixed character of, 121–2, 241, 258, 269, 271, 288–91, 392–3
and *see* Fairfax, Sir Thomas
Newport Pagnell, Bucks., 67, 231
Newton St Cyres, Devon, 160
Norden, John, 96, 97 n. 8, 99 n. 15
Norfolk, 66, 316 n. 17, 318
Northampton, Spencer Compton, 2nd earl of, Col., 223
Northumberland, Algernon Percy, 10th earl of, Gen., 6–7, 147–8, 171, 174, 185
Norwich, 38, 65, 91, 315
Norwich, George Goring, 1st Baron Goring and 1st earl of, 7, 26, 81, 315–82 passim, 397–8, 400
Nuremberg defence, 22
Nye, Nathaniel, 84–6

Oath of Supremacy, 153 n. 62
obedience, 21–2, 148–9, *and see* articles of war; courts martial
officers, 129, 140, 150, 153 n. 62, 167, 197, 221–2, 224–57 passim, 266, 279–81, 285–6, 316, 317, 319, 361–2, 392
honour, 154–6, 187–8, 360–3
professional formation, 13, 40–4, 47–9, 51, 58–61, 149, 219 n. 14, 285–6
and *see* courage; honour; mercenaries; soldiers; turncoats
Ogle, Col. Sir William, 1st Viscount, 188
Ordnance Office, 78
Orrery, Roger Boyle, 1st earl of, 251

Osborne, William, 337, 370, 382, 390–1
Owen, Sir John, 398 n. 15
Oxford, 2, 8–9, 10, 65, 67, 81 n. 31, 85, 98, 104, 136, 188, 242, 295–6, 298, 302, 305, 308, 309

pacificism, 16–7
Palatinate, 20, 25, 27, 28
Parker, Geoffrey, 49, 134
parliament
allegiance and sovereignty, 8–9, 21, 130–2, 396–7
committees:
Complaints for Breach of Articles, 166
Compounding, 309–10
Derby House, 349, 371
Indemnity, 395–6
ordinances:
'Golden Ordinance' for killing Irish prisoners, 206–8
martial law, 172
Militia Ordinance, 218, 394
paroles, 364
Self Denying Ordinance, 231
Vote of No Addresses, 315
Parliament Joan, 105
parole, 105, 106, 140–1, 162 n. 24, 167, 210, 303, 314, 326, 349–50, 362, 364, 394
Paty, —(prisoner), 157–8
Pell, Capt. William, 267 n. 41
Pembroke Castle, 65, 320, 352
Penruddock's rising, 380, 400
Peter, Hugh, 204, 260–1
Petition of Right (1628), 171–3
Peyton, Sir Thomas, 42 n. 37
Pickering, Col. John, 239 n. 59
Pit, Francis, 111
Pitt, Abigail, 401
Pitt, Edward, 400–1
Pitt, George, 401
Pitt, William, 400
plunder, 146, 149, 168, 179–85 passim, 191, 202–3, 231, 239, 254, 261, 262, 274, 281–2, 290, 292, 392, 393
Plymouth, Devon, 91 n. 79, 98, 105
Poland, 41
Pontefract, Yorks., 316, 392, 396
Porter, Endymion, 249
Porter, Lieut. Col. George, 249
Potley, Maj. Gen. Andrew, 49, 233
Powick Bridge, Worcs., 76
Poyer, Col. John, 158, 192, 319
Poyntz, Maj. Gen. Sydenham, 41, 45, 233, 234
Preston, Lancs., 75–6, 242, 279 n. 89, 292, 328, 353, 354, 356, 378, 380, 393

Pride's Purge, 397, 401
prisoners, civilian, 70, 100–1, 317, 328, 336, 339, 340, 344, 347–50, 354, 359, 377, 381
prisoners of war (soldiers), 106–8, 112, 136, 139, 140, 143–4, 153, 179, 376–82, 396–8
    exchange and re-enlistment, 8–9, 199, 226, 228, 277, 297, 302–3, 304, 348–9, 362, 377
    Irish, 206–8
    legal status, 131–2, 377, 396–8
    protections under articles of war, 146, 149
    protections under laws of war (customary), 139, 140, 157–8, 166–7, 207, 210, 314
provost marshals, 146, 150, 168, 175, 179, 184, 274
Prude, Lieut. Col. William, 45–6
Pudding, Capt. Jack (rope-dancer), 310
punishment and deterrence, 103, 145, 149, 158, 181–4, 192–4
Putney debates, 357
Pym, John, 129, 220–1

Quarles, John, 386
quarter and mercy
    mercy defined, and consequences, 164, 358, 377
    quarter defined, 329, 357, 363, 367–8
        granted or denied, 4, 139, 149, 198, 201, 203, 377, 388, 396–7
        Irish excluded from, 206–7
        storm, consequences of, 29, 157, 163–4, 201
quartermasters, 273–4
Quartermaster's Map, 97, 99

radicalism, 2, 6 n. 5, 11, 291, 314, 371, 383, 398
Raglan Castle, Wales, 245, 299, 305
Rainsborough, Col. Thomas, 116, 340, 357, 359, 385, 387, 388
Ram, Robert, 290 n. 140
ransom, 140, 143–4, 145 n. 43, 149, 153, 162, 379
rape, 25, 139, 142, 146, 149, 164–5, 169, 180, 185–6, 261, 262
Ravenna, 327, 374
Rawdon, Col. Marmaduke, 60
Ré, Isle of, 20, 25–6, 28, 50, 145, 319
Reading, Berks., 104, 122, 176, 187, 239, 241, 259
reciprocity and reprisal, 128–32, 157–8, 166–7, 207, 208, 210, 377, 397
regicides, 383, 402

religion, 9–10, 15–23, 122, 153–4, 290–1
renegades, *see* turncoats
Reresby, Sir John, 93
Restoration, 4–5, 146, 301
Rich, Col. Sir Charles, 26, 196
Richmond, James Stuart, 1st duke of and 4th duke of Lennox, 210
Rivers, Elizabeth Savage, Countess, 198–9
Robartes, John, 2nd Baron, 191, 204, 246
Roberts, John, 35
Roseworm (Rosworm), Capt. Johan, 235
Roy, Ian, 43, 45, 46, 176
Rump parliament, 397
Rupert, Prince, 3, 52, 65–6, 68–9, 77, 90, 99, 106, 110 n. 65, 118, 120 n. 113, 129 n. 6, 198–200, 234–5, 245, 272, 283, 299
    atrocities attributed to, 135, 138
    on killing prisoners, 166–7, 201, 207–8, 210, 229–30, 276
    and surrender of Bristol, 10, 66, 151–2, 187–8, 232, 296
Rushworth, John, 332, 342, 374, 390
Russell, Col. Sir William, 192, 247, 248
Rye, Sussex, 370

sacrilege, 86, 154, 159–61, 344
Saltash, Corn., 76
Sanders, Maj. Thomas, 120
Sandford, Capt., 232
Sandys, Col. Samuel, 248
Sarpi, Paolo, 22–3, 42
Saxton, Christopher, 96–8, 99 n. 15
Saye and Sele, William Fiennes, 1st Viscunt, 304
Sayers, Col., 319
Scarborough, Yorks., 208, 370
Scots, 40–51 passim, 105, 163, 200–1, 216, 217 n. 5, 226, 232–4, 248, 262, 314, 316, 320, 328, 380–1, 400
Scott, Thomas, 112
Scudamore, Sir John, 248, 400 n. 20
Sedascue, Maj. George, 197, 198 n. 11
Sedgwick, John, 7
Selden, John, 397 n. 14
Seneca, 15
Sexby, Col. Edward, 187, 188
sexual regulation, 142–3, 149, 169, 185–7, 209
Seymour, Col. Edward, 80 n. 26, 113
Shaftesbury, earl of, *see* Cooper, Anthony Ashley
Shakespeare, William, *Henry V*, 25, 34, 139–40, 158, 252, 259
Shambrooke, Lieut. Col. William, 342
Shelford, Notts., 76, 78 n. 18, 84 n. 47
Sherborne Castle, Dorset, 76, 79, 86, 226, 283

Shilborne, Col. Thomas, 299, 303–4, 306, 309
Shrewsbury, Shrops., 167 n. 43, 207
sieges, 2, 66, 89–90, 151–2, 158, 297–8, 310, 320–41 passim, 371–6
and see Boarstall; civilians; Colchester; disease; plunder
Skippon, Maj. Gen. Philip, 39, 73 n. 34, 193, 202 n. 22, 222, 243, 251–2, 257, 296, 317
Slade, Maj. Henry, 59
Slaning, Col. Nicholas, 48
Slingsby, Sir Henry, 52
Smith, Richard, 103, 110
soldiers, 'other ranks'
    and civil society, 25, 28–30, 65–71, 125, 149, 176–7, 259–62, 282, 383, 391–2
    conduct, ideal and actual, 18, 21–2, 40–54 passim, 128, 148–9, 218–20, 223–4, 235–6, 258–70 passim, 278–9, 286, 289–92, 393
    discipline and training, 125–6, 145, 147–50, 157, 169–70, 174, 181–4, 219, 225, 238, 286–90
    incentives, 86, 185, 219–20, 276 n. 78, 281–4, 392
    non-commissioned officers, duties of, 285–8
    pay and arrears, 238–9, 264–5, 281–2
    professionalism, 40–54, 235–6
    proximity to enemies, 71–4, 88, 102
    religion, 15–23, 159, 261, 280, 289
Solemn League and Covenant, 107, 201, 276
sovereignty, parliamentary, 8–9, 397
Spain, 20, 196–7, 254
Speed, John, 96–8
spies, 36, 94–5, 99, 102–6, 163, 255
Spinola, Ambrosio, marquess of Los Balbases, 50 n. 77
Sprigge, Joshua, 165, 290–1
St George, Col. William, 78, 229
Stamford, Henry Grey, 1st earl of, Gen., 223
Staples, Capt., 236
Star Chamber, 396
St Augustine, 17
St Fagan's, Wales, 378
St Neots, Cambs., 316
St Paul, vicomte de, 197
Strafford, Thomas Wentworth, 1st earl of, 44, 58
straggling, 149, 192, 263, 268–9, 272–5, 278
Stuart, Capt. Gen. Lord Bernard (titular earl of Lichfield), 277
St Werburgh, Chester, 105
Styward, Thomas, 144 n. 36, 145
Suckling, Sir John, 259–60

Suffolk, 68, 318, 326, 351, 370
surrender, 164, 197–8, 202–3, 293–5
    acceptable conditions for, 146, 148, 151–3, 181, 187–8
    and honour, 360–3
    negotiations and terms, 64, 82, 166, 167, 210, 232, 239, 306–9, 320
    as public performance, 308, 311, 355
Surrey, 378
Sussex, 378
Sutcliffe, Matthew, 15–6, 22, 215 n. 1
Swadlin, Thomas, 290 n. 140
Symonds, Richard, 68, 103, 193 n. 118, 201–2, 220, 249, 276
Syms, John, 72 n. 32, 98, 103, 117, 246
Syppens, Capt., 193

Tadcaster, Yorks., 240
Talbot, Lieut. Col. John, 48
Taylor, John, 99 n. 15
telescopes, 90, 95
Tertullian, 15
Thirty Years' War, 24–32 passim, 43–53 passim, 61, 127, 128, 135, 160, 199, 204–5, 216, 227, 333, 374
Thornhill, Col. Richard, 304
Tillier, Maj. Henry, 56
Tilly, Jean 't Serclaes, count of, 2
Tonbridge, Kent, 277
Torrington, Devon, 91, 120
torture, 135 n. 5, 164, 197, 343, 384
Tower of London, 112
trained bands, 34, 54–5, 67 n. 7, 218–9, 237, 317, 318
    and see Artillery Gardens
treason, 130–2, 243–4, 365, 394, 396–7
trees, protections of, 157, 160–1
Trelawny, Col. Jonathan, 221
Trevor, Arthur, 113
Tuke, Col. Sir Samuel, 249, 356
Turks, 135–6, 196–7, 199, 280, 381
turncoats, 49, 94–5, 106, 107, 198, 243–4, 263, 276–8, 316–7, 319–20, 355, 356, 381, 399
Turnham Green, London, 67
Tynemouth, Northumb., 81, 328

Upnor Castle, Kent, 121
Urry, Henry, 49 n. 70
Urry, Maj. Gen. Sir John, 49, 276 n. 76
Urry, Capt. William, 49 n. 70
Uxbridge, London, 70

Vane, Sir Henry, 49
Vavasour, Col. Sir William, 245, 400 n. 20
Venn, Col. John, 59, 86, 99

Venn, Thomas, 111 n. 71
Vere, Sir Francis, 47, 111 n. 71
Vere, Sir Horace, 1ˢᵗ Baron Vere, 18, 44, 47, 48 n. 67, 52
Vere, Sir John, 45
Vermuyden, Col. Cornelius, 110, 198 n. 11, 235
Verney, Sir Edmund, 140, 165, 229
Vicars, John, 28, 197
victuallers, 143, 150, 171, 273
Vincent, Philip, 29–30, 31 n. 28
Virginia, laws of (1612), 164 n. 34, 197

Wales and the Welsh, 65, 199–200, 209 n. 51, 259, 316, 318, 320, 378, 381
Walker, Sir Edward, 7–8, 28, 51–2, 82, 99, 130–1, 172, 245, 252, 268 n. 45, 276 n. 76
Walker, Dr Walter, 175 n. 63
Wallace, John, 7
Wallenstein, Albert, duke of Friedland and Mecklenburg, 41
Waller, Gen. Sir William, 41, 50, 92–3, 121, 122, 184, 197, 198, 201, 245, 400
  court martial records of, 174–9, 244, 270, 272
  generalship, 35, 86, 90, 101, 237, 256, 268
  and reconciliation, 12, 119, 133
  and soldiers, 118, 230, 242, 244, 266–7, 282
Wallington, Nehemiah, 390, 402
Wallis, John, 402
Walloons, 197, 208, 318
Wanfry, Capt., 250
Wardour Castle, Wilts., 161
Wareham, Dorset, 101, 117
Warwick, Robert Rich, 2ⁿᵈ earl of, Lord Admiral, 3, 81, 199, 226, 233, 244, 263, 316–7, 381, 399, 400
Washington, Col. Henry, 250
Watson, Leonard, 112
weather and war, 63, 77, 118–20, 239–40, 292, 319, *and see* Colchester
Weldon, Col. Ralph, 177
Wemyss, James, 90, 237, 244
Wentworth, Michael (brother of earl of Strafford), 44
Weymouth, Dorset, 81, 98

Whalley, Col. Edward, 317, 324
Wharton, Nehemiah, 68, 116 n. 94, 118, 220, 221, 270 n. 51, 281, 284
Whitbroke, Col., 235
Whitchurch, Shrops., 117
Whitelock, Bulstrode, 244 n. 84
Whitestone, Devon, 160
Whiteway, William, 26, 27, 31
Wilde, George, 17, 20, 127
Williams, Sir Roger, 40–1
Willoughby, Francis, 5ᵗʰ Baron Willoughby of Parham, 116, 264
Wilmot, Henry, 1ˢᵗ Baron Wilmot (later 2nd Viscount), 242, 244, 245
Wilson, Mr (minister), 99
Wilson, Lieut. Col. Rowland, 59
Winchester, Hants., 188
Windebank, Lieut. Col. Francis, 188, 193, 306
Wingate, Capt. Edward, 396
Windsor Castle, Berks., 377, 379
women, 202, 297–8, 300, 390–1, 399–400
  Irish, 208–10
  offences against, 162–5, 180, 201
  protections due to, 125, 137–8, 142, 145, 146
  sexual legislation and prosecution, 142–3, 145–6, 179–87 passim
  vulnerability, 132, 205, 314, 327, 339–41, 343, 354
  and see civilians; spies; *and see also* Lady Bankes; Lady Campion; countess of Derby; Lady Harley; Parliament Joan; Countess Rivers
Wood, Anthony, 311
Worcester, 3 n. 2, 5, 75, 84, 87, 92, 105, 166, 226, 305, 380
Worcester, Edward Somerset, 6ᵗʰ earl and 2ⁿᵈ marquess, 43 n. 43, 234, 245
Wortley, Col. Sir Francis, 248
Wrangel, Gen. Karl Gustav, 47 n. 66
Wrexham, Wales, 86
Wynd, Lieut. Col. Henry, 48
Wynne, Humphrey, 401–2

Yarmouth, Great, Norf., 107, 370, 371

Zouche, Richard, 132 n. 17